Return to an Address of the Honourable the House of Commons
dated 28th January 2004
for the

Report
of
the Inquiry into the Circumstances
Surrounding the Death of Dr David Kelly C.M.G.

by

Lord Hutton

Ordered by the House of Commons to be printed 28th January 2004

HC 247   London: The Stationery Office   £70.00 (inc VAT)

CONTENTS

Chapter 4

Chapter 5

Chapter 6

To the Rt Hon Lord Falconer of Thoroton, the Secretary of State for Constitutional Affairs.

CHAPTER 1

The sittings of the Inquiry

1. On 18 July 2003 I was requested by the Rt Hon Lord Falconer of Thoroton, the Secretary of State for Constitutional Affairs, to conduct an Inquiry into the death of Dr David Kelly. My terms of reference were:

   "urgently to conduct an investigation into the circumstances surrounding the death of Dr Kelly."

   Lord Falconer further requested me to deliver my report to him.

2. Mr Lee Hughes, a senior civil servant in the Department for Constitutional Affairs, was appointed as Secretary to the Inquiry. I requested Mr James Dingemans QC and Mr Peter Knox to act as counsel to the Inquiry, Clifford Chance LLP were appointed to act as solicitors to the Inquiry and the responsible partner, Mr Michael Smyth, assigned Mr Martin Smith, a senior associate, to act for them. The names of counsel and solicitors appearing for parties represented at the Inquiry are set out in appendix 1.

3. I held a preliminary sitting of the Inquiry on 1 August and I stated:

   [1 August, page 1, line 16]

   At the commencement of the Inquiry I wish to state the objectives which it should seek to achieve. First of all, my primary task is to investigate the circumstances surrounding the death and that will involve a detailed and careful examination of the relevant facts. Secondly, my terms of reference require me to conduct the investigation urgently, and that means that I must proceed with expedition, and I have no doubt that it is in the public interest that I should do so. Thirdly, I must ensure that the procedures at the Inquiry are fair to those who give evidence.

4. I also stated that the Inquiry would be held in two stages. The first stage would consist of calling witnesses to give evidence in chronological order as to the sequence of events insofar as that was possible. The witnesses would be examined by counsel to the Inquiry in a neutral way to elicit their knowledge and understanding of the facts and they would not be examined by counsel representing them or cross-examined by counsel representing other parties.

5. There would then be a period of adjournment after which the second stage of the Inquiry would commence. In the second stage I would ask persons, who had already given evidence and whose conduct might possibly be the subject of criticism in my report, to come back to be examined further by counsel to the Inquiry and, subject to my permission, by their own counsel and, subject also to my permission, to be cross-examined by counsel for other parties. I also stated that in the second stage I might call witnesses who had not been called in the first stage and against whom there might be no possible criticism.

1

6. The first stage of the Inquiry commenced on 11 August 2003 and concluded on 4 September 2003. The second stage of the Inquiry commenced on 15 September 2003 and concluded on 25 September 2003, save that the Inquiry sat on 13 October 2003 to hear further evidence from a witness who had been ill during the second stage.

7. During the period of adjournment between the first and second stages of the Inquiry I caused the solicitor to the Inquiry, Mr Martin Smith, to write to a number of witnesses informing them of possible criticisms of them arising from the evidence heard in the first stage and informing them that if they wished to dispute these possible criticisms they would have the opportunity to submit written representations and to make oral submissions at the second stage of the Inquiry. They were also informed that they would have the opportunity, if they wished, to give further evidence relating to those possible criticisms on examination by their own counsel and that they might be subject to cross-examination by legal representatives for other interested parties and counsel to the Inquiry. They were also informed that if, as a result of hearing further evidence in the second stage of the Inquiry, I was minded to make other possible criticisms which might affect them, they would be informed in the course of the second stage in order to allow them to deal with those new matters.

8. In the course of the second stage a number of witnesses were examined by their own counsel, and some of them were cross-examined by counsel for other interested persons or bodies and by counsel to the Inquiry. At the commencement of the second stage counsel to the Inquiry made an opening statement and at the close of the second stage counsel for the interested parties and counsel to the Inquiry made closing statements.

The terms of reference

9. My terms of reference were "urgently to conduct an investigation into the circumstances surrounding the death of Dr Kelly". In my opinion these terms of reference required me to consider the circumstances preceding and leading up to the death of Dr Kelly insofar as (1) they might have had an effect on his state of mind and influenced his actions preceding and leading up to his death or (2) they might have influenced the actions of others which affected Dr Kelly preceding and leading up to his death. There has been a great deal of controversy and debate whether the intelligence in relation to weapons of mass destruction set out in the dossier published by the Government on 24 September 2002 was of sufficient strength and reliability to justify the Government in deciding that Iraq under Saddam Hussein posed such a threat to the safety and interests of the United Kingdom that military action should be taken against that country. This controversy and debate has continued because of the failure, up to the time of writing this report, to find weapons of mass destruction in Iraq. I gave careful consideration to the view expressed by a number of public figures and commentators that my terms of reference required or, at least, entitled me to consider this issue. However I concluded that a question of such wide import, which would involve the consideration of a wide range of evidence, is not one which falls within my terms of reference. The major controversy which arose following Mr Andrew Gilligan's broadcasts on the BBC Today programme on 29 May 2003 and which closely involved Dr Kelly arose from the allegations in the broadcasts (1) that the Government probably knew, before it decided to put it in its dossier of 24 September 2002, that the statement was wrong that the Iraqi military were able to deploy weapons of mass destruction within 45 minutes of a decision to do so and (2)

that 10 Downing Street ordered the dossier to be sexed up. It was these allegations attacking the integrity of the Government which drew Dr Kelly into the controversy about the broadcasts and which I consider I should examine under my terms of reference. The issue whether, if approved by the Joint Intelligence Committee and believed by the Government to be reliable, the intelligence contained in the dossier was nevertheless unreliable is a separate issue which I consider does not fall within my terms of reference. There has also been debate as to the definition of the term "weapons of mass destruction" (WMD) and as to the distinction between battlefield WMD and strategic WMD. Mr Gilligan's broadcasts on 29 May related to the claim in the dossier that chemical and biological weapons were deployable within 45 minutes and did not refer to the distinction between battlefield weapons, such as artillery and rockets, and strategic weapons, such as long range missiles, and a consideration of this issue does not fall within my terms of reference relating to the circumstances surrounding the death of Dr Kelly.

10. I further consider that one of my primary duties in carrying out my terms of reference is, after hearing the evidence of many witnesses, to state in considerable detail the relevant facts surrounding Dr Kelly's death and also, insofar as I can determine them, the motives and reasons operating in the minds of those who took various decisions and carried out various actions which affected Dr Kelly.

11. In order to enable the public to be as fully informed as possible I have also decided, rather than set out a summary of the evidence, to set out in this report many parts of the transcript of the evidence so that the public can read what the witnesses said and can understand why I have come to the conclusions which I state.

12. Whilst I stated at the preliminary sitting on 1 August that I did not sit to decide between conflicting cases advanced by interested parties who had opposing arguments to present, it has been inevitable in the course of the Inquiry that attention has focussed on the decisions and conduct of individual persons, and therefore I think it is right that I should express my opinion on the propriety or reasonableness of some of those decisions and actions.

The facts

13. I propose to commence by stating the facts which I consider have been established by the evidence which I have heard and by the documents put in evidence and many of these facts have not been in any real dispute. After stating the facts, I propose to turn to consider the issues which arise from those facts and to express my opinion in relation to them.

14. At the outset I state, for reasons which I will set out in greater detail in a later part of this report, that I am satisfied that Dr Kelly took his own life by cutting his left wrist and that his death was hastened by his taking Coproxamol tablets. I am further satisfied that there was no involvement by a third person in Dr Kelly's death.

15. I also consider it to be important to state in this early part of the report that I am satisfied that none of the persons whose decisions and actions I later describe ever contemplated that Dr Kelly might take his own life. I am further satisfied that none of those persons was at fault in not contemplating that Dr Kelly might take his own life. Whatever pressures and strains Dr Kelly was subjected to by the decisions and actions taken in the weeks before his death, I am satisfied that no one realised or should have realised that those pressures and strains might drive him to take his own life or contribute to his decision to do so.

16. The facts which I consider have been established by the evidence given in the course of the Inquiry are the following and I shall return to discuss some of these facts in greater detail in later parts of this report.

Dr Kelly's employment in the Civil Service

17. Dr Kelly was a biologist by training, who held degrees from a number of universities and he was a very highly qualified specialist in the field of biology. In 1984 he joined the Ministry of Defence (MoD) and was appointed to head the microbiology division at the chemical and biological defence establishment at Porton Down in Wiltshire. The nature of Dr Kelly's employment within the Civil Service later became somewhat complex. In April 1995 the Defence Evaluation and Research Agency (DERA) was established as an agency of the MoD and Dr Kelly's personnel management and employment formally passed from the MoD to DERA. In 1996 Dr Kelly was appointed on secondment to the Proliferation and Arms Control Secretariat (PACS) within the MoD and he worked as an adviser to PACS and to the Non-Proliferation Department of the Foreign and Commonwealth Office (FCO) on Iraq's chemical and biological weapons capabilities and on the work of the United Nations Monitoring, Verification and Inspection Commission (UNMOVIC). Dr Kelly was also responsible for providing advice to the Defence Intelligence Staff (DIS) of the MoD and to the Secret Intelligence Service (SIS) on Iraq. Dr Kelly's secondment was principally funded by the FCO for whom Dr Kelly carried out a substantial proportion of his work. From 1991 to 1998 Dr Kelly made 37 visits to Iraq in the course of his duties and took very few holidays. In 2001 the part of DERA which employed Dr Kelly became part of Defence Science and Technology Laboratory (DSTL) which is a Trading Fund of the MoD and DSTL became Dr Kelly's employer during the remainder of his secondment to the MoD which continued until his death.

18. In the mid 1990s Dr Kelly became dissatisfied with his salary and grading after DERA had created a new salary and grading structure and moved away from the general Civil Service structure. It appears that Dr Kelly had not been properly assimilated within the DERA salary scales and it appears that this may have happened because he was working abroad so much. Dr Kelly sought assistance on a number of occasions from the officials who were then his line managers. They intervened on his behalf and Dr Kelly was eventually regraded and advanced to a higher grade in February 2002. One of his line managers, Dr Shuttleworth described Dr Kelly as being concerned and frustrated but not bitter about his salary and grading.

19. In the early 1990s Dr Kelly became involved in the analysis of information about the biological and warfare programme of the Soviet Union and he went to Russia as a member of the Anglo American team visiting biotechnology facilities in different parts of Russia and played a leading role in that inspection. His work in Russia was most successful and he was highly respected by both the British and American members of the team.

20. In 1991 Dr Kelly became one of the chief weapons inspectors in Iraq on behalf of the United Nations Special Commission (UNSCOM) and from 1991 onwards was deeply involved in investigating the biological warfare programme of the Iraqi regime. These investigations resulted in 1995 in UNSCOM making a breakthrough and forcing the Iraqi regime to admit that it did have a biological warfare programme. During the 1990s Dr Kelly built up a high reputation as a weapons inspector, not only in the United Kingdom but internationally, and he was described in evidence by the journalist and author, Mr Tom Mangold, who knew him well, as the "inspector's

inspector". The contribution made by Dr Kelly and the importance of his work was recognised by the Government and in 1996 he was appointed Companion of the Order of St Michael and St George (C.M.G.), the material part of the citation for the award stating:

> ... he devised the scientific basis for the enhanced biological warfare defence programme and led strong research groups in many key areas. Following the Gulf War he led the first biological warfare inspection in Iraq and has spent most of his time since either in Iraq or at various sites in the former Soviet Union helping to shed light on past biological warfare related activities and assisting the UK/US RUS trilateral confidence building process. He has pursued this work tirelessly and with good humour despite the significant hardship, hostility and personal risk encountered during extended periods of service in both countries. In 1991 he was appointed adviser to the UN Special Commission (UNSCOM). His efforts in his specialist field have had consequences of international significance.

21. It appears that in May 2003 Dr Kelly was being considered for a further award (which might well have been a knighthood as he had already been awarded the C.M.G.) because a minute to Heads of Department in the FCO dated 9 May 2003 requested recommendations for the Diplomatic Service List and on 14 May an official wrote the following manuscript note on the minute:

> How about David Kelly? (Iraq being topical).

The Government's Dossier on Weapons of Mass Destruction

22. On 24 September 2002 the Government published a dossier entitled:

IRAQ'S

WEAPONS OF MASS

DESTRUCTION

THE ASSESSMENT OF THE BRITISH

GOVERNMENT

This dossier contained a foreword by the Prime Minister:

> The document published today is based, in large part, on the work of the Joint Intelligence Committee (JIC). The JIC is at the heart of the British intelligence machinery. It is chaired by the Cabinet Office and made up of the heads of the UK's three Intelligence and Security Agencies, the Chief of Defence Intelligence, and senior officials from key government departments. For over 60 years the JIC has provided regular assessments to successive Prime Ministers and senior colleagues on a wide range of foreign policy and international security issues.
>
> Its work, like the material it analyses, is largely secret. It is unprecedented for the Government to publish this kind of document. But in light of the debate about Iraq and Weapons of Mass Destruction (WMD), I wanted to share with the British public the reasons why I believe this issue to be a current and serious threat to the UK national interest.
>
> In recent months, I have been increasingly alarmed by the evidence from inside Iraq that despite sanctions, despite the damage done to his capability in the past, despite the UN Security Council's Resolutions expressly outlawing it, and despite his denials, Saddam Hussein is continuing to develop WMD, and with them the ability to inflict real damage upon the region, and the stability of the world.
>
> Gathering intelligence inside Iraq is not easy. Saddam's is one of the most secretive and dictatorial regimes in the world. So I believe people will understand why the Agencies cannot be specific about the sources, which have formed the judgments in this document, and why we cannot publish everything we know. We cannot, of course, publish the detailed raw intelligence. I and

other Ministers have been briefed in detail on the intelligence and are satisfied as to its authority. I also want to pay tribute to our Intelligence and Security Services for the often extraordinary work that they do.

What I believe the assessed intelligence has established beyond doubt is that Saddam has continued to produce chemical and biological weapons, that he continues in his efforts to develop nuclear weapons, and that he has been able to extend the range of his ballistic missile programme. I also believe that, as stated in the document, Saddam will now do his utmost to try to conceal his weapons from UN inspectors.

The picture presented to me by the JIC in recent months has become more not less worrying. It is clear that, despite sanctions, the policy of containment has not worked sufficiently well to prevent Saddam from developing these weapons.

I am in no doubt that the threat is serious and current, that he has made progress on WMD, and that he has to be stopped.

Saddam has used chemical weapons, not only against an enemy state, but against his own people. Intelligence reports make clear that he sees the building up of his WMD capability, and the belief overseas that he would use these weapons, as vital to his strategic interests, and in particular his goal of regional domination. And the document discloses that his military planning allows for some of the WMD to be ready within 45 minutes of an order to use them.

I am quite clear that Saddam will go to extreme lengths, indeed has already done so, to hide these weapons and avoid giving them up.

In today's inter-dependent world, a major regional conflict does not stay confined to the region in question. Faced with someone who has shown himself capable of using WMD, I believe the international community has to stand up for itself and ensure its authority is upheld.

The threat posed to international peace and security, when WMD are in the hands of a brutal and aggressive regime like Saddam's, is real. Unless we face up to the threat, not only do we risk undermining the authority of the UN, whose resolutions he defies, but more importantly and in the longer term, we place at risk the lives and prosperity of our own people.

The case I make is that the UN Resolutions demanding he stops his WMD programme are being flouted; that since the inspectors left four years ago he has continued with this programme; that the inspectors must be allowed back in to do their job properly; and that if he refuses, or if he makes it impossible for them to do their job, as he has done in the past, the international community will have to act.

I believe that faced with the information available to me, the UK Government has been right to support the demands that this issue be confronted and dealt with. We must ensure that he does not get to use the weapons he has, or get hold of the weapons he wants.

The Executive Summary stated:

4. As well as the public evidence, however, significant additional information is available to the Government from secret intelligence sources, described in more detail in this paper. This intelligence cannot tell us about everything. However, it provides a fuller picture of Iraqi plans and capabilities. It shows that Saddam Hussein attaches great importance to possessing weapons of mass destruction which he regards as the basis for Iraq's regional power. It shows that he does not regard them only as weapons of last resort. He is ready to use them, including against his own population, and is determined to retain them, in breach of United Nations Security Council Resolutions (UNSCR).

5. Intelligence also shows that Iraq is preparing plans to conceal evidence of these weapons, including incriminating documents, from renewed inspections. And it confirms that despite sanctions and the policy of containment, Saddam has continued to make progress with his illicit weapons programmes.

6. As a result of the intelligence we judge that Iraq has:

....

- military plans for the use of chemical and biological weapons, including against its own Shia population. Some of these weapons are deployable within 45 minutes of an order to use them.

Chapter 3 headed: "THE CURRENT POSITION: 1998-2002" stated:

1. This chapter sets out what we know of Saddam Hussein's chemical, biological, nuclear and ballistic missile programmes, drawing on all the available evidence. While it takes account of the results from UN inspections and other publicly available information, it also draws heavily on the latest intelligence about Iraqi efforts to develop their programmes and capabilities since 1998. The **main conclusions** are that:

....

- Iraq's military forces are able to use chemical and biological weapons, with command, control and logistical arrangements in place. The Iraqi military are able to deploy these weapons within forty five minutes of a decision to do so.

....

Recent intelligence

5. Subsequently, intelligence has become available from reliable sources which complements and adds to previous intelligence and confirms the JIC assessment that Iraq has chemical and biological weapons. The intelligence also shows that the Iraqi leadership has been discussing a number of issues related to these weapons. This intelligence covers:

....

- **Saddam's willingness to use chemical and biological weapons:** Intelligence indicates that as part of Iraq's military planning, Saddam is willing to use chemical and biological weapons, including against his own Shia population. Intelligence indicates that the Iraqi military are able to deploy chemical or biological weapons within forty five minutes of an order to do so.

The rules governing the disclosure of information by civil servants

23. The rules governing the disclosure of information by civil servants in the MoD are set out as follows in Volume 7 of the MoD Personnel Manual:

Section 6: **Disclosure of Information**

6.1 Principles governing disclosure of information

This section describes the principles governing the public disclosure of information by serving or former members of the Department and sets out the rules that apply those principles to specific cases. The activities governed by this section are:

public lectures and speeches, interviews with or communications to the press or other media, film, radio and television appearances and statements to non-Governmental bodies, including MOD-sponsored conferences and seminars; .....

You must not make comment on, or make disclosure of:

classified or "in confidence" information;

relations between civil servants and Ministers, and advice given to Ministers;

politically controversial issues; ......

information that would conflict with MOD interests .....

anything that the MOD would regard as objectionable about individuals or organisations;

24. Paragraph 10 of Annex A to the Civil Service Code states:

Civil servants should not without authority disclose official information which has been communicated in confidence within the Administration, or received in confidence from others. Nothing in the Code should be taken as overriding existing statutory or common law obligations to keep confidential, or to disclose, certain information. They should not seek to frustrate or influence the policies, decisions or actions of Ministers, Assembly Secretaries or the National Assembly as a body by the unauthorised, improper or premature disclosure outside the Administration of any information to which they have had access as civil servants.

25. The DSTL procedure for conduct rules (which say on the title page that DSTL is part of the MoD) state:

8.4 Media activities

8.4.1 It is important to dispel any impression, however unfounded, that there is a conflict of interest between a particular activity and the responsibilities of an employee. There is no exhaustive list of activities that fall into this category, but it is in everyone (sic) interest for individuals to seek approval before indulging in any such activity and to ensure that records are kept.

8.4.2 Examples of activities that may conflict with the responsibilities of employees are:

- press announcements (these should be referred to Head of Corporate Affairs);

- broadcasts and media interviews and public speaking (these should be referred to Head of Corporate Affairs);

- lecturing or speaking at conferences and seminars, especially on matters of political sensitivity. The procedure for public disclosure of Dstl official information is to be followed. Employees should not attend political conferences in their official capacity without prior permission from their Department Manager;

- completing external questionnaires (e.g. those asking for detailed information about the organisation). Any doubts should be referred to Head of Corporate Affairs;

- publishing books, writing papers for publication. Applications to publish are to be made on a completed Dstl application for permission to publish (Form 199 – reference 10).

26. One of Dr Kelly's roles in the course of his work was to speak to the media and institutions on Iraq issues and parts of his Performance and Development Assessment for the year April 2002 to March 2003 dated 12 April 2003 are as follows:

Statement of your roles and responsibilities:

Adviser to Proliferation Arms Control Secretariat, MOD and Non-proliferation Department, FCO on Iraq's chemical and biological weapons capabilities, UNMOVIC activities, and CWC/BWC issues. Adviser to DIS and SIS on Iraq.

Adviser to UNMOVIC on chemical biological weapons and inspector training.

Communicating Iraq issues to the media and Institutions

....

Objective	Communication of Iraq issues externally	Date & initial
Your comments	To continue making contributions to the deliberations of International Institutions and providing informed contributions to the international media and press.	
Managers' comments	David has lectured widely on Iraqi WMD issues, is much sought for attendance at international conferences and as appropriate has provided media briefings	

Annexed to Dr Kelly's Performance and Development Assessment for April 2002 to March 2003 was the following list of attendance at conferences and contacts with the media:

11th & 12th November 2002

Organization for the Prohibition of Chemical Weapons, The Hague, The Netherlands "Protection Network"

18th to 20th November 2002

International Institute for Strategic Studies, London: Conference "Iraq: Invasion or inspections" 31st January and 1st February 2003

Media

Attributable and unattributable briefings plus interviews on Iraq, Russia, Weapons, Anthrax and Smallpox.

Television & Radio: Channel Four, Australian Broadcasting Company, Canadian Broadcasting Company, Tokyo Broadcasting Systems, CNN, CBS, ABC, Radio Netherlands, BBC four, BBC 24hours/World Service, BBC local radio (London, Wales).

News Media: Guardian, Daily Telegraph, The Times, New York Times, Washington Post, Los Angeles Times, Newsweek, Herald Tribune, and Wall Street Journal.

27. On 10 October 2002 Sir Kevin Tebbit, the Permanent Under-Secretary of State at the MoD, sent a minute to senior officials in the MoD in relation to contacts with the media:

CONTACTS WITH THE MEDIA

For a number of reasons the MOD and the Armed Forces are likely to find themselves the subject of more than usual media interest over the next six months. We ought to be as open as we can in explaining what we are doing and why. Equally, there is some information which must remain confidential if the Department and the Armed Forces are properly to perform their functions. It would be timely to restate the basic principles.

2. First, there are clear rules about seeking approval for media interviews and other contacts which must be followed in all cases. These are set out in DCI 313/99. In particular, proposals for contact by 2 Star officers/officials and above must be approved by Ministers. It is the responsibility of the officers/officials concerned to ensure that DGCC and his staff and/or the Corporate Communications and Media Ops staff embedded in TLB areas are informed of proposed media contacts so that appropriate guidance and advice can be provided. Unless there are very good reasons otherwise, communications staff should be present during interviews.

3. Second, submissions to Ministers and others must include a section on presentation covering both external and internal audiences, that is drawn up in conjunction with DGCC staffs. In particular, it must be explicitly acknowledged in the advice that goes forward that D News (or DGCC himself) has been consulted and is content.

4. Finally, a reminder of what CDS and I stated on 12 June about unauthorised leaks to the media. These are counterproductive and damaging to the reputation of the MOD in the eyes of the public and other Government Departments. They are also unprofessional and corrosive of trust and morale. In addition to being disciplinary offences, they could also lead to prosecution after criminal investigation.

5. I look to DMB members, TLB Holders and all senior line managers to enforce these guidelines.

The Intelligence and Security Committee

28. The Intelligence and Security Committee (ISC), a Committee of Members of Parliament, in its Report of September 2003 described its functions as follows:

   i.   The Intelligence and Security Committee (ISC) is established under the Intelligence Services Act 1994 to examine the expenditure, administration and policy of the United Kingdom's three intelligence and security Agencies: the Security Service, the Secret Intelligence Service (SIS) and the Government Communications Headquarters (GCHQ). The Committee also takes evidence from the Security and Intelligence Co-ordinator, the Chairman of the Joint Intelligence Committee (JIC) and the Defence Intelligence Staff (DIS), as well as departments and other organisations that receive secret intelligence from the Agencies.

   ii. The Prime Minister, in consultation with the leaders of the two main opposition parties, appoints the ISC members. Nominations for the membership of the Committee are put forward by the Government and Opposition whips, in a broadly similar way to the nomination of select committee members.

   iii. The Committee reports directly to the Prime Minister and through him to Parliament by the publication of the Committee's Reports. The members are notified under the Official Secrets Act 1989 and, as such, operate within "the ring of secrecy". The Committee sees significant amounts of classified material in carrying out its duties and it takes evidence from Cabinet Ministers and senior officials – all of which is used to formulate its Reports.

   iv. When laying a Report before Parliament, the Prime Minister, in consultation with the Committee, excludes any parts of the Report (indicated by the *** in the text) that would be prejudicial to the continuing discharge of the functions of the three intelligence and security Agencies. To date, no material has been excluded without the Committee's consent.

   It appears from that Report that the ISC decided about the start of May 2003 to examine the intelligence relating to Iraq's Weapons of Mass Destruction (WMD) and paragraph 12 of its Report states:

   On 8 May 2003, the Committee Chairman, the Rt. Hon. Ann Taylor, MP, wrote to the Chairman of the JIC to request all the JIC Assessments relating to Iraq and its WMD dating back to August 1990 and supporting intelligence.

CHAPTER 2

Dr Kelly's discussions with Ms Susan Watts on 7 May 2003 and with Mr Andrew Gilligan on 22 May 2003

29. On 7 May 2003 Ms Susan Watts, the Science Editor of BBC Newsnight telephoned Dr Kelly and had a discussion with him about a number of matters relating to Iraq. Ms Watts' brief shorthand notes made in the course of the discussion record that Dr Kelly said to her in respect of the statement in the Government's dossier that chemical and biological weapons were deployable within 45 minutes of an order to use them:

> mistake to put in ….. A Campbell seeing something in there … NB single source … but not corroborated … sounded good

30. On 22 May 2003, by prior arrangement, Dr Kelly met Mr Andrew Gilligan, the defence and diplomatic correspondent of the Today programme on BBC Radio 4, in the Charing Cross Hotel, London, and had a discussion with him. I will return to this discussion in more detail in a later part of this report.

31. On the evening of 28 May Mr Gilligan telephoned Mrs Kate Wilson the chief press officer at the MoD and spoke to her about the Today programme to be broadcast the next morning. I will return to this telephone conversation in more detail in a later part of this report.

The BBC Today programme and the BBC Five Live Breakfast programme on 29 May 2003

32. On 29 May 2003 in the Today programme on BBC Radio 4 Mr Gilligan broadcast a number of reports relating to the dossier published by the Government on 24 September 2002. These reports were preceded at 6.00am by the following headlines read by Mr John Humphreys and Ms Corrie Corfield:

> JH: Tony Blair is going to Iraq today. There have been new accusations over the reasons for fighting the war….
>
> CC: Tony Blair will set foot on Iraqi soil today – just seven weeks after Saddam Hussein was swept from power. His visit comes amid continuing controversy about the likelihood of weapons of mass destruction being found. The US Defence Secretary, Donald Rumsfeld, has suggested that the weapons might have been destroyed before the fighting began. This report is from our political correspondent, John Pienaar ("JP"), who's travelling with the Prime Minister.
>
> JP: This morning, Tony Blair becomes the first Western leader to land in Iraq since the war, a symbolic appearance and one that will test his political skills as well as his flair for presentation. The visit is about thanking the troops and weighing up the task of reconstruction, according to Mr Blair, not triumphalism. Even so, he and his team will want to cultivate the images that will tell the tale of a liberated people. The problems and bitterness of the aftermath of war will be discussed behind the scenes in talks with British officials, Iraq civilians and the military. Today's visit will be brief. The business of

rebuilding Iraq, politically and economically, and the search for the elusive weapons of mass destruction, looks like continuing perhaps for rather longer than Mr Blair might have hoped.

CC: A senior official involved in preparing the Government's dossier on Iraqi weapons of mass destruction has told this programme that the document was rewritten just before publication – to make it more exciting. An assertion that some of the weapons could be activated within 45 minutes was among the claims added at a late stage. The official claimed that the intelligence services were unhappy with the changes, which he said were ordered by Downing Street.

At 6.07am the following was broadcast:

JH: The government is facing more questions this morning over its claims about weapons of mass destruction in Iraq. Our defence correspondent is Andrew Gilligan. This in particular Andy is Tony Blair saying, they'd be ready to go within forty five minutes.

Andrew Gilligan (AG): That's right, that was the central claim in his dossier which he published in September, the main erm, case if you like against er, against Iraq and the main statement of the British government's belief of what it thought Iraq was up to and what we've been told by one of the senior officials in charge of drawing up that dossier was that, actually the government probably erm, knew that that forty five minute figure was wrong, even before it decided to put it in. What this person says, is that a week before the publication date of the dossier, it was actually rather erm, a bland production. It didn't, the, the draft prepared for Mr Blair by the Intelligence Agencies actually didn't say very much more than was public knowledge already and erm, Downing Street, our source says ordered a week before publication, ordered it to be sexed up, to be made more exciting and ordered more facts to be er, to be discovered.

JH: When you say 'more facts to be discovered', does that suggest that they may not have been facts?

AG: Well, erm, our source says that the dossier, as it was finally published, made the Intelligence Services unhappy, erm, because, to quote erm the source he said, there was basically, that there was, there was, there was unhappiness because it didn't reflect, the considered view they were putting forward, that's a quote from our source and essentially, erm, the forty five minute point er, was, was probably the most important thing that was added. Erm, and the reason it hadn't been in the original draft was that it was, it was only erm, it only came from one source and most of the other claims were from two, and the intelligence agencies say they don't really believe it was necessarily true because they thought the person making the claim had actually made a mistake, it got, had got mixed up.

JH: Does any of this matter now, all this, all these months later? The war's been fought and won.

AG: Well the forty five minutes isn't just a detail, it did go to the heart of the government's case that Saddam was an imminent threat and it was repeated four times in the dossier, including by the Prime Minister himself, in the foreword; so I think it probably does matter. Clearly, you know, if erm, if it, if it was, if it was wrong, things do, things are, got wrong in good faith but if they knew it was wrong before they actually made the claim, that's perhaps a bit more serious.

JH: Andrew, many thanks; more about that later.

At 7.32am the following was broadcast:

JH: Twenty eight minutes to eight. Tony Blair had quite a job persuading the country and indeed his own MPs to support the invasion of Iraq; his main argument was that Saddam had weapons of mass destruction that threatened us all. None of those weapons has been found. Now our defence correspondent, Andrew Gilligan, has found evidence that the government's dossier on Iraq that was produced last September, was cobbled together at the last minute with some unconfirmed material that had not been approved by the

Security Services. Now you told us about this earlier on the programme Andy, and we've had a statement from 10 Downing Street that says it's not true, and let me just quote what they said to you. 'Not one word of the dossier was not entirely the work of the intelligence agencies'. Sorry to submit you to this sort of English but there we are. I think we know what they mean. Are you suggesting, let's be very clear about this, that it was not the work of the intelligence agencies.

AG: No, the information which I'm told was dubious did come from the agencies, but they were unhappy about it, because they didn't think it should have been in there. They thought it was, it was not corroborated sufficiently, and they actually thought it was wrong, they thought the informant concerned erm, had got it wrong, they thought he'd misunderstood what was happening.

I mean let's, let's go through this. This is the dossier that was published in September last year, erm, probably the most substantial statement of the government's case against Iraq. You'll remember that the Commons was recalled to debate it, Tony Blair made the opening speech. It is not the same as the famous dodgy dossier, the one that was copied off the internet, that came later. This is quite a serious document. It dominated the news that day and you open up the dossier and the first thing you see is a preface written by Tony Blair that includes the following words, 'Saddam's military planning allows for some weapons of mass destruction to be ready within forty five minutes of an order to deploy them'. Now that claim has come back to haunt Mr Blair because if the weapons had been that readily to hand, they probably would have been found by now. But you know, it could have been an honest mistake, but what I have been told is that the government knew that claim was questionable, even before the war, even before they wrote it in their dossier.

I have spoken to a British official who was involved in the preparation of the dossier, and he told me that until the week before it was published, the draft dossier produced by the Intelligence Services, added little to what was already publicly known. He said: 'It was transformed in the week before it was published, to make it sexier. The classic example was the statement that weapons of mass destruction were ready for use within forty five minutes. That information was not in the original draft. It was included in the dossier against our wishes, because it wasn't reliable. Most things in the dossier were double source, but, that was single source, and we believed that the source was wrong.

Now this official told us that the transformation of the dossier took place at the behest of Downing Street, and he added: 'Most people in intelligence weren't happy with the dossier, because it didn't reflect the considered view they were putting forward'. Now I want to stress that this official and others I've spoken to, do still believe that Iraq did have some sort of weapons of mass destruction programme. 'I believe it is about 30% likely there was a chemical weapons programme in the six months before the war and considerably more likely, that there was a biological weapons programme. We think Hans Blix down-played a couple of potentially interesting pieces of evidence, but the weapons programmes were small: sanctions did limit the programmes'.

The official also added quite an interesting note about what has happened as a result since the war, of the capture of some Iraqi WMD scientists: 'We don't have a great deal more information yet than we had before. We have not got very much out of the detainees yet.'

Now the forty five minutes really is, is not just a detail, it did go to the heart of the government's case that Saddam was an imminent threat, and it was repeated a further three times in the body of the dossier, and I understand that the parliamentary intelligence and security committee is going to conduct an enquiry in to the claims made by the British Government about Iraq, and it is obviously exactly this kind of issue that will be at the heart of their investigation.

JH: Andrew Gilligan, many thanks.

Later in the Today programme Mr Adam Ingram MP, the Armed Forces Minister, was interviewed by Mr John Humphreys and in the course of the interview Mr Humphreys put to him the following allegation:

Can I tell you what the allegation was because I think you may have been a little misled on that. The allegation was not that it was concocted by Number 10, the allegation was that a report was produced. It went to Number 10. It was then sent back to be sexed up a little, I'm using not my own words, but the words of our source, as you know. Now, given that, is it possible that …..

AI: Well it's not true that, that allegation.

JH: That isn't true.

AI: No, it's not true. And you know Number 10 has denied that.

33. Also on 29 May on BBC Radio 5 Live Breakfast programme at 7.50am Mr Gilligan broadcast a report relating to the September dossier in which he said:

Presenter (P): Good Morning.

A senior official involved in preparing the Government's dossier on Iraqi weapons of mass destruction has said the document was rewritten just before it was published to apparently "make it more exciting". The official said the intelligence services were unhappy with the changes. Let's talk to Andrew Gilligan our defence correspondent.

Hello Andrew.

Andrew Gilligan: Hello

P: This was the dossier published what, last September by the Government?

Andrew: That's right. This is not the famous "dodgy dossier" that was copied off the internet, that came later. This was a much more substantial effort. Parliament was recalled to discuss it. Tony Blair made the opening speech in Parliament, em and, and it dominated the news that day. It was, it's the most substantial statement of the Government's case against Iraq.

P: And what, according to the intelligence services were the problems with it?

Andrew: Well, the draft they originally produced they tell me was actually not terribly exciting, it didn't add very much to what we already knew publicly. What any, kind of anyone who'd followed the story would know publicly, and it didn't satisfy Downing Street and they said eh, look, you know, is there anything more this – can, can we make this a bit more exciting please.

Em, and er, they mentioned a few things which they weren't very happy with and at Downing Street's insistence those were written into the document and one of the main things that em, that they weren't very happy with was this claim that Iraq could deploy its biological and chemical weapons within 45 minutes.

Now we now (sic), we can be pretty sure now that that claim was actually wrong. Because if they could deploy within that short a time we'd have found the weapons by now, you know if they were that handy then they would have been more or less lying around er, and easily, easy for the troops to find in six weeks. Em, now, you know, what I thought to be honest was that that eh, that claim was wrong in good faith. Em, but er, what my intelligence service source says is that em essentially they were always suspicious about this claim, they did not want it to appear in the document, they did not put it in their original draft because em most of the assertions in the dossier were double sourced, this was only one source, and they didn't believe the source, they thought he had got mixed up. They thought he had got mixed up between the time it took to assemble a conventional er missile assembly and em aa and the idea that em Saddam had a er weapons of mass destruction missile assembly.

P: So, I mean the implications that the, that Downing Street asked for it to be hyped up to help convince the doubters.

Andrew: Yeah, and, and they're not very happy. I mean the actual quote from my source was "most people in intelligence weren't happy with the dossier because it didn't reflect the considered view they were putting forward" and it was a matter of language and nuance as much as em er as actual detail. But the 45 minutes was very important because it went to the heart of the Government's case that Saddam was an imminent threat.

P: Absolutely. But, fundamentally, the intelligence services did believe, did have intelligence that Iraq did have weapons of mass destruction.

Andrew: Yeah, they, they do believe that Iraq had a programme and what my source said was that he believed it was about 30% likely that there was a chemical weapons programme even in the six months before the war, and more likely considerably more likely, that there was a biological weapons programme. But he said the programmes they thought were small and not necessarily an imminent threat and sanctions did limit the programmes and, and eh, you know that, that the the issue is about tone and, er and nuance, ….[Presenter: hmmm] … … it really is as much as anything else and, and really had they said all that in, in the way they wanted to it wouldn't have been nearly as compelling a case.

P: And, and in a word, the intelligence services, do they still believe weapons of mass destruction will be found in Iraq at some point?

Andrew: They believe there were some. Em, their (sic) not sure what to believe now to be honest, because what they are saying is, em, you know, they were int…, they have been interrogating all these em, all these people that they have captured and, and they are not telling them very much.

P: Thank you very much Andrew.

Dr Kelly's discussions with Mr Gavin Hewitt on 29 May 2003 and with Ms Susan Watts on 30 May 2003

34.   On 29 May around 2pm London time Mr Gavin Hewitt, a special correspondent for BBC News, telephoned Dr Kelly who was in New York and had a telephone conversation with him in relation to matters in Iraq. In his evidence to the Inquiry Mr Hewitt described what Dr Kelly told him as follows:

[13 August, page 79, line 9]

we got straight on to the question of his kind of overall view of the dossier and very early on in the conversation—and these are his precise words. He said:"No. 10 spin came into play". I asked him what he meant by this and he elaborated and he said he felt the essential quality of the intelligence provided by the Intelligence Services was fundamentally reasonable. That is the phrase, "fundamental information reasonable"; but—and this is where his reservation came in—he felt that the dossier had been presented in a very black and white way. He expressed some caution about that. I think he would have liked more caveats. I think he would have been comfortable, from what he said, that it would have been more measured, in his view. He then went on to give me his views about weapons of mass destruction and he was clear, throughout this fairly brief conversation, he believed that weapons of mass destruction did exist in Iraq, but he did not feel that they constituted a major threat and he felt that even if they were found they would not be found as a massive arsenal.

35.   On 29 May on BBC Television 10pm News Mr Hewitt broadcast the following report in relation to the September dossier:

This is really a story about trust. It begins here at MI6, the headquarters of the intelligence service. Some of those who work here are said to be uneasy about what the government did with information they passed on about Iraq. There were claims today that when Downing Street received the dossier it wanted it toughened up. When it was eventually published it did contain some dramatic warnings…..

The government acknowledged today that the forty five minute threat was based on a single source, it wasn't corroborated. This has rattled some MPs who are calling for an investigation…..

The government said today that every word within the dossier was the work of the security services. There had been no pressure from Number 10…..

But others with experience in the intelligence community say there were some murmurings about the final wording of a dossier……

I have spoken to one of those who was consulted on the dossier. Six months work was apparently involved. But in the final week before publication, some material was taken out, some material put in. His judgment, some spin from Number Ten did come into play. Even so the intelligence community remains convinced weapons of mass destruction will be found in Iraq. Only then will all the doubts go away.

The entirety of what was said in the 10pm news in relation to the September dossier is set out in appendix 2.

36. On 30 May 2003 Ms Susan Watts contacted Dr Kelly and had a lengthy telephone conversation with him which she recorded on a tape recorder and I am satisfied that she made an accurate transcript of that conversation. Part of that transcript is as follows:

SW: OK, um While I'm sure since you've been in New York I don't know whether you've been following the kind of the rumpus that's erupted over here over the … spat between the intelligence service and the umm…

DK: I guessed something was up – I read the Times this am and I could see there was something there and I think this follows on from what was happening in the states with Rumsfeld's comments.

SW: yes it's partly prompted by Rumsfeld – two statements by Rumsfeld – the first one saying that it was "possible" the weapons were destroyed before the war started and then he went on I think in another speech yesterday to say that the use of the argument on the position on WMD was for bureaucratic reasons rather than being the prime motive for the war, which is a rather vague statement.

DK: yes

SW: But what intrigued me and which made, prompted me to ring you, (huh) was the quotes yesterday on the Today programme about the 45 minutes part of the dossier.

DK: yep. We spoke about this before of course….

SW: We have

DK: I think you know my views on that.

SW: Yes, I've looked back at my notes and you were actually quite specific at that time – I may have missed a trick on that one, but err

(both laugh)

SW: you were more specific than the source on the Today programme – not that that necessarily means that it's not one and the same person … but, um in fact you actually referred to Alastair Campbell in that conversation….

DK: err yep yep …. with you?…

SW: yes

DK: I mean I did talk to Gavin Hewitt yesterday – he phoned me in New York, so he may have picked up on what I said … because I would have said exactly the same as I said to you….

SW: Yes, so he presumably decided not to name Alastair Campbell himself but just to label this as Number 10….

DK: yep yep

SW: are you getting much flak over that?

DK: me? No, not yet anyway I was in New York… (laughs)

SW: yes good timing I suppose

16

DK: I mean they wouldn't think it was me, I don't think. Maybe they would, maybe they wouldn't. I don't know.

SW: um so is that the only item in the report that you had concerns over being single-sourced rather than double-sourced?

DK: You have to remember I'm not part of the intelligence community – I'm a user of intelligence … of course I'm very familiar with a lot of it, that's why I'm asked to comment on it … but I'm not deeply embedded into that …xxx… So some of it I really can't comment because I don't know whether it's single-sourced or not

SW: but on the 45 minutes

DK: oh that I knew because I knew the concern about the statement … it was a statement that was made and it just got out of all proportion … you know someone … They were desperate for information … they were pushing hard for information which could be released .. that was one that popped up and it was seized on … and it was unfortunate that it was … which is why there is the argument between the intelligence services and cabinet office/number ten, because things were picked up on, and once they've picked up on it you can't pull it back, that's the problem…

SW: but it was against your advice that they should publish it?

DK: I wouldn't go as strongly as to say … that particular bit, because I was not involved in the assessment of it … no… I can't say that it was against MY advice … I was uneasy with it … I mean my problem was I could give other explanations … which I've indicated to you … that it was the time to erect something like a scud missile or it was the time to fill a 40 barrel, multi-barrel rocket launcher

…. (Next 5 words physically removed from tape … not present on Monday 14/7/03 …. assume due to rubbing as tape constantly re-wound)

…("all sorts of reasons why") 45 minutes might well be important and … I mean I have no idea who de-briefed this guy quite often it's someone who has no idea of the topic and the information comes through and people then use it as they see fit ….

SW: so it wasn't as if there were lots of people saying don't put it in don't put it in … it's just it was in there and was seized upon … rather than number ten specifically going against …?

DK: there were lots of people saying that – I mean it was an interesting week before the dossier was put out because there were so many things in there that people were saying well… we're not so sure about that, or in fact they were happy with it being in but not expressed the way that it was, because you know the word-smithing is actually quite important and the intelligence community are a pretty cautious lot on the whole but once you get people putting it/presenting it for public consumption then of course they use different words. I don't think they're being wilfully dishonest I think they just think that that's the way the public will appreciate it best. I'm sure you have the same problem as a journalist don't you, sometimes you've got to put things into words that the public will understand.

SW: simple

DK: in your heart of hearts you must realise sometimes that's not actually the right thing to say… but it's the only way you can put it over if you've got to get it over in two minutes or three minutes

SW: did you actually write that section which refers to the 45 minutes Or was it somebody else?

DK: errr. I didn't write THAT section, no. I mean I reviewed the whole thing, I was involved with the whole process … In the end it was just a flurry of activity and it was very difficult to get comments in because people at the top of the ladder didn't want to hear some of the things

SW: so you expressed your unease about it? Put it that way

DK: errr well… yes yep yes

SW: so how do you feel now number ten is furiously denying it and Alastair Campbell specifically saying it's all nonsense it was all in the intelligence material?

DK: well I think it's matter of perception isn't it. I think people will perceive things and they'll be, how shall I put it, they'll see it from their own standpoint and they may not even appreciate quite what they were doing

SW: do you think there ought to be a security and intelligence committee inquiry?

DK: yes but not now. I think that has to be done in about six months time when we actually have come to the end of the evaluation of Iraq and the information that is going to come out of it. I still think it's far too early to be talking about the intelligence that is there … a lot of intelligence that would appear to be good quality intelligence, some of which is not and it take a long long time to get the information that's required from Iraq. The process has only just started. I think one of the problems with dossier – and again I think you and I have talked about it in the past is that it was presented in a very black and white way without any sort of quantitative aspects of it. The only quantitative aspects were the figures derived essentially from UNSCOM figures, which in turn are Iraq's figures presented to UNSCOM – you know the xxx litres anthrax, the 4 tonnes VX – all of that actually is Iraqi figures – but there was nothing else in there that was quantitative or even remotely qualitative – I mean it was just a black and white thing – they have weapons or they don't have weapons. That in turn has been interpreted as being a vast arsenal and I'm not sure any of us ever said that …. people have said to me that that was what was implied, Again we discussed it… and I discussed it with many people, that my own perception is that yes they have weapons but actually not xzxxxx (xxx not problem) at this point in time. The PROBLEM was that one could anticipate that without any form of inspection, and that forms a real deterrence, other than the sanctions side of things, then that that would develop. I think that was the real concern that everyone had, it was not so much what they have now but what they would have in the future. But that unfortunately wasn't expressed strongly in the dossier because that takes away the case for war … (I cough) to a certain extent

SW: a clear and present, imminent threat?

DK: yes

....

SW: ok… just back momentarily on the 45 minute issue … I'm feeling like I ought to just explore that a little bit more with you … the um… err So would it be accurate then, as you did in that earlier conversation, to say that it was Alastair Campbell himself who…?

DK: No I can't. All I can say is the Number Ten press office. I've never met Alastair Campbell so I can't … (SW interrupts: they seized on that?) But … I think Alastair Campbell is synonymous with that press office because he's responsible for it.

The entire transcript of this telephone conversation is set out in appendix 3.

Further broadcasts and Mr Gilligan's article in the Mail on Sunday

37. On 31 May 2003 on the Today programme Mr Gilligan broadcast the following report which was introduced as "The Andrew Gilligan Essay":

In show biz they say you should never work with children or animals. In politics, may be the rule should be never work with children, animals or dossiers.

On Iraq, Tony Blair has issued three and they've all been questioned. The one on Saddam's security apparatus, famously largely copied of (sic) the internet. The one criticising Iraq's human rights record, which achieved the unusual feat for something on that subject of being attacked by Amnesty International. But it's the first, and the most substantial of the dossiers that's now, potentially, the most troublesome.

The first mention of it was on the 25th February 2002. A BBC poll had shown that 86 out [of] 100 Labour backbenchers didn't think there was enough evidence of the threat posed by Saddam. The dossier would, it was promised, provide that evidence. It was written during March; publication was promised for the end of the month but was shelved. The Government said it didn't want to alarm people. The papers said that it was because the dossier wasn't alarming enough. The BBC's intelligence and technical sources agreed. They told us that it didn't add much to what any well-informed layman already knew.

'What you have to understand is that 10 to 15 years ago, there was a lot of information. With a concealment and deception operation by the Iraqis, there's far less material.'

Other media heard the same. On August 29th, senior Whitehall sources told Michael Evans, Defence Editor of the Times, that the dossier was 'not revelatory'. On September 2nd, a Whitehall source told Richard Norton-Taylor, Security Editor of the Guardian: 'The dossier will no longer play a role. There's very little new to put in it.'

The very next morning, however, Mr Blair announced that the dossier would after all be published, and it was, on September 24th. By that day, the dossier, described as unrevelatory only 4 weeks before, had suddenly become very revelatory indeed. A senior figure involved in compiling it, told this programme two days ago that Downing Street had applied pressure to make it sexier. This quote from a British official appeared in yesterday's Washington Post:

'They were pressured and super-heated debates between Downing Street officials and intelligence officials over the contents of the dossier.'

The Prime Minister and his staff have spent the last two days denying claims that nobody has actually ever made, such as that material from the dossier was invented; that it came from sources other than the intelligence agencies; and that Downing Street wrote the dossier. They have, however, failed to deny several of the claims which the BBC source did make. There's been no denial of his allegation that the dossier was re-written the week before publication, nor has there been any denial that the line about Iraq's 45 minute deployment of biological weapons was added to the dossier at a late stage. When we put both these questions to Downing Street, they replied that they refused to discuss processology.

On both sides of the Atlantic, relations between intelligence professionals and their political masters are at a low ebb. In Washington, retired spies have written to President Bush saying the American public was misled. In Britain we've now seen two unprecedented intelligence leaks, directly challenging the Prime Minister. Time, perhaps, to take stock.

38. On 1 June 2003 The Mail on Sunday published an article written by Mr Gilligan. The first two columns of the first page of the article carried a photograph of Mr Alastair Campbell (the Prime Minister's Director of Communications) with a smaller photograph of Mr Gilligan below with the words in the nature of a headline:

I asked my intelligence source why Blair misled us all over Saddam's WMD. His response? One word … CAMPBELL

39. In the article Mr Gilligan wrote (inter alia):

The location was a central London hotel and the source was waiting as I got there. We'd both been too busy to meet for nearly a year, but there was no sign this would be anything more than a routine get-together.

We started off by moaning about the railways. Only after about half-an-hour did the story emerge that would dominate the headlines for 48 hours, ruin Tony Blair's Basra awayday and work the Prime Minister into a state of controlled fury.

The source agreed with Blair about one thing. He, too, was adamant that Iraq had had a Weapons of Mass Destruction programme in the recent past. He pointed out some tell-tale signs that the chief UN weapons inspector, Hans Blix, seemed to have missed. But he knew, better than anyone, that it didn't amount to the 'imminent threat' touted by Ministers.

And he was gently despairing about the way No.10 had spoiled its case by exaggeration. 'Typical Downing Street', he said, half smiling, half annoyed.

We'd discussed the famous Blair dossier on Iraq's weapons at our previous meeting, a few months before it was published last September. 'It's really not very exciting, you know,' he'd told me. So what, I asked him now, had changed?

'Nothing changed', he said. 'Until the week before, it was just like I told you. It was transformed the week before publication, to make it sexier.'

What do you mean? Can I take notes? 'The classic', he said 'was the statement that WMD were ready for use in 45 minutes. One source said it took 45 minutes to launch a missile and that was misinterpreted to mean that WMD could be deployed in 45 minutes. There was no evidence that they had loaded conventional missiles with WMD, or could do so anything like that quickly.'

I asked him how this transformation happened. The answer was a single word. 'Campbell'.

What? Campbell made it up? 'No, it was real information. But it was included against our wishes because it wasn't reliable.'

40. On 2 June 2003 in the BBC Newsnight programme at 10.30pm Ms Susan Watts broadcast a report in relation to the September dossier. The transcript of the relevant part of the Newsnight programme is as follows:

SW:

Over the weekend the storm over the missing weapons of mass destruction focused down on one key point: was the British public duped over the urgency of dealing with Iraq's banned weapons? The government's claim that Saddam could mobilise these within forty five minutes is already looking shaky, but on the Today programme this morning the Foreign Secretary, Jack Straw, suggested it had never been a key part of the argument.

JACK STRAW:

If you look at for example the key speech that the Prime Minister made on the 18th of March before the House of Commons, from my quick re-reading of it this morning, I can for example find no reference to this now famous forty five minutes.

SW:

But the reference to forty five minutes was there in the Prime Minister's speech to the Commons on the day he published his famous weapons dossier.

TONY BLAIR:

It concludes that Iraq has chemical and biological weapons, that Saddam has continued to produce them, that he has existing and active military plans for the use of chemical and biological weapons, which could be activated within forty five minutes including against his own Shia population.

SW:

And it features in the dossier itself four times, notably in the Prime Minister's forward and the executive summary.

SW:

Today, at the GH (sic) summit in Evian, Tony Blair once again found himself in rebuttal mode.

TONY BLAIR: The idea that we doctored such intelligence is completely and totally false, every single piece of intelligence that we presented was cleared very properly by the Joint Intelligence Committee.

SW:

It's a surprising claim to make given that it encompasses the other so called dodgy dossier, part of which was plagiarised, and in any case today Tony Blair appeared irritated that the weapons issue won't go away.

TONY BLAIR:

I think it is important that if people actually have evidence, they produce it, but it is wrong frankly for people to make allegations on the basis of so called anonymous sources when the facts are precisely the facts that we've stated.

SW:

But in some cases anonymous sources could be the only way to gain an insight into the intelligence world. We've spoken to a senior official intimately involved with the process of pulling together the original September 2002 Blair weapons' dossier. We cannot name this person because their livelihood depends on anonymity. Our source made clear that in the run up to publishing the dossier the government was obsessed with finding intelligence on immediate Iraqi threats and the government's insistence the Iraqi threat was imminent was a Downing Street interpretation of intelligence conclusions. His point is that, while the intelligence community was agreed on the potential Iraqi threat in the future, there was less agreement about the threat the Iraqis posed at that moment. Our source said:

SOURCE:

That was the real concern, not so much what they had now but what they would have in the future, but that unfortunately was not expressed strongly in the dossier, because that takes away the case for war to a certain extent. But in the end it was just a flurry of activity and it was very difficult to get comments in because people at the top of the ladder didn't want to hear some of the things.

SW:

Our source talks of a febrile atmosphere in the days of diplomacy leading to the big Commons debate of September last year; of the government seizing on anything useful to the case, including the possibly (sic) existence of weapons that could be ready within forty five minutes.

SOURCE:

It was a statement that was made it just got out of all proportion. They were desperate for information, they were pushing hard for information that could be released. That was one that popped up and it was seized on, and it's unfortunate that it was. That's why there is the argument between the intelligence services and Cabinet Office number 10, because they picked up on it, and once they've picked up on it you can't pull it back from them.

SW:

And again, specifically on the forty five minute point:

SOURCE:

It was in (sic) interesting week before the dossier was put out because there were so many people saying 'well I'm not so sure about that', or in fact they were happy with it being in, but not expressed the way that it was, because the word-smithing is actually quite important. The intelligence community are a pretty cautious lot on the whole but once you get people presenting it for public consumption then of course they use different words.

SW:

The problem is that the forty five minutes point was not corroborated. For sceptics it highlights the dangers of relying too heavily on information from defectors. Journalists in America are being accused of running propaganda from the Iraqi National Congress.

The Foreign Affairs Select Committee and MoD concern about leaks to the press

41. The Foreign Affairs Select Committee (FAC) is a Committee of Members of Parliament appointed by the House of Commons to examine the expenditure, administration and policy of the FCO and its associated public bodies. On 3 June 2003 the FAC announced that it would hold an inquiry into "The Decision to go to War in Iraq". The announcement stated:

> The inquiry will consider whether the Foreign and Commonwealth Office, within the Government as a whole, presented accurate and complete information to Parliament in the period leading up to military action in Iraq, particularly in relation to Iraq's weapons of mass destruction. The Committee will hear oral evidence from several witnesses in June and will report to the House in July.

In his evidence Mr Donald Anderson MP, the Chairman of the FAC, stated that Mr Gilligan's "revelations" in the Today programme were part of the context in which the Committee's decision to hold an inquiry was taken.

42. On 4 June 2003 Sir Kevin Tebbit wrote to the Chief of Defence Intelligence about the intense level of concern in respect of leaks or unauthorised statements made to journalists by members of the intelligence services or those close to them:

> **WMD: LEAKS**
>
> We spoke about this in the margins of the COS meeting this morning. There is clearly an intense level of high level concern about leaks or unauthorised statements made to journalists by members of the intelligence services or those close to them. While I have no reason to suspect anyone from the DIS, it is important that we do all we can to be satisfied that this is the case, and to remind staff of their professional obligations.
>
> 2. I discussed this with Sir David Omand last night and would be grateful if you could ensure that the following action is taken:
>
> - a notice to all staff (however discreetly handled) to report to you any suspicions as to the identity of any leaker. Of particular concern will be anyone known to be unhappy about the use made of the intelligence about '45 minute' WMD readiness. Please report any findings to me in the first instance;
>
> - any information we have about particular known contacts in the MOD;
>
> - a reminder to staff of the need to observe confidentiality in line with their professional obligations and to report any concerns about the use of intelligence to the management/command chain only;
>
> 3. I stress that I do not have any specific suspicions of the DIS. The information in the press is so generalised that it could have come from a much wider group, beyond DIS and the Agencies. For that reason, neither Sir David Omand nor I believe a formal leak inquiry is indicated, certainly at this stage. But we need to do all we can to investigate and tighten up.
>
> 4. As we discussed, DCDI may be the best person to handle this, particularly given Martin Howard's past experience as DGCC.

A further broadcast by Ms Susan Watts

43. On 4 June 2003 in the BBC Newsnight programme at 10.30pm Ms Susan Watts broadcast a further report relating to the September dossier. The transcript of the relevant part of the programme is as follows:

> SW:
>
> The questions for any inquiry are piling up. First, how sound was the Government's assertion that Saddam could launch banned weapons at 45 minutes' notice. The issue dominated today's debate. Tony Blair flatly denied that the 45-minute claim had unsettled the intelligence services.

TONY BLAIR

The claim about 45 minutes provoked disquiet amongst the intelligence community who disagreed with its inclusion in the dossier. Again, this is something I've discussed again with the chairman of the Joint Intelligence Committee. That allegation also is completely and totally untrue.

SW

But a source we've spoken to, a senior official intimately involved with the process of pulling together the original weapons dossier in which the claim was made, told us that he and others felt considerable discomfort over it.

ACTOR'S VOICE

I was uneasy with it. My problem was I could give other explanations which I've indicated to you, that it was the time to erect something like a Scud missile or it's the time to full a multi-barrel rocket launcher. All sorts of reasons why 45 minutes might well be important.

SW

In other words he is saying that Saddam might have rocket hardware that takes 45 minutes to assemble but not necessarily the weapons of mass destruction to which Tony Blair referred in his weapons dossier, when he said of Saddam: The document discloses that his military planning allows for some of the WMD to be ready within 45 minutes of an order to use them. The Prime Minister appeared to want to shift the focus of the argument, moving away from how the 45 minute claim was used to who put it in the weapons dossier.

TONY BLAIR

.... including the judgment about the so-called 45 minutes was a judgment made by the Joint Intelligence Committee and by them alone.

SW

Our source was not disputing that the 45-minute assessment was included in the dossier by the intelligence services although he did say he felt that to have been a mistake. His point was that the emphasis placed on that element of the intelligence in the foreword to the dossier went too far. He felt this emphasis turned a possible capability into an imminent threat and a critical part of the Government's case for war. Our source cannot be described as a rogue element. On the contrary, he is exceptionally well placed to judge the prevailing mood as the dossier of September last year was put together.

The evidence of Mr Andrew Gilligan and Mr Alastair Campbell to the FAC

44. On 19 June 2003 Mr Gilligan gave evidence to the FAC in relation to his reports in respect of the dossier on the Today programme on 29 May 2003. In his evidence he stated that these reports were based on a single source but he did not identify this source.

45. On 25 June Mr Alastair Campbell gave evidence in relation to the September dossier to the FAC. In the course of his evidence he said that it was untrue for the BBC to allege that the Prime Minister took the country into military conflict on the basis of a lie and he further said:

...the story that I "sexed up" the dossier is untrue: the story that I "put pressure on the intelligence agencies" is untrue: the story that we somehow made more of the 45 minute command and control point than the intelligence agencies thought was suitable is untrue.

CHAPTER 3

Dr Kelly's letter of 30 June 2003 to the MoD and the MoD interview with Dr Kelly on 4 July 2003

46. On 30 June 2003 Dr Kelly wrote a letter to Dr Bryan Wells, his line manager in the MoD. Dr Wells held the post of Director of Counter Proliferation and Arms Control in the MoD. The letter was received by Dr Wells in the late afternoon of 1 July. The letter was as follows:

Andrew Gilligan and his single anonymous source

Over the past month controversy has raged over the September 2002 Iraq WMD Dossier primarily because Andrew Gilligan of the BBC has claimed that the dossier was "sexed up" at the behest of Alastair Campbell the Prime Minister's press officer.

Andrew Gilligan is a journalist that I know and have met.

As you know I have been involved in writing three "dossiers" concerning Iraq – the 1999 UNSCOM/Butler Status of Verification Report, the September 2002 International Institute of Strategic Studies "Iraq WMD" report, and the UK Government "Iraq's Weapons of Mass Destruction". My contributions to the latter were in part 2 (History of UN Inspections) and part 1 chapter 2 (Iraq's programmes 1971-1998) at the behest of the FCO and I was not involved in the intelligence component in any way nor in the process of the dossier's compilation. I have not acknowledged to anyone outside FCO my contribution to any [of] these reports although it is easy to assume and conclude that I made contributions because of my substantial role in elucidating Iraq's biological weapons programme. I am not a member of the intelligence community although I interact with that community and I am essentially, as an inspector, a consumer of intelligence not a generator of intelligence.

The contents of both IISS and UK Government dossiers, which both rely heavily on the 1999 Butler report, I have discussed with many individuals drawn from the UN, "Think Tanks" academia, the arms control community, together with the media. My discussions have been entirely technical and factual and although the "45 minute deployment" issue has obviously been raised I have always given the honest answer that I do not know what it refers to and that I am not familiar with an Iraqi weapons system that it matches. The latter is of significance to the UN since they had to take it into account in their work. The UK Dossier was of general interest for about ten days after publication and, with the exception of UNMOVIC, was not a topic later raised with me. After that my discussions about Iraq's WMD centred on UNMOVIC's re-engagement with Iraq, the "enhanced" inspection process and UNVMOVIC's findings. Since the war I have discussed with some of those same individuals the failure to use chemical and biological weapons by Iraq and the apparent lack of success in finding such weapons after the war. It is natural to do so since I am one of the few who knows Iraq's programmes in detail and my information is derived from my United Nations work.

I have not had extensive dealings with Andrew Gilligan. As I recall I first met him at the IISS "Global Strategic Review" in September 2002 after the IISS dossier was published but before the UK Government dossier appeared. We would have discussed the IISS dossier since it was at the forefront of delegates discussions but the detail is now forgotten. I cannot recall meeting him before that although it is entirely possible that we have attended the same meetings at Chatham House or IISS. I next met with him in February 2003 at his request because he was about to depart to Iraq to cover the forthcoming war. I cannot recall any contact in the interim and do not believe that contact was made. It is some time since that meeting but I believe that we covered the topics of Hans Blix and UNMOVIC inspections, Iraqi individuals associated with the WMD programmes and sites associated with the programme. I also spoke separately with Linsey Hilsum (Channel 4), Carolyn Hawley and Jane Corbin (BBC) about the same issues before they went to Iraq. Gilligan said that he would informally tell me about his experiences in Iraq on his return (as did Jane Corbin). I have spoken to both since the war. I have had a number of telephone exchanges with Jane Corbin principally because she is keen to do a follow up to her UNMOVIC "fly on the wall" with the Iraq Survey Group (and my comments to her have been neutral) but none with Gilligan other than one made by him to arrange to meet to discuss his experience in Iraq. I also speak irregularly with Susan Watts the BBC Science Editor and Andrew Veitch the Channel Four Science Editor about scientific and technical aspects of Iraq's weapons and UN inspections.

I met with Gilligan in London on May 22nd for 45 minutes in the evening to privately discuss his Iraq experiences and definitely not to discuss the dossier (I would not have met with him had it been the case). As I recall, we discussed his ability to report before, during, and after the war in the presence of minders and freedom to move around Baghdad; accommodation at the Palestine Hotel; his impression of the coalition attacks; US military protection of journalists; the revelations likely to be made by Amer Al-Sa'adi, Huda Amash, Rihab Taha, Tariq Aziz and Ahmed Murtadda who are individuals associated with Iraq's "past" programme. He was particularly intrigued by Huda since he visited her home and met her husband but not Huda after the war and found her home guarded by "regime" Iraqis. We also discussed the failure of Iraq to use WMD and the inability to find them. I offered my usual and standard explanations (conditions early in the war not favourable to CB use and lack of command and control late in the war; that the small arsenal of weapons (or its destroyed remnants) compared to 1991 would be difficult to find without human information). The issue of 45 minutes arose in terms of the threat (aerial versus land launch) and I stated that I did not know what it refers to (which I do not). He asked why it should be in the dossier and I replied probably for impact. He raised the issue of Alastair Campbell and since I was not involved in the process (not stated by me) I was unable to comment. This issue was not discussed at any length and was essentially an aside. I made no allegations or accusations about any issue related to the dossier or the Government's case for war concentrating on his account of his stay in Iraq. I did not discuss the "immediacy" of the threat. The discussion was not about the dossier. Had it been so then I would have indicated that from my extensive and authoritative knowledge of Iraq's WMD programme, notably its biological programme, that the dossier was a fair reflection of open source information (ie UNSCOM/UNMOVIC) and appreciations.

I most certainly have never attempted to undermine Government policy in any way especially since I was personally sympathetic to the war because I recognised from a decade's work the menace of Iraq's ability to further develop its non-conventional weapons programmes.

I have had no further contact with Andrew Gilligan since May 22nd.

I did not even consider that I was the "source" of Gilligan's information until a friend in RUSI said that I should look at the "Oral Evidence provided to the Foreign Affairs Committee" on 19th June because she recognised that some comments were the sort that I would make about Iraq's chemical and biological capacity. The description of that meeting in small part matches my interaction with him especially my personal evaluation of Iraq's capability but the overall character is quite different. I can only conclude one of three things. Gilligan has considerably embellished my meeting with him; he has met with other individuals who truly were intimately associated with the dossier; or he has assembled comments from both multiple direct and indirect sources for his articles.

I should explain my "unusual" interaction with the media. In August 1991 I led the first biological weapons inspection in Iraq. I had no media exposure before that although anticipating that it would be inevitable I attended at my request the MOD Senior Officers TV course at Wilton Park which served to make me aware of some of the pitfalls of journalism. During and after the first inspection as Chief Inspector I conducted a number of major press conferences including the internationally covered midday press briefing at UN Headquarters in New York. That meant that the media were very much aware of me thereafter. Over the next ten years I undertook at the request of MOD, FCO, CBD Porton Down, and the (sic) especially the UN press office and UNSCOM/ UNMOVIC press officer both attributable interviews and occasionally unattributable briefings. All such interactions were cleared by the appropriate authority. As my contact details became known it became inevitable that direct approaches were made and I used my discretion as [to] whether I provided information. My interaction with the media helped keep the issue of Iraq's WMD a live issue. I interact with the media on four issues – Iraq, Soviet/Russian biological warfare, smallpox and anthrax. If it was technical information available from open sources (and nearly all requests were such) then I provided details or more realistically a clarification and explanation of that information (I tend to be a human archive on Iraq's chemical and biological programmes). If it was about individuals (Iraqi or UN) I would comment only on their role and not their personality. Comment on other matters were declined although in the case of Iraq it is impossible to draw a clear distinction between the truly technical and Iraq's political concealment.

I have appeared on many British and foreign television programmes including Today, Panorama, Channel 4 News, Newsnight, ABC, CBS sixty minutes, CNN etc. and I continue to get requests to do so. Since September 11th I no longer talk to camera about Iraq and rarely on other issues. All media requests are referred to James Paver of the FCO Press Office and most are now discouraged from approaching him by my stating that I doubted that it would be possible.

I have never served as a designated spokesperson for any organisation, never initiated the release of information on behalf of any organisation, and never discussed a JIC report. I have never contacted any journalist to claim that a newspaper report was correct (or incorrect). I have never made a claim as to the timing of when any part of the dossier was included. I have never acted as a conduit to release or leak information. I have never discussed classified information with anyone other than those cleared so to do. I do not feel "deep unease" over the dossier because it is completely coincident with my personal views on Iraq's unconventional weapons capability.

With hindsight I of course deeply regret talking to Andrew Gilligan even though I am convinced that I am not his primary source of information. At the time of considerable disarray in Iraq I was eager to gain whatever first hand information I could about the circumstances in Iraq and individuals associated with Iraq's WMD programme. I anticipated, incorrectly, that I would shortly return to Iraq to debrief some of those individuals and this is why I have spoken to some journalists who have also interacted with them recently.

I hope this letter helps unravel at least a small part of the "45 minute story". It was a difficult decision to make to write to you because I realise that suspicion falls on me because of my long association with Iraq's WMD programme investigation and the acknowledgement that I know Andrew Gilligan. I can only repeat that I do not believe that I am the single source referred to and that much of the information attributed to that source I am completely unsighted on and would not be able to provide informed comment about.

Communications and discussions within the Government in respect of Dr Kelly, 2 to 6 July

47. On 2 July Dr Wells wrote to Mr Martin Howard, the Deputy Chief of Defence Intelligence:

DR DAVID KELLY

You will wish to be aware of the attached letter that David Kelly has sent me. I am planning to speak to David about it on the afternoon of 4 July, and would welcome the opportunity to discuss with you beforehand. You may wish to pass a copy to the leak inquiry personnel.

48. Mr Howard received Dr Wells' letter on 3 July and he informed Sir Kevin Tebbit of Dr Wells' letter and of Dr Wells' intention to speak to Dr Kelly on the afternoon of 4 July. Sir Kevin then decided that Dr Kelly should be interviewed by Mr Richard Hatfield, the Personnel Director of the MoD together with Dr Wells. Sir Kevin also informed the Secretary of State for Defence, Mr Geoffrey Hoon MP,

that an official, whom he did not name, had admitted speaking to Mr Gilligan and that he would be interviewed the next day.

49. On 4 July Mr Hatfield interviewed Dr Kelly at 11.30am and Dr Wells also attended the interview. On 7 July Mr Hatfield prepared a note of the interview. The note was as follows:

NOTE OF INTERVIEW WITH DR DAVID KELLY

I interviewed Dr Kelly about his letter dated 30 June to his line manager, Dr Bryan Wells, at 11.30 on Friday 4 July. Dr Wells was present. The interview ended at approximately 13:15.

I began by explaining to Dr Kelly that his letter had serious implications. First, on the basis of his own account, it appeared that he breached the normal standards of Civil Service behaviour and departmental regulations by having had a number of unauthorised and unreported contacts with journalists. Regardless of the detail of what had passed, this opened up the possibility of disciplinary action. Second, his unauthorised discussion with Andrew Gilligan on 22 May appeared to be directly relevant to the controversy surrounding allegations made by Gilligan about the government's WMD dossier even if, as he had said in his letter, this had not been the discussion described by Gilligan at the FAC hearing.

I had two objects in the interview. First, I was looking to form a view of whether there was evidence to suggest that a sufficiently serious offence might have been committed to warrant formal disciplinary action. If I so concluded, the next step would be to initiate a formal fact-finding hearing in accordance with departmental procedures at which he could be accompanied by a colleague or TU representative if he so wished. Alternatively, I might conclude that a lesser offence had been committed which could be dealt with informally or that no offence had been committed. Second, I wished to try to establish if his meeting with Andrew Gilligan was likely to form the basis of evidence given by Gilligan to the FAC about the WMD dossier.

Dr Kelly said that he understood this.

I then asked him briefly to clarify one or two points in his letter which were not entirely clear before asking him to explain more fully the account on the second page of his dealings with journalists.

Dr Kelly said that he was widely known as an expert on Iraqi WMD, not least because of his extensive experience as a UN inspector. During his period with the UN he had often been asked to act as an expert spokesman. Subsequently, he continued to participate in many seminars and similar events concerning this and related subjects. He was often approached by academics, journalists and others operating in the field for background information and technical advice at such events and, sometimes, outside them. When a journalist approached him, he usually consulted the FCO press office, but on occasions he used his own judgment as explained in his letter.

I asked why he consulted the FCO press office rather [than] the MOD. Dr Kelly said that his salary was paid by the FCO. I said that was irrelevant – he was seconded to MOD. I asked who had given him authority to exercise his own judgment about contacts with journalists on defence related business, since this was contrary to standing departmental instructions. Dr Kelly said that he had never read those instructions, nor sought to discover what guidance existed about contact with journalists. He said that he had not really regarded his discussions [with] journalists, academics etc as being about defence business but as a continuation of his role as UN expert. I said that that was, at best, extraordinarily naïve – journalists were not seeking information out of academic interest but to construct stories. It was important to know the context of their enquiries and any particular sensitivities before speaking to them. I asked Dr Kelly whether, for example, he knew that one of the other journalists to whom he had spoken, was married to a member of the FAC. He said he did not. This was an illustration of why people were required to seek advice and permission from the press office before speaking to journalists. It was also very important to report back after contacts.

I then asked Dr Kelly to summarise his contacts with Gilligan. He said that he had first met and spoken to Gilligan at the IISS seminar on WMD in September 2002 which took place just before publication of the government dossier. He was unaware of having spoken to Gilligan previously, although it was possible that they might both [have] been at other similar events without being aware of each other. Gilligan had telephoned in February 2003 to say that he was going to Iraq and would like to meet for some background briefing. I asked Dr Kelly why, given that there was an interval of 24 hours before the meeting, he had not contacted even the FCO press office. He said that he had regarded it as non-sensitive because it was the sort of background that he would have given to any academic or journalist.

Dr Kelly said his next contact with Gilligan was in May. Gilligan rang him to offer feedback from his experiences in Iraq. He had accepted, for the reasons set out in his letter. They met on 22 May in the Charing Cross Hotel. [Dr Kelly later said that the meeting took place about 1745 and lasted until approx 1830]. Gilligan took notes but did not appear to have a tape recorder (although Kelly did not ask and there was no discussion of the basis of the meeting). The vast bulk of the conversation was about Iraqi individuals associated with WMD programmes, the course of the war, and why WMD had not been used. In the course of the latter, as recorded in his letter, Gilligan had raised the reference in the September dossier to the possibility of weapons being deployed in 45 minutes. Kelly had commented that this did not correspond with any weapon system that he knew. Gilligan had asked why he thought the claim had been included in the dossier. Kelly had said that he had assumed that it was for impact. Although he did not know what the claim was based on, it emphasised the immediacy of the threat. [I have prepared a detailed comparison of Kelly's account of his conversation with Gilligan's FAC evidence based on the second part of the interview.] I asked why he had not even reported the conversation afterwards, given the public debate about the two government dossiers. Kelly repeated that the discussion had not really been about the dossier and he had not said anything controversial. Indeed, even after Gilligan made his allegations, he had not made any association with their May 22 meeting. It was only when a colleague remarked to him that some of the comments attributed to Gilligan's source sounded similar to his own views that he realised that others might make similar connections, which was why he had written to his line manager. As he had said in his letter, however, he did not believe that he could be Gilligan's primary source because he had not made any allegations against the government and his views also differed from those attributed to the source in other ways.

At this point I asked Dr Kelly whether he was confident that he had accurately reflected the meeting with Gilligan and whether there was anything he had omitted about this other meetings (sic). I stressed that whatever the actual significance of anything he had said to Gilligan, their meeting could turn out to be very important in relation to the public dispute between the government and the BBC about Gilligan's claims. It might become necessary to consider a public statement based on his account. Gilligan's reputation was at stake and he would be bound to challenge any inaccuracies – and I reminded Dr Kelly of the possibility that he might have been tape-recorded. Dr Kelly said that he understood this but stood by his account.

I said that I was prepared to accept his account in good faith. On the basis of what his letter and what he had said, it was clear that he had breached departmental instructions on numerous occasions by having conversations with journalists which had been neither unauthorised (sic) by or reported to the MOD press office, although on most occasions he had consulted the FCO press office. His contact with Gilligan was particularly ill-judged. Even if he was not Gilligan's primary source, it had had very awkward consequences both for him and the department, much of which could have been avoided even if he had reported the contact immediately afterwards. Someone who had dealt regularly with the press in a previous capacity should have known better. This was a potentially very serious matter. Nevertheless, I accepted his assurance that there has been no malicious intent and there appeared no reason to believe that classified material had been revealed. On that basis, I judged that it would not be appropriate to initiate formal disciplinary proceedings. I would, however, write to him shortly to record my displeasure at his conduct. I went on to instruct him to familiarise himself with departmental guidance about dealings with the media, to report all contacts to his line manager and never to agree to an interview without explicit authority. Finally, I warned Dr Kelly that any further breaches would be almost certain to lead to disciplinary action and the possibility of disciplinary action could of course be re-opened if further facts came to light that called his account and assurances into question.

The second part of the interview was devoted to a more detailed comparison of Dr Kelly's interview with Gilligan's FAC appearance. I will summarise my conclusions – my detailed analysis is appended. (Dr Wells also took notes.)

It is very difficult to reconcile Dr Kelly's account of his May 22 discussion with the evidence given to the FAC by Gilligan, if this is indeed all attributable to a <u>single</u> source. Kelly's account is consistent with some aspects of the FAC evidence and some of the discrepancies might be attributable to exaggeration, misrepresentation or misunderstanding by Gilligan and/or Kelly. Although Kelly admits to two comments that might lend credence to a claim that the dossier had been "sexed-up", he denies making such a claim and the related allegations which Gilligan attributed to his 'single source' and Kelly was not involved in the preparation of the intelligence part of the dossier. The focus of the two discussions also appears different – the dossier is only a small part of the Kelly discussion and Kelly specifically denies telling Gilligan (or anyone else outside government) that he had had <u>any</u> involvement with the dossier. Moreover, some of the views attributed to the source appear directly contrary to those expressed by Kelly.

There is also some evidence that does point to the existence of a different source for these allegations. Some aspects of Gilligan's description of his source do not properly match Kelly (although exaggeration and misrepresentation to try to protect the identity of the source are both possible.). And, if Gilligan's answer to Q550 from the chairman is accurate, the source is a member of the intelligence services, which cannot be a description of Kelly. Another serious discrepancy is that both Gilligan's FAC evidence and the original article suggest that he had a discussion with his source in May 2002, several months before he met Kelly.

Gilligan refers to four sources in the FAC session. There does not have to be a fifth person. It is possible that there is no single source and that the allegations are a collage, to which Kelly's interview contributed but the specific allegations about interference with the dossier come from somewhere else. Another possibility is that there are really only three sources: the "single source" might actually be one of the other three sources referred to by Gilligan as providing different information.

<u>If</u> both Gilligan's and Kelly's accounts are essentially truthful, perhaps the most likely supposition is that Kelly appeared to provide broad collateral for Gilligan's "single source" claims about the dossier, although not for the specific allegations about political interference. During his FAC hearing Gilligan talks about the "single source" as the centre of his 45-minute story but comments that this is supported by other evidence.

50. Dr Wells prepared a note of the interview on 4 July which was as follows:

NOTES OF A MEETING ON DAVID KELLY'S MEETING WITH
ANDREW GILLIGAN – 4 JULY 2003

Present:

Mr Richard Hatfield, Personnel Director

Dr Bryan Wells, DCPAC

Dr David Kelly, CPAC Special Adviser

Gilligan's evidence to the FAC

1. Hatfield said that he wanted to go through the Transcript of Gilligan's evidence to the Foreign Affairs Committee and ask Kelly whether he could have been the source of what Gilligan said. He went through Gilligan's answers seriatim.

2. Q398 answer. Hatfield observed that Gilligan's meeting with his source might match his meeting with Kelly. In particular, the meeting had been Gilligan's initiative, and the source was quite closely connected with the issue of Iraqi WMD. Hatfield acknowledged that Kelly's account did not match Gilligan's descriptions of the source as someone he had known for some time, and that he had met several times and spoken on the phone from time to time; but Gilligan could have been embellishing.

3. Q417. Hatfield observed that the description of the source as a "British official who was involved in the preparation of the Dossier" matched Kelly. Kelly accepted this, but said that he had never acknowledged his role in the Dossier to anyone outside Government, although some might have guessed.

4. Q418 answer. Hatfield observed that the description of the source as "longstanding" and "one of the senior officials in charge of drawing up the Dossier" did not match Kelly, but again Gilligan could have been exaggerating.

5. Q449. Hatfield asked direct if Kelly had ever said that the "45 minute" assessment was put into the Dossier at a late stage (ie the week before publication, as Gilligan had alleged). Kelly replied that he had not been aware of the assessment (that some of Iraq's WMD could be ready within 45 minutes of an order) until he read it in the published version of the Dossier. He had not been involved in the final preparations of the Dossier (he had not been in London during August, but had been in September). The only late issue he had been involved in was responding to a request on whether from his perspective there was anything else to add to the Dossier. He had suggested adding passages on smallpox, but this had not been taken up. Hatfield double-checked – Kelly was saying that he was not aware of the 45 minute assessment until it was published and had no knowledge of the process by which it had been brought into the Dossier. Kelly confirmed.

6. Q451 answer. Hatfield asked again if Kelly was the source of the "allegations" about the sexing-up of the Dossier. Kelly replied that he was not.

7. Q453 answer. Hatfield asked if Kelly had discussed (he had) (sic) discussed with Gilligan the issue of Uranium being sought from Niger. Kelly said he thought he had, but he was not involved in the issue and would not have offered his own view (his own position was that he had nothing other than the IAEA view). Hatfield asked again in relation to Q454 answer: Kelly replied that he did not (and would not have) offered the view that this assessment was based on "unreliable information".

8. Q455. Hatfield asked again if Kelly had been the source of the allegations about the "45 minute claim". Kelly reiterated that he was not.

9. Q457 answer. Hatfield asked if there had been an exchange in which he identified Alastair Campbell as the person from No.10 who had asked for the Dossier to be changed to include the "45 minute claim". Kelly said that he had not said anything like the quotation that Gilligan attributed to the source: he did not have "wishes" in relation to the contents of the Dossier.

10. Q461 answer. Hatfield asked if the source's quote (that the "45 minute claim" had confused conventional and CBW deployment times) reflected Kelly's views. Kelly replied that he had no opinion on the "45 minute claim". He did not know what the original source was.

11. Q463 answer. Hatfield asked if Kelly shared the source's view that Downing Street had spoiled its case by exaggeration. Kelly replied that he had not said that the Dossier was exaggerated. He had taken the line that the threat from Iraqi WMD was current and specific.

12. Q478. Hatfield observed that Kelly had already denied alleging that the 45 minute claim was unreliable.

13. Q486 answer. Hatfield asked if Kelly shared the source's views that weapons at 45 minutes deployment would have been found by now because they could not be deeply concealed. Kelly replied that this was not a statement he would make.

14. Q511 answer. Hatfield asked if Kelly was of the view that Iraq had not been able to weaponise CBW. Kelly replied that this was not his assessment. Hatfield asked if Kelly shared the source's views that it was 30% likely that there had been an Iraqi CW programme in the 6 months before the conflict. Kelly replied that he had no doubt that Iraq had a CW programme, but this was the sort of assessment he might make purely

to weapons production. <u>Hatfield</u> probed: Gilligan was specifically quoting his source – had Kelly used those actual words? <u>Kelly</u> said that he had not, but accepted that it could be an inaccurate summation of what he might have said. <u>Hatfield</u> asked whether Kelly could have been the source of Gilligan's quotation in the <u>Q545 answer</u> (that it was more likely that Iraq had a BW programme, but that it was small). <u>Kelly</u> replied that he would not have used those terms, but that the statement could be a loose paraphrase of his views.

15. <u>Q559.</u> <u>Hatfield</u> observed that Kelly did not match Gilligan's confirmation that his source was someone in the intelligence services.

16. <u>Q565 answer.</u> <u>Kelly</u> observed that Gilligan's description of the meeting's duration as being "a couple of hours, perhaps, an hour and a half" did not match the meeting he had been at: his strong recollection was that it had been around 45 minutes.

17. <u>Hatfield</u> summed up. There appeared to be consistencies between parts of Gilligan's testimony to the Foreign Affairs Committee, and what Kelly says that he said to Gilligan. In particular, the meeting was set up at Gilligan's initiative, and Kelly had acknowledged that the statement that it was 30% likely that there was a CW programme in the 6 months before the conflict was consistent with his views. But there were significant discrepancies. In particular, Kelly denied having any knowledge of the "45 minutes claim" until after the Dossier was published, and denied having any knowledge of the process by which that assessment was included; he also denied giving any opinion that the evidence that Uranium had been sought from Niger was based on unreliable information. In addition, Kelly was not of the view that Iraq had not been able to weaponise CBW. There were other, minor inconsistencies with Gilligan's testimony: Kelly had not met Gilligan "several times", was not "long-standing, well-known" to Gilligan, and was not in the intelligence services, but Gillian might well have wished to embellish. <u>Hatfield</u> said that overall, his judgment was that if there were a single source for Gilligan's information, then it was not Kelly. Kelly's words may have been part of the background to Gilligan's stories, but on the basis of what he had testified, he was satisfied that Kelly was not the source of the most significant allegations.

51. On 4 July Sir Kevin Tebbit wrote to Sir David Omand, the Security and Intelligence Co-ordinator and Permanent Secretary of the Cabinet Office as follows:

ANDREW GILLIGAN AND THE SINGLE SOURCE

An official in the MOD had volunteered that he had a discussion with Andrew Gilligan on 22 May, one week before Gilligan's allegation about the interference in the production of the September dossier and the '45 minute story'. He is an FCO official seconded to the MOD's Proliferation and Arms Control Secretariat, with a long history of authorised dealing with the press in the course of his duties, though <u>not</u> in this case.

He was interviewed today by his line manager and my Personnel Director for two hours. The official claims that he met Gilligan to discuss Gilligan's experiences in Baghdad because he believed it would be helpful to him in his own role as a BW expert with long scientific/academic association with the Iraqi weapons programme, past experience as a UN Inspector and an expectation that he would be returning to Iraq to debrief Iraqis associated with their WMD programme shortly. It would appear, from what he had told us, that their discussion touched on some of the issues subsequently referred to by Gilligan in the press in a number of ways:

- in response to a question from Gilligan about the failure of Iraq to use WMD and the inability to find them, he said that conditions early in the war were not favourable and that there were command and control problems subsequently, and that the small arsenal of WMD remaining would be difficult to find without human information;

- on the issue of the 45 minutes, raised by Gilligan, he said that he did not know to what it refers (not having access to the intelligence report);

- asked why it should be in the dossier, he said that he replied "probably for impact";

- on the role of Alastair Campbell, he said he was unable to comment (not being involved in the process).

My immediate reaction was that this must be the "single source" to whom Gilligan referred to in his testimony to the FAC as the origin of the story that the Government exaggerated intelligence contained in the September dossier. Certainly, his comments to Gilligan could have been incorporated into Gilligan's 29 May story. However, closer examination, following today's interview suggests that this would not necessarily be a reliable conclusion. A significant element of the information that Gilligan attributes to this source in his FAC testimony would not have been known to this individual: he was not, for example, involved in, or claims to have been involved in, the intelligence component of the dossier or the process of the dossier's compilation. There are also discrepancies, over the circumstances of the meeting, the length of their relationship, and, indeed, about the nature of the individual: Gilligan claims that this source was a senior official in charge of drawing up the dossier. This official – although an acknowledged expert on Iraqi WMD – patently was not so involved; nor does he subscribe to views attributed to Gilligan's source.

So, there are three possibilities:

(a) that Gilligan has embellished this official's meeting with him, but that he is the 'single anonymous source';

(b) that Gilligan's source is someone else;

(c) that no one 'source' exists and is in fact a hotchpotch of comments from numerous individuals and articles.

In the case of (a), we would have the strongest possible reason for publicly correcting the misrepresentation made by Gilligan in the interests of factual accuracy. However, we do not have sufficient evidence to reach such a conclusion with any degree of safety. The official himself is adamant that he is not the single source. Were we to accuse Gilligan and the BBC of misrepresenting the official's remarks, it would be easy for Gilligan to claim that his source was someone else and that the Government was pursuing a vendetta.

For these reasons, I do not recommend that we use what the official has told us to seek to correct the public record further.

I do, however, believe it necessary to have defensive material available should the story leak. Of this there must be a possibility. The official himself says he came forward, not because he considered that he was the source of Gilligan's information, but because a contact in RUSI suggested that Gilligan's evidence to the FAC looked as if it drew on the sort of comments he might make about Iraq's CW and BW capability. In general, there must, therefore, be some speculation already. Contingent lines have, therefore, been prepared by officials here. These are enclosed. [The contingent lines, which appear from the enclosure to the letter to have been a press statement, are set out in appendix 4].

I should add that the official has clearly breached the MOD's rules about unauthorised contact with the media. There is no reason to suspect a breach of the OSA [Official Secrets Act] or compromise of security information, but discipline is being reinforced.

I am copying this letter to Andrew Turnbull, David Manning (No.10), Michael Jay (FCO), Eliza Manningham-Buller (Security Services) and John Scarlett (JIC).

52. On the evening of Thursday 3 July Mr Hoon telephoned Mr Jonathan Powell, the Prime Minister's Chief of Staff and told him that an official had come forward to say that he had spoken to Mr Gilligan. Later on that evening in the course of a general conversation on the telephone with the Prime Minister, who was in the North West of England, Mr Powell passed on to the Prime Minister the information about an official having come forward. On the afternoon of Friday 4 July Sir David Manning, Head of the Overseas and Defence Secretariat of the Cabinet Office, held a meeting in his

office in 10 Downing Street with Sir David Omand, Mr Powell and Mr John Scarlett, the Chairman of the Joint Intelligence Committee, to discuss the course of action which should be followed in light of the knowledge that an official had come forward to say that he had spoken to Mr Gilligan.

53. On 5 July Sir Kevin Tebbit sent a further letter to Sir David Omand in which he wrote:

ANDREW GILLIGAN AND THE SINGLE SOURCE

Since my letter to you yesterday afternoon, there has been a further development which points more strongly to our official as being the "source" for the Gilligan allegation about the dossier (albeit with plenty of room still for the possibility of embellishment from other sources and misrepresentation by the journalist).

Today's Times carries an article by Tom Baldwin which contains further hints as to Gilligan's informant. There are three new pointers, specifically:

- "BBC journalists have been told that Mr Gilligan's anonymous source is among the 100 British intelligence and weapons specialists currently in Iraq as part of the ISG";

- "Attempts to contact …. source in the past month to ask supplementary questions has proved unsuccessful because of the nature of his position";

- Asked if now based abroad the executive replied "Something like that".

Although the official is not in Iraq at present I understand that he was there recently, after his conversation with Gilligan on 22 May and was planning to visit again later this month as an expert helping with the work of the Iraq Survey Group searching for WMD. The fact that the BBC are uncertain of his precise whereabouts, is consistent with the official's statement at the MOD's interviews yesterday that he has had no contact with the BBC since 22 May. Gilligan will have been aware of his general plans to visit – the official states that this was the reason why he agreed to meet Gilligan in the first place – but the cutting of contact since then would explain the BBC's lack of precision in their knowledge about the exact timings of his presence in Iraq itself.

There remain many discrepancies between Gilligan's account of what he claims to have been told by the official and the official's own version of what transpired. We still cannot exclude the possibility that the main source, or other sources, are elsewhere. But it may be possible to explain and reconcile at least some of the mismatches. An official who denies having had access to the intelligence reporting or a hand in the production of the intelligence part of the dossier, as the official does, may nevertheless have said enough based on his expert knowledge of the earlier Iraqi programme, for someone of Gilligan's methods to claim that the official discredited the "45 minutes" intelligence eg by stating that such a high level of readiness did not correspond to the Iraqi systems of which he was aware.

Records of the MOD's interview with the official are still being prepared. I have asked that they be forwarded to us as soon as possible. But I wanted you and colleagues to be aware of this development immediately. The Times story today, whether accurate or not, will increase the likelihood that over the weekend other journalists will indeed identify and name the BBC's source as our official. (He is as I indicated in my earlier letter well known in media/academic circles).

There are also considerations, as we discussed yesterday, whether the Foreign Affairs Committee Chairman should be informed of what we now know, however inconclusive, before their report is published on Monday. And there is the question of whether this plays into the continuing impasse between the Government and the BBC.

I am copying this letter to Andrew Turnbull, David Manning (No.10), Michael Jay (FCO), Eliza Manningham-Buller (Security Service) and John Scarlett (JIC).

54. On 6 July Sir David Omand sent a letter to Sir Kevin Tebbit (dated 5 July) which Sir Kevin received on Monday 7 July in which Sir David wrote:

ANDREW GILLIGAN AND THE SINGLE SOURCE

Thank you for your letter of Friday afternoon. I discussed the contents with Jonathan Powell, David Manning and John Scarlett that evening. We recognised that at least part of the explanation of the Gilligan story could rest on the discussion he had had with the official who has now come forward. At the appropriate point it would be incumbent upon us to inform the FAC (and the ISC) so that they were not placed in a false position. But we also noted your caveat about the need to be more certain of the facts before reaching any firm conclusion, given certain apparent discrepancies. The Prime Minister subsequently saw your letter and spoke to Jonathan Powell, and as I relayed to you, he agreed that as you had recommended no immediate action should be taken to try to correct the record with the FAC or with the BBC until we were more sure of our ground.

The Prime Minister asked for a deeper analysis of what the official has actually said, read against the account Gilligan himself has given the FAC and other statements by the BBC. You agreed to put this in hand, in the light of the record being prepared by Richard Hatfield. When we spoke later yesterday evening, we recognised that it might be necessary for the individual to be re-interviewed on Monday.

Your follow-up letter on Saturday has also been seen by the Prime Minister, who was grateful for the further information in it. He discussed the options with me on Sunday morning. I was able to pass on to him the view of the Foreign Secretary, relayed to me by the FCO Resident Clerk on Saturday evening, against any immediate action with the FAC in advance of the publication of their report on Monday (their Report is complete and some members of the Committee are now abroad). The Prime Minister concluded that notwithstanding the further circumstantial details in your second letter he agreed with your recommendation that there were still too many unknowns for us to approach the FAC now. But we may need to react quickly if the meeting of BBC Governors tonight or comment on the FAC Report changes the position. As I reported to you this afternoon the PM is appearing before the Liaison Committee on Tuesday and you will need to submit updated advice for that appearance in any case.

We agreed that you will circulate the detailed account of the first interview as soon as possible, and consider whether to reinterview the individual on Monday. I should add that the Prime Minister was minded to ask that the ISC be fully briefed in confidence on the case – the timing we can consider in the light of your further advice.

I am copying this letter to Andrew Turnbull, David Manning and Jonathan Powell, Eliza Manningham-Buller and John Scarlett, and to the Private Secretary to Michael Jay (whom you contacted yesterday).

55. In the course of Saturday and Sunday 5 and 6 July, a number of these senior officials had discussions on the telephone with each other as to the course which should be followed and some of them also had telephone conversations with the Prime Minister. In addition Mr Hoon and Mr Alastair Campbell had discussions on the telephone (see paragraph 307).

The special meeting of the BBC Governors on Sunday 6 July 2003 and the telephone conversation between the Prime Minister and Mr Gavyn Davies on Monday 7 July 2003

56. On the evening of Sunday 6 July at 6.30pm there was a special meeting of the BBC Governors to consider (inter alia) the issues arising from Mr Gilligan's reports on the Today programme on 29 May 2003. I shall return to consider this meeting in greater detail at a later stage in this report. After the meeting Mr Gavyn Davies, the Chairman of the BBC issued the following statement:

The BBC Board of Governors met this evening [Sunday 6 July 2003] to discuss the allegations made by Alastair Campbell against the BBC's overall coverage of the Iraq war, and its specific coverage of the September intelligence dossier by Andrew Gilligan in the Today programme.

The Governors questioned Greg Dyke, the Director-General, and Richard Sambrook, the Director of News, about Mr Campbell's allegations. The Board reached the following conclusions.

First, the Board reiterates that the BBC's overall coverage of the war, and the political issues surrounding it, has been entirely impartial, and it emphatically rejects Mr Campbell's claim that large parts of the BBC had an agenda against the war.

We call on Mr Campbell to withdraw these allegations of bias against the BBC and its journalists.

Second, the Board considers that the Today programme properly followed the BBC's Producers' Guidelines in its handling of the Andrew Gilligan report about the September intelligence dossier, which was broadcast on 29 May.

Although the Guidelines say that the BBC should be reluctant to broadcast stories based on a single source, and warn about the dangers of using anonymous sources, they clearly allow for this to be done in exceptional circumstances. Stories based on senior intelligence sources are a case in point.

We note that an entirely separate story was broadcast by an unconnected BBC journalist on Newsnight on 2 June. This story reported very similar allegations to those reported by Andrew Gilligan on the Today programme, but the story has not been singled out for similar criticism by government spokesmen.

Moreover, as these reports fitted in to a general pattern of concern, conveyed to a number of BBC journalists with good contacts in the security services, we consider that it was entirely proper to reflect some unease about the presentation of the Government's arguments in the disputed dossiers.

The Board is satisfied that it was in the public interest to broadcast Mr Gilligan's story, given the information which was available to BBC News at the time. We believe it would not have been in the public interest to have suppressed the stories on either the Today programme or Newsnight.

Third, the Board considers that the Today programme should have kept a clearer account of its dealings with the Ministry of Defence on this story and could have also asked the No 10 Press Office for a response prior to broadcasting the story.

However, we note that firm government denials of the story were broadcast on the Today Programme within 90 minutes of the original broadcast by Andrew Gilligan, and these were followed soon after on the same programme by equally firm denials by a defence minister.

Fourth, the Board intends to look again at the rules under which BBC reporters and presenters are permitted to write for newspapers, once it has received recommendations from the Director of News. This examination will be conducted during the summer.

Finally, the Board wishes to place on record that the BBC has never accused the Prime Minister of lying, or of seeking to take Britain into war under misleading or false pretences.

The BBC did not have an agenda in its war coverage, nor does it now have any agenda which questions the integrity of the Prime Minister.

In summary, the Governors are ultimately responsible for ensuring that the BBC upholds the highest standards of impartiality and accuracy. We are wholly satisfied that BBC journalists and their managers sought to maintain impartiality and accuracy during this episode.

Early on the morning of 7 July between 7 a.m. and 8 a.m. the Prime Minister and Mr Gavyn Davies had a private telephone conversation at the request of the former. The discussion was an amicable one in which each expressed his point of view on the dispute which had arisen between the Government and the BBC but they were unable to reach agreement.

The FAC Report dated 7 July 2003

57. On the morning of Monday 7 July the FAC issued their report on The Decision to go to War in Iraq. At the commencement of their report they set out their Conclusions and Recommendations which included the following:

> 9. We conclude that the 45 minutes claim did not warrant the prominence given to it in the dossier, because it was based on intelligence from a single, uncorroborated source. We recommend that the Government explain why the claim was given such prominence. (Paragraph 70)
>
> ....
>
> 11. We conclude that Alastair Campbell did not play any role in the inclusion of the 45 minutes claim in the September dossier. (Paragraph 77)
>
> 12. We conclude that it was wrong for Alastair Campbell or any Special Adviser to have chaired a meeting on an intelligence matter, and we recommend that this practice cease. (Paragraph 79)
>
> 13. We conclude that on the basis of the evidence available to us Alastair Campbell did not exert or seek to exert improper influence on the drafting of the September dossier. (Paragraph 84)
>
> 14. We conclude that the claims made in the September dossier were in all probability well founded on the basis of the intelligence then available, although as we have already stated we have concerns about the emphasis given to some of them. We further conclude that, in the absence of reliable evidence that intelligence personnel have either complained about or sought to distance themselves from the content of the dossier, allegations of politically inspired meddling cannot credibly be established. (Paragraph 86)
>
> 15. We conclude that without access to the intelligence or to those who handled it, we cannot know if it was in any respect faulty or misinterpreted. Although without the Foreign Secretary's degree of knowledge, we share his confidence in the men and women who serve in the agencies. (Paragraph 90)
>
> 16. We conclude that the language used in the September dossier was in places more assertive than that traditionally used in intelligence documents. We believe that there is much value in retaining the measured and even cautious tones which have been the hallmark of intelligence assessments and we recommend that this approach be retained. (Paragraph 100)
>
> 17. We conclude that continuing disquiet and unease about the claims made in the September dossier are unlikely to be dispelled unless more evidence of Iraq's weapons of mass destruction programmes comes to light. (Paragraph 108)
>
> ....
>
> 26. We recommend that Andrew Gilligan's alleged contacts be thoroughly investigated. We further recommend that the Government review links between the security and intelligence agencies, the media and Parliament and the rules which apply to them. (Paragraph 154) [152].

Communications and discussions within the Government in respect of Dr Kelly, 7 and 8 July

58. On the morning of Monday 7 July Mr Scarlett sent the following note to Sir David Omand:

ANDREW GILLIGAN AND THE MOD SINGLE SOURCE

I agree with Kevin Tebbit's letter of Saturday that the finger points strongly at David Kelly as Gilligan's source. I have been through the Gilligan/FAC transcript again. I attach copies of two pages in particular which seem to make it clear that Gilligan has only talked to one person about the September dossier. If he could have referred to any corroborating information he would have done so. If this is true, Kelly is not telling the whole story.

Gilligan must have got the 45 minute single intelligence report item from somewhere, presumably Kelly. Conclusion: Kelly needs a proper security-style interview in which all these inconsistencies are thrashed out. Until we have the full story, we cannot decide what action to take. I think this is rather urgent. Happy to discuss.

59. Further meetings took place in 10 Downing Street on Monday and Tuesday 7 and 8 July to discuss the course to be followed in the light of Dr Kelly having come forward, and the Prime Minister was present at some of these meetings.

60. On 21 July 2003 Sir David Omand made a note for the record which was as follows:

MEETINGS IN THE PRIME MINISTER'S STUDY, 7 AND 8 JULY 2003

7 July

1. I was pulled out of a CMPS [Centre for Management and Policy Studies] lecture at 09.15 on Monday morning, 7 July, with a request to go straight to No.10. I joined a discussion in progress in the PM's study, with the PM, Foreign Secretary, David Manning, Jonathan Powell, Nigel Sheinwald, Sally Morgan. John Scarlett and Kevin Tebbit arrived a little late. Alastair Campbell was also present for part of the meeting.

2. The main subject was discussion of the FAC Report about to issue. There were various advance copies in the room. Lines to take were being prepared. It was noted that the FAC had split largely on party political lines, as the Appendices to the Report showed.

3. There was also a review of the weekend decision not to inform the FAC before the publication of their Report that Dr Kelly had come forward to say that he had met Mr Gilligan. Kevin Tebbit ran over the ground he had covered in his two letters (of Friday 4 and Saturday 5 July). There was some questioning from the PM about what we knew about Dr Kelly, and whether we could find out more about his views. Kevin Tebbit agreed to report back. Kevin Tebbit warned that Dr Kelly was an expert on Iraqi WMD and if he was summoned to give evidence some of it might be uncomfortable on specifics such as the likelihood of there being weapons systems being ready for use within 45 minutes. But he believed from what he had said to Richard Hatfield that Dr Kelly had no doubts that there were Iraqi WMD programmes being concealed from the inspectors. Kevin Tebbit also expressed the view that we would have to face up to the fact that Dr Kelly's name was likely to become public at some point soon, given the number of people he would have talked to. MOD were preparing contingency statements just in case.

4. There was complete agreement that the inconsistencies in Dr Kelly's story needed to be subject to more forensic examination, and that MOD ought to be considering re-interviewing him. Kevin Tebbit said that MOD were considering calling him back from a conference he was at in order to talk to him again. He reiterated that Dr Kelly had come forward of his volition, and that as far as MOD was concerned there was no question of any offence having been committed under the Official Secrets Act. Dr Kelly's continued co-operation was therefore essential. The Prime Minister made it clear that MOD should continue to handle the case properly, and should follow whatever internal procedures were normal in such cases.

8 July

5. John Scarlett and I were in a videoconference [*****] when we were asked to see the PM. I reported orally on further information received from the MOD to the effect that the re-interview had confirmed the earlier story as reported by Kevin Tebbit in his letter on Saturday. It looked as if the main explanation for the Gilligan story of a single source was Dr Kelly, but that Mr Gilligan may well have heavily embellished the conversation, or be drawing on other uncited sources, for the controversial parts of his story.

6. There was discussion (which I may have initiated) of the difficulty that Government witnesses before the ISC would be in if, as was very likely, they were asked whether we had a clue as to the identity of the Gilligan source. I said I would have to reply that we did have someone who had come forward – we could not attempt to cover up this important fact. And I was uneasy that we

could be accused of a cover up if we did not tell the FAC, subject to whatever came out of a re-interview. I suggested that we should write to the Chairman of the ISC to tell them that an MOD official had come forward, and thus enable them to interview the individual if they thought fit. We could provide the actual name in confidence. The ISC took evidence in private, so confidentiality could be maintained. If we wrote to the FAC (which the FAC might feel was appropriate given that they had just completed a report on the subject) then this could be read as an invitation by them to summon Dr Kelly. We all agreed that the ISC was the proper forum for investigation of this lead, and not the FAC. But the Prime Minister made clear that if, as he suspected, the FAC insisted on calling Dr Kelly to give evidence then we could not in conscience order him not to appear given the relevance of the information he had given us to the FAC's own inquiry. It was accepted at the meeting that copying any ISC letter to the FAC would be tantamount to a public statement, and therefore we should make public in a straightforward way the letter to the ISC. I agreed to write the letter given my position as Security and Intelligence Co-ordinator. MOD would draft with the Cabinet Office. I would make the ISC aware of the actual name of Dr Kelly separately and in confidence.

7. There was also discussion, briefly, of whether the BBC should be informed in advance that a public announcement of an MOD official coming forward was about to be made. We felt there should be, as a courtesy. There was reference to an idea (possibly from MOD) that Mr Hoon should write to either the DG or the Chairman of Governors of the BBC, and after some discussion it was felt that the Chairman was the appropriate person given the Governors' meeting later that evening. It was felt that it would be fair to Dr Kelly to give the BBC the chance to clear his name but it was unreasonable to press the BBC to go further and reveal the name of their source if it was not Dr Kelly. We were clear that they would not do that.

8. Immediately after the meeting at about midday I went to see the Clerk to the ISC, and explain that I was minded to write to the Chairman in those terms. The Clerk expressed some concern, saying that the ISC would not want to be put in a position publicly of having to see an individual; they would make their own mind up on the progress of their inquiry. He was sure that Ann Taylor would not want to break the Committee rule that they were not giving a public commentary on the progress of their inquiry, and a publication of a letter from me to her might be seen as just that. I then had to leave immediately for Heathrow airport for an official visit to Ottawa. I was informed by telephone that Ann Taylor had confirmed she definitely did not want to receive any letter that was going to be made public. There was confirmation that she however would be prepared to see a reference to the ISC possibly interviewing the individual, if that came at the end of a press statement from Government.

61. Also on 21 July 2003 Mr John Scarlett made a note which was as follows:

AIDE-MEMOIRE: MEETINGS AT WHICH I WAS PRESENT

<u>Friday 4 July</u>

Approx 1800: DO [David Omand], DM [David Manning], JSc [John Scarlett], JP [Jonathan Powell]. DO and JSc report from Kevin Tebbit that an MOD official has come forward. Name given. Sounds like Gilligan's source. Noted that normal MOD personnel procedures must be followed and appropriate legal advice taken. Need to think about whether BBC Governors and/or FAC (both of whom deliberate or report in the next three days) should be informed. JP to report to PM [Prime Minister].

<u>Monday 7 July</u>

0900: 10 minute meeting, PM with JP and JSc. Brief discussion of whether Dr K [Dr Kelly] could be the source. PM states that it must be handled according to proper MOD and Civil Service procedures. We need to know more before deciding next steps.

0930: PM meeting with JP, J Straw [Jack Straw], JSc, DO, DM, NS [Nigel Sheinwald], TK [Tom Kelly], AC [Alastair Campbell], SN [Sally Morgan], KT [Kevin Tebbit]. Main purpose to discuss FAC report. Brief discussion of MOD source. If he appeared before a Committee, would he be likely to support or otherwise the Government position? JSc to seek advice from MOD. Was he or was he not the source? No further decision possible without knowing more about his contact with Gilligan. KT asked to arrange a further interview as soon as possible. On leaving meeting KT to issue instructions for Dr K to come to London for interview.

Tuesday 8 July

0815: PM internal meeting to prepare for Liaison Committee. JP, AC, JSc, CS [Claire Sumner], CR [Catherine Rimmer], J Straw, DM, MR [Matthew Rycroft], TK (not all at once as I recall). At end PM wonders what to say if LC [Liaison Committee] asked about leak inquiries. Does PM have any idea about source? PM anxious not to be misleading if some kind of statement likely later in the day or next day. Eventually conclude that he must not trail a possible statement about anyone coming forward. He would reply, if asked, that we were taking the possibility of leaks seriously and looking at this in the normal way.

Circa 1145: PM meeting. DO, JSc, DM, JP, AC. Discussed informing ISC. SDO to send letter, JSc to draft. Do not want to involve FAC but if name becoming public they would be bound to ask to interview him. Agreement that the issue would inevitably become public. We were already open to criticism for not coming clean about the existence of a possible source. Not much time left. Also discussion of a letter from GH [Geoff Hoon] to Chairman BBC Governors.

1330: PM meeting. JP, JSc, AC, TK. Discussed draft letter to ISC. Word received from Ann Taylor that she does not want to receive it. Do press statement instead. Decide to draft press statement with separate private letter from GH to BBC Chairman giving the name. Discussion of how BBC will react (will they be ready to discuss this in businesslike way). If Dr K name becomes public will Government be criticised for putting him under "wider pressure"? PM repeats that MOD must remain in charge and follow their procedures.

62. At a meeting in 10 Downing Street on 7 July at which the Prime Minister and the Foreign Secretary, Mr Jack Straw MP, were present it was decided that Dr Kelly should be further interviewed to find out more about what he had said to Mr Gilligan. Mr Dominic Wilson, the Private Secretary to Sir Kevin Tebbit sent Mr Hatfield the following minute which was also sent to Mr Martin Howard and Dr Wells. The minute was dated 8 July but it was drafted by Mr Wilson on 7 July and was read over to Mr Hatfield before the interview with Dr Kelly on that day. The minute was as follows:

GILLIGAN: INTERVIEW WITH DR KELLY

PUS was grateful for your minute of 7 July and record of your discussions with Dr Kelly.

2. What is now needed is a more intensive interview with Kelly. The objective would be to establish what transpired between him and Gilligan, with a reliability that will stand up to the intense glare of public scrutiny. The core issue in this respect is whether it was Kelly who alleged that the 45 minute intelligence was inserted into the dossier against the wishes of the intelligence community and at the behest of the Government in general and Alastair Campbell in particular.

3. PUS believes that this must be pinned down as clearly as possible because of the continuing problem with the BBC and the FAC's recommendation that Gilligan's contacts should be investigated. It should also be in Kelly's own interest for this to occur, given that at least one of his colleagues has already speculated that he could indeed be Gilligan's 'single anonymous source' and Kelly's own view (as we understand it) that this would be a misrepresentation of the position.

4. Against this background I understand that arrangements have been made for the further interview to be carried out by you and addresses (sic) at 1600 today. The PUS would like to consider in the light of this whether to recommend a public announcement. The key issues will be:

    a.   a judgment of the probability that Kelly is in (sic) the principal source of Gilligan's allegations – wittingly or otherwise (and the credibility of alternative explanations);

    b.   Kelly's readiness to be associated with a public statement that names him and carries a clear and sustainable refutation of the core allegation on the '45 minute' intelligence;

c. our view about the robustness of the rest of his position, including on Iraq's WMD programmes generally.

5. In all this PUS remains concerned to ensure that Dr Kelly's rights are respected – it is important that he understands he is cooperating voluntarily. There is also the different angle that in the event that it becomes evident that he may have divulged classified or privileged information contrary to the position so far, proceedings would need to be stopped immediately to avoid prejudicing any case that might then need to be brought.

Press statements by Mr Alastair Campbell and the BBC on 7 July 2003

63. On Monday 7 July Mr Alastair Campbell issued the following press statement:

I am very pleased that the FAC (Foreign Affairs Select Committee) inquiry has found that the allegations made against me broadcast by the BBC are untrue.

These allegations were that I was responsible for the insertion of the 45-minute intelligence into the WMD (weapons of mass destruction) dossier, against the wishes of the Intelligence Agencies, whilst probably knowing it to be wrong.

This was then repeated over five weeks. These allegations are all false as the FAC has found. Indeed, even Sir John Stanley has said on this, the BBC was wrong.

I want to make it clear yet again that I fully respect the independence of the BBC.

There can be a dispute between us as to whether they should ever have run the original story.

But surely there can be no dispute that the allegations, whether or not sources, are untrue.

Even now, all that I ask is that the BBC accept this, and I note that at no point did the BBC Governors in their statement last night claim that the story was true, merely that the BBC were within their rights to run it. This issue – the truth of the claims – is the only issue, and the one that the BBC should be addressing.

I am saddened that, for whatever reason and despite overwhelming evidence, they still refuse to admit that the allegations they broadcast were false.

On 7 July the BBC also issued the following press statement:

The BBC believes today's report from the Foreign Affairs Committee justifies its decision to broadcast the Today programme story of 29 May and the Newsnight story of 2 June and shows that both were in the public interest.

In particular, we believe the decision to highlight the circumstances surrounding the 45 minute claim has been vindicated.

We would point to the unanimous conclusion of the Foreign Affairs Committee in paragraphs 70 and 71, which says:

"We conclude that the 45 minute claim did not warrant the prominence given to it in the dossier, because it was based on intelligence based on a single uncorroborated source. We recommend that the Government explain why the claim was given such prominence."

The committee continues: "We further recommend that in its response to this report, the Government set out whether it still considers the September dossier to be accurate in what it states about the 45 minute claim, in the light of subsequent events."

It is because of BBC journalism that the problems surrounding the 45 minute claim have come to light and been given proper public attention.

We note that the committee was deeply divided on the role Alastair Campbell played in the compilation of the September dossier and only reached a decision which supported his position on the casting vote of the Labour chairman. We also note that not all the Labour MPs on the committee supported this decision.

We also consider it important, in the context of our reporting, that in paragraph 100 the committee says unanimously:

"The language used in the September dossier was more assertive than that traditionally used in intelligence documents."

And in paragraph 107, the committee says: "We conclude that the continuing disquiet and unease about the claims made in the September dossier are unlikely to be dispelled unless more evidence of Iraq's WMD programmes come to light."

We are pleased that Alastair Campbell said this morning that his complaint is about one story only and was no longer an attack on the whole of the BBC's journalism or coverage of the war.

On whether or not it was right for the BBC to broadcast the Today programme story on 29 May, the BBC will have to agree to disagree with Mr Campbell. The Foreign Affairs Select Committee makes no comment on this.

The MoD interview with Dr Kelly on 7 July 2003

64. On Monday 7 July Dr Kelly was attending a course of pre-deployment training at the RAF station at Honington in Suffolk prior to leaving for Baghdad later that week. Dr Kelly was asked to return to London to be interviewed and he was interviewed on the afternoon of 7 July by Mr Hatfield and Mr Howard in the presence of Dr Wells. On 8 July Mr Hatfield wrote to Sir Kevin Tebbit as follows:

DR DAVID KELLY AND ANDREW GILLIGAN

1. I saw Dr Kelly again yesterday afternoon in company with Martin Howard and Bryan Wells.

2. As I told you last night, there was no change in the essentials of his story and in particular he stoutly maintains that, as in his original letter, he did not make accusations about the dossier and, in particular, did not suggest that any material had been added by Downing Street. Some of his other replies suggested that he had become rather more concerned that some of his background comments might have been regarded by Gilligan as providing collateral for his thesis and may well have been incorporated with information from other sources. As Kelly himself put it, "I am beginning to realise that I might have been led on!"

3. I made it clear to Dr Kelly that, given the FAC outcome and particularly the recommendation to try to follow up Gilligan's contacts, it was likely that the MOD would have to reveal that someone had come forward to admit talking to Gilligan. I said that I did not think that it would be necessary to reveal his name or to go into detail beyond indicating that the account given to us did not match Gilligan's PAC account, at least initially. It was, however, quite likely that his name would come out, not least because speculation about the nature of the source (eg the Times of 5 July 2003) might lead in his direction. It was also possible that, depending on further developments, the FAC might seek to call him as a witness. It was therefore very important that he should tell us if there was anything that he had omitted or was unsure about. Dr Kelly confirmed that there was nothing that he wanted to change or add. He also agreed that the attached draft press statement accurately reflected his position and that he would stand by it if questioned. I gave him a copy and said that we would try to give him advance warning of any announcement but circumstances might make this impossible. (I re-confirmed this understanding on the telephone this morning, when agreeing that he could complete his training at RAF Honington today).

4. I also attach a slightly updated version of my comparative analysis which reflects clarifications to some of the detail as a result of the second interview with Kelly. I have also tidied up serials 2 and 3, where my original comment was slightly misleading. Kelly first remembers speaking to Gilligan at the IISS seminar in September 2002 in a coffee break but his two arranged meetings with Gilligan were both this year, in February and May, before and after Gilligan's trip to Iraq. On reflection, the discrepancy with Gilligan's evidence to the FAC that he had not seen his contact face to face for 'about a year' is even greater. If the contact is Kelly this would mean that Gilligan was overlooking the meeting this February, as well as referring to a meeting which appears to have taken place in May 2002 before Kelly had met him.

65. The draft press statement attached to Mr Hatfield's letter of 8 July was as follows:

An individual working in the MOD has volunteered that he met with Andrew Gilligan on 22 May to discuss Gilligan's experiences as a correspondent in Iraq. This was one week before Gilligan's story claiming that the September 2002 Iraq dossier had been "sexed up". The account of the meeting given by this official does not match the account given by Gilligan to the Foreign Affairs Committee of his "single source". The official has told up that he made no allegations or accusations about the dossier and, in particular, did not suggest that any material had been added to the dossier by Alastair Campbell or Downing Street against the wishes of the intelligence community. He is not a member of the Intelligence Services or the Defence Intelligence Staff.

This discussion was not authorised in accordance with departmental guidance for contact with the media. This is being dealt with appropriately by line management.

There is no reason to suspect that a breach of security is involved.

66. Dr Wells made the following note of the meeting:

NOTES OF A MEETING ON DAVID KELLY'S MEETING WITH ANDREW GILLIGAN – 7 JULY

Present:

Mr Martin Howard, DCDI

Mr Richard Hatfield, Personnel Director

Dr Bryan Wells, DCPAC

Dr David Kelly, CPAC Special Adviser

1. Hatfield started by saying that he wanted the meeting to cover two issues. The first was to follow up the discrepancies between Gilligan's account of the meeting with his source, and Kelly's account of his meeting with Gilligan. The second issue was that MOD may wish to make a public statement, and he wished to discuss that with Kelly. The meeting was structured to follow Hatfield's comparative analysis circulated under his minute of 8 July to PS/PUS.

2. Serials 2 and 3. Hatfield said that Kelly had described the IISS Seminar in September 2002 as being the first time that he had consciously met Gilligan. Hatfield probed whether Kelly had indeed never met Gilligan before. Kelly replied that he could not recall having spoken to Gilligan before then. They certainly had not had a meeting or a purposeful discussion. Hatfield probed further; surely Kelly could not have forgotten such a meeting. Kelly replied that he could not recall one.

3. Hatfield then asked about the meeting between Kelly and Gilligan in February 2003. Kelly replied that the meeting was held at the Charing Cross Hotel and lasted for 45 minutes to 1 hour. It had taken place at Gilligan's suggestion. He could not recall having had any further contact until May.

4. Howard asked whether Kelly talked to journalists a lot. Kelly replied that he would have people contact him 3-4 times a week. Many of the calls were quite simply asking technical details. Howard commented that a non-technical discussion with Gilligan would therefore have stuck out.

5. Serials 4 and 5. Hatfield asked Kelly to describe in detail his involvement in the government's dossier of September 2002. Kelly said that to his recollection the idea of a dossier arose in April 2002. He had drafted his contributions (described in his letter of 30 June) during May and June 2002. He then recalled that the subject went into limbo. He was on leave for two weeks in August and then on duty in New York and consequently was not involved in any work during that month. His only subsequent involvement was when he was asked by DIS (in September) to look at the passages on biological weapons and consider whether anything extra could be added. He had suggested including a discussion of Smallpox, but that was subsequently rejected on the grounds of there being inadequate intelligence. That was the sum of his involvement. Howard asked if he had [been] contacted in order to check textual amendments. Kelly replied that he had

not. Howard also asked if Kelly had discussed the dossier with DIS staff. Kelly replied that he could not recall any in depth discussion. He recalled that there had not in any case been much discussion of the dossier at the time. He reminded the meeting that he had never acknowledged outside Government that he had contributed to the dossier.

6. Serial 6. Hatfield asked how Kelly described himself to Gilligan. Kelly replied that he assumed Gilligan would know that he was a senior adviser to DPACS/DCPAC. People had all sorts of ideas about his role; he continued to have a high profile on UNSCOM/UNMOVIC work; and a number of people believe that he was an intelligence officer. Hatfield asked if Gilligan thought that he was part of the intelligence agencies. Kelly replied that he could not exclude that possibility although he would not describe himself as such and would not have encouraged Gilligan to think it.

7. Serial 10. Howard asked if Gilligan had taken notes of the meeting. Kelly replied that Gilligan had produced a small notebook and pencil and had taken some notes but these were not copious.

8. Serial 8. Hatfield recalled that Kelly had been clear that the May meeting with Gilligan lasted 45 minutes. He asked the basis for this. Kelly replied that the meeting had been fixed for 17.00 hours. He clearly recalled Gilligan turning up at 17.15. He believed that he left at about 18.00 to catch the 18.30 Paddington train.

9. Serial 11. Hatfield referred to the quotation from Gilligan's source that the dossier was "transformed the week before it was published to make it sexier". He asked Kelly if he had said this or something similar. Kelly said that he had not described the dossier as having been transformed the week before publication, and could not recall using the term "sexier". Hatfield probed: had Kelly said anything that could be construed as being that quotation? Kelly said that he could not recall; his memory was that discussion of the dossier was fleeting. Hatfield commented that the flavour of Gilligan's evidence to the FAC was that the meeting concentrated on the dossier: that was why the differing accounts of the meeting's length were important: a longer meeting would have allowed more discussion of the issues. Howard referred to the passage in Kelly's letter of 30 June where he said that the "45 minutes claim" was included in the dossier for "impact". Was this the exact word used or was it a paraphrase? Kelly replied that he would use that word on occasion, but could not recall if he had said it to Gilligan. But he would not use the phrase to imply criticism: he meant it in the sense that the claim was in the forward (sic) signed by the Prime Minister, rather than simply in the body of the text. It therefore had "impact" in that sense.

10. Serial 13. Howard asked if Kelly had seen the intelligence report relating to the "45 minutes claim". Kelly replied that he had not. Howard asked if Kelly was aware that there was intelligence on the subject. Kelly replied that he was not, until the issue was in the public domain. Hatfield referred to the quote from Gilligan's source which said that "WMD were ready for use in 45 minutes … not in original draft … included against their wishes because it wasn't reliable". Did Kelly say this? Kelly replied that he could not believe that he would have said this: he did not say that it was not in the original draft; and he didn't know the wishes of the intelligence services. Hatfield asked what question Gilligan was asking Kelly to respond to when the "45 minute claim" came up. Kelly replied that they were discussing why WMD had not been used during the conflict. He had explained his own view which was that weather conditions had prevented use early in the campaign, and breakdown of C2 had prevented its use in the later commented (sic) that this was different from Gilligan's description to the FAC. Kelly continued that he wondered now if he had been led on by Gilligan. His stock answer on the "45 minutes claim" that was in the early 90s, Iraq had a policy to fill to use. But this still required transportation of the stored armaments to launch sites for their use. All this was time-consuming. He therefore could not relate the claim to anything he knew of. But he recognised that he was not familiar with all the systems.

11. Serial 14. Hatfield asked Kelly about his discussions on uranium imports from Niger. Kelly said that so far as he could recall it was not discussed in depth. He would not have said anything other than to note the IAEA observations on the issue.

12. Serial 16. Hatfield asked if Kelly had discussed with Gilligan the role of Alastair Campbell in the dossier. Kelly replied that, as he had said in his letter of 30 June, Gilligan did raise the

involvement of Campbell and Kelly said that he was unable to comment. Hatfield asked in what context the role of Alastair Campbell had been raised. Kelly replied that it was in the context of the editing process of the dossier. Hatfield asked what Kelly meant by being "unable to comment". Kelly replied that it would have been a dismissive response. Hatfield asked specifically if Kelly had himself referred to "Campbell". Kelly replied that he had not.

13. Serial 17. Hatfield asked if Kelly had said that Downing Street "had asked repeatedly if anything could be added to the original draft". Kelly replied that he had not.

14. Serial 18. Hatfield asked if there had been any discussion of the Iraqi source for the "45 minutes claim". Kelly replied that he had no idea who the source was and did not speculate on that source with Gilligan. Hatfield asked Kelly if he had told Gilligan that Iraq had not been able to weaponise CBW. Kelly replied that he had not said this and he believed otherwise.

15. Serial 24. Hatfield asked Kelly if he would have said whether (sic) that there was a 30% probability of there being a CW programme in the six months before the war. Kelly replied that 30% was the sort of figure he would use as the probability for there having been a current production programme. He was 100% certain that there had been a chemical weapon programme.

16. Serial 25. Hatfield asked if Kelly had said or believed that the Iraqi WMD threat was smaller and less imminent than that claimed by the government. Kelly replied that he believed the threat was both current and specific.

17. Howard asked if Kelly was aware of anyone else who could have been a source for Gilligan. Kelly replied that he was not aware of any sources. He was aware that some points of his description of the meeting with Gilligan matched those of Gilligan's description of his meeting with the source. Kelly said that he was concerned that Gilligan would try to hang the other stories on to him.

18. Howard asked if anybody from the BBC, and in particular Gilligan, had tried to contact Kelly since the meeting on May 22. Kelly replied that Gilligan had not tried to contact him. The only BBC person he could recall having contacted him was Susan Watts, a science editor.

19. Hatfield said that it was likely that the department would need to make some public statement on Kelly's involvement with Gilligan. He passed Kelly a draft press release and Kelly confirmed that he was content with its terms. Hatfield said that although Kelly was not named in the press release his identity may become known in due course. Kelly replied that he acknowledged this: in his letter of 30 June he had said that a friend at RUSI had alerted him to the possibility of his being considered as Gilligan's source.

67. On 8 July Mr Hoon had a lunchtime meeting with Mr Richard Sambrook, the Director of News at the BBC, to discuss the MoD's concern that Mr Gilligan had not forewarned it of the WMD allegations which he broadcast on 29 May.

68. At a meeting in 10 Downing Street on Tuesday 8 July commencing at 1.30pm it was learnt that Mrs Ann Taylor MP, the Chairman of the ISC did not want to receive a letter informing her that the civil servant had come forward (see Mr Scarlett's note set out in paragraph 61). It was then decided to issue a press statement that a civil servant working in the MoD had come forward to say that he had met Mr Gilligan on 22 May. A group of officials comprising Sir Kevin Tebbit, Mr John Scarlett, Mr Jonathan Powell, Mr Alastair Campbell and Mr Tom Kelly then began to draft the statement in 10 Downing Street.

69. During the first part of the afternoon of 8 July Dr Kelly was at RAF Honington and just after 3.30pm Mr Hatfield was telephoned by Mr Wilson, the Private Secretary to Sir Kevin Tebbit, who told him that it was expected that the MoD would need to make a statement about Dr Kelly that evening and that he (Mr Hatfield) was going to be asked to clear the text with Dr Kelly when it was available. At that point the text had not been sent to Mr Hatfield but Mr Wilson read the text over to him.

Mr Hatfield then rang Dr Kelly hoping to speak to him before he left RAF Honington but he got Dr Kelly's mobile telephone voicemail and left him a message saying that he wanted to talk to him as soon as possible about the possible release of a statement and about the text of that statement. Dr Kelly called Mr Hatfield back at 4.14pm and Mr Hatfield repeated the message which he had previously left on his voicemail. Mr Hatfield also told Dr Kelly that the statement was likely to be slightly longer than the one which they had discussed on the previous day because the text was going to say a little more about what Dr Kelly had told the MoD officials he had said to Mr Gilligan. Mr Hatfield still did not have the text of the statement which was to be issued and he said to Dr Kelly that they would need to talk again in half an hour or so. Soon after that telephone conversation Mr Hatfield received the text of the press statement. Mr Hatfield telephoned Dr Kelly again at 5.10pm and read through the statement to him paragraph by paragraph and when Mr Hatfield had finished reading the text Dr Kelly said that he was content with it. Mr Hatfield told Dr Kelly that the statement would be issued very soon and that he was certain it would be out by 7.00pm. Mr Hatfield also told him in that conversation or in the earlier telephone conversation at 4.14pm that he should talk to the press office and to Dr Wells about support.

The press statement issued by the MoD on 8 July 2003

70. The press statement was issued by the MoD about 5.45pm on Tuesday 8 July in the following terms:

> An individual working in the MOD has come forward to volunteer that he met Andrew Gilligan of the BBC on May 22. It was an unauthorised meeting. It took place one week before Mr Gilligan broadcast allegations against the Government about the WMD dossier on the Today programme.

> The person who has come forward has volunteered that he has known Mr Gilligan for some months. He says that he met Mr Gilligan in a central London hotel at Mr Gilligan's request. During the conversation Mr Gilligan raised the Iraqi WMD programme, including the "45 minutes" issue. The official says that Mr Gilligan also raised the issue of Alastair Campbell.

> The individual is an expert on WMD who has advised ministers on WMD and whose contribution to the Dossier of September 2002 was to contribute towards drafts of historical accounts of UN inspections. He is not "one of the senior officials in charge of drawing up the dossier". He is not a member of the Intelligence Services or the Defence Intelligence Staff.

> He says that when Mr Gilligan asked about the role of Alastair Campbell with regard to the 45 minute issue, he made no comment and explained that he was not involved in the process of drawing up the intelligence parts of the Dossier.

> He says he made no other comment about Mr Campbell. When Mr Gilligan asked him why the 45 minute point was in the Dossier, he says he commented that it was "probably for impact". He says he did not see the 45 minute intelligence report on which it was based.

> He has said that, as an expert in the field, he believes Saddam Hussein possessed WMD.

> We do not know whether this official is the single source quoted by Mr Gilligan. Mr Gilligan told the FAC he had only one source for his story, and that the other three sources he mentioned to the FAC did not talk to him about the September Dossier, or did so after the broadcast.

> The MOD, with the individual's agreement, intend to give his name to the Chairman of the Intelligence and Security Committee, in confidence, should they wish to interview him as part of their inquiry.

71. On the evening of Tuesday 8 July, after the press statement had been issued, Ms Pamela Teare, the Director of News in the MoD, and Mrs Kate Wilson, the chief press officer in the MoD, had a discussion and agreed that the latter should telephone Dr Kelly to alert him to the high level of media interest in the statement and to advise him that he might want to consider staying with friends. Accordingly, Mrs Wilson telephoned Dr Kelly on his mobile. She called him at 8.26pm when he said he was out walking and asked her to call him back. She then called Dr Kelly back about twenty minutes later and told him that the statement had been put out. She wanted to make sure that he had her contact numbers but he said that he did not have anything to write with and so he could not take her numbers down. Mrs Wilson then asked him if he had the number for the duty press officer and he said he did. Mrs Wilson told him that the MoD press office had had a lot of follow up questions and that he needed to think about alternative accommodation. She did not offer him accommodation because her view was that it was better to go and stay with family or friends than to go to a hotel, and that is what she recommended to him. She asked him if there was anything he wanted from her and he said there was not. Mrs Wilson said in evidence that it was a brief conversation. When asked how Dr Kelly sounded at the time she replied that he was not surprised by anything she said and he seemed very calm.

The press statement issued by the BBC on 8 July 2003 and correspondence between the MoD and the BBC

72. On 8 July Mr Hoon wrote to Mr Gavyn Davies, the Chairman of the Board of Governors of the BBC, enclosing the MoD's statement and saying:

> I am writing to draw to your attention an MOD statement which we shall be issuing later today about Andrew Gilligan's 'single source'. This is enclosed.

> You will see that we have not named the official within the MOD who has come forward. We would, however, be prepared to disclose his name to you in confidence, on the basis that you would then immediately confirm or deny that this is indeed Mr Gilligan's source, in the interests of resolving what has become a management problem for both our organisations.

> I am sure you will understand that this is not the same as divulging a source since the individual has come forward.

73. Mr Gavyn Davies replied to Mr Hoon on the 8 July and stated:

> Thank you for today's letter, which I believe you have now released to the press.

> I have to say that the offer in your letter seems to be an attempt to force the BBC News Division to reveal the name or names of the source(s) used by Andrew Gilligan on Today and Susan Watts on Newsnight. You will recognise that it is a cardinal principle of good journalism that sources should never be revealed, no matter how intense the pressure may be. As Chairman of the BBC, I support this principle.

> In line with this principle, I do not myself know the identity [of] the source(s) mentioned above, so I am unable to accept your offer of confirming whether their name(s) match the person who has come forward at the Ministry of Defence.

> I will be releasing this letter to the press.

74. On the evening of 8 July the BBC issued a press statement:

> We note that today, the Ministry of Defence has issued a statement saying that an individual working in the Ministry of Defence has come forward to volunteer information about an unauthorised meeting he says he had with Andrew Gilligan on May 22.

The description of the individual contained in the statement does not match Mr Gilligan's source in some important ways.

Mr Gilligan's source does not work in the Ministry of Defence and he has known the source for a number of years not months.

As we have said before, Mr Gilligan met several people in the period before the story was broadcast and discussed Weapons of Mass Destruction in various ways with a number of them.

His Today programme story was based on only one of those conversations.

'Comprehensive notes'

For the single conversation which led to the Today story, Mr Gilligan took comprehensive notes during the meeting with his source which do not correspond with the account given in the MoD statement.

These notes have already been deposited with the BBC legal department.

We note that the MoD statement says that "we do not know whether this official is Mr Gilligan's source".

Neither do we.

What we do know is that Mr Gilligan's notes and account of what he was told are very similar to the notes of a conversation Susan Watts, Science Editor of Newsnight, had with her source which led to the Newsnight reports of June 2 and 4.

These reports contained allegations consistent with the Gilligan report and she described her source as "a senior official intimately involved with [the] process of pulling together the September dossier".

Sources

We reiterate the point we made last week that Susan Watts and Andrew Gilligan have never met, spoken or corresponded about any issues let alone this particular matter.

We do not know whether their respective sources are the same person, as Susan Watts and George Entwhistle, the Editor of Newsnight, are unwilling to reveal her source.

However, if it is the same source, it is quite clear that the information he is now giving to the Ministry of Defence is not a full and frank account of the conversation with Mr Gilligan and that he has failed to mention the conversation with Susan Watts.

If it is a different source, it means that the original Gilligan story was separately corroborated by a second source – the person who spoke to Susan Watts.

Either way, we stand by Mr Gilligan's reporting of his source.

75. On 9 July Mr Hoon wrote to Mr Davies and stated:

Thank you for your letter of 8 July replying to mine of the same day.

This is not about the divulging of sources.

So that you can establish whether the name of the person who has come forward is the same as the name given to BBC Management by Andrew Gilligan, I am now prepared to tell you that his name is David Kelly, advisor to the Proliferation and Arms Control Secretariat in the MOD.

I trust that the BBC Internal Inquiry into Mr Gilligan's dealings with the MOD Press Office will be broadened to include this matter.

Mr Davies' office was informed by the MoD that it would not be releasing this letter to the press.

76. On 10 July Mr Davies replied to Mr Hoon stating:

> Thank you for your letter of 9th July. I have discussed the matter with Greg Dyke as Editor-in-Chief. Although I did not originally show him the name contained in your letter, I am sure he will have now seen the name in most of this morning's newspapers.

> The BBC will not be making any more comments about, or responding to any claims concerning, the identity of Andrew Gilligan's source for his story on the Today programme on May 29, or the identity of Susan Watts' source for her story on Newsnight on 2nd June.

The confirmation of Dr Kelly's name to the press and Dr Kelly's sudden departure from his home

77. On the afternoon of Friday 4 July Ms Pamela Teare, the Director of News in the MoD and Mrs Wilson, the Chief Press Officer in the MoD, prepared contingent briefings which might be used by MoD press officers in the form of Questions and Answers in case the press became aware in some way over the weekend that a civil servant had come forward to say that he had met Mr Gilligan on 22 May. In the course of the next few days until Tuesday 8 July these Questions and Answers were revised by Ms Teare and Mrs Wilson a number of times but they were not given to senior officials for their approval. On 8 July Ms Teare and Mr Martin Howard did further work on the Q and A material and after the decision had been taken to issue a press statement that an unnamed civil servant had come forward it was decided by the MoD that if the press put the correct name, ie Dr Kelly's name, to a government press officer the press officer would confirm it. The first draft of the Question and Answer material contained the following sentences:

> **Who is the official?**

> We are not prepared to name the individual involved.

> **Why not?**

> We have released all the relevant details. There is nothing to gain by revealing the name of the individual who has come forward voluntarily.

The final form of the Question and Answer material contained the following sentence:

> If the correct name is given, we can confirm it and say that he is senior advisor to the Proliferation and Arms Control Secretariat.

The different drafts of the Question and Answer material are set out in appendix 5.

78. After the MoD had issued the press statement in the late afternoon of 8 July the MoD press office was inundated with calls seeking more information but no member of the press suggested Dr Kelly's name.

79. On Wednesday 9 July there continued to be a great volume of press interest in the name of the civil servant who had come forward and the MoD press office received many calls from the media seeking more information and trying to identify the civil servant. Press officers in the MoD used the Question and Answer material which had been given to them and did not volunteer Dr Kelly's name. In the late afternoon, about 5.30pm, the Financial Times put Dr Kelly's name to Ms Teare who confirmed it. Shortly afterwards, the Guardian, the Daily Mail and the Daily Telegraph put Dr Kelly's name to a press officer and the name was confirmed. The Times put twenty names until Dr Kelly's name was put and confirmed.

80. About 6.00pm on 9 July Mrs Wilson heard that Dr Kelly's name had been confirmed to the press. She then telephoned Sir Kevin Tebbit's office about 6.15pm and requested his Private Secretary, Mr Wilson, to ask Dr Wells to ring Dr Kelly to tell him that his name had been confirmed to the press. It appears that Mr Wilson tried to contact Dr Wells by telephone for about half an hour and finally got in touch with him about 7.00pm when Dr Wells was on a train travelling home. Mr Wilson passed on to him the message from Mrs Wilson requesting him to tell Dr Kelly that the press office had confirmed his name to the press. Dr Wells then rang Dr Kelly at 7.03pm from the train on his mobile telephone and told him that he had been asked to pass on the message that the press office had confirmed his name to the press and Dr Wells advised him to get in touch with the press office. This call lasted for 46 seconds, it was a bad line and Dr Wells thought that they were cut off. Dr Kelly rang Dr Wells back at 7.09pm when Dr Wells was still on his train. Dr Wells thought that Dr Kelly had called him back because the earlier telephone call had been cut off and he repeated to Dr Kelly that the press office had confirmed his name.

81. In the late afternoon of 9 July Mr Nicholas Rufford, a reporter from the Sunday Times, who had met Dr Kelly at his home on previous occasions to discuss his work, drove to Dr Kelly's house in Oxfordshire because he suspected that Dr Kelly might be the person who had spoken to Mr Gilligan. He arrived at Dr Kelly's house about 7.30pm and saw him in the garden. The first words which Dr Kelly spoke to him were that he had just had a call from the MoD telling him that he would be named in national newspapers the following day. Mr Rufford told him that the press were on their way in droves and offered to provide him with hotel accommodation on behalf of his newspaper. Mr Rufford had some further conversation with Dr Kelly and left his garden about 7.45pm.

82. At 7.54pm when Dr Wells had got off his train and when communication was clearer between the two of them, Dr Wells called Dr Kelly again on his mobile telephone to check that he had got his earlier message and that he was acting on it and Dr Kelly told him that Nick Rufford had appeared on his doorstep.

83. After having spoken to Mr Wilson about 6.30pm, Mrs Wilson took steps to arrange that a press officer would be ready to go to Dr Kelly's house if Dr Kelly wanted him. She was about to telephone Dr Kelly about 8.00pm when Dr Kelly telephoned her and said that Nick Rufford had been in contact with him and asked him why he was not now in a hotel. Dr Kelly told Mrs Wilson that he was now minded to go to family or friends and he would be heading to the West Country, but he would let her know where he was when he got there.

84. Dr Kelly and his wife then packed some clothes very quickly and left their house in a rush within ten minutes. They drove towards Weston-Super-Mare and on the way they stopped just outside Swindon about 8.45pm and Dr Kelly telephoned Dr Wells and told him that he was travelling to Cornwall. Dr and Mrs Kelly spent the night of 9 July in Weston-Super-Mare. On the morning of Thursday 10 July Dr Kelly telephoned Dr Wells and they agreed to keep in touch.

CHAPTER 4

Requests by the FAC and the ISC that Dr Kelly should appear before them

85. On 10 July Mr Donald Anderson MP, the Chairman of the FAC, wrote to Mr Hoon stating:

    The Decision to go to War in Iraq

    The Foreign Affairs Committee wishes to receive an answer to the following question.

    - On what date, and at what time, did the meeting take place between Dr David Kelly and Mr Andrew Gilligan at which the conversation referred to in the MoD statement of 9 July (sic) took place?

    You will wish to know that the Clerk is writing to Dr Kelly today, inviting him, to appear before the Committee to give oral evidence in public on Tuesday 15 July, on questions directly relevant to the Committee's Report published earlier this week, arising from the MoD statement of 9 July (sic).

    I am copying this letter to Jack Straw and to Bruce George. I would be obliged if you were to reply to it not later than 4 o'clock tomorrow, 11 July.

    On 10 July the Clerk of the FAC wrote to Dr Kelly stating:

    The Decision to go to War in Iraq

    The Foreign Affairs Committee wishes to hear oral evidence from you in public at 3 o'clock on Tuesday 15 July, to answer questions directly relevant to the Committee's Report published earlier this week, arising from the MoD statement of 9 July (sic).

    I would be obliged if you were to reply to this letter not later than 4 o'clock tomorrow, 11 July.

86. On 10 July the Clerk of the ISC made an oral request to the MoD that Dr Kelly should give evidence before that Committee on 15 July.

87. On 10 July Sir Kevin Tebbit wrote to Mr Hoon stating:

    <u>DR KELLY</u>

    There have been requests to you for Dr Kelly to appear before both the FAC and the ISC (on the same day, 15 July).

    2. We had already offered him to the ISC and I recommend that you agree to that request, although to avoid setting a precedent, you should stress that you only are content for such a relatively junior official to appear given the exceptional nature of the evidence that Dr Kelly could offer. As regards the FAC, however, I recommend that you resist, on grounds that the FAC inquiry is completed (their report was finalised on 3 July, before we had been able to talk to Kelly ourselves) and that a separate session to question Kelly would attach disproportionate importance to him in relation to the subject of their inquiry as a whole. The ISC, on the other hand, are only just beginning their work and are better placed to ensure that Kelly's views are placed in the proper context (he is, after all, not the Government's principal adviser on the subject, nor even a senior one). A further benefit of an ISC hearing is that they can more easily handle national security dimensions, should they wish to cover intelligence material with Kelly, although they might be prepared, given the public interest, to hold most of their hearing in open session, although this could be unprecedented.

3. A further reason for avoiding two hearings, back to back, is to show some regard for the man himself. He has come forward voluntarily, is not used to being thrust into the public eye, and is not on trial. It does not seem unreasonable to ask the FAC to show restraint and accept the FAC hearing as being sufficient for their purposes (eg testing the validity of Gilligan's evidence).

4. It will, of course, be important to ensure that views that Kelly may express are not necessarily taken to represent HMG's policy, or even the collective view of either our intelligence or military expert communities. The ISC will be suitably placed to deal with this through the further witnesses they already plan to call, eg John Scarlett. The FAC, with their hearing ended and report produced, would not be in that position.

5. This line may not be sustainable in strict institutional terms: the FAC report to Parliament, whereas the ISC, although drawn from Parliament, report formally to the Prime Minister. And I do not believe that the ISC have taken testimony in public before.

But I think it worth a try at least. The individual himself is, I understand, prepared to appear before both bodies.

88.   On Friday 11 July Mr Hoon's Private Secretary wrote to Mr Straw's Private Secretary as follows:

FOREIGN AFFAIRS COMMITTEE: DR KELLY

As you know, the Defence Secretary received a letter yesterday afternoon from the Chairman of the Foreign Affairs Committee, Donald Anderson, asking that Dr David Kelly should appear before the FAC on Tuesday 15 July at 1500. At about the same time, we received an oral request from the Clerk to the Intelligence and Security Committee (ISC) asking for Dr Kelly to appear before them on the same day at 1230 for about 45 minutes. Donald Anderson has asked for a reply by 1600 today. The Government has already indicated, in the MOD press statement issued on Tuesday 8 July, that it would not object if the ISC asked to see Dr Kelly as part of their current inquiry.

The Defence Secretary has given the request from the FAC careful consideration. There are reasons for resisting this request:

- The FAC have already completed their inquiry. (Indeed, their report was finalised on 3 July before MOD officials had interviewed Dr Kelly themselves.)

- A separate session to question Dr Kelly would attach disproportionate importance to him in relation to the subject of the FAC's inquiry as a whole.

- The ISC is better placed than the FAC to handle the national security dimensions should the question of intelligence material arise.

- It is fairer on the man himself not to expect him to appear before two Parliamentary Committees within the space of 3 hours.

On the other hand:

- It is not unreasonable for the FAC to feel that Dr Kelly's account may call into question the evidence that they were given by Andrew Gilligan and that they should therefore have an opportunity to see him themselves. (It is conceivable, that having done so, they may decide to recall Gilligan.)

- Presentationally, it would be difficult to defend a position in which the Government had objected to Dr Kelly appearing before a Committee of the House which takes evidence in public in favour of an appointed Committee which meets in private. Although the ISC has considered taking evidence in public before and might decide to do so on this occasion, this could set an unwelcome precedent for both the Committee itself and for us.

The Defence Secretary has, therefore, concluded that on balance we should agree to the FAC's request. Given that Dr Kelly is a relatively junior official who played only a limited role in the preparation of the Dossier, we should invite Donald Anderson to agree that the Committee will confine its questioning to matters directly relevant to Andrew Gilligan's evidence. I understand that No.10 would be content with this approach.

Attached are drafts of the letters which the Defence Secretary proposes to send to Donald Anderson and Ann Taylor later today. I should be grateful for any comments that you may have by no later than 1430 today.

I am copying this letter to Jonathan Powell and Alastair Campbell (No.10) and to Sir David Omand and John Scarlett (Cabinet Office).

89. On 11 July Mr Hoon wrote to Mr Donald Anderson, the Chairman of the FAC, as follows:

Thank you for your letter of 10 July about Dr David Kelly.

I understand that Dr Kelly met Mr Gilligan on 22 May at about 1700 at the Charing Cross Hotel.

You also ask that Dr Kelly appears before the FAC on Tuesday 15 July at 1500. As you know, the Government has already suggested that the Intelligence and Security Committee (ISC) might wish to interview Dr Kelly as part of their continuing inquiry. (A copy of the MOD's press statement of 8 July is attached for convenience.) The Chairman of the ISC has now asked that Dr Kelly appears before them, also on next Tuesday, at 1230 for about 45 minutes. I am writing to Ann Taylor today agreeing to this request.

Although the FAC has now completed its own inquiry, I can understand why you also wish to see Dr Kelly. I am prepared to agree to this on the clear understanding that Dr Kelly will be questioned only on those mattes which are directly relevant to the evidence that you were given by Andrew Gilligan, and not on the wider issue of Iraqi WMD and the preparation of the Dossier. Dr Kelly was not involved in the process of drawing up the intelligence parts of the Dossier.

As I noted above, Dr Kelly will have appeared earlier the same day before the ISC. I hope that you will bear this in mind and not detain him for longer than about the same period of time indicated by the ISC. As he is not used to this degree of public exposure, Dr Kelly has asked if he could be accompanied by a colleague. MOD officials will discuss this further with the Clerk.

I should be grateful if you could confirm that you are content to proceed on this basis.

90. On 11 July Mr Hoon wrote to Mrs Ann Taylor, the Chairman of the ISC as follows:

I understand that the Clerk has asked whether I would be content for Dr David Kelly to appear before the ISC on Tuesday 15 July at 1230 for about 45 minutes to give evidence about his meeting with Andrew Gilligan on 22 May. As the Ministry of Defence indicated in the statement it issued on Tuesday 8 July, there are no objections to Dr Kelly appearing.

I should point out that it is unusual for an MOD official of Dr Kelly's grade to appear as principal witness before the ISC. Given the exceptional circumstances, I am content for Dr Kelly to appear but I would not regard this as setting a precedent. I presume that Dr Kelly will be questioned only on those matters which are directly relevant to the claims made by Andrew Gilligan, and not on the wider issue of Iraqi WMD and the preparation of the Dossier on which you have already arranged to take evidence from a range of more senior and qualified witnesses. Dr Kelly was not involved in the process of drawing up the intelligence parts of the Dossier.

91. Dr and Mrs Kelly spent the 11 and 12 July at the house of friends in Cornwall.

92. On 11 July Dr Wells and Dr Kelly had a telephone conversation in which Dr Wells told Dr Kelly of the request that he should appear before the FAC and the ISC and Dr Kelly stated that he would be prepared to appear before both Committees although he expressed concern about the publicity which would arise from appearing before the FAC. He also requested that he should be accompanied by a colleague who should give him guidance on procedures, should that be required.

93. On the afternoon of Sunday 13 July Dr Kelly drove to the house of his daughter, Miss Rachel Kelly, in Oxford, leaving Mrs Kelly at their friend's house in Cornwall. In her evidence Miss Kelly described her assessment of her father's appearance and feelings on the evening of 13 July and parts of her evidence were as follows:

> [1 September, page 127, line 20]
>
> And when I first looked at him there was a really strong expression on his face that really shocked me and I was actually quite distressed to see the hurt that I could see in his face. It was a particular look. There was a lot of distress and anxiety, perhaps a bit of humiliation.......
>
> [1 September, page 129, line 3]
>
> By that time I knew, from Mum and from Dad, that he would have to face these two Committees the coming week. And I think both of us accepted he did not have any choice but to go in front of them. And Dad certainly saw it as his duty.
>
> I mentioned earlier about his strong sense of duty as a civil servant. He would not have questioned that. He would have done what he had to do in order to fulfil that role for him.
>
> Q. Did he talk about the Select Committees?
>
> A. He did, yes. He seemed particularly – he really was quite distressed. He was composed on the outside but underneath I could see he was really very, very deeply traumatised by the fact that the second one would be televised live, and that did seem to be playing on his mind.
>
> Q. What did he say about the second one?
>
> A. Just he told me in very simple terms it would be televised live.......
>
> [1 September, page 130, line 4]
>
> Q. Did you talk to him about the Ministry of Defence or the circumstances in which his name had come out?
>
> A. A little. I think my question was along the lines of: was he getting much support from them? He replied he was getting support from friends and colleagues. He was not really able to articulate any actual support. I just remember feeling there was a lack of moral support for him because he could not tell me about it. He certainly said that people were recognising he had been through the mill. He just seemed very, very tired, very exhausted and under a lot of pressure.

94. On Monday 14 July Mr Donald Anderson wrote to Mr Hoon stating:

> Thank you for your letter of Friday, confirming the attendance of Dr David Kelly before the Committee tomorrow and answering the Committee's questions about the meeting between Dr Kelly and Andrew Gilligan.
>
> I share your clear understanding of the scope and duration of the questioning to which Dr Kelly will be subject, and will draw it to the attention of my colleagues on the Committee.

95. At breakfast on 14 July Miss Rachel Kelly described her father's state of mind:

> [1 September, page 132, line 10]
>
> He again seemed quite quiet, quite nervous, but composed on the outside. I just felt there was a huge amount of tension within him.

96. Later that morning Dr Kelly travelled from his daughter's home to London where he met Dr Wells in the MoD. Dr Wells told Dr Kelly that the MoD would arrange hotel accommodation for him in London that night so that he would not have to travel up the next day from Oxfordshire to give evidence before the two Committees but Dr Kelly said that he would prefer to stay with his daughter in Oxford and would again travel up to London on the next morning. In the course of this discussion Dr Wells gave Dr Kelly a letter which Mr Hatfield had written to him dated 9 July stating that he had breached departmental guidelines on contacts with journalists, but that formal

disciplinary proceedings would not be initiated. Mr Hatfield had given this letter to Dr Wells for him to give to Dr Kelly. The letter was in the following terms:

DISCUSSIONS WITH THE MEDIA

1. I interviewed you with your line manager, Dr Bryan Wells on Friday 4 July, about your letter to him of 30 June in which you described your contacts with the media in general and Andrew Gilligan in particular. I explained that your letter had serious implications since, on the basis of your own account, you appeared to have broken departmental regulations in having unauthorised and unreported conversations with journalists. Your conversation with Andrew Gilligan also appeared to be relevant to the controversy surrounding allegations made by Gilligan about the Government's September 2002 dossier WMD. This letter is not concerned with those wider aspects, although we discussed them during the latter part of the interview on 4 July and at a subsequent meeting on 7 July.

2. During our interview you clarified and expanded on what you had said in your letter of 30 June and I asked you a number of follow-up questions. At the end, I concluded that you had indeed breached departmental instructions on numerous occasions by having conversations with journalists which had been neither authorised by nor reported to the MOD press office. I accepted your assurance that in general these were essentially background, technical briefings and that on many – but not all – occasions you had consulted the FCO press office informally. In the case of Gilligan, you had had two arranged meetings (in February and May 2003) subsequent to your initial contact in the margins of an IISS seminar last September. You had not sought permission or advice prior to either of these meetings and, until your letter of 30 June, had not thought to report them subsequently.

3. As I made clear, these are serious breaches of standard departmental procedure and you were unable to give me any satisfactory explanation for your behaviour. Your contact with Gilligan was particularly ill-judged. Your discussion with him in May has also had awkward consequences for both yourself and the department which could easily have been avoided. I accept your assurance that these consequences were unforeseen and unintended and, in particular, that as you state in your letter you did not make any allegations or accusations about the preparation of the September 2002 dossier. I also concluded on the basis of your account that you had not divulged any classified or otherwise privileged information. On this basis, I have concluded that although your behaviour fell well short of the standard that I would expect from a civil servant of your standing and experience, it would not be appropriate to initiate formal disciplinary proceedings. You should, however, understand that any further breach of departmental guidelines in dealing with the media would almost certainly result in disciplinary action, with potentially serious consequences.

4. You should be absolutely clear that while you are working in the MOD you are required to seek explicit authority from your line manager and the MOD press office before agreeing to talk to journalists, even if there may be occasions when there may be advantage, additionally, in consulting the FCO. I would also urge you to be very cautious in any comments you might make at or in the margins of public seminars and the like. There is always the dangers (sic) that such remarks may be taken out of context.

5. I should also remind you that the possibility of disciplinary action could be reopened if any facts were to come to light which appeared to call into question the account and assurances that you gave to me.

6. I am sending a copy of this letter to Dr Wells as your line manager and a copy to Richard Scott at Dstl which will be placed on your personal file.

This letter in its unopened envelope was found in Dr Kelly's study in his home in Oxfordshire after his death. The police examined the letter and found none of Dr Kelly's fingerprints on the letter. Therefore it appears that Dr Kelly had not opened the envelope and had not read the letter.

97. After his discussion with Dr Wells, Dr Kelly attended a meeting with Mr Martin Howard, Dr Wells and Ms Heather Smith, a personnel officer in the MoD, to discuss his appearance before the FAC and the ISC. Dr Wells made a typewritten record of the meeting on 22 July which was as follows:

NOTES OF A MEETING WITH DR KELLY – 14 JULY

Present

Mr Martin Howard, DCDI

Dr David Kelly

Dr Bryan Wells, DCPAC

Ms Heather Smith, DGCP CHRO Cond/AD

1. <u>Howard</u> started the meeting by saying that he wanted to ensure that Kelly understood the procedures that the FAC and ISC were likely to following during their evidence sessions, and that he was comfortable with what was required of him. There was no question of the MOD seeking to impose Departmental lines: Kelly was free to tell his own story. Howard outlined the different bases on which the FAC and ISC were constituted, and their current interests in the Government's policy towards Iraq and WMD.

2. <u>Howard</u> then outlined the areas that the two Committees might be free to question Kelly. These were:

   (a) his role in Government, and relationship with the media;

   (b) his role in drawing up the Government's September 2002 Dossier;

   (c) his meeting with Gilligan: what transpired, and why he subsequently decided to inform his line management;

   (d) (for the ISC) his access to intelligence in general;

   (e) (for the ISC) his access to intelligence on the "45 minute claim".

Howard emphasised that the Committee's questioning in these areas would be eliciting essentially factual answers, and Kelly should feel free to give his own story. <u>Kelly</u> confirmed that he was happy about this.

3. <u>Howard</u> then outlined other areas where the Committees might probe, which were at the margins of what the Defence Secretary had defined when agreeing that the Committees could interview Kelly, but which were nevertheless hard to refuse. These areas were:

   (a) what Kelly thought of Government Policy on Iraq. Kelly said that his was a matter for Ministers;

   (b) whether Kelly thought he was Gilligan's source. <u>Kelly</u> asked if he could say "I don't believe I am"; <u>Howard</u> replied that Kelly was free to decide how to answer this to his own conscience: the Department was not telling him what to say;

   (c) what disciplinary action was being taken against Kelly. Kelly said that this was a matter for MOD.

4. <u>Kelly</u> asked what he might say about the issue of Uranium imports from Niger. <u>Howard</u> noted that Kelly had already said that in his meeting with Gilligan he had confined himself to repeating the IAEA observations on the matter. Kelly should feel free to repeat the same line if that was his position.

5. <u>Howard</u> asked Kelly about his contacts with Susan Watts; Kelly said that they had not spoken about the September Iraq Dossier.

6. <u>Wells</u> asked Kelly how he wanted to take forward his wish to be accompanied by a colleague to the FAC. <u>Kelly</u> replied that, on the basis of this present meeting, he did not feel the need to

have a colleague alongside him. He was aware that Wells would be accompanying him to the evidence sessions.

7. At the end of the meeting, <u>Kelly</u> said that he would welcome the chance to see Howard later in the week or early the following, to discuss Howard's recent visit to Iraq. He (Kelly) was looking forward to returning to theatre (sic). <u>Howard</u> said he would be pleased to see Kelly, to discuss Iraq and for a general discussion after the evidence sessions. <u>Kelly</u> concluded by saying that he appreciated Howard's giving up so much time to discuss his appearances before the Committees.

98. Dr Wells' typewritten record made on 22 July was based on a handwritten note which he had made at the meeting on 14 July and his handwritten note contained the words "tricky areas" which were not included in the typewritten record. A handwritten note made at the meeting by Dr Kelly also contained the words "tricky areas" as did a handwritten note made at the meeting by Ms Heather Smith. It appears that the "tricky areas" were the three areas set out in paragraph 3 of Dr Wells' typewritten record. The three handwritten notes of Dr Wells, Dr Kelly and Ms Smith respectively are set out in appendix 6.

99. After this meeting Dr Kelly returned to his daughter's home in Oxford on Monday afternoon. When she first saw him that evening she described him as follows:

[1 September, page 133, line 4]

He was as normal really, quite composed, quite relaxed.

But she said that later that evening:

[1 September, page 133, line 21]

Dad just seemed lost in his thoughts……….

[1 September, page 133, line 24]

He just seemed under an overwhelming amount of stress, that is the only I can describe it, that there was something on his mind. I would guess he was contemplating the day ahead of him the next day, but he also seemed to be finding it almost painful to think about it. He was just very withdrawn, and I was just very, very concerned about him.

100. On the afternoon of 14 July Mr Gilligan sent an e-mail to Mr Greg Simpson, an official of the Liberal Democrat Party, in relation to Dr Kelly's appearance before the FAC on the next day and later in the afternoon Mr Simpson sent on that e-mail to Mr David Chidgey MP, a member of that party and a member of the FAC. The e-mail was in the following terms:

We have been doing some research on David Kelly. Aside from the red herring of a source-hunt, he is an extremely interesting witness in his own right – probably, if he answers fully, the best you'll have had.

He is described in one of the standard reference works (Tom Mangold and Jeff Goldberg, Plague Wars) as "the senior adviser on biological warfare to the MoD … the West's leading biological warfare inspector" with "world-recognised expertise in every aspect of biological warfare [whose] knowledge cannot be overtrumped.

- As has been reported, he was the chief field inspector of UNSCOM, the predecessor to UNMOVIC. He led the first and last BW inspections in Iraq carried out by UNSCOM.

- He was one of three officials who accompanied Jack Straw when Straw gave evidence to the FAC about Iraq's WMD programmes on September 25 2002, one day after publication of the Blair dossier. He said hardly anything, however; Straw did all the talking.

- We believe he is currently the chief British inspector on the Iraq Survey Group (the No.2 Brit in the Group under Brigadier John Deverell, the British contingent commander.)

Questions for Kelly

What is the current state of the Iraq Survey Group's knowledge about Iraq's BW programme? Have you found anything? Did you believe in September 2002 that Iraq was an immediate danger? Was everyone happy about the inclusion of the 45 minute point in the dossier in the light of what's been discovered since? Did you know the 45-minute point was single-source? Were there any arguments between the intelligence services and No 10 over the dossier?

Above all, he should be asked to say what kind of a threat Iraq was in September 2002 in his opinion. If he is able to answer frankly it should be devastating. Obviously he works for the Government and who pays the piper calls the tune. But if you could put some of these quotes (particularly the Watts) to him I think it would have some impact.

He is on record as saying that Iraq was NOT the greatest WMD threat. Leakage from the Russian programmes, he believed, was a greater threat.

For instance, CBC (Canadian TV), 23 October 2002: "Leakage from Russia is the greatest threat, because Russia had a dedicated programme and a great understanding of how you use smallpox as a volatile weapon."

On 18 Oct 2001, at the height of the US anthrax scare, Kelly told The Independent that if suspicion fell on any country as the source of the US anthrax "the obvious one is Russia, it's a league ahead of Iraq." He also said that Iraq had "too much at stake" to take part in any action against the West.

He also told my colleague Susan Watts, science editor of Newsnight (who described him as " a senior official intimately involved with the process of pulling together the dossier"):

"In the run-up to the dossier, the Government was obsessed with finding intelligence to justify an immediate Iraqi threat. While we were agreed on the potential Iraq threat in the future, there was less agreement about the threat the Iraqis posed at that moment.

That was the real concern – not so much what they had now, but what they would have in the future. But that unfortunately was not expressed strongly in the dossier, because that takes the case away for war to a certain extent....

[The 45 minutes point] was a statement that was made and it got out of all proportion. They were desperate for information. They were pushing hard for information that could be released. That was one that popped up and it was seized on, and it's unfortunate that it was. That is why there is the argument between the intelligence services and No 10, because they picked up on it and once they'd picked up on it you can't pull it back from them.... So many people were saying 'well, we're not sure about that'.... because the word-smithing is actually quite important."

Does he still agree with this?

Is Kelly our source? We are not ruling anyone in or out as the source. I had many conversations with people inside and outside the intelligence community about the issue of Iraqi WMD and the dossier. We suspect the MoD of playing games to try to eliminate names.

However: if, as the MoD has said, Kelly's involvement in the dossier was only tangential, he cannot be our source. Two of my source's claims which have proved to be true – that the 45-minute point derived from a single informant, and that it came in late – have been shown to be true. Such facts could only have been known to someone closely involved in compiling the dossier until a late stage.

It is clear that Mr Chidgey made use of the quotation of what Dr Kelly said to Ms Susan Watts set out in the e-mail when he questioned Dr Kelly the next day when he appeared before the FAC.

101. After breakfast the next morning, Tuesday 15 July, Miss Kelly said that her father seemed:

[1 September, page 135, line 24]

> ... fine. We had coffee and normal breakfast. He was – I think he was just trying to enjoy his time with me possibly rather than think ahead to the day. He had done his thinking perhaps the night before.

102. After breakfast Dr Kelly travelled up to London from Oxford and met Dr Wells in the MoD in the mid morning. It had been arranged that Dr Kelly would give evidence before the ISC in the Cabinet Office in Whitehall at noon on Tuesday 15 July and would give evidence before the FAC at 2.30pm on that afternoon. In the course of the morning the clerk to the ISC informed Mr Hoon's office that Dr Kelly's appearance before that Committee had to be postponed to the next day, but there was a misunderstanding about which hearing by a Committee had been postponed and Dr Kelly, accompanied by Dr Wells and Wing Commander John Clark, who was a friend and colleague of Dr Kelly in the MoD, went to the Cabinet Office and then returned to the MoD on learning of the misunderstanding. In the afternoon Dr Kelly, accompanied by Dr Wells, Wing Commander Clark and Mrs Wilson, the chief press officer of the MoD went to the House of Commons and Dr Kelly gave evidence to the FAC.

Dr Kelly's appearances before the FAC and the ISC

103. The 15 July was an extremely hot day in London, a bomb scare in Whitehall prevented Dr Kelly being driven to the House of Commons in a government car as had been arranged, and he had to walk there in a rush. In his appearance before the FAC Dr Kelly gave the following evidence:

> **Q15 Mr Hamilton:** May I ask which drafts of the final September dossier did you see and were drafts sent back to you at every stage for your comment?
>
> **Dr Kelly:** No, I was not involved in that process at all.
>
> **Q16 Mr Hamilton:** So you made your contribution and that went into it subsequently?
>
> **Dr Kelly:** Yes. My contribution was not to the intelligence dimension.
>
> **Q17 Mr Hamilton:** Can I ask what meetings you attended at which the dossier was discussed?
>
> **Dr Kelly:** I attended no meetings at all at which the dossier was discussed.
>
> **Q18 Mr Hamilton:** So you were asked to prepare a section?
>
> **Dr Kelly:** I was.
>
> **Q19 Mr Hamilton:** You prepared that section, you had access to the relevant intelligence material and that was submitted to the person compiling the dossier?
>
> **Dr Kelly:** The component that I wrote did not require intelligence information, let us get that straight. It was not the intelligence component of the dossier, it was the history of the inspections, the concealment and deception by Iraq, which is not intelligence information.
>
> **Q20 Mr Olner:** Dr Kelly, could you speak up, please. The problem is these microphones do not amplify the noise.
>
> **Dr Kelly:** I apologise. I have a soft voice, I know.
>
> **Q21 Chairman:** One final question under this heading. Presumably you did discuss this with other colleagues who were involved themselves in the preparation of the dossier, so you knew what was going on?

Dr Kelly: I was familiar with some of it. Actually I was either on leave or working abroad in the August and earlier September of that time frame. That component, no, I really was not involved.

Q22 Mr Chidgey: I just want to move on to the section of our inquiry dealing with contacts with Andrew Gilligan and journalists, but before we talk about Andrew Gilligan can I just confirm that you have also met Susan Watts?

Dr Kelly: I have met her on one occasion.

Q23 Mr Chidgey: Thank you. I would just like to read out to you a statement in the notes that were made: "In the run-up to the dossier the Government was obsessed with finding intelligence to justify an immediate Iraqi threat. While we were agreed on the potential Iraqi threat in the future there was less agreement about the threat the Iraqis posed at the moment. That was the real concern, not so much what they had now but what they would have in the future, but that unfortunately was not expressed strongly in the dossier because that takes the case away for war to a certain extent". Finally, "The 45 minutes was a statement that was made and it got out of all proportion. They were desperate for information. They were pushing hard for information that could be released. That was one that popped up and it was seized on and it is unfortunate that it was. That is why there is an argument between the intelligence services and Number 10, because they had picked up on it and once they had picked up on it you cannot pull back from it, so many people will say 'Well, we are not sure about that' because the word smithing is actually quite important." I understand from Miss Watts that is the record of a meeting that you had with her. Do you still agree with those comments?

Dr Kelly: First of all, I do not recognise those comments, I have to say. The meeting I had with her was on November 5 last year and I remember that precisely because I gave a presentation in the Foreign Office on Iraq's weapons of mass destruction. I cannot believe that on that occasion I made that statement.

Q24 Mr Chidgey: That is very helpful. Can I just be clear on this: I understand that these notes refer to meetings that took place shortly before the *Newsnight* broadcasts that would have been on 2 and 4 June.

Dr Kelly: I have only met Susan Watts on one occasion, which was not on a one-to-one basis, it was at the end of a public presentation.

....

Q43 Ms Stuart: I may not have heard something you said in response to Mr Chidgey's question. You did confirm that you had a meeting and talked with Susan Watts?

Dr Kelly: I have met with her personally once at the end of a seminar I provided in the Foreign Office on November 5.

Q44 Ms Stuart: You have neither met nor talked to her since?

Dr Kelly: I have spoken to her on the telephone but I have not met her face-to-face.

Q45 Ms Stuart: When have you talked to her on the telephone?

Dr Kelly: I would have spoken to her about four or five times.

Q46 Ms Stuart: During May at all?

Dr Kelly: During May? I cannot precisely remember. I was abroad for a fair part of the time in May, but it is possible, yes.

Q47 Ms Stuart: Have you had any conversations or meetings with Gavin Hewitt?

Dr Kelly: Not that I am aware of, no. I am pretty sure I have not.

....

Q56 Mr Olner: Really Mr Gilligan's story was basically about drafts of dossiers being changed, being "sexed-up". Did you infer to Mr Gilligan in any way, shape or form that he might have misrepresented what you said?

Dr Kelly: My conversation with him was primarily about Iraq, about his experiences in Iraq and the consequences of the war, which was the failure to use weapons of mass destruction during the war and the failure by May 22 to find such weapons. That was the primary conversation that I had with him.

Q57 Mr Olner: You certainly never mentioned the "C" word that he went on to explain in his column?

Dr Kelly: The "C" word?

Q58 Mr Olner: The Campbell word.

Dr Kelly: The Campbell word did come up, yes.

Q59 Mr Olner: From you? You suggested it?

Dr Kelly: No, it came up in the conversation. We had a conversation about Iraq, its weapons and the failure of them to be used.

Q60 Mr Olner: How did the word "Campbell" come to be mixed up with all of that? What led you to say that?

Dr Kelly: I did not say that. What I had a conversation about was the probability of a requirement to use such weapons. The question was then asked why, if weapons could be deployed at 45 minutes notice, were they not used, and I offered my reasons why they may not have been used.

Q61 Chairman: Again, I am finding it very difficult to hear. The fans have been turned off, could you do your very best to raise your voice, please.

Dr Kelly: It came in in that sense and then the significance of it was discussed and then why it might have been in the dossier. That is how it came up.

Q62 Mr Pope: Mr Gilligan said in his article in the *Mail on Sunday* of 1 June "I asked him", the source, "how this transformation happened. The answer was a single word. 'Campbell'." In your conversation with Mr Gilligan did you use the word "Campbell" in that context?

Dr Kelly: I cannot recall using the name Campbell in that context, it does not sound like a thing that I would say.

Q63 Mr Pope: Do you believe that the document was transformed, the September dossier, by Alastair Campbell?

Dr Kelly: I do not believe that at all.

Q64 Mr Pope: When you met Mr Gilligan on 22 May he says in his article that he met a source in a central London hotel on that day. Did you meet him in a central London hotel?

Dr Kelly: I did.

Q65 Chairman: Which hotel was that?

Dr Kelly: The Charing Cross Hotel.

Q66 Mr Pope: Did you begin your conversation with Mr Gilligan by discussing the poor state of Britain's railways?

Dr Kelly: No.

Q67 Mr Pope: The reason I ask is because he said "We started off by moaning about the railways" and what I am trying to get to the bottom of is whether or not you were the source, the main source, of Mr Gilligan or whether you were one of the other three minor sources which Mr Gilligan has told us he had. I am really trying to get to the bottom of that. Mr Gilligan will not answer this Committee's questions on those specific points. I just want to know, in your own opinion do you believe that you were the main source of Mr Gilligan's article on 1 June?

Dr Kelly: My believe is that I am not the main source.

Q68 Mr Pope: Do you know who the main source is?

Dr Kelly: No.

Andrew Mackinlay: Any idea?

Q69 Mr Pope: I want to be absolutely clear on this. You do not believe that you are the main source, that it is someone else?

Dr Kelly: From the conversation I had with him, I do not see how he could make the authoritative statement he was making from the comments that I made.

Q70 Mr Maples: Dr Kelly, just following on from what Mr Pope was saying. Mr Gilligan told us that he had four sources in this area and we are trying to find out whether you are the one or whether you are one of the other three. Did you know about this 45 minute claim before the dossier was published?

Dr Kelly: No, it became apparent to me on publication.

Q71 Mr Maples: So you did not know about it before you, like all of us, read the dossier?

Dr Kelly: No. I might have appreciated it 48 hours beforehand but not before that.

Q72 Mr Maples: You would not have known about it significantly in advance. You were never part of any discussions about whether this should or should not be included in the dossier?

Dr Kelly: No.

....

Q101 Andrew Mackinlay: So you made no comments about the veracity of [the dossier] at all to Gilligan, you did not say it was exaggerated, embellished, probably over-egged?

Dr Kelly: No, I had no doubt that the veractiy of it was absolute.

Q102 Chairman: Sorry, I had no doubts?

Dr Kelly: On the veracity of the document.

Q103 Andrew Mackinlay: Did you express any view about that document at all to him which you can share with this Committee?

Dr Kelly: We are talking of a conversation we had six weeks ago and for me it is very difficult to recall that, so I cannot recall the comments that I made. All I can say is that the general tenet of that document is one that I am sympathetic to. I had access to an immense amount of information accumulated from the UN that complements that dossier quite well, remarkably so, and although the final assessment made by the United Nations was status of verification documentation, not a threat assessment, the UN did not make a threat assessment, put the two together and they match pretty well.

Q104 Andrew Mackinlay: Okay. Dr Kelly, a few moments ago I asked you for the names of other journalists you have had contact with in the timescale we were talking about and you said you have not got access to your home. We are going to write formally to the MoD and by that time you will have done your homework and sent it to us in an envelope, but this afternoon can you tell me those journalists who you do recall having met in the timescale? What are their names?

Dr Kelly: Having met?

Q105 Andrew Mackinlay: Yes.

Dr Kelly: I have met very few journalists.

Q106 Andrew Mackinlay: I heard "few", but who are the ones in your mind's eye at this moment? What are their names?

Dr Kelly: That will be provided to you by the Ministry of Defence.

Q107 Andrew Mackinlay: No, I am asking you now. This is the high court of Parliament and I want you to tell the Committee who you met.

Dr Kelly: On this occasion I think it is proper that the Ministry of Defence communicates that to you.

Chairman: But it is a proper question.

Andrew Mackinlay: You are under an obligation to reply.

Chairman: If you have met journalists there is nothing sinister in itself about meeting journalists, save in an unauthorised way.

Q108 Andrew Mackinlay: Who are they?

Dr Kelly: The only people that I can remember having spoken to in recent times about this particular issue – not about this particular issue – is Jane Corbin and Susan Watts.

....

Q116 Richard Ottaway: Dr Kelly, you confirmed in response to questions from Mr Pope that in your opinion you do not think that you were the central source of Mr Gilligan's report?

Dr Kelly: That is my belief.

Q117 Richard Ottaway: In Mr Gilligan's report there were two fundamental assertions which have subsequently been proved correct. One is that the 45 minute assertion was entered late into the September dossier and, secondly, that the 45 minute assertion came from a single, uncorroborated source. I think we can safely say from what you have been saying that you were unaware of either of those two things?

Dr Kelly: Correct.

Q118 Richard Ottaway: Given that Mr Gilligan's source of the story has proved to be correct, do you think it is fair to say that you could not have been the source? It is not jut a question of your opinion, but you could not have been the source.

Dr Kelly: It is very difficult for me to be that strong. I do realise that in the conversation that I had there was reinforcement of some of the ideas he has put forward.

Q119 Richard Ottaway: Given that there were two assertions which have been proved correct, which you did not know about, you clearly were not the source of those assertions.

Dr Kelly: Correct.

Q120 Richard Ottaway: So, therefore, you could not have been the central source?

Dr Kelly: Correct.

Q121 Richard Ottaway: When it was announced that the MoD put out a statement that you had been in contact with the press, in the penultimate paragraph the MoD says: "We do not know whether this official is the single source quoted by Mr Gilligan". Given what you have said today, why did you allow that statement to be made?

Dr Kelly: Can you repeat the statement, please?

Q122 Richard Ottaway: "We do not know whether this official is the single source quoted by Mr Gilligan".

Dr Kelly: Because I think that is the MoD's assessment.

Q123 Richard Ottaway: Did you know that they were going to say that?

Dr Kelly: I did.

Q124 Richard Ottaway: Did you tell them that it was an incorrect statement?

Dr Kelly: No. The whole reason why this has come up and the reason why I wrote to my line management was because I had a concern that because I had met with Andrew Gilligan in fact

I may have contributed to that story. When I reflected on my interaction with him and realised the balance between the general conversation and the very specific aspect we are now discussing today, which was a very, very minor part of it, I did not see how on earth I could have been the primary source. I did not see how the authority would emanate from me.

Q125 Richard Ottaway: I share your analysis, I do not see how you could have been the primary source. Why did you not complain to the MoD that this was an inaccurate statement they were making?

Dr Kelly: Because, as I have just explained, I did realise that in fact I may have inadvertently, if you like, contributed to that.

Q126 Richard Ottaway: You reached the conclusion that you were not the source?

Dr Kelly: I do not believe I am the source.

Q127 Richard Ottaway: You have just concurred with me that you could not have been the source.

Dr Kelly: Following the logic I agree with that, yes.

Q128 Richard Ottaway: In that, the MoD says they do not know of the source and it was knowingly said by you.

Dr Kelly: That is the situation.

Q129 Richard Ottaway: Do you think possibly the MoD knowingly got it wrong?

Dr Kelly: No, I am saying that the MoD cannot make the categorical statement that you want it to make based on my information provided to them.

Q130 Richard Ottaway: I have to say that there seems to be an inconsistency between your two statements. Would you agree that there is an inconsistency between your belief that you were not the single source and the MoD's statement?

Dr Kelly: There is an element of inconsistency there, I have to agree with you.

Q131 Richard Ottaway: In response to my colleague, David Chidgey, he gave you a quote which appeared on *Newsnight* in a programme introduced by Susan Watts. You have confirmed that you have spoken to Susan Watts. Can I take you through the quote again that was read out. You said you did not recognise it. Could you just concentrate on it. It is talking about the 45 minute point. It said: "The 45 minute point was a statement that was made and it got out of all proportion. They were desperate for information. They were pushing hard for information that could be released. That was the one that popped up and it was seized on and it is unfortunate that it was. That is why there is the argument between the intelligence services and Number 10, because they picked up on it and once they had picked up on it you cannot pull back from it, so many people will say 'Well, we are not sure about that' because the word smithing is actually quite important." There are many people who think that you were the source of that quote. What is your reaction to that suggestion?

Dr Kelly: I find it very difficult. It does not sound like my expression of words. It does not sound like a quote from me.

Q132 Richard Ottaway: You deny that those are your words?

Dr Kelly: Yes.

....

Q155: Sir John Stanley: Who made the proposition to you, Dr Kelly, that you should be treated absolutely uniquely, in a way which I do not believe any civil servant has ever been treated before, in being made a public figure before being served up to the Intelligence and Security Committee?

Dr Kelly: I cannot answer that question. I do not know who made that decision. I think that is a question you have to ask the Ministry of Defence.

Q156 Sir John Stanley: So you did not make it yourself?

Dr Kelly: Certainly not.

Q157 Sir John Stanley: We have to assume therefore that your ministers then are responsible for treating you uniquely as a civil servant in highly publicising you before going to the Intelligence and Security Committee?

Dr Kelly: That is a conclusion you can draw.

Q158 Sir John Stanley: Why did you go along with it, Dr Kelly? You were being exploited, were you not?

Dr Kelly: I would not say I was being exploited.

Q159 Sir John Stanley: You had been before them to rubbish Mr Gilligan and his source, quite clearly?

Dr Kelly: I just found myself to be in this position out of my own honesty in acknowledging the fact that I had interacted with him. I felt obliged to make that statement once I realised that I may possibly be that source. Until then, I have to admit that I was out of the country for most of the time this debate was going on so I was not following the actual interactions that were going on. It was not until I was alerted to the transcript by a friend that I actually even considered that I might be the source.

Q160 Sir John Stanley: If I may say so, I think you have behaved in a very honourable and proper manner by going to your departmental line managers in the circumstances you describe. That does not get away from the key issue, which is why did you feel it was incumbent upon you to go along with the request that clearly had been made to you to be thrown to the wolves, not only to the media but, also, to this Committee?

Dr Kelly: I think that is a line of questioning you will have to ask the Ministry of Defence. I am sorry.

Sir John Stanley: I am grateful.

Q161 Chairman: Do you feel any concern at the way the Ministry of Defence responded after you volunteered your admission?

Dr Kelly: I accept what has happened.

Q162 Andrew Mackinlay: The feeling I have, and you might be able to help me with this, was that there was no serious attempt by the security or intelligence services or the Ministry of Defence Police to find out Gilligan's source. Did they come knocking at your door or that of your colleagues, to your knowledge at all, to discover that?

Dr Kelly: I have no knowledge of that whatsoever.

Q163 Andrew Mackinlay: Since you wrote to your superiors in the way you have done, have you met Geoff Hoon?

Dr Kelly: No.

Q164 Andrew Mackinlay: Any Ministers?

Dr Kelly: No.

Mr Pope: Any special advisers?

Q165 Andrew Mackinlay: Any special advisers?

Dr Kelly: No.

Q166 Andrew Mackinlay: Do you know of any other inquiries which have gone on in the department to seek the source – to clarify in addition to you or instead of you or apart from you?

None whatsoever?

Dr Kelly: No.

Q167 Andrew Mackinlay: I reckon you are chaff; you have been thrown up to divert our probing. Have you ever felt like a fall-guy? You have been set up, have you not?

Dr Kelly: That is not a question I can answer.

Q168 Andrew Mackinlay: But you feel that?

Dr Kelly: No, not at all. I accept the process that is going on.

Q169 Chairman: I am sorry. You accept...?

Dr Kelly: I accept the process that is happening.

Q170 Mr Hamilton: Dr Kelly, I am sorry to go back to something that I know you have already answered or partially answered, but I just want to clarify. My colleague, Mr Ottaway, did refer to this earlier. I just want to come back to this question of Alastair Campbell and Mr Gilligan. The MoD statement states that when Mr Gilligan asked about the role of Alastair Campbell with regard to the 45 minute issue "he made no comment and explained that he was not involved in the process of drawing up the intelligence parts of the dossier" – that is you, of course. Just for the record, can you tell me absolutely whether you named or otherwise identified Alastair Campbell or did you say anything which Mr Gilligan might reasonably have interpreted as identifying Mr Alastair Campbell as wanting to change the dossier or "sex it up" in any way or make undue reference to the 45 minute claim?

Dr Kelly: I cannot recall that. I find it very difficult to think back to a conversation I had six weeks ago. I cannot recall but that does not mean to say, of course, that such a statement was not made but I really cannot recall it. It does not sound like the sort of thing I would say.

....

Q172 Sir John Stanley: How do you explain the reasons for the delay between the letter you wrote on 30 June and the release of the Ministry of Defence statement throwing you to the wolves?

Dr Kelly: I cannot explain the bureaucracy that went on in between. I think it went through the line management system and went through remarkably quickly.

Q173 Sir John Stanley: Did you get any impression that the statement was delayed by the Ministry of Defence in order to ensure that it went out only after our report was published?

Dr Kelly: I cannot answer that question. I really do not know.

Q174 Mr Olner: You work for the MoD, Dr Kelly, but work obviously very closely with the intelligence and security services. Did you suggest to anyone at all that the intelligence and security services were unhappy about the September dossier?

Dr Kelly: Unhappy? I do not think they were unhappy. I think they had confidence in the information that was provided in that dossier.

Q175 Mr Olner: So there was no, if you like, feeling within the security services that this was a piece of work that had been "sexed-up" and it was going to be rubbished at the end of the day?

Dr Kelly: I think there were people who worked extremely hard to achieve that document and the calibre of the document that was produced.

Q176 Mr Pope: When you met Mr Gilligan on 27 May did you feel at the time that you were doing anything untoward, that you were breaching the confidence that is expected of you within your job?

Dr Kelly: No. I think it has been agreed by the Ministry of Defence there was no security breach involved in the interactions I had.

Q177 Mr Pope: Do you think, in your experience, that there is a widespread culture in the MoD and, perhaps, in the intelligence and security services of people speaking in an unofficial capacity to journalists? Certainly the impression I got from Mr Gilligan was that that was a widespread culture that journalists would have a number of contacts in the MoD or in the security services. Is that your experience?

Dr Kelly: It is not my experience but I think you have to recognise that I have a strange background in the sense that I operated for ten years internationally interacting with international press and was well-known to the press and had quite a lot of contact. I think I am somewhat unusual in terms of the people who have an interest in that situation.

Q178 Mr Pope: Finally, were you aware of any widespread unease about the accuracy of the September dossier, at the time it was published, amongst people who were involved in providing information for it?

Dr Kelly: I do not believe there was any difficulty over the accuracy of that document.

104. In his evidence Wing Commander Clark was asked if Dr Kelly had said anything to him in the afternoon after he had given evidence to the FAC. Wing Commander Clark's evidence was:

[27 August, page 125, line 1]

Q. Did Dr Kelly comment on any of the questions that he had been asked?

A. Yes. He was totally thrown by the question or the quotation that was given to him from Susan Watts. He spoke about that when he came back to the office. He did say that threw him. He had not expected or anticipated that that would have come to the fore at that forum.

Q. When you say the question about Susan Watts, can you be a bit more precise about what that questions was?

A. I cannot remember exactly which member of the Committee, but a member of the Committee read out a very long quotation from Susan Watts – well, no, it was a quotation that had been reported on by Susan Watts which apparently David or Dr Kelly had said. Now, in response to that Dr Kelly said it was not his quote. That had come on quite early. That had really surprised him, that that quote had been tabled to him.

Q. So after the hearing he says to you: that really threw me?

A. Yes he did.

Q. Did he say why it really threw him?

A. No, I have no recollection of that.

105. On 15 July 2003, after the FAC had heard evidence from Dr Kelly, the Chairman of the Committee, Mr Donald Anderson, wrote to Mr Jack Straw and stated:

The Decision to go to War in Iraq

As you know, the Committee heard oral evidence today from Dr David Kelly of the Ministry of Defence.

The Committee deliberated after hearing Dr Kelly's evidence, and asked me to write to you, expressing their view that it seems most unlikely that Dr Kelly was Andrew Gilligan's prime source for his allegations about the September dossier on Iraq. Colleagues have also asked me to pass on their view that Dr Kelly has been poorly treated by the Government since he wrote to his line manager, admitting that he had met Gilligan.

I am copying this letter to Geoff Hoon and to Bruce George.

This letter was released to the press.

106. In response to the letter from Mr Anderson the MoD issued the following statement on the evening of 15 July:

The Foreign Affairs Committee has said that it seems most unlikely that Dr David Kelly was Andrew Gilligan's "prime" source for his allegations.

As was made clear in our statement of 8 July, the MoD does not know whether Dr Kelly is the "single" source referred to by Andrew Gilligan before the FAC.

The FAC use the phrase "prime" source. Does this mean that the FAC doubt Mr Gilligan's story? If Dr Kelly is not the source, why does the BBC not say so now? The BBC has the opportunity to clear up this issue. Their silence is suspicious. Their appeal to the principle of source protection is clearly bogus in this case, as Dr Kelly came forward voluntarily.

We also note the FAC's view that Dr Kelly has been "poorly treated" by the Government. We do not accept this. Dr Kelly came forward voluntarily with information on a matter of public interest. He has been properly treated in accordance with Departmental procedures. He has expressed no complaint to us or the FAC, who took the initiative to call him as a witness.

107. In the late afternoon of 15 July Dr Kelly returned to his daughter's home in Oxford. She said in her evidence:

[1 September, page 136, line 19]

he just seemed utterly exhausted. He was really, really tired......

[1 September, page 139, line 5]

He seemed relieved that it was over. I think he was still on some sort of adrenalin high almost. He was – it was – he was happy to be home and happy to receive phone calls from friends to express how it had gone.

Miss Kelly said that on that evening her father was eating well. She was asked whether he was sleeping well and she said:

[1 September, page 142, line 20]

Yes, I actually asked him directly because I was concerned that he might not be, and his reply to me was that he was so exhausted he was sleeping very well indeed.

108. Miss Kelly and her father had breakfast together on the morning of Wednesday 16 July. Her evidence was:

[1 September, page 145, line 1]

Q. And how was he feeling about the Select Committee that was going to take place on the 16th July?

A. On that day he did seem more relaxed, mainly because it was going to be behind closed doors. I think he thought it would be a lot more along technical lines, so he was more comfortable with what he would have to say to them.

109. On that morning Mr David Wilkins, Miss Rachel Kelly's fiancé had breakfast with Miss Kelly and Dr Kelly. His evidence was:

[1 September, page 158, line 25]

Q. And how did he seem in the morning?

A. My recollection is that again it was fairly normal.

Q. And did he comment about the support or absence of support he was getting?

A. Yes, he did. He said that his colleagues – he said that colleagues had been "tremendously supportive", that is a direct quote. I remember him saying that, that they had been tremendously supportive. I did get the impression that it was not all colleagues. I cannot remember his exact wording, but the implication and the impression I was left with was that it was some but not all.

Q. And did he mention anything at all about the Ministry of Defence or how his name had come out, at this stage?

A. I have to say he did not, no, not to me.

110. On 16 July the Clerk of the FAC wrote to the Private Secretary to Mr Hoon:

> At his appearance yesterday before the Foreign Affairs Committee, Dr David Kelly was asked to supply a list of journalists with whom he has had contact. He pointed out that he will be unable to answer this question immediately, because he does not at present have access to his personal diaries. The Committee accepted that its question should be pursued through MoD.
>
> I would be grateful to receive the information for which the Committee has asked as soon as you are able to supply it, accepting that it may be necessary to consult the transcript in order to confirm exactly what was sought. I will try to ensure you receive a copy of the transcript as soon as possible after it has been received in this office, which I expect to be either later today or early tomorrow.

111. On the morning of Wednesday 16 July Dr Kelly travelled up to London from Oxford and gave evidence before the ISC and he was accompanied by Dr Wells and Wing Commander Clark.

112. In his appearance before the ISC Dr Kelly gave (inter alia) the following evidence:

> **MICHAEL MATES:** If you have a long history of dealing with the press and are an officer of the Ministry of Defence and understand that you are experienced in doing this and doing it on a regular basis what is then the difference to person like you to having an authorised meeting with him and an unauthorised meeting, surely in the olden days you didn't get authority every time you spoke to a person of the press?
>
> **DR KELLY:** Yes. The situation is that in the very early days I only spoke to the press, either when they approached me in the Middle East when I had, I just had to react to it there and then, or if I was either in the United Kingdom or the United States at the behest of the United Nations, the Ministry of Defence and the Foreign Office. As time went by, of course, you have follow-up questions, you'd have clarification, individual reporters, individual companies, media companies would have my contact details and of course I would be contacted directly, and I'd use my discretion as to whether I responded to that or responded to which ever Ministry or Agency demanded and essentially that's what I've done ever since, I have used my discretion. Now as the years have gone by, of course, I've got 'cold calls' sometimes I've been asked about things which I haven't been dealing with before and again I used my judgment.
>
> **MICHAEL MATES:** But specifically it has been, has it got this wrong, the MoD said that your contact with Andrew Gilligan was 'unauthorised'.
>
> **DR KELLY:** That's correct.
>
> **MICHAEL MATES:** But then doesn't the MoD expect you to use your judgment about these things or is there an absolute prohibition?
>
> **DR KELLY:** I think in practice there's an absolute prohibition, but I also believe that of course there is an element of reality in all of this, and although there's an absolute prohibition, technically, in terms of the guidance that is provided one.
>
> **MICHAEL MATES:** And on the occasions when you have spoken to the press, and it has been known you've spoken to the press, because for whatever reason have you been reprimanded?
>
> **DR KELLY:** This is the first time I've ever got into any trouble.
>
> **ANN TAYLOR:** Is it that the first, because it was the first time you've done something that is so clearly unauthorised, or is it because it's the first time it's been a problem?
>
> **DR KELLY:** I think it's the first time it's been a problem! ....
>
> ....
>
> **DR KELLY:** I was aware of the general debate that was going on between those who were supporting the war and those who were against the war and the justification for war and I saw this as being part of that debate. The reference was to a senior intelligence officer who'd been involved, primarily in drafting the dossier, that didn't match me, I'm not an intelligence officer,

I was not involved, I mean I was involved in aspects of drafting the dossier but in the non-intelligence dimension but I certainly wasn't responsible for the final content of that dossier, so the alarm bells didn't start ringing. A friend of mine at RUSI suggested, and I don't think she suggested because she identified me, but she said I should read that, and when I read it there was one phrase in there that I read as being a 'Kelly' statement, which was a statement about the probability that Iraq had, the probability was that Iraq had chemical weapons and that probability was about 30%. That is something that I say and so I then re-read it and thought 'well is this what I've been saying all the way through' and I think there is a blend of what I have said and what someone may have said.

MICHAEL MATES: You've said always that the probability is 30% that they had chemical weapons?

DR KELLY: The probability is 100% that they had a programme and I think it's about 30% that they have chemical weapons.

MICHAEL MATES: And you said that too, to Gilligan?

DR KELLY: I said that to many people.

....

MICHAEL MATES: And, just the last point, are you surprised at the public MoD reactions or was it that the statement made with your agreement?

DR KELLY: The official MoD press statement was made with my agreement, yes.

MICHAEL MATES: So you weren't surprised, okay.

ANN TAYLOR: Can I just ask before I move on to James, you mentioned the transcript of the FAC and you said that you weren't an intelligence officer and that whilst you were involved in drafting the dossier you weren't involved in the applying or editing or decisions on it, do you thinks that Andrew Gilligan regarded you as an intelligence officer and did you at any stage tell him that you'd been involved in the drafting or the writing about this document, or information for it?

DR KELLY: I've not acknowledged to anyone that I was involved in the drafting of the dossier, I meant, that essentially, my component which was the non-intelligence component which was done at the request of the Foreign Office so not even Brian Wells' predecessor as the Director of PAC was aware that I wrote that part.......

....

JAMES ARBUTHNOT: May I ask, the allegation that Andrew Gilligan made that someone had said that the forty-five minutes, that the issue of forty-five minutes was over-hyped in the document. That's not something that you recognised as having come from you?

DR KELLY: No I think I may well have said that the forty-five minute mention was there for impact, yes, because it came out of a conversation, not about the dossier, but about Iraq, 'why weapons had not been used and why they had not been found subsequently' and then the question was 'well if you have something that is available in forty-five minutes surely it would have been used' and then, I can't identify such a system that you could use within forty-five minutes and then the question was 'why would it be included' and I can't give an answer as to why it would be included?

JAMES ARBUTHNOT: So if you might have said that it was there for impact, you can't be firmer than that as to whether you did or did not say that it was there for impact?

DR KELLY: No I'm pretty sure I said it was there for impact, I've acknowledged that.

MICHAEL MATES: As opposed to being factually correct?

DR KELLY: It depends on how you interpret what I've said. I have said that I don't, I can't identify a weapons system that could be used within forty-five minutes of deployment.

MICHAEL MATES: To Gilligan?

DR KELLY: Yes, I've said it to many people, but to Gilligan, yes.

JAMES ARBUTHNOT: So if that was a statement that was there for impact was it a statement that you think should not have been there?

DR KELLY: I think I'd like to quote Hans Blix who at the weekend said that he thought it was unwise to have it there, I think that's probably the correct statement to make. I can't, I really can't say that I thought it should not be there because I'm actually not aware of the intelligence behind it.

JAMES ARBUTHNOT: But you did feel that it unwise to it there?

DR KELLY: Now I do, yes. At the time, when it came out, I really didn't make a judgment on it, it was there, it was a statement, I was puzzled but it by I didn't make a judgment on it.

JAMES ARBUTHNOT: Did you think when you were speaking to Andrew Gilligan that you gave him the impression that you felt it was unwise for it to have been there?

DR KELLY: That's a possibility, I can't, really can't, because you are talking about a dynamic and I really can't recall … I have to admit it's a possibility, yes.

JAMES ARBUTHNOT: Did you or he mention Alastair Campbell in your discussions in May?

DR KELLY: Alastair Campbell came up – because the question was then 'well why was it there?' and he asked that question, now I was not involved in the process of assembling the dossier, my contribution to the dossier was in May/June of last year, after that I had no involvement in the compilation of the dossier, the drafting of it, the synthesis of it, so I was not in a position to comment on that.

JAMES ARBUTHNOT: So when he said 'why was it there?' what did you say, if you can remember?

DR KELLY: I can't recall accurately because, but, I mean essentially it would be words to the effect that I could not comment, I really cannot remember the exact phrase that I used because I was not in a position to comment.

JAMES ARBUTHNOT: Might it have been that you said, you said Alastair Campbell came up in the context of 'why was it there?'; How did Alastair Campbell come up in the context of that?

DR KELLY: I'm having great difficulty to clearly remember this, but my feeling is the question was asked by Gilligan.

JAMES ARBUTHNOT: What question?

DR KELLY: When you asked about 'why it was there' and then the successive question was about Campbell.

JAMES ARBUTHNOT: So might Andrew Gilligan have said, did Andrew Gilligan say 'why was it there?' and then did he say 'was it Campbell who put it in'.

DR KELLY: I mean that's the sequence that occurred, I mean the exact phrasing I regret I cannot remember, on this occasion this was not something of deep significance to me, you have to remember and so….

JAMES ARBUTHNOT: But if he had said 'was it Campbell who put it in' what do you think you would have said in reply?

DR KELLY: Well I would have no knowledge of that, I just did not have any knowledge about that, so I could not have responded positively or negatively for that matter.

GAVIN STRANG: Could I just ask you know, what is your view of that September dossier?

DR KELLY: My view of the dossier?

GAVIN STRANG: Yes, standing back a bit and giving a view based on your experience and knowledge of that subject.

DR KELLY: I think it is an accurate document, I think it is a fair reflection of the intelligence that was available and it's presented in a very sober and factual way. It's presented in a way that is not an intelligence document or a technical document, I think it is presented in a way that can be consumed by the public, it is well written.

GAVIN STRANG: And you think that precisely what's there will stand the test of time?

DR KELLY: Yes I think so and of course there are certain features that have been confirmed, the extended range missiles, UNMOVIC have found certain weapons albeit not many of them which were capable of dealing either chemical or biological materials so that, to a certain extent has been substantiated, but I'd have to admit that the substantiation is quite small at the moment.

ANN TAYLOR: Just as a follow-up to that, what level of understanding of the document did you think that Andrew Gilligan had when you were discussing these matters with him?

DR KELLY: We didn't really discuss the dossier, the conversation I had was about Iraq and many aspects of that, it came up in the context of weapons, whey they had not been used, why they'd not been found; and in the course of that discussion the question came up about why the forty-five minutes was there, when that came into the dossier, and for me, I mean it's very difficult now to know whether it was a fleeting moment, whether it was two minutes, three minutes, I really can't recall, it may be that he was focused on that issue, but I certainly wasn't I was more focused on acquiring information about Iraq immediately post-conflict which would be useful to my work in the future.

ALAN HOWARTH: You said to us that you thought that there was an absolute prohibition on a person in your position talking to the media, but you suggested that this more or less happens more as a notion than absolute prohibition. Were you in breach of normal practice in doing what you did?

DR KELLY: My understanding now is that I was in breach of normal practice.

ALAN HOWARTH: But you weren't aware at the time that you were in breach of normal practice?

DR KELLY: No, because essentially on this, I actually very rarely meet journalists although I do talk to them on the telephone and on this occasion, I must admit, I'd regarded it more as being more a private conversation than I had a briefing or in any way a disclosure at all.

ALAN HOWARTH: And you didn't report back to any colleagues on the fact of your conversation and what had been said.

DR KELLY: No.

ALAN HOWARTH: When you went to meet Andrew Gilligan, at the Charing Cross Hotel, did you enter the discussion with an agenda of your own, you've mentioned that you were anxious to learn what you could from him, but did you also go to meet him with a view to conveying any particular points to him.

DR KELLY: No, it was very much with the intention of being in receive mode – to understand his experience he had in Iraq.

ALAN HOWARTH: So did you feel justified in talking to him as you did at the time?

DR KELLY: I felt comfortable, I'm not sure what you mean by justified.

ALAN HOWARTH: Do you still feel comfortable about the fact that you did so?

DR KELLY: Had this not all have arisen then yes I would have, because I actually did derive information from him, which was useful. I of course deeply regret it, with hindsight, but yes, if this had not arisen it would have been a useful meeting for me.

ALAN HOWARTH: And you regard him as a reliable witness, you've derived information from him, are you satisfied as to the quality, reliability of what you learned from him?

DR KELLY: I am, the information that I derived from him which I found interesting was that he was actually accessing individuals who had not surrendered and he visited them at their homes, he did not physically gain access to them, which was surprising to me, first of all, was that he knew where they were and apparently the Security Services didn't, whether they did or not, and were eavesdropping, I just don't know, and that those individuals were being protected by the regime, or the residue of the regime and so I found that quite fascinating as to why particular individuals would be protected in such a way.

ALAN HOWARTH: And do you know how to take good advantage of such contacts?

DR KELLY: I don't know is the answer to that. They are people that he had apparently had spoken to before the war.

JOYCE QUIN: Can I ask you how you respond to the letter that the Chairman of Foreign Affairs Committee has apparently written to the Foreign Secretary expressing the view that it seems most unlikely that you were Andrew Gilligan's prime source for his allegation about the September dossier on Iraq.

DR KELLY: Well that's what I believe myself, I mean I do not believe that I'm the prime source, regrettably I've discussed with him issues that are – now – controversial, but I did not do that, my instigation that I raised, it was not something that I felt particularly strongly about, and people who know me know that I feel quite strongly that Iraq had weapons programmes, that they had such weapons and my whole background working for both the Ministry of Defence and the United Nations really supports the position of the dossier, and one of the comments I made yesterday to the Foreign Affairs Committee was that in essence you take a report produced in 1999 by Richard Butler, which was a status of verification achieved by UNSCOM and put that alongside the dossier, they match quite well and the two together essentially comprise quite a reasonable definition of the problem, the threat presented by Iraq, and I also hasten to add that it was not of course the UN's job to do a threat assessment, it was very much a status of verification, but you can read that in another way, assess it as a threat.

JOYCE QUIN: When you volunteered the information to the MoD that you had met Andrew Gilligan did you at that time feel you might be the prime source, or again did you just come forward with that information because you felt it was better given that Andrew Gilligan's story was getting such prominence that you ought to make it clear that you had met him?

DR KELLY: I felt uncomfortable with the situation that I found myself in and so the only way of resolving that problem, because I thought, for three days before deciding to write, and my conscience dictated that I communicated what I had done in the best way that I could, and that's exactly what I did.....

....

ANN TAYLOR: Do you think that the dossier was a sound document?

DR KELLY: Yes........

....

ALAN BEITH: In the course of the discussion it was assumed you would have people of your level of technical knowledge of these things, were you conscious that there were other people who shared your very, very specific reservations, that is for example that you couldn't conceive a weapon system which could have fitted this description or who voiced other reservations about either the dossiers or the general drift of government statements about Iraq?

DR KELLY: Three very different questions. My discussions are primarily technical, I think in terms of the latter part, no, I didn't discuss that with anyone, it wouldn't be my remit or interest to do so. In terms of the forty-five minutes, yes that was very seriously discussed, particularly with people in the United Nations, in UNMOVIC who were desperately trying to think about what system is it they should be looking for when they went back into Iraq, because it doesn't fit any of the known Iraqi systems, so yes, that was talked about and discussed very seriously.

ALAN BEITH: And with that kind of discussion very understandably, particularly UNMOVIC or ex-inspector colleagues, was that, did that in any way fit the description of 'turbulence in the system' which for example Pauline Neville-Jones used although she was presumably talking primarily about intelligence work, that is, which I interpret to be a lot of people having a lot of discussions are saying 'oh, we've got serious doubts about this or that'.

DR KELLY: I wouldn't describe it as 'turbulence in the system' when the people that I talked to when one was seriously trying to think about what it can refer to, and of course it stimulated talk about the systems that we know about as well, it was a serious discussion, I wouldn't describe it as 'turbulence', it's the sort of vigour of discussion you'd have as a consequence of a statement that's not well understood.

ALAN BEITH: Seen as an 'unconcluded' discussion.

DR KELLY: So far, yes....

....

KEVIN BARRON: ....Did Gilligan have a pencil and paper with him, when you were chatting?

DR KELLY: He had a notebook with him, yes..........

....

JOYCE QUIN: And in the transcript of Gilligan's – in the final segment he said the words of his source were that it was transformed in a week before it was published to make it 'sexier', that didn't come from you then?

DR KELLY: The word 'transformed' is not something that would have occurred to me in terms of the document, first of all I had not seen the earlier drafts of it, so I wouldn't know whether it had been transformed or not, the document itself is a very sober, well written, there is no emotive language in it, it's factual, I don't see it as being 'transformed'.

MICHAEL MATES: But you wouldn't describe it as 'sexy'?

DR KELLY: I think the 'forty-five minutes' for impact is the only, that's the only bit that that would be the case.

JAMES ARBUTHNOT: But 'sexier' is that a word you would use?

DR KELLY: It is a word I would use, I use it on occasions.

JAMES ARBUTHNOT: Is it a word you did use?

DR KELLY: I cannot recall on that occasion.

JAMES ARBUTHNOT: But you might have done?

DR KELLY: It's possible, yes.......

....

ANN TAYLOR: Can I ask, at the beginning you mentioned that you do see certain intelligence reports but you haven't been very specific about that, can you give us some idea of what you see by way of JIC papers, what you see from DIS, you mentioned that you did see some *intelligence* reporting could you give us a fuller picture please, of what they might be?

DR KELLY: Certainly. I see all the *intelligence* reporting concerned with both Iraq and ***, with regard to chemical and biological weapons, that arrives in the Proliferation and Arms Control Secretariat and I have full access to that. Within the Defence Intelligence Services I liaise with the Rockingham cell which used to service UNMOVIC and UNSCOM and now will service the Iraq Survey Group and I don't go through all the information that they have but, almost on a weekly basis I'll sit down with the principal officer there and he will alert me to anything that he thinks is of relevance to my work. I also liaise with SIS, they call me in if they want to discuss any raw intelligence with me in if they want any assistance in interpreting intelligence. I see them every two months or so.

Dr Kelly's actions after he had given evidence to the ISC on 16 July 2003

113. After giving evidence to the ISC Dr Kelly returned to his daughter's home in Oxford where he was joined by Mrs Kelly who had travelled from Cornwall. In her evidence Miss Kelly said that when her father arrived back in Oxford he seemed:

[1 September, page 146, line 21]

Again just exhausted. The pressure seemed to have lifted a little bit when he met me at the station, he seemed more relaxed........

[1 September, page 148, line 5]

During the evening he had seemed more relaxed, but when he left – it is hard to describe, I think I recognised that the pressures seemed to be returning to him a little bit. He seemed to be looking ahead to the next day, and I again felt that that he was under this enormous stress and tension and I was a little bit concerned about him once again as he left.

Before Dr Kelly left his daughter's home he had arranged with her that she would meet him the next evening at his home to go for a walk to see a foal near his house.

114. Mrs Kelly said in her evidence that on Wednesday evening on the drive home from her daughter's house, Dr Kelly was very tense and very very tired. When they arrived back at their home Dr Kelly went into his study and switched on his computer and downloaded e-mails and then soon went to bed.

115. Prior to Dr Kelly's appearance before the FAC on 15 July Mr Andrew Mackinlay MP, a member of that Committee, had tabled two Parliamentary Questions for answer by the Secretary of State for Defence.

The first Parliamentary Question was:

To ask the Secretary of State for Defence, when over the past two years Mr David Kelly has met Andrew Gilligan of the BBC.

The second Parliamentary Question was:

To ask the Secretary of State for Defence, which journalists Mr David Kelly has met over the past two years; other than Andrew Gilligan of the BBC, (a) for what purpose each meeting was held, (b) when each meeting took place.

116. Dr Kelly was aware of these Parliamentary Questions before he went back to Oxford from London on the afternoon of 16 July and it had been arranged that on the next day, working from home, Dr Kelly would send the necessary details to the MoD before 10am on 17 July to enable answers to be prepared to those Questions. On Thursday 17 July at 9.22am Dr Kelly sent the following e-mail to Wing Commander Clark and Dr Wells:

John and Bryan,

I have compiled the information as best I can. The list of journalists is the most difficult because some may date before 2002 and some may have nothing to do with Iraq whatsoever! Attached is the information in Word.

Regards,

Attached to this e-mail was the following information:

IISS meeting was 12 to 14th September 2002

I have records of meeting:

Nick Rufford (Sunday Times) 14th March 2002 (discussing Al-Manal)

Alex Nicholl (Financial Times) 15th May 2002 (Iraqi WMD in general)

Phillip Sen (The Engineer) 3rd October 2002 (Inspection technology)

(Other than Andrew Gilligan I know that I have met Jane Corbin and Tom Mangold in the past year but have not recorded those meetings in my diary.)

Letter to Peter Watkins

I have contact with the following journalists:

Tamar Weinstein, CBC Radio Canada

Anna Maria Tremonti, CBC Radio Canada

Bernard Edinger, Reuters

Andrew Veitch, ITN

Mark Worthington, TBS News

Tetsuya Chikushi News, 23 TBS News

Koichiro Yoneda, TBS News

Paul Lashmar, The Independent

Susan Lambert, Australian Broadcasting Corporation

Jeremy Webb, New Scientist

James Bone, The Times

Marilyn Chase, Wall Street Journal

Jeff Goldberg, Freelance journalist

Tom Mangold, BBC Panorama

Judith Miller, New York Times

Calum Lynch, Washington Post

Nick Rufford, Sunday Times

Helen Vyner, Simon Prentice Associates

Susan Wells, BBC*

Carolyn Hawley, BBC

Lynsey Hilsum, Channel Four News

Jane Corbin, BBC

Stephen Endelberg, New York Times

Sean O'Neill, Daily Telegraph

(note this is essentially a list of those journalists that I have business cards for or have recorded in my electronic contacts list, some may date from earlier than 2002; I will have had contact with others but I have no record).

---

* The reference to "Susan Wells, BBC" was very probably intended as a reference to Susan Watts, BBC.

117. On the morning of Thursday 17 July about 8.30am Dr Wells' office received four Parliamentary Questions tabled by Mr Bernard Jenkin MP.

The first Parliamentary Question was:

> To ask the Secretary of State for Defence, whether his Department has complied with Dr David Kelly's terms and conditions of employment in handling the matter of his discussions with Andrew Gilligan.

The second Parliamentary Question was:

> To ask the Secretary of State for Defence, on how many occasions Dr David Kelly spoke to BBC radio 4 defence correspondent Andrew Gilligan; and whether his line managers were aware of this.

The third Parliamentary Question was:

> To ask the Secretary of State for Defence, what (a) civil service and (b) MoD rules and regulations may have been infringed by Dr David Kelly in talking to BBC radio 4 defence correspondent Andrew Gilligan.

The fourth Parliamentary Question was:

> To ask the Secretary of State for Defence, what disciplinary measures his Department will take against Dr David Kelly.

118. At 9.28am on 17 July Mr James Harrison, Dr Wells' deputy, sent these four Parliamentary Questions to Dr Kelly attached to an e-mail which stated:

> David
>
> more PQs! But plenty of time for reply. I expect that Bryan will deal tomorrow.
>
> James

119. After receipt of Dr Kelly's e-mail sent at 9.22am, Wing Commander Clark helped to draft replies to the two Parliamentary Questions tabled by Mr Andrew Mackinlay and to the letter dated 15 July from the Clerk of the FAC requesting details of Dr Kelly's contacts with journalists. These replies were seen by the Parliamentary Under-Secretary's office which contacted Wing Commander Clark and suggested (inter alia) that as Ms Susan Watts had been referred to in the hearing when Dr Kelly appeared before the FAC, her name should be taken out of the general list of journalists to whom Dr Kelly had spoken and put into the paragraph which referred to the specific contacts that Dr Kelly had had with journalists. Accordingly Wing Commander Clark prepared a draft reply to the letter from the Clerk of the FAC dated 16 July which referred to a meeting with Ms Susan Watts on 5 November 2002. The draft was as follows:

> Thank you for your letter of 16 July, asking for a list of journalists with whom Dr David Kelly has had contact.
>
> As Dr Kelly explained in his evidence to the Foreign Affairs Committee, the presence of the press outside his house has meant that he has not in recent days been able to gain access to the personal records he holds there. He was able to gain access to them last night. Mr Hoon wanted me to write to you as quickly as possible with this information, noting that it is drawn from a rapid analysis by Dr Kelly of his records.

Dr Kelly has records of having held one-to-one meetings with the following journalists over the past 2 years at their request:

Name	Date	Purpose
Nick Rufford	14/03/02	Discussing Al-Manal (Sunday Times)
Alex Nicoll	15/5/02	Iraqi WMD in general (Financial Times)
Phillip Sen	3/10/02	Inspection technology (The Engineer)
Andrew Gilligan	Feb 2003	Iraqi WMD in general (BBC)
Andrew Gilligan	22/05/03	Iraqi WMD in general (BBC)

Dr Kelly has also had such meetings during the period with Jane Corbin (BBC) on general UN Inspections and Tom Mangold (BBC) on UNSCOM Inspections, but has no record of the dates.

In addition, Dr Kelly has spoken with journalists about Iraq at a range of seminars and similar events, and on the telephone. He has also discussed non-Iraq WMD matters, on which he is an acknowledged expert. For example, he had a conversation about Iraq WMD with Andrew Gilligan at the IISS seminar 12-14 September 2002 and, as mentioned at the Foreign Affairs Select Committee hearing, he met with Susan Watts (BBC), following his presentation at the Foreign Office Open Day on the 5 November 2002. Other than those noted above, Dr Kelly does not have records of contacts with journalists. However, those journalists whose business cards (or other contact details) Dr Kelly has in his possession are listed below: he believes that he has met them, either one-to-one or in the margins of seminars or other events, and in some cases possibly many years ago.

Tamar Weinstein, CBC Radio Canada

Anna Maria Tremonti, CBC Radio Canada

Bernard Edinger, Reuters

Andrew Veitch, ITN

Mark Worthington, TBS News

Tetsuya Chikushi News, 23 TBS News

Koichiro Yoneda, TBS News

Paul Lashmar, The Independent

Susan Lambert, Australian Broadcasting Corporation

Jeremy Webb, New Scientist

James Bone, The Times

Marilyn Chase, Wall Street Journal

Jeff Goldberg, Freelance journalist

Judith Miller, New York Times

Calum Lynch, Washington Post

Helen Vyner, Simon Prentice Associates

Carolyn Hawley, BBC

Lynsey Hilsum, Channel Four News

Stephen Endelberg, New York Times

Sean O'Neill, Daily Telegraph

120. Wing Commander Clark gave the following evidence in respect of this change in the draft answer:

[27 August, page 137, line 9]

Q. Did Dr Kelly ever see this draft with Susan Watts' name in the body of the paragraph?

A. It was discussed with him, yes, but he would not have seen it, no; he did not physically see it.

121. Wing Commander Clark was asked what conversations he had had with Dr Kelly in the course of 17 July:

[27 August, page 137, line 18]

Q. Can you recall what conversations you had with Dr Kelly in the course of the 17th July apart from specifically on the e-mails?

A. Yes. We had a number of calls. The first one was obviously about 10 o'clock in the morning to say the information required is on the Internet machine. The reason he would make that call is the Internet machine is a stand alone machine in an office some 30 yards from where I work, so you had to know it was on there to go and find it.

We also had a general discussion of developments, how he was feeling. He was feeling still tired but in good spirits, although at that stage – and David Kelly was a very private man and very rarely mentioned his family – I mentioned he had come in later on the 16th because of a personal problem at home. That was because he had obviously come back from Cornwall and his wife had been left in Cornwall and he some way had to work out how to get his wife, who has arthritis, back from Cornwall. That is why he had been making arrangements on the 16th and that is why he was somewhat later in. On the 17th, when I asked him how he was going, he basically said he was holding up all right but it had all come to a head and his wife had taken it really very badly. Whether that was in association with the additional pressure of having to get back the day before under her own steam, I do not know, but he did say that his wife had been very upset on the morning of the 17th.

Q. Did you discuss going back to Iraq at all?

A. Yes, it was something we discussed regularly because Dr Kelly was very keen to get back to Iraq to support the ISG and on that morning, because we thought that really we were clearing the workload associated with PQs and with the Select Committees, we looked at a reasonable date for him going back. Having discussed it with Dr Wells, we came up with the date of the 25th which basically gave him just slightly over a week to get his personal effects sorted out and then he would fly out. So that – I spoke to him on the Thursday and it was going to be a week the following Friday that he would fly out.

Q. Did you book a flight for him?

A. Yes, I did. Having agreed that then he was booked on a flight.

LORD HUTTON: So that was a definite plan, Wing Commander, was it, that he would go out on the 25th?

A. It was my Lord.

LORD HUTTON: He knew that?

A. Provided basically we would seek authority from the Deputy Chief of Defence Intelligence that he was happy we had received it, it was a definite plan. He had agreed that Dr Kelly himself could easily make that date.

122. During the course of 17 July Wing Commander Clark was also contacted by the Private Secretary to Mr Hoon who referred to an article written by Mr Nick Rufford in the Sunday Times on 13 July referring to Dr Kelly. Dr Kelly had made no reference to that meeting with Mr Rufford in the details he had given of meetings with journalists and Wing Commander Clark was asked to check with Dr Kelly if that meeting had taken place and, if it had, to include it in the reply. Wing Commander Clark telephoned Dr Kelly to speak to him on this point about 3.20pm. His evidence was:

[27 August, page 140, line 17]

Q. At what time did you attempt to ring Dr Kelly?

A. It was – I have since been told by the police – I thought it was close to 3 o'clock but it was about 3.20, and I was told by his wife who answered the telephone that Dr Kelly had gone for a walk at 3 o'clock.

Q. Can you recall what the last telephone conversation you actually had with Dr Kelly was before that attempt to get hold of him?

A. Yes, I had a call with him which was just before 3 o'clock. Again I thought it was earlier but we have been able to track that down from investigating my log of e-mails and the telephone log that the police were able to provide. So about 6 or 7 minutes before 3 o'clock was the last conversation. That was the one where we discussed Susan Watts and the business cards.

Q. When you say Susan Watts, i.e. appearing in the body of the text?

A. Absolutely right. So that had been agreed.

123. On the morning of 17 July at 11.18am Dr Kelly sent a number of e-mails to friends and colleagues who had sent him, by e-mail, messages of support. The e-mails sent by Dr Kelly were as follows:

To Ron Manley:

Ron

Many thanks for your thoughts. It has been difficult. Hopefully it will all blow over by the end of the week and I can travel to Baghdad and get on with the real work.

Best wishes

David.

To Geeta Kingdon:

Geeta,

Many thanks for your thoughts and prayers. It has been a remarkably tough time. Should all blow over by early next week then I will travel to Baghdad a week Friday.

I have had to keep a low profile which meant leaving home for a week! Back now.

With best wishes and thanks for your support.

David

To Debra Krikorian:

Deb,

Many thanks for the email. GKW let me know that you had been trying to contact me but I have been keeping low on MOD advice. If all blows over by the beginning of next week I will get to Baghdad soon.

Regards,

David.

To Alastair Hay:

Dear Alastair,

Many thanks for your support. Hopefully it will soon pass and I can get to Baghdad and get on with the real job.

Best wishes,

David

To Philippe Michel:

Philippe,

Many thanks for your email. I know that I have a lot of good friends who are providing support at a difficult time.

Hope to see you soon.

Regards,

David

To Malfrid Braut:

Malfrid,

Thanks. It has been difficult. I hope to get to Baghdad soon to really work. I will then probably be out of email contact but send me whatever you wish and I will respond as soon as I can.

I am sure that Cairo remains absorbing.

Best wishes,

David

To Dick Foster:

Dick,

Quite a week. If all blows over I will be in Baghdad next Friday. Hope to see you shortly after that.

All the best,

David

124. On 16 July Judith Miller, a reporter on the New York Times had sent Dr Kelly the following e-mail:

David,

I heard from another member of your fan club that things went well for you today. Hope it's true. J.

125. On 17 July at 11.18am Dr Kelly sent Judith Miller the following e-mail:

Judy,

I will wait until the end of the week before judging – many dark actors playing games.

Thanks for your support. I appreciate your friendship at this time.

Best,

David

The e-mail was sent in the context of Judith Miller's reference to his appearance before the FAC but it is not possible to draw any clear inference as to whom Dr Kelly was referring in his reference to "many dark actors playing games".

126. In her evidence Mrs Kelly described Dr Kelly's state of mind and actions on the morning and early afternoon of 17 July as follows:

[1 September, page 43, line 16]

Q. 17th July is a Thursday. What time did you get up that day?

A. About half past 8. It is rather later than normal. We were both tired.

Q. How did he seem?

A. Tired, subdued, but not depressed. I have no idea. He had never seemed depressed in all of this, but he was very tired and very subdued.

Q. Did he have any work to do that day?

A. He said he had a report to write for the MoD. This is the one that somebody on the Foreign Affairs Committee referred to as his "homework" I think.

Q. Some Parliamentary Questions that were tabled?

A. That is right.

Q. How did he seem about that?

A. He just got on with it, basically.

Q. What time did he start work?

A. Probably about 9 o'clock, quarter to 9.

Q. Where physically did he work in the house?

A. In his study. It was a downstairs room to the left of the front door, one side of the dining room.

....

[1 September, page 45, line 5]

Q. He went into his study I think you told us about 9 o'clock?

A. That is right.

Q. Did he come out of his study at all?

A. He came out for coffee. We had a quick word.

Q. What time was that?

A. That would be about 11 I think, something of that order.

Q. Do you know whether he made any telephone calls that day?

A. Yes, he was certainly on the phone quite a bit I think, not as much –

Q. Could you hear that?

A. Yes, I could hear the phone ringing from time to time, but he picked it up. We did not actually sit together to have coffee then and we did not really talk at that stage.

Q. So after his coffee at 11 o'clock he went back to carry on?

A. He went back to carry on. I left the house for a few minutes to meet somebody and pick up some photographs. I came back, went into his study to try and lighten the atmosphere a bit by showing him some photographs and some other data I had got for the History Society. He smiled, stood up and then said he had not quite finished. But a few minutes later he went to sit in the sitting room all by himself without saying anything, which was quite unusual for him, but he went and sat in the sitting room.

Q. And what time had you gone out to get the photographs?

A. Not absolutely certain, it was something like quarter to 12, I think.

Q. So if you were 10 minutes doing that, you must have been back just shortly before 12, is that right?

A. I was a bit longer than that. I was about half an hour.

Q. So about a quarter past 12. When was he sitting in the sitting room?

A. From about 12.30 I would think.

Q. Did he say anything?

A. No, he just sat and looked really very tired. By this time I had started with a huge headache and begun to feel sick. In fact I was physically sick several times at this stage because he looked so desperate.

Q. Did he have any lunch?

A. Yes, he did. I said to him – he did not want any but he did have some lunch. I made some sandwiches and he had a glass of water. We sat together at the table opposite each other. I tried to make conversation. I was feeling pretty wretched, so was he. He looked distracted and dejected.

Q. How would you describe him at this time?

A. Oh, I just thought he had a broken heart. He really was very, very – he had shrunk into himself. He looked as though he had shrunk, but I had no idea at that stage of what he might do later, absolutely no idea at all.

Q. And that was how he was looking and seeming to you. Did you talk much at lunch?

A. No, no. He could not put two sentences together. He could not talk at all.

Q. You said, I think, you were feeling unwell that day?

A. That is right.

Q. What did you do?

A. I went to go and have a lie down after lunch, which is something I quite often did just to cope with my arthritis. I said to him, "What are you going to do?" He said, "I will probably go for my walk".

Q. I think you told us you heard the phone ringing during the day. Had you seen his reaction to any phone calls during the day?

A. No, no.

Q. You had only seen his reaction when he had gone into the sitting room?

A. That is right.

Q. And then at lunchtime?

A. That is right.

Q. What time do you think you went upstairs, so far as you can remember?

A. It would be about half past 1, quarter to 2 perhaps.

Q. Where was he at that time?

A. He went into his study. Then shortly after I had laid down he came to ask me if I was okay. I said: yes, I will be fine. And then he went to change into his jeans. He would be around the house in a tracksuit or tracksuit bottoms during the day. So he went to change and put on his shoes. Then I assumed he had left the house.

Q. Because he was going for a walk?

A. That is right. He had intended to go for this regular walk of his. He had a bad back so that was the strategy for that.

Q. And did he, in fact, go straight off for his walk?

A. Well, the phone rang a little bit later on and I assumed he had left so I suddenly realised I had not got a cordless phone and I thought it might be an important call for him, perhaps from the MoD. So I went downstairs to find the telephone in the dining room. By this time the ringing had stopped and I was aware of David talking quietly on a phone. I said something like: I thought you had gone out for a walk. He did not respond of course because he was talking on the phone.

Q. Where was he at this time?

A. In his study.

Q. Do you know what time this was?

A. Not exactly, no. Getting on for 3, I would think.

Q. Do you know who the caller was?

A. I assumed it was the MoD, I am not sure.

Q. And did Dr Kelly go out for his walk?

A. Well, the phone rang again at about 3.20, after which – it was a call for me – a return call for me, and I could not settle in bed so I got up at that stage and I was aware that definitely David had left by this time.

Q. So he had gone?

A. He had gone by 3.20.

Q. So between 3 and 3.20 he had gone for a walk?

A. That is right, yes.

It appears to be clear that the telephone call which Dr Kelly answered just before 3pm was from Wing Commander Clark (see para 122).

127. After leaving his house to go for a walk Dr Kelly met an elderly neighbour whom he knew, Mrs Ruth Absalom who had taken her dog out for a walk. She said that she met Dr Kelly around 3pm on a lane about a mile away from his home. She described their meeting as follows:

[2 September, page 2, line 14]

Q. What did you say to him?

A. He said, "Hello Ruth" and I said, "Oh hello David, how are things?" He said, "Not too bad". We stood there for a few minutes then Buster, my dog, was pulling on the lead, he wanted to get going. I said "I will have to go, David". He said, "See you again then, Ruth" and that was it, we parted.

Q. How did he seem to you?

A. Just his normal self, no different to any other time when I have met him.

CHAPTER 5

The search for Dr Kelly and the finding of his body

128. Dr Kelly did not return from his walk and Mrs Kelly, who was joined by two of her daughters during the course of the evening (her third daughter being in Scotland) became increasingly worried about him. Mrs Kelly's two daughters went out separately in their cars to look for their father on the roads and lanes along which he might have been walking, but when they had found no trace of him they rang the police about 12.20am on Friday 18 July.

129. The Thames Valley Police began an immediate search for Dr Kelly and the search operation was carried out with great efficiency. A police dog was used to assist in the search and a police helicopter with heat seeking equipment was called in. Assistant Chief Constable Michael Page was informed that Dr Kelly was missing at 3.09am and he arranged a meeting of key personnel at Abingdon Police Station at 5.15am. By 7.30am 40 police officers were engaged in the search and Assistant Chief Constable Page was advised by two police specialists in the location of missing persons that Harrowdown Hill, which was an area where Dr Kelly had often walked, was an area to which particular attention should be given in the search. Assistant Chief Constable Page then directed that the area of Harrowdown Hill should be searched and members of the South East Berks Emergency Volunteers and the Lowland Search Dogs Association, who had joined the search, were deployed to Harrowdown Hill.

130. Two of the volunteers taking part in the search were Ms Louise Holmes, with her trained search dog, and Mr Paul Chapman. They worked together as a team and began their search about 8am and after a time they went into the wood on Harrowdown Hill from the east side. The dog picked up a scent and Ms Holmes followed him. Ms Holmes saw the dog go to the bottom of a tree and he then ran back to her barking to indicate that he had found something. She then went in the direction from which the dog had come and she saw a body slumped against the bottom of a tree. She shouted to Mr Chapman, who was behind her, to ring control to tell them that something had been found and she went closer to see if there was any first aid which she could administer. She saw the body of a man at the base of the tree with his head and shoulders slumped back against it. His legs were straight in front of him, his right arm was at his side and his left arm had a lot of blood on it and was bent back in a strange position. It was apparent to her that the man was dead and there was nothing she could do to help him. The person matched the description of Dr Kelly which she had previously been given by the police. Ms Holmes then went back to Mr Chapman retracing the route by which she had come into the wood although there was no definite path or track by which she had approached the tree.

131. Mr Chapman had been unable to contact control so he made a 999 call to speak to Abingdon Police Station and arranged to walk back to where he and Ms Holmes had parked their car in order to meet the police officers who were coming to meet them.

On the way back to their car they met three other police officers who themselves had been engaged in searching the area and Mr Chapman told them that they had found the body. Mr Chapman then took one of the police officers, Detective Constable Coe, to show him where the body was. Mr Chapman showed Detective Constable Coe the body lying on its back and Detective Constable Coe said that the body was approximately 75 yards in from the edge of the wood. Detective Constable Coe saw that there was blood around the left wrist and he saw a knife, like a pruning knife, and a watch on the left side of the body. He also saw a small water bottle. He remained about seven or eight feet away from the body and stayed in that position for about 25 or 30 minutes until two other police officers arrived who made a taped off common approach path to be used by everyone who came to the place where the body was lying. Two members of an ambulance crew, Ms Vanessa Hunt and Mr David Bartlett arrived at the scene about 9.55am. They checked the body for signs of life and found none. They then placed four electrodes on the chest to verify that life was extinct and the monitor showed that there was no cardiac output and that life was extinct. They then disconnected the four electrodes from the heart monitor and left them on the chest and they themselves left the scene.

The investigations into the death of Dr Kelly

132. Assistant Chief Constable Page was informed at 9.20am that the body had been found. In his evidence he described the actions which he took and which were taken by others on his instructions as follows:

[3 September, page 26, line 8]

Q. What happened after that information had come to your attention?

A. Well, from my perspective I appointed a senior investigating officer, a man who would, if you like, carry out the technical issues around the investigation. I met fairly quickly with my Chief Constable and we decided what levels of resourcing and what levels of investigation we should apply to these circumstances.

Q. The fact that a body had been discovered, what sort of inquiry did you launch at the start?

A. We determined from the outset because of the attendant circumstances that we would apply the highest standards of investigation to this particular set of circumstances as was possible. I would not say I launched a murder investigation but the investigation was of that standard.

Q. We have heard how a common access path was established yesterday.

A. Yes.

Q. And the fingertip searching was carried out. Did forensic pathologists become involved?

A. Yes. We were very anxious, from the outset, to ensure the most thorough possible examination of the scene. I spoke to the Oxfordshire coroner, Mr Gardiner, and we agreed between us that we would use a Home Office pathologist, which is a very highly trained pathologist. It was also agreed with the senior investigating officer that we would use forensic biologists who are able to look at the scene and, in particular, blood splashes and make certain determinations from those in relation to what may have happened. As you say, a common approach path had been established; and it was determined that for that common approach path and for a distance of 10 metres either side and for a radius of 10 metres around Dr Kelly's body that we would carry out a fingertip search. It was also agreed that Dr Kelly's body would be left in situ so that the pathologist and the biologists could visit the scene with the body in situ to make their own assessment of the scene, which is not always the case but in this case we decided it would be wise to do so.

Q. Why was that, just to ensure –

A. Just to ensure that they could look at the environment and the surroundings and take in the full picture.

133. The detailed examinations which were carried out on the body at the place where it was found and of the area surrounding the body in the wood were as follows. Police search teams led by Police Constable Franklin and Police Constable Sawyer conducted a thorough fingertip search of the common approach path of the area surrounding the body and of the area on either side of the approach path. After the body had been moved they also conducted a fingertip search of the ground on which the body had been lying. This search lasted from 12.50pm to 4.45pm and the search of the ground on which the body had lain lasted from 7.24pm to 7.45pm. Nothing of significance was found in the searches and Constable Sawyer said:

[2 September, page 56, line 25]

When I first saw Dr Kelly I was very aware of the serious nature of the search and I was looking for signs of perhaps a struggle; but all the vegetation that was surrounding Dr Kelly's body was standing upright and there were no signs of any form of struggle at all.

134. Dr Nicholas Hunt, a Home Office accredited forensic pathologist arrived at the place where the body was lying at 12.10 pm and at 12.35pm he confirmed that the body was dead. He then waited whilst the police carried out a fingertip search of the common approach path and he then began a thorough investigation of the body at 2.10pm. After this examination of the body at the scene and after a post mortem examination Dr Hunt furnished a detailed post mortem report dated 25 July 2003 to the Oxfordshire coroner and at the Inquiry he gave evidence in accordance with his findings set out in that report.

135. Dr Kelly was right handed. In a statement furnished to the Inquiry Police Constable Roberts stated:

On Saturday 19th July 2003, I was on duty performing the role of Family Liaison Officer for Thames Valley Police.

On this date I spoke to Sian KELLY, the daughter of Dr David KELLY who confirmed that her father was right handed.

136. In the course of his evidence Dr Hunt gave (inter alia) the following evidence:

[16 September, page 9, line 14]

A. He was wearing a green Barbour type wax jacket and the zip and the buttons at the front had been undone. Within the bellows pocket on the lower part of the jacket there was a mobile telephone and a pair of bi-focal spectacles. There was a key fob and, perhaps more significantly, a total of three blister packs of a drug called Coproxamol. Each of those packs would originally have contained 10 tablets, a total of 30 potentially available.

Q. And how many tablets were left in those packs?

A. There was one left.

LORD HUTTON: Did you actually take those blister packs out? Did you discover them in the pocket yourself?

A. Yes, as part of the search, my Lord.

....

[16 September, page 12, line 5]

Q. Did you notice anything about the face?

A. His face appeared, firstly, rather pale but there was also what looked like vomit running from the right corner of the mouth and also from the left corner of the mouth and streaking the face.

Q. What would that appear to indicate?

A. It suggested that he had tried to vomit whilst he was lying on his back and it had trickled down.

....

[16 September, page 12, line 22]

Q. Did you investigate the scene next to the body?

A. Yes.

Q. And what did that show?

A. There was a Barbour flat-type cap with some blood on the lining and the peak near his left shoulder and upper arm. In the region of his left hand lying on the grass there was a black resin strapped wristwatch, a digital watch, which was also bloodstained.

Q. Was the watch face up or face down?

A. It was face down.

Q. What about next to the watch?

A. Lying next to that was a pruning knife or gardener's knife.

Q. Can you describe what type of pruning knife it was?

A. The make was a Sandvig knife. It was one with a little hook or lip towards the tip of the blade. It is a fairly standard gardeners' type knife.

Q. Were there any bloodstains on that knife?

A. Yes, over both the handle and the blade.

Q. Was there any blood beneath the knife?

A. Yes, there was. There was blood around the area of the knife.

Q. How close to the knife was the blood?

A. It was around the knife and underneath it.

Q. Did you notice a bottle of water?

A. Yes, there was a bottle of Evian water, half a litre.

Q. Was there any water in that bottle?

A. Yes, there was some remaining water. I do not recall what volume exactly.

Q. Can you remember precisely where the bottle was in relation to the bottle? (sic)

A. Yes, it was lying propped against some broken branches to the left and about a foot away from his left elbow.

Q. And did you notice anything in particular about the bottle?

A. Yes, there was some smeared blood over both the bottle itself and the bottle top.

Q. Did that indicate anything to you?

A. It indicated that he had been bleeding whilst at least placing the bottle in its final position. He may already have been bleeding whilst he was drinking from it, but that is less certain.

Q. Was there any other bloodstaining that you noticed in the area?

A. There was. There was an area of bloodstaining to his left side running across the undergrowth and the soil and I estimated it was over an area of 2 to 3 feet in maximum length."

[16 September, page 15, line 13]

Q. Did you notice any signs of visible injury to the body while you were there?

A. Yes. At the scene I could see that there were at least five what I would call incised wounds or cuts to his left wrist over the what is anatomically the front of the wrist, but that is the creased area of the wrist.

Q. Were there any other visible signs of injury to the body?

A. No, there was nothing at the scene.

137. At 7.19pm Dr Hunt ended his examination of the body at the scene where it was found and the body was moved to the John Radcliffe Hospital in Oxford where Dr Hunt commenced a post mortem examination at 9.20pm. The examination concluded at 12.15am on 19 July. In describing what he found on his post mortem examination Dr Hunt gave (inter alia) the following evidence:

[16 September, page 17, line 1]

Q. On this further examination, did you find any signs of injury to the body that you have not already mentioned?

A. I did. I was able to note in detail the injuries over his left wrist in particular.

Q. You have made a report, a post-mortem examination report?

A. Yes.

Q. Would you just like to read from the significant parts of that in relation to the injuries you found?

A. Certainly. There was a series of incised wounds, cuts, of varying depth over the front of the left wrist and they extended in total over about 8 by 5 centimetres on the front of the wrist. The largest of the wounds and the deepest lay towards the top end or the elbow end of that complex of injuries and it showed a series of notches and some crushing of its edges. That wound had actually severed an artery on the little finger aspect of the front of the wrist, called the ulnar artery. The other main artery on the wrist on the thumb aspect was intact. There were a number of other incisions of varying depth and many smaller scratch-like injuries over the wrist. The appearance that they gave was of what are called tentative or hesitation marks, which are commonly seen prior to a deep cut being made into somebody's skin if they are making the incision themselves.

....

[16 September, page 19, line 5]

Q. Did you see any signs of what are called defensive injuries?

A. No, there were no signs of defensive injuries; and by that I mean injuries that occur as a result of somebody trying to parry blows from a weapon or trying to grasp a weapon.

Q. What injuries would you normally expect to see of that type?

A. If somebody is being attacked with a bladed weapon, like a knife, then cuts on the palm of the hand or over the fingers where they are trying to grasp the knife, or cuts or even stabs on the outer part of the arm as they try to parry a blow.

138. In his evidence Dr Hunt stated that he had sent a sample of the stomach contents to a forensic toxicologist, Dr Alexander Allan, and he received a toxicology report back from Dr Allan. He described what this report showed as follows:

[16 September, page 21, line 13]

Q. In summary what did it show?

A. It showed the presence of two compounds in particular. One of them is a drug called dextropropoxyphene. That is an opiate-type drug, it is a mild painkiller, and that was present at a concentration of one microgramme per millilitre in the blood.

Q. Did it show anything, this report, in summary?

A. Yes, it did. It showed the presence of paracetamol.

Q. The concentration of that?

A. 97 milligrammes per millilitre.

Q. Where was that present in the body?

A. It was also present in the stomach contents, as well as the blood.

139. With reference to the estimated time of death Dr Hunt's evidence was as follows:

[16 September, page 22, line 8]

Q. Were you able to estimate the time of death?

A. Yes, within certain limits, using a particular technique based upon the rectal temperature.

Q. What time of death did you estimate as a result of that?

A. The estimate is that death is likely to have occurred some 18 to 27 hours prior to taking the rectal temperature, and that that time range was somewhere between quarter past 4 on 17th July and quarter past 1 on the morning of the 18th July.

Q. You took the rectal temperature at what time?

A. That was taken at quarter past 7 in the evening of the 18th.

140. In his evidence Dr Hunt summarised his conclusions as a result of his examinations as follows:

[16 September, page 22, line 22]

I found that Dr Kelly was an apparently adequately nourished man in whom there was no evidence of natural disease that could of itself have caused death directly at the macroscopic or naked eye level. He had evidence of a significant incised wound to his left wrist, in the depths of which his left ulnar artery had been completely severed. That wound was in the context of multiple incised wounds over the front of his left wrist of varying length and depth. The arterial injury had resulted in the loss of a significant volume of blood as noted at the scene. The complex of incised wounds over the left wrist is entirely consistent with having been inflicted by a bladed weapon, most likely candidate for which would have been a knife. Furthermore, the knife present at the scene would be a suitable candidate for causing such injuries.

The orientation and arrangement of the wounds over the left wrist are typical of self inflicted injury. Also typical of this was the presence of small so-called tentative or hesitation marks. The fact that his watch appeared to have been removed deliberately in order to facilitate access to the wrist. The removal of the watch in that way and indeed the removal of the spectacles are features pointing towards this being an act of self harm.

Other features at the scene which would tend to support this impression include the relatively passive distribution of the blood, the neat way in which the water bottle and its top were placed, the lack of obvious signs of trampling of the undergrowth or damage to the clothing. To my mind, the location of the death is also of interest in this respect because it was clearly a very pleasant and relatively private spot of the type that is sometimes chosen by people intent upon self harm.

Q. Is that something you have found from your past experience?

A. Yes, and knowledge of the literature. Many of the injuries over the left wrist show evidence of a well developed vital reaction which suggests that they had been inflicted over a reasonable period of time, minutes, though, rather than seconds or many hours before death.

LORD HUTTON: What do you mean by a "vital reaction"?

A. A vital reaction, my Lord, is the body's response to an area of damage. It manifests itself chiefly in the form of reddening and swelling around the area.

LORD HUTTON: I interrupted you. You were at 9 and you are coming on to 10, I think.

A. Thank you, my Lord. There is a total lack of classical defence wounds against sharp weapon attack. Such wounds are typically seen in the palm aspects of the hands or over the outer aspects of the forearms. It was noted that he has a significant degree of coronary artery disease and this may have played some small part in the rapidity of death but not the major part in the cause of death.

Given the finding of blister packs of Coproxamol tablets within the coat pocket and the vomitus around the ground, it is an entirely reasonable supposition that he may have consumed a quantity of these tablets either on the way to or at the scene itself.

Q. What did the toxicology report suggest?

A. That he had consumed a significant quantity of the tablets.

Q. I am not going to trouble you with the details of the toxicology report. Was there anything else in addition to the toxicology samples that you noticed?

A. (Pause). Really the only other thing in addition to that was the coronary artery disease that could have had a part in the rapidity of death in these circumstances.

Q. You have mentioned the minor injury to the inner aspect of the lip.

A. Yes.

Q. Moving on from that, you mentioned the abrasions to the head. Would you like to resume your summary at that point?

A. Yes. The minor injuries or abrasions over the head are entirely consistent with scraping against rough undergrowth such as small twigs, branches and stones which were present at the scene.

LORD HUTTON: Did you give any consideration or do anything in relation to the possibility of Dr Kelly having been overpowered by any substance?

A. Yes, indeed, my Lord. The substances which one thinks of, as a pathologist, in these terms are volatile chemicals. Perhaps chloroform is a classic example. So in order to investigate that-

LORD HUTTON: you need not go into the detail but if you state it in a general way.

A. I retained a lung and also blood samples until the toxicology was complete.

LORD HUTTON: And the purpose of that toxicology being?

A. To examine for any signs of a volatile chemical in the blood or, failing that, in the lungs.

LORD HUTTON: Yes, I see. Thank you.

Yes, Mr Knox.

MR KNOX: If you move on to conclusion 18.

A. Certainly. The minor reddened lesions on the lower limbs are typical of areas of minor hair follicle irritation or skin irritation, so they were not injuries in particular. They were not puncture wounds.

Q. Conclusion 19?

A. I had undertaken subcutaneous dissection of the arms and the legs and there is no positive evidence of restraint-type injury.

Q. Conclusion 20?

A. There is no positive pathological evidence that this man had been subjected to a sustained violent assault prior to his death.

LORD HUTTON: Just going back to your previous observation, a restraint-type injury of someone who has been held by the arms and the legs.

A. Yes, my Lord. Yes, particularly around the areas of the ankles and the wrists.

LORD HUTTON: Yes. Yes. Thank you.

MR KNOX: Conclusion 21?

A. There was no positive pathological evidence to indicate that he has been subjected to compression of the neck, such as by manual strangulation, ligature strangulation or the use of an arm hold.

Q. And next?

A. There is no evidence from the post-mortem examination or my observations at the scene to indicate that the deceased had been dragged or otherwise transported to the location where his body was found.

141. Dr Hunt summarised his opinion as to the major factor involved in Dr Kelly's death as follows:

[16 September, page 28, line 5]

Q. And in summary, what is your opinion as to the major factor involved in Dr Kelly's death?

A. It is the haemorrhage as a result of the incised wounds to his left wrist.

Q. If that had not occurred, would Dr Kelly have died?

A. He may not have done at this time, with that level of dextropropoxyphene.

Q. What role, if any, did the coronary disease play?

A. As with the drug dextropropoxyphene, it would have hastened death rather than caused it, as such.

Q. So how would you summarise, in brief, your conclusions as to the cause of death?

A. In the formulation, the cause of death is given as 1(a) haemorrhage due to 1(b) incised wounds of the left wrist. Under part 2 of the formulation of the medical cause of death, Coproxamol ingestion and coronary artery atherosclerosis.

Q. You have already dealt with this, I think, but could you confirm whether, as far as you could tell on the examination, there was any sign of third party involvement in Dr Kelly's death?

A. No, there was no pathological evidence to indicate the involvement of a third party in Dr Kelly's death. Rather, the features are quite typical, I would say, of self inflicted injury if one ignores all the other features of the case.

142. A forensic biologist, Mr Roy Green, arrived at the scene where the body was lying at 2pm on 18 July. He examined the scene with particular reference to the blood staining in the area. The relevant parts of his evidence are as follows:

[3 September, page 144, line 9]

Q. Did you examine the vegetation around the body?

A. Yes.

Q. Did you form any conclusions from that examination?

A. Well, the blood staining that was highest from the ground was approximately 50 centimetres above the ground. This was above the position where Dr Kelly's left wrist was, but most of the stainings were 33 centimetres, which is approximately a foot above the ground. It was all fairly low level stuff.

Q. What does that mean?

A. It meant that because the injury – most of the injuries would have taken place while Dr Kelly was sitting down or lying down.

Q. Right. When you first saw the body, what position was it in?

A. He was on his back with the left wrist curled back in this sort of manner (Indicates).

Q. Did you make any other relevant discoveries while you were looking around the area?

A. There was an obvious large contact bloodstain on the knee of the jeans.

Q. What do you mean by a "contact bloodstain"?

A. A contact stain is what you will observe if an item has come into contact with a bloodstained surface, as opposed to blood spots and splashes when blood splashes on to an item.

Q. Which means at some stage his left wrist must have been in contact with his trousers?

A. No, what I am saying, at some stage he has knelt – I believe he has knelt in a pool of blood at some stage and this obviously is after he has been injured.

Q. Any other findings?

A. There were smears of blood on the Evian bottle and on the cap.

Q. And what did that indicate to you?

A. Well, that would indicate to me that Dr Kelly was already injured when he used the Evian bottle. As an explanation, my Lord –

LORD HUTTON: Yes.

A. – when people are injured and losing blood they will become thirsty.

MR DINGEMANS: They become?

A. Thirsty, as they are losing all that fluid.

Q. You thought he is likely to have had a drink then?

A. Yes.

Q. What else did you find?

A. There was a bloodstain on the right sleeve of the Barbour jacket. At the time that was a bit – slightly unusual, in that if someone is cutting their wrist you wonder how, if you are moving across like this, how you get blood sort of here (Indicates). But if the knife was held and it went like that, with the injury passing across the sleeve, that is a possible explanation. Another possible explanation is in leaning across to get the Evian bottle that the two areas may have crossed.

Q. Had crossed?

A. Yes.

Q. We know, in fact, the wrist which was cut was the left wrist, is that right?

A. That is correct.

Q. And we know that Dr Kelly was right handed.

A. I was not aware of that, but yes.

Q. Were those all your relevant findings?

A. The jeans, as I have talked about, with this large contact stain, did not appear to have any larger downward drops on them. There were a few stains and so forth but it did not have any staining that would suggest to me that his injuries, or his major injuries if you like, were caused while he was standing up, and there was not any – there did not appear to be any blood underneath where he was found, and the body was later moved which all suggested those injuries were caused while he was sat or lying down.

143. Dr Alexander Allan, a forensic toxicologist, was sent blood and urine samples and stomach contents taken from the body of Dr Kelly in the course of Dr Hunt's post mortem examination which he then analysed. Dr Allan found paracetamol and dextropropoxyphene in the samples and stomach contents. He described paracetamol and dextropropoxyphene as follows:

[3 September, page 8, line 2]

The two components, paracetamol and dextropropoxyphene, are the active components of a substance called Coproxamol which is a prescription only medicine containing 325 milligrammes of paracetamol and 32.5 milligrammes of dextropropoxyphene.

Q. What sort of ailments would that be prescribed for?

A. Mild to moderate pain, typically a bad back or period pain, something like that. And the concentrations of both drugs represent quite a large overdose of Coproxamol.

Q. What does the dextropropoxyphene cause if it is taken in overdose?

A. Dextropropoxyphene is an opioid analgesic drug which causes effects typical of opiate drugs in overdose, effects such as drowsiness, sedation and ultimately coma, respiratory depression and heart failure and dextropropoxyphene is known particularly in certain circumstances to cause disruption of the rhythm of the heart and it can cause death by that process in some cases of overdose.

Q. And what about paracetamol, what does that do?

A. Paracetamol does not cause drowsiness or sedation in overdose, but if enough is taken it can cause damage to the liver.

Q. If enough? I think you mean if too much is taken.

A. If too much is taken. I beg your pardon.

Q. What about the concentrations you have mentioned that you found in the blood? What did that indicate?

A. They are much higher than therapeutic use. Typically therapeutic use would represent one tenth of these concentrations. They clearly represent an overdose. But they are somewhat lower than what I would normally expect to encounter in cases of death due to an overdose of Coproxamol.

Q. What would you expect to see in the usual case where dextropropoxyphene has resulted in death? What types of proportions or concentrations would you normally expect to see?

A. There are two surveys reported I am aware of. One reports a concentration of 2.8 microgrammes per millilitre of blood of dextropropoxyphene in a series of fatal overdose cases. Another one reports an average concentration of 4.7 microgrammes per millilitre of blood. You can say that they are several fold larger than the level I found of 1.

Q. What about the paracetamol concentration you found?

A. Again, it is higher than would be expected for therapeutic use, approximately 5 or 10 times higher. But it is much lower or lower than would be expected for paracetamol fatalities normally unless there was other factors of drugs involved.

Q. What sort of level would you normal (sic) expect for paracetamol fatalities?

A. I think if you can get the blood reasonably shortly after the incident and the person does not die slowly in hospital due to liver failure, perhaps typically 3 to 400 microgrammes per millilitre of blood.

Q. About four times as much in other words?

A. Yes.

Q. Putting it in short terms, you would expect there to be about four times as much paracetamol and two and a half to four times as much dextropropoxyphene?

A. Two, three, four times as much paracetamol and two, three, four times as much dextropropoxyphene in the average overdose case, which results in fatalities.

Q. You have mentioned that it seemed that a number of Coproxamol drugs were taken. Was it possible, from your examination, to estimate how many tablets must have been taken?

A. It is not possible to do that, because of the complex nature of the behaviour of the drugs in the body. I understand that Dr Kelly may have vomited so he would have lost some stomach contents then. There was still some left in the stomach and presumably still some left in the gastrointestinal tracts. What I can say is that it is consistent with say 29/30 tablets but it could be consistent with other scenarios as well.

144. Dr Allan also said in his evidence that the only way in which paracetamol and dextropropoxyphene could be found in Dr Kelly's blood was by him taking tablets containing them which he would have to ingest.

145. In relation to an examination of Dr Kelly's body Assistant Chief Constable Page said in evidence:

[23 September, page 201, line 1]

Q. We heard about investigations that have been carried out in the post-mortem and toxicology reports.

A. Yes.

Q. And the pathologist said that Dr Kelly's lung had been removed for tests. Have you discussed that matter with the toxicologist?

A. I have discussed that matter with the toxicologist. The lung was not subjected to tests, and the rationale given to my team by the toxicologist is that the blood was tested for an entire range of substances including volatile substances and stupefying substances. No trace whatsoever was found and therefore they considered that examining the lung would not be relevant because if it was not in the blood, it would not be in the lung.

146. Very understandably the police did not show the knife found beside Dr Kelly's body to his widow and daughters but the police showed them a photograph of that knife. It is clear that the knife found beside the body was a knife which Dr Kelly had owned since boyhood and which he kept in a desk in his study, but which was found to be missing from his desk after his death. In her evidence Mrs Kelly said:

[1 September, page 53, line 22]

Q. We have heard about the circumstances of Dr Kelly's death and the fact that a knife was used. Were you shown the knife at all?

A. We were not shown the knife; we were shown a photocopy of I presume the knife which we recognised as a knife he had had for many years and kept in his drawer.

Q. It was a knife he had had what, from childhood?

A. From childhood I believe. I think probably from the Boy Scouts.

And in a statement furnished to the Inquiry Police Constable Roberts stated:

The knife found in possession of Dr David Kelly is a knife the twins, Rachel and Ellen recognise (from pictures shown by Family Liaison Officers). It would not be unusual to be in his possession as a walker. They have seen it on their walks with him. He would have kept it in his study drawer with a collection of small pocket knives (he did like gadgets) and the space in the study drawer where a knife was clearly missing from the neat row of knives is where they believe it would [have] lived and been removed from.

147. It also appears probable that the Coproxamol tablets which Dr Kelly took just before his death came from a store of those tablets which Mrs Kelly, who suffered from arthritis, kept in their home. In a statement furnished to the Inquiry Detective Constable Eldridge stated:

At 1000hrs on Thursday 7th AUGUST 2003 I was on duty at Long Hanborough Incident Room when I removed from secure storage the following items for examination:—

1. Exhibit SK/2 CO-PROXAMOL BOX AND STRIP OF TEN TABLETS taken from Janice KELLY

2. Exhibit NCH/17/2 CO-PROXAMOL BLISTER PACKETS FRONT BOTTOM BELLOWS POCKET these had been removed from Dr KELLY'S coat pocket by the Pathologist

On examining both items I saw that they were identical. They were marked M & A Pharmacy Ltd and had the wording CO-PROXAMOL PL/4077/0174 written on the foil side of each of the blister type packs.

I can say that enquiries have been made with M & A PHARMACHEM who are the manufacturers of CO-PROXAMOL. The batch number shown on the tablets in our possession was checked with a view to tracing the chemist that these tablets had been purchased from. I can say that this batch number relates to approximately 1.6 million packets of tablets that will have been distributed to various chemists throughout the country.

148. In relation to the question whether Dr Kelly took his own life the opinion of Dr Hunt was as follows:

[16 September, page 23, line 14]

The orientation and arrangement of the wounds over the left wrist are typical of self inflicted injury. Also typical of this was the presence of small so-called tentative or hesitation marks. The fact that his watch appeared to have been removed whilst blood was already flowing suggest that it had been removed deliberately in order to facilitate access to the wrist. The removal of the watch in that way and indeed the removal of the spectacles are features pointing towards this being an act of self harm.

Other features at the scene which would tend to support this impression include the relatively passive distribution of the blood, the neat way in which the water bottle and its top were placed, the lack of obvious signs of trampling of the undergrowth or damage to the clothing. To my mind, the location of the death is also of interest in this respect because it was clearly a very pleasant and relatively private spot of the type that is sometimes chosen by people intent upon self harm.

Q. Is that something you have found from your past experience?

A. Yes, and knowledge of the literature.

149. Professor Keith Hawton was requested by the Inquiry to give evidence in relation to the death of Dr Kelly. Professor Hawton is an eminent expert on the subject of suicide and is the Professor of Psychiatry at Oxford University and is the Director of the Centre for Suicide Research in the University Department of Psychiatry in Oxford. He stated in his evidence that the majority of those who commit suicide do not leave a suicide note or message. He further stated:

[2 September, page 101, line 25]

Q. Did you form any assessment of whether Dr Kelly's death was consistent with suicide?

A. I think all the information we have about his death and the circumstances of his death strongly point to his death having been by suicide.

Q. And what would you say drives you to that conclusion?

A. Well, the first thing is the site in which the death occurred. We have heard that it occurred in an isolated spot on Harrowdown Hill. In fact it was, as I think you have been told, in woodland about 40 or 50 yards off the track taken by ramblers. The site is well protected from the view of other people.

Q. Have you been to the site?

A. I have visited the site, yes.

Q. And what did you notice there then?

A. Well, I noticed, first of all – what struck me was it is a very peaceful spot, a rather beautiful spot and we know that it was a favourite – it was in the area of a favourite walk of Dr Kelly with his family.

Q. What other factors have you considered relevant?

A. The nature of his injuries is very consistent with an act of self cutting. The doctor – I have read Dr Hunt's report , who is the Home Office forensic pathologist. I have also seen the photographs of the injuries to Dr Kelly's body; and the nature of the injuries to his wrist are very consistent with suicide.

Q. Why do you say that? We have heard from some of the ambulance personnel who did not themselves see very much blood. We have heard from others who did see more blood. What is relevant here?

A. Well I am referring here particularly to the nature of the cutting which perhaps I would prefer not to describe in detail.

Q. Right.

A. But it –

Q. Perhaps you can just explain why you do not want to describe these matters in detail.

A. Well, one of the concerns I have is that there is now good evidence that reporting and portrayal of detailed methods of suicide in the media can actually sometimes facilitate suicide in other people.

Q. So it is perfectly obvious there are lots of members of the press here. If you had to say anything to them about the reporting of your evidence today, what would it be?

A. I think with regard to the specific method of suicide, I would prefer that that was kept as general as possible.

Q. For those reasons?

A. Yes.

Q. You have talked about the cutting. What else do you consider to have been consistent with suicide?

A. Well, the situation or the circumstances in which Dr Kelly's body was found are consistent, in that he had apparently removed – his glasses were found by his body in a way - in a manner suggesting that they had been taken off by him, as was his cap; his watch had been taken off, was removed from the body.

Q. What does that indicate?

A. It suggests that he removed the watch to give him better access to be able to carry out the cutting.

Q. And was there anything else that you saw from the pathologist's report that assisted you in your conclusion?

A. Well, the instrument that was used, which I have seen a photograph of, and the family, as you know, I think, have been shown a copy of a similar instrument, a large penknife – I will call it a penknife, but it is a rather primitive style of penknife – is very similar to one that he had in his drawer in his study, and it was one I think you heard yesterday he had had since his childhood.

Q. Yes.

A. When considering something like this, one obviously has to think about whether there could have been some other person or persons involved in the act, and the circumstances suggest that this was not the case.

Q. What, whether some third parties were involved in Dr Kelly's death?

A. Yes.

Q. And what circumstances do you consider show that there were not?

A. Well, there were no signs of violence on his body other than the obvious injury to his wrist that would be in keeping with his having been involved in some sort of struggle or a violent act. There was no sign I understand of trampling down of vegetation and undergrowth in the area around his body. So that makes it highly unlikely that others could have been or were involved.

Q. We are going to hear from a toxicologist. Have you had a chance to read that report?

A. I have.

Q. Does that assist you in your determinations?

A. Well, we know that evidence was found in Dr Kelly's body and also on his person of him having consumed some particular medication.

Q. Right. And what medication was that?

A. That is Coproxamol.

Q. And why does that assist in your determination?

A. Well, it in itself is quite a dangerous medication taken in overdose because it can have particular effects on both breathing and also on the heart rhythm.

LORD HUTTON: Just going back to the knife, Professor Hawton, you said it was very similar to one in his drawer. Now, we have been told, for very understandable reasons, that Mrs Kelly was not shown the knife. But when you say "very similar", are you drawing the inference that in fact it was probably a knife that had been in his drawer, is that what why you say "very similar"?

A. Yes, I am my Lord.

LORD HUTTON: Yes, quite. Thank you very much. Yes.

MR DINGEMANS: We were dealing with the toxicologist's report. What do you understand the position to be in relation to that Coproxamol?

A. Well, I understand that the evidence found from blood levels and from the contents of Dr Kelly's – in Dr Kelly's stomach suggests that he had absorbed – he had taken approximately 30 tablets – I am sorry, the number of tablets is based on the number that were missing from the sheets he had with him.

Q. Right.

A. But that he had consumed well in access of a therapeutic dose of Coproxamol and given the blood levels and the relatively small amounts in his stomach, although he had vomited, I believe you have heard evidence he has vomited, but this would suggest he had consumed Coproxamol some time before death.

Q. Does that assist you in determining whether or not any third party was involved?

A. Well, for a third party to have been involved in the taking of the Coproxamol would, I imagine, have involved a struggle. I mean if somebody was forced to take a substantial number of tablets, it is difficult to believe there would not have been signs of a struggle.

Q. That is a factor you have borne in mind?

A. Yes.

Q. Did you come, then, to any overall conclusion about whether or not Dr Kelly had committed suicide?

A. I think that taking all the evidence together, it is well nigh certain that he committed suicide.

150. In his evidence Assistant Chief Constable Page stated:

[23 September, page 195, line 13]

Can you just briefly outline to his Lordship the lines of inquiry that you set out when confronted with the discovery of Dr Kelly's body?

A. Yes, certainly. Very early on in the inquiry one sets up a series of hypotheses which one tries then to knock down. For the sake of completeness the first of these would be: was the death natural or accidental? In this case it is fairly obvious that was not the case. The next question is: was it murder? I think as I pointed out in my last evidence, the examination of the scene and the supporting forensic evidence made me confident that actually there was no third party involved at the scene of the crime and therefore, to all intents and purposes, murder can be ruled out. One is then left with the option that Dr Kelly killed himself.

LORD HUTTON: Sorry, may I just ask you Mr Page, you say no third party was involved at the scene of the crime. Did you consider the possibility that Dr Kelly might have been overpowered and killed elsewhere and his body then taken to the wooded area where it was found?

A. Yes, my Lord; and I think, again, upon examination of the pathologist's evidence and of the biologist's evidence, it is pretty clear to me that Dr Kelly died at the scene.

LORD HUTTON: Yes. Thank you.

MR DINGEMANS: You were going on to say having ruled out natural causes, having ruled out murder.

A. One is left with the fact that Dr Kelly killed himself. My duty in that respect is to establish to the best of my satisfaction that there was no criminal dimension to Dr Kelly's death.

Q. Have you found any evidence suggesting that there was a criminal element?

A. Based on the extensive inquiries that we have undertaken thus far, I can find no evidence to suggest any criminal dimension to Dr Kelly's death.

Q. Can you give his Lordship, and everyone else, some idea of how many people you have interviewed in the course of your inquiries?

A. Yes, certainly. We have made contact with somewhere in the region of 500 individuals during the course of our inquiry.

Q. How many statements have you taken?

A. We have taken 300 statements and we have seized in excess of 700 documents in addition to the computer files I referred to when I gave evidence last time.

LORD HUTTON: Mr Page, could you just elaborate just a little on what you mean by no criminal dimension?

A. Well, again, my Lord, I would – I suppose being a police officer and I am inherently suspicious and I would look at the circumstances and ask myself a range of questions as to why Dr Kelly would have taken his own life.

LORD HUTTON: Yes.

A. And very early on in the inquiry, based on early discussions with the inquiry it seemed entirely out of character for Dr Kelly to take that move. Therefore, my view of whether there was a criminal dimension to this would centre around: was he being blackmailed? Was he being put under some other criminal behaviour that would have prompted him to take this action?

LORD HUTTON: Thank you for that, I just wanted you to elaborate that. And you have excluded that in your inquiries?

A. We have carried out extensive inquiries and based on those inquiries, I can find no evidence that he was being blackmailed or indeed any other evidence of any other criminal dimension.

151. Those who try cases relating to a death or injury (whether caused by crime or accident) know that entirely honest witnesses often give evidence as to what they saw at the scene which differs as to details. In the evidence which I heard from those who saw Dr Kelly's body in the wood there were differences as to points of detail, such as the number of police officers at the scene and whether they were all in uniform, the amount of blood at the scene, and whether the body was lying on the ground or slumped against the tree. I have seen a photograph of Dr Kelly's body in the wood which shows that most of his body was lying on the ground but that his head was slumped against the base of the tree - therefore a witness could say either that the body was lying on the ground or slumped against the tree. These differences do not cause me to doubt that no third party was involved in Dr Kelly's death.

The evidence of Mr David Broucher

152. Mr David Broucher, a member of the Diplomatic Service, gave evidence that in February 2003 he was the United Kingdom's Permanent Representative to the Conference on Disarmament in Geneva. He said that he had met Dr Kelly once in connection with his duties. He had not made a minute of the meeting or recorded it in his diary and doing the best that he could he thought that the meeting was in February 2003 in Geneva. He said that he wanted to pick Dr Kelly's brains because he knew that he was a considerable expert on compliance with the biological weapons convention in relation to Iraq. He had a meeting with Dr Kelly for about an hour. They talked about the history of Iraq's biological weapons capability, about Dr Kelly's activities with UNSCOM, about what he thought might be the current state of affairs, and they also talked about Iraq and the biological weapons convention.

153. Mr Broucher was asked:

[21/8, page 142, line 13]

Q. Did you then go on to discuss the possible use of force in Iraq?

A. We did.

Q. Can you tell us, in your own words, what was said?

A. I said to Dr Kelly that I could not understand why the Iraqis were courting disaster and why they did not cooperate with the weapons inspectors and give up whatever weapons might remain in their arsenal. He said that he had personally urged – he was still in contact with senior Iraqis and he had urged this point on them. Their response had been that if they revealed too much about their state of readiness this might increase the risk that they would be attacked.

Q. Did Dr Kelly say how he was in contact or not?

A. He did not give any details of names or places or times; and I did not ask him that.

Q. Did he say what he had said to those persons that he had contacted?

A. He said that he had tried to reassure them that if they cooperated with the weapons inspectors then they had nothing to fear.

Q. Which, as I understand it, was the position adopted by the United Nations.

A. So I understand, yes.

Q. And did he disclose how he felt about the situation?

A. My impression was that he felt that he was in some personal difficulty or embarrassment over this, because he believed that the invasion might go ahead anyway and that somehow this put him in a morally ambiguous position.

Q. Did he say anything further to you?

A. I drew some inferences from what he said, but I cannot recall the precise words that he used.

Q. What inferences did you draw?

A. Well, I drew the inference that he might be concerned that he would be thought to have lied to some of his contacts in Iraq.

Q. Did you discuss the dossier at all in this conversation?

A. We did discuss the dossier. I raised it because I had had to – it was part of my duties to sell the dossier, if you like, within the United Nations to senior United Nations officials; and I told Dr Kelly that this had not been easy and that they did not find it convincing. He said to me that there had been a lot of pressure to make the dossier as robust as possible; that every judgment in it had been closely fought over; and that it was the best that the JIC could do. I believe that it may have been in this connection that he then went on to explain the point about the readiness of Iraq's biological weapons, the fact they could not use them quickly, and that this was relevant to the point about 45 minutes.

Q. Did you discuss Dr Kelly's position in the Ministry of Defence?

A. He gave me to understand that he – it was only with some reluctance that he was working in the Ministry of Defence. He would have preferred to go back to Porton Down. He felt that when he transferred into the Ministry of Defence they had transferred him at the wrong grade, and so he was concerned that he had been downgraded.

Q. Right. Did you have any other conversation with Dr Kelly that day?

A. As Dr Kelly was leaving I said to him: what will happen if Iraq is invaded? And his reply was, which I took at the time to be a throw away remark – he said: I will probably be found dead in the woods.

Q. You understood it to be a throw away remark. Did you report that remark at the time to anyone?

A. I did not report it at the time to anyone because I did not attribute any particular significance to it. I thought he might have meant that he was at risk of being attacked by the Iraqis in some way.

Q. And you, at the time, considered it to be a sort of general comment one might make at the end of a conversation?

A. Indeed.

Q. Where were you in July this year on about 17th/18th July?

A. I was on leave in Geneva.

Q. And did you hear of Dr Kelly's death at all?

A. I believe I heard about it on the television news.

Q. Right. And did you see a picture of Dr Kelly on the news?

A. Yes.

Q. What was your reaction to that?

A. I recognised him, I realised that I knew him.

Q. And as a result of that what happened?

A. Nothing happened immediately because I was aware that I knew him but it was not until later that I became aware of the circumstances of his death and realised the significance of this remark that he had made to me, seemingly as a throw away line, when we met in February.

Q. Did you contact anyone about your recollection?

A. Yes, I did, not immediately but when the Inquiry began on 1st August it seemed to me that I needed to make known this fact.

Q. Can I take you to CAB/10/9? How did you make this fact known?

A. I sent an e-mail to my colleague, the press officer for biological weapons in the Foreign Office, Patrick Lamb.

Q. And you say to Patrick Lamb: "Is the FCO preparing evidence for the Hutton Inquiry?" We have heard from Mr Lamb: "If so, I may have something relevant to contribute that I have been straining to recover from a very deep memory hole." Is that right, that at the time your impression was that it was a throw away remark, and is it also fair to say that it was deeply buried within your memory?

A. Yes, that is fair to say, and the other facts of the meeting took some time for me to remember; and it took a long time to establish when the meeting took place because it was not noted in my diary.

154. Mr Broucher was clear in his evidence that he had only met Dr Kelly on one occasion. After he had given evidence Dr Kelly's daughter, Miss Rachel Kelly, looked at her father's diary and found that it contained an entry that he had met Mr Broucher in Geneva on 18th February 2002. In her evidence Miss Kelly said:

[1 September, page 97, line 6]

Q. We have heard from your mother this morning. She has given us some of the background. Can I ask you to look at a diary entry for 2002? Before I ask you to look at that, can you just tell me where you found the diary?

A. Yes. The diary was in my father's study –

Q. It is FAM/1/1. If we look at the entry for February, what does it tell us?

A. It mentions specifically a meeting with David Broucher on 18th February 2002, and the interesting thing with my father's diaries is he tended to write entries in them after the event and this would have been a meeting that he actually had because it is in his diary.

Q. It does not look like we have been able to get the diary on the screen, but if I look at the diary that I have in front of me, it says: "Monday 18th February 2002, 9.30, David Broucher, US mis."

A. Yes, US mission.

Q. It gives details of his flights into Geneva the day before.

A. Yes, the day before.

Q. And out of Geneva on 20th February; is that right?

A. Yes, that is correct, on the 20th.

Q. And that is February 2002?

A. It is a year earlier than the date that David Broucher gave as being this year, the conversation he had with my father.

Q. And I think Mr Broucher told us he had only had one meeting with your father.

A. Yes, that is what made me look at it. I actually thought that was the case.

Therefore it appears to be clear that Dr Kelly's one meeting with Mr Broucher was in February 2002 and not in February 2003.

155. In his evidence Professor Hawton said:

[2 September, page 122, line 21]

Q. We have heard evidence from a Mr Broucher, who relayed a comment about Dr Kelly being found "dead in the woods" and he had at the time thought it was a throwaway remark. He had attributed it, if he attributed it at all, to Iraqi agents. Then after hearing of Dr Kelly's suicide he thought perhaps it was something else. Can you assist with that at all?

A. Well, I gained the impression talking to family members about that particular alleged statement that it was not a typical – not that he would say that particularly – communicate that, but it was the sort of throwaway comment he might make. I have also gathered that it is quite possible that it was not made at the time that was initially alleged but possibly a year beforehand.

Q. We have seen now diaries. Mr Broucher thought it was February 2003. He did say it was a deep memory pocket. We have seen diaries which suggest that he has met Mr Broucher in February 2002 and Mr Broucher has said they only met once. So that may mean it is February 2002. Does that assist?

A. I think it is pure coincidence. I do not think it is relevant to understanding Dr Kelly's death.

156. It is a strange coincidence that Dr Kelly was found dead in the woods, but for the reasons which I give in paragraph 157 I am satisfied that Dr Kelly took his own life and that there was no third party involvement in his death.

The cause of the death of Dr Kelly

157. In the light of the evidence which I have heard I am satisfied that Dr Kelly took his own life in the wood at Harrowdown Hill at a time between 4.15pm on 17 July and 1.15am on 18 July 2003 and that the principal cause of death was bleeding from incised wounds to the left wrist which Dr Kelly inflicted on himself with the knife found beside his body. It is probable that the ingestion of an excess amount of Coproxamol tablets coupled with apparently clinically silent coronary artery disease would both have played a part in bringing about death more certainly and more rapidly than would have otherwise been the case. Accordingly the causes of death are:

1a Haemorrhage

1b Incised wounds to the left wrist

2   Coproxamol ingestion and coronary artery atherosclerosis

I am satisfied that no other person was involved in the death of Dr Kelly for the following reasons:

(1) A very careful and lengthy examination of the area where his body was found by police officers and by a forensic biologist found no traces whatever of a struggle or of any involvement by a third party or third parties and a very careful and detailed post mortem examination by Dr Hunt, together with the examination of specimens from the body by a forensic toxicologist, Dr Allan, found no traces or indications whatever of violence or force inflicted on Dr Kelly by a third party or third parties either at the place where his body was found or elsewhere.

(2) The wounds to his wrist were inflicted by a knife which came from Dr Kelly's desk in his study in his home, and which had belonged to him from boyhood.

(3) It is highly unlikely that a third party or third parties could have forced Dr Kelly to swallow a large number of Coproxamol tablets.

These conclusions are strongly supported by the evidence of Professor Hawton, Dr Hunt and Assistant Chief Constable Page.

158. I am further satisfied from the evidence of Professor Hawton that Dr Kelly was not suffering from any significant mental illness at the time he took his own life.

The statement issued by the BBC after Dr Kelly's death

159. On Sunday 20 July the BBC issued the following statement:

> The BBC deeply regrets the death of Dr David Kelly. We had the greatest respect for his achievements in Iraq and elsewhere over many years and wish once again to express our condolences to his family.
>
> There has been much speculation about whether Dr Kelly was the source for the *Today* programme report by Andrew Gilligan on May 29th. Having now informed Dr Kelly's family, we can confirm that Dr Kelly was the principal source for both Andrew Gilligan's report and for Susan Watts reports on Newsnight on June 2nd and 4th.
>
> The BBC believes we accurately interpreted and reported the factual information obtained by us during interviews with Dr Kelly.
>
> Over the past few weeks we have been at pains to protect Dr Kelly being identified as the source of these reports. We clearly owed him a duty of confidentiality. Following his death, we now believe, in order to end the continuing speculation, it is important to release this information as swiftly as possible. We did not release it until this morning at the request of Dr Kelly's family.
>
> The BBC will fully co-operate with the Government's inquiry. We will make a full and frank submission to Lord Hutton and will provide full details of all the contacts between Dr Kelly and the two BBC journalists including contemporaneous notes and other materials made by both journalists, independently.
>
> We continue to believe we were right to place Dr Kelly's views in the public domain. However, the BBC is profoundly sorry that his involvement as our source has ended so tragically.

CHAPTER 6

The issues which arise

160. In my opinion my terms of reference require me to consider a number of issues which arise from the evidence which I have summarised in the preceding paragraphs of this report. They are issues which counsel addressed in their examination and cross-examination of witnesses and in their statements at the conclusion of the evidence. The issues may be grouped under five main headings:

I Issues relating to the preparation of the dossier of 24 September 2002.

II Issues relating to Dr Kelly's meeting with Mr Gilligan in the Charing Cross Hotel on 22 May 2003.

III Issues relating to the BBC arising from Mr Gilligan's broadcasts on the BBC Today programme on 29 May 2003.

IV Issues relating to the decisions and actions taken by the Government after Dr Kelly informed his line manager in the MoD that he had spoken to Mr Gilligan on the 22 May 2003.

V Issues relating to the factors which may have led Dr Kelly to take his own life.

Issues relating to the preparation of the dossier of 24 September 2002

161. These issues are the following:

(a) How was the dossier of 24 September 2002 prepared and who was responsible for drafting it?

(b) What part (if any) did the Prime Minister or Mr Alastair Campbell or other officials in 10 Downing Street play in the preparation of the dossier?

(c) Were the Prime Minister or Mr Alastair Campbell or other officials in 10 Downing Street responsible for intelligence being set out in the dossier which they knew or suspected was incorrect or misleading?

(d) Was it improper for Mr Scarlett, the Chairman of the JIC, and the other members of the JIC to take into account suggestions as to the wording of the dossier from 10 Downing Street?

(e) Were Mr Scarlett and the other members of the JIC influenced by pressure from 10 Downing Street to make statements in the dossier that were stronger than were warranted by the intelligence available to them?

162. These issues arise for consideration because in his broadcasts on the Today programme on 29 May 2003 Mr Gilligan reported that according to his source "the government erm, probably knew that the forty five minute figure was wrong, even before it decided to put it in ..... Downing Street ... ordered a week before publication, ordered [the dossier] to be sexed up, to be made more exciting and ordered more facts to be err, to

be discovered" and that at the behest of 10 Downing Street the dossier "was transformed in the week before it was published, to make it sexier …. and the reason [the 45 minutes claim] hadn't been in the original draft was that it was, it was only erm, it only came from one source and most of the other claims were from two, and the intelligence agencies say they don't really believe it was necessarily true because they thought the person making the claim had actually made a mistake, it got, had got mixed up". In addition in his article in the Mail on Sunday on 1 June 2003 Mr Gilligan wrote that his source told him "[the dossier] was transformed a week before publication, to make it sexier", and when he asked how this transformation happened his source answered with a single word "Campbell".

The drafting of the dossier

163. In order to consider the drafting of the dossier it is necessary to go back to February 2002. In February 2002 the Overseas and Defence Secretariat in the Cabinet Office commissioned a paper on the weapons of mass destruction capabilities of four countries of concern, including Iraq. This paper was for possible use in the public domain. The paper on the four countries of concern was prepared by the assessment staff in the Cabinet Office which prepares intelligence assessments for the Joint Intelligence Committee (JIC).

164. The JIC, which meets once a week in the Cabinet Office, is responsible for the presentation of assessed intelligence to the Prime Minister and the Government. Since September 2001 the Chairman of the JIC has been Mr John Scarlett and the other members of that Committee are the heads of the three intelligence agencies, the Secret Intelligence Service (SIS), the Security Service and the Government Communications Headquarters (GCHQ), together with the Chief of Defence Intelligence (CDI), the Deputy Chief of Defence Intelligence (DCDI), and senior officials from the major policy departments of the Government, the FCO, the MoD, the Home Office, the Treasury and the Department of Trade and Industry. Sir David Omand is also a member of the JIC. The JIC is therefore composed of very senior and experienced persons in the field of intelligence and is the most senior body in the country concerned with the assessment and presentation of intelligence to the Government.

165. In mid March 2002 it was decided by the Prime Minister's Office and by the FCO not to continue work on the paper relating to the WMD capabilities of four countries. At that time increasing attention was being given to Iraq and its WMD capabilities and the assessment staff were therefore asked to continue with the drafting of a paper relating to Iraq alone. The paper relating to Iraq alone was completed by assessment staff and confirmed by the JIC, and was then passed to the Prime Minister's Office on 21 March 2002.

166. In late March 2002 it was decided by the Prime Minister's Office that the time was not right to proceed with publication of the Iraq paper, but it was kept in being for possible use in the future and during the spring and summer of 2002 the draft paper was regularly updated by the assessment staff.

167. In April 2002 the Counter-Proliferation Department (CPD) at the FCO was asked by the Cabinet Office to prepare a short paper for possible eventual publication on the history of UNSCOM inspections in Iraq. The Head of CPD prepared an initial text which he showed to Mr Patrick Lamb, the Deputy Head of CPD, and Dr Kelly for comment. It was agreed that it would be useful if the paper could include a case-study, within the historical element, focussed on the Iraqi biological weapons programme.

Dr Kelly wrote the first draft of four paragraphs relating to Inspection of Iraq's biological weapons programme which appeared on page 38 of the published dossier as follows:

Inspection of Iraq's biological weapons programme

In the course of the first biological weapons inspection in August 1991, Iraq claimed that it had merely conducted a military biological research programme. At the site visited, al-Salman, Iraq had removed equipment, documents and even entire buildings. Later in the year, during a visit to the al-Hakam site, Iraq declared to UNSCOM inspectors that the facility was used as a factory to produce proteins derived from yeast to feed animals. Inspectors subsequently discovered that the plant was a central site for the production of anthrax spores and botulinum toxin for weapons. The factory had also been sanitised by Iraqi officials to deceive inspectors. Iraq continued to develop the al-Hakam site into the 1990s, misleading UNSCOM about its true purpose.

Another key site, the Foot and Mouth Disease Vaccine Institute at al-Dawrah which produced botulinum toxin and probably anthrax was not divulged as part of the programme. Five years later, after intense pressure, Iraq acknowledged that tens of tonnes of bacteriological warfare agent had been produced there and at al-Hakam.

As documents recovered in August 1995 were assessed, it became apparent that the full disclosure required by the UN was far from complete. Successive inspection teams went to Iraq to try to gain greater understanding of the programme and to obtain credible supporting evidence. In July 1996 Iraq refused to discuss its past programme and doctrine forcing the team to withdraw in protest. Monitoring teams were at the same time finding undisclosed equipment and materials associated with the past programme. In response, Iraq grudgingly provided successive disclosures of its programme which were judged by UNSCOM and specially convened international panels to be technically inadequate.

In late 1995 Iraq acknowledged weapons testing the biological agent ricin, but did not provide production information. Two years later, in early 1997, UNSCOM discovered evidence that Iraq had produced ricin.

At the end of April 2002 Mr Lamb took over primary responsibility for the further elaboration of the historical UNSCOM element and he attended regular meetings of officials in the Cabinet Office in order to review and amend the text as necessary. Dr Kelly did not attend any of these meetings but Mr Lamb regularly reported any developments to him and routinely sought his advice on any proposed changes in the text.

168. During May 2002 Mr Lamb was requested by the Cabinet Office to add further material to the UNSCOM text covering three main areas: a reference to the military significance of Iraq's "Presidential Palaces", inclusion of background material on "Operation Desert Fox", and the provision of examples of the extent of Iraqi deception and obstruction to the work of the UNSCOM inspectors. In drafting this material and before submitting it to the Cabinet Office Mr Lamb discussed the draft with Dr Kelly and sought his views.

169. Dr Kelly saw the evolving draft of the briefing papers being put together by the Cabinet Office during May and June 2002 entitled "Iraqi WMD Programmes", "the history of UN weapons inspections in Iraq" and "the Iraqi regime: Crimes and Human Rights Abuses".

170. By 20 June 2002 a dossier had been prepared entitled BRITISH GOVERNMENT BRIEFING PAPERS ON IRAQ. Its contents were:

Executive Summary

Iraqi Weapons of Mass Destruction Programmes

History of UN Weapons Inspections in Iraq

Iraqi Regime: Crimes of Human Rights Abuses

The dossier contained no reference to Iraq's ability to deploy chemical or biological weapons within 45 minutes of an order to use them (which I shall hereafter term "the 45 minutes claim"). This dossier dated 20 June 2002 is set out in appendix 7.

171. On 3 September 2002 the Prime Minister announced that the Government would publish a paper on Iraq's WMD capability in the next few weeks. On 4 September the Overseas and Defence Secretariat of the Cabinet Office arranged for the three papers on Iraq's WMD capabilities, on the history of UN weapons inspections in Iraq and on abuse of human rights by the Iraqi regime to be recirculated to senior officials at 10 Downing Street, the FCO and the MoD to remind them of the current state of knowledge on those issues. The assessment staff also put in hand the updating of their existing draft on Iraqi WMD.

172. On 5 September 2002 a meeting was held in the Cabinet Office to consider the preparation of the paper announced by the Prime Minister. The meeting was chaired by Mr Alastair Campbell and was attended by Sir David Manning, Mr John Scarlett, Mr Julian Miller and other officials from the Cabinet Office, the FCO and the MoD. A further meeting chaired by Mr Campbell was held in his office in 10 Downing Street on 9 September. In his evidence Mr Scarlett described the purpose of the meeting on 5 September as follows:

[26 August, page 39, line 23]

The meeting was to discuss the overall presentation of the Government assessment which the Prime Minister had referred to. So it was intended to discuss how this would be done, what the overall format – the best structure for the assessment should be, and how responsibilities for preparing it, drafting it, taking it forward, should be allocated."

He described the purpose of the second meeting on 9 September as follows:

[26 August, page 53, line 22]

It was a continuation of a discussion we had had on 5th September. It had had the same agenda, but in this case to finalise the arrangements for the format, the structure, and sort of taking forward the presentation of the Government's assessment. I would like to say here, that both this meeting, on 9th September, and the meeting on 5th September, were chaired by Alastair Campbell because they were unique – they were wholly and only concerned with those issues. There was no discussion of intelligence issues, intelligence matters, intelligence at all, at that meeting or at those meetings so it was wholly appropriate, in my view, that they should be chaired by Alastair Campbell. It was not, in any sense of the term at all, an intelligence – neither of them were intelligence meetings.

173. After the meeting of 9 September Mr Campbell sent a memorandum to Mr Scarlett, which was circulated to Sir David Manning, Mr Jonathan Powell and a number of other officials. Relevant passages in the memorandum are as follows:

At our discussion this morning, we agreed it would be helpful if I set out for colleagues the process by which the Iraq dossier will be produced.

The first point is that this must be, and be seen to be, the work of you and your team, and that its credibility depends fundamentally upon that.

The second is that you are working on a new dossier, according to the structure we agreed at the meeting last week, to meet the new circumstances which have developed over recent weeks and months. Therefore, the rush of comments on the old dossier are not necessary or totally relevant. People should wait for the new one, which will be more detailed and substantial.

The structure we agreed last week was roughly as follows:

- why the issue arose in the first place

- why the inspection process was necessary

- the history of concealment and deception

- the story of inspectors, leading to their departure

- the story of weapons unaccounted for, and what they could do

- a section on ballistic missile technology

- CW/BW

- nuclear

- the sanctions regime, and how the policy of containment has worked only up to a point

- illicit money

- the repressive nature of the regime

- why the history of the man and the regime (Iraq/Iran; chemical weapons on his own people; Kuwait; human rights) makes us worried he cannot be allowed further to develop these weapons.

Much of this is obviously historical, but the history is a vital part of the overall story. This is something the IISS Report deals with very well.

The media/political judgment will inevitably focus on "what's new?" and I was pleased to hear from you and your SIS colleagues that, contrary to media reports today, the intelligence community are taking such a helpful approach to this in going through all the material they have. It goes without saying that there should be nothing published that you and they are not 100% happy with.

....

We agreed that by the end of today, you should have most of the draft material together, with the Agencies providing the sections relevant to the middle part of our structure, and the FCO providing the more historical material.

You will want to go through this material before submitting a consolidated draft to No.10 and others. You will also take this to the US on your visit at the end of the week.

In the meantime, I will chair a team that will go through the document from a presentational point of view, and make recommendations to you. This team, I suggest, will include John Williams (FCO) Paul Hamill (CIC) and Phil Bassett and David Bradshaw from here. Writing by committee does not work but we will make recommendations and suggestions, and you can decide what you want to incorporate. Once they are incorporated, we need to take a judgment as to whether a single person should be appointed to write the final version.

The full terms of the memorandum are set out in appendix 8 to the report.

174. With reference to this memorandum Mr Scarlett gave the following evidence:

[26 August, page 55, line 7]

Q. That left you dealing with the intelligence, is that right?

A. It left me in charge of the drafting of those parts of the dossier that were related to intelligence in any way at all or were intelligence based. I and my team were responsible for that, of course answering to the JIC.

Q. Mr Campbell I think used the expression, or it may have been in the documents one has read, of "ownership", the document being owned by you. What did you understand that to mean?

A. Ownership, that I was absolutely to be in charge.

LORD HUTTON: Well, you said Mr Scarlett that you were to be in charge of the document in any way relating to intelligence.

A. Hmm.

LORD HUTTON: But presumably someone must have had overall charge and responsibility. I mean, someone must have been concerned with the final product. Was that to be you or someone else or was it the position that there were a number of people who were concerned with the final shape of the dossier as it would be made available to the public?

A. Well, my Lord, why I made the slight qualification that I did is for that reason, that it was almost completely clear by this stage, by the time this note went out, that I was that person.

LORD HUTTON: Yes.

A. But there was still some slight ambiguity about who would be responsible for the parts of the dossier which were not going to be intelligence based. This relates to human rights and weapons inspections, in particular, where the FCO had been seen to be the lead department. In fact in this text here I think it says at the end: "Writing by Committee does not work but we will make recommendations and suggestions, and you can decide what you want to incorporate. Once they are incorporated, we need to take a judgment as to whether a single person should be appointed to write the final version." There was still a slight ambiguity there as to who would write the final version. The reason why I had had discussion with Alastair Campbell at the beginning of the meeting on my own was to say to him that it was very important that only one person and one unit had ownership and command and control of this exercise, that that should be me, that I wanted it stated clearly in writing; and I wanted that to be the outcome of our meeting, which, with the slight qualification at the end there, it was.

LORD HUTTON: Yes.

MR DINGEMANS: The slight qualification, what, being at the bottom of page 3 of that?

A. I say qualification, it is a slight ambiguity.

Q. That he was dealing with documents from a presentational point of view as it were?

A. No –

LORD HUTTON: How does the paragraph begin?

A. The page on my screen, it begins, the paragraph: "In the meantime, I will chair a team…", that is fine. That was going to look at the presentational point of view, fine. That was going to make recommendations to me, fine. There is a reference as to a further judgment to be made "as to whether a single person should be appointed to write the final version."

LORD HUTTON: I see.

MR DINGEMANS: In fact no other person was appointed, is that right?

A. I made sure that was me.

LORD HUTTON: Was there a later decision to that effect or was it simply understood, or in the way that matters worked out it was you, was that the position?

A. No – well, my Lord, I do not want to make too much of this point because there was really not too much discussion about it. It is just that there was an ambiguity in the way that note was written. In practice, and I am sure it was Alastair Campbell's understanding at the time that I went away as the person in charge of the whole exercise.

175. When he gave evidence on 23 September Mr Scarlett was asked by counsel for the Government about a passage in the record of a meeting in his office on 18 September attended by Mr Tom Kelly, Ms Clare Sumner, Mr Danny Pruce, Mr Julian Miller and Mr Scarlett himself together with a number of officials from the FCO and the MoD headed:

IRAQ DOSSIER: PUBLIC HANDLING AND BRIEFING

The record set out the main points agreed at the meeting, the first of which was:

Ownership of the dossier

- Ownership lay with No.10.

MR SUMPTION: Could we have CAB/27/2, please? This is the first of three documents that was disclosed at the end of August, after you gave your evidence first time round. It is a note of a meeting in your office on 18th September. What was the meeting about; can you tell us?

A. This was a meeting held under my Chairmanship to discuss and agree, looking ahead by this stage to the production process, at the issues relating to the actual production of the document, the briefing which would need to happen alongside it, issues such as press lines and dissemination. So it was a series of practical issues, quite separate from the drafting of the text itself.

Q. Is that answer affected by the text which is redacted?

A. What is redacted are either sort of individual names, as you can see at the top there, which would add nothing to the understanding of the document; and there is also separate redaction in addition to names which relates to briefing arrangements for foreign governments and sensitive recipients.

Q. If you look on the first page, you will see: "Ownership of the dossier. "Ownership lay with No.10." Why did that appear there?

A. Right. We had one previous meeting on this subject, on 16th September, and that was also talking about production arrangements; and at that stage there had not been any discussion of: well, which Government Department was going to be taking the lead on presenting this document on behalf of the Government? So this point was raised straight away at the 18th September meeting; and it was immediately agreed that this was a document which was going to be presented – or since this was a document that was going to be presented by the Prime Minister to Parliament on behalf of the Government, its ownership, in that sense, looking ahead to that moment, lay with No.10 and the JIC itself does not produce documents for public dissemination and there had never been any intention that it would do so. So it is ownership in that sense and it is a forward looking statement.

176. Drafts of assessments on Iraqi WMD Programmes were prepared dated 5 and 9 September 2002. Drafts of the complete dossier were prepared dated:

10/11 September

16 September

19 September

20 September

These four drafts are set out in appendices 9, 10, 11 and 12.

The intelligence in relation to the 45 minutes claim

177. Before describing the drafting of the dossier from 5 September 2002 onwards it is relevant to refer to the intelligence received by the SIS in relation to the 45 minutes claim. The intelligence was received by the SIS on 29 August 2002. In his evidence Sir Richard Dearlove, the Chief of the SIS, who was also a member of the JIC, described the intelligence as follows:

> **[15 September, page 84, line 25]**
>
> Q. Can I ask you about the intelligence leading up to the 45 minutes claim. When did you first become aware of this?
>
> A. Can I just say, you use the word "claim"; I think I would prefer to refer to it as a piece of well sourced intelligence.
>
> Q. Right. When did you first become aware of this well sourced piece of intelligence?
>
> A. It first came to my attention when it was reported towards the end of August. I think the precise date is 29ᵗʰ August.
>
> Q. And what was the process which this intelligence underwent after it was reported?
>
> A. Well, the normal SIS procedure would be to put this into what we call a CX report and send it out to customers who would be on the distribution, normal distribution for this type of intelligence.
>
> Q. In the Foreign Affairs Committee report at FAC/3/26 we can see, at paragraph 62, that the Foreign and Commonwealth Office had told the Committee that the intelligence on which the claim was based came from "an established, reliable and long-standing line of reporting". Can you comment on that?
>
> A. Well, I can except I would not normally comment in public on the status of an SIS source; but a certain amount of this is already in the public domain.
>
> Q. I am only seeking comments that are already in the public domain.
>
> A. Yes, it did come from an established and reliable source equating a senior Iraqi military officer who was certainly in a position to know this information.

178. This intelligence was sent to the assessment staff of the JIC on 30 August 2002. The JIC meets on a Wednesday and the assessment staff prepared an assessment on Iraqi WMD Programmes for the meeting of the JIC on Wednesday 4 September 2002. The assessment staff had not had time to include in that assessment the intelligence on the 45 minutes claim sent to it by the SIS before the meeting on 4 September. After that meeting the assessment was then reworked to take account of this fresh intelligence and the new assessment dated 5 September was circulated to JIC members with a request for comments by 9 September. This draft contained the following passage in relation to the 45 minutes claim:

> Iraq has probably dispersed its special weapons, including its CBW weapons. Intelligence also indicates that from forward-deployed storage sites, chemical and biological munitions could be with military units and ready for firing within 45 minutes.

179. An e-mail dated 6 September was sent by the biological weapons branch in the DIS to the assessment staff making comments on the JIC draft assessment dated 5 September. This e-mail was as follows:

> a good paper. Some minor comments from the BW side.
>
> Para 2 4ᵗʰ sentence – not sure we can be as categorical as "never", SIS may have something which means we need to fudge this slightly but they weill (sic) talk to you.

Para 3 final bullet last line. The intelligence refers to a maximum time of 45 minutes, the average was 20 minutes. This could have important implications in the event of a conflict.

Para 8 – First sentence – There is specific intelligence that Iraq plans to use CBW, it is just that there is no specific intelligence of their plans as to how/when/with what they would do so. As stated in para 4 there is intention to use during this phase.

Para 8 6th line – delete biological. It is difficult to see how persistent biological could shape the battle field.

Para 8 line 10 replace chemical munitions with CB munitions (which is what the intelligence states).

Para 10, we would like a more specific reference to possibility of sabotage/terror on lines of supply/homeland.

180. All but one of these suggestions were accepted and reflected in a fresh assessment issued on 9 September. The assessment of 9 September contained the following passage in relation to the 45 minutes claim:

> Iraq has probably dispersed its special weapons, including its CBW weapons. Intelligence also indicates that chemical and biological munitions could be with military units and ready for firing within 20-45 minutes.

181. Sir Richard Dearlove described the process by which the 45 minutes claim became included in the JIC assessments and in the dossiers as follows:

[15 September, page 88, line 18]

Q. We can see that at CAB/17/3.

A. Yes. Yes. And, in fact, what we are looking at there is a change in the drafting, which I think was recommended by my staff to ensure that the inclusion of intelligence on 45 minutes reflected more accurately the wording of the original CX report – CX is the phrase we use to refer to the intelligence reports produced by SIS.

....

[15 September, page 90, line 2]

Q. Did you see the dossier drafted on 10th or 11th September?

A. Yes, I certainly would have done, in preparation for the JIC meeting that took place on 11th September. I mean, it is normal practice for me to be closely briefed by my staff before attending the full JIC meeting; and, in fact, the process of putting together the dossier was covered very closely on a day-to-day basis by the team that I had working on it. Although it is some time ago and I do not have a precise recollection of every exchange, I was kept closely involved.

Q. Was there any discussion of the draft dossier on 11th September?

A. At the JIC meeting?

Q. Yes, sorry, at the JIC meeting.

A. Yes. There certainly was.

Q. What was the nature of that discussion?

A. As far as I recall, it was how to incorporate into the dossier the previous JIC judgments on Iraqi WMD and the addition to that picture of any new intelligence that might be available.

Q. Was there any unhappiness expressed at the JIC meeting in relation to the dossier and the drafting process?

A. No, I do not think there was. I mean, there was obvious concern on my part, as the chief of the service, that the fact of moving in the direction of publication should take full account of our concerns on issues of operational security.

Q. And at that stage had anyone mentioned any comments on the 45 minute section of the dossier which had been included for the draft of the 11th September JIC meeting?

A. No, they certainly had not. I think it is worth me adding that when we circulate a report there is a procedure by which any reader can comment on the report or question its contents; and that is a mechanism that is frequently used. The circulation of the report that included the piece about 45 minutes did not evoke any comment from customers at all.

....

[15 September, page 92, line 18]

Can I take you to DOS/2/58, which was the dossier part or the main part of the dossier dated 16th September 2002. We can see that in the top right-handed corner. We get the 45 minute source at DOS/2/72 at the bottom: "The Iraqi military may be able to deploy chemical or biological weapons within 45 minutes of an order to do so."

A. Yes.

Q. Did you pick up any differences or inconsistencies between the foreword and the executive summary, on one side, and the main text of the dossier on the other?

A. My understanding is that these were discussed in the drafting committee and in fact I was briefed for the JIC meeting on 17th September. My reaction was that all of these statements are in fact, despite the differences of nuances, they are consistent with the original intelligence report.

Q. The meeting on 17th September, was that a full JIC meeting?

A. Yes, it was a full JIC meeting.

Q. Are you sure about the date? We have had one on 4th September, one on the 11th. I think we heard from another witness –

A. Yes. Yes, I am sorry, it is the 18th. It is the 18th. My apologies.

Q. Was this considered on the 18th September in committee?

A. Yes, it was, at the end of the meeting, as far as I recall.

Q. We have seen a number of memoranda that were produced on 17th September, one from Mr Campbell, which was CAB/11/66, and he introduces it by saying: "Please find below a number of drafting points. As I was writing this, the Prime Minister had a read of the draft … and he too made a number of points." Then some specific general comments are made. More detailed comments are made later on in the memorandum. We know that there was a reply to that memorandum by Mr Scarlett on 18th September. That is CAB/11/70. We can see the first page of that there. Did you see Mr Campbell's memorandum?

A. I did not see that memorandum; but in fact I was aware, from my senior officer who was working on the drafting, that there had been, for example, a debate over the amount of time it might take the Iraqis to develop a nuclear weapon; and I know that there was, let us say, a rigorous response to questions in terms of sticking with the original intelligence in recording those issues in the dossier.

Q. We are not interested in any disputes beyond the 45 minutes source because that was what Dr Kelly appears to have commented on. Were you aware of any commentary in relation to the 45 minute point, at this stage?

A. When you say any commentary, any commentary exactly –

Q. Any commentary from Defence Intelligence Staff, for example?

A. No, I was not.

Q. Was that raised at all at the JIC meeting on 18th September?

A. Not that I can recall. It was not raised.

Q. After the meeting on 18th September, was there another JIC meeting at which the dossier was considered before publication?

A. No. The last formal meeting of the JIC at which it was considered was the 18th.

Q. Do you know whether or not it was considered by your service after 18th September?

A. Yes. After the JIC meeting I met the senior officer involved in the drafting committee and expressed to him satisfaction from the SIS point of view at the state of the draft at that stage. He then had authority delegated from me to agree the dossier but subject to the fact that there were no further what I would describe as substantive changes in the text.

Q. From what you had seen of the draft which you considered on 18th September and the draft as published, did you consider that there had been any substantive changes in the text?

A. No, I do not think after that there were substantive changes that changed it significantly.

Q. We know that the wording in the dossier, the inconsistency or apparent inconsistency between the executive summary and the foreword having been pointed out, we know that the wording of the dossier was strengthened to mirror that within the foreword and the executive summary. Did you know of that at the time?

A. I was aware what the final version was going to be, yes.

Q. And how were you made aware of the final version?

A. Well, by talking to my – I had copies of it, plus the amount of contact I had with those SIS staff working on the dossier.

………

[15 September, page 98, line 7]

LORD HUTTON: Sir Richard, could we just go back a little, please, to the final draft? You said that you delegated to one of your officers the signing off of the draft provided there were no substantive changes in it. Did you in fact see a copy of the final draft? Was it circulated to you or was it the earlier draft of 18th September which you saw?

A. I would have seen a final draft, my Lord.

182. Mr Scarlett gave a similar description of the process whereby the 45 minutes claim became included in the drafts of the assessments and the dossiers:

[26 August, page 46, line 9]

At this time, in the first week of September, the JIC was considering a classified assessment, which was completely separate as an exercise from a public assessment, of chemical and biological weaponry and possible scenarios for use, including in the event of a conflict in Iraq, or by the Iraqi regime. That assessment – or that subject had been commissioned by the JIC itself in late August. The normal JIC process had applied. There had been a meeting of the interdepartmental Current Intelligence Group headed, as normal, by a deputy head of assessment staff on 28th August, to consider a first draft of that classified assessment. That first draft had then been considered in a full meeting of the JIC on 4th September, which was Wednesday, as normal. The JIC had discussed that draft, had noted that important new intelligence was coming in, which was relevant to this subject, and had asked assessment staff, again as is quite normal, to go away, to reconsider their existing draft, in particular to reconsider the important new intelligence from various sources and to prepare a new draft.

Assessment staff had taken that task away. On 5th September they had produced a revised draft which they had sent, as is normal, to the participating working level members, who would be represented in the Current Intelligence Group and which would include Defence Intelligence Staff, DIS. This e-mail is the response from DIS to the main drafter of the paper. This is part of the classified process.

Q. Can I take you to CAB/17/3 which I think are redacted extracts from JIC papers. We can see the 5th September JIC draft which provided, at page 4, paragraph 3, final bullet: "Iraq has probably dispersed its special weapons, including CBW weapons. Intelligence also indicates that from forward deployed storage sites, chemical and biological munitions could be with military units and ready for firing within 45 minutes." Was that the first time that intelligence had featured in the JIC assessments?

A. Yes, that intelligence was based on a report which was issued on 30th August.

Mr Scarlett described the drafts of 5 September and 9 September as assessments. On 10/11 September a draft dossier was circulated to interested groups.

183. In his evidence Sir Richard Dearlove commented on the reliability of intelligence coming from a single source. In the course of his examination by counsel to the Inquiry he was referred to an internal DIS memorandum dated 20 September 2002 commenting in relation to the 45 minutes claim:

[15 September, page 97, line 12]

This is reported as fact whereas the intelligence comes from a single source. In my view the intelligence warrants no stronger a statement than '... Intelligence suggests that military planning allows .....'

In relation to this point Sir Richard stated:

[15 September, page 97, line 19]

I have to say I am rather bemused by the sentence "this is reported as fact whereas the intelligence comes from a single source". It rather implies that a single source cannot report a fact. I mean, if I can add to that.

Q. Yes, of course.

A. CX reports as produced by my service are essentially single source; and much high quality intelligence which is factual or proved to be factual is single source material. So I do not really understand that comment.

Q. Were you aware of any unhappiness with the 45 minutes point within your service?

A. No, I certainly was not.

184. In his evidence Mr Scarlett commented on the intelligence in relation to the 45 minutes claim being single sourced as follows:

[26 August, page 48, line 9]

Q. Was this intelligence single-sourced?

A. This was a report from a single source. It was an established and reliable line of reporting; and it was quoting a senior Iraqi military officer in a position to know this information.

Q. And were people unhappy about the use of single-sourced as opposed to double-sourced material?

A. Not at all, because the use of those terms in this context represents a misunderstanding of the assessment process. The assessment process takes into account a large number of considerations when it is considering intelligence against the background of other information which is available and what has already been assessed, and also, of course, the reliability and record of the particular line of reporting in question. In this particular case, it was judged straight away that the intelligence was consistent with established JIC judgments on the command, control and logistical arrangements and capabilities of the Iraqi armed forces and their experience and capabilities in the area of use of CP ammunitions. It brought an additional detail because for the first time in our reporting it gave a particular time, gave some precision.

185. The actual drafting of the dossier was carried out by a small number of members of the assessment staff who were answerable to Mr Julian Miller, the chief of the assessment staff, who in turn was answerable to Mr Scarlett, who in turn obtained the approval of the JIC to the issuing of the dossier. Mr Scarlett described the process of drafting the dossier as follows:

[26 August, page 72, line 2]

LORD HUTTON: Was the position, then, that a number of members of your assessment staff were engaged in the drafting? It came to you and ultimately you took responsibility for the final draft?

A. Yes.

LORD HUTTON: But do I understand that a number of hands might have been involved in the preparation of the draft by the assessment staff?

A. The work in assessment staff was being carried out by a small unit, mainly of two people, who were answering to one of the deputy heads of the unit.

LORD HUTTON: Yes.

A. In fact, I can correct that, at that particular moment the deputy head was absent; and then answering to the chief of assessment staff who was in charge of the drafting group.

LORD HUTTON: Yes.

A. So this detail was in the hands, in terms of the central drafting process, of assessment staff under the leadership of Julian Miller.

The concerns of Dr Brian Jones, the head of the nuclear, chemical and biological weapons section in the Scientific and Technical Directorate of the Defence Intelligence Analysis Staff

186. In his evidence Mr Anthony Cragg explained that his principal task as Deputy Chief of Defence Intelligence was to manage the work of the Defence Intelligence Analysis Staff (DIAS) which was responsible for producing military intelligence assessments for the Chiefs of Staff and was also responsible for contributing to the central intelligence analysis arrangements under the JIC. There were three directorates in DIAS, one dealing with regional affairs which was a geographically based organisation, one was a generically based organisation looking at issues such as weapons of mass destruction, terrorism, proliferation, export control and the grey arms market on similar matters and the third directorate was the Scientific and Technical Directorate of DIAS, DIAS being part of the Defence Intelligence Staff (DIS). Dr Brian Jones in September 2002 supervised the nuclear, chemical and biological weapons section in the Scientific and Technical Directorate and he reported to the Director of that Directorate who in turn reported to Mr Cragg.

187. From early 1989 Dr Jones' section often received advice from Dr Kelly. In his evidence Dr Jones described Dr Kelly's relationship with his section as follows:

[3 September, page 61, line 8]

A. At some early stage we arranged that David could come regularly into the secure area which the DIS occupies, and I encouraged him to do so, and he had a pass that meant he did not have to be accompanied when he came in, so he could walk in, and I encouraged him to do that, to talk to my staff and talk to me.

Q. What was the purpose of encouraging him to do that?

A. Primarily it would be – I mean, this sort of approach we used because the staff within the intelligence community is obviously very limited, we cannot know all that we need to know, so we need professional advisers from outside. So that sort of relationship was encouraged. We would consult with him. He would come in and chat to us about things he had spotted. It was the normal exchange, when those sort of relationships are developed.

Q. What was he consulted on? What areas was he consulted on?

A. Well, obviously Iraq was a – was something – we were always interested to hear what David said about Iraq. He was a considerable expert on Iraq, from his visits there. We also needed his advice, from time to time, on detailed microbiological matters, technical – scientific, technical matters that came up in information we were looking at when perhaps we could not understand it fully and we needed to ask him, you know, if he could interpret, if he could tell us what he thought was going on.

188. In the summer of 2002 Dr Jones went on holiday on 30 August and returned to work on 18 September. Dr Jones described the situation when he returned to work as follows:

[3 September, page 68, line 18]

Q. Before you went on holiday, was the dossier on your workload?

A. Not on mine personally; and I was not aware that anyone in the branch was working hard on it.

Q. When you came back, was it still the same situation?

A. No, the situation had changed a great deal and on my return to work one of the first things that my staff had told me was that the dossier had suddenly become very active and that they had been very busy working on the dossier, looking at several drafts and responding to drafts in very, very short timescales and it really had dominated their workload while I had been away.

189. In his evidence Dr Jones described how on 18 September he saw Dr Kelly in the office of one of his staff in the DIS looking at the latest draft of the dossier:

[3 September, page 72, line 6]

Do you know whether Dr Kelly had seen the earlier drafts of the dossier? You go on holiday on 30th August, nothing mentioned about the dossier. We have then seen various drafts starting with 4th September and running through. Do you know whether he had seen all those drafts?

A. I cannot say whether he had seen all of them. The impression I gained on my return, although such was the nature of the relationship it was not something I felt I had to ask about, was that he had looked at other drafts than the one – I mean he was actually – I discovered on 18th September, when I met him then, that he was actually looking at the latest draft at that time.

Q. He was looking at the latest draft, what, sitting in someone's office and looking at the latest draft?

A. Yes.

Q. I think you told us he had been asked because of his chemical and biological warfare expertise. Was he looking at those aspects of it?

A. I think he had a general interest. He had, I understand, provided information. I mean, he had a particular expertise about one section of that dossier and had made a contribution to it; and that really related to the work he had done from the early 1990s up to 1998 when the UNSCOM inspectors left Iraq.

Q. Did you discuss with Dr Kelly his view of the dossier as so far drafted?

A. At that point, I did. I asked him what he thought: what do you think of the dossier, David? You know.

Q. And what did he say?

A. He said he thought it was good.

Q. And were there others in your group who had differing views?

A. There were, yes.

Q. And what did you do, having heard of these different expressions of support for the dossier?

A. Well, maybe I can just explain that some of my staff had said that they were unhappy with all the detail that was in the dossier. My expert analyst on CW expressed particular concern. I had,

I think, at the time I spoke to David, begun to look at his problems, to look at the bits of the dossier that he had problems with.

Q. And what was your CW expert's particular concern?

A. Well, at its simplest he was concerned that some of the statements that were in the dossier did not accurately represent his assessment of the intelligence available to him.

190. In relation to the 45 minutes claim Dr Jones described the concerns as follows:

[3 September, page 85, line 19]

A. I think there were – the problems we had fell into three categories. I mean, firstly we had problems about the source. Indeed, as you have heard, the primary source was described as reliable and – who had reported regularly in the past, I think.

Q. So why did you have any concerns?

A. Well, our concern was that what we were hearing was second-hand information.

Q. Right.

A. He was not the originator of the information we heard; and I cannot recall knowing then as much as I know now about that secondary source. I mean, maybe we did.

Q. Was Dr Kelly aware of these concerns at the time?

A. He was certainly aware at that time or shortly afterwards that there were concerns over the 45 minute claim.

Q. Shared by persons such as yourself?

A. Yes, I mean – yes, I think from contact with myself and people in my branch. I do not think that at that stage he would have seen the original reporting.

Q. Right.

A. My recollection is that it was something that we could not automatically show to him; and I cannot recall that permission was asked for that material to be shown to him. So he did not – he was not aware, I think, from reading the material. But he would have been aware of – at some stage, whether before or after the dossier, that there was a problem with the sourcing, I think, just from chatting to us.

LORD HUTTON: Yes. Dr Jones, the Inquiry has been shown this intelligence report that a person in Iraq had been told by another person in Iraq that these weapons could be deployed within 45 minutes. Had you, at any time, prior to 24th September, actually seen that report, seen its wording or seen a summary of it?

A. Yes, I had seen that report.

LORD HUTTON: You had seen that report. And also presumably other members of your staff had seen that report?

A. Yes. In fact they drew it to my attention on my return, as part of their briefing me on the problems they were having with the dossier, with the drafts of the dossier. I think it had actually arrived whilst I was on leave, you know.

....

[3 September, page 90, line 1]

A. The second category was the content of the information. I have already touched on that slightly but maybe I can expand a little. And this was that the information did not differentiate between whether these were chemical weapons or whether they were biological weapons; and that is an important matter.

Q. Why is that?

A. Really because if one is thinking in terms of biological warfare agents that fall into this category of being reasonably described as weapons of mass destruction, then they would have to be live biological warfare agents.

Q. Is it easy to keep biological –

A. The important point is that from the time of delivery to the time that they have an effect there is an appreciable delay. So the circumstances in which 45 minutes to deliver them would be fairly special circumstances where that 45 minutes mattered. So that was an issue, an issue that concerned us. And there was also – that sort of pushed us to thinking perhaps we were talking about chemical weapons here. It is easy to put them together in a collective term, chemical and biological weapons is something that rolls off the tongue. But there was an element of doubt coming into our analysis on that. We would have looked, normally, for further definitions to feel really comfortable with a report of this sort as to which particular agents were involved, because as I have said, different agents behave in different ways. And the way in which they behave will relate to whether it is important that you can launch these things within 45 minutes.

....

[3 September, page 92, line 7]

A. The third area was we felt that we did in fact lack the collateral intelligence that allowed us to add confidence, if you like, to this single source. I mean, that is part of the analysis process. One casts around to see whether information from other sources or of other types actually fits that information; and there were some reports on plans and logistics and you could say that the military experience might be there that matched such capabilities. But the sort of thing we would normally look for is – I have mentioned before – these things come together. The evidence of agent production and the absence of CW agent production was – evidence of that worried us. We had not seen the weapons being produced. We had no evidence of any recent testing or field trials and things like that. So that all cast some doubts in our mind on that particular piece of intelligence. There is an important point to make, I think – I mean it might be your next question.

Q. Well, you tell me.

A. The important point is that we at no stage argued that this intelligence should not be included in the dossier.

Q. Right.

A. We thought it was important intelligence. I personally thought that the word used in the main body of the text, that the intelligence indicated this was a little bit strong but I felt I could live with that, but I thought that the other references to this intelligence in the dossier –

Q. Which were?

A. They were references, I think, in a conclusion in the executive summary.

Q. In the executive summary – there was no conclusion. There was at one stage, but …

A. And indeed in the foreword. I thought they were too strong.

Q. If one looks on the page, there is Saddam and the importance of CBW. Was there anything that you knew of concerning that matter?

A. Yes, I think we felt that it was reasonable to say that the intelligence indicated that this was the case; and I think I felt it was a reasonable conclusion to draw; but we did not think – we did not think the intelligence showed it absolutely beyond any shadow of doubt.

Q. And there is a difference, I take it, from your answer between "indicates" and "shows"?

A. Yes.

191. On 17 September a member of Dr Jones' staff sent a memorandum to the assessment staff of the JIC making a number of comments on the dossier. The memorandum is headed:

IRAQI WMD DOSSIER – COMMENTS ON REVISED DRAFT (15 SEPT 2002)

[The reference to "REVISED DRAFT (15 SEPT 2002)" appears to refer to the draft dossier which was then in circulation and which on the next day was dated 16th September.]

The memorandum makes the following comment in relation to the Executive Summary, para 3 – 2nd bullet point:

The judgment "has military plans for the use of chemical and biological weapons, some of which could be ready within 45 minutes of an order to use them." Is also rather strong since it is based on a single source. "Could say intelligence suggests….

192. It appears that this concern about the 45 minutes claim was already known to the assessment staff of the JIC on 16 September and on that day was considered by them in the Cabinet Office and subsequently at a DIS meeting called by Mr Cragg, the Deputy Chief of Defence Intelligence on 17 September which was attended, among others, by two of the directors of DIS, the Director of Global Issues and the Director of Science and Technology, who was Dr Jones' line manager. Mr Cragg's evidence in relation to Dr Jones' concerns was as follows:

[15 September, page 26, line 20]

Q. On the same day you have the Defence Intelligence Staff putting in its response saying: we are not so happy with the executive summary, we do not mind the dossier. And you have Mr Campbell putting in: we are quite happy with the summary, not so happy with the dossier.

A. Yes.

Q. If you then go on to page 70 you can see the response, which is dated 18th September 2002. This is from Mr Scarlett. If you go over to 71 at 10 you we can see: "The language you queried on the old page 17 has been tightened", which picks up the point in the dossier.

A. Hmm.

Q. It seems, therefore, that Mr Scarlett was taking on-board the comment from Mr Campbell but not necessarily taking on-board the comment from the Defence Intelligence Staff.

A. Yes.

Q. Do you know whether or not that caused any unhappiness amongst the Defence Intelligence Staff?

A. I think that the Defence Intelligence Staff, as you say, were concerned about the executive summary and its discontinuity with the main text. I put this down to the fact that the executive summary pulled together or reflected not merely recent intelligence which was being – which was contained in the main text, but also the general context of the new intelligence which had been received, such as knowledge, which we had had for many years, of the capabilities of the Iraqis in their use of chemical weapons and also our knowledge that they had commander control arrangements for the use of these weapons in place. These other issues informed the judgment in the executive summary to which the Defence Intelligence Staff were objecting slightly or wanting to modify the wording.

Q. On 18th September, after 16th September, the next dossier which is produced appears to be dated 19th September in the morning.

121

A. Correct.

Q. No-one has had a chance to note that at the 18th September JIC meeting.

A. Hmm.

Q. With that to refresh your memory, was there any discussion on 18th September about the inconsistency or apparent inconsistency between the executive summary and the wording of the dossier?

A. At the JIC meeting?

Q. Yes.

A. Not to my recollection. If I can just track back a little.

Q. Yes, of course.

A. I apologise. The assessment staff reviewed the text of 16th September at a meeting which they chaired, at which the DIS were present. The points raised about the concerns on the executive summary, about the 45 minutes, were raised at that meeting and the argumentation I have just deployed to you was used to explain why the executive summary said what it did. This was reported back to me at a meeting which I held, I think, on the afternoon of 17th September.

Q. So when was the date of this meeting, then?

A. Which meeting? I am sorry.

Q. When this inconsistency was being reviewed, as it were.

A. At a Cabinet Office assessment staff meeting on 17th September.

Q. On the 17th?

A. Correct.

LORD HUTTON: Then, in the light of what you were told at that meeting, you decided to call a meeting yourself, is that correct, Mr Cragg?

A. No, my Lord, I was interested in the comments which had been made by the staff on the draft dossier and I wanted to have a session with those who had attended the Cabinet Office meeting to talk through that. That was one purpose of the meeting. A second purpose was that we were expecting, and I think by then -

LORD HUTTON: Sorry, you arranged that meeting, did you?

A. I did. It was an internal DIS meeting attended by the two directors most concerned, plus those who had attended the meeting in the Cabinet Office.

LORD HUTTON: Who were those two directors?

A. The Director of Global Issues and the Director of Science and Technology, my Lord.

LORD HUTTON: Yes, thank you.

A. The second purpose of the meeting was to review the way ahead, in the sense that we were expecting there to be a statement in Parliament the following week and we needed to make sure that we were prepared to provide back up for the issuing of that statement. So that, in a sense, was the main purpose of that, the meeting on 17th.

Q. MR DINGEMANS: What did those who had attended the Cabinet Office assessment tell you about the discussion of the inconsistency that we can see between the documents on 16th September?

A. They said firstly, on the actual detailed intelligence, recent intelligence underpinning the main text and partly the executive summary, that the Secret Intelligence Service, SIS, were satisfied that the source was established and reliable and they were – they supported the reporting, which had itself already been included in a JIC assessment on 9th September.

Q. I do not want to ask you about the wording of the recent intelligence.

A. No.

Q. Or indeed where it had come from.

A. Right.

Q. But is this right: the recent intelligence did not deal with the 45 minute issue?

A. It did.

Q. It did?

A. Yes. If I could just track back again. My staff also reported to me there had been a discussion, as I say, of the general context in which the new intelligence had appeared which convinced them that it was quite reasonable to take the line they did in the executive summary concerning the likelihood or the capability of the Iraqis to deploy weapons of mass destruction within 45 minutes of a decision to do so.

LORD HUTTON: Mr Cragg, did part of this discussion relate to the point that I think Dr Jones had been concerned that the intelligence about the 45 minutes claim was single sourced, but then, as I follow the evidence, the SIS, at the meeting that you conducted or at the meeting in which you took part, said that they were satisfied about the reliability of that source? Was that what occurred? Have I understood it correctly?

A. SIS were present at the Cabinet Office meeting, my Lord. At that point – I was not there myself, but I understand from my staff that there was a discussion on the validity of the source, which would almost certainly have included whether it was single source.

LORD HUTTON: Yes.

A. And the answer, I think, on the single source issue is that, as I believe Mr Scarlett said in his first appearance, my Lord, that single source clearly has to be looked at with some care; but this was a known sourced, established and reliable with a good reporting record. And the statements he was making, the intelligence he was providing was well in context of known Iraqi approaches.

LORD HUTTON: Yes. I see. Yes.

A. So in that sense – I think Mr Scarlett said it fairly clearly – there were no qualms about including this reporting.

LORD HUTTON: I see. Yes. Thank you.

MR DINGEMANS: What was your understanding about ownership of the dossier –

LORD HUTTON: Just before you ask that, may I ask you: at the conclusion of the meeting which you attended, and you had knowledge that Dr Jones and his staff were concerned about the wording relating to the 45 minutes claim, what was your conclusion about the validity of their concerns?

A. I felt, my Lord, bearing in mind the views expressed by SIS and supported by the assessment staff, that their concerns had been dealt with satisfactorily. That was my judgment.

LORD HUTTON: Yes. I see. Yes. Yes.

MR DINGEMANS: And your view was then made known to the two directors who had attended?

A. We discussed this round my table, so they knew.

Q. The Director for Science and Technology was the line manager for Dr Jones, is that right?

A. He was, correct.

193. Therefore Mr Cragg's evidence was that Dr Jones' concerns were considered by the assessment staff and by SIS and also at a meeting which he called attended by Dr Jones' line manager in the DIS, the Director of Science and Technology, and that the view

was taken that it was proper to approve the wording in respect of which Dr Jones had raised reservations. Dr Jones continued to have reservations and in a minute to Mr Cragg and others dated 19 September 2002 he stated:

IRAQ DOSSIER

Reference: Iraq Dossier Draft issued on 19 Sept 02

1. [***] has been involved in the generation of the Iraq dossier which, in the last two weeks has involved a number of iterations which have incorporated new intelligence. It is my understanding that some of the intelligence has not been made available to my branch. Because of this they have had to express their reservations on several aspects of the dossier. Most of these have been resolved. However, a number remain in the document at reference and it is important that I note for you at this stage the remaining areas where we are unable to confirm the statements made on the basis of the information available to my branch.

2. Although we have no problem with a judgment based on intelligence that Saddam attaches great importance to possessing WMD we have not seen the intelligence that "shows" this to be the case. Nor have we seen intelligence that "shows" he does not regard them only as a weapon of last resort, although our judgment is that it would be sensible to assume he might use them in a number of other scenarios. The intelligence we have seen indicates rather than "shows" that Iraq has been planning to conceal its WMD capabilities, and it would be a (sic) reasonable to assume that he would do this.

3. We have a number of questions in our minds relating to the intelligence on the military plans for the use of chemical and biological weapons, particularly about the times mentioned and the failure to differentiate between the two types of weapon.

4. We have not seen intelligence which we believe "shows" that Iraq has continued to produce CW agent in 1998 – 2002, although our judgment is that it has probably done so. Whilst we are even more convinced that Iraq has continued to produce BW agent (on the basis of mobile production intelligence) we would not go so far as to say we "know" this to be the case.

5. Finally, I note we are pleased that the claim that Iraq used aflatoxin against the Shia uprising in 1991 has been excluded from the dossier but we are concerned that the claim in relation to mustard remains as we consider the evidence to be weak.

194. In his evidence Mr Cragg referred to Dr Jones' minute of 19 September 2002 as follows:

[15 September, page 38, line 4]

Q. Is this strong language for intelligence personnel?

A. Yes. I was quite surprised to receive the minute, because we had gone – we had tried to explain what the situation was, certainly on the production issue and, as far as I can tell also perhaps, although I am not certain, on the 45 minutes.

Q. And having received a document that surprised you, what did you do as a result of that?

A. Well, it arrived late on 19th September. I cannot be sure, but it would have been my normal practice to try to discuss it with him, but I did not. I think, and I cannot be sure about this, because by then he had left the office and I was faced with the document itself.

Q. Were you given another version after 19th September?

A. Of the dossier?

Q. Yes.

A. There was another version on the 20th, but I was on leave on the 20th September. What I was referring to was I found myself with Dr Jones' minute, which I had to decide what to do with.

Q. So, for the reasons you have given, you do not do anything about it on the 19th?

A. Oh I did.

Q. Sorry?

A. In the sense that I reflected on Dr Jones' concerns and decided that on the issues he raised I was satisfied with the actual text of the dossier, which I had in front of me. I can expand further if you wish.

Q. Yes, please do.

A. Dr Jones, quite rightly – I have no problems with him raising issues, indeed I have always encouraged debate in the DIS on these issues. On the question that – I took the view that on the question of the 45 minutes and of the chemical weapons production, this had already been considered at length with the Cabinet Office in their meeting of 17th September and that I was satisfied with the decisions reached and consequently with the wording of the dossier at that point. On the other issues raised, which I think relate to the importance attached to the possession of chemical weapons, the absence of proof that they are seen as a – they are not seen, excuse me, as a weapon of last resort. And the absence of proof, definitive proof, that efforts are being made to conceal them. I took the view that on each of those there had been much intelligence over the years, not merely in the past few weeks but over a long period, which sustained the view taken in the dossier.

LORD HUTTON: Did you consider, Mr Cragg, whether you should report Dr Jones' concerns to the Chief of Defence Intelligence or to the JIC? In a sense, I think you have perhaps given an explanation already, but I would just like you to respond to that particular question, if you would please.

A. Well, certainly my Lord, the Chief of Defence Intelligence, who was not in the office on the Thursday, was in the office on the Friday and himself took a view on Dr Jones' concerns. No doubt you will hear from him on that point.

LORD HUTTON: Yes.

A. On the question of approaching the Chairman of the JIC, I took the view that since all of the issues had either been discussed with the Cabinet Office or were well within the general thrust of known intelligence that it was not necessary to raise the issue with Mr Scarlett. If I had done, I am as sure as I can be that he would have asked: what is the view of yourself and the Chief of Defence Intelligence on this issue?

The approval of the dossier by the JIC

195. In September 2002 Air Marshal Sir Joseph French was Chief of Defence Intelligence and was a member of the JIC. He stated in his evidence that he was content that the 45 minutes claim should be included in the dossier and he was content that the dossier should be issued. Air Marshal French stated:

[15 September, page 64, line 7]

Q. After the meeting of 11th September, did you attend any other JIC meetings before the dossier was published?

A. No, I was not in [the] office on the 18th and was represented by Mr Cragg, who is a member of the JIC himself.

Q. And we have heard from Mr Cragg.

A. Yes, you have. Yes.

Q. On 11th September you say you had a meeting beforehand to discuss any issues that had been raised. On 10th to 11th September there is the first draft of the dossier, which is produced after the 45 minutes claim has been finally assessed by the JIC. Was the 45 minutes claim raised at that stage?

A. Not in the JIC on the 11th, no.

Q. Was it raised in the meeting with you beforehand?

A. I am not aware at this stage. Obviously the assessment went through. It could well have been brought to my attention, but I would have not been surprised nor do I go against the mention of 45 minutes.

Q. If it had been mentioned to you, would you have raised it at the Joint Intelligence Committee?

A. No, because from a military perspective the 45 minutes is something that I would fully understand that in certain circumstances forces could be well able of actually starting to deliver systems within that timeframe.

....

[15 September, page 71, line 18]

Q. Having seen Dr Jones' memorandum, what did you do as a result of that?

A. We were on the 20th, which was the final draft day.

Q. Yes.

A. And that ultimately I had to make the decision whether or not the DIS was content for the document to go to print; and I was content for it to go to print.

Q. Were you sent a copy of the dossier that was produced on 20th September?

A. Yes, I was.

Q. Did the JIC meet in committee to approve that dossier on the 20th?

A. No, in that we have gone through several iterations and, as is normal Government practice, something that had been in the drafting that long quite often we would have out of committee clearance and sometimes that clearance would be on silence procedures, i.e. if you have not reported by the due date time then it would be recognised that you were content for the document to go forward.

Q. So a copy was distributed and it was up to you to make any objections known?

A. Yes.

196. In September 2002 Mr Anthony Cragg was the Deputy Chief of Defence Intelligence and a member of the JIC. In his evidence he also stated that he was content that the 45 minutes claim should be included in the dossier and that he was content that the dossier should be issued. He stated:

[15 September, page 49, line 11]

the dossier reflected the JIC assessments on the recent intelligence; and the JIC assessments were an accurate reflection, put into context, of the intelligence itself. So it was a flow of perfectly reputable intelligence conveyed by the assessment staff and ourselves into the JIC assessment and thence into the dossier.

....

[15 September, page 52, line 24]

I was, myself, perfectly satisfied with the way in which the drafting of the document, the dossier, was taking place under the management of the assessment staff, supervised by John Scarlett. I am quite sure, from having read the dossier many times, it does not go beyond the remit, as it were, of available intelligence.

....

[15 September, page 56, line 6]

In my view, from my perspective, the dossier was prepared and produced by a rigorous process of drafting. I myself saw what you might call the rolling draft as being the principal means by which the JIC membership, the individuals, contributed to and exercised influence over the process. It is certainly the case that as drafting proceeded, some points were accepted and some were not. That is the nature of drafting of course. But I am quite sure, in my own mind, that the reasons for accepting or rejecting were rational and good reasons, it was not done in an arbitrary way.

....

[15 September, page 56, line 19]

I and my senior managers were satisfied with the outcome. I have no reason to believe that Air Marshal French himself was not personally satisfied with the outcome. If I had not been satisfied, I would have said so.

197. At the conclusion of his evidence Sir Richard Dearlove stated:

[15 September, page 107, line 18]

I think the only one point I would like to make in relation to our earlier discussion, I reported to my directors I think on 19th September that we had had full visibility of the process of preparing the dossier and that the whole process had gone extremely well.

Q. And did you do anything after the publication of the dossier to record that?

A. Yes, I did. At the JIC meeting, I think on 25th September –

Q. Yes, we have heard there is one on the 18th, so it must be the 25th.

A. – I proposed a vote of thanks to the Chairman on behalf of the JIC members for the way in which he and the assessment staff had conducted a difficult exercise and the integrity with which it had been done, and it was done spontaneously of course.

Q. Was the vote of thanks passed?

A. Yes, it was.

The differing wording of the 45 minutes claim in the draft dossiers

198. The draft dossier of 20 June 2002 and the assessment for the JIC meeting on 4 September 2002 contained no reference to the 45 minutes claim. This was because the intelligence which was the basis for the 45 minutes claim was not received by the SIS until 29 August 2002 and the assessment staff did not have time to include it in the assessment for the meeting of 4 September 2002.

<u>The draft assessment dated 5 September 2002</u>

199. It contained a reference to the 45 minutes claim:

Iraq has probably dispersed its special weapons, including its CBW weapons. Intelligence also indicates that from forward-deployed storage sites, chemical and biological munitions could be with military units and ready for firing within 45 minutes.

<u>The assessment dated 9 September 2002</u>

200. It contained a reference to the 45 minutes claim:

Iraq has probably dispersed its special weapons, including its CBW weapons. Intelligence also indicates that chemical and biological munitions could be with military units and ready for firing within 20-45 minutes.

The draft dossier dated 10/11 September 2002

201. The Executive Summary stated:

6. Recent intelligence adds to this picture. It indicates that Iraq:

....

- envisages the use of weapons of mass destruction in its current military planning, and could deploy such weapons within 45 minutes of the order being given for their use;

Section 6 headed:

"IRAQI CHEMICAL, BIOLOGICAL, NUCLEAR AND BALLISTIC MISSILE PROGRAMMES: THE CURRENT POSITION" stated:

"13. Special Security Organisation (SSO) and Special Republican Guard (SRG) units would be involved in the movement of any chemical and biological weapons to military units. The Iraqi military holds artillery and missile systems at Corps level throughout the Armed Forces and conducts regular training with them. The Directorate of Rocket Forces has operational control of strategic missile systems and some Multiple Rocket Launcher Systems. Within the last month intelligence has suggested that the Iraqi military would be able to use their chemical and biological weapons within 45 minutes of an order to do so.

The draft dossier dated 16 September 2002

202. The Executive Summary stated:

[intelligence] allows us to judge that Iraq

- has military plans for the use of chemical and biological weapons, some of which could be ready within 45 minutes of an order to use them. Saddam and his son Qusay have the political authority to authorise the use of these weapons;

203. Chapter 3 headed:

THE CURRENT POSITION: 1998-2002 stated:

1. This chapter sets out what we now know of Saddam's chemical, biological, nuclear and ballistic missile programmes, drawing on all the available evidence. While it takes account of the results from UN inspections and other publicly available information, it also draws heavily on intelligence about Iraqi efforts to develop their programmes and capabilities since 1998. The **main conclusions** are that:

....

- Iraq's military forces maintain the capability to use chemical and biological weapons, with command, control and logistical arrangements in place. The Iraqi military may be able to deploy these weapons within forty five minutes of a decision to do so;

....

Recent Intelligence

5. Subsequently, intelligence has become available from reliable sources which complements and adds to previous intelligence and confirms the JIC assessment that Iraq has chemical and biological weapons. The intelligence also shows that the Iraqi leadership has been discussing a number of issues related to these weapons. This intelligence covers:

....

- **Saddam's willingness to use chemical and biological weapons:** intelligence indicates that Saddam is prepared to use chemical and biological weapons if he believes his regime is under threat. We also know from intelligence that as part of Iraq's military planning, Saddam is willing to use chemical and biological weapons against any internal uprising by the Shia population. The Iraqi military may be able to deploy chemical or biological weapons within forty five minutes of an order to do so.

204. The Executive Summary stated:

> 4. ...As well as the public evidence, however, significant additional information is available to the government from secret intelligence sources, described in more detail in this paper. This intelligence cannot tell us about everything. But it provides a fuller picture of Iraqi plans and capabilities. It shows that Saddam Hussein attaches great importance to possessing weapons of mass destruction which he regards as the basis for Iraq's regional power. It shows that he does not regard them only as weapons of last resort. He is ready to use them, including against his own population, and is determined to retain them, in breach of United Nations Resolutions. Intelligence also shows that Iraq is preparing plans to conceal evidence of these weapons from renewed inspections, including by dispersing incriminating documents. And it confirms that despite sanctions and the policy of containment, Saddam has continued to make progress with his illicit weapons programmes.

> 5. As a result of this intelligence we judge that Iraq has:

> ....

> - military plans for the use of chemical and biological weapons, some of which are deployable within 45 minutes of an order to use them. The authority to use chemical and biological weapons ultimately resides with Saddam, but he may have delegated this authority to his son Qusai;

205. Chapter 3 headed: "THE CURRENT POSITION: 1998-2002" stated:

> 1. This chapter sets out what we know of Saddam's chemical, biological, nuclear and ballistic missile programmes, drawing on all the available evidence. While it takes account of the results from UN inspections and other publicly available information, it also draws heavily on the latest intelligence about Iraqi efforts to develop their programmes and capabilities since 1998. The **main conclusions** are that:

> ....

> - Iraq's military forces are able to use chemical and biological weapons, with command, control and logistical arrangements in place. The Iraqi military are able to deploy these weapons within forty five minutes of a decision to do so.

> ....

> **Recent intelligence**

> 5. Subsequently, intelligence has become available from reliable sources which complements and adds to previous intelligence and confirms the JIC assessment that Iraq has chemical and biological weapons. The intelligence also shows that the Iraqi leadership has been discussing a number of issues related to these weapons. This intelligence covers:

> ....

> - **Saddam's willingness to use chemical and biological weapons:** intelligence indicates that Saddam is prepared to use chemical and biological weapons if he believes his regime is under threat. We also know from intelligence that as part of Iraq's military planning, Saddam is willing to use chemical and biological weapons against an internal uprising by the Shia population. Intelligence indicates that the Iraqi military are able to deploy chemical or biological weapons within forty five minutes of an order to do so.

The draft dossier dated 20 September 2002

206. This dossier contained a foreword by the Prime Minister which included the statement:

> In recent months, I have been increasingly alarmed by the evidence from inside Iraq that despite sanctions, despite the damage done to his capability in the past, despite the UNSCRs [Security Council Resolutions] expressly outlawing it, and despite his denials, Saddam Hussein is

continuing to develop WMD, and with them the ability to inflict real damage upon the region, and the stability of the world.

Gathering intelligence inside Iraq is not easy. Saddam's is one of the most secretive and dictatorial regimes in the world. So I believe people will understand why the Agencies cannot be specific about the sources, which have formed the judgments in this document, and why we cannot publish everything we know. We cannot, of course, publish the detailed raw intelligence. I and other Ministers have been briefed in detail on the intelligence and are satisfied as to its authority. I also want to pay tribute to our Intelligence and Security Services for the often extraordinary work that they do.

What I believe the assessed intelligence has established beyond doubt is that Saddam has continued to produce chemical and biological weapons, that he continues in his efforts to develop nuclear weapons, and that he has been able to extend the range of his ballistic missile programme. I also believe that, as stated in the document, Saddam will now do his utmost to try to conceal his weapons from UN inspectors.

The picture presented by JIC papers in recent months has become more not less worrying. It is clear that, despite sanctions, the policy of containment has not worked sufficiently well to prevent Saddam from developing these weapons.

I am in no doubt that the threat is serious, and current; that he has made progress on WMD, and that he has to be stopped.

Saddam has used chemical weapons, not only against an enemy state, but against his own people. Intelligence reports make clear that he sees the building up of his WMD capability, and the belief overseas that he would use these weapons, as vital to his strategic interests, and in particular his goal of regional domination. And the document discloses that his military planning allows for some of the WMD to be ready within 45 minutes of an order to use them.

The Executive Summary stated:

4. As well as the public evidence, however, significant additional information is available to the Government from secret intelligence sources, described in more detail in this paper. This intelligence cannot tell us about everything. However, it provides a fuller picture of Iraqi plans and capabilities. It shows that Saddam Hussein attaches great importance to possessing weapons of mass destruction which he regards as the basis for Iraq's regional power. It shows that he does not regard them only as weapons of last resort. He is ready to use them, including against his own population, and is determined to retain them, in breach of United Nations Security Council Resolutions (UNSCR).

5. Intelligence also shows that Iraq is preparing plans to conceal evidence of these weapons, including incriminating documents, from renewed inspections. And it confirms that despite sanctions and the policy of containment, Saddam has continued to make progress with his illicit weapons programmes.

6. As a result of the intelligence we judge that Iraq has:

....

- military plans for the use of chemical and biological weapons, including against its own Shia population. Some of these weapons are deployable within 45 minutes of an order to use them.

207. Chapter 3 headed "THE CURRENT POSITION: 1998-2002" stated:

1. This chapter sets out what we know of Saddam's chemical, biological, nuclear and ballistic missile programmes, drawing on all the available evidence. While it takes account of the results from UN inspections and other publicly available information, it also draws heavily on the latest intelligence about Iraqi efforts to develop their programmes and capabilities since 1998. The **main conclusions** are that:

- Iraq's military forces are able to use chemical and biological weapons, with command, control and logistical arrangements in place. The Iraqi military are able to deploy these weapons within 45 minutes of a decision to do so.

Recent intelligence

5. Subsequently, intelligence has become available from reliable sources which complements and adds to previous intelligence and confirms the JIC assessment that Iraq has chemical and biological weapons. The intelligence also shows that the Iraqi leadership has been discussing a number of issues related to these weapons. This intelligence covers:

....

- **Saddam's willingness to use chemical and biological weapons:** intelligence indicates that as part of Iraq's military planning, Saddam is willing to use chemical and biological weapons, including against its own Shia population. Intelligence indicates that the Iraqi military are able to deploy chemical or biological weapons within 45 minutes of an order to do so.

The dossier published by the Government on 24 September 2002

208. The relevant parts of the dossier which included a foreword by the Prime Minister are set out in paragraph 22.

209. The first draft of the foreword by the Prime Minister had been worded as follows:

> The document published today is the work of the Joint Intelligence Committee (JIC), which is made up of the heads of the UK's three Intelligence and Security Agencies, the Chief of Defence Intelligence, and senior officials from those government departments. The JIC provides regular assessments to me on a wide range of foreign policy and international security issues.
>
> Its work, like the material it analyses, is largely secret. It is unprecedented for them to publish this kind of document, but in light of the debate about Iraq and Weapons of Mass Destruction (WMD), I wanted to share with the British public the reasons why I believe this issue to be a current and serious threat to the UK's national interests.
>
> In recent months, I have been increasingly alarmed by the evidence from inside Iraq that despite sanctions, despite the damage done to his capability in the past, and despite the UNSCR's expressly outlawing it, Saddam Hussein is continuing to develop WMD, and the ability to inflict real damage upon the region, and the stability of the world.
>
> Gathering intelligence inside Iraq is not easy. Saddam's is one of the most secretive and dictatorial regimes in the world. So I believe people will understand if the agencies cannot be specific about the sources, human and technical, which have formed the judgements in this document. I and other ministers have been briefed in detail on the sources, and are satisfied as to their authority, and the authority of the information they have disclosed.
>
> What I believe they established beyond doubt is that Saddam has continued to produce chemical and biological weapons that he continues in his efforts to develop nuclear weapons, and to extend the range of his ballistic missile programme.
>
> This picture is every month has become more not less worrying. Faced with the picture put before me on seeing a succession of JIC papers on the subject, as Prime Minister I have a choice: do I ignore this evidence; or do I act to address the threat?
>
> I am in no doubt that the threat is serious, and current; that he has made progress on WMD and that he has to be stopped.
>
> Alone among leaders, Saddam has used chemical weapons. Intelligence reports make clear that he sees the possession of WMD as vital to his strategic internal of regional domination. And the document discloses that his military planning allows for some of the WMD to be ready within 45 minutes of an order to use them.

In today's integrated world, a major regional conflict does not stay confined to the region in question. Faced with someone who has shown himself capable of using WMD, I believe the international community has to stand up for itself and ensure its authority is upheld.

The threat posed to international peace and security, when WMD are in the hands of a dangerous and unstable regime like Iraq's is real. Unless we face up to the threat, we place at risk the lives and property of our own people.

The case I make is not that Saddam could launch a nuclear attack on London or another part of the UK (He could not). The case I make is that the UN resolution demanding that he stops his WMD programme are being flouted; that since the inspectors left four years ago, he has continued with this programme; and the inspectors must be allowed back in to do their job properly.

The sentence in this first draft "The case I make is not that Saddam could launch a nuclear attack on London or another part of the UK (he could not)." was not included in the dossier published on 24 September.

The allegation that the dossier was sexed-up

210. In his broadcasts on the Today programme on 29 May 2003 one of the allegations made by his source which Mr Gilligan reported was that the dossier had been "sexed-up" on the orders of 10 Downing Street. In his broadcast at 6.07am Mr Gilligan said:

> … Downing Street, our source says, ordered a week before publication, ordered it to be sexed-up, to be made more exciting and ordered more facts to be er, to be discovered.

In his broadcast at 7.32am Mr Gilligan said:

> … I have spoken to a British official who was involved in the preparation of the dossier, and … He said 'it was transformed in the week before it was published, to make it sexier.'

211. It is clear from the evidence which I have heard and from the documents which have been put in evidence that 10 Downing Street took a very close interest in the drafting of the dossier and was concerned that the intelligence set out in it should be presented in a way which made as strong a case against Saddam Hussein as the intelligence properly permitted. On 11 September 2002 a member of the JIC assessment staff sent the following e-mail to the intelligence agencies:

> Dear all
>
> We have now received comments back from No 10 on the first draft of the dossier. Unsurprisingly they have further questions and areas they would like expanded.
>
> The main comments are:
>
> 1. They liked the use of a specific personality, Haidar Taha, in the paras on CW. Can we add any more personalities, related to BW, nuclear, BM, who are doing jobs now that are suspicious (sic) because of their previous role. (Can we say anything about Dr Rihab Taha for instance?)
>
> 2. Is there any intelligence that Iraq has actively sought to employ foreign experts, in particular in the nuclear field?
>
> 3. They want more details on the items procured for their nuclear programme – how many did they buy, what does this equate to in terms of significance to a nuclear weapons programme?
>
> 4. Can we say how many chemical and biological weapons Iraq currently has by type! If we can't give weapons numbers can we give any idea on the quantity of agent available!
>
> I appreciate everyone, us included, has been around at least some of these buoys before, particularly item 4. But No 10 through the Chairman want the document to be as strong as

possible within the bounds of available intelligence. This is therefore a last (!) call for any items of intelligence that agencies think can and should be included.

Responses needed by 1200 tomorrow.

Thanks

PS

[***] we have already discussed the continuing need to say something about Iraq's capability to make INDs (as per March JIC paper).

212. **On 17 September Mr Campbell sent the following minute to Mr Scarlett:**

Please find below a number of drafting points. As I was writing this, the Prime Minister had a read of the draft you gave me this morning, and he too made a number of points. He has also read my draft foreword, which I enclose (he will want another look at it before finally signing it off but I'd appreciate your views at this stage).

He said he thought you'd done a very good job and it was convincing (though I pointed out that he is not exactly a "don't know" on the issue).

He feels that Chapter 3 should be re-ordered, to build towards the conclusions through detail ie. start with paragraph 8 (chemical agent) through to paragraph 16, then do paragraphs 2-7, then paragraph 1. If you agree, it would need a little re-writing.

He, like me, was worried about the way you have expressed the nuclear issue particularly in paragraph 18. Can we not go back, on timings, to "radiological device" in months; nuclear bomb in 1-2 years with help; 5 years with no sanctions.

He wondered if there were any more pictures that could be used.

He thought we should make more of the "no civil nuclear" point, and list dual use products.

He felt we don't do enough on human rights, and Saddam's disregard for human life is an important point. He felt there should be more made of the points in the box on page 45.

My detailed comments on the draft, which is much stronger.

1. In light of the last 24 hours, I think we should make more of the point about <u>current</u> concealment plans. Also in the executive summary, it would be stronger if we said that despite sanctions and the policy of containment, he has made real progress, even if this echoes the Prime Minister.

2. In the summary you are clear that Saddam's sons have authority to authorise CW/BW use. In the text (Page 23) it is weaker "may have".

3. Can we say he has <u>secured</u> uranium from Africa.

4. Could we use the 60,000 figure in the executive summary, re aluminium.

5. Also in executive summary, can we be clear about the distances by which he is seeking to extend missile range.

6. "Vivid and horrifying", re human rights, doesn't fit with the dry text around it.

7. Re illicit earnings, how much of the 3 billion is illegally gained.

8. On page 15 can we list quantities of eg. Shells, sprays etc.

9. On page 16, bottom line, "might" reads very weakly.

10. On page 17, 2 lines from the bottom, "may" is weaker than in the summary.

11. On page 19, top line, again "could" is weak "capable of being used" is better.

12. Re FMD vaccine plant. It doesn't need the last sentence re "probable" renovation.

13. On page 24, 3rd line, you say 1991 when I think you mean 1998.

14. The nuclear timelines issue is difficult. I felt it worked better in the last draft. Julian showed me: namely "radiological devices" in months: nuclear bomb 1-2 years with help; 5 years with no sanctions.

15. It would be stronger if you could be more explicit about when a JIC assessment has gone to the PM, and the basis upon which it has been published.

16. I've seen Ed Owen's comments, and don't agree that there are too many bullet points in the executive summary.

In addition officials in 10 Downing Street and officials in the FCO sent a number of e-mails to their colleagues about drafting points in the dossier. These e-mails are set out in appendix 13.

213. On 18 September Mr Scarlett sent Mr Campbell the following minute:

IRAQ: WEAPONS OF MASS DESTRUCTION

1. Thank you for your minute of 17 September.

2. The Prime Minister suggested that Chapter 3 should be re-ordered. We have looked at this, but found that the restructured text has less impact than the original. Nonetheless, I attach for you only a version amended along the lines proposed.

3. On the nuclear timings, I explained yesterday the decision to drop earlier references to an improvised nuclear device, on which there is no intelligence. I have retained paragraph 18, which factually summarised the JIC position. But I have amended the latest sections (now paragraph 24) to bring out more clearly the current judgements. I hope you will find this makes the position clearer.

4. We are continuing to look for more pictures, but as yet have nothing that adds usefully to the text.

5. On the civil nuclear point, we have brought out the position on the Iraqi programme article clearly in a box. Dual use products are also now listed separately in bullet point form. The impact here is much improved. Finally, the Prime Minister had asked for more on human rights. We have added to the text in part 3, and also given this a little more prominence in executive summary.

6. Turning to your details points, we have been able to amend the text in most cases as you proposed. Taking your points in sequence:

    1. we have strengthened language on current concerns and plans, including in the executive summary. The summary also bring out the point on sanctions and containment, as you proposed.

    2. on the position of Saddam's sons, the intelligence supports only 'may have'.

    3. on the uranium from Africa, the agreed interpretation of the intelligence, brokered with some difficulty with the originators and owners of the reporting allows us only to say that he has 'sought' uranium from Africa.

    4. we have introduced the reference to 60,00 aluminium tubes into the executive summary.

    5. also in the executive summary, we now refer to the 200km range of the smaller missiles.

    6. "vivid and horrifying" has been dropped.

    7. I can confirm that all of the £3 billion is illegally gained; the text now makes this clear.

    8. we do not have intelligence which allows us to list quantities on the old page 15 for the various delivery means.

    9. we cannot improve on the use of 'might' on the old page 16.

10. the language you queried on the old page 17 has been tightened.

11. your proposal to replace could by capable of being used has been incorporated.

12. we have deleted the sentence referring to the probable renovation of the FMD plant.

13. the date has been corrected.

14. see my previous comments.

15. we have discussed separately the references to JIC assessments.

7. Additionally, we have looked at the executive summary in the light of Ed Owens comments. While we have not reduced the number of bullet points, we have taken some of his other drafting and structural arrangements.

214. Mr Scarlett was questioned about his response to Mr Campbell's point 10 in the latter's minute of 17 September and this questioning related to changes in the wording of the draft dossiers, the changes being these: in the draft dated 16 September the executive summary stated that recent intelligence indicates that Iraq "could deploy [WMD] within 45 minutes of the order being given for their use", whereas the main text of the draft stated that the Iraqi military "may be able to deploy chemical or biological weapons within forty five minutes of an order to do so." However in the drafts of 19 and 20 September and in the dossier published on 24 September the executive summary stated that some chemical and biological weapons "are deployable within 45 minutes of an order to use them" and the main text stated that the Iraqi military "are able to deploy chemical or biological weapons within 45 minutes of an order to do so". In his evidence Mr Scarlett said:

[23 September, page 98, line 11]

Q. Point 10 is about the 45 minutes point.

A. Yes.

Q. What do you say about that?

A. Right. Well, that is a reference to the fact that in the text as drafted on 16th September there was a clear inconsistency between the way in which the 45 minutes point was expressed in the executive summary, where for the first time in the drafting it was being expressed as a judgment, not as a reference to recent intelligence; the way it was expressed in the conclusions, the main conclusions in that part of the dossier dealing with chemical and biological weaponry, and also in the body of the text for that part, and then in the main conclusions, a box, which at that stage was in the draft at the end; and in the executive summary at the beginning and in the conclusion at the end it was stated that the chemical and biological weapons could be ready for use within 45 minutes; and in the body – in that main conclusions part in the body of the text and also in the text it was "may". This was clearly an inconsistency which was unbalanced and needed to be addressed.

As it happened, completely separate from this point, the DIS had raised the question in advance of the drafting meeting which was taking place under Julian Miller's Chairmanship at 0900 hours on 17th September, had raised the wording in the 16th September draft of the executive judgment, and had said that they thought it was rather strong. They did not think that the point should not be in the dossier, they thought that the judgment was rather strong. So that was the subject of discussion at the 17th September meeting before this memo was received.

Q. Yes.

A. It was decided that, after the end of the discussion that the assessment staff would go away and look at the 9th September classified assessment and also at the intelligence and bring the wording of the text, the two middle sort of points, into line with what the assessment and the intelligence said. The assessment staff also pointed out that the executive summary was worded in the form of a judgment, which was a different point, and the DIS proposal had been it should

135

be qualified "intelligence suggests that". The assessment staff view was you could not do that with a judgment, a judgment is either a judgment or it is not there at all. It is not possible to qualify it with "intelligence indicates" or "intelligence suggests" or whatever. So that was their – that was how they left it. Subsequently –

Q. Just pausing there, were those decisions you have just described made before or after those involved learned of this comment?

A. Yes, that discussion took place before this comment was received; and that work was undertaken before this comment was received. As I now know, and we did not at the time, the meeting was discussed within the DIS at a meeting chaired by Tony Cragg in the afternoon of the 17th September when it was decided not to pursue the point raised by the DIS any further. So the action that was taken by assessment staff, consistent with what they had said at the morning meeting, was to amend the draft, and when the new draft was circulated it had been amended to take account of the action that they had taken. This had absolutely nothing to do with any of this. When I replied on this point on the 18th, I said that I think the wording had been tightened. What that meant, quite clearly, was that the wording had been brought into line so the inconsistency had been removed, and it had been brought into line with the underlying intelligence.

Q. It has been suggested, on behalf of the BBC, that if there is an inconsistency you should tone down the executive summary rather than tone up the text.

A. But as of course I have explained, the executive summary for the dossier, in paragraph 6, which is the relevant part, took the form of a judgement. It was not a summary of the main points in the text, it was a judgment.

When cross-examined by Mr Caldecott QC for the BBC Mr Scarlett said:

[23 September, page 126, line 15]

Q. Now the only assessment element of the 45 minute claim in the 9th September final assessment is in the main text, is it not?

A. Yes.

Q. And it says that it is merely an indication.

A. Yes.

Q. If that was the agreement, how is it reflected by strengthening the word "may" to the word "are"?

A. Because the intelligence contained no indication of "may", no indication of uncertainty. It was a statement in the intelligence report that they had this capability. But the JIC assessment of the 9th September put in terms of intelligence indicates that they have that capability, and that was therefore reflected in exactly those terms in the main body of the redrafted text, which is what the assessment staff said they would do.

Q. But that, with respect, is to – I do not know what the wording of the raw intelligence is but of course I take it from you.

A. Yes.

Q. But –

A. Thank you.

Q. – that is slightly to look, is it not, at the wording of the raw intelligence without taking into account the assessment element and the choice of the word "indicates"? We have had a lot of evidence about the importance of precision and the significance of words like "indicates".

A. Indeed.

Q. If you do go back you do not just look at the raw intelligence, you look at how it was assessed; and it was assessed as "indicates", not "shows". Why does it therefore get put up to "are" if you are implementing this agreement?

A. The 9ᵗʰ September assessment that intelligence indicates that chemical and biological munitions could be with military units and ready for firing within 20 to 45 minutes – that was the wording, the sense of which was accurately reflected in the redrafting on the 17ᵗʰ September of the dossier. That is the point I am making. They went back to the intelligence, the original intelligence, which contained no caveat of uncertainty. They went back to the way in which it was phrased in the 9ᵗʰ September assessment and they redrafted their main body of the dossier to come into line with that, which it had not been before, including the words "intelligence indicates that".

Q. You say there was no element of uncertainty in this intelligence?

A. Report, yes.

Q. Report. Well, can I just put to you some possible elements of uncertainty which might have influenced the assessors to say "indicates" and not "shows"? Firstly, you did not know what munitions the Iraqi officer was specifically referring to, did you?

A. No, that is right.

Q. You did not know from where or to where the munitions might be moved within 45 minutes?

A. That is right.

Q. Indeed, it was thought at one point that it must mean that these munitions were at forward depots but it was thought that was too uncertain so it was removed?

A. No, that was removed because it was not stated as such in the intelligence report; but that was the assessment at the time of what it did refer to, and indeed remains the assessment of what it did refer to, that these were munitions at forward deployed points.

Q. You see, "forward deployed points" is removed. If they are not at forward deployed points, one asks oneself: where are they?

A. At forward deployed points, that is where we assessed them to be.

Q. Why remove "forward deployed points" in that sense?

A. We were being accurate and precise and not putting into the 9ᵗʰ September assessment wording which was not actually in the assessment. We could have left it in, it was a fine point but it was decided not to put it in, so it was not.

Q. Do you accept that assessors could have regard to the fact, for example, that they did not know from where to where exactly what was covered by this period of 45 minutes? They did not know the specific weapons referred to. It was relayed to them through an intermediary – I appreciate a reliable one, but nonetheless it is a second-hand. All these were matters properly to take into account in deciding whether it indicated or showed a particular state of affairs.

A. You are talking as if the assessors sit there and operate in a vacuum. They do not. They are assessing individual intelligence reports against the background of their knowledge. This was a point of precision which was being given, a timing which was being given for the first time with precision, to an assessment which already existed about the capability of the Iraqi armed forces in this area. That is what assessment is about. There is too much emphasis on sources, single reporting. Assessment is a much more complicated thing than that and it takes many aspects into account, as has been explained many times to this Inquiry.

Q. Mr Scarlett I am entirely with you about that and I readily accept that the assessment staff doing their exercise on 9ᵗʰ September took into account all these matters, but the fact is that their conclusion was "indicates".

A. The sentence in the assessment was referring to the intelligence report as such. It was not looking at it in the wider context. The JIC had instructed the drafters to incorporate and take account and assess recent intelligence which was coming in, the 45 minutes report clearly fell into that category and under that rubric the assessment staff drafted, on 16ᵗʰ September, for the first time, a judgment, drafted a judgment, which was then discussed at the 17ᵗʰ September meeting, which was then circulated to JIC members, was accepted by JIC members, explicitly in the case of DIS and SIS, and therefore had the full authority of a JIC assessment.

Q. But, you see, if the word "indicates" in the 9th September assessment is a mere word of a narrative and not a word of judgment, why, on 17th September, is it agreed that you will have regard to what the assessment said on this subject?

A. We did, and that was what was taken into account in the main body of the text; but what was in the executive – what was in the judgment was a different point. As I have said, the judgment is a judgment taking into account the factors I have already indicated to you. It is not a summary of the main points in the text. The word "indicates" relates to the specific intelligence report. The judgment does not just confine itself to one intelligence report.

Q. Much as I would like to spend the afternoon continuing on this, I think I had better move on.

215. On 19 September the draft of the dossier of that date was circulated to Mr Jonathan Powell, Sir David Manning, Sir David Omand and the members of the JIC by Mr Scarlett asking for any essential further comments from members of the JIC by 3pm. The memorandum from Mr Scarlett was as follows:

IRAQI WMD: PUBLIC PRESENTATION OF INTELLIGENCE MATERIAL

1. I attach the draft dossier on Iraq. It reflects a number of comments from you and others received over the last day or so, and takes account of the most recent intelligence.

2. I should draw your attention to some changes to the Executive Summary, reflecting comments from the Foreign Office; to a simplified account of Saddam's nuclear programme; and to a restructuring of the final section on Saddam's Iraq to bring out human rights issue more clearly. In particular you should note that we have toned down the reference to aluminium tubes in paragraph 22 on page 28, and removed it from the Executive Summary. This reflects some very recent exchanges on intelligence channels. Finally, I have recast the conclusion to remove the chart, which a number of readers considered to lack impact.

3. Copies go to JIC members on a personal basis, reflecting the continuing sensitivity of the document and the imperative need to avoid leaks. If they have any essential further comments on this draft, I will need to receive them by 15:00 today, 19 September.

At 3.45pm Mr Jonathan Powell sent the following e-mail to Mr Campbell and to Mr Scarlett:

Found my copy. I think it is good.

I agree with Alastair you should drop the conclusion.

Alastair – what will be the headline in the Standard on day of publication?

What do we want it to be?

I think the statement on p19 that "Saddam is prepared to use chemical and biological weapons if he believes his regime is under threat" is a bit of a problem. It backs up the Don McIntyre argument that there is no CBW threat and we will only create one if we attack him. I think you should redraft the para. My memory of the intelligence is that he has set up plans to use CBW on western forces and that these weapons are integrated into his military planning.

It needs checking for typos, eg Iraqi in middle of page 27.

The relevant passage in the dossier dated 19 September was as follows:

Saddam's willingness to use chemical and biological weapons: intelligence indicates that Saddam is prepared to use chemical and biological weapons if he believes his regime is under threat. We also know from intelligence that as part of Iraq's military planning, Saddam is willing to use chemical and biological weapons against an internal uprising by the Shia population. Intelligence indicates that the Iraqi military are able to deploy chemical or biological weapons within forty five minutes of an order to do so.

Having considered Mr Powell's e-mail Mr Scarlett changed the passage in the draft dated 20 September to read:

Saddam's willingness to use chemical and biological weapons: intelligence indicates that as part of Iraq's military planning, Saddam is willing to use chemical and biological weapons, including against an internal uprising by the Shia population. Intelligence indicates that the Iraqi military are able to deploy chemical or biological weapons within forty five minutes of an order to do so.

Mr Caldecott suggested to Mr Scarlett in cross-examination that this change was made as a result of intervention by 10 Downing Street, and Mr Scarlett replied that he and his assessment staff were prompted to look again at this passage by Mr Powell's e-mail and the change was made as a result of the exercise of his professional judgment and that of his colleagues in the assessment staff. The relevant passage in the cross-examination is as follows:

[23 September, page 156, line 20]

Q. I want to ask you about a change we have not yet looked at in evidence. Could we, please, look at CAB/11/103? This is a suggestion that comes in from Downing Street –

A. Yes.

Q. – after your deadline of 3 o'clock. It is timed at 3.45 from Mr Powell, the Downing Street Chief of Staff.

A. Yes.

Q. Sent only to you and Mr Campbell and copied to Sir David Manning.

A. Yes.

Q. "Found my copy. I think it is good. "I agree with Alastair you should drop the conclusion." That we know is done.

A. Yes.

Q. "Alastair – what will be the headline in the Standard on day of publication? "What do we want it to be?" I will not ask you about that.

A. No.

Q. "I think the statement on page 19 that 'Saddam is prepared to use chemical and biological weapons if he believes his regime is under threat' is a bit of a problem. It backs up the Don McIntyre argument that there is no CBW threat and we will only create one if we attack him." Now, Don McIntyre is a chief political columnist at the Independent.

A. Yes.

Q. "I think you should redraft the para. My memory of the intelligence is that he has set up plans to use CBW on Western forces and that these weapons are integrated into his military planning." Right?

A. Yes.

Q. The suggestion there, is it not, is that the dossier should be redrafted to remove an express suggestion that Saddam Hussein is a defensive threat?

A. Hmm.

Q. And leave an implication that, in fact, he is an offensive threat; is that right?

A. No. It is not right. It is not to leave the implication that he is an offensive threat, it is to take away the explicit, as it were, limitation that it is a defensive – not a defensive threat, but it is a defensive sort of point.

139

Q. Do you accept you can transform a dossier by omission, Mr Scarlett?

A. Well, omission is –

Q. Taking out what was in it before?

A. Of course, that is – it is important what you take out as well as what you put in.

Q. You see, such a change would make a great effect, would it not, on the threat in fact presented by Saddam Hussein in the eyes of the public?

A. Shall I say what I did about this?

Q. Yes, please do.

A. Yes. This e-mail did prompt me and the assessment staff to look again at that particular passage. Now, we were acting under the instructions from the JIC to keep what we were writing in line with standing JIC assessments and also with recent intelligence. As I recall this particular paragraph – obviously this particular paragraph was under the heading of what recent intelligence was showing. Now, there had been an intelligence report which made that point, I mean a recent intelligence report which is why it was phrased like this.

When we looked at it again, we also realised two things: first of all, that there was no standing JIC assessment which made it clear whether we were defining Saddam's threat, if you like, as defensive or CW posture as defensive or offensive. More to the point, there was recent reporting, in addition, which was not reflected here, but which was quite clear reporting, which placed his attachment to CBW and the importance that he placed on it very much in the context of his perception of his regional position, his plans to acquire and maintain regional influence and, as one report, and maybe more, put it: dominate his neighbours. In other words, the recent intelligence was more complex than that phrase implied. Bearing those points in mind, we concluded that this was not right, the way this was phrased; and therefore we took that out. That is what I did.

Q. This formula had appeared in the draft of the 11th September, circulated to JIC members and approved. It had appeared in the draft of the 16th September, circulated to JIC members and approved. It appeared in the draft of the 19th September, circulated to JIC members and approved. Why the change? Only the reason you have given.

A. Well that is an important reason and I was acting under JIC instructions, and within our authority and delegated authority, as I have explained, in basing what we did on the recent intelligence.

Q. Can we, please, look at BBC/30/8 as to what the intelligence did say on this subject, so far as we can work it out? This is an extract, again, of the ISC report.

A. Hmm.

Q. BBC/30/8, please. Scroll down a little bit, please, to 119. "The assessments staff produced an intelligence update on 27 November 2002."

Q… That is obviously after publication.

A. Yes.

Q. "It reiterated an earlier JIC assessment that if Saddam were to be faced with the likelihood of military defeat and removal from power, he would be unlikely to be deterred from using chemical and biological weapons by any diplomatic or military means."

A. Yes.

Q. Now that is consistent, is it not, with the original wording?

A. What that says – it says what he would do if he was – and he would use these weapons if he were faced with these circumstances. It does not say, at all, that those are the only circumstances in which he would use those weapons and the reporting definitely did not say that.

Q. Can we look at what I assume is, in fact, the later intelligence update on 27th November at paragraph 120? I accept this is post publication.

A. Hmm.

Q. "It was assessed that Saddam was prepared to order missile strikes against Israel, with chemical or biological warheads, in order to widen the war should hostilities begin. Saddam had also identified [other countries] as targets. The update also contained recent intelligence that Saddam would use chemical or biological weapons if allied forces approached Baghdad, if Basra, Kirkuk and Mosul fell to allied control, or if Iraqi military units rebelled." All of those states of affairs are triggered by a defensive position of extreme danger for Saddam Hussain, are they not?

A. Yes, because that assessment in that update is relating to that specific set of circumstances, the likelihood of an invasion of Iraq. It is the same point as I have just made.

Q. Can we just finish this by looking at the changes that were made in the dossier as a result of this intervention from Downing Street at BBC/29/19?

A. Sorry, can I just interrupt to say, before I forget, that it was not as a result of the interventions from Downing Street, it was as a result of the exercise of my professional judgment and that of my colleagues in assessment staff for the reasons I have just given.

Q. It would not have occurred without Mr Powell's memorandum, would it?

A. I said we were prompted to look again at this by the memorandum. I was exercising my judgment as I was authorised to do entirely in line with the existing intelligence – the recent intelligence which indeed had come in and which was not taken into account properly by that phrase.

Q. I think it is right we should look at the change to complete this. Bottom of BBC/29/19.

A. Yes.

Q. The strike through is what was deleted and the underling what was put in. We see the most important words deleted are "if he believes his regime is under threat". Again one sees "including against his own people" replaces the fact that it would only happen if there was an internal uprising by the Shia population.

A. It does not say it would only happen, it says against an internal uprising. Again the same point, there was intelligence which said that, but there was also intelligence which said that he was prepared to use CBW against the Shia in circumstances other than the internal uprising, which was why that change was made. It is the same point.

216. However, although it is clear that 10 Downing Street took a close interest in the drafting of the dossier and made a number of suggestions on the drafting which Mr Scarlett accepted, I am also satisfied that 10 Downing Street recognised that the wording of the dossier had to conform with the intelligence as assessed by the JIC and that the wording had to be approved by the JIC. In his minute to Mr Scarlett dated 9 September 2002 which has been set out at greater length in paragraph 173 Mr Campbell stated:

the media/political judgment will inevitably focus on

"what's new?" and I was pleased to hear from you and your SIS colleagues that, contrary to media reports today, the intelligence community are taking such a helpful approach to this in going through all the material they have. It goes without saying that there should be nothing published that you and they are not 100% happy with.

217. I am further satisfied that Mr Scarlett did not accept drafting suggestions emanating from 10 Downing Street unless they were in keeping with the intelligence available to the JIC and he rejected any suggestions which he considered were not supported by such intelligence. This is demonstrated by his minute to Mr Campbell dated 18 September 2002 in reply to Mr Campbell's minute of 17 September. It is clear

from Mr Scarlett's minute that whilst he accepted some of Mr Campbell's suggestions he rejected others where the intelligence did not support a strengthening of the language: see paragraph 6 subparagraphs 2, 8 and 9 (set out in paragraph 213 of this report). I am also satisfied that the dossier was published with the full approval of the JIC as was stated in evidence by Mr Scarlett, Sir Richard Dearlove (the Chief of SIS), Sir David Omand, Air Marshall Sir Joseph French (the Chief of Defence Intelligence) and Mr Anthony Cragg (the Deputy Chief of Defence Intelligence).

218. The e-mail from a member of the assessment staff to the Intelligence Agencies dated 11 September 2002 stating that "No. 10 through the Chairman want the document to be as strong as possible within the bounds of available intelligence" was put to the Prime Minister. He stated in evidence to the Inquiry:

[28 August, page 5, line 22]

Q. Were you aware that this process was going on?

A. Yes, of course, and it was important that it made the best case that we could make subject, obviously, to it being owned by the Joint Intelligence Committee and that the items of intelligence should be those that the agencies thought could and should be included. So if you like it was a process in which they were in charge of this, correctly, because it was so important to make sure that no-one could question the intelligence that was in it as coming from the genuine intelligence agencies, but obviously I mean I had to present this to Parliament. I was going to make a statement. Parliament was going to be recalled. We were concerned to make sure that we could produce, within the bounds of what was right and proper, the best case.

LORD HUTTON: So you would agree, Prime Minister, that the wording that "No.10 through the Chairman want the document to be as strong as possible within the bounds of available intelligence" is a fair way of putting your view and the view of your staff in No.10?

A. Provided that is clearly understood as meaning that it is only if the intelligence agencies thought both that the actual intelligence should be included and that there was not improper weight being given to any aspect of that intelligence. In other words, given that the process was that they had to decide what it was we could properly say, then obviously we wanted to – we had to make this case because this was the case that we believed in and this was the evidence that we had, because all of this stuff was obviously stuff that had come across my desk.

219. The minute to Mr Campbell from Mr Scarlett dated 18 September was put to the Prime Minister. He stated:

[28 August, page 12, line 5]

Q. Were you aware of these type of responses from Mr Scarlett?

A. No, I was not aware of the absolute detail of it; but on the other hand, I mean, having read it, it seems to me a perfectly right way of proceeding. In other words, there are certain things that we are asking if they can improve on this or improve on that and they say: well, we can or we cannot. I think the important thing I would say is that once the decision had been taken that, as it were, John Scarlett and the JIC should actually own this document, it should be their document, then I think everything that was done was subject to that. Obviously it was vitally important when we got to Parliament and produced this document that I was able to stand up absolutely clearly and say: look, this is the work of the joint intelligence agencies, they stand behind the intelligence that is here.

The minute which Mr Campbell sent to Mr Scarlett on 17 September 2002 was put to Mr Campbell in cross-examination by Mr Caldecott QC for the BBC:

[22 September, page 166, line 17]

Q. What you were concerned to do was to strengthen the language of the dossier, were you not, through these suggestions or at least most of them?

A. I was keen, and this is the job the Prime Minister asked me to do, to make sure that the dossier as presented to Parliament was a strong, clear, consistent document that allowed him effectively to explain to the British public the reality of the threat posed by Saddam Hussein's WMD. That is my job in these circumstances; and I think if you are saying "strong" equals "sexed-up", I do not accept that at all. If you are saying "strong" equals a good, solid piece of work that does the job that the Prime Minister wants it to do, then I agree with that.

Q. Would it be sexing up – sorry.

LORD HUTTON: Carry on, Mr Caldecott.

MR CALDECOTT: Would it be sexing up the dossier to change the text, to strengthen the text to match the summary rather than to lower the summary to match the text, Mr Campbell?

A. It would depend on the circumstances that you were putting. None of it would be sexing up unless you were doing something improper in relation to the intelligence judgments. This dossier could only be as strong as a public document as the underlying intelligence assessments allowed it to be.

Q. Why were you commenting on the intelligence judgments at all?

A. I was not. I was commenting upon a draft of a document that the Prime Minister was expected to present to Parliament and the public. And I was doing so in my capacity as the Prime Minister's adviser, and in this instance John Scarlett's adviser because that is what he had asked me to do, on presentational issues.

Q. The response you got from Mr Scarlett on the 45 minutes point is at CAB/11/71; and obviously I accept that this is mainly a point for him, but all he says is: "The language you queried on the old page 17 has been tightened".

A. Hmm, hmm.

Q. Do you see that?

A. I do. I am aware of that.

Q. He had adopted a change which you had initiated, had he not?

A. No. May I say, I do not think there would have been anything improper had he done so because I had pointed out an inconsistency and it was for John Scarlett to resolve that in whatever way he and Julian Miller and Julian Miller's team wanted. But, as I understand it from Mr Scarlett, that is a point Mr Miller had already spotted. I do not accept that in me saying on page 17, two lines from the bottom, "may" is weaker than in the summary" I am doing anything more than pointing out what is an inconsistency, which is one of the points the Prime Minister had asked me to undertake.

Q. I do not understand what it was that Mr Miller had spotted.

A. The inconsistency.

Q. Okay, he spotted an inconsistency between the main text and the summary of the main text?

A. Correct.

Q. The answer is perfectly obvious, you have to downplay the summary so it matches the text, it is very simple, is it not?

A. No, the answer depends –

Q. The summary is too strong.

Q. The answer depends upon the underlying intelligence assessments which Mr Scarlett and Mr Miller have. They are not a matter for me.

Q. But you knew it had been round to JIC members, it had been round the agencies, and we have a draft on 16th September which talks about "may". What business was it of yours to suggest that "may" might be strengthened?

A. I am not suggesting "may" might be strengthened. I am pointing out that in one place it is more definitive than in another. That is an inconsistency. And this is a document which – I mean the JIC, their job, most of the time, is obviously to prepare assessments to be read by small numbers of other experts. This was a document to be read by the public. And that – it was being presented by the Prime Minister. It was going to attract massive attention around the world. I was doing the job on this the Prime Minister asked me to do. And this was a very, very, very small part of it. This was not an important part of those discussions.

Q. You were writing a foreword at this time, were you not, for the –

LORD HUTTON: Mr Caldecott, before we proceed, could we just try to see where we are on this point because I think it is of some importance. As I understand it, you are suggesting to Mr Campbell that if he strengthens the document from the point of view of presentation that is, to use the term that was used in Mr Gilligan's report, "sexing-up" the dossier. Mr Campbell, as I understand his evidence, is saying that if he makes presentational points which, I think he accepts, may strengthen the document, that is permissible provided it does not alter the intelligence. Mr Campbell, I think, is suggesting that on his understanding that is not sexing up the document. First of all, is that the way in which you are putting the point to Mr Campbell?

MR CALDECOTT: My Lord, I fully accept that to a substantial degree this must be a point for Mr Scarlett because after all he is responsible for the ultimate draft.

LORD HUTTON: Yes.

MR CALDECOTT: However, there is a point which I have yet to come to, which is why I will be –

LORD HUTTON: I do not want to anticipate, but I think it is an important point and I want just to be clear what the difference between you and Mr Campbell so far is. Mr Campbell, have I correctly summarised the point that you have been making in the point I put to Mr Caldecott?

A. You have.

LORD HUTTON: Yes.

MR CALDECOTT: the point I want to develop with you – actually, if the stenographers want a break now, it would be convenient, if they want one.

LORD HUTTON: Yes. I will rise.

220. The term "sexed-up" is a slang expression, the meaning of which lacks clarity in the context of a discussion of the dossier. It is capable of two different meanings. It could mean that the dossier was embellished with items of intelligence known or believed to be false or unreliable to make the case against Saddam Hussein stronger, or it could mean that whilst the intelligence contained in the dossier was believed to be reliable, the dossier was drafted in such a way as to make the case against Saddam Hussein as strong as the intelligence contained in it permitted. If the term is used in this latter sense then, because of the drafting suggestions made by 10 Downing Street for the purpose of making a strong case against Saddam Hussein, it could be said that the Government "sexed-up" the dossier. However, having regard to the other allegations contained in Mr Gilligan's broadcasts of 29 May I consider that those who heard the broadcasts would have understood the allegation of "sexing-up" to be used in the first sense which I have described, namely that the Government ordered that the dossier be embellished with false or unreliable items of intelligence. Thus Mr Gilligan reported that the source said that:

… the government probably erm, knew that the forty-five minute figure was wrong, even before it decided to put it in,

that

… the dossier, as it was finally published, made the Intelligence Services unhappy, erm, because, to quote erm the source he said, there was basically, that there was, there was, there was unhappiness because it didn't reflect the considered view they were putting forward, that's a quote from our source and essentially, erm, the forty-five minute point er, was, was probably the most important thing that was added,

that

... the intelligence agencies say they don't really believe it was necessarily true because they thought the person making the claim had actually made a mistake, it got, had got mixed up,

and that

... the information which I am told was dubious did come from the agencies, but they were unhappy about it, because they didn't ... think it should have been in there. They thought it was, it was not corroborated sufficiently, and they actually thought it was wrong, they thought the informant concerned erm, had got it wrong, they thought he had misunderstood what was happening.

Therefore, in the context of Mr Gilligan's broadcasts, I consider that the allegation that the Government ordered the dossier to be "sexed-up" was unfounded.

The meaning of the term "Weapons of Mass Destruction"

221. Mr Gilligan's broadcasts on 29 May related to the claim in the dossier that chemical and biological weapons were deployable within 45 minutes and did not refer to the distinction between battlefield weapons, such as artillery and rockets, and strategic weapons, such as long range missiles. A consideration of this distinction does not fall within my terms of reference, but the distinction was noted and commented on by the ISC in paragraphs 111 and 112 of its report presented to Parliament by the Prime Minister in September 2003:

111. Saddam was not considered a current or imminent threat to mainland UK, nor did the dossier say so. As we said in our analysis of the JIC Assessments, the most likely chemical and biological munitions to be used against Western forces were battlefield weapons (artillery and rockets), rather than strategic weapons. This should have been highlighted in the dossier.

112. The dossier was for public consumption and not for experienced readers of intelligence material. The 45 minutes claim, included four times, was always likely to attract attention because it was arresting detail that the public had not seen before. As the 45 minutes claim was new to its readers, the context of the intelligence and any assessment needed to be explained. The fact that it was assessed to refer to battlefield chemical and biological munitions and their movement on the battlefield, not to any other form of chemical or biological attack, should have been highlighted in the dossier. The omission of the context and assessment allowed speculation as to its exact meaning. This was unhelpful to an understanding of this issue.

In the course of the Inquiry some evidence was given in relation to the distinction between battlefield weapons and strategic weapons and I set this evidence out.

222. In his evidence on 26 August Mr Scarlett said:

[26 August, page 144, line 16]

A.... Andrew Gilligan, when quoting his source, said that the source believed that the report was relating to warheads for missiles.

LORD HUTTON: Yes.

A. Which, in fact, it was not; it related to munitions, which we had interpreted to mean battlefield mortar shells or small calibre weaponry, quite different from missiles.

LORD HUTTON: Yes.

A. So it is possible that Dr Kelly, who, as I still understand it, never did see or probably did not see the original report, was in a state of genuine confusion about what the report actually said.

223. In his evidence on 3 September Dr Jones said:

[3 September, page 63, line 10]

Q. Were there any reorganisations, at any time, in your role?

A. Yes, there were. In about 1996 there was a fairly major reorganisation; and that involved drawing together the analysis, activities on chemical warfare, on biological warfare and on nuclear aspects into one branch.

Q. Who was heading that branch?

A. I took charge of that branch when it was formed.

Q. If you have chemical, biological and nuclear, are those the weapons of mass destruction?

A. That is a term that is often applied to them, yes. I have some problems with the term myself.

Q. I am sorry, I was going to ask you what the term actually meant, what you understood the term meant.

A. "Weapons of mass destruction"?

Q. Yes.

A. Well, it is used to – if it is used too loosely it is used to represent all nuclear, chemical and biological weapons.

Q. You say "used too loosely", which rather suggests you think it ought to be used in a more restrictive way?

A. That is a personal opinion, yes.

Q. What is your personal opinion about weapons of mass destruction?

A. My personal opinion is that almost all – almost all – nuclear weapons truly fit this concept of being a weapon of mass destruction, that some biological weapons are perhaps reasonably described in that way because they could be used to produce very large numbers of casualties on the same sort of scale perhaps even as nuclear weapons, but there are many biological weapons that struggle to fit into that. Some are incapacitants for example rather than lethal.

Q. What is an incapacitant?

A. An incapacitant is something in a weapon sense designed to make someone unable to conduct their duties rather than to actually kill them.

Q. Making them sick or giving them diarrhoea et cetera?

A. Exactly so.

Q. Those are biological weapons you think do not fit into that character. What about the chemical weapons?

A. I think chemical weapons almost struggle to fit into that category. There are certain agents and certain scenarios where I would think that chemical weapons truly are describable as weapons of mass destruction. Sorry, could I take a sip of water?

Q. Yes of course.

A. We are getting into considerable detail here. I think the sort of scenarios where I think that chemical weapons might be described as a weapon of mass destruction are where they might be used in enclosed spaces. An example might be the somewhat unsuccessful attempt to use them in that way by Aum Shinri-kyo on the Tokyo underground in the mid 1990s, where if large amounts of the nerve agent they tried to use had entered the atmosphere then many more people would have died. But it is rather more difficult to think of them in those terms really on the battlefield perhaps where to produce large numbers of casualties you need very large amounts of material.

Q. Obviously if you are an infantry solider in the front line and subject to a nerve agent artillery attack you have to put on your gas mask, if you get it on in time. Is that sort of artillery shell delivery of chemical weapons something you would term a weapon of mass destruction?

A. No, I think personally I would struggle to make that particular scenario really fit into an equivalence of them facing a nuclear blast.

LORD HUTTON: Do I gather, Dr Jones, that there is perhaps some debate in intelligence circles then about the precise meaning of "weapons of mass destruction"? You are expressing your own view. Do I take it that there are others that might take a different view?

A. There may be. I mean, I think "weapons of mass destruction" has become a convenient catch-all which, in my opinion, can at times confuse discussion of the subject.

LORD HUTTON: Yes, I see. Thank you, yes.

MR DINGEMANS: You say there may be. Are you aware of anyone who does have a different view?

A. That is difficult. I do not think I was ever in a situation where it was discussed in quite those terms. I think it was quite a frequent comment from myself and my staff about particular issues, that it is perhaps not right to use that general term to describe something that is more specific.

Q. Mr Scarlett, I think, told us that Dr Kelly may have been confused about the difference between missile delivery of chemical weapons and artillery delivery. Do you think there is a difference between the two, in terms of weapons of mass destruction?

A. Yes. I think I would struggle to describe either as a true weapon of mass destruction.

224. In his evidence on 15 September Sir Richard Dearlove said:

[15 September, page 100, line 17]

Q. Can I ask you about some criticisms that have been made of the 45 minutes source and take you to FAC/3/28? This is paragraph 69 of a report from the Foreign Affairs Committee.

A. Hmm.

Q. And at the bottom of the page, paragraph 69, they say this, having reported what the Foreign Secretary says: "This answer begs the question why the 45 minutes claim was highlighted by the Prime Minister when he presented the dossier to the House, and why it was given such prominence in the dossier itself, being mentioned no fewer than four times, including in the Prime Minister's foreword and in the executive summary? We have not seen a satisfactory answer to that question. We have been told that the entire document, including the executive summary, was prepared by the Chairman of the JIC, except for the foreword, which he approved. We note with disappointment that we were unable to find out why Mr Scarlett chose to give the 45 minutes claim such prominence, as we have been prevented from questioning him." Did you consider that the 45 minutes – and they say "claim" – was given undue prominence?

A. Well, I think given the misinterpretation that was placed on the 45 minutes intelligence, with the benefit of hindsight you can say that is a valid criticism. But I am confident that the intelligence was accurate and that the use made of it was entirely consistent with the original report.

LORD HUTTON: Would you just elaborate what you mean by the misinterpretation placed on the 45 minutes claim, Sir Richard?

A. (Pause). Well, I think the original report referred to chemical and biological munitions and that was taken to refer to battlefield weapons. I think what subsequently happened in the reporting was that it was taken that the 45 minutes applied, let us say, to weapons of a longer range, let us say just battlefield material.

MR DINGEMANS: Can I ask you to comment on paragraphs 108 to 112 of the Intelligence and Security Committee report. We do not have that yet scanned in. I think you have a copy of the conclusions from 108 to 112; is that right?

A. Yes, I have.

Q. At 108 it is made clear that there were a wide range of departments and agencies commenting on the draft and they say that the dossier was not sexed up by Alastair Campbell or anyone else. At 109 it is said that Alastair Campbell did not chair meetings on intelligence matters. At 110 it is said that the use of the phrase "continued to produce chemical and biological weapons" could give the impression that Saddam was actively producing both chemical and biological weapons and makes comments about the JIC knowledge there. At 111 it deals with the question of whether or not Saddam Hussein was considered a current or imminent threat.

With that introduction can I turn to 112 which says: "The dossier was for public consumption and not for experienced readers of intelligence material. The 45 minutes claim, included four times, was always likely to attract attention because it was arresting detail that the public had not seen before." It then goes on to say that it was unhelpful to an understanding of the issue. Do you agree with that comment?

A. Well, not entirely. But I think I would repeat what I said in answer to the last question. Given the misinterpretation of the original piece of intelligence, particularly as it was not qualified in terms of its relationship to battlefield munitions, this now looks a valid criticism; but I think the intelligence was accurate and that it was put to legitimate use in the drafting process.

Q. Can I take you back to the document I think you have at about page 3 of the bundle you have, which is CAB/17/3, extracts from the JIC assessment relating to 45 minutes; then just read to you the extract from the foreword to the dossier. Although I do not ask for this to be called up, it is at DOS/1/59 at the top. It says this: "And the document [i.e. the dossier] discloses that his military planning allows for some of the WMD to be ready within 45 minutes of an order to use them." Do you consider that to have been a fair reflection of the JIC assessments of 5th and 9th September?

A. Yes, I think it is.

Q. And in what way would you reconcile the two statements?

A. (Pause). Can you repeat that question?

Q. Certainly. I am sorry you have not got it in front of you. "And the document [the dossier] discloses that his military planning allows for some of the WMD to be ready within 45 minutes of an order to use them."

A. I do not quite see what you are driving at in asking me this question, but in fact I think one has to see this piece of intelligence against the background of Iraqi armed forces having in the past used chemical munitions, and this, in that context, not being a surprising piece of intelligence.

225. In his evidence on 22 September when cross-examined by Mr Caldecott, Mr Hoon said:

[22 September, page 80, line 16]

Q. Did you know that the 45 minute claim in the dossier was taken from a JIC assessment which does not in fact identify any particular weapon?

A. Well, I recall at the time having some discussion in the Ministry of Defence about the kinds of weapons that could be deployable within 45 minutes; and I think the assumption was made that they would be, for example, chemical shells, which were clearly capable of being deployed, as I think Mr Scarlett has indicated to the Inquiry, in a time even less than 45 minutes; I think he suggested 20 minutes.

Q. So you knew, did you, that the munitions referred to were only battlefield munitions?

A. I was certainly aware that that was one suggestion, yes.

Q. Was there any other suggestion that they were not battlefield munitions but strategic munitions?

A. I recall asking what kind of weapons would be deployable within 45 minutes; and the answer is the answer that I have just given to you.

Q. Which was shells, battlefield mortars, tactical weapons of that kind?

A. Yes.

Q. Would your Department be responsible for correcting any false impression given by the press on an issue of this importance?

A. I think on an issue of this importance it would not simply have been the Ministry of Defence that was solely responsible. There would have been an effort across Government.

Q. Are you aware that on 25th September a number of newspapers had banner headlines suggesting that this related to strategic missiles or bombs?

A. I can recall, yes.

Q. Why was no corrective statement issued for the benefit of the public in relation to those media reports?

A. I do not know.

Q. It must have been considered by someone, must it not?

A. I have spent many years trying to persuade newspapers and journalists to correct their stories. I have to say it is an extraordinarily time consuming and generally frustrating process.

Q. I am sorry, are you saying that the press would not report a corrective statement that the dossier was meant to refer, in this context, to battlefield munitions and not to strategic weapons?

A. What I am suggesting is that I was not aware of whether any consideration was given to such a correction. All that I do know from my experience is that, generally speaking, newspapers are resistant to corrections. That judgment may have been made by others as well.

Q. But, Mr Hoon, you must have been horrified that the dossier had been misrepresented in this way; it was a complete distortion of what it actually was intended to convey, was it not?

A. Well, I was not horrified. I recognised that journalists occasionally write things that are more dramatic than the material upon which it is based.

Q. Can we forget journalists for the moment and concentrate on the members of the public who are reading it? Will they not be entitled to be given the true picture of the intelligence, not a vastly inflated one?

A. I think that is a question you would have to put to the journalists and the editors responsible.

Q. But you had the means to correct it, not them. They could not correct it until they were told, could they?

A. Well, as I say, my experience of trying to persuade newspapers to correct false impressions is one that is not full of success.

Q. Do you accept that on this topic at least you had an absolute duty to try to correct it?

A. No, I do not.

Q. Do you accept that you had any duty to correct it?

A. Well, I apologise for repeating the same answer, but you are putting the question in another way. I have tried on many, many occasions to persuade journalists and newspapers to correct stories. They do not like to do so.

Q. Can I suggest to you a reason why this was not done? It would have been politically highly embarrassing because it would have revealed the dossier as published was at least highly capable of being misleading.

A. Well, I do not accept that.

Q. So your suggestion is that this was a disgraceful exaggeration by the press of what was clear in the dossier as a reference to battlefield munitions?

A. I am certainly suggesting that it was an exaggeration, but it is not unusual for newspapers to exaggerate.

Q. Can you tell me, if you happen to have it to hand, where in the dossier it is made clear that the CBW weapons which were the subject of the 45 minute claim were only battlefield munitions?

A. Well, I do not have it to hand; and I do not know whether it was made clear.

226. In his evidence on 23 September when examined by counsel for the Government Mr Scarlett said:

[23 September, page 111, line 1]

Q. Dr Jones gave evidence also about another matter, namely the definition of weapons of mass destruction, the definition of weapons of mass destruction.

A. Yes.

Q. And, in particular, he gave evidence about whether they included battlefield munitions. Is there an accepted definition of weapons of mass destruction?

A. Well, the best I can do here is to quote the most recent statement made on behalf of the British Government on this issue which was by the Foreign Office Minister Mr O'Brien in answer to a Parliamentary Question on 28th January this year, in which he said there is no universally accepted definition of the phrase "weapons of mass destruction" but it is generally held to refer to nuclear, chemical and biological weapons.

Q. Does that include battlefield munitions or not?

A. Yes, it does.

227. When cross-examined by Mr Caldecott, Mr Scarlett said:

[23 September, page 136, line 24]

Q. I just want to deal with one very short point. I think it was your own conclusion, I do not know whether it is reflected in the full JIC paper, which I have not seen, that the 9th September 45 minute claim related to battlefield munitions?

A. It did, yes.

Q. I think we can see how you might well have reached that conclusion if we look at BBC/30/ 3, very quickly. This is an extract from the Intelligence and Security Committee Report.

A. Hmm.

Q. It deals with delivery systems.

A. Yes.

Q. The potential systems are set out in 46.

Q. Yes.

Q. A number of serious doubts about almost all of them, except for artillery shells and so on, are expressed in 47. Then in 48. "The JIC assessed that the Iraqis might use chemical and biological weapons against neighbouring states or concentrations of Western forces. We were told that the weapons systems most likely to be used to deliver chemical and biological munitions against Western forces were artillery and rockets."

A. Yes.

Q. "These are battlefield weapons, which can be used tactically to great effect, but they are not strategic weapons." Firstly, was that made clear to the Prime Minister?

A. There was no discussion with the Prime Minister that I can recall about the 45 minutes point in connection with battlefield or strategic systems. Indeed I do not remember a discussion with the Prime Minister about the 45 minutes point at all.

150

Q. Who, apart from the internal assessment staff, was this message conveyed to?

A. Sorry, what message?

Q. Only battlefield munitions, not strategic weapons.

A. You say "only battlefield munitions". Do you know what a battlefield munition, a battlefield weapon, might actually involve? I can tell you the assessment from the DIS of what the most likely delivery system for chemical and biological, particularly chemical weapons, would be, and this was based on the experience of the Iran/Iraq War. Multiple rocket launchers, in particular the BM21 with a range of 20-kilometres or artillery up to the 155 millimetre artillery, which would have a range of 40 kilometres. In the Iran/Iraq War 20,000 Iranians were killed or wounded through the use of chemical weapons, so the difference between strategic and tactical in those contexts is quite difficult to draw, particularly as Iran's use of chemical weapons in the Iran/Iraq War had a strategic effect of halting a major Iranian advance. I just thought I would say that.

Q. Mr Scarlett, I totally take the point but you are well aware, are you not, of the distinction between range and casualty?

A. Yes.

Q. Yes. Strategic weapons have a far longer range, they could reach British bases in Cyprus, for example, which is what the newspaper said on 25th September.

A. A small number of newspapers said it on 25th September and not thereafter.

Q. A small number of newspapers with a readership of millions.

A. On the 25th September there were a small number of headlines about that; and afterwards virtually no reference to it.

Q. Were you concerned that that should be corrected, Mr Scarlett?

A. No, I was not and I will tell you why not. First of all, as regards my own assessment staff, we were ready to field enquiries from the press offices of No. 10, the MoD, the FCO with anything relating to issues of this kind. We received no enquiries whatsoever about the 45 minute point. The second point was I was of course following the press coverage of the dossier and I was interested to note that immediately after the headline flurry on various points on the 24th and 25th September the press coverage fell quickly into assessing the dossier as a sober and cautious document that most explicitly did not make a case for war, if anything it made a case for the return of the inspectors and it focused in particular, quite rightly in my view, on the importance of what the dossier had to say about the nuclear issue. I was content with the way that coverage came out; and that is – that was my attitude over many months indeed.

Q. Do I understand you to say that you do not correct it because no questions had been asked about it?

A. No, you may understand it but that would be wrong, but I have explained that the reason why that was not an issue in my mind was because of the very sober and sensible way in which media coverage of the dossier fell into place immediately after the 25th September.

Q. Well, what about the 25th September itself? This is the day it is announced in the House of Commons by the Prime Minister, and certainly a number of newspapers, with mass readerships throughout the country, have misunderstood it. Why was it not put right and why were you not concerned to put it right?

A. Because it was a fleeting moment and then the underlying assessment by the media of the dossier was as I have just described, and beyond that, of course, it is not my immediate responsibility to correct headlines and if I did that, I certainly would not have time to do my job.

151

Summary of conclusions on the issues relating to the preparation of the dossier of 24 September 2002

228. The conclusions which I have come to on these issues are the following:

(1) The dossier was prepared and drafted by a small team of the assessment staff of the JIC. Mr Scarlett, the Chairman of the JIC, had the overall responsibility for the drafting of the dossier. The dossier, which included the 45 minutes claim, was issued by the Government on 24 September 2002 with the full approval of the JIC.

(2) The 45 minutes claim was based on a report which was received by the SIS from a source which that Service regarded as reliable. Therefore, whether or not at some time in the future the report on which the 45 minutes claim was based is shown to be unreliable, the allegation reported by Mr Gilligan on 29 May 2003 that the Government probably knew that the 45 minutes claim was wrong before the Government decided to put it in the dossier was an allegation which was unfounded.

(3) The allegation was also unfounded that the reason why the 45 minutes claim was not in the original draft of the dossier was because it only came from one source and the intelligence agencies did not really believe it was necessarily true. The reason why the 45 minutes claim did not appear in draft assessments or draft dossiers until 5 September 2002 was because the intelligence report on which it was based was not received by the SIS until 29 August 2002 and the JIC assessment staff did not have time to insert it in a draft until the draft of the assessment of 5 September 2002.

(4) The true position in relation to the attitude of "the Intelligence Services" to the 45 minutes claim being inserted in the dossier was that the concerns expressed by Dr Jones were considered by higher echelons in the Intelligence Services and were not acted upon, and the JIC, the most senior body in the Intelligence Services charged with the assessment of intelligence, approved the wording in the dossier. Moreover, the nuclear, chemical and biological weapons section of the Defence Intelligence Staff, headed by Dr Brian Jones, did not argue that the intelligence relating to the 45 minutes claim should not have been included in the dossier but they did suggest that the wording in which the claim was stated in the dossier was too strong and that instead of the dossier stating "we judge" that "Iraq has:- military plans for the use of chemical and biological weapons, including against its own Shia population. Some of these weapons are deployable within 45 minutes of an order to use them", the wording should state "intelligence suggests".

(5) Mr Campbell made it clear to Mr Scarlett on behalf of the Prime Minister that 10 Downing Street wanted the dossier to be worded to make as strong a case as possible in relation to the threat posed by Saddam Hussein's WMD, and 10 Downing Street made written suggestions to Mr Scarlett as to changes in the wording of the draft dossier which would strengthen it. But Mr Campbell recognised, and told Mr Scarlett that 10 Downing Street recognised, that nothing should be stated in the dossier with which the intelligence community were not entirely happy.

(6) Mr Scarlett accepted some of the drafting suggestions made to him by 10 Downing Street but he only accepted those suggestions which were consistent with the intelligence known to the JIC and he rejected those suggestions which were not consistent with such intelligence and the dossier issued by the Government was approved by the JIC.

(7) As the dossier was one to be presented to, and read by, Parliament and the public, and was not an intelligence assessment to be considered only by the Government, I

do not consider that it was improper for Mr Scarlett and the JIC to take into account suggestions as to drafting made by 10 Downing Street and to adopt those suggestions if they were consistent with the intelligence available to the JIC. However I consider that the possibility cannot be completely ruled out that the desire of the Prime Minister to have a dossier which, whilst consistent with the available intelligence, was as strong as possible in relation to the threat posed by Saddam Hussein's WMD, may have subconsciously influenced Mr Scarlett and the other members of the JIC to make the wording of the dossier somewhat stronger than it would have been if it had been contained in a normal JIC assessment. Although this possibility cannot be completely ruled out, I am satisfied that Mr Scarlett, the other members of the JIC, and the members of the assessment staff engaged in the drafting of the dossier were concerned to ensure that the contents of the dossier were consistent with the intelligence available to the JIC.

(8) The term "sexed-up" is a slang expression, the meaning of which lacks clarity in the context of the discussion of the dossier. It is capable of two different meanings. It could mean that the dossier was embellished with items of intelligence known or believed to be false or unreliable to make the case against Saddam Hussein stronger, or it could mean that whilst the intelligence contained in the dossier was believed to be reliable, the dossier was drafted in such a way as to make the case against Saddam Hussein as strong as the intelligence contained in it permitted. If the term is used in this latter sense, then because of the drafting suggestions made by 10 Downing Street for the purpose of making a strong case against Saddam Hussein, it could be said that the Government "sexed-up" the dossier. However in the context of the broadcasts in which the "sexing-up" allegation was reported and having regard to the other allegations reported in those broadcasts I consider that the allegation was unfounded as it would have been understood by those who heard the broadcasts to mean that the dossier had been embellished with intelligence known or believed to be false or unreliable, which was not the case.

CHAPTER 7

Issues relating to Dr Kelly's meeting with Mr Gilligan in the Charing Cross Hotel on 22 May 2003

229. These issues are the following:

(a) What did Dr Kelly say to Mr Gilligan in the course of the meeting?

(b) At the time of his meeting with Mr Gilligan and discussing the dossier with him was Dr Kelly having a meeting which was unauthorised and in breach of the Civil Service rules of procedure which applied to him?

(c) At the time of the meeting or subsequently to it did Dr Kelly realise that the meeting was unauthorised and in breach of the Civil Service rules of procedure which applied to him?

(a) What did Dr Kelly say to Mr Gilligan in the course of the meeting?

230. In his evidence to the Inquiry Mr Gilligan said that in the course of his meeting with Dr Kelly on 22 May in the Charing Cross hotel he made notes on his personal organiser (an electronic notebook). The version of his notes which Mr Gilligan first referred to in his evidence was as follows (Exhibit JP/15):

20030522 kelly 22.5.03 transformed wk befo €re pub to make it sexier

the classic was the 45 mins. mst thn €gs inndossier wre dbl sc but that was single-source one source €e said it took 4 minutes to set up a missile assembly, that wa - €s misinterpreted

most people in intel werent happy with it, € beause it didnt refect the considere view they were putting f€orward

campbell

real info but unr, incl agaisnt ur wishes

no €t in orig draft – dull, he asked ifanything else cd go in

u f €rom africa – not nuke xpert but was v suspect, documents certa €inly forges,

10-15 yrs go there was a lot of info, with the c €oncelment anddeception op there was far less infomration

it w €as small because you dnt conceal a lg prog, and because it was € actually quite hard toimport things. the sanctions were effect €tive, they did limit programme

no usable wpns

in one of the ja €n - chemical reactors not destroyed by unscom, gla lined chamb €er to promote chme rections – were being used again by the ira €qis, recovered, taken

at al muthanna, not properly destoyed b €y un, recovred y iraqis, taken to fallujah, and used for no-ba €nned purposes.

the 18 chem missiles wre reportedby blix, but € downplayed blix thought they wre leftovers

i thin it 30pc €likely that iraq had active cw prog in the 6 m to a year like €lier that ther was bw

not much coming out of detainees, desp €ite financal inventives … they are in qt gd conds in me

there € has been prolif – not in terms of people walking across the i€raqi border with 20 shells, but supply chain knowedge, -plans

€isg headed by a major general, below him 2 one starts, british € an australian

we dont have a gt deal of knowldege than we ha €d before

1500 – 100 brits, 10-20 aussies – not all experts, ab €out 20 of the brits are

it is a big handicap not to be able t €o draw on the eertise of russian and german et exprts

isq baŸ

kelly cont real debate as to w €hether the mobile labs are what they appear to be - i is an od €d pieceof kit, feeling is it cdbe made into a fermenter, but i €s it a fermenter

enormosu qual of documents to be explouted- €

saadi and taha were taken out of the problm… because they €interfaced with the un

weve got 10-20 in custody..

why didnt € they use them? in the early stges, you just have to look at t €he weather conds, by the end the c2 was in total disarray.

hi €s prog was small – he couldnt have killed very many people, ev €en if everything had gone right for him – not really md in tru €e meaning of ord

british 1-star is john deverell, kelly will Ÿ be senior brit inspector Ÿ%

231. This was an abbreviated note. In order to assist the Inquiry Mr Gilligan expanded this note in order to give a fuller version of abbreviated words and to correct obvious typographical errors. This expanded version was as follows:

transformed week before publication to make it sexier

the classic was the 45 mins most things inn dossier were double source but that was single-source. one source said it took 45 minutes to set up a missile assembly, that was misinterpreted..

most people in intelligence weren't happy with it, because it didn't reflect the considered view they were putting forward

campbell

real info but unreliable, included against our wishes

not in original draft – dull, he asked if anything else could go in

uranium from Africa – not nuke expert but was very suspect, documents certainly forgeries,

10-15 years ago there was a lot of information, with the concealment and deception operation there was far less information

it was small because you don't conceal a large programme, and because it was actually quite hard to import things. the sanctions were effective, they did limit programme

no usable weapons

in one of the january – chemical reactors not destroyed by unscom, glass lined chamber to promote chemical reactions – were being used again by the Iraqis, recovered, taken

at al mutahanna, not properly destroyed by un, recovered by Iraqis, taken to fallujah, and used for no-banned purposes

the 18 chemical missiles were reported by blix, but downplayed..blix thought they were leftovers

I think it 30percent likely that iraq had active chemical weapons programme in the

6 months to a year

likelier that there was biological weapons

not much coming out of detainees, despite financial incentives.. they are

in quite good conditions

in middle east

there has been proliferation – not in terms of people walking across the Iraqi border with 20 shells, but supply chain knowledge, - plans

iraq survey group headed by a major general, below him 2 one starts, british and australian

we don't have a great deal of knowledge than we had before

1500 – 100 brits, 10-20 aussies – not all experts, about 20 of the brits are

it is a big handicap not to be able to draw on the expertise of russian and german et experts

isq ba

real debate as to whether the mobile labs are what they appear to be – it is an odd piece of kit, feeling is it could be made into a fermenter, but is it a fermenter

enormous qual of documents to be explouted

saadi and taha were taken out of the problem..because they interfaced with the un

we've got 10-20 in custody

why didn't they use them? in the early stages, you just have to look at the weather conditions, by the end the c2 was in total disarray.

his programme was small – he couldn't have killed very many people, even if everything had gone right for him – not really mass destruction in true meaning of word

british 1-star is john deverell, kelly will be senior brit inspector

232. In his evidence Mr Gilligan said that on the next day, 23 May, he made a manuscript note of his conversation with Dr Kelly:

[12 August, page 29, line 20]

A. The first thing I did was I sat down and did a sort of manuscript note of my full recollection of the conversation, because the trouble with making notes on one of these little keyboards is, as you see, they are abbreviated, so while it was still in fresh in my mind I actually sat down and did a full manuscript note of what I remembered my questions had been and what his answers had been; and the answers, the sentences are slightly fleshed out a little. Some of the sentences in the notes were abbreviated and these sentences fleshed them out. So that was the first thing I did.

233. However Mr Gilligan said in evidence that he could not now find that note and that he thought he had mislaid it. Mr Gilligan said that he had offered the Today programme the story about Dr Kelly and that the programme wanted a summary of Dr Kelly's main quotes and he then sent to a producer of the Today programme a note of Dr Kelly's main quotes on 28 May which was as follows:

WHAT MY MAN SAID

Q. What about the Blair dossier {Sept 2002}? When we last met {in spring 2002} you said the dossier wouldn't tell us anything we didn't already know.

A. Until the week before it was just the same as I told you. It was transformed in the week before it was published, to make it sexier.

Q. What do you mean?

A. The classic was the statement that WMD were ready for use within 45 minutes. Most things in the dossier were double-source but that was single source. And we believed that the source was wrong. He said it took 45 minutes to construct a missile assembly and that was misinterpreted {in the dossier} to mean that WMD could be deployed in 45 minutes. What we thought it actually meant was that they could launch a conventional missile in 45 minutes. There was no evidence that they had loaded missiles with WMD, or could do so anything like that quickly.

Q. So how did this transformation happen?

A. Campbell.

Q. What do you mean? They made it up?

A. No, it was real information. But it was included in the dossier against our wishes because it wasn't reliable. It was a single source and it was not reliable.

He said Downing Street had asked if there was anything else on seeing the dull original dossier and had been told about this and other things.

Other examples – he mentioned the African uranium, although said he had no personal knowledge of that because he doesn't do nuclear.

Other quotes: "What you have to understand is that 10-15 years ago there was a lot of information. With the concealment and deception operation {by the Iraqis} there was far less material."

"I believe it is 30 per cent likely there was a CW programme in the six months before the war, and more likely that there was a BW programme, but it was small because you couldn't conceal a larger programme. The sanctions were actually quite effective. They did limit the programme."

"Most people in intelligence weren't happy with it {the dossier}, because it didn't reflect the considered view they were putting forward."

On the aftermath: "We don't have a great deal more information yet than we had before. We have not get (sic) very much out of the detainees yet."

234. After Mr Gilligan had first given evidence to the Inquiry on 12 August it emerged from an inspection of his personal organiser carried out by two computer experts, Professor Anthony Sammes instructed by the Inquiry and Mr Edward Wilding instructed by Mr Gilligan who gave evidence on 18 September, that there were two versions of his notes of his conversation with Dr Kelly. It appeared that the note on his personal organiser to which Mr Gilligan had referred when he had first given evidence and which is set out in paragraph 230 above was not the first note which he had made but that there was an earlier note which was as follows (Exhibit JP/11):

20030521 kelly 22.5.03 in one of the jan - € chemical reactors not destroyed by unscom, gla lined chamber €to promote chme rections – were being used again by the iraqis €, recovered, taken at al muthanna, not properly destoyed by u €n, recovred y iraqis, taken to fallujah, and used for no-banne €d purposes.

the 18 chem missles wre reportedby blix, but do €wnplayed…blix thought they wre leftovers

i thin it 30pc lik €ely that iraq had active cw prog in the 6 m to a year likely €that ther was

not much coming out of detainees, despite finan €cal inventives…they are

the dossier was transformed in the € wek before it was published, to make it sexier

the classic w €as the 45 mins…one source said it to took 4 minutes to set up a € rocket launcher… and that was misinterpreted

i alwsy said t €he programme was small

most people in intel werent happy with € it, beause it didnt refect the considere view they were putti €ng forward

45 min was single-source

10-15 yrs go there was a €lot of info, with the concelment anddeception op there was far € less infomration

iraq survey group- 1500 – six months to 2 y €ears

war was a tragic failure of diplomacy, no direct ffort t €o engg iraq

it was a football for everyone

it was small becau €se you dnt conceal a lg prog, and because it was actually quit €e hard toimport things

the sanctions were effective, they di €d limit programme

saddam

there has been proliferation – not € in terms of people walking across the iraqi border with 20 sh €ells, but supply chain knowedge,-plans

isg headed by a major €general, below him 2 one starts, british an australian

we don €t have a gt deal of knowldege than we had before

1500 – 100 b €rits, 10-20 aussies- not all experts, about 20 of the brits ar €e

it is a big handicap not to be able to draw on the eertise €of russian and german et exprts

real debate as to whether th €e mobile labs are what they appear to be – i is an odd pieceof € kit, feeling is it cdbe made into a fermenter, but is it a feŸ rmenter

isq ba Ÿ

kelly cont enormosu qual of do €cuments to be explouted

saadi and taha were taken out of the € problem…because they interfaced with the un

weve got 10-20 €in custody

why didnt they use them? in the early stges, you j €ust have to look at the weather conds, by the end the c2 was i €n total disarray.

his arsenal was small – he couldnt have kil €led very many people, even if everything had gone right for hi €m

british 1-star is john deverall, kelly will be senior brit Ÿ inspector Ÿ4

235. There are two significant differences between these two versions of the note. The earlier version is dated in the top left hand corner 20030521 indicating that it was made on 21 May 2003, and it does not contain the name "Campbell", whereas the later version to which Mr Gilligan referred when he first gave evidence is dated in the top left hand corner 2003 05 22 and contains the name "Campbell".

236. When he was recalled on 18 September to give evidence to explain these two versions of the notes Mr Gilligan's evidence was as follows:

[18 September, page 192, line 14]

Q. Can you tell us when JP15 was created, first of all?

A. Yes. JP15 was created at the meeting with David Kelly. There were two saves of this file in the organiser. The one on the left that you see which has the date of the 21st on it, and the one on the right which has the date of the 22nd, indicating that the organiser's clock crossed midnight during the meeting. The one on the right, the 22nd, is the final saved version of the notes taken at that meeting.

Q. When did you create that document?

A. At the end of the meeting with David Kelly, when I was agreeing the quotes I would use with him. It was the result of the checks I did with Dr Kelly at the end of the meeting. It overwrote the version of 21st May.

....

[18 September, page 197, line 1]

MS ROGERS: Can I just ask you this: as you are taking notes during the conversation, are you getting down every word verbatim?

A. No.

Q. So on the text on the right-hand page we see the words "[most things in] dossier were [double source] but that was single-source", and on the left-hand side of the page in the paragraph marked 1 those words are not there but there are three dots.

A. That is right.

Q. Can you explain the change?

A. Yes. Essentially this is me going over the quotes I wanted to use with David Kelly. I read them to him and he expanded on them for me in a couple of points. For instance, in that section about the 45 minutes, you will see that the original text says "the classic was the 45 [minutes] … one source said it took 4" should be 45 minutes "to set up a rocket launcher … and that was misinterpreted".

When I read back that quote he said "the classic was the 45 minutes" was fine; and then he said: Yes, most things in the dossier were double source but that was single source, and he asked me to change "rocket launcher" to "missile assembly", so – which I did. And the rest of the quote is as he originally gave it.

Q. Looking at the second paragraph on the right-hand page, can you look over to the left-hand side and about a third of the way down you see the words "most people in [intelligence] weren't happy". So will you put a 2 beside that? We know that there are no changes there. Paragraphs 3 and 4 and 5 do not appear on the left-hand page. Can you explain why it is that they do not appear on the left but they do appear on the right?

A. Yes. This is the passage about Campbell, among other things. I cannot remember how far into the conversation that Campbell came up. This suggests it came up near the end, in the quote checking process, but I cannot be absolutely sure about that. What I do know is that when we were going over the checks then the words that appear there were spoken by David Kelly. We expanded on this section. He said – this is when he made the point about it being real information but unreliable and "included against our wishes".

LORD HUTTON: I am sorry, does that mean that the name "Campbell", whether it was first uttered by you or by Dr Kelly, only arose when you were going through, at the end, with Dr Kelly, what he had already told you?

A. I cannot remember why I did not note it in the first version. It may be that he was going too fast, I did not get it down the first time. But what happened at the end was that the – that when we were going over the quotes I was asking him whether there were – whether I could use the Campbell quote, as I mentioned in my earlier evidence, and he said the words that appear in those notes.

LORD HUTTON: May it have been that the word "Campbell" was not uttered by you or by Dr Kelly until you were going over what he had previously told you at the end of your discussion?

A. That may be the case; but again, at this distance of four months I cannot remember. I was going on the JP15 note, which is the only sort of extant version in the organiser.

LORD HUTTON: But why does "Campbell" then appear towards the start of that note?

A. This is – the notes are – the notes are in the order of – in which I discussed them with Dr Kelly, the quotes. Clearly the key quote of the exchange from my point of view was "transformed the week before it was published to make it sexier" and the second most important quote was "the classic was the 45 minutes". Those were the first two quotes I sought to check with David Kelly. So there the second, the JP15 version, shows the order in which I discussed them with Dr Kelly when I was checking them.

237. After the two computer experts and Mr Gilligan (for the second time) had given evidence on 18 September the computer experts at the request of the Inquiry made efforts by a specially devised computer software programme to access Mr Gilligan's personal organiser in order to show the sequence in which the files were generated regardless of their position in the memory as their recorded date. However it has not been possible for them to arrive at any positive conclusion on this matter.

238. Mr Gilligan said in his evidence on 12 August that it was he who introduced the term "sexier" into the conversation:

[12 August, page 25, line 16]

A. We started by talking about other things and then we got on to the dossier; and I said: What happened to it? When we last met you were saying it was not very exciting. He said: Yes, that is right, until the last week it was just as I told you. It was transformed in the week before publication. I said: To make it sexier? And he said: Yes, to make it sexier. Then I said: What do you mean? Can you give me some examples? And he said the classic – he did not use the word example, he said the classic was the 45 minutes, the statement that WMD could be ready in 45 minutes, and most things in the dossier were single source.

But Mr Gilligan was definite in his evidence that it was Dr Kelly and not he who introduced the name "Campbell" into the discussion:

[12 August, page 26, line 24]

Q. Then there is the entry which is just a single word, "Campbell". Was there any question that gave rise to that entry?

A. Yes, it was something like: how did this transformation happen?

Q. Right.

A. And then the answer was that, one word.

Q. He said just "Campbell"?

A. Yes.

Q. And what question led to the next entry?

A. Well I was surprised and I said: What, you know, Campbell made it up? They made it up? And he said: No, it was real information but it was unreliable and it was in the dossier against our wishes.

LORD HUTTON: May I just ask you, Mr Gilligan, looking at the first paragraph, you put the question: Was it to make it sexier? And Dr Kelly replied: Yes, to make it sexier?

A. Yes, to make it sexier, yes, so he adopted my words.

LORD HUTTON: Now are you clear in your recollection that you asked how was it transformed, and that the name Campbell was first spoken by Dr Kelly?

A. Yes, absolutely.

LORD HUTTON: It was not a question by you: was Campbell involved in this?

A. No, it was him. He raised the subject of the 45 minutes and he raised the subject of Campbell.

239. In his letter to his line manager, Dr Wells, dated 30 June 2003 Dr Kelly wrote:

> The issue of 45 minutes arose in terms of the threat (aerial versus land launch) and I stated that I did not know what it refers to (which I do not). He asked why it should be in the dossier and I replied probably for impact. He raised the issue of Alastair Campbell and since I was not involved in the process (not stated by me) I was unable to comment. This issue was not discussed at any length and was essentially an aside.

240. Ms Olivia Bosch, who had been a UN Inspector in Iraq in 1996, was a trusted friend and colleague of Dr Kelly and she frequently spoke to him on the telephone. In her evidence she told the Inquiry what Dr Kelly had said to her about his meeting with Mr Gilligan:

[4 September, page 10, line 11]

It was another time towards mid May he told me he had an unauthorised meeting with Andrew Gilligan, someone he had met a couple of times before but did not know that well. And he said he was – he was taken aback by the way Andrew Gilligan tried to elicit information from him. I said: yes, but that is what journalists do. He understood that, but he said he had never experienced it in the way that Gilligan had tried to do so, by a name game was the term.

Q. Just pause there for a moment. Did he explain what he meant by "name game"?

A. Yes.

Q. Well, what did he say?

A. Okay, and this was with reference to the September dossier and I do not recall exactly what aspect of it. It was the name game bit was what reminded – what sticks in my mind. He said that Gilligan wanted to play a name game as to who was responsible for inserting information into the dossier, and that if I understand correctly Gilligan said to him: I will name you some names. Apparently David had said that Gilligan very quickly – the first name he mentioned very quickly and immediately was Campbell. David told me he could neither confirm nor deny. David said as he was a civil servant he could not provide Government names, least of all to a journalist. We kind of laughed there. Nor could he deny as Gilligan would continue listing names or could continue listing names until the right name came up.

Q. Did Dr Kelly then say what he had actually said to Gilligan?

A. Yes, then he said what he actually said. Because he could not confirm or deny but he thought he had to give an answer so he said "maybe".

Q. So in other words what had happened is Gilligan had come up with the name Campbell and then Dr Kelly had said: maybe?

A. Right.

LORD HUTTON: Did you understand if Mr Gilligan had given more names – you said he came up almost immediately with that name.

A. Right. It is part of this name game that Campbell – sorry, that Gilligan had quickly put up Campbell. It did not give David time really to think about what was going on in that way.

LORD HUTTON: Did you understand that was the first name?

A. Yes, the very first name.

MR KNOX: I just want to get this right: did Dr Kelly say he had given Gilligan this explanation about not being able to name civil servants or did Dr Kelly say: he said Campbell, I said maybe, and the reason I did that is because I am a civil servant.

A. I am not clear. He might have said to Gilligan that he cannot give names but I am not clear. I cannot remember exactly.

Q. You cannot remember precisely what he said he had said to Gilligan?

A. Yes, right on that. In terms of this kind of process.

241. Having heard and considered Mr Gilligan's evidence about how there came to be two versions of his discussion with Dr Kelly on his personal organiser, and how he lost his manuscript note which he made the next day, and how his memory of his discussion with Dr Kelly is not now entirely clear, I have considerable doubt as to how reliable Mr Gilligan's evidence is as regards what Dr Kelly said to him and, in the state of the evidence, including the absence of any conclusive evidence from the two computer experts, I am unable to come to a definite conclusion as to whether or not Mr Gilligan's account of how he made the two versions of the notes of his discussion with Dr Kelly is correct. It may be that his account of how he came to make the two versions of his discussion on his personal organiser in the course of his meeting with Dr Kelly is basically correct. It may be that the fact that the first version is dated 21 May and the second version is dated 22 May is due to the clock on the personal organiser being slow and that the clock changed from 21 May to 22 May in the course of the meeting.

242. On the question whether in their discussion Mr Gilligan first suggested the name "Campbell" to Dr Kelly or whether it was Dr Kelly who first spoke the name "Campbell" to Mr Gilligan, it may be that it was Dr Kelly who first spoke the name "Campbell", having regard to the evidence of Ms Susan Watts, whom I regard as an accurate and reliable witness. In a telephone conversation which she had with Dr Kelly on 7 May 2003 she made a shorthand note that Dr Kelly said to her regarding the 45 minutes claim "…mistake to put in … A Campbell seeing something in there … NB single source … but not corroborated … sounded good." I think it is also reasonably clear from the transcript of Ms Watts telephone conversation with Dr Kelly on 30 May that he accepted in that conversation that he had mentioned the name of Alastair Campbell to her in relation to the 45 minutes claim in their earlier telephone conversation on 7 May. The relevant parts of the transcript are:

SW: But what intrigued me and which made, prompted me to ring you, (huh) was the quotes yesterday on the Today programme about the 45 minutes part of the dossier

DK: yep. We spoke about this before of course…

SW: We have

DK: I think you know my views on that.

SW: Yes, I've looked back at my notes and you were actually quite specific at that time – I may have missed a trick on that one, but err

(both laugh)

SW: you were more specific than the source on the Today programme – not that that necessarily means that it's not one and the same person …but, um in fact you actually referred to Alastair Campbell in that conversation…

DK: err yep yep … with you?…

SW: yes

DK: I mean I did talk to Gavin Hewitt yesterday – he phoned me in New York, so he may have picked up on what I said… because I would have said exactly the same as I said to you…

SW: Yes, so he presumably decided not to name Alastair Campbell himself but just to label this as Number 10…

DK: yep yep

....

SW: ok... just back momentarily on the 45 minute issue...I'm feeling like I ought to just explore that a little bit more with you...the um... err. So would it be accurate then, as you did in that earlier conversation, to say that it was Alastair Campbell himself who...?

DK: No I can't. All I can say is the Number Ten press office. I've never met Alastair Campbell so I cant.... (SW interrupts: they seized on that ?) But... I think Alastair Campbell is synonymous with that press office because he's responsible for it.

Therefore the fact that Dr Kelly had mentioned the name of Alastair Campbell to Ms Watts in relation to the 45 minutes claim in their telephone conversation on 7 May tends to suggest that it might have been Dr Kelly who introduced the name "Campbell" into his discussion with Mr Gilligan.

243. In his evidence Mr Gavin Hewitt, whom I also regard as an accurate and reliable witness, said that he spoke on the telephone to Dr Kelly on the afternoon of 29 May about the dossier and that Dr Kelly said to him "No. 10 spin came into play". As Dr Kelly made this comment to Mr Hewitt on 29 May it may be that when Mr Gilligan suggested to him that the dossier had been transformed to make it "sexier", he replied "yes, to make it sexier".

244. However two of the most serious allegations reported in Mr Gilligan's broadcasts on the 29 May were the claim that "actually the Government probably knew that that the forty five minute figure was wrong, even before it decided to put it in" and the claim that "the reason it [the 45 minute figure] hadn't been in the original draft was that ... it only came from one source and most of the other claims were from two, and the intelligence agencies say they don't really believe it was necessarily true because they thought the person making the claim had actually made a mistake, it got, had got mixed up". Mr Gilligan's notes of his discussion with Dr Kelly contained no entries which suggest that Dr Kelly made either of these allegations to Mr Gilligan. In relation to the allegation that the 45 minutes claim had not been inserted in the original draft of the dossier because it only came from one source, Mr Gilligan accepted in answer to his own counsel that the allegation was wrong:

[17 September, page 7, line 21]

Q. In terms, also, of the reason for the non-inclusion of the 45 minutes, you say in this part of the broadcast, it is at the top of BBC/4/223, which I think is up, that the reason for the non-inclusion was that it had only come from one source.

A. Yes. As I have said in my witness statement, that was wrong, although I do not attribute that particular view to David Kelly in fact. But that is clearly incorrect. The reason it came in late, which is now accepted, was that it simply was a matter of the timing when it arrived.

Q. It arrived late, but it was single sourced?

A. Yes.

245. In relation to the allegation that the Government probably knew that the 45 minutes claim was wrong even before it decided to put it in the dossier, Mr Gilligan also accepted in cross examination by Mr Sumption QC for the Government that his words were imperfect and he should not have said them:

[17 September, page 14, line 20]

Q. Mr Gilligan, I would like to ask you first about your 6.07 broadcast, where you said that the Government probably knew that the 45 minutes figure was wrong even before they put it in. You made a point a few minutes ago about the difference between dishonesty and spin. If a

164

Government puts into a dossier which it lays before Parliament a statement which it probably knows to be wrong, is that an allegation that they are dishonest, in your book?

A. I think the allegation here that I was trying to convey was that the claim in the form in which it was made was considered to be wrong, considered to be unreliable and considered to be misinterpreted by many in the intelligence community; and that form being that Saddam's military planning allows some WMD to be ready within 45 minutes of an order to use them.

Q. But when you said that the Government probably knew that it was wrong, you were actually saying, whether you intended to or not, that they were dishonest, were you not?

A. The allegation I intended to make was of spin, but as I say, I do regard those words as imperfect and I should not have said them.

Q. And the reason why you should not have said them is that they did, in fact, accuse the Government of dishonesty, whether or not that was your intention.

A. I think that is probably right, yes. But I really did try and repeatedly make it clear on subsequent occasions that I was not accusing the Government of lying or fabrication. I said that the intelligence was real. I said at 7.32 – I said on subsequent broadcasts on 31st May that I was not accusing the Government of lying or fabrication or of making this up. I said it also repeatedly to the Foreign Affairs Committee, to the Spectator and in The Mail on Sunday.

Q. I think you accepted on the last occasion that you gave evidence here, and more or less accepted this morning, that that particular allegation, that the Government probably knew that the 45 minutes figure was wrong, was something that you could not support?

A. It was not sufficiently supported. It did not have no support. David Kelly did not say it in terms but he did say that the statement that WMD were ready for use in 45 minutes was unreliable. He said it was wrong. He said it was included "against our wishes". And the conclusion I drew from that was that the wishes had been expressed and the wishes had been made known, which is something we do now know to be the case.

Q. You accept, I think, that it was expressed by you as something that your source had said, whereas in fact it was an inference of your own?

A. Yes, that is right, that was my mistake.

Q. The same is true, is it not, of the word "ordered"; that was not something that Dr Kelly had said, it was Gilligan speaking not Kelly, was it not?

A. Yes. It was my interpretation of what he had said.

246. When questioned by Mr Dingemans QC, counsel to the Inquiry, Mr Gilligan said:

[17 September, page 77, line 12]

Q. I will not repeat my earlier questioning nor indeed the earlier cross-examination. Can I just take you to some passages of the 29th May broadcast at the start and ask whether you contend these were accurate representations of what Dr Kelly had told you? BBC/1/4, if I may. The first part I want to draw your attention to is in the first paragraph: "… what we've been told by one of the senior officials in charge of drawing up that dossier was that, actually the Government probably erm knew that that 45 minutes figure was wrong, even before it decided to put it in." Do you now accept that was not based on what Dr Kelly had told you?

A. I accept that it was not the – I accept that it was not the right form of words to use because it gave listeners the impression that he had said that in terms. He did not say it in terms.

Q. And he did not suggest that to you?

A. Well, he said that the statement that WMD were ready for use in 45 minutes was unreliable, it was wrong, it was misinterpreted and he said that it had been included "against our wishes". I concluded from that that the wishes had been made known, but it was wrong to ascribe that statement that they had been made known to Dr Kelly.

Q. The bottom of the page: "… and the reason it hadn't been in the original draft was that it was, it was only erm, it came from one source and most of the other claims were from two, and the intelligence agencies say they don't really believe it was necessarily true…" That was not the reason it had not been in the original draft, do you now accept that?

A. Yes, I do.

Q. And Dr Kelly gave you nothing to suggest that was the reason.

A. That is correct, and I did not ascribe it in fact to him either.

Q. The next page. Just before "End of first recording": "Clearly, you know, if erm, if it, if it was, if it was wrong, things do, things are, got wrong in good faith but if they knew it was wrong before they actually made the claim, that's perhaps a bit more serious." Suggesting that Dr Kelly had suggested to you that the claim was false.

A. I think the operative word here is "if". This does suggest that I am not suggesting it is true. But, you know, as I have said to you before, the statement that – the statement "probably knew it was wrong" was – was not something that Dr Kelly had said in terms.

Q. If you knew that this was not right you would have said so. It was not your suggestion that they knew that it was wrong, was it?

A. No, my error in this was in ascribing that – you know, expressing my understanding as something which Dr Kelly had actually said in terms, which he had not.

Q. And neither had he suggested it?

A. Well, he said things which had led me to conclude it, but he had not suggested it directly, no.

Q. Scrolling down the page, Mr Humphrys picking up on what you are saying, fourth line down: "Now our defence correspondent, Andrew Gilligan, has found evidence that the Government's dossier on Iraq that was produced last September, was cobbled together at the last minute with some unconfirmed material that had not been approved by the Security Services." Dr Kelly did not say that to you, did he?

A. No. These were not my words, these were John Humphrys' words. I would not have said those words and did not write them for him.

Q. That was Mr Humphrys' understanding of your earlier broadcast no doubt.

A. I do not believe it was –

Q. He is hardly likely to have made it up.

A. The cues – the things that the presenter says, the cues are actually written by the presenters before the programme even starts, so he would not have heard the earlier broadcast at the time that he devised this particular cue.

Q. BBC/1/6 towards the bottom of the paragraph: "Now that claim has come back to haunt Mr Blair because if the weapons had been that readily to hand, they probably would have been found by now but you know, it could have been an honest mistake, but what I have been told is that the Government knew that claim was questionable, even before the war, even before they wrote it in their dossier." Dr Kelly never told you that, did he?

A. No. Again, my error there was expressing that understanding, and I defend the use of "knew it was questionable" but expressing it as something which Dr Kelly had told me in terms, which he had not – but it was not the main thrust. It was not the main import of the broadcast. The broadcast was summarised probably most – in its essentials by the news bulletin piece which I wrote, and that did not mention any "Government knew" type things.

[17 September, page 83, line 22]

MR DINGEMANS: So there are those errors you accept in your transmission on 29th May?

A. Yes, I do. Yes.

Q. In fact, on 29th May there was an allegation made against the Government of conscious wrongdoing; do you accept that?

A. My feeling on this was that it was an allegation less serious than that; that it was part of a political debate. As I say, I mean, the Ministry of Defence press log is – has got – I have just got a – I mean, the stories in the newspapers in the morning of 29th May, that was before a word had been spoken by me, included the Independent splash "Labour rebels threaten to report Tony Blair for misleading Parliament"; the Mirror "War of Lies"; the Guardian "Tony Blair faces growing crisis over failure to uncover WMD"; The Times "Inquiry into arms dossier claim". So this was seen –

Q. So you thought you would join in?

A. This was seen as part of –

Q. Is that right, Mr Gilligan?

A. This was seen as part of a continuing debate. It was not something we created. It was not something we started.

Q. I did not say you created it, Mr Gilligan. I am asking you about 29th May. Did you think you would join in with that morning's headlines?

A. No, that was not the intention. The intention was to report what Dr Kelly had told me; and I regret that on those two occasions I did not report entirely carefully and accurately what he had said. My error was to ascribe that statement to him when it was actually a conclusion of mine.

247. Therefore it is clear that Dr Kelly did not tell Mr Gilligan that 10 Downing Street probably knew that the 45 minutes claim was wrong before it decided to put it in the dossier. The true position was that the 45 minutes claim was inserted in an assessment by the assessment staff of the JIC based on intelligence received by the SIS and the 45 minutes claim was then inserted in the dossier with the full approval of the JIC, and at the time of the publication of the dossier the JIC, the assessment staff and the SIS believed that the intelligence relating to the 45 minutes claim was reliable.

248. It is also clear that the reason why the 45 minutes claim was not in the original draft of the dossier was not that it only came from one source. The reason why the 45 minutes claim was not included in the original draft was because the relevant intelligence was not received until 29 August 2002.

Issues (b) and (c)

(b) In meeting Mr Gilligan and discussing the dossier with him was Dr Kelly having a meeting which was unauthorised and in breach of the Civil Service rules of procedure which applied to him?

(c) At the time of the meeting or subsequent to it did Dr Kelly realise that the meeting was unauthorised and in breach of the Civil Service rules which applied to him?

249. Referring to the list of Dr Kelly's contacts with the press for the year April 2002 to March 2003 (see paragraph 26) counsel to the Inquiry put the following questions to Mr Hatfield:

[11 August, page 59, line 4]

Q. He is talking here about on 11th and 12th November 2002 there is the Organisation for the Prohibition of Chemical Weapons, The Hague, The Netherlands, "Protection Network". He deals with that from 18th to 20th November. Then he deals with the International Institute for Strategic Studies, London, a conference, talking about invasion or inspections, that is January and February 2003. That is shortly before the war. "Media. "Attributable and unattributable briefings plus interviews on Iraq, Russia, weapons, anthrax and smallpox. "Television and radio: Channel 4, Australian Broadcasting Company, Canadian Broadcasting Company, Tokyo Broadcasting Systems, CNN, CBS, ABC, Radio Netherlands, BBC 4, BBC 24 hours/World Service, BBC local radio (London, Wales)." Then the news media, he seems to go through the whole of Fleet Street: Guardian, Daily Telegraph, The Times, New York Times, Washington Post, Los Angeles Times, Newsweek, Herald Tribune and Wall Street Journal. So he was having extensive contact with them.

A. He had an extensive number of contacts with them, yes.

Q. Yes.

A. But it does not also make clear over what period, but nevertheless.

Q. It also appears to make clear that some of the contact was on an unattributable basis.

A. Yes.

Q. Is that something that is authorised, as it were, by the Ministry of Defence?

A. Yes, it should be.

Q. Right.

A. Indeed, his own letter, which started the events as far as I was concerned, makes it clear that they normally were cleared. In fact, slightly unusually but nonetheless cleared through the FCO press office usually rather than the MoD press office. That clearly reflects a lot of it is briefing in relation to his role in support of what he did in relation to UNMOVIC, where the Foreign Office were in the lead. I would assume every one of those listed on there had been cleared either on an individual basis or if you like especially in relation to the appearances at conferences on a block basis that: this is the sort of conference you do and you know the rules.

Indeed, the general rules we started with make it quite clear that, for example, contact with IISS does not have to be cleared on an individual basis because it is an established institution with which MoD deals. But there are rules about how you behave at such conferences where you are speaking.

250. Sections of the Civil Service rules of procedure relating to civil servants speaking to journalists are set out in paragraphs 23, 24 and 25. Mr Patrick Lamb, the deputy head of the Counter Proliferation Department in the FCO, gave evidence as to how the system of authorising Dr Kelly to speak to the press operated. In cross-examination by Mr Gompertz for Dr Kelly's family he stated:

[24 September, page 79, line 19]

Q. Can I invite you to recollect your evidence on a previous occasion? You said, in answer to Lord Hutton, that in theory and properly he, Dr Kelly, should have approached the press office about each and every request. I am looking at page 102 if you have it in front of you. I am sorry, I do not have a copy to show you. In practice, you then said, as I think we all know: '... once a journalist has a number they will tend to pursue that person or ring that person without – off the cuff. Dr Kelly worked from home, to a very large extent; and so that meant that often, I presume, he would receive calls at home having exchanged a card with a journalist. And certainly there were instances where, for reasons I perfectly understand, he had no opportunity to seek prior authorisation or clearance. But in my experience he was also very scrupulous about informing us after the event. That in itself was helpful, very helpful in the event that something arose following that particular interview' – Is that a fair summary?

A. I think that is an accurate reading of what I said on that occasion.

Q. Thank you. Is it a fair summary of what happened?

A. It is a summary of what happened. Let me explain. The point is that I recognise perfectly that Dr Kelly was attending seminars, he was attending receptions, as I do, and there were occasions when journalists will meet with him and those are not occasions when this procedure can be followed, self-evidently. There are also instances where Dr Kelly would have exchanged a card or a telephone number with a journalist, a meeting with that journalist may have been approved by the Foreign Office, and that journalist rings Dr Kelly to clarify a particular point or pursue some other item. I would not expect Dr Kelly to put down the phone and say: sorry, I cannot speak about this issue until I have spoken to the Foreign Office. There is an element whereby – as I said, I believe, elsewhere in my evidence, there is an element of self-discipline and judgment involved in all of these matters, and that self-discipline is imposed on all of us involved, including Dr Kelly. I believe that if he were contacted by a journalist say two or three months after an initial contact, he should at that point have referred that to the Foreign Office, because the whole point of getting policy and press office agreement is to take account of events as they are today and not events as they were two or three months ago.

Dr Kelly, I think, understood very clearly that he should not become involved on commenting on current UK Government policy.

Q. The words you use there, "self-discipline" and "judgment", are an echo from a document I think you prepared, CAB/1/115. If we can scroll down to paragraph 4 – having described the system, I am not going to go through it because we have looked at this document before, but you say this: "This system, which ultimately relied on self-discipline and judgment on all sides, worked well and provided the media with expert background briefing and led to no embarrassments for HMG over the period 2000-2002." That is fair, is it?

A. It is fair, yes. It is an accurate reading of what I said.

251. Mr Lamb also stated that sometime in late May 2003 Dr Kelly briefly mentioned to him that he had spoken to Mr Gilligan and Ms Watts:

[24 September, page 64, line 14]

Q. Can I move on to the second topic I wish to cover. When did you first become aware that Dr Kelly had spoken to Mr Gilligan and Ms Watts?

A. I believe that this took place or rather I believe he spoke to me some time in late May. I say this for two reasons. I believe it had to be subsequent to his conversations with Ms Watts, which I now know took place on 7th and 12th May. I believe it had to be subsequent to his conversation with Mr Gilligan which took place on 22nd May, because Dr Kelly referred, very fleetingly and very briefly, to the fact that he had spoken to both those journalists in a conversation that took place in my office. He did not elaborate. He made no further comment or explanation or exposition as to what had taken place, if anything. And I noted, very specifically, those two names and that I remember specifically – the only element of the conversation I now retain is the fact, and retained even at the time, that he had spoken to two named journalists and that I was unaware that he had sought authorisation.

Q. Why did you not follow it up at the time that Dr Kelly made those comments?

A. I did not follow it up at the time because he did not specifically say to me that he wished to raise a matter with me. He did not specifically say: I would like to discuss with you what took place, or give me any run through as to what had happened, as he had done previously in the case of the German TV radio interview where he had gone through it in detail. Dr Kelly, I should add, on that occasion, and because I was extremely busy with covering two posts within the Proliferation and Arms Control Department at that time and was dealing with another meeting which I cannot refer to here but was a bilateral meeting with another country, an issue that country had raised already at Prime Minister level, I was the lead FCO official dealing with that meeting, which took place eventually on 28th May, and running with all the arrangements for it and preparations for it. That is why I was extremely busy, as I now recall. It was that particular issue that was dominating my attention. Dr Kelly, I think, could and should have spoken to either of my three colleagues, possibly four colleagues, to whom he could have drawn this – he could have drawn this to their attention and any one of them would have realised what needed to be done. He could and should primarily have spoken, in my judgment, to the press office as well. He did not.

This was a fleeting reference and comment made to me at a time when he knew and saw that I was busy. Dr Kelly and I normally sat down at the table in my office when he came to call. On this occasion my distinct recollection is of being behind my desk, totally preoccupied with the work I was doing, and of him standing in the doorway. It was most unusual for us to have such an exchange. It was a very fleeting and brief exchange.

252. In her evidence, in describing a conversation which she had had on the telephone with Dr Kelly, his friend and colleague Ms Olivia Bosch said:

[4 September, page 9, line 4]

Q. What did Dr Kelly say about his relationship with the press generally?

A. He seemed fairly relaxed about it. He seemed to enjoy talking with the press and giving them background information. He knew that they were seeking information to better understand what some of the processes were that were going on in Iraq. And if I refer to my second statement, where I mention that in terms of an approach he said that the Foreign Office and Ministry of Defence had different approaches. And I started – and I kind of led – I said: do you mean that you do not talk – sorry: with respect to the Ministry of Defence, is it that you do not talk to journalists or the press unless there was a reason to do so, whereas the Foreign Office was more relaxed? And in effect – and then I started – that you could speak – he was saying: unless there was a reason not to. So they had slightly different emphasis in terms of what it was. But, on the whole, I understood that he recognised – and he said he would need pre-authorisation for that but on occasion, sometimes, he would speak on the telephone for a quick answer or something like that that he might not get that pre-authorised, but the Foreign Office was much more relaxed in his dealings with them.

253. Mr Gompertz submitted that as Dr Kelly was employed by DSTL and sometimes worked for the FCO and for the MoD it was difficult for him to know from whom he should seek authorisation to speak to the press. Dr Kelly's precise employment situation in May 2003 was somewhat complex, and there could be debate as to which of the sets of rules forbidding speaking to journalists set out in paragraphs 23, 24 and 25 applied to him. But it is clear that one of those sets of rules applied to him and that in making the comments which he probably did to Mr Gilligan about the 45 minutes claim being single sourced and that there was unhappiness in the intelligence community about the phraseology employed in the dossier in relation to that claim, Dr Kelly was in breach of one or other of those sets of rules.

254. Dr Kelly must have learned of some of the matters on which he commented to Mr Gilligan when he had discussions with Dr Jones and other DIS officials in the DIS offices on 18 and 19 September 2002. In respect of the propriety of discussing such matters with a journalist Sir Richard Dearlove stated in his evidence in relation to Dr Kelly's conversation with Ms Watts on 30 May:

[15 September, page 106, line 22]

A. Can I also say in respect of this recorded conversation here?

Q. Yes.

A. As chief of the service, I am shocked to see someone discussing one of our CX reports, which is what he is discussing, with a journalist without authorisation.

Q. I appreciate he was not within your specific area, which is why I have not asked you about it, but what would your reaction have been to finding out about these discussions?

A. That it is a serious breach of discipline.

Dr Brian Jones stated:

[3 September, page 137, line 8]

Q. If members of your staff had given this sort of information to journalists about the discussions that had taken place in your branch relating to concerns about the dossier, what would your reaction have been to that?

A. (Pause). I would have thought that they were acting well beyond the bounds of what they should have been doing. I would have been very disappointed and very annoyed.

255. Under Parts IV A and V of the Employment Rights Act 1996 an employee is protected from being subjected to any detriment by his employer if he makes a "protected disclosure" of information as defined in that Act. I consider that the information which Dr Kelly disclosed to Ms Susan Watts on 7 and 30 May and to Mr Gavin Hewitt on 29 May and whatever information he disclosed to Mr Gilligan on 22 May was not "protected disclosure" of information within the meaning of the 1996 Act. In his evidence to the ISC Dr Kelly said:

ALAN HOWARTH: When you went to meet Andrew Gilligan, at the Charing Cross Hotel, did you enter the discussion with an agenda of your own, you've mentioned that you were anxious to learn what you could from him, but did you also go to meet him with a view to conveying any particular points to him.

DR KELLY: No, it was very much with the intention of being in receive mode – to understand his experience he had in Iraq.

I am further of the opinion that in relation to such information there was no provision of the 1996 Act which operated to relieve Dr Kelly from the duty imposed on him in relation to the non-disclosure of information by the Civil Service rules of procedure set out in paragraphs 23, 24 and 25. It is also clear that after his meeting with Mr Gilligan on 22 May 2003 Dr Kelly never sought to suggest that he had been entitled to discuss intelligence matters with Mr Gilligan.

256. It may be that in his meeting with Mr Gilligan Dr Kelly said more to him than he intended to say. As Ms Watts said in her evidence, Dr Kelly could be gossipy and chatty with a journalist. It may be that at the time of the meeting Dr Kelly did not realise the gravity of the situation which he was helping to create by discussing intelligence matters with Mr Gilligan. His discussion with Ms Watts on 30 May suggests that he treated an unauthorised discussion with a reporter about intelligence matters in a somewhat lighthearted way:

DK: I mean I did talk to Gavin Hewitt yesterday – he phoned me in New York, so he may have picked up on what I said … because I would have said exactly the same as I said to you…

SW: Yes, so he presumably decided not to name Alastair Campbell himself but just to label this as Number 10…

DK: yep yep

SW: are you getting much flak over that?

DK: me? No, not yet anyway I was in New York… (laughs)

SW: yes good timing I suppose

DK: I mean they wouldn't think it was me, I don't think. Maybe they would, maybe they wouldn't. I don't know.

257. But whatever Dr Kelly thought at the time of his meeting with Mr Gilligan it is clear that after Mr Gilligan's broadcasts on 29 May Dr Kelly must have come to realise the gravity of the situation for which he was partly responsible by commenting on intelligence matters to him. In his letter to Dr Wells dated 30 June he wrote: "With hindsight I of course deeply regret talking to Andrew Gilligan even though I am convinced that I am not his primary source of information.", and I have no doubt that this regret weighed on his mind during June and July.

258. It is also clear that Dr Kelly himself recognised that his meeting with Mr Gilligan was unauthorised. In her evidence Ms Bosch said:

[4 September, page 10, line 4]

Q. You have mentioned one occasion when Dr Kelly found his name in the press, which he was upset by, which perhaps is the article I took you to. Did Dr Kelly around this time, April or May, around that type of time, did he have any further discussion with you about his contacts with the press?

A. Well, he mentioned in his – I am not sure of the time sequence but if I go through here. It was another time towards mid May he told me he had an unauthorised meeting with Andrew Gilligan, someone he had met a couple of times before but did not know that well. And he said he was – he was taken aback by the way Andrew Gilligan tried to elicit information from him. I said: yes, but that is what journalists do. He understood that, but he said he had never experienced it in the way that Gilligan had tried to do so, by a name game was the term.

....

[4 September, page 12, line 20]

LORD HUTTON: Ms Bosch, you said Dr Kelly told you he had an unauthorised meeting with Mr Gilligan.

A. Yes.

LORD HUTTON: Did he use the word "unauthorised"?

A. Yes, he did.

LORD HUTTON: How did he come to say that? Did he just say to you: I had an unauthorised meeting with Mr Gilligan?

A. Yes, because we would just talk kind of freely about journalists who you would see, whatever, and I believe that he had come back – I do not know if it was that very night he mentioned it or whatever. But we had – he had, in previous conversations, mentioned authorised and unauthorised.

LORD HUTTON: Yes.

A. And he had mentioned this was an unauthorised meeting.

LORD HUTTON: Yes.

A. So confiding, I suppose, in a way.

Summary of conclusions on the issues relating to Dr Kelly's meeting with Mr Gilligan in the Charing Cross Hotel on 22 May 2003

259. The conclusions which I have come to on these issues are the following:

(1) In the light of the uncertainties arising from Mr Gilligan's evidence and the existence of two versions of his notes made on his personal organiser of his discussion with Dr Kelly on 22 May it is not possible to reach a definite conclusion as to what Dr Kelly said to Mr Gilligan. It may be that Dr Kelly said to Mr Gilligan that

Mr Campbell was responsible for transforming the dossier, and it may be that when Mr Gilligan suggested to Dr Kelly that the dossier was transformed to make it "sexier", Dr Kelly agreed with this suggestion. However I am satisfied that Dr Kelly did not say to Mr Gilligan that the Government probably knew or suspected that the 45 minutes claim was wrong before that claim was inserted in the dossier. I am further satisfied that Dr Kelly did not say to Mr Gilligan that the reason why the 45 minutes claim was not included in the original draft of the dossier was because it only came from one source and the intelligence agencies did not really believe it was necessarily true. In the course of his evidence which I have set out in paragraphs 244, 245 and 246, Mr Gilligan accepted that he had made errors in his broadcasts in the Today programme on 29 May 2003. The reality was that the 45 minutes claim was based on an intelligence report which the Secret Intelligence Service believed to be reliable and the 45 minutes claim was inserted in the dossier with the approval of the Joint Intelligence Committee, the most senior body in the United Kingdom responsible for the assessment of intelligence. In addition the reason why the 45 minutes claim was not inserted in the first draft of the dossier was because the intelligence on which it was based was not received by the SIS in London until 29 August 2002. Therefore the allegations reported by Mr Gilligan that the Government probably knew that the 45 minutes claim was wrong or questionable and that it was not inserted in the first draft of the dossier because it only came from one source and the intelligence agencies did not really believe it was necessarily true, were unfounded.

(2) Dr Kelly's meeting with Mr Gilligan was unauthorised and in meeting Mr Gilligan and discussing intelligence matters with him, Dr Kelly was acting in breach of the Civil Service code of procedure which applied to him.

(3) It may be that when he met Mr Gilligan, Dr Kelly said more to him than he had intended to say and that at the time of the meeting he did not realise the gravity of the situation which he was helping to create by discussing intelligence matters with Mr Gilligan. But whatever Dr Kelly thought at the time of his meeting with Mr Gilligan, it is clear that after Mr Gilligan's broadcasts on 29 May Dr Kelly must have come to realise the gravity of the situation for which he was partly responsible by commenting on intelligence matters to him and he accepted that the meeting was unauthorised, as he acknowledged in a telephone conversation with his friend and colleague Ms Olivia Bosch after his meeting with Mr Gilligan.

CHAPTER 8

Issues relating to the BBC arising from Mr Gilligan's broadcasts on the BBC Today programme on 29 May 2003

260. These issues are the following:

> (1) Was there a failure by the BBC to exercise proper editorial control over Mr Gilligan's broadcasts on the Today programme on 29 May?

> (2) Was the BBC management at fault in failing to investigate properly and adequately the Government's complaints that the report was false that the Government probably knew that the 45 minutes claim was wrong even before it decided to put it in the dossier?

> (3) Was there a failure by BBC management to inform the Governors of the BBC of the extent of editorial concerns about Mr Gilligan's broadcasts in relation to the 45 minutes claim?

> (4) Whilst the Governors were under a duty to protect the independence of the BBC from Government interference, were the Governors at fault in failing to investigate properly and adequately the Government's complaints about the report on the Today programme in relation to the 45 minutes claim, and were the Governors too ready to accept the opinion of BBC management that the broadcasts were proper ones for the Today programme to make.

261. Before considering these issues it is relevant to set out in greater detail what occurred during and after Mr Gilligan's broadcasts on 29 May.

Denials by the Government

262. The Government strongly denied the truth of the allegations reported by Mr Gilligan in the Today programme and the 10 Downing Street duty press officer who heard the broadcast at 6.07am, having spoken to the Prime Minister's press officer travelling with him in the Middle East and having spoken also to Mr John Scarlett, issued a denial of the allegations at 7.15am, the denial stating:

> These allegations are untrue, not one word of the dossier was not entirely the work of the intelligence agencies. The suggestion that any pressure was put on the intelligence services by Number Ten or anyone else to change the document are (sic) entirely false.

This denial was reported by Mr John Humphreys on the Today programme in the broadcast beginning at 7.32am when, speaking to Mr Gilligan he said:

> Now you told us about this earlier on the programme Andy, and we've had a statement from 10 Downing Street that says it's not true, and let me just quote what they said to you. 'Not one word of the dossier was not entirely the work of the intelligence agencies'. Sorry to submit you to this sort of English but there we are. I think we know what they mean. Are you suggesting, let's be very clear about this, that it was not the work of the Intelligence Agencies.

AG: No, the information which I am told was dubious did come from the agencies, but they were unhappy about it, because they didn't think it should have been in there. They thought it was, it was not corroborated sufficiently, and they actually thought it was wrong, they thought the informant concerned erm, had got it wrong, they thought he'd misunderstood what was happening.

263. Later on 29 May an official in the Prime Minister's press office wrote to the BBC stating that Mr Gilligan's broadcast on the Today programme had made serious and untrue allegations about 10 Downing Street over the presentation of the dossier.

264. On 25 June Mr Campbell gave evidence to the FAC. In the course of his evidence he asserted in strong terms and on a number of occasions that the report broadcast by the BBC on 29 May was untruthful and that it was a lie that he (Mr Campbell) or the Prime Minister or 10 Downing Street overrode the judgment of the intelligence agencies to insert intelligence in the September 2002 dossier which was exaggerated or with which the intelligence agencies were not 100 per cent content. Part of his evidence was as follows:

Q986 Richard Ottaway: The second main conclusion that is being queried is the 45-minute point, which you have dealt with quite extensively in your memorandum. The Foreign Secretary made a similar point yesterday about the 45 minutes. Are you saying the same today that this is what the intelligence people are telling you and it must be true?

Mr Campbell: When the first draft of the September 2002 dossier was presented to Number 10, I think I am right in saying that was the first time I had seen that and again, as I say, having seen the meticulousness and the care that the Chairman of the JIC and his colleagues were taking in the whole process, I really did not think it was my place, to be perfectly frank, to say, "Hold on a minute, what is this about?" What is completely and totally and 100 per cent untrue – and this is the BBC allegation, which is ostensibly I think why the Chairman called me on this – what is completely and totally untrue is that I in any way overrode that judgment, sought to exaggerate that intelligence, or sought to use it in any way that the intelligence agencies were not 100 per cent content with.

Q987 Richard Ottaway: You use some rather interesting wording in your memorandum that to suggest it was inserted against the wishes of the intelligence agencies was false. Was it put in at your suggestion?

Mr Campbell: No, otherwise – It existed in the very first draft and, as far as I am aware, that part the paper stayed like that.

Q988 Richard Ottaway: Have you gone back to the JIC on that point since publication?

Mr Campbell: I can assure you that I have had many, many discussions about this issue with the Chairman of the JIC, not least in preparation for this hearing.

Q989 Richard Ottaway: And they are still standing behind it?

Mr Campbell: Absolutely, absolutely. In relation to that particular story, which as Sir John Stanley said to the BBC correspondent last week, is about as serious an allegation as one can make, not just against me but against the Prime Minister and the intelligence agencies, they are basically saying that the Prime Minister took the country into military conflict and all that entails – loss of military and Iraqi civilian life – on the basis of a lie. Now that is a very, very serious allegation.

Q990 Richard Ottaway: Can I suggest it is Parliament that took the country into war.

Mr Campbell: The allegation against me is that we helped the Prime Minister persuade Parliament and the country to go into conflict on the basis of a lie. I think that is a pretty serious allegation. It has been denied by the Prime Minister, it has been denied by the Chairman of the Joint Intelligence Committee, it has been denied by the Security and Intelligence Co-ordinator and it has been denied by the heads of the intelligence agencies involved, and yet the BBC continue to stand by that story.

Q991 Richard Ottaway: You believe that time will prove you right on that one?

Mr Campbell: I know that we are right in relation to that 45-minute point. It is completely and totally untrue, and I do not use this word –

Q992 Richard Ottaway: I am talking about the substance.

Mr Campbell: It is actually a lie

....

Q1007 Mr Pope: Thank you, Chairman. Mr Campbell, the charges against you really are of the gravest nature: that you exaggerated the evidence to persuade a reluctant Parliament to vote for a war which was not popular. We heard in evidence from Mr Gilligan of the BBC last week and he alleged that you transformed the original September dossier, and if I can just quote what he said in evidence, my "source's claim was that the dossier had been transformed in the week before it was published and I asked " – that is Gilligan – "'So how did this transformation happen?', and the answer was a single word, which was 'Campbell'". That is an incredibly damaging allegation. Could you comment on its veracity?

Mr Campbell: As I explained earlier, the story that I "sexed-up" the dossier is untrue: the story that I "put pressure on the intelligence agencies" is untrue: the story that we somehow made more of the 45 minute command and control point than the intelligence agencies thought was suitable is untrue: and what is even more extraordinary about this whole episode is that, within an hour of the story first being broadcast, it was denied, emphatically: it then continued. We were in Kuwait at the time – the Prime Minister was about to get a helicopter to Basra – it was denied: the story kept being repeated: the following day the BBC returned to it and it was denied – by now we were in Poland and I remember being called out of a breakfast with the Prime Minister and the Polish Prime Minister because I had asked to speak to John Scarlett, the Chairman of the Joint Intelligence Committee, just to absolutely double/triple check that there was nothing in this idea that the intelligence agencies were somehow unhappy with the way that we behaved during the thing and that there was no truth at all that anybody at the political level put pressure on the 45 minute point and John said, "Absolutely. It is complete and total nonsense and you can say that with my authority". Then the Prime Minister had to come out of the breakfast with the Polish Prime Minister; he was about to do a press conference about the Polish EU referendum campaign and, of course, the British media are all asking about this lie, which is what it was.

Q1008 Mr Pope: On the 45 minutes, what you have refuted up until now is the allegation that you inserted the 45 minute claim into the dossier and I am trying to make a different point which is that there is an allegation not that you inserted it but you gave it undue prominence; that this was a background piece of information; it was based on a single piece of uncorroborated intelligence advice and yet it was given undue prominence. It is mentioned in the foreword by the Prime Minister and it is mentioned three other times throughout the document and it is a chilling allegation – that our troops in Cyprus or our troops perhaps if they went into Iraq could face a 45 minute threat of the deployment of a chemical attack?

Mr Campbell: Well, it is true that when the BBC representative came to the Committee last week he claimed that all he had ever alleged was that we had "given it undue prominence". I am afraid that is not true. What he said last week was not true. It was a complete backtrack on what he had broadcast and written about in the *Mail on Sunday, The Spectator* and elsewhere. Now the reason why I feel so strongly that we, the government, from the Prime Minister down deserve an apology about this story is it has been made absolutely clear not just by me – you can put me to one side and I am well aware of the fact that I am defined in a certain way by large parts of the media, but when you put in the Prime Minister, the Foreign Secretary, the Chairman of the Joint Intelligence Committee, the Head of the Secret Intelligence Service, the Government Security and Intelligence Co-ordinator all saying emphatically "This story is not true" and the BBC defence correspondent on the basis of a single anonymous source continues to say that it is true, then I think something has gone very wrong with BBC journalism.

Q1009 Mr Pope: Are you saying that he lied not just to the Committee but on the radio? I have the transcript of the Today programme of 4 June. He said, "The reason why this story has run so as long" – and this is a direct quote – "is nobody has actually ever denied the central charge made by my source".

Mr Campbell: The denial was made within an hour of the lie being told on the radio. Now, I am not suggesting that he has not had somebody possibly say something to him but whatever he has been told is not true, and I think in relation to the briefing paper, when that mistake was discovered, we put our hands up and said "There is a mistake here" and we found out where it happened and we dealt with it, and I would compare and contrast with an organisation which has broadcast something – not just once but hundreds of times since – that is a lie.

....

Q1101 Mr Maples: … What I put to you is that what will probably happen is that it is perfectly possible you, and Andrew Gilligan, actually told the truth and what happened here was that everybody slightly exaggerated their position.

Mr Campbell: I did not. I did not have a position. This is the Joint Intelligence Committee. Andrew Gilligan's allegations were about the Joint Intelligence Committee paper, not the other one.

Q1102 Mr Maples: He said that you sought to change it –

Mr Campbell: No, he said, I sexed it up and I made changes against the wishes of the agencies. That is a lie.

Q1103 Mr Maples: I am suggesting to you it is possible that you sought changes to this document which did not involve countermanding intelligence. After all, your craft is presentation, that is what you are extremely good at, and it would be almost unbelievable if you did not have some input into how this document was presented.

Mr Campbell: As I have said many times before, there is a legitimate place in the political process for dealing with issues of presentation and communication now we have a 24-hour media, round the world, round the clock. He did not say that. He said that I abused British Intelligence. He went further and said it was done against the wishes of the intelligence agencies; not true. I think that is a pretty serious allegation which is why I am very, very grateful for the opportunity to rebut it.

265. In his evidence to the FAC Mr Campbell also attacked the BBC by alleging that there was an anti-war agenda in large parts of the BBC.

Q1104 Mr Maples: The same allegation has apparently been made – I do not know whether you have seen it – in yesterday's *New York Times.* It says, 'A top State Department expert on chemical and biological weapons told Congressional Committees in closed oral hearings last week that he had been pressed to tailor his analysis on Iraq and other matters to conform with the Bush Administration's views', several Congressional officials said today. You may say, "Here is some rogue agent in the State Department saying this to a rogue journalist", but it is interesting, is it not, how this allegation crops up here and now it has cropped up in Washington as well.

Mr Campbell: Can I explain why I think the allegation crops up. Again, I think this goes to the heart of the way some of these issues are covered by the media. I do not think we should make any bones about this. There are large parts of the media which have an agenda on the issue of Iraq. For most of those parts of the media their agenda is open, it is avowed. If you bought the *Daily Mirror* in the run-up to the conflict, you knew that paper was against our position. If you bought *The Sun*, you knew that paper was passionately supportive of our position on dealing with Saddam. I would identify three stages in this. In the run-up to conflict there was an agenda in large parts of the BBC – and I think the BBC is different from the rest of the media and should be viewed as different from the rest of the media because it is a different organisation in terms of its reputation, in terms of its global reach and all the rest of it – and there was a disproportionate focus upon, if you like, the dissent, the opposition, to our position. I think that in the conflict itself the prism that many were creating within the BBC was, one, it is all going wrong, and I can give you an example –

Q1105 Mr Maples: Well, I think probably many of us would agree with that.

Mr Campbell: And now what is happening now, the third, the conflict not having led to the Middle East going up in flames, not having led to us getting bogged down for months and months and months, these same people now have to find a different rationale. Their rationale is that the Prime Minister led the country into war on a false basis, that is what this is about.

266. On 26 June Mr Campbell wrote to Mr Greg Dyke, the Director General of the BBC and to Mr Sambrook, the Director of News at the BBC about Mr Gilligan's broadcasts on 29 May. Mr Sambrook replied to Mr Campbell on 27 June and on 27 June, after receiving Mr Sambrook's reply, Mr Campbell issued a statement to the press. The correspondence between the Government and the BBC from 29 May to 27 June, together with Mr Campbell's press statement of 27 June is set out at appendix 14.

267. On 27 June at 7.10pm Mr Campbell appeared on the Channel 4 television news programme when he took part in a heated interview with Mr Jon Snow, the presenter of the programme. The interview commenced as follows:

> **Jon Snow:** Well now we are joined by Alastair Campbell, a rare moment, thank you for, for coming in. This row between you and the BBC, I mean, many will see it as a diversionary tactic to prevent people actually seeing the real issue here which is that MPs are not getting to the root of whether in fact the intelligence we were provided with was the real intelligence provided by the intelligence services.

> **Alastair Campbell:** Well if people wish to see it as a diversionary tactic they may. The media are constantly telling people never to take things at face value. This isn't a row between me and the BBC this is an attempt by the Government to get the BBC to admit that a fundamental attack upon the integrity of the Government, the Prime Minister, the intelligence agencies, let alone people, the, sort of, evil spin doctors in the dark who do their dirty works in the minds of a lot of journalists, let them just accept for once they have got it wrong. The allegation, let's just understand what this allegation amounted to, and these weasel words in Richard Sambrook's letters, letter today (indistinct) says to me we didn't make the allegation we reported a source making the allegation. What does that say about journalism? You've been a journalism for decades, I was a journalist for quite a long time, I respect a huge number of journalists including many at the BBC...

> **JS:** But I have to say

> **AC:** ... but they're now saying I, you can say anything you want on the television because somebody said it to you, doesn't matter if it's true...

> **JS:** ... yes...

> **AC:** doesn't matter if you check it, doesn't matter if it's corroborated....

> **JS:** ... however the BBC's ...

> **AC:** ... you can say it.

> **JS:**... the BBC's riposte to you is very reasoned. It is set in the context of all the other information which was in the public domain, it's entirely consistent with that information. It credits the Guardian, the Observer, the Independent, the Times, I mean, most of Fleet Street had similar accounts of what intelligence sources were telling them. The BBC doesn't seem to be out of step with anybody else.

> **AC:** The BBC in their letter to me, and it's fascinating, they have post facto justification of a story by citing sources in newspapers which wrote stories subsequent to their, to the story that they had done. Some of those stories I know for a fact are incorrect. One of them, there's no point going through all the detail I think the public are probably bored rigid with this already, one of those stories I know for a fact is wrong and I've addressed in evidence to the select committee.

JS: I think the public is more likely to be concerned at the extraordinarily intemperate language which is coming out on behalf of the Prime Minister in your name. 'The story was a lie, it is a lie …

AC: Correct.

The full transcript of the interview is set out in appendix 15.

268. On 29 June Mr Campbell wrote to Mr Sambrook. In addition to the correspondence between Mr Campbell and Mr Sambrook correspondence took place between Mr Ben Bradshaw MP, who wrote on behalf of the Government, Mr Hoon and the BBC from 28 June until 10 July in relation to Mr Gilligan's broadcasts on the Today programme on 29 May. This correspondence is set out in appendix 16.

269. On 1 July Mr Gavyn Davies sent the following e-mail to the Governors of the BBC:

> I am sure we have all had a trying weekend, reading the press and listening to broadcasts on the Campbell/BBC row. The press commentary over the weekend has not been uniformly good for the BBC position, but it has certainly been very bad from the government point of view, as was the opinion poll data in the News of the World today. My hunch is that the government would now like the row to go away, and this has been reinforced by the fact that Alastair Campbell has said that he will return to "business as usual", at least until he sees the report of the Foreign Affairs Committee on Monday week. It is clear that some Labour MPs feel that Campbell did himself and the government damage by his performance on Channel 4 news on Friday, and they now want to calm things down.
>
> Having said that, I think it is unknowable whether the FAC will rule in the BBC's favour on the 45 minute claim in the September dossier. They might do so, but it is also possible that they will say that the truth is confused, since early drafts within the intelligence community did not include the 45 minute claim, while later ones did. Or they may conceivably just conclude that the first draft which was seen by Mr Campbell did indeed include the 45 minute claim, as he has always argued. This latter form of judgment would be problematic, especially if Campbell then files a formal complaint which goes for adjudication either to the Governors or the BSC.
>
> Some may therefore argue that there could be advantage for the BBC in reaching a settlement with No 10 which both sides can live with, perhaps in advance of, or shortly after, the publication of the FAC report. However, I remain firmly of the view that, in a big picture sense, it is absolutely critical for the BBC to emerge from this row without being seen to buckle in the face of government pressure. If the BBC allows itself to be bullied by this sort of behaviour from No 10, I believe that this could fatally damage the trust which the public places in us. Furthermore, I think we should remember that the main historic role of the Governors has been to shield the BBC from this sort of attempt to exert political muscle over our news output. This, it seems to me, really is a moment for the Governors to stand up and be counted. So, I hope you will agree that, whatever emerges about the precise details of the 45 minute claim, we must not give any ground which threatens the fundamental independence of our news output, or suggests that the Governors have buckled to government pressure.
>
> My last thought is this. It may never be definitively proven whether the details of the claim made by Andrew Gilligan's source were 100% accurate or not. And of course I recognise that the Producers' Guidelines must been seen to be upheld. But I do not believe that the BBC has lied to the public, or that it has accused the Prime Minister of lying, or that it has been wrong to place a great deal of scrutiny on the validity of the government's intelligence dossiers. Such have been the proven failings in these dossiers, I wonder whether the Today programme could conceivably have suppressed the Gilligan story, coming as it did from a credible and senior source. Would suppression of the views of such an important source have been a valid thing to do in such circumstances?
>
> I put this only as a question, not least because we may have to adjudicate on the matter at a later date. But I feel very comfortable that the BBC did not knowingly mislead the public; and equally comfortable that our news department was pursuing a matter which it was wholly in the public interest to pursue.

Please either ring me or send me a quick e-mail if you would like to register any views. I feel in need of some guidance about your broad feelings, without of course wishing to hold anyone to a definitive position in advance of any subsequent judgments we may need to make.

With best wishes

The special meeting of the Governors of the BBC on 6 July 2003

270. On 4 July Mr Gavyn Davies called a special meeting of the Governors of the BBC for 6.30pm on Sunday 6 July and sent them the following e-mail:

> As you know I have decided to call a Governors' meeting for 6.30pm on Sunday 6th July in Room 2364, Broadcasting House to discuss the Campbell affair. I do not think that we can wait until the next monthly Governors' meeting to discuss this subject, especially in view of the fact that the publication of the Annual Report will precede the July Governors' meeting, and we need an agreed line to take in public before then.
>
> This is an unusually important moment in our careers as Governors. I am pleased that you have all made yourselves available for this meeting – two of you by phone. We shall be joined by Greg, Richard Sambrook, Caroline Thomson and Stephen Whittle. Sally Osman, Head of Communications, will also be available once we are in a position to agree a statement and to discuss communications. Simon has compiled a pack of background papers which will be issued to you later today.
>
> I do not think that we should seek to take a view during this meeting on whether the Gilligan story was accurate. This is not a question on which we need to take responsibility. Instead, I think we should concentrate on the following three questions:
>
> 1. Mr Campbell has made allegations of systemic bias in the BBC's coverage of the war. Should we reiterate our already-published view that these criticisms are invalid, and are therefore rejected by the Board?
>
> 2. Mr Campbell has also alleged that the Today programme breached the BBC's producers' guidelines. I believe that we should investigate this allegation, which has been repeatedly made in public, without waiting for an official complaint from Mr Campbell. We can do this on Sunday. We need to consider whether to publish our verdict following the meeting.
>
> 3. We should also consider whether to initiate investigations into any other matters of concern. These could include: the rules under which BBC journalists are allowed to publish newspaper articles under their names; the nature of the producers' guidelines on the use of single-source, and anonymous-source material; and the training of BBC journalists, especially in matters relating to regulation, accuracy and impartiality. If we do decide to initiate any such investigations, we may or may not wish to publish that decision now.
>
> I am aware that the Foreign Affairs Committee will be reporting on Monday morning, but I do not think we need to wait for that report, since I hope that we are not going to try to give a verdict of our own on the accuracy of the Gilligan story. In addition, I think that the BBC may be under pressure on Monday, and I think that the Governors should be visible during this time. Whatever we decide at our meeting, we should not be absent from the debate next week.
>
> I look forward to seeing you on Sunday.
>
> With best wishes

271. Prior to the special meeting of the Governors of the BBC on the evening of 6 July Mr Campbell wrote on the 5 July to Mr Gavyn Davies and to all the other Governors the following letter:

> In advance of your meeting to discuss the allegations that were made against the Government on the Today programme on May 29, and subsequent events, I thought it would be helpful to send you the enclosed.
>
> It sets out, as fully as possible, how the Government has sought to deal with this issue since the allegations were first broadcast. I have included all the correspondence between myself and the

BBC, and between colleagues in Government and the BBC. You will see from this that these serious allegations were not put to us in advance. You will see the swift denial, made with the backing of the Chairman of the Joint Intelligence Committee, which had little or no effect upon subsequent reporting. You will see also that we did strive to resolve this privately. You will also see, from the exchanges the BBC has had both in correspondence and on air with Geoff Hoon and Ben Bradshaw, that we strongly dispute the BBC claims that the allegations were put to us before broadcast.

I am assuming that you will have been provided with all the relevant transcripts of evidence through the Foreign Affairs Committee. You will find in this file documentation referred to in the paragraph above and a transcript of the Thursday May 29 broadcast. I have also attached the text of Mr Gilligan's Mail on Sunday article of Sunday 1 June.

I am sorry to have sent you so much material, but I think it important, particularly in light of the way recent BBC reporting following Mr Gilligan's evidence to the FAC has sought to redefine the allegations, that you have all this material to hand.

I note from press cuttings that the BBC views my complaint as an attack upon the independence of the BBC. I want to assure you that is not the case. I respect the BBC's independence. I believe the BBC is one of the country's greatest assets and I have long been an admirer of its ethos, much of its journalism and many of its journalists.

It is also being said that I intend to use this issue as the basis of a broader attack upon the BBC. Let me assure you that whatever concerns we have expressed about coverage of Iraq, or about what we see as the agenda-driven journalism of some journalists and some parts of the BBC, they are not the issue here.

At issue here is one specific set of allegations, profoundly damaging to the Prime Minister, the Government and our Intelligence Agencies, which we know to be false and which we have sought, first privately and then publicly, to have corrected. It is about one story, the procedures that were or were not followed, pre and post broadcast, and the difficulties we have had in seeking redress for the broadcast of such a serious and false allegation, which has since been repeated, because of the BBC's reach and deserved reputation, in hundreds of media outlets in dozens of countries around the world – some examples of which are attached.

I hope this is helpful. I do not intend to inform the press that we have sent this to you.

272. The Governors met on the evening of 6 July and the minutes of the meeting were as follows:

BOARD OF GOVERNORS

MINUTES OF AN EXTRAORDINARY MEETING

HELD IN PRVIATE SESSION

Sunday 6 July 2003, 6.30pm to 8.50pm

in Room 2364 Broadcasting House

PRESENT:

Gavyn Davies – Chairman

Richard Ryder – Vice-Chairman

Ruth Deech

Dermot Gleeson

Sarah Hogg (by phone)

Merfyn Jones

Fabian Monds

Pauline Neville-Jones

Angela Sarkis

Robert Smith (by phone)

Ranjit Sondhi

Simon Milner – The Secretary

Tina Stowell – Head of Business Administration

APOLOGIES

There were no apologies.

Gavyn Davies opened this Extraordinary Meeting of the Board by thanking Governors for attending on a Sunday evening. He noted that no member of management, including the Director-General, was present.

1. OVERVIEW AND CONTEXT

Gavyn Davies outlined the background to the meeting. The BBC had been criticised by Alastair Campbell, some members of the Government – and that morning by the Prime Minister in a newspaper interview – for reporting an allegation made by an intelligence source that the September 2002 Intelligence Dossier had been "sexed-up" to strengthen the Government's case for war in Iraq.

The Foreign Affairs Select Committee of the House of Commons (FAC) had conducted an inquiry into the Government's case for war in Iraq and – amongst other witnesses – Andrew Gilligan, the BBC's Defence Correspondent had given evidence about his report of 29 May 2003 on Radio 4's *Today* covering an Intelligence source's allegation that "45 mins to deploy weapons of mass destruction" had been inserted into an Intelligence Report against the wishes of the Intelligence Services. Alastair Campbell had rejected this story in the strongest terms, calling on the BBC to apologise for making untrue allegations against him, the Prime Minister and the Government in general. Since then the row between the BBC and Alastair Campbell had escalated, with Mr Campbell criticising the BBC's coverage of the war more generally as biased against the Government. The following morning, the FAC was scheduled to publish its conclusions.

Gavyn Davies said that, following notification to Governors on Friday 4 July the meeting had become public. Therefore, a public statement following the meeting on conclusions reached was expected. He believed this was right, as any attempt not to provide a statement would be interpreted as the Governors being indecisive and perhaps in disagreement with management. That said, the Board was operating independently of management and it was possible to demonstrate this without any sign that Governors were 'caving in' to either BBC management or the Government.

Prior to the meeting, the Secretary had circulated to Governors:

- The transcript of the relevant sections of *Today* on 29 May 2003

- Andrew Gilligan's *Mail on Sunday* article of 1 June 2003

- The Official Report of Andrew Gilligan's evidence to the Foreign Affairs Select Committee of 19 June

- The Official Report of Alastair Campbell's evidence to the Foreign Affairs Select Committee of 25 June

- Alastair Campbell's letter of 26 June to Richard Sambrook (released to the media)

- Richard Sambrook's reply of 27 June (released to the media)

- An open letter from Alastair Campbell of 29 June in response

- Richard Sambrook's letter to the Chairman of the Foreign Affairs Select Committee of 30 June (not published)

- A further letter from Richard Sambrook to the Chairman of the Foreign Affairs Select Committee of 4 July (not published).

In addition, Alastair Campbell had written personally to each Governor on Saturday 5 July under cover of similar material, plus copies of private correspondence between him and other Government representatives and Ministers with Richard Sambrook and other BBC News senior managers.

Gavyn Davies asked the Board to consider the following issues before management were invited to join the meeting and be questioned by Governors:

- The BBC's coverage of the war in Iraq in general terms. Gavyn Davies did not believe the Board should reopen this issue as it had stated publicly twice before that it considered the BBC's coverage to be impartial. Furthermore, evidence existed through public opinion polls and a study by Cardiff University that the BBC's coverage was not perceived to be biased. If Governors remained convinced of their previously published view, should they repeat it?

- Had Andrew Gilligan's report on *Today* breached the BBC's Producers' Guidelines? And in particular, was the BBC wrong not to inform Number 10 of the story in advance of broadcast?

- Should Governors comment on the Prime Minister's comments about the BBC's story being an attack on his personal integrity? Gavyn Davies hoped it would be possible to include something in the statement that would set the record straight and provide an olive branch in this respect.

- Whether an investigation into any other matters of concern should be instigated. For example, the rules under which BBC journalists were allowed to publish newspaper articles; the nature of the Producers' Guidelines on the use of single-source and anonymous-source material; and the training of BBC journalists, especially in matters relating to regulation, accuracy and impartiality.

Gavyn Davies confirmed that the Board's public statement would not necessarily comment on all issues discussed at the meeting. During discussion, the following points were made:

a. Coverage of the War in Iraq

- Most Governors did not support reopening their assessment the BBC's coverage of war in Iraq, remaining convinced that it was impartial.

- There was a suggestion that Governors should not offer immediate support to the management, however. Although there was no reason to doubt the BBC's coverage of the war, the Board could request the Director-General to undertake a review with external experts. This would demonstrate that the BBC was not arrogant and avoid accusations of a whitewash by the Governors; providing an opportunity to raise questions with management in light of the review's conclusions. Indeed, the report by Cardiff University into broadcast coverage of the war only served to reassure the BBC that an external review was not something to worry about.

Gavyn Davies noted the intention of such a review was to verify Governors' judgment, rather than reopen the debate. But the majority of the Board did not support this proposal. However, in line with the new arrangements for monitoring impartiality, the Board could, for example, request that coverage of the war in Iraq be the next subject for external review by experts when the next quarterly report on impartiality came forward to the Board in October. However, this should not be referred to publicly at this time.

b. Producers' Guidelines

- It was clear that the Board was being asked to consider whether it was right to broadcast the allegation as an allegation and not decide whether that allegation was true.

- Governors' initial view was that the Producers' Guidelines on single sources were clear and there was sufficient evidence that due consideration had been applied before the report was broadcast.

- Some Governors were less sure about whether the BBC had acted in line with the Guidelines in relation to consulting Number 10 prior to and following broadcast of the story. Indeed, there was a view that the BBC had been naïve to broadcast this allegation without expecting a powerful reaction and therefore should have been more careful in his consultations with Government.

- On the Guidelines more generally, the Board might consider commenting publicly that these were being re-examined in light of this episode, not least because the Intelligence Services now operated in a more open fashion. Also, there had been management activity since the broadcast that required examination. For example, careful language had not been applied by Andrew Gilligan throughout.

- Gavyn Davies was absolutely firm that the Board should not seek to widen the debate to the Producer Guidelines more generally. The Board was being asked at this meeting to determine whether the Guidelines as currently published had been upheld. Alastair Campbell had criticised the BBC's coverage of the war and this must be refuted. Likewise, if the Board agreed, it should make clear why it believed the BBC was right to broadcast Andrew Gilligan's report. He noted that the Governors' Programme Complaints Committee was a vehicle for handling complaints of this nature, but it was perfectly proper and in the public interest for the Board as a whole to consider this matter. In any case, a formal complaint had not been received about the Andrew Gilligan report.

- If there was a convincing argument that the BBC should back down from its confrontation with the Government then it should do so. However, there was none, so Governors should support the BBC's journalists unless it was felt that proper procedures had not been followed.

- The Board's discussion should be considered in the context of what the FAC's report might conclude. It would probably criticise the Government about the February "dodgy dossier" and to some extent also the September dossier. But it was likely also to criticise the BBC for its reporting thereof.

c. Newspaper articles by BBC journalists

- There was some support for commenting more generally on proposals to tighten the guidelines in relation to BBC journalists writing newspaper articles and creating, rather than reporting the news.

Summarising this part of the discussion, Gavyn Davies said the Board remained of the view that the BBC's coverage of war in Iraq was impartial. Most Governors were somewhat concerned about *Today's* contacts with Number 10 and the need to establish if proper procedures had been followed. On the other hand, some were not convinced that *Today* was required to contact Number 10. There was a lack of clarity on whether this was appropriate or not.

The Board of Governors was then joined by the following:

Greg Dyke   Director- General

Richard Sambrook   Director, News

Caroline Thomson   Director, Policy & Legal

Mark Damazer   Deputy Director, News

Stephen Whittle   Controller, Editorial Policy

Gavyn Davies welcomed the senior managers and said that the mood amongst Governors was supportive and the Board had agreed there was no need to reopen the question of whether the BBC's reporting of the war in Iraq was biased. Governors wished to ask management questions about the following issues relating to or arising from the Andrew Gilligan report on the *Today Programme:*

- If the Producers' Guidelines were upheld

- If sufficient warning was given to Number 10 in advance of the broadcast

- What opportunities were available to the Government to deny the story

- If the rules relating to BBC journalists writing newspaper articles should be re-examined

2. PRODUCERS' GUIDELINES

Richard Sambrook said the Guidelines related to three issues in this case:

- Anonymity: where he believed no action taken demonstrated non-compliance.

- Single-sourcing: where the Guidelines requested "reluctance". The context of management's decision to go ahead with the story based on a single source was made clear in Richard Sambrook's open letter to Alastair Campbell.

- Fairness: whether sufficient warning was provided to Government about the story and if due prominence was afforded to their denials.

On the latter, there was a separate story running on *Today* on 29 May about cluster bombs and the editorial team had asked Adam Ingrams' office (a Defence Minister) if his interview could be extended to include weapons of mass destruction (WMD) at around 5.30pm the previous day. Whilst the programme team had been clear in recalling what it said to the Minister's office, it was not clear from the notes taken how much detail was provided on the WMD story. The normal practice in these circumstances was for ministers' offices to confer with other Government departments to seek their agreement of a minister commenting on a subject outside their area of responsibility.

The Board noted that inadequate note-taking was a common problem amongst programme-makers and this sometimes made it difficult for the GPCC to adjudicate on complaints.

a. Single Source

On the use of a single source, Stephen Whittle said from his inquiries he was confident that the appropriate editorial processes had been followed robustly before the item was broadcast. He confirmed he did not know the identity of the source, but the editor of the programme was informed as was the Head of Radio News and both were convinced that the source was credible and reliable. Since the item was broadcast, Richard Sambrook had been informed of the source's identity and Greg Dyke had been told what position the source held.

In response to questions, Richard Sambrook said it was not known if the source used by Susan Watts for a similar item on *Newsnight* was the same as that used by Andrew Gilligan. If it was the same – as it appeared to be – this confirmed the accuracy of Andrew Gilligan's reporting of the source. If it was a different source, this served to reinforce the story further.

On anonymity of sources, Stephen Whittle said the Guidelines were more relevant to contributors who provided themselves on air but required protection because the allegations they were making could put them in danger. Mark Damazer noted a comment that the Guidelines on anonymity did not appear to apply in this case. He said it was very difficult to have a guideline that applied to off-the-record sources as the key judgment in deciding whether to use them was consideration of the context of the information they were providing. Greg Dyke added that in this case, it was already public that the Government had wrongly presented evidence as official intelligence when it was in fact material retrieved from the internet (known as the "dodgy dossier").

Governors responded that this line of defence was not convincing. The context in this case created an obligation on the BBC to report, but was not the justification for it. The key argument was the judgment of senior editorial staff that the source was credible and on that basis the Board was content that management had acted appropriately.

Mark Damazer said that in judging the credibility of a source, the following factors were considered:

- their relationship to the journalist; ie how well known they were

- whether information provided previously had been proven to be correct

- the plausibility of the information they were providing.

In this case, the source met all these criteria and therefore the context of the "dodgy dossier" only added weight to the decision to use the information.

Concluding this part of the discussion, Gavyn Davies said the Board was content that the BBC had acted appropriately in reporting the information provided by a single source.

b. Contacts with the Government

Stephen Whittle said achieving clarity on the contacts between the *Today* team and Government departments on this occasion was difficult because a full note had not been kept. He ran through the sequence of contacts established from his inquiries. In addition to the information already provided by Richard Sambrook about requests for an interview with Adam Ingram, he reported that Andrew Gilligan spoke to a MOD press officer (mobile-to-mobile) at around 6.30pm to inform them that the interview would be extended to include WMD. The MOD's account of this contact was different, claiming that Andrew Gilligan mentioned only the cluster bomb story and only upon being asked said there was another issue but this was not a matter for the MOD. Andrew Gilligan agrees he said something to indicate that the WMD issue was not principally a MOD story, but claims that he only spoke about WMD during the conversation and not cluster bombs. It was possible that he might have said something like: "we've asked for an interview on cluster bombs, but we also want to talk about WMD".

Stephen Whittle said it was unlikely that Andrew Gilligan would have discussed the cluster bomb story beyond a passing reference as it was not something he was working on and therefore something he knew nothing about it.

Following a further exchange between another member of the programme team and the MOD, the department confirmed that Adam Ingram would appear the following morning and be prepared to talk about both issues (having consulted the FCO about cluster bombs). The night editor spoke further to the MOD at around 10.30pm and sought confirmation that Adam Ingram would take questions on WMD in addition to cluster bombs. He concurs with the MOD's recollection that no detail was provided on the WMD issue, but the night editor assumed that the detail had already been covered in earlier conversations.

Stephen Whittle said the BBC's weakness in this area was the lack of solid and reliable notes about what was said to the MOD about the allegations made by Andrew Gilligan's source. At that time, the *Today Programme* was not planning to run the WMD story as a scoop, but more as a "chatter in the air" issue. The programme's running order showed it was not the lead item and this might explain why the notes kept were not as contemporaneous and complete as they might have been.

In response to questions, he confirmed that the Gilligan story was broadcast first at 6.05am and Number 10's response at 7.40am. Caroline Thomson said a potential difficulty for the BBC was not contacting Number 10 in advance to provide an opportunity for them to deny the story in advance of broadcast.

In response to further questions, Stephen Whittle said that Producers' Guidelines were not explicit about advance notification. The Guidelines required programme-makers to provide an opportunity to those named to respond.

During discussion, Governors made the following points:

- The culture of *Today* had become one of creating rather than reporting news. It had moved in line with tabloid and Sunday newspaper journalism where contacting people who might deny a story were avoided. This should be examined in due course to determine if the BBC should operate in this fashion. That said this general view did not diminish the opinion that the BBC was right to broadcast the story.

- There was a view expressed that *Today* had been naïve about the potential power of this story, but this was not widely shared. Furthermore, it was not surprising that the BBC had become wiser after the event to the importance of the story as other events had increased its significance.

- That said some Governors did believe that Number 10 should have been contacted prior to broadcast as it would have placed the BBC in a much stronger position to defend its decision. On the other hand, caution was expressed in creating a situation where any report that might upset Number 10 required the BBC to contact the Prime Minister's office in advance.

Gavyn Davies concluded this part of the discussion saying that the majority view of the board was that the allegations should have been put to Number 10 in advance of the broadcast. However, he noted the strong concerns expressed by some Governors about including this in the statement that would follow this meeting and said it would not be included in strong terms.

Broadcast of denials

Richard Sambrook said BBC News disputed the claim that it had alleged the "45 minutes" had been inserted against the wishes of the Chairman of the JIC and Intelligence Chiefs. The source had said "against our wishes" and this had not been extrapolated to any individual. As to denials of the story, the Prime Minister, John Reid, Jack Straw and Baroness Amos were all provided the opportunity on air over the following days. But each time this occurred, it was necessary to repeat the allegations for them to deny.

Following an account from Mark Damazer about how the "45 minute claim" had been disputed by the Government since the broadcast, and a discussion by Governors about the accuracy of the report, Gavyn Davies reminded the Board that it was not a matter for them. He noted that Pauline Neville-Jones did not believe the Intelligence denials have been given due prominence and her criticisms of BBC News for the balance of its reporting in this particular area. In response, Richard Sambrook said he would undertake a detailed review of the JIC denials that had been broadcast. Gavyn Davies said however that the majority of the Board had not expressed doubt about the coverage of Intelligence denials and therefore the review that Richard Sambrook had promised would not be made public. Indeed, doing so would indicate a "climb-down" by the BBC.

In response to questions about whether management was comfortable that the required high standard of reporting had been retained throughout *Today* on 29 May, Richard Sambrook said that Andrew Gilligan had been very clear about his report being based on a single source. John Humphreys had, however, used some phrases that were infelicitous, but Andrew Gilligan had but [sic: put] him back on track during their exchanges.

Gavyn Davies reminded the Board that a formal complaint had not been received about *Today*, even though Richard Sambrook had made sure Alastair Campbell was aware of the route he could follow should he wish to do so.

Concluding this part of the discussion, Gavyn Davies said the Board agreed that the Producers' Guidelines had been upheld. The majority view of the Board was that the allegations should have been put to Number 10 in advance of broadcast. However, in light of some concern expressed by Governors about including this in the statement, he would ensure the wording in relation to this aspect was carefully drafted to avoid any indication that this was a requirement for any story that might offend Number 10 in the future. But he believed it important to "nod in the direction" of Number 10 that the notes kept by the programme-makers on contacts with the Government were inadequate for the Board to confirm that every effort had been made to inform the Government appropriately. Finally, the majority view of the Board was that the Government had received sufficient opportunities to deny the story.

3. RULES PERMITTING BBC JOURNALISTS TO WRITE NEWSPAPER ARTICLES

Gavyn Davies asked the Board to consider whether it should request a review of the rules that currently permit BBC journalists to write newspaper articles.

In response to questions about whether Andrew Gilligan's *Mail on Sunday* article, published on 1 June, had been vetted in accordance with the rules, Richard Sambrook said it had not. Originally, he had been informed that Kevin Marsh (Editor of Today) had vetted the article and this would have been in line with procedures. However, more lately, it had transpired this had not occurred. Richard Sambrook added that he was on record as saying the rules associated with writing newspaper articles would be reviewed.

Greg Dyke said he was against allowing BBC journalists to write newspaper articles, but it was difficult to prevent in many circumstances because of the freelance contracts most journalists concerned had with the BBC. In any case, he believed it was an issue to be examined at a later date and separately to that currently before the Board. Gavyn Davies disagreed, saying it was relevant because Andrew Gilligan had gone further in the *Mail on Sunday* in reporting his source's allegations.

Other Governors agreed, saying it was an important issue and the principle of it required examination. Richard Sambrook's public commitment was helpful, but it was important that the Governors themselves were seen to be examining the issue as it was a matter that concerned the Board.

Gavyn Davies agreed and said the statement would say that the Board would look again at the rules that permitted this following the study already promised by the Director of News.

The meeting was suspended at around 8.10pm whilst Gavyn Davies prepared a statement for publication.

273. After the Governor's meeting Mr Davies issued the statement set out in paragraph 56. On 7 July Mr Davies sent the following e-mail to the Governors:

> I attach a clean copy of the Statement which I issued on the Board's behalf last night.

> I was aware during the meeting that I may have been rushing the discussion more than usual, because there was a hard deadline around 9pm. If we had missed this deadline, the Governors' conclusions would have missed the morning papers completely, and would then have been swamped by the news about the FAC report on Monday. This explains why it was so important to get the statement agreed quickly in our final meeting. (Thanks to Pauline's eagle eye, we narrowly avoided the cardinal error of writing the mistaken words "allegations made by Andrew Gilligan" in the final draft; in the end, it correctly said "allegations reported by Andrew Gilligan".)

> Chairing the meeting, I was very impressed by the seriousness and toughness displayed by the Governors. My view is that we demonstrated that the Board of Governors is not a body which can be easily bullied, either by politicians or the management. I am sure that we will benefit from demonstrating this in the long run, even if we get some of the familiar flak in the immediate future.

> There were two traps which we could have fallen into on Sunday - caving in to No 10, or caving in to the executive. I strongly believe that we did neither.

> I asked someone who has worked for the BSC how other regulators would have reacted to having to rule on the Campbell allegations, if Ofcom were ever to get responsibility for BBC impartiality. He said simply: "In my experience, they would run a mile."

> As I write this e-mail, the FAC report has just been published. Given that the key conclusion, "clearing" Alastair Campbell survived only on the casting vote of the chair, and much of the rest of the report was highly critical of Mr Campbell's role, it looks as though the BBC has emerged

intact from the report, though some will say that it is still very messy. I hope, perhaps optimistically, that this may give us a chance to move on to other matters.

Alastair Campbell and Jack Straw have both now withdrawn their general claims that the BBC was systemically biased during the war. This is a major step forward, and a victory for the Governors, since this would not have happened without our intervention. It also suggests there may be a willingness to de-escalate the overall row with the BBC. But the government is still adamant that the Gilligan report, in its specific allegation, was plain wrong, and have – very sensibly from their point of view – noted that the Governors did not substantiate the accuracy of this report. Richard Sambrook has said in public that the government and BBC News may have to "agree to disagree" on this. Since there is nothing much more to be said on this until the intelligence committee reports in September, the row may begin to move off the front pages.

Thank you once again for the solidity displayed yesterday.

The gravity of the allegation reported in the Today programme

274. Before considering the issues relating to the BBC set out in paragraph 260 it is also appropriate to comment again on the distinction (referred to in paragraph 9) between an allegation that the Government probably knew at the time of publication that intelligence contained in the dossier was wrong or questionable and an allegation that intelligence contained in the dossier, which the Government believed to be reliable, was in reality unreliable. Although to some extent the latter allegation is implicit in the former allegation and future discoveries or the absence of discoveries in Iraq may show the latter allegation to be correct (an issue which does not come within my terms of reference and on which I express no opinion), the former allegation is a much graver one and is an attack on the integrity of the Government itself, and Mr Gilligan's broadcasts on 29 May reported this express allegation. I consider that the view of Sir David Manning (in the summer of 2003 Foreign Policy Adviser to the Prime Minister and Head of the Overseas and Defence Secretariat in the Cabinet Office) as to the gravity of this allegation was fully justified. He said:

[18 August, page 178, line 19]

A. I should say there was strong feeling about the accusations that had been made by Andrew Gilligan.

Q. Can you perhaps tell us about your feelings in that respect?

A. I think because it was seen as a pretty direct attack on the integrity of the Prime Minister and officials at No.10, in the sense that they would try to persuade the chairman of the Joint Intelligence Committee to massage or to revise his conclusions, his recommendations, for political convenience, I saw it personally as also an unjustified attack on John Scarlett personally, the chairman of the JIC, because implicit in this is the assumption that he is willing to do this. But having myself, in a previous incarnation, sat on the Joint Intelligence Committee, I also thought it absolutely inconceivable that even if there were to be such collusion between officials in No.10 and the chairman of the JIC, it was absolutely inconceivable that the senior figures around the JIC table would agree to this. So I felt it was a very serious attack, not only, however, upon the integrity of individuals but a very serious attack on the integrity of the processes of Government. The JIC process is of no use if it is one that can be moulded or massaged by political fiat. It must be seen to be the best and most scrupulous assessment possible. Therefore there were very strong feelings about this attack. I think that is how I perceived it. I did not see it, myself, as a row between two particular individuals or between No.10 and a particular part of the media. I saw it as something where it was important that we tried to restore elements of trust, which had been challenged by this very direct assault on the integrity both of people and of process.

Q. You mentioned that it was not perceived as such amongst the senior civil servants, effectively, which is where you were dealing with it from.

A. Yes.

Q. But you obviously had substantial interaction with those who are not civil servants. Was it perceived as such amongst them, do you know, from your own knowledge?

A. Well, I think there were certainly moments of personal anger. I do not want to pretend they were not personally affronted by some of these attacks. But I think there was a sense this was an attack or a charge or an allegation of a different kind. It struck the very heart of whether or not you believe that the Prime Minister is going to tell the chairman of the Joint Intelligence Committee that his conclusions of his Committee are inconvenient and they must be changed for the political convenience of the Prime Minister of the day. And I think that was a charge that went beyond the usual, if I can put it like this, sparring that goes on and was seen as a very fundamental attack on the processes of Government and trust therein.

Although the question whether intelligence approved and provided to the Government by the JIC was reliable is a very important question, it is not one which involves the integrity of the Government: there is a great difference between broadcasting an allegation that intelligence provided to the Government was unreliable and broadcasting an allegation that the Government knew that intelligence set out in the dossier was wrong or questionable before it published it in the dossier, and it was the broadcasting of the latter allegation by the BBC which drew Dr Kelly into the controversy about Mr Gilligan's broadcasts.

275. The issues which arise in relation to the BBC have to be decided against the background of three matters which I have already decided have been established:

> (1) Dr Kelly did not say to Mr Gilligan that the Government probably knew that the 45 minutes claim was wrong or questionable before it was included in the dossier or that the 45 minutes claim was not included in the original draft because it only came from a single source. The allegations reported by Mr Gilligan that the Government probably knew that the 45 minutes claim was wrong or questionable before the dossier was published and that it was not inserted in the first draft of the dossier because it only came from one source and the intelligence agencies did not really believe it was necessarily true, were unfounded.

> (2) Mr Gilligan accepted in his evidence that his broadcast at 6.07am gave the wrong impression on these matters and that he should have scripted the broadcast before he made it.

> (3) The report that the Government probably knew that the 45 minutes claim was wrong or questionable before it was inserted in the dossier was an extremely grave allegation which attacked the integrity of the Prime Minister and the Government and it did not constitute merely a piece of political debate or the normal type of comment which is made in relation to a matter of great public interest on which other reporters are commenting.

The case made by the BBC and Mr Gilligan

276. Both the BBC and Mr Gilligan accepted that there could be criticism of the 6.07am broadcast, and the BBC also accepted that there could be criticism of the way in which the BBC treated the broadcast thereafter, but the case which was made on behalf of both the BBC and Mr Gilligan, although with some differing emphases, was that notwithstanding those criticisms, there was great public interest in the September 2002 dossier and serious issues of great public importance arose in relation to the reliability of the intelligence contained in it, and therefore it was right for the BBC and Mr Gilligan to report the concern of Mr Gilligan's source that the dossier

had been sexed up and that there was concern in intelligence circles about the way in which the 45 minutes claim was worded in the dossier. The point was further made that there had been a number of similar claims in the media and that the evidence of Dr Brian Jones showed that the report that there was concern in intelligence circles was correct.

277. Stress was also laid on the point that the criticisms of Mr Gilligan's broadcast very largely related to what he said in the broadcast commencing at 6.07am and to the part of the broadcast commencing at 7.32am in which he said that the Government probably knew that the 45 minutes claim was questionable, and that in his broadcast commencing at 7.32am and in subsequent broadcasts Mr Gilligan made it clear that the information which he had been told was dubious did come from the intelligence agencies. The point was also made that Mr Gilligan's report that the intelligence relating to the 45 minutes claim was only single sourced was shown to be correct. Therefore the BBC and Mr Gilligan contended that, despite the flaws which they accepted in Mr Gilligan's reports, they were nevertheless performing an important public service in reporting the doubts and reservations which existed in the intelligence agencies, as established by Dr Jones' evidence, about the wording of the 45 minutes claim in the dossier.

278. The BBC and Mr Gilligan also laid stress on the point that in his broadcast Mr Gilligan did not report that he or the BBC believed that the Government probably knew that the 45 minutes claim was wrong, rather he reported that this was the belief of a source who, because of his knowledge of intelligence matters and the preparation of the dossier, was well placed to express such a view and whom Mr Gilligan was entitled to view as a credible source. The point was further made, particularly on behalf of Mr Gilligan, that insofar as he could, Mr Gilligan had found confirmation for what his source had told him in reports in other newspapers stating that intelligence sources were unhappy about the contents of the dossier and in the fact that the Government had had to admit that the dossier which it had issued in February 2003 (about links between Saddam Hussein and Al Quaeda) was flawed. Mr Gilligan also said in evidence on 12 August:

[12 August, page 30, line 6]

A... Then I basically sought to corroborate the story. I went to see –

Q. How did you try to do that?

A. I went to see a couple of people. I saw the – well, I will call them senior contacts in Government; and I asked them about this. I did not tell them obviously that David Kelly had said it but I said I have been told this and was there any truth in it. And neither of them would confirm or deny –

Q. Sorry to interrupt. What did you say you had been told?

A. I said I had been told that the dossier had been transformed the week before it was published and that this was done at the behest of Alastair Campbell.

Q. So those two things were what you put to the two senior Government contacts?

A. Yes, that is right.

Q. What did they say?

A. Neither of them denied it. One of them said something I could not take as a confirmation but said, you know: I think you should keep digging, something like that. But when somebody says something like that, it is not a confirmation and it cannot be taken as such but it is obviously not a denial either. And then the others just refused to talk about it. I know both of these people – I believe anyway both of these people would have been in positions to know about the dossier.

279. Both the BBC and Mr Gilligan relied on the recognition in the jurisprudence of the United Kingdom and also in the jurisprudence of the European Court of Human Rights that the press and other parts of the media have a vital role to play in a democratic society in fully reporting on matters of public concern and public interest and in exposing to public gaze matters which the Government might wish to remain hidden. Mr Caldecott commenced his closing statement on behalf of the BBC by saying:

[25 September, page 94, line 7]

...there can be few subjects of greater public interest than reasons presented by a Government to its own people as possible grounds for war. That – let there be no doubt about it – was the purpose of the September dossier. It was an assessment of the threat posed by a foreign power against whom hostilities were in serious contemplation.

It was advertised by a label which is almost unique in British political history. The Prime Minister was to share with the people the gist of the formal intelligence assessments he had received from the Joint Intelligence Committee. The invitation was to share the Prime Minister's conclusion, having shared the intelligence.

Mr Caldecott concluded his statement by saying:

[25 September, page 124, line 3]

...the BBC anticipates criticism of the 6.07 broadcast in particular and its treatment thereafter, but they do ask the Inquiry to have in mind the public interest in the remainder of its extensive coverage of Dr Kelly's concerns about the dossier, which the BBC believes the public had a right to know.

In her closing statement, on behalf of Mr Gilligan, Ms Rogers said:

[25 September, page 134, line 7]

The decision to go to war, the Government's justification for it, deserves the closest possible scrutiny. A defence correspondent who failed to raise these matters in the continuing public debate would be failing in his duty.

It is the role of the journalist to investigate and report upon matters of legitimate public interest. This journalism was not an unwarranted intrusion into someone's private life, it was not celebrity gossip. It was a classic example of working journalism reporting on a matter of public interest.

Freedom of expression is a fundamental right. It is a right to receive as well as a right to communicate information. The media play a vital role in a democracy as the eyes and ears of the public. The law protects freedom of expression not just as a lofty principle, not just as a matter of theory, but as a matter of practical reality.

....

[25 September, page 137, line 9]

Today we do not take the word of public figures automatically at face value. We question what we are told. It is right that we should. It is healthy for society that we do. It is by public debate, vigorous open debate, that we are all better informed. The issues raised in this reporting were big issues, serious issues of substance. The reporting of claims and responses to claims is the common currency of political debate. The Government, doing its job, responded to Andrew Gilligan's story swiftly and as fully as it wanted. The Government has a vast dedicated and sophisticated communications machinery. It had no difficulty in getting what it wanted to say reported in the media, both on 29th May and after it made press statements, statements in Parliament, and what it said was reported just as widely as what Dr Kelly had said.

280. Counsel for the BBC and for Mr Gilligan were right to state that the communication by the media of information (including information obtained by investigative reporters) on matters of public interest and importance is a vital part of life in a

democratic society. However the right to communicate such information is subject to the qualification (which itself exists for the benefit of a democratic society) that false accusations of fact impugning the integrity of others, including politicians, should not be made by the media. Where a reporter is intending to broadcast or publish information impugning the integrity of others the management of his broadcasting company or newspaper should ensure that a system is in place whereby his editor or editors give careful consideration to the wording of the report and to whether it is right in all the circumstances to broadcast or publish it. The issue of untruthful allegations of fact in relation to political matters made by the media has been considered recently by the House of Lords in Reynolds v Times Newspapers Ltd [2001] 2 AC 127 and I set out relevant passages in the judgments of Lord Nicholls of Birkenhead, Lord Cooke of Thorndon and Lord Hobhouse of Woodborough in appendix 17.

281. The allegations in Mr Gilligan's broadcast on 29 May that the Government probably knew that the 45 minutes claim was wrong or questionable and that the 45 minutes claim was not included in the first draft of the dossier because it was only single sourced were unfounded. Whatever doubts there may now be about the reliability of the intelligence in relation to the 45 minutes claim, and whether Dr Brian Jones' concerns about the wording of the 45 minutes claim in the dossier are ultimately shown to have been valid, the claim in the dossier was sanctioned at the time of publication by the JIC. Mr Scarlett (the Chairman of the JIC), Sir Richard Dearlove (the Chief of SIS), Sir David Omand, Air Marshall Sir Joseph French (the Chief of Defence Intelligence), and Mr Anthony Cragg (the Deputy Chief of Defence Intelligence), all gave evidence that the JIC gave its approval to the claim being set out in the dossier, the claim itself having first appeared in a normal assessment prepared by the JIC assessment staff. A report by Mr Gilligan that the 45 minutes claim in the dossier was sanctioned by the JIC but that a source had told him that one section in the DIS had expressed concern about the wording of the claim would have been an accurate report. But Mr Gilligan broadcast a very different and much graver allegation which was unfounded.

282. I am unable to accept, in the context of Mr Gilligan's broadcasts, the distinction which he and the BBC rely on, between a report that the BBC believed that the Government probably knew that the 45 minutes claim was wrong and a report that a source had told the BBC that the Government probably knew that the 45 minutes claim was wrong. This is not a distinction recognised by the law in relation to actions for defamation. In relation to some spheres of public life on which the BBC reports it may be permissible to report what an anonymous but apparently credible source had said. But I consider that when a charge of such gravity is made, as that the Government probably knew that the 45 minutes claim was wrong, the impression created in the mind of the listener and the harm done to confidence in the integrity of the Government differs little whether the allegation is made directly by the BBC or is reported by the BBC as an allegation made by an apparently credible and well informed source.

283. Mr Gilligan's broadcast at 6.07am was unscripted and made from his own home and he accepts that it should have been scripted. In many cases it will be necessary for a BBC reporter to broadcast a report which has not been previously scripted and approved by the editors of the programme. But the BBC knew that in his broadcast on 29 May Mr Gilligan was going to report serious allegations against the Government. This was clear from one of the headlines read by Corrie Corfield at 6.00am on 29 May:

A senior official involved in preparing the Government's dossier on Iraqi weapons of mass destruction has told this programme that the document was rewritten just before publication – to make it more exciting. An assertion that some of the weapons could be activated within 45 minutes was among the claims added at a late stage. The official claimed that the intelligence services were unhappy with the changes, which he said were ordered by 10 Downing Street.

284. Therefore I consider that in relation to a subject of such importance and of such gravity the BBC should not have permitted Mr Gilligan to broadcast his report at 6.07am without editors having seen the script of what he was going to say and having considered whether it should be approved. I think that the validity of this view is confirmed by the e-mail which Mr Kevin Marsh, the editor of the Today programme, sent to Mr Stephen Mitchell, the Head of Radio News, on 27 June 2003:

> Some thoughts … clearly I have to talk to AG [Andrew Gilligan] early next week: I hope that by then my worst fears - based on what I'm hearing from the spooks this afternoon – aren't realised. Assuming not, the guts of what I would say are:
>
> • This story was a good piece of investigative journalism, marred by flawed reporting – our biggest millstone has been his loose use of language and lack of judgment in some of his phraseology.
>
> • It was marred also by the quantity of writing for other outlets that varied what was said or was loose with the terms of the story.
>
> • That it is in many ways a result of the loose and in some ways distant relationship he's been allowed to have with *Today*.
>
> I will propose that we change that:
>
> • That he works substantially in the office.
>
> • That he comes in to TVC to put his pieces together and to file (he usually files from home)
>
> • That all his proposed stories are discussed with me, in detail as early as possible in the process – face to face if possible
>
> • That anonymous sources pass an explicit credibility test with me.
>
> • That his material is filed/assembled in time to be heard by me or a senior Ass Ed in time to make changes.
>
> • That we agree on a script or on core elements of a script that he does not subsequently vary.
>
> • That he stops writing for non-BBC outlets?? OR
>
> • That all writing for non-BBC outlets is seen 24 hours in advance of copy time and before it is filed by two editors/managers – if changes are necessary, the changed copy is seen, again before being filed??
>
> Does this sound too harsh?? Thoughts?? I'd like anything I say to him to be consistent with anything anyone else above me in the hierarchy…

The relevance of this e-mail is not diminished by the e-mail of congratulations which Mr Marsh had previously sent to Mr Gilligan dated 30 May 2003:

> Statement of the obvious, I guess, but it's really good to have you back here in the UK. Great week; great stories, well handled and well told. 'Course it's meant Today has had a great week too…. and that's lifted everyone. We still have to have that conversation – but since you're entirely nocturnal while I'm a normal human being, we don't seem to meet too often. Maybe you could creek the coffin lid open next week during daylight hours??? Anyhow, it's great to have you back on your beat. Talk soon.

285. As I have stated, Mr Gilligan accepted in his evidence that he had made errors in his broadcast at 6.07am on 29 May, and a number of witnesses from the BBC accepted in the course of their evidence that the BBC had made errors in relation to Mr Gilligan's broadcast on 29 May and in dealing with the Government's complaints about those broadcasts.

The evidence of Mr Gavyn Davies, the Chairman of the Board of Governors of the BBC, Mr Greg Dyke, the Director General of the BBC, and Mr Richard Sambrook, the Director of News of the BBC

286. At the end of his evidence Mr Gavyn Davies said:

[28 August, page 166, line 17]

Q. And is there anything else that you wanted to add?

A. I think on behalf of the whole BBC I would like to put on record that we enormously regret the death of Dr Kelly. The BBC has the deepest sympathy for Dr Kelly's family; and all of us in the BBC are profoundly sorry about the tragic events of the last two months and we will do our utmost to learn important lessons for the future.

287. At the end of his evidence Mr Greg Dyke said:

[15 September, page 183, line 23]

Q. Is there anything else that you know of the circumstances surrounding Dr Kelly's death that you can assist his Lordship with or anything else you would like to say?

A. Well, I think I would say this: that, as I have said earlier, what the processes of the last few weeks have certainly exposed is that politics and journalism are far from exact sciences, and the forensic examination really of the events of May, June and July has revealed I think areas where in hindsight we would have – we might have behaved differently. We might have done things differently. Obviously we should learn from that. Naturally we will not prejudge the findings of the Inquiry before settling on any changes but I have asked our General Counsel Nicholas Eldred to begin to look at some of the lessons which we might learn from this. For instance, I have asked him with assistance from senior editorial figures in the BBC to look at aspects of the producer guidelines, particularly concerning anonymous sources and the description of them. I have certainly asked that in future whether the first of all broadcasts of controversial items should in future be scripted as opposed to – we will look again at the use of the – the concept of the two-way, in terms of controversial pieces.

....

[15 September, page 185, line 4]

A. Richard Sambrook, as I think Gavyn Davies has already told you, is himself looking and the whole executive will discuss what should be the rules on BBC journalists writing for other newspapers. As I say, I have no doubt there will be lessons for us all to learn, but there will certainly be lessons for the BBC to learn and we will take account of those.

288. In his evidence when examined by counsel for the BBC, Mr Caldecott, the Director of News of the BBC, Mr Sambrook, said:

[17 September, page 107, line 1]

Q. Are you aware that both Mr Dyke and Mr Davies have given evidence to the effect that there are lessons to be learnt by the BBC?

A. I am, yes.

Q. Is that a view you share?

A. Yes, it is. I think there are a number of lessons that the BBC will have to take from this.

Q. Can I just run through some possibilities and get your comments on them? Mr Gilligan referred, this morning, to the fact that the 6.07 broadcast was in fact produced live and not scripted. Have you any comment to make about that?

A. I think it is clear that any report which sets out a set of serious allegations should be carefully scripted in advance.

289. Whilst accepting that there were some grounds for criticism of its conduct the case made by the witnesses for the BBC consisted of six main points:

(1) In the weeks immediately after the broadcast on 29 May the Government had complained about those broadcasts in general terms and had not complained specifically about the report that the Government probably knew that the 45 minutes claim was wrong and the complaints which the Government did make were distorted by the aggressive tones in which they were made by Mr Campbell and by his attack on the integrity and independence of the BBC. In his evidence Mr Dyke said:

[15 September, page 150, line 20]

MR DINGEMANS: We have seen some of the extracts from Mr Campbell's evidence where he said that the story was a lie and those aspects. I will not take you to those because I think we have seen them enough before. But what was your reaction to those attacks on the stories?

A. Well obviously this was a pretty unprecedented – as I said, an unprecedented attack.

LORD HUTTON: Well, did you consider, Mr Dyke, whether Mr Campbell's complaint to the FAC related to the entirety of Mr Gilligan's broadcast on 29th May or whether his complaint related, in particular, to this allegation: the Government probably knew that the 45 minutes claim was wrong?

A. Well, that had not been the nature of the complaints up until that time, in the two letters that we had got.

LORD HUTTON: Yes.

A. So it seemed to me a much more general attack based around a particular story or based around a story, but a general attack on the BBC. So, remember he was accusing us of lying; he was saying that we had run an agenda against the war or certain parts of the BBC had run an agenda against the war. These are very serious charges to make against a broadcasting organisation.

LORD HUTTON: Yes.

A. So it seemed – he had also said we had effectively accused the Prime Minister of lying, which Richard Sambrook said to me was not – it would be almost impossible to construe what we said as that. That is why I agreed that Richard should go back to London and go on to the Today Programme to put our case.

(2) In his broadcast at 6.07am Mr Gilligan was not making a direct allegation on his own part or on the part of the BBC that the Government probably knew that the 45 minutes claim was wrong, but was reporting the allegation of a source whom he regarded as credible and well placed to make the allegation.

Mr Davies said:

[28 August, page 117, line 13]

…I believe that if the BBC News reports that the BBC believes something, the requirement for certainty is much greater on behalf of the broadcaster. If the BBC reports that a credible and reliable source believes something, then it is clearly thought to be something that should be put into the public domain, a valid remark to put into the public domain, but it is clearly hinged on one person's view. And I think that that was what this was.

(3) Mr Gilligan's report was supported by Ms Watts' broadcast which contained similar allegations. Mr Davies said:

[24 September, page 38, line 14]

A. The Governors had a great deal of information going into the meeting and they had an important corroboration for the Gilligan report, which continues to slip out of the mind of the Government; and that is the Susan Watts reports. I said in my first appearance before this Inquiry that the Susan Watts report was not identical to the Gilligan report. I actually studied both before I went into the meeting and I knew they were not identical, but I equally knew that the burden of what Mr Gilligan had reported in his many broadcasts on the subject at the end of May was a close match to the burden of what Ms Watts reported on 2nd and 4th June. And I do not think it should be forgotten that that is the case, because certainly in my mind, and in several other Governors' mind, maybe the whole of the Board of Governors who received the information before they went into the meeting, that was seen as an important corroboration of the Gilligan story.

(4) The Government failed to make use of the complaints procedures which are available to those who consider that they have been unfairly criticised in the BBC broadcast. In his evidence Mr Davies said:

[28 August, page 110, line 10]

Q. Were there any avenues, so far as you were concerned, that might have been used to resolve the dispute?

A. Well, another troubling aspect of this, to me, was that the Director General had told me that in a previous letter to Mr Campbell, I think on 16th June or thereabouts, the Director of News had suggested to Mr Campbell that if he felt he had a complaint about inaccuracy of a particular broadcast or unfairness, he should approach the BBC Programme Complaints Unit, which I think would have given him due process for resolving his complaint in a non-conflictual and non-public manner. He also had the option, which I do not think he was told in that letter specifically, of complaining to the Broadcasting Standards Commission about unfairness. That is a body that is entirely independent of the BBC and has the power, if it finds on the side of the complainant, to ask the BBC to broadcast a correction.

(5) In his evidence to the FAC Mr Campbell had launched an unprecedented attack on the integrity and independence of the BBC and the Governors were under a duty in the public interest to resist that attack:

In his evidence on 28 August Mr Davies said:

[28 August, page 109, line 12]

…I felt this was an extraordinary moment. I felt it was an almost unprecedented attack on the BBC to be mounted by the head of communications at 10 Downing Street. Mr Campbell accused the BBC of lying directly. He accused Mr Gilligan of lying directly. He alleged that the BBC had accused the Prime Minister of lying, something which I never believed the BBC had done. And he accused the BBC of having followed an anti-war agenda before, during and after the Iraqi conflict. I must say, I took this as an attack on the impartiality of the BBC and the integrity of the BBC, done with great vigour.

And in his evidence on 24 September Mr Davies said:

[24 September, page 25, line 14]

…we were faced with such an intemperate attack on our impartiality and our integrity, Mr Sumption, that I think it was perfectly reasonable for me to take the view that the public were looking to the Governors to stand up for the independence of the BBC, not to stand up for the management but to stand up for the public interest.

Q. What you were saying was that whatever details might emerge about the precise facts about the 45 minutes claim, (1) there should be no compromise of the kind you refer to at the beginning of that paragraph and (2) the Governors must not give way but must be seen to support the management.

A. Absolutely not saying that whatsoever. It does not say anything about supporting the management in there. Nor would I accept your interpretation of the first part of that paragraph. The first part of that paragraph, I can tell you, meant: we must not do a "behind the stairs" deal with No.10 Downing Street which the public will see as a means of taking off the public agenda a matter of legitimate public interest.

Q. You were so concerned about creating the outward appearance of succumbing to political pressure that you were urging the Governors that they should not give an inch whatever a further investigation of the facts might show. Is that not the position?

A. It is absolutely not the position, Mr Sumption. I do not, at any stage in my life, ignore the facts. And the most important thing, undoubtedly, is to tell the truth to the public. But what I was concerned about here – and I can tell you it was in the face of absolutely unprecedented pressure from the Director of Communications at 10 Downing Street, not an insignificant figure in the Government at the time. In the face of that pressure, I then believed and I now believe, and I had the full support of all of the Board in saying that it was a legitimate public duty of the Board to say that that pressure was intolerable.

(6) It was not feasible for the Governors to investigate themselves the accuracy of Mr Gilligan's report. Mr Davies said in his evidence on 24 September:

[24 September, page 13, line 3]

MR SUMPTION: Mr Davies, you mentioned, in answer to my question, the point that the Governors do not want to duplicate the judgment of the executives. No doubt in investigating matters that come before them the Governors will depend on the assistance of senior executives to provide them with information, but you will surely agree that their role is to form an independent judgment and not simply to act as amplifiers for views which the BBC staff have already formed?

A. I agree with that, Mr Sumption; and if you knew my colleagues you would not think they were acting as amplifiers to anybody.

Q. Let us look at what did happen in this case. You have given evidence at phase 1 that it would not have been possible for the BBC Governors to investigate the accuracy of Mr Gilligan's report. Did you mean by that that the Governors had no means of deciding whether the dossier had actually been sexed up or not and, if so, by whom?

A. I think I made it clear in my evidence that what I was referring to there is what I have come to know as the intrinsic accuracy of what the source said. I felt, going into the meeting, and I still feel today even more strongly having seen what has happened at this Inquiry, that it was extremely complicated, difficult and, as I said last time, actually literally impossible for the Governors to get the information required to determine the intrinsic accuracy of the source's allegations. Therefore, we focused on whether the source was credible and reliable, whether procedures had been followed and whether the source had been accurately reported.

Q. Let us look at what they were in a position to look into, because I think your last answer suggests that there may be some common ground on that. The Governors were in a position, were they not, to consider whether the journalist had a proper support from his own source for what he had broadcast. They could consider that, could they not?

A. The Governors could and did consider that and asked management about it.

Q. In your phase 1 evidence you said that the BBC had to be absolutely clear – these are your words – that they were reporting the words of the source. That is the point that the Governors could have investigated, is it not?

A. Mr Sumption, the word "investigated" is a strong word here. The Governors questioned the management on that aspect. It was not actually, at that stage, thought to be the central issue facing the Governors, but they did question management on that aspect.

Q. The Governors were in a position, were they not, to consider whether the status of the source was such that he could be expected to know the facts?

A. They were certainly in a position to determine that, with the proviso that I do not think it would have been right and proper, it would have been highly irregular for them actually to have known who the source was.

Q. They could have been told what the status of the source was without being told his name.

A. I do not believe that would have made any sense at all. I think if they had been told what the status of the source was in any precise terms they would effectively, almost certainly, have been told who the source was. It would have been quite easy, I think, as we have seen recently, to have deduced who Dr Kelly was from an accurate description of what he did.

Consideration of the issues relating to the BBC

290. Having considered the evidence given by the witnesses from the BBC (leaving aside the evidence given by Mr Gilligan) I consider that the BBC was at fault in a number of respects as follows:

(1) I have already stated that the BBC failed to ensure proper editorial control over Mr Gilligan's broadcasts on 29 May and, in particular, over his first broadcast at 6.07am.

(2) I consider that the BBC management was at fault in failing to investigate properly and adequately the Government's complaints that the report was false that the Government probably knew that the 45 minutes claim was wrong even before it decided to put it in the dossier, in the following reports. The BBC management failed, before Mr Sambrook wrote his letter of 27 June to Mr Campbell, to make an examination of Mr Gilligan's notes on his personal organiser of his meeting with Dr Kelly to see if they supported the allegations which he had reported in his broadcast at 6.07am. When the BBC management did look at Mr Gilligan's notes after 27 June it failed to appreciate that the notes did not fully support the most serious of the allegations reported in the 6.07am broadcast, and it therefore failed to draw the attention of the Governors to the lack of support in the notes for the most serious of the allegations. A factor which contributed to these failures was the failure of the BBC management to appreciate the gravity of the allegations reported in Mr Gilligan's broadcast at 6.07am and I consider that the allegations made against the Government in the broadcast at 6.07am were so grave and gave rise to such a serious public controversy that it was unreasonable for the BBC management to expect the Government to pursue its complaint about them through the usual channels of the BBC Programme Complaints Unit or the Broadcasting Standards Commission, procedures which could take weeks or, perhaps, months before a conclusion was arrived at. These failures are shown in the evidence of Mr Dyke, Mr Sambrook and Mr Davies.

Mr Dyke said:

[15 September, page 148, line 22]

A. On 25th and 26th June I was chairing a BBC – we have twice a year a BBC Executive Committee conference, this was in Surrey – when the news came through of a pretty ferocious attack which Alastair Campbell had launched not just against the particular report broadcast by Andrew Gilligan, but on the BBC's journalistic integrity and in particular on our coverage of the war.

Q. Your coverage of the?

A. Of the war, sorry.

Q. And what was your reaction to that?

A. Well, I discussed it with Richard Sambrook who was also at the conference. He had been invited by that time to appear on the Today Programme the following day to answer Mr Campbell's allegations and we both agreed that he should leave the conference and go. I mean, an attack of this sort of scale from the Government's Director of Strategy and Communications was pretty near unprecedented, I would have thought.

LORD HUTTON: Had you, by this stage, read the details of Mr Gilligan's broadcast report on 29th May, Mr Dyke?

A. (Pause). I do not remember.

LORD HUTTON: Yes.

A. I think probably not.

LORD HUTTON: Yes.

A. Probably not.

LORD HUTTON: You see, I have read already part of the report which said that actually the Government probably knew that the 45 minutes figure was wrong even before it decided to put it in. Would you regard that as a very grave charge indeed against the Government?

A. Well, of course it – it was a charge being made not by the BBC but by a source to the BBC; but at that stage I would not have read that. I would have received Stephen Whittle's account of our process. The process was going pretty well. I would have talked about this with Richard Sambrook. By this time remember the story had died away. This had not been brought on to our radar screen over the previous 10 days at all, 14 days.

LORD HUTTON: Whether the charge was made by the BBC or by a source which the BBC was reporting, would you regard it as a very serious allegation?

A. Oh, it is pretty serious charge. But there is a distinction between a charge made by the BBC and a charge made by a source to the BBC.

LORD HUTTON: Yes.

A. They are very – a very different – they carry a different degree of gravity.

....

[15 September, page 157, line 2]

Q… When you were helping draft [Mr Sambrook's letter of 27 June in reply to Mr Campbell's letter of 26 June], did you, at that stage, listen to a tape of the broadcast on 29th May?

A. (Pause). I think we read the transcript.

Q. You read the transcript. I think we have that at BBC/1/5 onwards. What was your reaction, if we look at BBC/1/4, to the opening of the piece which Mr Gilligan has told us was unscripted and had followed a more neutral introduction by the news reader?

A. Well, I think we – during that day we had all the transcripts of not just the early piece, but we had all the different pieces that were run throughout the morning; and I read through them. What I did was to largely get involved in the writing of the first half of the reply.

Q. Right. But having read, for example, this bit at BBC/1/4 where it was said "the Government probably knew that the 45 minute figure was wrong", I can take you to other bits later on.

A. Sure. I cannot say that particular piece jumped out at me. I mean, clearly we knew there were fairly serious allegations, the point has been made, but I do not think that piece particularly jumped out."

Mr Dyke, referring to the drafting of Mr Sambrook's reply to Mr Campbell dated 27 June, said:

[15 September, page 161, line 6]

Q. Did you ask or were you shown, at this stage, Mr Gilligan's notes of his meeting?

A. No.

Q. Were they available to the meeting that was drafting this reply?

A. No. Mr Gilligan was there, but – he was in the part of the meeting in the other part of the office, he was not at the meeting where I was. But we assumed that these replies were accurate.

LORD HUTTON: Why did you assume they were accurate, Mr Dyke? I mean very strong protests were being made by the Government on this particular point and the Chairman of the Joint Intelligence Committee had said that the report was wrong. Now, why did you not consider the accuracy of it?

A. Because we were reporting a source. I mean, there is a real distinction, and it has been, I think, muddled in a lot of the reporting, including I would say some of our own reporting of this issue.

MR DINGEMANS: Will you explain the distinction?

A. The distinction was whether this was the BBC saying this or whether this was the BBC reporting the source. We were reporting a source. There are questions that have to be asked when you are doing that, but that work had been done and the view was that this was a credible source to report.

Mr Sambrook said:

[17 September, page 110, line 17]

Q. Can I, please, just move on to some matters involving you rather more closely? The reply to Mr Campbell's substantially long letter of complaint of 26th June was, in part, drafted by you?

A. It was, yes.

Q. Do you accept that there were some errors in that letter [of 27 June] as to what Dr Kelly had in fact said to Mr Gilligan?

A. Yes, I do.

Q. Had you looked at Mr Gilligan's notes at the time that you drafted that reply?

A. No, I had not, no.

Q. Do you accept, with hindsight, that you should have done?

A. Yes, I think if I had been able to go through Andrew Gilligan's notes in some detail and gone through them with him in some detail, we might have got to a point where we realised these were not comments that were directly attributable to Dr Kelly; and clearly I regret that.

Q. Was Mr Gilligan involved in the drafting process of that letter?

A. Yes, he was.

Q. I do not think we need turn the passages up, but did Mr Gilligan consent to the letter going out in the form that it did?

A. Yes he did. Indeed, part of the reason why Mr Gilligan spent most of that day in our offices, as the letter was being drafted, was that he could be consulted on matters such as that.

....

[17 September, page 122, line 3]

Q. Would you agree that the more serious the allegation, the greater the care which you would expect the BBC to take to ensure that it can be properly supported?

A. Yes.

Q. These were exceptionally serious allegations, were they not?

A. Well, I think one thing I should make clear is that I do not think the programme or indeed the BBC, in those early weeks, ever took the wording of the 6.07 broadcast or that phrase within the 6.07 broadcast to be the definitive version of the allegations that we were making. I think our view was the definitive version was the scripted version, in the news bulletins at 6 o'clock, 7 o'clock and 8 o'clock and at 7.32. The live two-ways at 6 o'clock are deemed by the programme, although it is certainly true the audience does not necessarily perceive them this way, as a sort of preview for the major reports that are coming up during that day's programme. So I think the mindset on the programme, and I think this continued for some time afterwards, was that the definition of this item, in the BBC's view, were the scripted versions of it and the 6.07 was something that had strayed from what we believed to be the core allegations we were making or that our source was making.

Q. Leaving aside the mindset of the programme, you very fairly accept the audience would not necessarily have perceived it the same way?

A. Indeed.

Q. In practice it is the most dramatic and gravest allegation which will attract the most attention rather than the allegation which is scripted?

A. Depending on how often it is repeated and how many people hear it, yes.

Q. Yes. But if you make a sufficiently dramatic allegation, other media will catch on to it, will they not?

A. They may do, yes.

Q. They are professional followers of each other's copy, are they not?

A. They are.

Q. Now, you have already I think agreed in your earlier evidence, and indeed I think it is implicit in the evidence you have given today, that the 6.07 allegation that the Government probably knew that the 45 minutes point was wrong before putting it into the dossier was, in fact, going to strike people as an exceptionally grave allegation. I think you have accepted that?

A. It clearly had that effect.

Q. Yes. It was an attack, was it not, on its face, on the integrity of those who had been involved at the highest levels in the production of the dossier?

A. In the way it was phrased, it clearly would have had that effect. It is a different question about intent.

Q. Yes, I understand that. Even in the 7.32 broadcast, the allegation was, was it not, that the Government had put the 45 minute point into the dossier against the advice of the Intelligence Services, who had told them that they regarded it as questionable?

A. Words to that effect, yes.

....

[17 September, page 160, line 8]

Q. Mr Dyke has given evidence and you I think have associated yourself this afternoon with that evidence, to virtually quote him, I think, that he wished that he had paused in late June and ordered a full investigation of the whole issue.

A. Yes.

Q. That is one of the points that Mr Dyke made which you associate yourself with?

A. I certainly think we should have paused and considered at greater length the charges that were being levelled against us. Whether that amounts to a full investigation of the whole issue, I am not sure. But I certainly think the letter of the 27th was written under considerable pressure, particularly the deadline imposed on us by Mr Campbell, and if we had not been under that pressure to respond then the errors in that letter of the 27th might not have been made.

Q. There was not in fact a careful examination of all the allegations that had been made, how far they could be supported by Mr Gilligan's notes and what conclusions should be drawn from that before the Governors' meeting, was there?

A. There was an investigation and examination. What we did not do was go through the personal organiser notes in point by point detail with Andrew. If we had done that, I think it might have pointed up the two errors that we made in that letter. But we certainly went through every point that Mr Campbell raised in his letter. We discussed them in some detail, both with Andrew Gilligan and with Kevin Marsh, and we just discussed them between ourselves as a senior editorial team before coming out with that letter. I would not want anybody to think that the letter was written purely in haste. We spent as much time as we had over it and we went into considerable detail on all the points that Mr Campbell made.

Q. The truth is that the investigation that had been carried out by the time the Governors met on 6th July was no fuller than the investigation that had been made before you wrote that letter, except in this respect: that you had, by now, looked at both versions of Mr Gilligan's notes?

A. We had seen Mr Gilligan's notes, that is true. We had also, by that time, identified many similarities in Ms Watts' reports as well with the reports Andrew Gilligan had made, which had taken us some time to get to because I was abroad when her broadcasts originally went out. I think that also lent some support to the broad thrust of the allegations that Mr Gilligan's source was making.

Q. In the press release following the meeting of the Governors, it was said that the BBC had never attacked the good faith of the Prime Minister.

A. That is also what I said in my Today interview on the 26th.

Q. Did anyone draw the Governors' intention to what Mr Gilligan had in fact said at 6.07?

A. No, it was not at the forefront of our minds. Indeed, it was not at the forefront of our minds in drafting the response of the 27th because it was raised there by Mr Campbell for the first time, as the third of those 12 questions, and indeed in the previous three letters from the Government the wording of the 6.07 broadcast had never been referred to you (sic) and their complaints were much more about whether we had abided by the producer guidelines, the strength given to denials and a number of other issues, such as the description of the JIC. They had never drawn the precise language of the 6.07 as being the core of their complaint. Indeed, even when we got the letter of the 26th where it was raised for the first time in that list of questions, I took the core of their complaint to be that John Humphreys paragraph on the front page.

Q. So nobody said, as I understand your evidence, to the Governors at that meeting: there is a problem about the 6.07 broadcast, which was unscripted, and where Mr Gilligan appears to have gone further than he should have done?

A. No, because at that time the Government's complaint was all-encompassing. They were not saying: we have a problem, we have a complaint about the 6.07 broadcast. They said: we have a complaint about the entirety of these allegations. I think Mr Campbell's letter to the Director General on the 26th said "the story is 100 per cent wrong". This was an all or nothing complaint, not a complaint about a phrase in one version of 19 broadcasts.

Q. It was a number of complaints, one of which related specifically to the 6.07 broadcast.

A. I accept that the wording of the 6.07 was raised for the first time in the letter of the 26th, yes.

Q. In fact you had at 6.07, whether you intended to or not, attacked the good faith of the Government, had you not?

A. On reflection I can see that. At the time, I do not think that was sufficiently recognised, no.

Q. Did anyone point out to the Governors that the dossier had said that it reflected the views of the JIC and Mr Gilligan had broadcast, at 7.32, an allegation that the Government had actually inserted things contrary to intelligence advice? Was that point made to the Governors?

A. No. As I have explained to you before, we saw the core allegations that were being made about the scripted items rather than 6.07, and again, even in that allegation we did not accept that the reservations of the Intelligence Services necessarily referred to the heads of those services or the JIC; and I believe we always thought of it in terms of people lower down the chain who had been involved in the assessment and production of the dossier, who were concerned, and at some level unspecified in the BBC's broadcast, that stuff had been included against their advice.

LORD HUTTON: May I just ask you on that point, Mr Sambrook, if we look at BBC/1/4, which is the first page of the transcript, if we can scroll down that, please. Yes, just there. You see the paragraph there beginning: "Well, erm, our source says that the dossier, as it was finally published, made the Intelligence Services unhappy…" Then if we go over to the next page which is the commencement of the broadcast at 7.32, about halfway down that passage: "… Andrew Gilligan has found evidence that the Government's dossier on Iraq that was produced last September was cobbled together at the last minute with some unconfirmed material that had not been approved by the Security Services." Now, there is a reference to the Intelligence Services being unhappy and then there is a reference to "had not been approved by the Security Services".

A. Hmm.

LORD HUTTON: I think later there is a reference at 006 to Mr Gilligan, where he said "most people in intelligence were not happy"; but if one looks at the first two references, that gives the picture, does it not, that it was the entirety of the Intelligence Services, or would it not apply certainly to the heads of the Intelligence Services?

A. I accept that reading can be taken from it.

LORD HUTTON: You say "can be taken from it". Is that not the only reading if you just look at those passages? Once they were heard by someone listening to the broadcast: "the Intelligence Services".

A. I think all I can say, my Lord, is that in the programme's mind, and indeed in ours for some time, that was not what we believed to be the allegation that had been made.

LORD HUTTON: Is the important thing not what the listeners take it to mean?

A. I agree with that, yes.

LORD HUTTON: Yes.

MR SUMPTION: You have accepted that there was no basis in Mr Gilligan's notes for the assertion that that point had been made to him by Dr Kelly, the conscious misfeasance point.

A. It was not in his notes, yes.

Q. Was that point made to the Governors?

A. Yes, I said to the Governors that his notes were not verbatim, were not – not every that he had broadcast was contained in his notes but that Mr Gilligan asserted that what was not there was a proper reflection of his conversation with Dr Kelly. The one point the Governors challenged me on was whether the name "Campbell" was represented in the notes and I told them that it was, next to a phrase about transformation of the dossier. And that was really the only point that they wanted to have more clarification about the notes on.

Q. You see, Mr Sambrook, when you wrote the 27th June letter you had not seen Mr Gilligan's notes; and when you subsequently saw them you realised that there might be a problem about the unequivocal way in which you had answered Mr Campbell's question whether the BBC stood by the 6.07 allegation.

A. When I saw his notes I had the conversation with Andrew about those elements of his broadcast which were not captured in his notes and he continued to assert that his conversation with Dr Kelly backed up those comments, and I took him at face value.

Q. So he continued to tell you that that was what Dr Kelly had actually told him?

A. He continued to say it was a proper – he did not say it was a direct quote at that point but he did say it continued to be a proper reflection and interpretation of what Dr Kelly had told him, which is what I think I said in my evidence on the 13th.

Mr Davies said:

[24 September, page 29, line 9]

Q. Well, were you aware, at the time of the meeting, that Mr Sambrook had not examined Mr Gilligan's notes at the time of writing his letter on 27th June?

A. I was aware of that. I also knew he had written the letter in the presence of Mr Gilligan for a large part of his writing.

Q. Were you aware he had examined them since writing that letter?

A. I was aware he had examined them before the Governor's meeting.

Q. Were you aware the notes did not support the most serious of the allegations, namely Mr Gilligan's source had accused the Government of putting material into the dossier knowing it was probably wrong?

A. None of the Governors were aware that the notes did not substantiate that, and nor did, I think – was Mr Sambrook aware of that. He had looked at the notes and he had not, I think, picked up – I believe he said this to the Inquiry – that parts of the 6.07 broadcast were not repeated in the notes formally. However, he had asked the journalist, Mr Gilligan, whether or not he fully stood by the reports and the answer was, "Yes, both factually and in terms of interpretation", and that is what he told us.

Q. So Mr Sambrook had looked at the notes but had not picked up the fact that the most serious of the allegations was not reflected in the note; that is your evidence, as I understand it, indeed it is Mr Sambrook's.

A. I think it was not repeated verbatim in the notes. I think Mr Sambrook had not noted that it was not repeated verbatim in the notes. I believe Mr Sambrook told the Inquiry that.

Q. The notes were not, of course, put before the Governors even in redacted form, were they?

A. No, they were not.

(3) The e-mail sent by Mr Kevin Marsh to Mr Stephen Mitchell on 27 June 2003 set out in paragraph 284 was critical of Mr Gilligan's method of reporting and was clearly relevant to the complaints which the Government was making about his broadcast on 29 May. Yet it appears that this e-mail of 27 June 2003 was never brought to the attention of Mr Sambrook or to the attention of the Governors. In his evidence Mr Dyke said:

[15 September, page 169, line 17]

Q. We have also seen an e-mail at BBC/5/118, in which comments were made about Mr Gilligan's reporting.

A. Yes.

Q. Did you see this e-mail?

A. No, I did not know of the existence of this e-mail until the day the Inquiry started. I should explain, I was away – I took a truncated holiday and therefore I came back and that was the first I knew of this e-mail.

LORD HUTTON: Do you think you should have been made aware of it before the Governors' meeting?

A. I do not think – my understanding, but you must confirm it with him, is that Richard Sambrook had not seen this e-mail before the Governors' meeting.

LORD HUTTON: Do you think he should have seen it?

A. There are a million e-mails a day inside the BBC. Unless somebody had referred it to him, he would not have seen it. But I certainly had not seen it; and I did not see it until the Inquiry started.

LORD HUTTON: But it is very critical of the broadcast about which the Government was making very serious complaints and about which there was a very serious controversy.

A. Sorry, can I just … (Pause). It says this – yes, it makes – it expresses certain concerns: "This story was a good piece of investigative journalism marred by flawed reporting."

LORD HUTTON: "Our biggest millstone has…"

A. Yes, on reading this I could not say I was not concerned.

LORD HUTTON: If I could ask you again Mr Dyke: do you not think that somebody in the BBC chain of management should have brought this to the attention of Mr Sambrook and/or yourself before the Governors' meeting?

A. They would not have brought it to my attention.

LORD HUTTON: Very well, that –

A. This is further down the chain, quite a long way down the chain.

LORD HUTTON: Yes.

A. But, well – whether they should have done, they did not.

In his evidence Mr Sambrook said:

[17 September, page 132, line 6]

Q. We have certain observations from Mr Marsh himself which are included in an e-mail on 27th June which you will find at BBC/5/118. When did you first see this e-mail?

A. When it was disclosed for the Inquiry.

Q. I see. Now, as I understand it, partly from documents and partly from Mr Dyke's evidence, Stephen Mitchell is somebody who, from time to time, looks into matters which one might loosely call regulatory for the senior executives; is that wrong?

A. No, Stephen Mitchell is the head of Radio News who reports to me. It is Stephen Whittle who is the controller of editorial policy.

Q. You are right to correct me on that. If we could look at what Mr Marsh says: "Some thoughts – clearly I have to talk to Andrew Gilligan early next week. I hope that by then my worst fears – based on what I'm hearing from the spooks this afternoon – aren't realised. Assuming not, the guts of what I would say are: "This story was a good piece of investigative journalism, marred by flawed reporting – our biggest millstone has been his loose use of language and lack of judgment in some of his phraseology. "It was marred also…" that is a point about the Mail on Sunday and the Spectator. "That is in many ways a result of the loose and in some ways distant relationship he's been allowed to have with Today." Have you discussed with Mr Marsh his views as reflected in this document?

A. I had discussed, before this document, in broad terms his views of Andrew Gilligan as a reporter and indeed with Stephen Mitchell as well, yes.

Q. Can you tell us why it is, what is the loose language which Mr Marsh is drawing attention to as possibly fulfilling his worst fears?

A. I am not sure that the loose language is related to the worst fears. I think that is a separate point.

Q. Leaving the fears, let us concentrate on the loose language.

A. As I said, this was not flagged up to me at the time. I only knew about it after it was disclosed to this Inquiry. My understanding of what Kevin was talking about is we should have had a consistent phrase for capturing the allegations that Dr Kelly was making, both for presenters and for reporters and within the report scripts, and it would have been a lot better if we had been entirely consistent on that.

Q. You had not seen this document, as I understand your evidence, by the time you briefed the Governors' meeting on 6th July?

A. That is correct.

Q. Do you think you should have done?

A. I think if Kevin Marsh or Stephen Mitchell had had real concerns about the nature of the reporting or indeed about the nature of the way we were dealing with the Government's complaint, I would have expected them to bring those to my attention. I am not clear that this e-mail necessarily represents serious concerns.

LORD HUTTON: You think it does not represent serious concerns?

A. My personal view about it is that it is much more saying – it is entitled "from here"; my personal view about it is that it is an e-mail from a programme editor to his line manager saying that in future we would be better to have a more disciplined use in terms of scripting materials and not doing live two-ways and so on; and it is an attempt to look forward at how things should be managed in the future. Again, this was not flagged up to me at the time. All I can say is that, I mean, I know both Kevin Marsh and Stephen Mitchell extremely well and I believe if they had serious concerns about the quality of the journalism or indeed our response to the Government, they would have raised it directly with me and they did not.

MR SUMPTION: Is it not a source of concern if grave allegations are made against public figures on the basis of loose use of language and lack of judgment in the phraseology? Is that not a source of concern?

A. If that is their view then it would be, yes.

Q. Well, it does seem to have been Mr Marsh's view; and what exactly did the Governors, when they came to consider this, know about the views of the editor of the programme itself, ie Mr Marsh?

A. Well, they – I do not think the Governors were particularly interested in the editor's view; they were interested in my view; and I shared with them the view I had had for a considerable period of time, and which was certainly partly informed by Mr Marsh and by Mr Mitchell, which was that Andrew Gilligan was in some respects a good reporter. There are two aspects to journalism. There is the finding out of the information and there is then how you present it. My view for some time would be that Andrew Gilligan is extremely good at finding out information but there are sometimes questions of nuance and subtlety in how he presents it which are not all that they should be. Indeed, in my evidence to the Inquiry on August 13th we talked a little bit about some of the issues that arose during his reporting of the Iraq War in that context, and I was frank with the Board of Governors about that, my view of Andrew Gilligan in those terms. I think I described him as a reporter who paints in primary colours rather than something more subtle.

Q. If you had known that Mr Marsh's views were as reflected in this e-mail at the time of the Governor's meeting, would you have thought it right to draw their attention to the fact?

A. I think it is hypothetical because I was not – I did not see this e-mail.

Q. Yes, I know it is hypothetical but I would still like your answer to the question.

A. No, I think the Governors would have wanted to know what my view was.

Q. Right. They would not have been interested in the views of Mr Marsh, as the editor of the programme that was being complained about?

A. Well, only if they significantly differed from mine.

Q. I see. Do you share the views expressed here?

A. I have already told you what my views of Andrew Gilligan's reporting were.

In his evidence Mr Davies said:

[28 August, page 135, line 18]

Q. Can I take you to BBC/5/118, where it was said : "…I have to talk to AG [that is Mr Gilligan] early next week. I hope that by then my worst fears … aren't realised. Assuming not, the guts of what I would say are: "This story was a good piece of investigative journalism, marred by flawed reporting – our biggest millstone has been his loose use of language and lack of judgment in some of his phraseology." Also the writing for other outlets and an explanation as to why that might have happened. Did you think you ought to have known of these comments at the Governors' meetings?

A. No, I did not honestly. These comments were between the editor of Today and, I think, the Director of Radio News. They are considerably below the Board of Governors level. What we needed to know at Board of Governors was what the considered judgment of the News Division and the Director General was of Mr Gilligan as a reporter; and these comments do not reflect their considered judgment – I think Mr Sambrook said that in evidence to this Inquiry; and certainly they do not reflect what the Director of News said about Mr Gilligan as a reporter to the Governors.

I am unable to accept these dismissive comments on the relevance and importance of Mr Marsh's e-mail. I consider the lack of knowledge on the part of Mr Sambrook and the Governors of Mr Marsh's e-mail containing criticisms of Mr Gilligan's method of reporting shows a defect in the BBC's management system for the consideration of complaints in respect of broadcasts.

(4)(a) I consider that the Governors found themselves in a difficult position at their meeting on the evening of 6 July as they were being told by the management of the BBC that they were satisfied as to the credibility and reliability of the anonymous source and that Mr Gilligan fully stood by his reports. The view taken by Mr Gavyn Davies is shown in the following passage of his evidence when cross-examined by Mr Sumption:

[24 September, page 30, line 20]

Q. Were you aware that since Mr Gilligan's original broadcast, statements had been made both by Mr Gilligan and himself [Mr Sambrook] that the source was in the Intelligence Services, but that by 6th July Mr Sambrook knew that that was not so?

A. No, I was not aware that – this intelligence source point, Mr Sumption, and the difference between intelligence sources and Intelligence Service sources, had not come across my radar screen in any detail by the time of the Governors' meeting.

Q. Do you not think it should have come across somebody's radar screen if the Governors were going to be properly informed about this?

A. It did come across somebody's radar screen. Both the Director of News and I should imagine the Director General, who broadly knew who the source was, would have thought about it in some detail. I think what Mr Sambrook said to the Inquiry was that when he described the source as an Intelligence Service source on his Today Programme interview, he subsequently realised that that was a mistake but that he did not feel that he could correct that mistake without pointing further fingers at the source. He did not mention any of that to the Governors.

Q. He did not, did he? So the Governors did not know that a part of what had been said about the status of the source on the BBC was known to the Director of News to be wrong; and they had no report on the extent to which Mr Gilligan's notes supported what he had broadcast. Those two points are factually correct, are they not?

A. The Governors did not know anything about the source other than the credibility and reliability of the source as attested by several editors.

Q. In other words, the answer to my question is: no, they did not know either of those two facts and nobody told them.

A. In terms of the notes that Mr Gilligan gave – kept of his meeting with Dr Kelly, the Governors were told that those notes substantiated the broadcast and, more to the point, that Mr Gilligan was standing fully behind his broadcast. Now, I do want to say a word about notes here, because these notes have adopted an extraordinarily large part of the discussions that have been had since.

Most journalists broadcast material based, to a large extent, on memory as well as notes; and most journalists do not make verbatim or anywhere near verbatim notes of their discussions. One of the reasons that is the case – and I can tell you this because I have worked, in my career, for a lengthy period of time as a part time journalist – is most journalists think that it puts off the person they are talking to if they either bring out a tape recorder or a notepad. Therefore it is very customary, Mr Sumption, for the journalist's memory to be every bit as important as the journalist's notes.

Q. We know that Mr Gilligan claims that he did, in fact, take notes during his meeting with Dr Kelly. So whatever the general position may be, that does not seem to be a relevant consideration in this case.

A. It does because he has always made it clear that this was not a verbatim set of notes.

Q. Let me take you up on what you said a moment ago, that the Governors were told that Mr Gilligan's notes supported the broadcast. As I understand what you said slightly earlier than that, they were told that even though Mr Sambrook had not examined the notes carefully enough to pick up the point that the 6.07 allegations were not reflected there.

A. As Mr Sambrook correctly told you, at the time the main interest in what the notes said appeared to be in two things: one was whether the notes substantiated The Mail on Sunday's article allegation by the source, that the source had used the word "Campbell" or had attributed to Alastair Campbell the transformation of the document. That was one thing. The second was whether the notes substantiated the "sexing up" or "making the document sexier" phrase. And those were the two things that I think Mr Sambrook said were particularly on his mind when he inspected the notes; and the notes did substantiate both those two things.

Q. Was nobody interested in the question whether the notes substantiated the suggestion broadcast by Mr Gilligan that the Government had put material into the dossier knowing that it was probably wrong? Was no one interested in that question?

A. The focus on the 6.07 broadcast, which has become very intense recently in the Government's case, was not actually reflected with the current degree of intensity at the time. Mr Sambrook has said to this Inquiry that it had not acquired the profile, in his thinking, that it has since acquired in the Government's case. I would argue, sir, that it had not acquired this profile in the Government's complaints prior to about the latter part of June either.

Q. I do not accept that, Mr Davies, but I am not going to go through that point with you. That too is a matter of record. But the fact is if Mr Sambrook had carefully gone through the notes and compared them with the transcript of what Mr Gilligan had said, it would have been absolutely apparent to him what all BBC witnesses have acknowledged so far in this Inquiry, namely that Mr Gilligan had gone too far, would it not?

A. He would have noted that the precise words used in the 6.07 broadcast were not duplicated in the notes, and I think he would then have asked Mr Gilligan why; and, in a sense, I would say that actually was – what Mr Gilligan said was that the 6.07 was an interpretation and not a direct quote from the source, he should not have suggested it was a direct quote. It was an interpretation from the source. And he was at that stage standing by it. One of the things I would say about the possibility of a complaints process, and one reason why I think that a full complaints process may have perhaps had problems sorting this particular issue out, is that I think the same thing may have happened. I think they may have looked at the notes, seen that they did not duplicate the words in the 6.07, asked Mr Gilligan why not and Mr Gilligan may well have said: that was a valid interpretation of what the source said to me. That is why I think some further concrete evidence may have been needed to sort this out.

Q. Are you saying that whatever Mr Gilligan said about things that were not in his notes would have been taken at face value by the Governors without further investigation?

A. I did not say anything about the Governors, I was talking about by the PCU.

Q. By the PCU then.

A. I do not think anything would have been taken at face value at all. It would have been taken as evidence, certainly.

[24 September, page 36, line 22]

Q. How were the Governors going to form an independent view of the question whether Mr Gilligan had gone further than his source and the question whether the source had been accurately described without having the information before them that was, in fact, in Mr Sambrook's head as this meeting took place?

A. I have already explained to you, I think that the focus on the notes is exaggerated to some degree. And what I think the Governors wanted – I speak for myself, Mr Sumption; what I wanted, as Chairman, was I wanted the considered judgment of the executives that we had appointed to run the news division and the Director General on whether the source was credible and reliable and whether the source was accurately reported. And short of seeking to duplicate their process in a way that would have suggested that we did not trust them, I am not sure what we could have done. Let me explain something to you: the Board of the BBC cannot operate, cannot operate, unless it is in a situation in which it can rely on the good faith and competence of its officers. I am absolutely certain that it can. If it sought to duplicate all of the actions of management it would indeed become the management. There is a gap between what the Board is and does and what the management is and does.

Q. Mr Davies, I quite understand that the Governors' board is a supervisory and, in some respects, an investigatory body. But surely the problem here was that the Governors did in fact duplicate what the executives had done instead of forming a view of their own which, if they had been properly informed, might have been very different?

A. No, they did not duplicate what the executive had done. They expressed the judgment, which I do not resile from at all, that it was in the public interest to put the words of the source into the public domain.

Q. They were put in a position where, for sheer want of information on the point, they had no alternative but to accept the views of the executives although those executives had dug themselves firmly into a position, is that not right?

A. The Governors had a great deal of information going into the meeting and they had an important corroboration for the Gilligan report, which continues to slip out of the mind of the Government; and that is the Susan Watts reports. I said in my first appearance before this Inquiry that the Susan Watts report was not identical to the Gilligan report. I actually studied both before I went into the meeting and I knew they were not identical, but I equally knew that the burden of what Mr Gilligan had reported in his many broadcasts on the subject at the end of May was a close match to the burden of what Ms Watts reported on 2nd and 4th June. And I do not think it should be forgotten that that is the case, because certainly in my mind, and in several other Governors' mind, maybe the whole of the Board of Governors who received the information before they went into the meeting, that was seen as an important corroboration of the Gilligan story.

Q. Would you turn to BBC/6/107, please? This is part of the official minute of the meeting in question. After the executives are drawn it says, second paragraph from the top of the page: "Following an account from Mark Damazer about how the '45 minutes claim' had been disputed by the Government since the broadcast, and a discussion by Governors about the accuracy of the report, Gavyn Davies reminded the Board that it was not a matter for them." So is the position that when the Governors did start discussing the accuracy of the report you intervened to stop them?

A. I think that is a very tendentious way of putting it. I was reminding them, as I had said to them in the e-mail on the Friday and had basically been agreed with by all Governors, that the intrinsic accuracy of the report, ie whether the source was telling, fundamentally, the truth or not, as opposed to whether we were accurately reporting him, was something that we were not in a position to determine. I therefore felt at this stage, and other Governors agreed with me, that the discussion was interesting but going down a by-way which we could not reach a conclusion on.

211

Q. I see. You could not, of course, without the information.

A. No, we could not have got the information, Mr Sumption. There was no way of obtaining the information.

(4)(b) The Governors were right to take the view that it was their duty to protect the independence of the BBC against attacks by the Government and there is no doubt that Mr Campbell's complaints were being expressed in exceptionally strong terms which raised very considerably the temperature of the dispute between the Government and the BBC, but Mr Campbell's allegation that the BBC had an anti-war agenda in his evidence to the FAC was only one part of his evidence. The Government's concern about Mr Gilligan's broadcast on the 29 May was a separate issue about which specific complaints had been made by the Government. Therefore I consider that the Governors should have recognised more fully than they did that their duty to protect the independence of the BBC was not incompatible with giving proper consideration to whether there was validity in the Government's complaints, no matter how strongly worded by Mr Campbell, that the allegations against its integrity reported in Mr Gilligan's broadcasts were unfounded and the Governors failed to give this issue proper consideration. The view taken by the Governors, as explained by Mr Gavyn Davies in his evidence, that they had to rely on the BBC management to investigate and assess whether Mr Gilligan's source was reliable and credible and that it was not for them as Governors to investigate whether the allegations reported were themselves accurate, is a view which is understandable. However I consider that this was not the correct view for the Governors to take because the Government had stated to the BBC in clear terms, as had Mr Campbell to the FAC, that the report that the Government probably knew that the 45 minutes claim was wrong was untruthful, and this denial was made with the authority of the Prime Minister and the Chairman of the JIC. In those circumstances, rather than relying on the assurances of BBC management, I consider that the Governors themselves should have made more detailed investigations into the extent to which Mr Gilligan's notes supported his report. If they had done this they would probably have discovered that the notes did not support the allegation that the Government knew that the 45 minutes claim was probably wrong, and the Governors should then have questioned whether it was right for the BBC to maintain that it was in the public interest to broadcast that allegation in Mr Gilligan's report from an anonymous source and to rely on Mr Gilligan's assurance that his report was accurate. Therefore in the very unusual and specific circumstances relating to Mr Gilligan's broadcasts, I consider that the Governors are to be criticised for themselves failing to make more detailed investigations into whether this allegation reported by Mr Gilligan was properly supported by his notes and for failing to give proper and adequate consideration to whether the BBC should publicly acknowledge that this very grave allegation should not have been broadcast.

Summary of conclusions relating to the BBC arising from Mr Gilligan's broadcasts on the BBC Today programme on 29 May 2003

291. (1) The allegations reported by Mr Gilligan on the BBC Today programme on 29 May 2003 that the Government probably knew that the 45 minutes claim was wrong or questionable before the dossier was published and that it was not inserted in the first draft of the dossier because it only came from one source and the intelligence agencies did not really believe it was necessarily true, were unfounded.

(2) The communication by the media of information (including information obtained by investigative reporters) on matters of public interest and importance is a vital part of life in a democratic society. However the right to communicate such information is subject to the qualification (which itself exists for the benefit of a democratic society) that false accusations of fact impugning the integrity of others, including politicians, should not be made by the media. Where a reporter is intending to broadcast or publish information impugning the integrity of others the management of his broadcasting company or newspaper should ensure that a system is in place whereby his editor or editors give careful consideration to the wording of the report and to whether it is right in all the circumstances to broadcast or publish it. The allegations that Mr Gilligan was intending to broadcast in respect of the Government and the preparation of the dossier were very grave allegations in relation to a subject of great importance and I consider that the editorial system which the BBC permitted was defective in that Mr Gilligan was allowed to broadcast his report at 6.07am without editors having seen a script of what he was going to say and having considered whether it should be approved.

(3) The BBC management was at fault in the following respects in failing to investigate properly the Government's complaints that the report in the 6.07am broadcast was false that the Government probably knew that the 45 minutes claim was wrong even before it decided to put it in the dossier. The BBC management failed, before Mr Sambrook wrote his letter of 27 June 2003 to Mr Campbell, to make an examination of Mr Gilligan's notes on his personal organiser of his meeting with Dr Kelly to see if they supported the allegations which he had reported in his broadcast at 6.07am. When the BBC management did look at Mr Gilligan's notes after 27 June it failed to appreciate that the notes did not fully support the most serious of the allegations which he had reported in the 6.07am broadcast, and it therefore failed to draw the attention of the Governors to the lack of support in the notes for the most serious of the allegations.

(4) The e-mail sent by Mr Kevin Marsh, the editor of the Today programme on 27 June 2003 to Mr Stephen Mitchell, the Head of Radio News, (see paragraph 284) which was critical of Mr Gilligan's method of reporting, and which referred to Mr Gilligan's "loose use of language and lack of judgment in some of his phraseology" and referred also to "the loose and in some ways distant relationship he's been allowed to have with Today," was clearly relevant to the complaints which the Government were making about his broadcasts on 29 May, and the lack of knowledge on the part of Mr Sambrook, the Director of News and the Governors of this critical e-mail shows a defect in the operation of the BBC's management system for the consideration of complaints in respect of broadcasts.

(5) The Governors were right to take the view that it was their duty to protect the independence of the BBC against attacks by the Government and Mr Campbell's complaints were being expressed in exceptionally strong terms which raised very considerably the temperature of the dispute between the Government and the BBC. However Mr Campbell's allegation that the BBC had an anti-war agenda in his evidence to the FAC was only one part of his evidence. The Government's concern about Mr Gilligan's broadcasts on 29 May was a separate issue about which specific complaints had been made by the Government. Therefore the Governors should have recognised more fully than they did that their duty to protect the independence of the BBC was not incompatible with giving proper consideration to whether there was validity in the Government's complaints, no matter how strongly worded by

Mr Campbell, that the allegations against its integrity reported in Mr Gilligan's broadcasts were unfounded and the Governors failed to give this issue proper consideration. The view taken by the Governors, as explained in evidence by Mr Gavyn Davies, the Chairman of the Board of Governors, that they had to rely on the BBC management to investigate and assess whether Mr Gilligan's source was reliable and credible and that it was not for them as Governors to investigate whether the allegations reported were themselves accurate, is a view which is understandable. However this was not the correct view for the Governors to take because the Government had stated to the BBC in clear terms, as had Mr Campbell to the FAC, that the report that the Government probably knew that the 45 minutes claim was wrong was untruthful, and this denial was made with the authority of the Prime Minister and the Chairman of the JIC. In those circumstances, rather than relying on the assurances of BBC management, I consider that the Governors themselves should have made more detailed investigations into the extent to which Mr Gilligan's notes supported his report. If they had done this they would probably have discovered that the notes did not support the allegation that the Government knew that the 45 minutes claim was probably wrong, and the Governors should then have questioned whether it was right for the BBC to maintain that it was in the public interest to broadcast that allegation in Mr Gilligan's report and to rely on Mr Gilligan's assurances that his report was accurate. Therefore in the very unusual and specific circumstances relating to Mr Gilligan's broadcasts, the Governors are to be criticised for themselves failing to make more detailed investigations into whether this allegation reported by Mr Gilligan was properly supported by his notes and for failing to give proper and adequate consideration to whether the BBC should publicly acknowledge that this very grave allegation should not have been broadcast.

CHAPTER 9

Issues relating to the decisions and actions taken by the Government after Dr Kelly informed his line manager in the MoD that he had spoken to Mr Gilligan on 22 May 2003

292. These issues are the following:

(a) Did the Government behave in a way which was dishonourable or underhand or duplicitous in revealing Dr Kelly's name to the media, thereby subjecting him to the pressure and stress which were bound to arise from being placed in the media spotlight?

(b) If the Government did not behave in a way which was dishonourable or underhand or duplicitous in revealing Dr Kelly's name to the media, did the Government fail to take proper steps to help and protect Dr Kelly in the difficult position in which he found himself?

Did the Government behave in a way which was dishonourable or underhand or duplicitous in revealing Dr Kelly's name to the media, thereby subjecting him to the pressure and stress which were bound to arise from being placed in the media spotlight?

293. The allegation has been made by a number of commentators, with varying degrees of force, that the Government devised and implemented an underhand strategy to name Dr Kelly whereby his name was deliberately but covertly leaked to the press in order to strengthen the Government's case in its battle with the BBC. In his cross-examination of the Secretary of State for Defence, Mr Gompertz QC, on behalf of Dr Kelly's family, put the following suggestion to him, which he denied:

> **[22 September, page 25, line 4]**
>
> What I suggest to you is that there was a deliberate Government strategy to leak Dr Kelly's name into the public arena without appearing to do so, by a combination of the press statement, the question and answer material, the Prime Minister's official spokesman press briefing and other leaks which appear to have taken place to the press. That is what I suggest.

Mr Gompertz in his closing statement said that one of the principal aims of Dr Kelly's family in the Inquiry was that "the duplicity of the Government in their handling of Dr Kelly should be exposed".

294. The issue whether the Government acted towards Dr Kelly in a manner which was dishonourable or underhand or duplicitous was one in respect of which Government witnesses were questioned at length in the course of the Inquiry, and I think it is desirable that parts of their evidence on this issue should be set out in chronological sequence at some length in this report so that the public can read their evidence and understand the conclusions to which I have come.

The evidence of Ms Pamela Teare, the Director of News at the MoD, on 18 August

295. Ms Teare gave evidence that at lunchtime on Tuesday 8 July she and Mr Martin Howard began a redraft of Question and Answer material. The redraft when completed was as follows:

> **Q & A**
>
> **Who is the official?**
>
> The official works in MoD.
>
> **What is his name and current post?**
>
> We wouldn't normally volunteer a name.
>
> <u>If the correct name is given,</u> we can confirm it and say that he is senior advisor to the Proliferation and Arms Control Secretariat.
>
> **How long has he been in MoD?**
>
> He has been in his current position for 3 to 4 years. Before that he was a member of UNSCOM.
>
> **Did the official play any part in drawing up the dossier?**
>
> He was involved in providing historical details of UNSCOM's activities prior to 1998.
>
> **Is he a senior figure?**
>
> He is not a member of the SCS – he is a middle-ranking official.
>
> **Is he still working for MoD?**
>
> Yes.
>
> **Is he in Iraq?**
>
> No, though he visited Iraq recently for a week.
>
> **Is he a member of the ISG?**
>
> No.
>
> **Do you believe he is the single source?**
>
> It is not for us to say – only the BBC can confirm that.
>
> **So he hasn't volunteered to being the source?**
>
> No. He volunteered that he met Mr Gilligan and discussed the September dossier.
>
> **It is unprecedented for a Government Department to make a statement of this sort. Why have you done it?**
>
> There is no comparable situation that springs to mind. We have set out the facts as they have been put to us, on an issue of considerable public concern. The official involved volunteered the information to us.
>
> **Can we interview the individual?**
>
> No – this is not appropriate as the consequences will be dealt with by MoD internally.
>
> **Will he be disciplined/sacked?**
>
> Appropriate management steps will be taken. On the basis of our current understanding of the situation, he will not be sacked.
>
> **Where did he meet Mr Gilligan?**
>
> He says they met in the Charing Cross Hotel, central London.
>
> **In what form did this official come forward?**
>
> The official approached his line manager, which is the standard procedure for raising concerns. He has also been interviewed by the relevant members of senior staff.

Why has the official come forward now?

It followed his reading of the detailed evidence Mr Gilligan gave to the FAC.

What was it in that evidence that made the official consider that his conversation might be relevant?

The official felt that a number of elements of the conversation he had with Mr Gilligan were consistent with Mr Gilligan's evidence to the FAC when describing his single source. Though a number were not. For details – see the statement.

Are you suggesting Mr Gilligan deliberately "sexed up" his story?

We are making no accusations. We are merely setting the information that has been put to us.

When did he come forward?

At the beginning of last week.

Why has it taken you a week to produce the information?

It was necessary to arrange for the official to be interviewed to establish, as far as we can, the details of his meeting with Gilligan.

When was he interviewed?

On Friday and Monday.

Which senior staff were informed?

The PUS was informed on Thursday. He informed the Secretary of State that evening.

When were No 10 told and if they were, why?

No 10 were told on Friday. It is only natural that they would be informed of a development on an issue of major concern.

Which other government departments were told?

As you would expect, Cabinet Office and FCO.

Why did you not tell the FAC over the weekend?

A further interview was required and that took place on Monday afternoon.

What if the BBC deny he is the source?

We have not claimed he is – I refer you back to our statement.

Can the FAC/ISC interview him?

We will be willing to consider any such request.

Were No 10 involved in this announcement?

The decision to issue a statement was made by the MoD.

How can you be sure that there has been no breach of the OSA?

On the basis of the information we have been given, there is no evidence to suggest a breach.

296. Ms Teare said:

[18 August, page 46, line 1]

A.... We had formed a view – I think there was a consensus amongst those closely involved in this issue in the department, really from the beginning, on two points: really that ultimately the MoD would have to make a public statement, would have to offer a public statement and that, secondly, Dr Kelly's name was likely to come into the public domain. If that is the case, which we believed it to be, we had to agree an approach whereby we could handle that situation.

217

A. We had discussed the whole issue of handling the name; and essentially Martin and I had – and essentially there were two issues. One, that it was possible that Dr Kelly's name would emerge; and the second issue was that during that process or at the same time as or even before, there were a group of other individuals who had similar backgrounds to him who might be identified incorrectly and on whom the media spotlight would fall and in a case related to this particular issue, that spotlight would be very strong. We agreed therefore that we were not prepared to have that situation, that it would be unfair on others.

LORD HUTTON: Yes.

A. So accordingly, if you decide on that policy that you cannot have a situation whereby people are wrongly identified and subjected to a lot of attention from the media, it follows, therefore, that if an incorrect name is put to you, that you will have to reject it.

MR KNOX: Is not all this a bit of a charade though, because as soon as you make it plain to the press: give me the right name and I will tell you if you have the right answer, you are doing effectively exactly the same thing by an incorrect means as what you could do directly and just give the name out?

A. No, I think we had – you know, we had not had Dr Kelly – the idea of Dr Kelly's name being made public had not been discussed with him. The time that you would have had to consider it, between when he was consulted about the final version of this statement and when it went out, would have been insufficient for him to consider it properly and to make what other arrangements he needed.

One of the purposes for saying to people that we would be prepared to confirm the right name was going back to what I have originally said, which was that we were seeking to avoid the people who were not involved being named in the media, and the only way we could seek to do that was to make it clear to journalists we would correct wrong names so they did not get into the public domain.

Q. Did you tell Dr Kelly as far as you were aware you would be adopting this strategy, namely confirming to journalists his name if they managed to come up with it?

A. I did not speak to Dr Kelly at any point.

Q. Do you have any reason to suppose he was told this?

A. He was certainly told on more than one occasion, as I understand, that his name was likely to come into the public domain.

Q. I know, but was he told that this strategy would be adopted by the MoD press office?

A. Not to my knowledge.

LORD HUTTON: I should make it clear perhaps to the press that if I put certain questions to you that it does not mean at all I have reached any conclusion on the point. I have to consider a number of possibilities. I understand your reasoning in saying if a number of names are considered and they are not the correct names, the spotlight would fall unfairly on them; and therefore the thinking was: well, to avoid that, if we are given names which are incorrect, we will say so. But another way of looking at it is that if you adopt that approach, when the press do learn the correct name the spotlight falls very fiercely indeed on that particular person. Let us say you have six people whose names are being discussed in the press. People will then realise that certainly it is very general speculation and the individuals named may well not be the correct people at all. Certainly there is no particular person who would be regarded necessarily as being the actual civil servant concerned. But did you give any consideration to the fact that by permitting Dr Kelly's name to come out, he would be subjected to very intense media speculation?

A. Yes, I mean, there are two points I would like to make.

LORD HUTTON: Yes. Certainly.

A. The first is that whilst you might suggest that if a number of names are bandied around they would not be subjected to a great deal of media interest and concentration, I think because the profile of this subject was so large, I think actually that it would have had a lot of media attention, which would have been most unhelpful and most unfair.

The second point is, though, that we were certainly concerned for Dr Kelly. It is not as if, you know, we agreed this approach just because it was purely the best way to avoid other people being named, and accordingly, as I say, he had been made aware on two occasions that we were likely to have to make a statement, his name would come into the public domain. On the evening of the 8th July, Dr Kelly was rung by the chief press officer to alert him to the level of media interest that had arisen following the issue of our statement, to make sure that she had – or rather he had her contact number, made clear she was available to offer advice 24 hours a day, and also to suggest to him he might wish to consider staying with friends. So we were very mindful of that, and for the reasons I have given why we did not think it was fair the media spotlight would fall on others, we were aware that spotlight would be heavy and he would need guidance on how to deal with that.

297. Ms Teare was asked whether the information contained in the Question and Answer material did not provide clues to the press as to Dr Kelly's identity:

> [18 August, page 65, line 17]
>
> Q. What I think might look strange is obviously you decide not to name him outright but you give all these clues and it is inevitable, is it not, once you have given all these clues, the press are going to get the right name if you have told them "I will confirm it"?
>
> A. As I say, I do not accept this material was offered on the basis of it offering clues. There are several other points I would make. One is if, as you seem to be trying to suggest or others may suggest, all we were doing was planting lots of hints about the real identity of the unnamed official, then it is surprising on the other hand that (a) it took journalists 24 hours at least to work it out and (b) that they were ringing, putting quite a large number of names to us. So those two things seem to be slightly contradictory.
>
> Q. It might be thought you did not want to be thought to be seen naming him directly, is that right?
>
> A. No, I do not accept that. As I say, we had taken a decision that he would not be named in the statement and therefore we were not – you know, we were not offering anything more that would seek to undermine that decision, I can assure you.

The evidence of Mr Jonathan Powell, the Chief of Staff, at 10 Downing Street, on 18 August

298. In his evidence Mr Powell described two meetings involving the Prime Minister which took place in 10 Downing Street on 8 July at 11.30am and 1.30pm. In the course of his evidence he was asked:

> [18 August, page 113, line 24]
>
> Q. ...can I just ask you a series of questions about Dr Kelly's name coming out into the public domain? I mean, was one of the reasons that Dr Kelly's name was wanted to be put into the public arena was to correct – was to show that Mr Gilligan was wrong about what he claimed to have been told?
>
> A. Not Dr Kelly's name. I mean, the fact that someone had come forward certainly, as again I referred to that Kevin Tebbit letter of Friday made it clear: if we had these facts, we should make them public. One just has to think for a second what would have happened if we had not made them public and what we would have been accused of in those circumstances in terms of a cover up.

299. In describing the meeting commencing at 1.30pm Mr Powell said:

[18 August, page 123, line 21]

A. You recall from the previous meeting what we had been discussing was how we should make the fact that someone had come forward public because we thought it would be wrong to withhold that information. So we were clear it was going to become public. The manner in which we had discussed doing it in the first meeting was that letter to the ISC. That was now no longer possible since the ISC did not want us to do it that way, so we had to look at other means of doing so.

Q. What were those other means? First of all with the ISC, how did you sort that out?

A. Well, with the ISC we adopted the idea that had been put to us by them, that we could refer at the end of our press release to the fact that this individual was willing to be interviewed by them. But in terms of how we would make it public we reverted to the idea of a press release, which is what had been sent to us by the MoD the previous evening.

Q. So the 8th July, because the ISC are not happy with you publicising the letter to them –

A. Hmm.

Q. – you are now going back to the Ministry of Defence press release?

A. That is correct.

Q. You, in fact, produced some Q and A material. Can I take you to CAB/1/59? You can see that there is an e-mail. Can you tell everyone who that e-mail is to and from?

A. Yes, the first one in the sequence is from our Parliamentary private secretary, the person who deals with Parliamentary affairs, to me. Then it is replied from me to her.

Q. Right. What is the first one about?

A. Well, they are both about a Q and A on the issue of this official coming forward.

Q. Right. And why were you drafting this?

A. Well, it turns out, having spoken to this official subsequently, this was actually a misunderstanding. There was – this official thought she was drafting a Q and A for the Prime Minister's questions on Wednesday, which is her job to prepare for that. I thought she was drafting a more general Q and A on this issue.

Q. Right. So these are draft – if you turn to page 60, you can see most of these will need to be answered by MoD: "When was the PM made aware that the individual had come forward? And by who?" You can see it appears to be directed towards questions to the Prime Minister.

A. Yes.

Q. So these are drafts of what was understood, then, to be an issue that might be raised at Prime Minister's Questions, is that right?

A. That is correct. It was a rather sort of a – not a terribly well-developed piece of work. It was a very rapid series of quick fire questions and even less series of responses which I e-mailed back very quickly, but this piece of work did not go anywhere subsequently.

The evidence of Sir David Manning, formerly Foreign Policy Adviser to the Prime Minister, and Head of the Overseas and Defence Secretariat in the Cabinet Office, on 18 August

300. In his evidence Sir David Manning said that he had had a meeting in 10 Downing Street with Sir David Omand and Mr John Scarlett on the evening of Friday 4 July to discuss the fact that an official in the MoD had come forward to say that he had been in contact with Mr Gilligan:

[18 August, page 148, line 8]

Q. You discussed it. Can you tell us what the gist of those discussions were?

A. Yes. I think there were two things that we discussed particularly. The first was whether or not we should make the fact that an official had come forward – whether we should make this available to the Foreign Affairs Committee and also to the ISC, the Intelligence and Security Committee, because we knew that they were both meeting to discuss the issue of the allegations in Mr Gilligan's broadcast.

....

[18 August, page 149, line 18]

MR DINGEMANS: And so there is discussion about the ISC and FAC. And were any conclusions reached?

A. The conclusions were that they should certainly consider whether we should make this information available to them. No conclusion was reached in the sense that we decided that we definitely should; but we were concerned that this was important, perhaps material, to their enquiries and we should therefore consider very carefully whether to make this information known to them.

301. The following question was put to Sir David Manning:

[18 August, page 152, line 6]

Q...... the sudden concern to ensure that Dr Kelly should appear before the FAC, or the Government should be seen to be cooperating with the FAC, seems on the face of it inconsistent with the attitude that had been displaced (sic) [displayed] before.

A. Well, I can only speak for myself but I would have thought that we should certainly make the fact available to the chairman of the Foreign Affairs Committee that this had happened. It would be for him then to decide what he wanted to do with that knowledge. But if I had been asked for my advice at that stage, I would have said that since there had been a major Public Inquiry conducted by the Foreign Affairs Committee on this issue, if someone had come forward who seemed to be potentially very important we must at least consider, which is what we were discussing on that Friday night, whether that fact should be made available to him.

302. In relation to the question whether it would be possible to shield Dr Kelly's name from public knowledge, Sir David Manning said the following:

[18 August, page 162, line 24]

Q. Did that influence your thinking of the matter, namely the understanding that Dr Kelly was happy for his name to go forward?

A. It seemed to me important that he should be consulted on this, yes.

Q. Important that he should be consulted; but his reported answer or the answer reported to you, that was obviously a factor in your approach to it, is that right?

A. Yes, it was a factor in my approach. But I have to be honest with you, I thought it very unlikely that if the conclusion was reached that Dr Kelly might well be Andrew Gilligan's source, that it would be possible to shield his name from public knowledge.

Q. Why is that?

A. Because I was struck by the article in The Times on Saturday the 5th which, if I recall, was a front page article which clearly showed that the press were very interested in who Andrew Gilligan's source or sources might be. And it seemed to me that it was unlikely given the level of press and public interest, that if somebody had come forward in this sort of way that their name was likely to remain secret.

Q. If you had known, for example, that Dr Kelly was less than happy about his name coming out, if that had been his view, would that have affected your views on whether his name should be given to the FAC or ISC?

A. I think if I had known he was unhappy about it, it would have perhaps qualified the way that we spoke or indicated to the chairs of those Committees; but I would still have taken the view that we should make it known to the chairman and the chair of the ISC, the chairman of the FAC, that someone had come forward.

303. In relation to the meeting which took place in 10 Downing Street on the morning of Tuesday 8 July Sir David Manning said:

[18 August, page 175, line 10]

Q....... what is concluded at this meeting that started at about 11.30 on Tuesday 8ᵗʰ July?

A. I think the conclusion was that we should inform the chair of the ISC, since the ISC was still conducting its enquiries and it was therefore a live Inquiry, and that this should be done by means of a letter to Ann Taylor, who is the chair, and that it should probably go from David Omand and that this letter, I think, should be copied to Donald Anderson, the chairman of the Foreign Affairs Committee.

Q. Right. I think you have explained why Ann Taylor is going to get the letter, because she has an ongoing Inquiry. Why is it going to be copied to Donald Anderson?

A. Because, as I think I said earlier, we felt that it was very important that we were not in the position of apparently withholding key information from the Foreign Affairs Committee, which had just spent several weeks investigating this matter when something that was perhaps very important had just emerged and that as a courtesy, to say the least, we should tell the chairman of the Foreign Affairs Committee what had happened.

The evidence of Mr Alastair Campbell, formerly the Prime Minister's Director of Communications and Strategy, on 19 August

304. Mr Campbell gave evidence that on Friday 4 July he was told by Mr Hoon that a person had come forward who had admitted meeting Mr Gilligan:

[19 August, page 137, line 4]

A. I was telephoned by Geoff Hoon about a different matter. He was actually just phoning up to offer his support and solidarity in advance of Monday. He asked me whether Jonathan Powell had mentioned I think from memory he thought the source issue. I said: no he had not, what is that? He explained somebody had come forward, that this person had admitted meeting Mr Gilligan in I think he said at that time in a hotel, that the person had acknowledged saying some of the things that had been reported by Mr Gilligan but had insisted that he had not said other things. Again, I cannot remember if this was what Mr Hoon said to me but certainly then or subsequently I was told that related specifically to this person, saying they had never said anything in relation to me.

Q. Right. And did Mr Hoon share what his initial instinct was in relation to this matter?

A. His initial instinct was I think he felt this was serious and this was a serious disciplinary matter and this person, if it was the source, had clearly caused the Government considerable difficulty and embarrassment by saying something to a reporter that was not true, but then went on to say – and this, I think, accorded with my instinct at the time – that he was in all probability telling the truth in saying that he did not say all of these things.

If I can just explain why I felt that. I had always felt about this story that Mr Gilligan probably did have a source, but that he exaggerated the source and he exaggerated what the source said. So it kind of fitted with the feeling I had had about this. I think what Mr Hoon was saying was his initial instinct was this person has to be dealt with severely but then actually thought: well, he has come forward, he has come forward in the spirit of openness and honesty and he is claiming he has been misrepresented if he is the source.

305. In his personal diary Mr Campbell had made the following entry for 4 July 2003:

> Spoke to Hoon who said that a man had come forward who felt he was possibly Gilligan's source, had come forward and was being interviewed today. GH said his initial instinct was to throw the book at him, but in fact there was a case for trying to get some kind of plea bargain. Says that he'd come forward and he was saying yes to speak to AG, yes he said intel went in late, but he never said the other stuff. It was double-edged but GH and I agreed it would f*** Gilligan if that was his source. He said he was an expert rather than a spy or a full-time MOD official. GH and I agreed to talk tomorrow.

306. Counsel to the Inquiry referred Mr Campbell to this entry and Mr Campbell said:

[19 August, page 138, line 15]

Q. You use a specific phrase in your diary. I am going to have to ask you just to relate that and explain it.

A. I have used in my diary – the reason I did not use it in answer to you now is I think it does risk being unfair to Mr Hoon. He actually said his initial instinct was, as I say, to be severe in this regard but there was a case for trying to get some kind of plea bargain. That is what I recorded.

Q. A plea bargain with?

A. In relation to the person who had come forward. In other words, the person had been honest and open in coming forward, had acknowledged some of the, if you like, offences that were being described, but was adamant he had not been responsible for others.

Q. Why do you say that is likely to be misinterpreted or unfair?

A. Because I think it carries a suggestion that Mr Hoon was saying to me: I think we can do some kind of deal with this guy, and that is not what he was saying.

Q. Did you have any view about what this was likely to do to Mr Gilligan?

A. I felt that if this person was the source, and Mr Hoon had explained to me that the person was not a member of the Intelligence Services, was not centrally involved in the drawing up of the dossier, I therefore felt that if this person was the source then it was probably the only way that we were actually going to be able to establish the truth, namely that the allegations of May 29th were false, because of course Mr Gilligan had told the Select Committee they were based on a single source.

307. Mr Campbell was asked about his view of the matter over the weekend of 5 and 6 July:

[19 August, page 144, line 24]

Q. Can I then turn to 6th July, which is the Sunday? How would you describe you spent most of this particular weekend? Who were you speaking to over this particular weekend?

A. Well, I was – the FAC was due to report on Monday so I was working on that, and certainly talking to Jack Straw, I think, at some point during the day on that. I also spoke, over that weekend, to the Prime Minister, Geoff Hoon and Jonathan Powell about the issue of the source.

Q. And what was your view about that matter?

A. My view was that, as I said earlier, it was probably – if this person was the source, it was probably the only way that this issue was going to be properly bottomed out. I suggested to the Prime Minister two proposals – I cannot remember exactly when these were, but the first – my first instinct, and I think Geoff Hoon's as well, was that if this development came out over that weekend the Foreign Affairs Committee were going to accuse us of having covered it up. And I was suggesting that, in confidence, not the name and I did not know the name at that point, but that Donald Anderson possibly be informed that there had been this development and that it might be relevant to the way that he framed his report on Monday which, as you say, had already gone to the printers by then.

And the second proposal I made was that the BBC governors be told in advance of their meeting on the Sunday evening.

Q. And why were you keen, as it were, to get the fact that a source or a possible source had come forward out to either the FAC or the BBC?

A. Because I thought that that development ought to have a material effect upon the outcome of those two events on the assumption that this was the source.

Q. And did the Prime Minister accept your advice in that respect, or yours and Mr Hoon's views in that respect?

A. No. No, he did not.

Q. What was his view?

A. His view – he could see the point and we had a discussion about it; and he said: I hear what you say, I can see that if it comes out – and the thing to understand about this, is that these – I mean, Government departments do leak and these kind of things can get out and he was worried that that might happen there over that weekend. So the Prime Minister said: I hear what you say about the cover-up point, I hear what you say about the BBC, but you have to leave this to Sir Kevin Tebbit and David Omand to handle. And I was guided by that instruction.

Q. Did you think that was the right approach?

A. I felt – at the time I am not sure that I did, but I think I do now.

Q. Did Mr Hoon think that was the right approach?

A. I think he felt, like I did, that the – this was a development that could, at that time, possibly have been communicated to these bodies. But he too – I think he discussed it – he certainly discussed it with Jonathan Powell. He may well have discussed it with the Prime Minister as well. The Prime Minister's view was very, very clear and everybody understood it from the word go.

308. Mr Campbell was asked what course, with hindsight, he thought should have been adopted in relation to Dr Kelly having come forward:

[19 August, page 150, line 9]

MR DINGEMANS: What are you saying should have been adopted?

A. I have to admit this is, in part, a hindsight point.

Q. Yes.

A. But it is a thought that I had at the time, which I probably did not articulate as forcefully as I normally do articulate proposals that I have, because I was being instructed by the Prime Minister just to stay a little bit distant from this, because I was so centrally involved in relation to the events concerning the Foreign Affairs Committee.

I feel, and I think this is something Godric Smith in his own way did articulate at the time but again maybe we did not push this in the way that we should, but in these difficult situations where you are dealing with individuals as well as institutions and individuals who are not necessarily, as Mr Dingemans said, used to dealing with some of the things that we are used to dealing with all the time, then clarity is always best, and I completely understand why the Ministry of Defence had the strategy that they had in relation to if you like the two stage statement because Dr Kelly had said he did not want to be in that first wave, he had made that clear, we were told.

But I think again, and I emphasise this is with an element of hindsight, that probably what I feel I maybe should have expressed more forcefully at that time is: look, if you are in this kind of situation you do have to have some element of control over the process here. You cannot just let this sort of dribble out in a way that you are not clear how it is then going to unfold. So I think the desired outcome, given that everybody, including it seems Dr Kelly, understood that it is likely because of the importance of this development he was likely to be identified, he was likely to have to appear at one or both Select Committees, far better it would have been for that to be announced properly, cleanly, straightforwardly and then you can actually put in place all the proper support that somebody who is not used to this kind of pressure can then maybe better deal with it.

LORD HUTTON: But that is going to subject the individual to very great pressure. He is going to be put into the full glare of the media.

A. I accept that, but I think the judgment that was being reached by everybody involved in these discussions is that was going to happen because since Dr Kelly's death, I mean, parts of the media have been trying to give the impression: you know that they would never have been interested in this issue if it had not been for this clue, that clue and all the rest of it. The media were in full pursuit of this story and it was going to happen. I am afraid it is just the way of the world that we are in that the – I do not know if – I saw an interview Tom Mangold did after Dr Kelly's death where he said Dr Kelly understood this. Maybe he did understand it but maybe he did not understand the ramifications of it, that it was going to happen.

[19 August, page 154, line 2]

A.... I felt, in some of those discussions that we were having, during that period, that there was an element of unreality about them; that any second there could have been a phone call.

Indeed, it seems that the report of Mr Rufford – the reporter Mr Rufford from the Sunday Times was already on to this. It was going to happen. I think what we – again, I say with the benefit of hindsight what we did not do was actually just acknowledge that and I think maybe more time could then have been taken with Dr Kelly to sit down and say: look, this is virtually inevitable, it is going to have to happen and therefore let us work out exactly all the steps that then have to be taken.

As I say, it is easy in a sense to – and I do not want to feel that I am criticising others in this, because I understand how these strategies can get drawn up in very difficult, fast moving situations. But I think that would have been a better approach.

309. Mr Campbell referred to the discussion which took place at 10 Downing Street on the morning of Tuesday 8 July:

[19 August, page 163, line 9]

Q. We then come on to the 8th July. The Prime Minister is prepared, in the morning, for the Liaison Committee. I think we have heard from Mr Powell about that yesterday. Then at 11.30am he returns from the Liaison Committee and there is a discussion about whether or not Dr Kelly's name should be made public. Were you party to that discussion?

A. I was party to parts of that discussion.

Towards the end of his evidence the following question was put to Mr Campbell:

[19 August, page 165, line 12]

LORD HUTTON: Mr Campbell, in a sense I think you have already given detailed answers to a number of matters relating to Dr Kelly's name being released, but appreciating that, I would just like to ask you another general question: suppose at this discussion on 8th July someone had said: let us just hold on for a minute, this is a civil servant who has given very distinguished service to his country, he has admittedly been indiscreet in speaking to a journalist as he has, but if we release his name we are going to subject him to very considerable strain. Is that right that we should do this? Can we not simply batten down the hatches? And there is a risk of a leak but perhaps it will not come out, or if the names are put to us we just say: we do not respond to questions about civil servants. I know you have in a sense already responded to that question, but I wondered if you could give a general answer, a general summary as to what the response would have been if that question had been raised?

A. I think you could have done that, but I think it would still have ended with all the media pressure – media and other pressure that you refer to, because I think it would have come out, because these things do. And again, I mean, I am slightly – I have given up reading newspapers in recent weeks but I have a slight concern that things I have said already will be taken as critical of others. I regret that if that is the case. I do want to say in all those discussions I was privy to

Kevin Tebbit in particular was absolutely solicitous. He did not make the point in exactly the way that you put it -

LORD HUTTON: No, I appreciate that.

A. – but he was constantly emphasising: this is an employee. Yes, he has clearly done something that he should not have done, but we are his employer and have a duty of care to him.

The other observation I would make from those discussions, again this clearly is a hindsight point, but the impression I got – I did not know Dr Kelly, but the impression I got was of, and the way that he was being described was actually of a very strong, resolute character, clearly of deep conviction and who had been in many difficult, stressful circumstances, and I just do not think it crossed anybody's mind that it might take the turn that it did.

310. Some questions were also put to Mr Campbell about the Government's concern that they would be accused of a cover-up:

[19 August, page 167, line 15]

LORD HUTTON: But a cover-up in what sense? What would have been covered up?

A. What would have been covered up would be the fact – bear in mind – and this is why it was so difficult to draft that press release that was finally released, because there were so many of these competing factors. Part of the discussion that I recall, involving Sir Kevin Tebbit, Sir David Omand, the Prime Minister and others, was Sir Kevin clearly not being 100 per cent sure about whether – what Dr Kelly had actually said, about what he might say if he was called before a Select Committee.

So I do not think people should imagine that we were sitting there thinking: well, Dr Kelly, up before the Select Committee, it is unadulterated, unalloyed good news for the Government. It was not necessarily going to be so because Kevin Tebbit had reported he did have concerns about some aspects of the Government's position.

LORD HUTTON: So the concern was that if his name was not given by the Government but it was later revealed, it might transpire that Dr Kelly had views which were quite or strongly critical of the Government?

A. That is right; and that is why the Government did not want to put him before public scrutiny. And I think if, for example, on that Saturday that I was talking to the Prime Minister and Jonathan Powell and the Defence Secretary about the issue, if one of the Sunday papers, on that Saturday, had discovered this development then I can guarantee you the headlines the next day would have been "Government cover-up on eve of FAC report".

The evidence of Sir Kevin Tebbit, Permanent Under-Secretary of State at the Ministry of Defence, on 20 August

311. In his evidence Sir Kevin Tebbit said that he thought it was inevitable that Dr Kelly's name would become public at some stage:

[20 August, page 58, line 23]

Q. Did you at this stage [7 July 2003] have any view about whether or not Dr Kelly's name should be made public?

A. I started from the premise that it was inevitable that his name would become public at some stage. He had implied as much in his own letter.

Q. We have seen the passages where he says someone at RUSI – you think it may be Chatham House –

A. Yes.

Q. – may have known him, and also that he thought that some suspicion might fall on him.

A. Yes.

Q. Is there not a difference between those two passages and actually giving the name out to the press?

A. There is indeed, but there are many other elements in between the two points. As I say, the comment from a member of staff who did not know about this beforehand, having read The Times on Saturday, saying: they have all but named him, was also very significant. I have learnt subsequently actually, I did not know at the time, that knowledge that Dr Kelly had had meetings with Andrew Gilligan were becoming discussed at cocktail parties that officials in the Ministry of Defence were having. I only learnt that subsequently but it gives, I think, a flavour of the sort of environment.

312. Later in the course of examination by counsel to the Inquiry Sir Kevin Tebbit gave the following evidence:

[20 August, page 72, line 1]

LORD HUTTON: ..... can you just elaborate a little more on the point: why, if the Government were aware that there was an official who had not been directly concerned in drawing up the intelligence part of the dossier, if they knew there was such an official, why would the Government feel obliged to put his views into the public arena?

A. The 45 minutes comment he would make, I think, was not a central point here. The central point was that if we were certain that Dr Kelly provided the explanation for a story which had a fundamental influence on public confidence and trust in the Government's policies, then there was a strong case, one might almost say a duty, to bring that information forward.

LORD HUTTON: Yes. So it was because he was the source of the story, not just that he was an official who may have held views that differed from the Government's views?

A. Absolutely. I think it was almost a unique and unprecedented case, my Lord. Here was a single anonymous source, we had learnt from Mr Gilligan, who was responsible for a judgment which had a major effect on the confidence in the Government and on the intelligence process. If we find that there is a single identified source who says, effectively, "It was I, but I did not say those things, they are" as Dr Kelly put it "a considerable embellishment on what I said", then that would be the only way of clarifying reliably the public record. It would have been no good for the Government to say: we have an anonymous source who we think might be the same one that said something different. The authenticity would have depended on the individual being named.

313. In relation to the Government's concern that it would be accused of a cover-up Sir Kevin Tebbit said:

[20 August, page 74, line 7]

MR DINGEMANS: So would the Government be accused of a cover up if Dr Kelly does not believe he is the source, and you may agree or disagree with him, and he has uncomfortable views on some aspects of the 45 minutes claim? Where is the cover up in that?

A. I think the cover up is: here we are, sitting on information of great relevance to the Foreign Affairs Committee, and indeed the Intelligence and Security Committee, which arrives in a letter dated 30th June and here we already are, 7th July, the Foreign Affairs Committee have reported without any knowledge of this. This was a critical adjunct to Andrew Gilligan's testimony, which was the main reason for the Foreign Affairs Committee's hearing and process. We had said nothing about it. Here we were, a week later. It did look as it we were withholding information of great public interest.

314. With regard to the Question and Answer material and the issuing of the MoD statement Sir Kevin Tebbit gave the following evidence:

[20 August, page 83, line 4]

Q. Can I also take you to the defensive Q and A material which is at MoD/1/62, which I think was prepared for the reaction to the press release, which I think we have been told went out at about quarter to 6 on Tuesday, 8th July. Were you aware of this defensive Q and A material?

A. Yes, I was aware of it.

Q. Were you party to any of the drafting of this defensive Q and A material?

A. No, I did not draft any of it. I did glance through it.

Q. Do you know whether or not Dr Kelly was aware, if this was all a voluntary process, of the defensive Q and A material?

A. No I do not think he would have – I am sure he did not see the Q and A.

Q. He did not see the Q and A?

A. I am pretty sure he did not.

Q. Perhaps you can tell me if this is right or wrong: if you go through the Q and A material, we have been told if they ask these questions, they get these answers; this is to prepare all the press officers so they are giving the same answers. That is right, is it not?

A. (Pause). Yes- well, I assume so. I mean, I did not spend time myself in going through the detailed Q and A. I regarded that as the normal backgrounding that is given on these sorts of issues. I spent more time over the actual statement itself.

Q. I understand that. But now that you have had a chance to look at the Q and A material.

[Part of the Q and A material was then read out by counsel.]

…it does seem, reading this, and certainly I think we are likely to hear this from journalists, that once you got these clues, if they can be so described, it is not going to be very difficult to identify Dr Kelly?

A. These were not intended to be clues.

315. With reference to discussions which took place in 10 Downing Street on 8 July Sir Kevin Tebbit said:

[20 August, page 85, line 22]

A… So my own view was always that it would be preferable for Dr Kelly to come forward with a clear statement. We had not reached that stage on the Tuesday evening, because the discussions with Dr Kelly had still been concentrating on the discrepancies between his account and Andrew Gilligan's. Nevertheless, it was felt, not just in the Ministry of Defence but very strongly in No.10 and in the Cabinet Office, that it was necessary for a statement to be made, that the information could not be held on to. I was not, myself, present during all the discussions on the Tuesday because I was in Portsmouth handing out awards for bravery for people who had managed to save the "Nottingham" from sinking, so it was an event that I could not really cancel. But I was aware of the discussions that were going on at No.10 and the Cabinet Office and there was a very strong feeling that we needed to come forward with the information. If –

MR DINGEMANS: Who did you understand that strong feeling to come from?

A. Well, it was a collective view of Sir David Omand, John Scarlett, the Prime Minister. It was one which I did not disagree with at all, but I was not there. And, as you recall, the first idea was that this should be sent in the form of a letter to the Intelligence and Security Committee for them to look at, and also that it should be put to the BBC in the context of: we are not asking you to say whether this is the source but only to say if it is not, so that we could be clear on our ground. As it happened, Ann Taylor decided she did not wish to receive this unless it was preceded by a public statement.

Q. Is that the reason that the impetus came for the public statement?

A. I think that was the reason, so that when I returned from Portsmouth it was quite clear that the view in Whitehall, which we shared in the Ministry of Defence, we did not dissent, was that we should indeed issue a public statement, and the sense was that that needed to be done more or less then on that date, the Tuesday or so. So we needed to issue a statement before we had got to a stage really where we could name Dr Kelly, because the last conversation we had had with him had not actually got to that point.

Q. He had not yet said: okay, give my name out?

A. He had not been asked that question.

Q. And so when the defence Q and A material is deployed and the material not intended to be clues is used as clues by journalists, and the journalists then come back with the right name, and the name is given out, was Dr Kelly, at this stage, voluntarily cooperating with the process?

A. I think again this is not the context that I would put it in. We needed to come up with the statement that was sufficiently informative to justify its existence. That is to say, it had to explain that the individual who had come forward had a status which was different from that alleged by Mr Gilligan and also that his views were not exactly the same as those claimed by Mr Gilligan on this critical issue of Government interference on the dossier, in order to justify the statement and the intention of it being discussed further in the Intelligence and Security Committee.

The need for a question and answer brief in the first instance was no more than that we had always expected that Dr Kelly's name would come out, at any moment, throughout this process from the receipt of his letter onwards, growing over time. So there was always a need to anticipate the prospect that journalists would say, anyone would say: you know, we know it is Kelly. And we could not deny that it was Dr Kelly if that circumstance arose. We could not deny it partly because this is not an issue on which to play games, it was an issue of vast public importance, and partly because it would have been wrong for other members of the Ministry of Defence to come under suspicion and media scrutiny, which indeed did happen.

I mean, this was not an abstract concern. This was a real point. We had journalists tapping on the windows of an individual's house trying to attract the attention of their children in order to talk to their father, who happened to be a member of the Ministry of Defence. Nothing to do with this issue at all. But the idea that we could not allow others to come under that sort of scrutiny was real. It was not an abstract point. And therefore we had to be prepared to say: no, it is not X or it is not Y.

Therefore, to the extent there was a strategy, it was simply that. The question and answers were guidance for backgrounding, but there was no intention of, as it were, volunteering the name or playing games with the press trying to help them get the name. They certainly worked hard enough to find it. In a way, I fear, the statement we made showed the futility really of trying to make a statement based on an anonymous source. If the name is not there, the press is not that interested. They spent huge efforts trying to find out who it was.

316. Sir Kevin Tebbit said in his evidence that he was concerned to know how Dr Kelly was coping:

[20 August, page 97, line 1]

Q. On 14th July I think you have a conversation with Mr Howard about whether Dr Kelly felt under stress. Do you –

A. Yes. I can remember – I mean, it was not prompted by anything other than a general concern that Dr Kelly should be coping and so I asked Mr Howard to make sure that he was okay.

317. At the conclusion of his evidence on 20 August Sir Kevin Tebbit summarised his views as follows:

[20 August, page 97, line 20]

Q. Is there anything else that you know of the circumstances surrounding Dr Kelly's death that you can assist his Lordship with?

A. I do not think there is. I have thought long and hard about this issue. As you can imagine, as Permanent Secretary I have felt deep sense of responsibility, not of culpability but of responsibility in this area, since he was a member of my staff and my staff were talking to him. So his death came as a terrible shock. I have thought long and hard about the approach that was taken, whether it was reasonable to ensure that Dr Kelly came forward to tell his story. I still believe that to have been the right course of action. I believe that was correct on a number of grounds. Firstly, on grounds of proportionality. I mean, this was not a minor issue. This was a major issue, in terms of Government reputation and in terms of the integrity of the whole way in which we handle intelligence. And in those circumstances one has to weigh that against individual considerations.

The second issue was the problem of having a single anonymous source, and then an individual comes forward who we have reason to believe is that source, or at least provides the explanation for what Andrew Gilligan reported. In other words, these are very special circumstances. So correcting the public record could only be achieved by that single anonymous source being named as the individual who can provide the explanation.

The third issue that I have thought about concerns accountability. I mean normally, as the Permanent Secretary, or indeed Ministers such as Geoff Hoon, if officials in our departments are carrying out our business, implementing Government policy, sometimes controversially, sometimes disagreeing, sometimes issues arising in the press, we still take responsibility for their actions and do not expect to put them in front of committees. I appear regularly in the Public Accounts Committee to answer for the actions of my officials, whether they are helpful or unhelpful, and I accept that responsibility because they are doing their job. This was a case where an individual had caused a great deal to happen, operating, as it were, outside his official responsibilities; and the only way, in a sense, that he could deal with that was under his own responsibility. So there was a different sense of accountability here. The attendance at Parliamentary Committees was something that Ministers had to decide. The issues were always bound to come out anyway and that was always underlying this point, that we expected the name to emerge at any stage throughout the process, and the concerns that despite your points that the Government would be criticised heavily for not bringing it forward, the problems of other members of the department coming under suspicion if we were not prepared to confirm that it was Dr Kelly once a public statement had been made.

But all these issues have gone round in my head, but I am satisfied that we did the right things, balancing very difficult issues.

The evidence of Mr Thomas Kelly, one of the Prime Minister's official spokesmen, on 20 August

318. Mr Kelly gave two lobby briefings to journalists on the morning and the afternoon of Wednesday 9 July. In his evidence on 20 August he described what he tried to do in those briefings:

[20 August, page 193, line 14]

Q. We know that during the course of the 9th July his name is obtained by various journalists. Were you party to that process at all?

A. No. I was asked questions at the Lobby and I tried – I felt uncomfortable doing the Lobbies that day because I think I was trying to juggle a number of different pressures, if you like. I was trying to juggle the need to try to protect Dr Kelly's name for as long as possible, though, again, I was aware that Dr Kelly had accepted that his name would become public.

Q. Who had told you that?

A. Kevin Tebbit. I had heard at one of the meetings.

Q. He had said that?

A. He had said that.

Q. Yes.

A. I accepted that as a realistic assessment of my own judgment as to what might happen. So I was trying to protect Dr Kelly's identity. But I was also trying to clarify the apparent discrepancies between the MoD statement and the BBC's response to it. And I was also being asked questions by journalists as well. So I was trying to juggle, if you like, a number of different pressures.

The evidence of Sir David Omand, the Security and Intelligence Co-ordinator in the Cabinet Office, on 26 August

319. In his evidence Sir David Omand was asked why a number of senior officials met on Friday 4 July to discuss the fact that Dr Kelly had told his line manager in the MoD that he had spoken to Mr Gilligan. Sir David's evidence was:

[26 August, page 167, line 5]

LORD HUTTON: I have asked at least one other witness, Sir David, as to the reason why these very senior officials, including yourself, all assembled to discuss this report with Sir Kevin Tebbit. I mean, it does seem a galaxy gathering to discuss this matter, if I may so put it. Do you have any comment on that?

A. I think the explanation lies in the front pages of the newspapers, that this was an issue which had dominated political debate in the country for a considerable time and showed no signs of diminishing. It was a matter of intense interest and concern to the Prime Minister, in view of the nature of the allegations which were being made. It was a matter of concern to me, because it was directly challenging the integrity of a process for which I was responsible.

320. Sir David was asked about a meeting which took place in 10 Downing Street on Tuesday 8 July and his evidence was:

[26 August, page 182, line 22]

Q. Did you express any views about the FAC or not, at that stage?

A. Yes, we discussed what should be done. I made clear my view, which was that there was now sufficient probability that he was the single source to warrant our informing the Parliamentary Committees; and that, in particular, the Intelligence and Security Committee needed to know they were about to take evidence from senior witnesses on these very matters, and we could not be in a false position of appearing before a Committee and not admitting to the fact that we now believed that it was likely we had an explanation for the stories that had appeared.

Q. What was said about the Foreign Affairs Committee?

A. As far as I can recall the logic of the discussion, we first considered the position of the Intelligence and Security Committee and agreed that we had to inform them. And certainly I made it clear that if I was giving evidence I would certainly have to admit to this knowledge; and that it would be very difficult, indeed, unthinkable, to inform one Committee, the Intelligence and Security Committee, and not inform the Foreign Affairs Committee, which is a Select Committee of Parliament, who had only just completed a report which touched on these matters; so that if we informed one we would have to inform the other. The logic then went on to debate: if we inform the Foreign Affairs Committee, is that tantamount to making the matter public? And we concluded that it was.

Q. Had not the Foreign Secretary given evidence in private to the Foreign Affairs Committee?

A. Yes, he had.

Q. The Foreign Affairs Committee had reported, had they not?

A. They had.

Q. And you were, as a Government, cooperating with the Intelligence and Security Committee in giving them drafts of the dossier, and you were less than cooperative to the Foreign Affairs Committee, you were not giving them any drafts of the dossier. Why did you need to tell them anything?

A. (Pause). The answer to that, I think, you have already had this morning from a member of the Committee and indeed from the Chairman of the Committee. For us to have deliberately withheld this information from a Select Committee, when it was relevant to a report they had just produced, whilst making it available to another Committee of Parliamentarians would have been, in my view, improper.

Q. Was any thought given to notifying the Foreign Affairs Committee in private?

A. Yes.

Q. I mean, like Mr Straw's evidence.

A. The evidence may have been given in private, but the fact that he was giving it certainly was not. That was very publicly known. And we thought it just inconceivable that we could inform the Chairman and the Chairman would not feel obliged to inform the Committee; and once we had told the Foreign Affairs Committee in full, that was tantamount to making the matter public.

The evidence of the Rt Hon Geoffrey Hoon MP, the Secretary of State for Defence, on 27 August

321. In his evidence Mr Hoon described his reaction when he heard that an official had come forward:

[27 August, page 11, line 19]

Q. Were you told anything about a letter that the official had written?

A. I was told that he had set out, in some detail, that he had had this meeting with Andrew Gilligan. There were various details put to me, but I – the significant thing was that although he had recognised some of the things that Andrew Gilligan subsequently broadcast as being attributable to him and to his conversation, he did not believe that he was Andrew Gilligan's single source because there were other things in the broadcast that he did not recognise as having said to Andrew Gilligan in the course of that meeting.

Q. Did you have any initial reaction to this information?

A. I think my first – my very first reaction was that this was something that could well lead to disciplinary proceedings, as far as the official was concerned. The Ministry of Defence, in the period – for some time, has had something of a reputation for unauthorised briefing and leaking to journalists; and it did appear that this was perhaps an opportunity to demonstrate that unauthorised contacts with journalists would be looked at seriously.

Q. Can I just there take you to a reference which is 5th June 2003, MoD/1/17? This is a memorandum from Martin Howard who the Deputy Chief of Defence Intelligence. He says, in paragraph 2, that the Ministry of Defence had a reputation as a "leaky" department.

Over the page at MoD/1/18, towards the bottom, he said this: "I repeat, that I have no reason to think that anyone in the DIS is responsible for the leak to Mr Gilligan. But if it turns out that this is the case and the individual is identified, the strongest possible action will be taken." Which I think you say accords with your initial thought?

A. That was certainly my very first thought, because over some time there had been warnings to – I will not just say officials, because this extended obviously as well to members of the armed forces. It was not simply a question of officials being warned, it was a concern generally about security, not least in times of conflict, that information should be held securely within the department.

Q. Your other reaction?

A. Immediately, perhaps almost at the same time, I was also concerned at the Foreign Affairs Committee hearings because my assumption was that any disciplinary process will take some considerable time to complete. On that Thursday, as far as I was aware, the Foreign Affairs Committee was still meeting, still hearing, as part of their investigation into the decision to take military action in Iraq, a significant part of which was concerned with the Andrew Gilligan broadcast and the role that he had played and Alastair Campbell had played. So I was very concerned, at that stage, that if an official had come forward who had relevant evidence to that inquiry, that that would be something that we would have to make known, quite quickly, to the Foreign Affairs Committee.

322. Mr Hoon stated that personnel issues in the MoD were the responsibility of the Permanent Secretary:

[27 August, page 15, line 14]

Q. Did you decide, when you were talking to Sir Kevin Tebbit, what to do in relation to Dr Kelly, about interviews or anything else?

A. Well, I did not decide because it has always been my practice, in the Ministry of Defence, to ensure that appropriate responsibilities are dealt with by appropriate people. When I first arrived in the Ministry of Defence I think it was the then Chief of Defence Staff described the leadership of the Ministry of Defence as a three legged stool. He had responsibility for military matters; the Permanent Secretary had responsibility for personnel matters, Civil Service; and I was responsible for political leadership of the department. Therefore, as far as any personnel issues were concerned, the responsibility was clearly that of the Permanent Secretary.

Q. Was anything said about interviews with Dr Kelly though, in your discussions?

A. The Permanent Secretary summarised the position consistently, I believe, with the thoughts that I have just set out to you in terms of my initial reaction, which was that either there could be a disciplinary process affecting the official or there could be what he described as a management process, reflecting the fact that the official had come forward, was apparently cooperating, and could, he believed at that stage, correct the public record, that is the material that Andrew Gilligan had broadcast. That was his analysis of the issue. That analysis I accepted because he was responsible for those personnel questions.

LORD HUTTON: Was correcting the public record a personnel matter?

A. As far as Sir Kevin was concerned, it was important to the Ministry of Defence and indeed to the Government as a whole that the public record should be corrected. I think he viewed that as a management issue, as far as dealing with the official was concerned.

323. Mr Hoon described his first discussion with Mr Campbell after he had heard that an official had come forward:

[27 August, page 21, line 2]

Q. Did you speak to Mr Campbell about your initial reactions on hearing the news of Dr Kelly coming forward?

A. Yes, I did. I described to him the process that I have set out to you now, which is what my initial reaction was, the importance of security of information in the Ministry of Defence and the possibility of there being disciplinary proceedings, but also I emphasised to him my concern about any suggestion that the Government should be covering up the fact of a potential witness coming forward, in the light of the continuing, as I felt at the time, Foreign Affairs Committee deliberations. So I went through precisely the process that I have gone through today of describing to him both my initial reaction and then my thoughts about the relevance of this to the Foreign Affairs Committee.

Q. I think Mr Campbell's recollection was that the conversation was on the Friday. He also mentioned that after you had spoken about your initial instincts in relation to disciplinary proceedings, you mentioned the words "plea bargain". Do you recollect mentioning that to Mr Campbell?

A. I do not remember using that particular phrase to him, but I can see that as a shorthand account of what I had described to him it would have summarised, in a sense, the alternatives available to the personnel director in the Ministry of Defence in dealing with Dr Kelly. But I would want to emphasise that it was never the case that Richard Hatfield or anyone else in the Ministry of Defence offered any kind of an arrangement or deal to Dr Kelly. I have subsequently read the accounts that Richard Hatfield has set out of the interviews he conducted with Dr Kelly. There was no mention of any kind of deal or plea bargain. It was simply perhaps Alastair's summary of the material that I had set out to him; and the material I had set out was entirely retrospective. It was not in any way suggesting how the matter would be taken forward.

Q. What had you said to Mr Campbell that could be written down in shorthand as a plea bargain?

A. I had taken him through, in precisely the way I have done today, my initial reaction, which was this was potentially a serious disciplinary issue. But equally my second thought, which was that this potential witness might have something to say relevant to the Foreign Affairs Committee hearing and that we would have to take care to avoid any suggestion that we might be seen to be covering up the fact of this witness, given the importance of the issue to the Foreign Affairs Committee.

LORD HUTTON: But Secretary of State, a plea bargain, as I understand it, usually means that a person charged with some sort of offence agrees to plead guilty on the understanding that he will not receive a very severe sentence.

A. That is also my understanding, my Lord.

LORD HUTTON: Yes. But do you think you might have used this term or do you think it is a term which Mr Campbell attributed to the sense of what you were saying to him?

A. Well, I do not recall using the phrase.

LORD HUTTON: Yes.

A. I can see that in the description that I gave of the process that had taken place up until then, that that might be a shorthand account, because normally disciplinary proceedings would follow from an investigation where the authorities inside the Ministry of Defence, as a result of their efforts, had identified a particular individual who might have broken the rules. In contrast, this particular individual had come forward. He had written quite a detailed letter, had volunteered information, was apparently cooperating. So, in a sense, my Lord, without it being in any way a formalised arrangement, and I would want to emphasise this was not in any way acted upon by Richard Hatfield or anyone else, that that might have been seen to be of that kind by Alastair in the course of his summarising our conversation.

324. Mr Hoon described his view of the matter during the weekend of 5 and 6 July:

[27 August, page 30, line 11]

Q. Did you have a view at that stage about whether or not it was desirable that Dr Kelly's name should be made public?

A. I was concerned at that stage that we did not have enough information to be able to be sure that Dr Kelly was the single source of Andrew Gilligan's material. And in those circumstances, and indeed throughout the history of this matter, because I was not sure that that was the case, I did not believe that it was appropriate to make his name public.

Q. Were you aware that throughout, whether rightly or wrongly, Dr Kelly was contending that he was not the single source?

A. That he was not?

Q. Yes.

A. Yes, I was aware of that and I have said so already to the Inquiry. I was aware of that because of the letter that he wrote to the Ministry of Defence and, indeed, because of the interview that he had conducted with Richard Hatfield. That was a significant factor in the material that Kevin Tebbit told me about following the interview.

325. Mr Hoon said that he was never sure before Dr Kelly's death that he was Mr Gilligan's single source:

[27 August, page 37, line 13]

MR DINGEMANS: Going forward, as it were, almost to the end of the story, before Dr Kelly's death were you ever sure that Dr Kelly was the single source?

A. Not before his death.

Q. But we also know that Dr Kelly's name did come out.

A. Yes, it did.

Q. So, I understood you to be saying that at that stage you were still concerned with ensuring, out of fairness to Dr Kelly, his name did not come out before you were sure he was the single source.

A. That is absolutely right. Indeed, I had a conversation with my private secretary on the day that the BBC made their announcement, still questioning whether in fact – because I had been told they were going to make an announcement but I did not know the nature of it at the time. I still was not sure on – when was it? – Sunday, about the 20th I should imagine, when they made their announcement, I still was not sure at that stage, before they made their announcement, that Dr Kelly was their single source.

326. Mr Hoon was asked which was the lead department in dealing with the situation which had arisen on Dr Kelly coming forward:

[27 August, page 46, line 25]

Q. Who did you understand to be the lead department? Had it now become No.10 or was it still the Ministry of Defence?

A. Well, the Ministry of Defence was the lead department as far as dealing with Dr Kelly on a personnel basis, as far his position, as far as the department were concerned, then I was concerned that the Permanent Secretary should look at that matter as an employment concern issue, to look at it from a point of view ensuring that Dr Kelly was properly and fairly treated. Equally, there were clearly wider implications in what was happening as far as the Government as a whole were concerned. That is why the Cabinet Office and Downing Street were engaged.

327. Mr Hoon was asked about the Question and Answer material:

[27 August, page 52, line 6]

Q..... Do you know whether or not Dr Kelly was told about the draft Q and A material and the Q and A material as deployed?

A. I do not, no. But can I make clear that I did not see either of these documents. They were not submitted to my office. That would not be something that I would normally deal with.

328. Mr Hoon was asked whether anyone from the MoD actually took an active role in the meeting in 10 Downing Street on the morning of Tuesday 8 July:

[27 August, page 55, line 5]

Q...... it rather looks like at the Tuesday morning meeting there is no-one from the Ministry of Defence actually taking an active role in it; is that fair or unfair?

A. Well, I think as a matter of fact it must be fair, although, as I understood it, Kevin Tebbit did come back from Portsmouth before that meeting concluded. So I thought that he was present for at least part of the meeting and certainly was present in the course of drafting material following on from that meeting.

329. Mr Hoon was asked in relation to the statement issued by the MoD on Tuesday 8 July:

[27 August, page 65, line 25]

Q…. So your understanding was that this was part of a fall back after the first public letter to the ISC had been rejected, to get the BBC to confirm whether or not Dr Kelly was the source; is that right?

A. Yes.

Q. And as far as you understood, it was not intended that Dr Kelly's name should ever be made public until he had been confirmed as the source; is that right?

A. That was certainly my concern, yes. That we should only act when we were sure about his role.

Q. What is also distributed for deployment that day and the following day when queries come in about the press statement are the Q and A that was actually finalised. That is at MoD/1/62. If we look at the second –

LORD HUTTON: Just before we go on to that, is it your evidence, Secretary of State, that this MoD statement was issued solely for the purpose of trying to persuade the BBC to reveal its source or was there another reason behind it?

A. That was certainly part of it, but throughout I had been concerned, as I think I have indicated, my Lord, to the Inquiry already, that we were in possession of significant information about a potential witness relevant to Parliamentary proceedings, relevant to the public debate; and I, as each day went by, was increasingly concerned that we were not making this information known, certainly to the Foreign Affairs Committee but to the wider public.

LORD HUTTON: Yes.

A. I was very conscious that we risked being accused of a cover-up. I remember having a conversation about what would happen if, say, a Sunday newspaper on the Sunday had got wind of the fact that someone had come forward in the Ministry of Defence. I am sure that they would have accused us of covering that fact up.

330. With reference to the Question and Answer material Mr Hoon said:

[27 August, page 69, line 22]

A.….. I did not see this Q and A and played no part in its preparation, so it is a little difficult for me to comment about any underlying purpose. But if you are suggesting that there was some deliberate effort here to identify Dr Kelly, I say that is absolutely wrong and certainly no effort by me or my office to do that. As I have emphasised throughout, my concern was to identify the facts, and the key fact was whether Dr Kelly was or was not Andrew Gilligan's single source.

LORD HUTTON: But you have also said that in your earlier discussions with Sir Kevin Tebbit he had said that the fact that Dr Kelly had come forward might enable the public record to be corrected. I think you had accepted that that was a consideration in your mind as well.

A. Yes, my Lord, but that was only on the basis that he was clearly Andrew Gilligan's single source.

LORD HUTTON: Yes. Yes. But we have heard that in the course of the week, and indeed over the preceding weekend, the feeling had been growing amongst some very senior officials that, in fact, Dr Kelly was the single source. Were you aware of that, and in the week beginning 7th July?

A. I cannot comment on – I think your Lordship is referring, probably, to David Omand's assumptions at that stage.

LORD HUTTON: Yes.

A. I was not aware of David Omand's thinking. I was aware that Sir Kevin Tebbit, having on the Friday evening readily accepted the advice from Richard Hatfield about his assessment of Dr Kelly's position, thought again on the Saturday, particularly after seeing the article by Tom Baldwin in The Times; and I think as a result of that he wrote a further letter to David Omand indicating that he felt there was now more evidence pointing to the fact that Dr Kelly was the single source. So there was a change in his thinking. But again, I do not think I or anyone else at that stage was sure enough, certainly from my position, to name Dr Kelly, because I think that would have been unfair to Dr Kelly.

331. With reference to the making of the statement by the MoD on Tuesday 8 July, Mr Hoon was asked:

[27 August, page 75, line 2]

MR DINGEMANS: One other way of battening down the hatches would have not been to make a press statement. At this stage you do not know it is Dr Kelly, you are making the press statement as part of the fall back plan to try to get the BBC to confirm whether it is or not. If you make the press statement, for all the reasons you have given, the press are going to go into a detailed hunt for that person; why not just avoid making the press statement?

A. Because of the need to acknowledge the fact that someone had come forward. There are a number of factors relevant to that. It is not only the attitude of the Foreign Affairs Committee; it is the fact that at some stage, for example, Government would have to respond to the Foreign Affairs Committee's conclusions and inevitably the timing of our knowledge about a potential witness would have to be made known. And I do not think it is – I do not think you should underestimate the view that Parliament would take of a Government department deliberately withholding such information.

332. With reference to Dr Kelly's name becoming public, Mr Hoon said:

[27 August, page 78, line 25]

A... I am sure from the moment they became aware that someone had come forward that journalists would be making determined efforts to discover his name. It was something Dr Kelly was warned about on the Friday when he first spoke to Richard Hatfield. I think it is something most people involved in this would think inevitable, that at some stages journalists would identify him. In a sense it is surprising, given the reason he came forward in the first place, that he was not identified sooner.

Q. Can I take you to 10th July, when his name does become public. There is a letter of request –

LORD HUTTON: Just before we go on to that. You said, Secretary of State, that people had assumed it was inevitable that his name would become public. Now, against that background, I appreciate you have emphasised that on a number of occasions, is it a fair summary then to suggest that Dr Kelly's name became public because of questions put by the press, not because it was the wish of the Government that the name should become public, and you hoped that the name would not become public for as long as possible but nonetheless it was always accepted that it was inevitable that it would become public? Just amplify that or qualify that in any way. I appreciate I have sought to summarise what has been quite lengthy evidence on your part.

A. I had from the beginning recognised that there was a significant probability that his name would become public, not least because the reason why he wrote to the Ministry of Defence in the first place, as I understand it, was because his views were so distinctive on a particular aspect on Iraq's weapons of mass destruction that a colleague had identified his views, in effect, in the mouth of Andrew Gilligan giving evidence to the Foreign Affairs Committee. So those close to Dr Kelly recognised that he must have had some contact with Andrew Gilligan because Andrew Gilligan was repeating well known views that Dr Kelly held.

That, I am sure, was the reason why Richard Hatfield warned Dr Kelly, on the Friday afternoon in the first interview, that there was every prospect of his name becoming known. It was obviously something, as well, that had been taken into account in securing Dr Kelly's consent to the issuing of the press statement.

So at each stage there was a recognition that his name would become known. What I am resisting, certainly as far as I am concerned, is any suggestion that there was some sort of conspiracy, some sort of strategy, some sort of plan covertly to make his name known. That was not the case.

333. With reference to Dr Kelly's name being confirmed to journalists Mr Hoon was asked:

[27 August, page 100, line 6]

Q. Were you aware that there has been some evidence that Mr Taylor, who I think is your special adviser, is that right?

A. Yes.

Q. Had confirmed Dr Kelly's name to journalists?

A. Hmm.

Q. Were you aware of that?

A. I was not specifically aware at the time but I – excuse me. I have learned since that that happened, yes.

Q. And what is your view on that?

A. Well, I assume that that was consistent with the question and answer process that had been agreed within the department. I do not think it occurred in any earlier timeframe.

Q. The question and answers material that your special adviser knows about but you did not?

A. I did not see the question and answer, but I was obviously aware of the advice that I had received that if the right name was given to an MoD press officer they should confirm it. I am not suggesting – I am not suggesting, for a moment, that I was not aware of that; and obviously my special adviser would have been aware of it as well.

Q. Do you know whether Dr Kelly was told that that was a proposed approach?

A. He was certainly told and agreed to the fact that a press statement was to be issued because that had been done on the – at least on the Tuesday, the day before the events you are describing.

Q. But I have taken you to the first draft of the Q and A which says: can't tell you anything until we have spoken to Dr Kelly and I have taken you to the second draft which appears to have been deployed which changes. Was Dr Kelly told of the change as far as you know?

A. Not as far as I know.

The evidence of the Rt Hon Tony Blair MP, Prime Minister, on 28 August

334. In the course of his evidence I asked the Prime Minister why so many senior officials should have been concerned in discussing what should be done after Dr Kelly had informed his line manager in the MoD that he had spoken to Mr Gilligan. The Prime Minister's evidence was as follows:

[28 August, page 49, line 20]

LORD HUTTON: Prime Minister, I have asked other witnesses why these very senior officials were all concerned with this matter. There was a discussion, and Mr Powell discussed with Sir David Manning, Sir David Omand and Mr John Scarlett. Why were so many senior officials concerned with this?

A. I think it was really that this was – I mean, this whole issue was still the dominant issue. You had the Foreign Affairs Select Committee report on the Monday into really the nature of the allegation. Then suddenly at the last minute comes forward somebody who might be the source. And I think there was a real concern on the part of everyone – we were in a quandary, frankly, right from the very beginning. The Foreign Affairs Select Committee is about to report on the Monday, the report is going to deal precisely with the Andrew Gilligan allegations and here is somebody who suddenly emerges as the person who may be the source of those allegations.

LORD HUTTON: Yes.

A. I think the reason why people were involved at a senior level in the Civil Service were first of all that it was very important. Secondly, certainly as the matter developed, I was very, very keen, indeed insistent, that we did have the senior people involved because I anticipated right from the very beginning that there were going to be a lot of questions asked afterwards about: when did you know? Why did you not tell the Chairman of the Foreign Affairs Committee? How could you let them make their report on Monday when you were in possession of information plainly relevant to their report? That was I think the explanation as to why people at a senior level were involved.

LORD HUTTON: Again, I think having heard a considerable amount of evidence the reason may be obvious, but why was this a quandary? What was the quandary which you were concerned had arisen?

A. The quandary really was this: we had never really wanted the Foreign Affairs Committee to look into this; we thought the ISC should do it. But they had and that is their right to do so and they had conducted their investigation. Suddenly, as I say, at the last minute forward comes somebody who may be the source of the allegation that was at the centre of the FAC report. What did you do? Did you inform the Chairman of the Foreign Affairs Committee immediately, which is one possibility and which I have no doubt afterwards people would have said to us we should have done. Did you try and get greater clarity of whether this was indeed the source or not? So how did you handle this? The reason why I thought it was very, very important to involve the senior officials is that the whole allegation around the Foreign Affairs Committee report and all the rest of it was about the propriety of the Government. Here is an issue that also seems to reflect on propriety and I am in receipt of that information.

So I thought it was essential not in a sense to pass the responsibility to them – in the end I have full responsibility for the decisions that are taken – but in order to make absolutely sure that when at a later point, as I thought there would be, not obviously in the context which we are talking now, but people would say: when did you know? What did you know? Who did you tell? I would be able to say: we handled this by the book, in the sense of with the advice of senior civil servants. Not, as I say, in order to pass responsibility to them, but in order to make sure that this was not, as it were, the politicians driving the system but us taking a consensus view as to what the right way to proceed was.

335. The Prime Minister was asked about a passage in Sir Kevin Tebbit's letter to Sir David Omand dated 5 July 2003 (set out in full in paragraph 53):

The Times story today, whether accurate or not, will increase the likelihood that over the weekend other journalists will indeed identify and name the BBC's source as our official. (He is as I indicated in my earlier letter well known in media/academic circles.)

The Prime Minister said with reference to this passage:

[28 August, page 55, line 7]

A. I mean, the two things that I took out of this were: (1) that it was more probable he was indeed the source; and (2), that this thing was already washing round the media.

Q. Or may well be washing round other parts of the media, as it were?

A. It was in The Times and, you know, I think that they were – I certainly took that as an indication that he thought this was – you know, that this thing could come out at any point.

Q. Had you been told that the matter might come out at any point at this stage?

A. I cannot recall, but I mean I think – I would use my own judgment about that, to be frank.

Q. Your own judgment was?

A. My own judgment was obviously there was a – with an issue with so much political focus on it as this, when someone was being interviewed and reinterviewed and presumably people were talking about it within the system, then you have an article in The Times, I think I would have thought there was a fair possibility it would leak in any event.

336. The Prime Minister later referred to his concern that the Government might be accused of a cover up:

[28 August, page 61, line 6]

Q. So you had understood, at this stage, that any public involvement of Dr Kelly was to be on the basis of his cooperation?

A. Yes. I mean, I think what was – look, right at the very outset, as I say, part of this difficulty was he had come forward. We were in receipt of this information. You know, the question was: what do we now do with that information, in particular in relation to the FAC, which was a concern; and I cannot recall exactly when I was told this, but I think there was certainly – it was said that he realised that he might end up having to give evidence.

Q. He realised he might end up giving evidence?

A. Yes.

Q. Do you recall who said that to you?

A. I do not but certainly by the time we got to 7th July, I mean the basis of the meeting was that he had already realised his name would in all likelihood come out.

Q. You have mentioned your concerns that the Government might be accused of a cover-up in relation to the FAC. Were you, at this stage, keen that the FAC reopen their inquiry or did you have any view on that?

A. No, I mean – look, if I had really wanted the FAC to do it, I think I could perfectly properly have put that information before the FAC actually on the Saturday or Sunday. I really was not sure what the right way to handle this issue was, but I knew that what we could not do was be in a situation where we were accused of misleading the FAC and that the reason why I thought it was so important to involve the senior officials, as I was saying to his Lordship just a moment or two ago, was in order to make it – you know, to make sure that we were operating in a way that they were content with, and therefore if at a later time people say: why on earth did you not give this information immediately to the FAC over the weekend, I could say: there were discussions going on. It was being handled by the MoD. This was the advice given to us by officials. Not as I say to put off responsibility. Responsibility is mine in the end. I take the decisions as Prime Minister. But in order to be able to say we had played it by the book.

337. Referring to a meeting which had taken place in 10 Downing Street on Monday 7 July after the FAC had reported the Prime Minister said:

[28 August, page 65, line 8]

Q. The outcome of that meeting was, I think, to conclude what had already been provisionally decided, that he should have a second interview. Do you recall that?

A. Yes. I mean, I think, as I recollect it, it was already the fact that he was going to be reinterviewed and I thought: well, that at least takes care of this for the moment. So, it is only after the reinterview you then reach the point when you really have to take a decision. But throughout Monday I should say that I mean the two things that seemed to us very, very clear, there was some surprise we expressed to each other on the Monday morning that it had not already leaked, and I think were was no doubt in anyone's mind that if on reinterview it was clear that he was in all probability the source then we were going to have to disclose that.

338. Referring to a meeting which took place in 10 Downing Street on Tuesday 8 July the Prime Minister said:

[28 August, page 71, line 22]

Q. So in the light of those considerations, who decided to do what?

A. Well, we decided that the – how do we then proceed? We cannot conceal this information. What is the best way of proceeding? And I mean it was a discussion about it and I think the consensus was that the best thing was that David Omand should write to the Chairman of the ISC, copy it to the FAC for courtesy and then make public the fact that the source had come forward.

Q. Why was there a need to make public the fact that a source had come forward?

A. For two reasons really. I think, first of all, we were at any point concerned, as I said a moment or two ago – I think we were quite surprised on the Monday it had not already come out, but we thought that it was likely to come out at any particular point. And, secondly, because once you had copied it to the FAC – I mean, I thought there was a remote possibility the FAC might decide not to interview him, but I rather thought that they would.

Q. And that was the reason that it was decided to publicise the ISC letter?

A. Well, that you had to at least – in respect of the fact that there was somebody who had come forward, my concern was to get that information not concealed but, as it were, out there so that no-one could say afterwards: look, this is something that you people were trying to cover up or conceal from a House of Commons Committee. And that was the view of the meeting. Again I say this in absolutely no sense to say this was the civil servants' decision rather than my decision. I take full responsibility for the decisions. I stand by them. I believe they were the right decisions. But the advice also of Sir David, in particular, who was, if you like, the key person for me, was that it would have been improper to have withheld this from the FAC.

339. In relation to the press statement issued by the MoD on 8 July and the Question and Answer material prepared by the MoD press officers the Prime Minister said:

[28 August, page 76, line 24]

Q.…. Were you aware of any assistance with the drafting of this press statement being given by officials within No.10?

A. I think certainly it came to Jonathan and I may have scanned my eye over it myself, but I cannot absolutely recall that.

Q. And I think we have heard that there was a drafting session in Mr Smith's room because this was on his computer.

A. Hmm, hmm.

Q. And that press statement was issued at about 5.45 on 8th July, and there has been evidence that it was read over to Dr Kelly.

A. Hmm, hmm.

Q. Also deployed was what was called defensive Q and A material.

A. Hmm.

Q. Were you aware of the existence of the defensive Q and A material?

A. I was not, but I, you know, would have thought it perfectly natural that the MoD had to prepare to field inquiries. I assume they had been doing that for several days.

[28 August, page 78, line 16]

Q. Now, these questions and answers, it appears, assisted the journalists in identifying Dr Kelly. Do you know whether any view had been taken that that should happen?

A. No, I do not; but I have to say that I think that the basic view of this was – you see, we were quite clear the name was going to come out in one way or another, and as far as I am aware, I think someone said this at the meetings, Dr Kelly was aware of that too. I think it was decided to do this by way of a public statement, not mentioning the name, (a) because we were not entirely clear, (b) I think to give at least a little bit of time to us; but the important thing was that at least the fact that someone had come forward saying I am the source was no longer something we possessed. We had actually been open and said: this is the case. As I say, I did not see the MoD Q and A, but I think the basic view would have been not to, as it were, offer the name but on the other hand not to mislead people. I think there was also some concern frankly if you ended up with a great scrabble as to who was the name, you know, other people might be thought of as the name who were not.

[28 August, page 80, line 9]

LORD HUTTON: Now, do you think, perhaps looking at it in retrospect, that it might have been a more appropriate procedure if the source had simply been named in the statement?

A. I have obviously thought very carefully about whether there were alternative ways of dealing with this. One alternative was certainly to make an open statement and name him upfront. I think the reason for the hesitation there was: well, we could not be absolutely sure about this. I seem to recollect, but I cannot be sure who said this and exactly when it was said, that there was some issue as to whether Dr Kelly himself did not want to be named in what I think was called the first wave of media focus on it. But I mean the only thing I would say, my Lord, is that if we had named him in the statement, I mean – I do not think the outcome in terms of him appearing in front of the FAC or any of the rest of it would have been any different.

[28 August, page 83, line 12]

Q. Was there any discussion about the pressure that Dr Kelly might be exposed to when you were having these meetings on 8th July?

A. Obviously one of the things that was part of the conversation that we were having was what Dr Kelly did, what sort of a person was he, what experience did he have. I mean, all I can say is that there is nothing in the discussion that we had that would have alerted us to him being anything other than someone, you know, of a certain robustness who was used to dealing with the interchange between politics and the media. Having said that, incidentally, it is never, ever a pleasant thing; indeed it is a deeply unpleasant thing for someone to come suddenly into the media spotlight. Certainly we were aware of that. It is one of the reasons why the press statement I think it was said at the meeting should be agreed with Dr Kelly. But there was in my view no way of avoiding the fact that you could not keep this information private.

340. It was put to the Prime Minister that the Government could have made a statement that a civil servant had come forward and then said nothing more about his status or his name:

[28 August, page 94, line 12]

Q. Or another way of proceeding may have been having disclosed that this person has come forward, not to say anything more either about his status or about his name?

A. Yes. The only difficulty there I think is that people would have felt that if you got a great swirl around, well, who is the person, you know, and a whole lot of people being named and identified, then before you know where you are, they have the wrong person. Remember this was still very much in the context this is somebody – I think they somewhat shifted the way they described him but the original allegation was this was someone in charge of the process of drawing up the dossier. Not who had contributed to the dossier, in charge of it.

So I think there was some anxiety within the MoD, I think I was not particularly aware of this but there was some anxiety in the MoD that in the difficult circumstances what you could not do is have a whole lot of speculation going on about a lot of other people being the source.

The evidence of Mr Richard Taylor, the special adviser to the Secretary of State for Defence, on 4 September

341. Mr Taylor gave evidence that on the morning of Wednesday 9 July he attended a routine meeting in Mr Hoon's office to discuss media issues of the day. The other persons present at the meeting were Mr Hoon, Mr Hoon's Private Secretary Mr Watkins, and the Director of News at the MoD Ms Pamela Teare. Mr Taylor said:

[4 September, page 77, line 11]

A. The meeting started, as always, with looking at the press cuttings, and the key issue that morning, the broadcast media as well, was the MoD statement of the previous evening and the BBC's reply, both to the press statement and in a separate parallel process Mr Davies' reply to Mr Hoon's letter of 8th July.

[4 September, page 81, line 8]

Q. Was anything mentioned about the Q and A material?

A. At the end of a discussion on how to follow up the letter to Mr Davies there was a brief discussion on what we should do if journalists were to ring and put the name directly to the Department of who the official was. I would not call it a discussion of the Q and A material. There was a discussion of one of the questions, which I have since learnt was in the Q and A material.

Q. Was there any discussion about the other questions in the Q and A material?

A. No, not –

Q. Was he a member of the UNSCOM et cetera?

A. No, to the best of my recollection we only discussed the rationale for what to do if the name was put directly to the department.

342. Mr Taylor was asked:

[4 September, page 83, line 2]

Q. Have you found out since whether or not Ms Teare discussed this Q and A material with anyone?

A. I have only learnt through the course of the Inquiry that she discussed it with the Permanent Secretary's office, but not at the time.

Q. Not from what the Inquiry has heard, from our own research at the Ministry of Defence. No-one has told you, as it were?

A. I did not see the question and answer brief until after Dr Kelly had died; and I did not therefore ask any questions about it in this timeframe.

[4 September, page 84, line 8]

Q. Why was it decided to confirm the name if the correct name had been put forward?

A. There was a discussion that morning about that approach; and we explicitly talked through if a direct name was put then it was agreed that it would be not tenable to say "no" because that would be to lie.

The evidence of Ms Pamela Teare, on 18 September

343. Ms Teare gave further evidence on 18 September when she was examined by counsel for the Government. Counsel asked her about the nature of Question and Answer briefings:

[18 September, page 85, line 8]

Q. I want to ask you first about the nature of Q and A briefings. Is there anything unusual about the production and use of Q and A briefings in Government departments?

A. No, far from that. The production of Q and A material is standard practice across Whitehall. The Q and A tries to anticipate the sort of questions that the media may ask the press office on a given issue and to provide factual information in answer to those.

Q. So what are they intended to achieve?

A. Essentially they are to provide or to enable – they are to enable press officers to handle media inquiries on a specific subject particularly when they may not be familiar with that subject. They also ensure consistency of approach. But the material is not deployed by the press office unless it has been cleared by the policy officials concerned; and you know they are used in a reactive way. They are not issued in their entirety in any way. So if a journalist asks a specific question, then that specific part of the Q and A will be used. But they are not issued as a whole.

344. She was then asked about Question and Answer material:

[18 September, page 88, line 6]

Q. Was that statement, the statement produced on 4th July, supported by a Q and A document?

[The statement produced on 4 July is set out in appendix 4.]

A. The statement was, as I understand it, prepared by Martin Howard and Richard Hatfield in the Permanent Secretary's office and was agreed there. The Chief Press Officer and I recognised that should we need to deploy this over the weekend, and it would only have been on a reactive basis, we would need -

LORD HUTTON: Sorry, I think it is clear but if you could explain a bit more what you mean by reactive basis.

A. Sorry my Lord.

LORD HUTTON: It is quite clear. I just want it for the sake of the record to be clear.

A. We would not have volunteered that statement. It would have only ever been used in whatever form if the story itself had broken in the media over the weekend.

LORD HUTTON: Yes.

MR LLOYD-JONES: So it is a reactive statement in that sense, does it need Q and A material?

A. If it got to the circumstances where it had to be deployed then, as is the norm, we would have to have some Q and A materials because inevitably we would be asked questions related to the statement. So yes, we would need to have some material.

Q. Was any Q and A material drawn up during the 4th July?

A. Yes, the Chief Press Officer and I did draw up a draft.

Q. The Chief Press Officer is Mrs Kate Wilson; is that right?

A. Yes.

Q. You drew up a draft. What was the source of the material in the draft?

A. The source of the material in the draft was the information that she had obtained from the meeting in the PUS's office she had attended earlier in the day. But the draft that we came up with was very raw, very green.

345. Ms Teare gave evidence that the draft Question and Answer brief was reworked on 7 July and she was asked:

> **[18 September, page 95, line 13]**
>
> Q. So what line was the draft Q and A brief intended to support?
>
> A. The line that the Q and A was intended to support was that, as I understood the policy at the time, we were not prepared to volunteer Dr Kelly's name; but also, as I say, I had had time to consider some of the implications of the situation of when names were actually put to us, which I felt was, you know – it would be impossible to escape if a statement was issued, because I felt that journalists would immediately work very, very hard to try to identify the person who was unnamed in the MoD statement.
>
> So we had to consider there what was the best way of trying to – and indeed the fairest way of trying to deal with the situations when names would be put to us. We felt it was possible that people who were not involved in this could wrongly be identified by the media. So we were seeking to prevent that happening. I think that that position is reflected in that second draft.

346. Ms Teare gave evidence that when she heard on the afternoon of 8 July that Mr Hatfield had cleared the press statement with Dr Kelly she asked Sir Kevin Tebbit to approve the Question and Answer material which she and Mr Martin Howard had prepared:

> **[18 September, page 107, line 17]**
>
> Q. So what did you do about that?
>
> A. I said to the Permanent Secretary that, you know: Martin and I have agreed between us a Q and A, you know, I need your approval before it could be used.
>
> Q. Did you show it to him?
>
> A. I did.
>
> Q. Did he read it?
>
> A. Yes he did.
>
> Q. What did he say?
>
> A. He read it through and gave me approval for it to be deployed.
>
> Q. Was anything said about asking Dr Kelly to approve the Q and A brief?
>
> A. No, that was not discussed, nor would I have expected it to be so.
>
> Q. Why do you say that?
>
> A. Well, Q and A, as I say – to prepare Q and A material in support of a statement is standard practice Whitehall-wide. It was essentially factual material, the contents of which I was sure it was accurate because I had agreed it with Martin Howard. As I say, Dr Kelly had also been made aware that his name was likely to enter the public domain.

347. Ms Teare was asked if she received any calls from the press on the evening of 8 July after the MoD statement had been issued:

> **[18 September, page 110, line 11]**
>
> Q. Before we get to the next day, during that evening did you receive any calls?
>
> A. I received a number of media enquiries, yes.
>
> Q. Were any of them enquiring about the identity?
>
> A. Some of them actually asked me what the name of the individual was.
>
> Q. Did you tell them?
>
> A. No.
>
> Q. Did you tell any of them that although you would not reveal the name, you would confirm it if they already knew it?

A. Yes.

Q. Why did you consider it appropriate to say that?

A. I felt it was necessary to explain that because I wanted to ensure a system where the media would actually check with us before they printed a name or broadcast a name.

Q. What interest were you seeking to protect by taking that course?

A. Essentially, it would have two purposes. One was that it would prevent those who were not involved from wrongly being named in the media; and, secondly, it would give us an indication, and therefore we could pass the information on, if Dr Kelly's name was coming forward.

LORD HUTTON: Pass information on to whom?

A. I am sorry, my Lord?

LORD HUTTON: Pass information on to whom that Dr Kelly name was coming up?

A. No, I mean we would get – if we had a system whereby journalists were coming to us to check the name first, we would get a heads up that Dr Kelly's name was likely to appear.

LORD HUTTON: I thought you said you could pass information on.

A. In that we could alert Dr Kelly, I mean, and alert others in the department.

348. Ms Teare described a briefing meeting which she had with Mr Hoon on the morning of 9 July:

[18 September, page 116, line 13]

Q. Moving on, then, to 9th July, was there a Secretary of State's briefing meeting that morning?

A. Yes, there was.

Q. Did you attend it?

A. Yes, I did.

Q. How clear is your recollection as to what was discussed at the meeting?

A. I mean, I recall there was a meeting. I can recall what the key topics of conversation were, but I do not recall exactly who said what.

Q. Do you recall who was there?

A. The Secretary of State, his principal private secretary, Richard Taylor, special adviser, myself. I think that was all.

Q. What is your recollection as to what was discussed?

A. Well, it was a fairly brief meeting, because I know we had another one that was about to start very shortly afterwards. But my recollection is that the bulk of the meeting was to do with discussions of how we might follow up with the correspondence with the BBC.

Q. Was anything said about the Q and A material?

A. I think it is likely that I might have run through the – an outline of the Q and A material and the approach that we were adopting.

Q. Would you have had any particular reason to do that?

A. No, other than at that meeting it has several purposes: one, I go through the press coverage of the morning and I would normally outline how we were handling sort of main issues of the day. And it would be in that line that I would have done so.

349. Ms Teare said that a press officer was ready to go to Dr Kelly's house on the evening of 9 July:

[18 September, page 121, line 22]

Q. Were you aware what the press office was doing on that evening of the 9th to assist Dr Kelly?

A. On the evening of the 9th, again once the name had been confirmed, we were anxious that we should identify and have ready to go, or in fact send, a press officer to Dr Kelly's house.

Q. What would have been the point of sending a press officer?

A. The point had been that had Dr Kelly chosen to stay there, the likelihood, in fact the certainty, was that large numbers of media would turn up outside his house, and the role of the press officer is to act as a buffer between the media and Dr Kelly and to give him advice on handling and to deal with the media on the scene.

Q. Do you know why that was not done sooner?

A. It was not done sooner because (a) the name had not been confirmed; but also we were working on the assumption that once the name had been confirmed it would take journalists a number of hours to work out where he lives because, in the normal way, they would go through the electoral roll and then operate a policy of elimination. We had assumed after the name had been confirmed there would be a couple of hours – a few hours, actually where we could arrange to send someone.

Q. Was a press officer in fact sent to Dr Kelly's home?

A. No, a press officer was not sent but one was identified and one was on standby ready to go.

350. Ms Teare also said that a press officer accompanied Dr Kelly when he went to give evidence to the FAC on 15 July:

[18 September, page 123, line 12]

Q. Finally, and very briefly, Ms Teare, the FAC hearing took place on 15th July and Dr Kelly appeared to give evidence. Did the press office provide any assistance to Dr Kelly in respect of that appearance?

A. Yes, a press officer was sent to accompany Dr Kelly.

Q. What was the press officer's role on that occasion?

A. Essentially to ensure that the media did not hassle or pester Dr Kelly in any way.

351. Ms Teare was cross-examined by Mr Gompertz as to what happened on 9 July:

[18 September, page 123, line 25]

Q. Ms Teare, let us start with the 9th July. The first identification was made at 5.30 approximately in the evening.

A. It was 5.30 or very shortly thereafter.

Q. Yes. Why was it that Dr Kelly was not notified of this fact at all until he telephoned at about 8 o'clock?

A. Well, as I say, the Chief Press Officer rang the Permanent Secretary's office and they were going to make the appropriate arrangements for him to be told. We felt that – it was certainly my view that there were two things: 1. It would be better for him to talk to someone who knew him about this; and also that while the press office role was there to provide practical media handling advice, you know, we did not have any responsibilities for a welfare role; and again, we thought it was better that his line manager should contact him so that he could also discuss, you know, availability of hotel accommodation if that was what Dr Kelly was seeking. Now, I understand that Dr Wells did speak to him but you would need to check the times with him.

Q. Had you alerted Dr Wells to the fact that he might be needed in order to inform Dr Kelly of his identification?

A. Not specifically, but –

Q. Why not?

A. Because I did not think that it –

Q. Why had he not been notified he might be needed as a matter or urgency to telephone Dr Kelly?

A. I think that the way the situation was unfolding at the time, Dr Kelly was in very regular contact with all of those involved – sorry, Dr Wells was in very regular contact with all of those involved, and that the Permanent Secretary's office had numbers to contact him in and out of working hours.

Q. I do not follow that. I am sure it is my fault. Had anybody contacted Dr Wells to say: you may be needed at short notice to contact Dr Kelly to tell him he has been identified by the press?

A. That had not been done so by the press office, that is all I can say.

Q. Why could not Mrs Wilson telephone Dr Kelly direct? She had done so the night before after all.

A. She could have done that but, as I have explained, we felt that it was better that Dr Kelly should receive this news from his line manager. As I say, we did not have in our gift any arrangements vis a vis hotel accommodation should Dr Kelly have decided that he wanted to take that up.

Q. You do not think, with the benefit of hindsight, it would have been very much better if Dr Kelly had had something like two hours' notice rather than 10 minutes' notice to leave the house?

A. I think that what was important in handling this situation and in the media advice he was given was the crucial time was when the statement was first issued on the 8th; and on that day Dr Kelly was contacted. He was told of the very high levels of media interest and he was advised, at that point, to consider staying with friends; and I think that actually was the most important time.

352. The draft Question and Answer brief prepared on 4 July contained the following draft questions and answers:

Who is the official?

We are not prepared to name the individual involved.

Why not?

We have released all the relevant details. There is nothing to gain by revealing the name of the individual who has come forward voluntarily.

353. The final Question and Answer brief prepared on 8 July and used by press officers on 9 July contained the following passage:

What is his name and current post?

We wouldn't normally volunteer a name.

If the correct name is given, we can confirm it and say that he is senior advisor to the Proliferation and Arms Control Secretariat.

354. Mr Gompertz questioned Ms Teare about this change in the Question and Answer brief:

[18 September, page 131, line 15]

Q. Let us go on to the draft as used. Would you like to look at that? It is MoD/1/62. Do you accept that there is a change between, at any rate, the first draft that you prepared and this draft with regard to the naming: "If the correct name is given [underlined] we can confirm it…", and so on. Do you accept there is a change there?

A. I will accept it reflects a different approach.

Q. Who authorised that approach?

A. As I say, these documents were evolving and reflecting my advice, at the time, on the basis of the information I had at the time.

Q. Would you like to answer the question?

A. I am trying to help you with the question. And accordingly no decision was taken – you say: who took the decision? I did not consider that any of this material was available for use by the press office until it had been agreed by a senior official and approved. Other than that, it was just a document that reflected my advice and my views and was subject to approval.

Q. Yes. Who approved it?

A. It was agreed with Martin Howard and it was approved by the Permanent Secretary.

Q. Thank you. Did the Secretary of State see this draft?

A. Not to the best of my knowledge.

Q. No?

A. No.

Q. What about the routine press meeting on 9th July which you attended and which other people attended as well?

A. That was the day after the draft had been approved.

Q. Yes. Did the Secretary of State see that document at that meeting?

A. I do not recall.

Q. You see, we have heard some evidence to suggest that he did, and that there was some brief discussion about this document at that meeting.

A. Hmm, hmm.

Q. You know that, I expect. Do you agree or disagree with that evidence or do you not remember?

A. I do not recall there being a long discussion about the Q and A.

Q. Nobody said that there was a long discussion.

A. No.

Q. A brief discussion is what I put to you.

A. I cannot recall the detail, though I think it is highly likely that I would have outlined some of the material in the Q and A, but I cannot give you a verbatim account.

Q. To the Secretary of State?

A. Yes.

Q. And no doubt in order to outline the material you would have had the document with you.

A. Yes, I suspect I would have done.

Q. And no doubt you would have shown it to him?

A. He may have already had it. He may have already –

Q. Do you know or not know?

A. I do not know. I did not show him a document at that meeting, because, as I say, the bulk of that meeting was about how to follow up the correspondence with the BBC.

355. Mr Gompertz then put these further questions to Ms Teare:

[18 September, page 135, line 18]

Q. ... One other matter. If the MoD did not wish to release Dr Kelly's name, could it not, in response to an enquiry, say this: we will neither confirm nor deny any name?

A. That is one approach, but I had considered -

Q. What is wrong with it? You were about to tell us, I apologise, I interrupted you.

A. It is one that I had considered; but again, it did not deal with the difficulty of other people who were involved in the similar field from being named in the media; and that was something we felt that was not acceptable.

Q. So on the one hand it was not acceptable that they might be wrongly identified.

A. It was not just a question of wrongly identified, because certainly my view was that anyone that was named would actually be subject to very high levels of media interest.

Q. Yes. Did you consider, though, that if that did happen it would not be through the agency of the MoD, would it, because you had not either confirmed nor denied their name?

A. but the effect would have been the same; and what I was seeking to avoid was that individuals who had nothing to do with this situation were subject to high levels of media intrusion.

Q. Do you know whether any assessment was undertaken as to the pros and cons of releasing information of the kind that appears in the statement and in the Q and As which would lead to Dr Kelly's identification, against adopting a stone wall attitude, if I can put it in that way, of declining to cooperate with the press at all? Was anything like that undertaken?

A. I am not aware of anything, no, nor would I expect to be.

356. Ms Teare was questioned by Mr Knox, counsel to the Inquiry:

[18 September, page 137, line 6]

MR KNOX: You said in your evidence that production of Q and A material is quite normal in a case when a press announcement is being put out, is that correct?

A. Yes. I think I said "standard practice".

Q. Is it standard practice that the following should happen: first, that a press announcement is agreed with a civil servant concerned in a story which contains some information about that civil servant but at the same time Q and A briefings are prepared which give more details about the identity of that civil servant over and above those agreed in the press statement?

A. I cannot agree with you that it is standard; and the reason that I cannot accept, you know – accept that, is that the situation with which we had to contend was totally without precedent, so there was not, you know, such as a thing as standard practice. There was no yardstick with which to judge it. That is one of the reasons why it was such a difficult situation.

357. Mr Knox questioned Ms Teare about the fairness of not telling Dr Kelly about the Question and Answer procedure:

[18 September, page 143, line 2]

Q. Let us just deal with the matter, as a matter of fairness. Dr Kelly is called in the afternoon in order to agree a press statement with him; that is right, is it not?

A. (Nods).

Q. He would naturally suppose from that that certain information is going to be released about him in that press statement.

A. Hmm, hmm.

Q. He is not told by the MoD that further information will be released about him by the MoD press office, is he?

A. No, he is not, but as I say –

LORD HUTTON: Yes, carry on Ms Teare. You were going to add something.

A. As I say, it is standard Civil Service practice when any statement is released that a Q and A is also produced to support it which contains some factual information related to the statement. That is not an unusual practice.

MR KNOX: I understand "unusual" or "not unusual". What I am trying to understand is this: why did you not tell Dr Kelly this is what you were proposing to do?

A. I saw there to be no reason to tell him, because the material that we had was in the Q and A, it was largely factual, and that Dr Kelly had already been forewarned that his name was likely to enter the public domain. And what is more, we – when – you know, in the run up to that happening we would – I knew that we would be in touch with Dr Kelly to provide him with advice on media handling. So I saw no role for me to insist that the Q and A should be run by him.

Q. Was there any reason for not telling Dr Kelly what you were intending to do in answer to questions from journalists?

A. No, there was not any reason why he could not have been told. As I say, there was no discussion of it because it was not felt to be an issue.

Q. Would it not have been better and fairer to Dr Kelly to give him the full picture? Namely: (1) we will put out this press statement; (2) if we get asked certain questions we are going to have to answer them this way and thereby reveal further details about you. Would that not have been the fairer way of dealing with it?

A. I do not actually accept it was unfair because Dr Kelly – for a start, I felt that Dr Kelly's name was likely to emerge because he was quite well known in media circles anyway. But on the substance of the Q and A material, I do not see that there was anything there that we needed to consult him about in any way. As I say, if he had not have been – if he had not been told and it had not been discussed with him and that he had no expectation of his name becoming public, if he in no way had been given to believe that might happen, then I think there would have been a question of fairness. But I do not see it at all in this case.

358. A draft Question and Answer brief prepared before the final draft contained the following:

Is it X (ie the correct name)?

If the correct name is put to us from a number of callers, we will need to tell the individual we are going to confirm his name before doing so.

359. Mr Knox asked Ms Teare:

[18 September, page 148, line 25]

Q. We know in the eventual Q and A you prepare there is no equivalent provision for telling Dr Kelly that his name is now being put to journalists.

A. Hmm, hmm.

Q. Presumably, therefore, there was a conscious decision to change from the approach you see in the first of these Q and As I have showed you to the eventual approach adopted in the final Q and A, is that right?

A. As I have tried to explain already, it is not – when you say there was a decision to move from one to the other, that suggests that the existing one was a freestanding approved document; it was not. The drafts of the Q and A represent the information and my thinking at that point in time –

LORD HUTTON: Ms Teare, I appreciate the point you have been making that the question and answer has to be approved by a policy maker –

A. And indeed it – sorry.

LORD HUTTON: - but if you would look at the question this way: was it the position that your thinking on this matter was changing, in that in this draft you had said: if the correct name is given we will have to tell the individual we are going to confirm his name before doing so; and there is a change from that to the latter draft where that does not appear. What was your thinking as to that change, contrary to anything – just what was in your mind?

A. Yes, to get from the second to the third?

LORD HUTTON: Yes.

A. That reflected the development of my thinking, also that I had acquired more knowledge about the situation, because I had been told, during the course of the 8th, that Dr Kelly had been forewarned that his name was likely to become public.

360. Mr Knox also put the following questions to Ms Teare:

[18 September, page 155, line 12]

Q. Ms Teare, with hindsight, thinking back on what happened, the inevitable effect of the Q and A approach was this surely: first, it was likely to increase the interest of journalists because you have this almost game of 20 questions; is that not right?

A. I do not accept that. I mean, I do not understand what you mean by why the Q and A would encourage that. As I said, the Q and A is produced in support of any statement; and in terms of the guessing game, the guessing game was of the journalists' own making, it was not ours.

Q. Do you think it did have the effect of increasing the journalists' interests, the way that information was gradually being given to them?

A. No, I do not. I think what stimulated the journalists' interest was the release of the statement; and it was on that same day that Dr Kelly was contacted by the press office, warned of the high level of media interest and, as I say, offered media handling advice there and then.

Q. Did not the approach also mean this: that Dr Kelly's name would come out at a wholly unpredictable time?

A. Short of actually including Dr Kelly's name in the original statement, I do not see how we could have controlled when his name would have emerged.

Q. It would follow, would it not, also, that Dr Kelly himself would not have any proper notice of the fact or time at which his name was going to be revealed? That must be right.

A. Dr Kelly was told on the evening of the 8th July that a statement had been issued, there were very high levels of media interest and that he might want to think about staying with friends. That to my mind was the key point, because once we had issued the statement then journalists from that point were going to try hard to identify the individual. He was made aware of that high level of interest.

Q. Yes. Would it not have been better to adopt a rather more upfront approach with Dr Kelly, in hindsight, and simply agree a particular time at which his name could be given to the press, so he would know exactly what was going on?

A. I think we certainly are talking hindsight there. The position that we were in was one where, as we have heard, although the idea of including Dr Kelly's name with the original statement that Kevin Tebbit had asked should be pursued, it was not in fact pursued. The position that we would have put Dr Kelly in is that we would have been finishing, finalising the statement and then sort of springing on him the notion of including his name in it. So I think that would not have been fair either.

Q. You did not want to spring anything on Dr Kelly, is that right?

A. I did not want to say to Dr Kelly, with a few moments – no more than a few moments to consider it: we are going to put your name in the statement.

LORD HUTTON: Just on that point, Ms Teare, and I appreciate you say we are discussing the matter with hindsight, looking at what happened and bearing in mind the point you made that Mrs Wilson in fact rang him on the evening of the 8th July and said to consider alternative accommodation. But looking back, with hindsight, might it not have been better to have said to Dr Kelly that the MoD were proposing to name him in the statement but it would not released for 24 hours and it would be released at a particular time? Suppose you would have said to him on the Monday afternoon: it will be released at 6pm on the Tuesday afternoon. Then he would have known precisely when his name was going to come into the public arena, and if he had wanted to leave home he would have had the time to do it.

A. Again, with hindsight, that could have been a possibility; but I do not think – again, to get to that position you would have to unpick so many of the things that had happened.

LORD HUTTON: Yes.

A. As I say, because the issue of including Dr Kelly's name in the original statement was never addressed with him.

LORD HUTTON: I quite appreciate that and you are making the point a lot of things would have to be unpicked. But even on that basis, it would have been open, let us say over the weekend, or on Monday 7th July, to have had a meeting with Dr Kelly and to have said to him: this is a matter of great public importance, the Ministry of Defence feels, because of the interests of the FAC and the general public interest, that we will have to put out a statement that you have come forward, and we consider that it would be better for you, as well as for the MoD, that we name you in the statement, and we are proposing to issue a statement in 24 hours' time. The point I am putting to you is, with hindsight, that that would have made it clear to him precisely when his name would become public and there would not have been the matter of him having to leave his home with Mrs Kelly in a rush, within about 10 minutes.

A. As I say, that would have been a possibility; but one of the reasons I felt that we did not get to that point was because there remained uncertainty as to whether Dr Kelly was Andrew Gilligan's source or not.

LORD HUTTON: Yes, I see. That has been mentioned by other witnesses. I appreciate that.

A. I think it was that uncertainty that sort of meant that a decision was not taken until sort of, you know, the Tuesday afternoon, really, to make a statement.

The evidence of the Rt Hon Geoffrey Hoon MP, on 22 September

361. Mr Hoon gave further evidence to the Inquiry on 22 September. He was first examined by counsel for the Government and in the course of that examination he said:

[22 September, page 1, line 1]

Q. Why did you consider, at that time, that it was right to publish that press statement?

A. Well, I had been concerned for some days by then that an official having come forward who had something relevant to say about the subject of two Parliamentary inquiries, at that stage we had still not identified that fact. I first became aware of it on the previous Thursday, but in fact Dr Kelly had first communicated his contact with Andrew Gilligan as long ago as Monday 30th June. Therefore, I was increasingly concerned about the amount of time that was passing without us acknowledging the fact that an official had come forward.

In addition, officials were due to give evidence the following day, the 9th, to the ISC; and therefore, again, there was some concern that if they had been asked questions about this matter they needed to be clear as to the position that the Government was taking. Above all else, because of both pressures, I was concerned that we should not be accused of covering up the fact that an official had come forward.

Q. With the benefit of hindsight, do you still consider that it was the right thing to do?

A. Yes, I do, because once an official had come forward, once he had made known the fact that he had had an unauthorised contact with Andrew Gilligan, then we had to deal with it. We did not have the option of doing nothing. We had to resolve this matter and use our best judgment to deal with the situation.

Q. The Inquiry has heard that in the early evening of 9th July the MoD press office confirmed to a journalist the identity of the person who had come forward, Dr Kelly. Were you aware, on 9th July, that the MoD press office was adopting an approach under which it was proposing to confirm the identity of the individual if the correct name was put?

A. Yes, I was. I had had a conversation earlier that day with Sir Kevin Tebbit, the Permanent Secretary, in which he had set out to me the concerns that he had as far as the press office were concerned, in particular that individual press officers should not be seen to be lying to journalists, and that it was better that they should, if the right name was put to them, acknowledge the fact. He was also very concerned that there was a risk to other members of staff, other officials, and he did not want anything said by the press office to lead journalists in the direction of the wrong official.

362. In the course of cross-examination Mr Gompertz put to Mr Hoon the interview which he had had with Mr Peter Sissons on BBC News 24 on 19 July 2003, the transcript of which was as follows:

Peter Sissons: The death was a great tragedy. Our thoughts of course are with his wife, with his family and with all his friends and colleagues at the MoD, and obviously in the wider scientific community, this is a very great personal tragedy. He killed himself after your department, indeed you personally outed him as the probable mole.

Geoff Hoon: I'm afraid that's simply not right, and as the evidence that the department will give to the inquiry will show, we followed very carefully established MoD procedures, and at all stages, certainly as far as I personally was concerned, we protected his anonymity.

Sissons: You're not saying you didn't name him in a letter to the Chairman of the BBC.

Hoon: I wrote a confidential letter to the Chairman of the BBC inviting the Chairman of the BBC to indicate whether Dr Kelly was or was not the primary source of Mr Andrew Gilligan's story. I think it's quite important to say at this stage that there will be, as the Prime Minister has indicated, a full inquiry. There will be an opportunity for everyone involved in this tragedy to set out the facts. I think it is important that we await the outcome of that enquiry before rushing to judgment.

Sissons: Whose idea was it to name him in the letter to the BBC which was subsequently leaked?

Hoon: As I say there was a careful procedure within the MoD, the procedures of the MoD were scrupulously followed. And it was, at an appropriate stage, judged that given the prospect of the name of Dr Kelly being revealed in any event, that it was better to invite the BBC to comment, rather than to allow there to be the kind of chase by the media that we've seen all too often in these kinds of circumstances. Again, these are matters for the inquiry.

Sissons: Why was his name then leaked?

Hoon: I'm not aware that his name was leaked. It was certainly not leaked by me, and I assure that we made great efforts to ensure Dr Kelly's anonymity.

Sissons: Were the finger prints of anyone in government on the leaking of his name?

Hoon: Not as far as I am aware. But again, these are obviously matters for Lord Hutton's inquiry.

Sissons: You also warned the Select Committee, did you not, in effect to be gentle with him.

Hoon: I was well aware that two committees had invited Dr Kelly to give evidence actually on the same day, although as I understand it subsequently he did not give evidence to both committees. But nevertheless at the time I was expecting that he would be required to give two sets of evidence to two different committees, and I certainly suggested by letter to the Chairman of the Foreign Affairs Committee that, as someone unused to the procedures of committees, that they should recognise that in the way in which they went about their questioning.

363. Some of the questions which Mr Gompertz put to Mr Hoon were as follows:

[22 September, page 23, line 23]

Q.… The first question I ask you about that is: what are these careful procedures of the MoD which were scrupulously followed?

A. Well, there were personnel procedures. As I indicated to the Inquiry before, it was my judgment that those were best left in the hands of those responsible, ultimately the Permanent Secretary. He delegated the responsibility of interviewing Dr Kelly to the personnel director, Richard Hatfield. I have read his evidence. It confirms it is consistent with what I was told at the time. He looked at this matter, first of all, on the basis of whether or not there was a disciplinary issue. Having decided that there was not, he then conducted a further interview with Dr Kelly. As I understand it, that is consistent with the Ministry of Defence personnel procedures.

Q. There are no procedures for naming civil servants, are there?

A. I did not name Dr Kelly other than in a private letter to –

Q. That is not the question I asked you, Mr Hoon. I am very sorry to interrupt you. There are no procedures for naming civil servants are there?

A. Well, I think that is not the fairest way of putting this issue. The issue is whether the procedures were followed. The procedures, as I have indicated, were followed. Since I did not name Dr Kelly other than in relation to the letter that I wrote privately to Gavyn Davies, I am not sure where your question takes us.

Q. Well, let us see. What I suggest to you is that there was a deliberate Government strategy to leak Dr Kelly's name into the public arena without appearing to do so, by a combination of the press statement, the question and answer material, the Prime Minister's official spokesman press briefing and other leaks which appear to have taken place to the press. That is what I suggest.

A. Well, you have put that point to a number of witnesses; they have all denied it; and I deny it.

Q. His name was leaked, was it not?

A. Not by me.

Q. No?

A. No.

Q. Because, let us just finish with this document on TVP/3 –

A. I apologise for interrupting you. But the suggestion you are making is there is some evidence that I leaked it. Perhaps you would indicate where it is so that I can comment on it.

Q. We will come to that in just a moment. What I am going to ask you next is this, Mr Hoon. You say about two-thirds of the way down that document: "I'm not aware that his name was leaked. It was certainly not leaked by me, and I assure ['you' it must be] that we made great efforts to ensure Dr Kelly's anonymity."

A. That is right, yes.

Q. What efforts did you make or did the MoD make to ensure Dr Kelly's anonymity?

A. Well, first of all, the knowledge of his name was limited to a very small number of people within the Ministry of Defence. I gave evidence on the last occasion that I was not told of his name until the Friday evening in a conversation with the Permanent Secretary. I did not tell my own special adviser until Wednesday 9th July. He learned about it from a news bulletin the previous evening. My principal private secretary did not tell other members of the office of what had occurred.

My office removed all identifying details from the copy of Dr Kelly's letter faxed to my constituency office on Friday 4th July because I did not have a secure line in my constituency office. Before we sent the private letter to Gavyn Davies we assured there was a fax line immediately available to him, again to ensure the letter did not fall into other hands. The press statement did not contain details about the name of Dr Kelly. Despite efforts by a number of journalists to require the press office to identify him by name, that was resisted. A whole series of steps were taken to protect Dr Kelly's anonymity.

364. Mr Gompertz then questioned Mr Hoon about the statement issued by the MoD in the late afternoon of Tuesday 8 July:

[22 September, page 28, line 6]

Q. This was a press statement, was it not?

A. Yes, it was.

Q. So journalists were going to receive it, obviously. And they were going to follow the leads given in it, were they not?

A. I have no doubt that journalists throughout this period were trying to identify who was the source of Andrew Gilligan when he had his conversations, yes.

Q. In your desire to protect Dr Kelly's anonymity at all times, did you consider that the press statement might alert journalists?

A. I did not consider that it would alert journalists in the sense you are suggesting. It certainly inevitably meant that their interest in this matter would be heightened, yes.

Q. I mean, for example, we have evidence from Mr Norton-Taylor of the Guardian. He said that it whetted his appetite, which I have no doubt is substantial. Did that occur to you?

A. I have just answered your question. I recognise that the issuing of a statement was likely to lead to journalists wanting even more than they had previously to identify Andrew Gilligan's source. But there is clear evidence that journalists were already looking for Andrew Gilligan's source. I accept that this was bound to increase their enthusiasm for making that identification.

[22 September, page 30, line 1]

Q. Yes. I am putting to you a rather wider point at the moment, that the Government as a whole had decided on a strategy which would lead Dr Kelly's name into the public arena, with a view to him giving evidence before the FAC. Now, is that a strategy that you recognise or not?

A. No, it is not; and indeed I do not believe that there is the slightest shred of evidence for that assertion.

365. Mr Gompertz then took Mr Hoon through the lobby briefing which Mr Tom Kelly, the Prime Minister's official spokesman, gave to journalists on 9 July. Mr Hoon said:

[22 September, page 33, line 13]

A. I am somewhat puzzled as to why I am being asked questions about what someone else said in relation to a briefing I had no part in and which I could not reasonably have anticipated was going to be given in this way.

MR GOMPERTZ: For the reason I have already put to you, that this was not just a strategy devised by the MoD, was it? This was a Government strategy.

LORD HUTTON: Is your evidence, Secretary of State, that whatever may have been the strategy in the minds of other people, you were not aware of this strategy and you were not aware that this information would be given out at the Lobby briefing? Is that what you are saying?

A. That is exactly my position, my Lord.

LORD HUTTON: Yes.

A. Learned counsel is suggesting there was some sort of a conspiracy right across Government for all these people to be involved in giving out small parts of information which he has concluded provided a picture. But there is just no evidence of that, my Lord. Certainly as far as I am concerned there was no such conspiracy.

LORD HUTTON: I think Mr Gompertz is putting to you that there was a conspiracy on the part of the Government as a whole. You have said, as far as you were concerned, you were not aware of that.

A. Yes.

LORD HUTTON: Do you want to add anything further on that point that Mr Gompertz has put to you?

A. Not only was I not aware of it, I would be extremely surprised, not only in the light of the evidence which your Lordship has heard but also what I knew of what was going on elsewhere in Government, if that is a possible argument that any reasonable person could make.

MR GOMPERTZ: Well, thank you for that, Mr Hoon. Are you suggesting that No.10 is in the habit of issuing press briefings concerning a particular Department, in this case your Department, without any consultation whatsoever?

A. That is a very difficult question to answer precisely. I am sure that as and when issues arise – bear in mind that journalists who attend these Lobby briefings are trying to catch out the briefers on a range of issues and will ask all sorts of questions, some of which may be anticipated given the news of the day, some of which may not. So I think strictly the answer to your question is that by and large it would not always be possible for, on every occasion, the briefers to consult with the Department. They would simply have no notice of the questions that were coming up.

Q. In this particular instance this was the story of the moment, was it not?

A. Yes, it was.

Q. Yes. So are you saying that what Mr Tom Kelly said on this occasion was without your knowledge in any shape or form?

A. It was without my knowledge in any shape or form, yes.

366. Mr Gompertz then questioned Mr Hoon about his knowledge of the Question and Answer material and the clear implication of some of his questions was that Mr Hoon had not been frank in his evidence to the Inquiry on 27 August that he had not seen the Question and Answer material. Mr Hoon rejected this suggestion and in the course of his answers on the point he said:

[22 September, page 41, line 17]

A. But I think, Mr Gompertz, if I may explain: you are not properly understanding the way in which a Q and A document works. A Q and A document is prepared for the use of press officers. It is not something that comes to my office. It is based on decisions that are taken by the Department as a whole as a guidance for press officers when they are answering questions put to them by journalists. If I may give you an example: at around this time we were taking a decision on which particular training aircraft should be purchased for the Royal Air Force. Eventually a decision was taken on which aircraft we would choose. That would have been, I am sure – I have never seen it, but I am sure that would have been incorporated into a question and answer document, but I would not have needed to see the answer to the question which I am sure was likely to be the first question: which training aircraft has the Ministry of Defence decided to purchase? It would have then given the answer. But I would not have needed to see that because in fact it was simply reflecting decisions previously taken by the Ministry of Defence, in exactly the same way that I take it that this question and answer document was reflecting the views taken in the Department.

MR GOMPERTZ: Can I ask you now, then, to look at another passage in your evidence on the previous occasion? Page 69, line 17 is the question. Do you have that?

A. Yes, I have.

Q. I do not think I need read the question, in fact. But at line 22 you say this: "I did not see this Q and A and played no part in its preparation, so it is a little difficult for me to comment about any underlying purpose". Is that an answer you stand by?

A. Well, the Q and A had been prepared the night before.

Q. Yes. So do you stand –

A. Therefore I played no part in its preparation.

Q. Even though there was discussion about it the following morning in your office?

A. I was asked by the Permanent Secretary whether I confirmed the document that had been prepared the night before, as far as one small aspect of it was concerned, which was the decision to confirm Dr Kelly's name if a journalist got it right, and I agreed to that. But that was the only issue that was raised with me by either the Permanent Secretary or indeed the subsequent press briefing meeting.

Q. So apart from those matters, you had no knowledge of the Q and A material being prepared in your Department at all?

A. Not until I saw the Q and A document much later, no.

Q. Did it occur to you that the material contained in the Q and A document might lead to the identification of Dr Kelly if the right questions were asked by journalists?

A. Well, with the benefit of hindsight I can see that the answers to some of those questions might have assisted journalists in that process, yes.

Q. But you did not, at the time, think to look through the document in its entirety in order to continue your avowed intention of protecting Dr Kelly's identity at all times?

A. Well, I have made clear on more than one occasion that this is a routine process entered into for the benefit of press officers answering questions put to them by journalists. It has never been my practice to go through the Q and As which I am sure are routinely prepared in relation to a whole range of subjects in the Ministry of Defence.

367. Mr Gompertz then questioned Mr Hoon about the words "plea bargain" in the entry in Mr Campbell's diary for 4 July:

[22 September, page 45, line 4]

Q. Somehow Mr Campbell came to write in his diary the two words "plea bargain".

A. Hmm.

Q. How did that come about?

A. Well, I cannot strictly answer that question but, as I indicated on the last occasion, we had a conversation about the process that I think I have already described to the Inquiry today; a process whereby initially there was a consideration of whether or not there were any disciplinary questions that Dr Kelly might face, followed by a recognition that having come forward voluntarily, apparently cooperating, that the matter could be dealt with in a different light. And I believe what I told the Inquiry on the last occasion, and I stand by, is that that description might have led Mr Campbell to see this in terms of, journalistic shorthand, a plea bargain.

Q. What Mr Campbell wrote in his diary, as I understand it, is this: "GH said his initial instinct was to throw the book at him but in fact there was a case for trying to get some kind of plea bargain." Do you recognise that statement?

A. Well, I have seen those words.

Q. Well, do you recognise those words as words spoken by you during this telephone conversation?

A. No, I do not. I indicated to the Inquiry on the last occasion that I recognised them as journalistic shorthand for rather a long explanation that I had given to Alastair about what had, by then, taken place.

Q. You know perfectly well the meaning of the expression "plea bargain", do you not? Lord Hutton took you through it last time, did he not?

A. He did.

Q. And you know it anyway having practised at the bar yourself.

A. I am well aware of it.

Q. Yes. How could that expression, on your account of matters, have any relevance to what you were discussing with Mr Campbell?

A. As I indicated on the last occasion, Dr Kelly was coming forward, he volunteered, he appeared to be cooperating. That – perhaps you would be best putting these matters to Mr Campbell, but that is an aspect, at any rate, of what happens when there is a plea bargain, someone cooperates with the authorities.

Q. What you are talking about, someone coming forward, cooperating and so on, that is mitigation, is it not? There is no element of a bargain there.

A. No, there is not; and I was at great pains to emphasise that there was no bargain; and indeed when you put that I think to Mr Hatfield, he said there was no bargain. Nothing followed from this conversation at all. There is no evidence at all anywhere that anyone entered into any kind of a bargain with Dr Kelly.

Q. The fact that he had come forward and said voluntarily what he had in his letter and then in the interview of 4th July, those were matters in the past, were they not, when you were speaking to Mr Campbell?

A. Well, to the best of my recollection, on the Saturday morning I was describing to him – I was relaying to him second-hand conversations because I was describing to him what I had been told by the Permanent Secretary.

Q. How could there be, I quote, "a case for trying to get some kind of plea bargain" in the future?

A. Sorry, I do not follow that.

Q. How could it be that you were saying that there was a case for trying to get some kind of plea bargain?

A. I was not.

Q. Did you say anything that might have led Mr Campbell to write down words of that kind?

A. Well, I think I have explained my understanding of this exchange. I took Alastair Campbell through what had occurred up until then. I explained that Dr Kelly – I am not even sure, to be quite – I am pretty confident I did not actually say it was Dr Kelly, I said "the official" or something of the kind. I have indicated previously, as far as I am concerned that that was his summary of the past. I do not understand that this was anything that was to be acted on for the future. Indeed, there is no evidence that anyone so acted.

Q. Did you think that Dr Kelly ought to give evidence in front of the FAC?

A. When I received a request from the Chairman of the Foreign Affairs Committee, I eventually concluded, with the benefit of the advice that I had received, that, yes, he should give evidence once his name was in the public domain, yes.

Q. And if he gave evidence in front of the FAC contrary to the account which Mr Gilligan had given, that would assist the Government, would it not?

A. I think it would assist everyone. I think it would have assisted-

Q. Never mind everyone, what about the Government?

A. I am including the Government in "everyone".

Q. Right.

A. The Government would have benefited; the BBC would have benefited; and I think, most importantly, the public would have benefited. And the point that I made right at the outset of my original evidence was that the difficulty with Andrew Gilligan's story was that we were not in a position to assess the nature, quality, status of his source. So that ultimately it was of benefit to everyone that he should give evidence once he had been identified.

Q. Was this a benefit which you were referring to in your conversation with Mr Campbell, when you said there was a case for trying to get some kind of plea bargain?

A. Perhaps I need to look at his diary in order to be sure about what you are saying. I have summarised, I think on more than one occasion, and I do not wish to try your patience by repeating it, but these were Alastair Campbell's words, they were not my words; and the best I can do is to say that they were a summary of the description of the process that by then I was aware had taken place.

Q. Because, of course, Dr Kelly did give evidence before both Committees.

A. Eventually, yes.

Q. With your encouragement?

A. With my agreement.

368. Mr Hoon was also questioned by counsel to the Inquiry. Mr Dingemans asked him about the meeting which took place with Ms Pam Teare and Mr Richard Taylor in his office on the morning of Wednesday 9 July:

[22 September, page 101, line 20]

Q. Did you not, when that discussion was taking place, ask whether or not Dr Kelly was happy with this proposed approach of the Ministry of Defence confirming his name?

A. I did not. But -

Q. Why not?

A. Well, because I believed that proper steps had been taken to apprise Dr Kelly of the consequences of, particularly, the press statement being issued on the Tuesday; and indeed felt that that was more than sufficient to make him aware of what was possibly going to follow.

Q. Do you think there is a difference between yourself being confirmed by an employer and other people working it out?

A. There is clearly a difference; but the assumption throughout, which Dr Kelly had accepted, was that at some stage his name would come out; and of course it did come out, and it came out as a result of various investigations by journalists who then put the name to the MoD press office.

Q. Did you not think that he ought to have been told about the Q and A material being deployed which would have given details in addition to that contained in the press statement?

A. Again, I think that is to misunderstand the nature of the Q and A. It was not deployed in the sense that your question implies. It was simply background advice for press officers to deal with anticipated questions being put by journalists.

Q. Mr Campbell said in his evidence, in hindsight – he used those words "in hindsight" – that it was wrong to have the name dribble out in this way. Do you agree with that?

A. No, I do not. I regret that perhaps Dr Kelly's name was bandied about amongst journalists in the way that it was, but I do not believe, given the way in which journalists operate, that there was much alternative. I do not see how it could have been the case that journalists determined to identify Dr Kelly could have been prevented from doing so.

Q. Why was he not named with his consent, after his consent had been obtained, in a press statement, if it was inevitably going to come out?

A. First of all, his consent had not been sought. And we do not know whether he would have consented to that process.

Secondly, we were still, at that stage, as I have said repeatedly, unsure as to whether Dr Kelly was or was not Andrew Gilligan's single source.

Q. But –

A. Therefore, it did not seem to me necessarily appropriate, at that point, to volunteer his name.

Q. But if the question and answer material is being drafted on the basis it is inevitable his name is going to come out, if the decision has been taken to confirm his name if given because it is inevitable his name will come out, why not actually tell him his name is going to come out, put it in a press statement and give him the express opportunity to consent? Because we have heard that Dr Kelly perceived, rightly or wrongly, he had been let down by his employers. That would have at least met that particular complaint.

A. Well, it would have met that particular complaint. Then perhaps if that course had been followed you would be putting to me a different complaint, which is that, for example, Dr Kelly was not given sufficient time to prepare himself; that he was not given sufficient opportunity to consider what course of action he should take. The approach that was taken, particularly on the evening of 8th July, to warn him that the press statement was being made, to give him the opportunity of going through all the details in the press statement and then to apprise him of the likely press interest following the issue of the press statement, at least gave him some time to think about what action he should take in order to protect himself against the enthusiasm of the press for seeing out his identity.

The evidence of Mr Alastair Campbell, on 22 September

369.   Mr Campbell was examined by counsel for the Government who asked him about his suggestion on the evening of 7 July 2003 that Dr Kelly's name should be given out to a newspaper:

[22 September, page 130, line 21]

Q. Can I ask you about another point please? Evidence has been given on the evening of 7th July 2003 you had a discussion with Godric Smith in which you suggested that Dr Kelly's name should be given out to an evening paper. Can you tell us, please, exactly what your suggestion was, why it was made and what became of it?

A. No, it was not a discussion with Godric Smith, it was a discussion with the Defence Secretary, part of which Godric Smith heard on my speaker phone in the office, and I was not suggesting to Godric or to Mr Hoon or to anybody else that the name of the person who had come forward be put into the public domain. I was suggesting in advance of the Prime Minister's Liaison Committee appearance that the fact of somebody coming forward should be put into the public domain. And there was a very – I hesitate even to call it a proposal, it was a thought which was very quickly rejected by the Defence Secretary, Godric and Tom Kelly both thought it was a bad idea. But more importantly I raised it with the Prime Minister, he thought it was a bad idea and nothing came of it.

Q. During the period between your having this thought and it being sat on by all those people, did you have a view about how the name would be conveyed to the press?

A. No, I was not suggesting the name be conveyed.

Q. Sorry, the fact that somebody had come forward.

A. What my thought was based on was the idea of whether this should happen, not how. Had the decision been taken that it should have been taken forward, then we would have had a

261

discussion about how to do that, but I was not envisaging doing it in anything other than an open way, making clear that this was information that would come from the Government.

Q. Mr Dingemans put to Mr Hoon that no doubt the suggestion was that it should be done anonymously. When Mr Dingemans puts that question to you, what will your answer be?

A. If he does put that question to me in those terms, that was not what I had in mind.

Q. What did you have in mind, if anything?

A. Well, what I had in mind at that point was – I mean bear in mind on 7th July I had been busy all day with if you like helping to organise the Government's response to the Foreign Affairs Committee report. Come the late afternoon, early evening, I am starting to turn my mind to the Prime Minister's forthcoming appearance at the Liaison Committee and what I had in mind was something, a plan, that allowed the Prime Minister when he appeared at the Liaison Committee to be able to avoid what I think could have been a very difficult situation had he been asked about this, the question whether we knew anything about the source.

What I had in mind was a chain of events which ended if you like with the Prime Minister being able to say: I am aware of these reports, I am aware somebody has come forward, it is being handled by the Ministry of Defence. My worry was if there was nothing in the public domain at that time, either he would be put in a position where he could leave himself open to the charge of being misleading, in other words if he said nothing when he did know something that would be difficult or he would be put in a position where he, the Prime Minister, would be launching if you like yet another fire storm around this issue.

370. Mr Campbell was cross-examined by Mr Caldecott on behalf of the BBC but he was not cross-examined by Mr Gompertz. Mr Campbell was also questioned by counsel to the Inquiry, Mr Dingemans. In the course of that examination the following questions were put to Mr Campbell about the entry in his diary of 4 July relating to "plea bargains":

[22 September, page 196, line 7]

LORD HUTTON: Can we just look at the slightly earlier part of that entry. I understood from your evidence on the first occasion, I think, that it is your recollection that the Secretary of State used the words "some kind of plea bargain"?

A. I do not know that he used those exact words. I used those words to convey there the sense of what I felt he was saying to me, which was that this person had come forward, the person had acknowledged that he had done something wrong in having the unauthorised contact with Mr Gilligan. What I felt Mr Hoon was saying was that the person was saying: yes, I did some of these things. I did not do these, and I hope that by being honest and straightforward in coming forward to you that will be taken into account in any disciplinary action that might follow. And that was my assessment of what Mr Hoon was saying to me.

LORD HUTTON: Well, then you, yourself, would sometimes use the word or the term a "plea bargain"?

A. No, I would not normally, no but I -

LORD HUTTON: Are you saying it is a term that is familiar to you?

A. It is not a term that I would normally use. It may be that the Secretary of State used that. It is certainly my sense of what he said. But I cannot vouch 100 per cent for the Secretary of State using those exact words.

371. Mr Campbell had made the following entries in his diary for 9 July and 15 July 2003:

9 July 2003

BBC story moving away because they were refusing to take on the source idea. There was a big conspiracy at work really. We kept pressing on as best we could at the briefings, but the biggest thing needed was the source out. We agreed that we should not do it ourselves, so didn't but later in the day the FT, Guardian after a while Evans [Defence Correspondent of the Times] got the name.

15 July 2003

Looking forward to Kelly giving evidence, but GS, CR and I all predicted it would be a disaster and so it proved. Despite MOD assurances he was well schooled...

372. Mr Dingemans asked Mr Campbell about the entry for 9 July:

[22 September, page 221, line 8]

Q. Mr Kelly we know in the afternoon of 9th July gives out some further information which helped Mr Blitz along the path to the identification of Dr Kelly: "We kept pressing on as best we could at the briefings." Is that a reference to any discussions you had had with Mr Kelly?

A. No, that I think is the point that I am making. We keep having to make the point to the press that in our view, if this is the source then the story is wrong and the BBC should acknowledge that. And that is the point that we are making; and I think that the – I know that Tom Kelly is before the Inquiry tomorrow so he will have to answer the questions that you put then. But the points that he made at that briefing were in response to a BBC response to the MoD statement that was seeking to put over the point that this could not possibly be the source and that is why he had to make the points that he did.

Q. In which case the BBC are saying it is not him. You think it is him because that is what Mr Howard thinks, and the biggest thing needed was a source out. Now I imagine that is the name of the source, is that right?

A. That is correct, yes.

Q. So in Government circles it was recognised that it would assist them to have Dr Kelly's name out; is that fair?

A. That was my view. There were – although again qualified by the observation that I made earlier, qualified further, I think you raised other parts of my diaries when I first gave evidence, it was never going to be unalloyed but I think the –

Q. I am going to take you to a bit which balances that.

A. But this had become the nub of the issue. That was not Dr Kelly's fault. He did not know that was going to happen when he met Mr Gilligan but that was the reality of the situation that now pertained.

LORD HUTTON: I know you have gone over it before but you say qualified the view expressed. Just remind me very briefly what you are referring to there.

A. That it was not clear that it was necessarily going to be unalloyed good news for Dr Kelly to appear in public because he may well have things to say that would not necessarily accord with Government policy.

LORD HUTTON: I see, thank you.

MR DINGEMANS: Of course if you prevent, not you personally, but if Government prevents him giving that evidence, keeps the Foreign Affairs Committee off it, it is all good news from the Government's point of view.

A. Well, you have probably, no doubt, read some of the transcripts and you may have seen some of the video coverage of the Foreign Affairs Committee. I do not believe the Foreign Affairs Committee would have held back from asking whatever questions they wanted.

Q. The biggest thing needed was the source out. You say that was your view. Do you know if anyone else had that view?

A. I think by now – I mean, I think the mood around No.10 and I suspect much of the rest of the Government by now is that this whole issue is taking up a huge amount of time and energy; the BBC clearly were not going to accept they were wrong. They were not investigating, in my view, the complaint. It was frankly just going nowhere.

Q. Without his name out?

A. No, just generally. And I think that what had happened is that the statement had gone out, everybody felt it was inevitable at some point he was going to be identified. It was probably certain that the FAC and the ISC would want to see him. That was where this was heading. But I think by now, frankly, everybody is thinking this whole thing is just – I do not think – I think everybody felt pretty dispirited by the whole thing.

Q. Did you agree or discuss with Ms Teare the proposition that the Ministry of Defence would confirm Dr Kelly's name if the correct name was given?

A. I was aware that that was the policy that they had agreed.

Q. Who told you that?

A. (Pause): I think I learnt it from Pam or from Kate Wilson at one of the morning meetings, that that was the approach they were taking.

Q. Do you know which morning meeting?

A. I do not know.

Q. What was your reaction: good, that is what I want, because I think you have said quite frankly you wanted his name out?

A. As I said when I first gave evidence, I had been asked by the Prime Minister to take pretty much of a back seat on all of this. I can see why that plan was put together. It is, as I explained earlier when I gave evidence before, the reality of a lot of press office work; but I think it would have been better if there had been greater clarity and control in the process. I think it is always a mistake to cede control on these issues to the press.

Q. You have seen the Q and A material now. You have heard that Dr Kelly was not told about that. As a press man yourself, what are your views on that? Do you think Dr Kelly ought to have been told about the proposal to confirm his name?

A. I thought he had been told, that – I thought he understood, certainly I understood that he understood that that was going to happen.

Q. That the Ministry of Defence would confirm his name?

A. That if it was put to them by the press.

Q. Who had told you that? I appreciate that you say was your understanding. Who had given you that understanding?

A. Again, specifically I think it was – it was within the context of those meetings then. I cannot specifically recall that.

Q. Because assume, just for the purposes of the argument, that he had not been told.

A. Had not?

Q. Had not. That would have been quite wrong, would it not?

A. Well, just to go back to the point I made earlier.

Q. Not going back to points.

A. Well, it is actually to answer the question. I think that in a situation like this, where you have a person there who whilst experienced with the press on one level has not necessarily experienced what it is like dealing when you personally are the centre of this sort of thing, then I think it is best that you are brought in and are part of an agreed plan and an agreed strategy which you then implement together.

Q. Indeed. And if you are not and you are told only about the press statement but not about the lines or the Q and A material or about the fact that your boss may confirm the name if the correct name is given to you, it is always likely to lead to problems, is it not?

A. Again, I can see why in the circumstances that existed at the time the plan that was put together was put together. As I said both times I have appeared now, I always think it is better in these difficult situations, you have a plan, you involve everybody in that, everyone knows what is going on. But, again the – I mean I read Kate Wilson's evidence for example. I never spoke to Dr Kelly. I do not know how he was reacting. I mean, I got the sense from the way she was describing those conversations that maybe he did not want the help that was being offered. I just do not know. But I do not think it is really fair for me to deliver judgment in the way that you are asking me to.

Q. "We agreed that we should not do it ourselves, so didn't but later in the day the FT, Guardian [and] after a while Evans [Defence Correspondent of the Times] got the name."

A. Hmm.

Q. After Mr Blitz from the Financial Times got the name, he was rang up by someone who gave him further information; he spoke with Miss Teare. Do you know anything about that?

A. I do not know.

Q. I imagine you would deprecate all this briefing off the record after the event beyond the Q and A and the press statement, is that right?

A. Well, there would not be any need for it. The statement had gone out. I have said, you know, what I think about the fact that this came out as it were in an uncontrolled way. Beyond that, there is no real purpose served. As I say, again, just to put the other side of this, there was a – this was a – the media were banging the phones of everybody the whole time, but I am not aware of what you are referring to in relation to what Mr Blitz was told after the name.

Q. Mr Blitz was given further information about the status of the individual providing further information, which was supporting the Government line that Dr Kelly could not have known what was said to have been said –

A. I see. I am not aware of that.

Q. And I have already asked you about the articles that Mr Baldwin wrote.

A. Yes.

Q. Did you have any knowledge of any information given to Mr Baldwin at this time about Dr Kelly's status or anything?

A. No.

Q. 15th July, finally: "Looking forward to Kelly giving evidence, but GS, CR and I all predicted it would be a disaster and so it proved." I think that was the point about it not always being good news.

A. I think it goes back to the point I made about 9th July. I mean, through this whole episode, really, what has been so – it has obviously been terrible and far worse for Dr Kelly and his family than for anybody else but what has been terrible from our perspective is that at every stage of this we have felt as it were to be the wronged party and yet nothing has really ever gone according to the outcome that we might have wished, and frankly I think it just reflected in the mood that then existed in Downing Street that this was something which we were going to have to sort of put behind us and forget.

Q. "Despite MoD assurance he was well schooled…" Who gave you those assurances?

A. Again I think that was a – myself and Jonathan Powell just wanted to be assured by the MoD that Dr Kelly was being prepared, as an FAC appearance does require a lot of preparation. I think it was Kate Wilson, at a morning meeting.

Q. I am sorry, I did say "finally" before. Going back to the 9th July, one question I forgot to ask. The last sentence : "We agreed that we should not do it ourselves…" Who is "we"?

A. No. 10, No.10.

Q. So that is No.10 – there are a lot of people in No.10.

A. That will be a reference – the discussions I have about these sorts of issues would be myself, Tom Kelly and Godric Smith.

Q. The Prime Minister?

A. The Prime Minister would not – I mean, I am not suggesting there that anybody is saying that we should be doing it ourselves. I am just making the point – the Prime Minister was clear we should be saying nothing about this at all and beyond the strategic points that I had been making earlier, namely if this is the person then the BBC story is wrong and the BBC should be big enough to accept that.

The evidence of Mr Thomas Kelly, on 23 September

373. In his evidence on 23 September Mr Kelly further described his preparation for the lobby briefings on 9 July:

[23 September, page 3, line 19]

Q. When you began to prepare for the Lobby briefings on 9th July, what were the matters that you expected to be asked about?

A. Well, obviously, the MoD statement which had been issued on the evening beforehand was going to be the major subject; but that was very much going to be conditioned by the BBC statement which had been issued just an hour afterwards, which had called into question two of the central elements of the MoD statement.

Q. What elements had that statement called into question?

A. Well, what they had called into question was the fact that Mr Gilligan, the MoD had said, had known or the official who had come forward had known Mr Gilligan for a matter of months; the BBC said it had been longer than that, it had been for years; and also the BBC stated that the official – Mr Gilligan's source – did not work for the MoD.

Q. What issues did those two statements give rise to that you thought were liable to provoke questions?

A. Well, clearly that the underlying theme was that the MoD statement lacked credibility, because if it was wrong about where the person worked, if it was wrong about how long the source had known Mr Gilligan, then the whole credibility of the MoD statement was at risk. If the whole credibility of the MoD statement was at risk then the idea that this official might be Mr Gilligan's source was completely at stake.

Q. What information did you seek in order to deal with the questions that you anticipated on that point?

A. I sought - at the 8.30 morning media meeting in No.10, I identified these two issues as two issues which I was going to have to address and I sought clarification of what the answers to those issues were from the FCO and the MoD; and I made it clear that, obviously, the answers I would have to give at 11 o'clock.

374. He described his objectives at the briefings as follows:

[23 September, page 5, line 19]

Q. What were your objectives in dealing with possible questions from Lobby journalists? Did you go into the Lobby briefings intending to make it easier to identify Dr Kelly?

A. Well, I have to stress that at no point did I try to give information or drop clues which I thought would lead to Dr Kelly's identification. There was no -

Q. If I can just stop you there, I am going to take you to the actual briefings in a moment. At the moment I would just like to be clear about the intentions that you had in mind when you went into that briefing before you said anything.

A. Well, the BBC statement had created considerable difficulty for me and I was under no illusion about the difficulties I faced. I had to balance what I thought were a number of competing pressures. I genuinely wanted to try to protect Dr Kelly's identity as much as possible but I had to explain the discrepancies between the BBC statement and the MoD statement; and I had to do so without misleading the Lobby, which is the golden rule for Prime Minister's Official Spokesman, you cannot mislead the Lobby. One other factor was that I did not want to implicate anybody else as being the possible source because that would put suspicion on other people as well.

375. Mr Kelly was asked how much information he gave out in the morning briefing:

[23 September, page 7, line 9]

Q. How much information did you give out in the morning briefing which was not already in the public domain?

A. Well, my intention was to give information but to do so in as limited a way as possible to address the discrepancies between the MoD statement and the BBC statement. So, I identified that I thought the important information was partly what this person was not. So I stressed that the source was not a member of the Intelligence Service, that the person was not a member of the military intelligence; and also I put the importance of that because the BBC had placed so much onus on that.

What I did try to explain was the discrepancy over which Department the person worked for, by explaining that he worked for the MoD but his salary was paid for by another Department, but despite repeated questioning I did not say which Department that was; and I also explained the discrepancy over how long Dr Kelly had known Mr Gilligan by saying that the person concerned had known Andrew Gilligan in a number of different guises, in a number of different ways over the years. I deliberately chose that euphemism to try to give as little information away as possible, whereas what I actually knew was that Mr Gilligan and Dr Kelly had come across each other in press briefings over the years. I thought that was too specific, so I chose the phrase "different guises".

Q. Yes. You have the morning briefing notes open. If there is anything you particularly wish to draw our attention to to fill out that summary, this is your or an opportunity to do so.

A. The one point I would like to underline is – well, there are two points really. Firstly, the impact of the BBC statement is obvious from the second paragraph of the summary, in which I am asked three times in the one paragraph how the source that we have identified, the person who had come forward, could possibly be Mr Gilligan's source, given what the BBC have said in response. So the effect of the BBC statement had been to seriously call into question the MoD's statement. That I had to deal with.

Secondly, the other issue, if I may deal with it, is in the middle of the first paragraph where I say that I address the question of the position of the source. As long ago as 4th June, a few days after we had returned from Iraq, I had identified the position of the source as being a key issue. I did so because my understanding was that only a member of the JIC had the full intelligence picture on which to make the kind of claim that the Today Programme had done. That is why I thought it was important to stress that the official who turned out to be Dr Kelly could not have been in a position to make that claim.

376. Mr Kelly then described the information he gave out in the afternoon briefing:

[23 September, page 9, line 12]

Q. I want to turn to the afternoon briefing. That starts at CAB/1/511. I do not want to take you through the whole of these rather long notes but if you look at the bottom of 511 and over to the middle of 512, and at pages 513 and the top of page 514, and then at the last paragraph to begin on page 514, you will find that you gave out more information in the afternoon briefing than you had done in the morning.

A. Again, I think what was important was that I knew I was going to come under persistent questioning, and indeed I did so. In the morning briefing and in the afternoon briefing I deliberately drew a line forward, a defensive line, if you like, forward of my actual state of knowledge and, therefore, what I tried to do was give away as little information as possible. Hence my description of Dr Kelly as a technical expert, because I thought if I described him as a WMD expert I would get persistent questioning on what kind of WMD expert, where he was, et cetera. Again, in the afternoon, I got persistent questioning on why we would not say what Department paid his salary and hence I tried to give away as little information as possible. But inevitably I did give away some information but I do not believe that that actually helped any of the journalists identify Dr Kelly.

Q. Can you summarise the additional information that you gave out in the afternoon briefing which you had not given out in the morning and which was not in the public domain?

A. The information I think I gave out in the afternoon briefing was the reason why I refused to say which Department paid for his salary, which was that there were only a few people who were paid in this way and therefore that is why I could not give it out because they would be able to identify Dr Kelly. I felt I had to do that because otherwise the Lobby would think that there was something underhand about us refusing to say. I had to give them an explanation. There are times in the Lobby when assertion is not enough. It was also put to me that was this person a secondee. If I had refused to address that issue the assumption would be – because people were putting to me that this person worked for the FCO or was paid for by the FCO, the assumption would be that he was a diplomat. I could not let that assumption rest because the FCO had made it very plain to me in the morning that they did not want people to assume he was a diplomat because they thought suspicion would fall on other people. So I had to describe him as a consultant. I thought consultant was a very vague term and I did not think it would help people identify Dr Kelly.

377. Mr Kelly was asked whether Dr Kelly was some kind of a pawn in a game which he was playing with the press:

[23 September, page 12, line 13]

MR SUMPTION: The suggestion has been made that Dr Kelly was some kind of pawn in a game that you were playing with the press. What do you say about that?

A. Absolutely not. There were lots of pressures on everybody at this time, but I genuinely feel that I and I do not believe others that I worked with lost sight of that there was an individual caught up in this controversy, in the middle of it, and that therefore we had to respect that individual. At the same time, there was a logic of events which stretched back to 29th May which unfortunately, and I did not like that logic, but there was a logic which was working its way through. Now, there were times whenever if the BBC had stepped back, I think that logic could have been stopped, but as the effect of the BBC statement on what I had to do on the 9th [July] showed, it was very difficult to get out of the pressure of those events.

Q. Finally, Mr Kelly, if I can turn to one matter arising after Dr Kelly's death. You have already made your position clear, very publicly, on the Walter Mitty remarks and you have apologised without reservation for that. What I want to ask you is this: it has been suggested that what you said on that occasion about Dr Kelly was part of a broader plan on the part of the Government or yourself to belittle him, so that his disclosures to Andrew Gilligan would seem less significant. Do you have any comment to make about that?

A. Well, I was not aware of or part of any strategy to demean or belittle Dr Kelly. I have accepted that my remark was wrong, it was a mistake, it was a too colourful phrase to use, but it was a mistake in what I thought was a private conversation. It was not part of any broad strategy and I would not have been part of any broad strategy.

378. In cross-examination Mr Gompertz put to Mr Kelly many of the answers which he had given to journalists in the two lobby briefings on 9 July and suggested that they constituted a great deal of information which helped to identify Dr Kelly:

[23 September, page 20, line 8]

Q. Can I put this suggestion to you: that if one combines what you said, I realise chronologically not in the right order, but what you said in the Lobby briefing with what was in the MoD statement, there was a great deal of information, I suggest, which would enable a journalist who knew about such matters to identify the person concerned very quickly?

A. Well, I think the problem is that we are talking about two separate events. I had to respond to the questions which journalists were asking as a result of the BBC statement. If the BBC had not put out their statement, I would not have had to respond to the questions. If I had not responded to the questions, then the impact of the BBC statement, as the seven questions I got during the morning and the afternoon made clear, would have been to totally discredit the MoD statement.

Q. So the problems were all of the BBC's making, were they?

A. I am simply explaining the context in which I had to operate on the morning and the afternoon of the 9th June. As I have already said, I was under no illusion as to the difficulty I had in balancing the competing pressures that faced me that day. Those difficulties were real and I was fully aware of them.

379. Referring to Mr Campbell's diary entries for the 7 and 9 July Mr Gompertz put to Mr Kelly:

[23 September, page 26, line 25]

Q. Because the whole purpose of the statement, the Lobby briefings and the Q and A material is demonstrated in these notes, is it not, Mr Kelly? Namely, that there was a strategy to reveal Dr Kelly's name without appearing to do so?

A. Categorically not.

380. With reference to Mr Kelly's "Walter Mitty" remark to a journalist on The Independent after Dr Kelly's death, Mr Gompertz put the following question:

[23 September, page 35, line 16]

Q. But can I just say this: that the suggestion is that this was not just a single off the cuff remark to Mr Waugh, it was a scene setting remark, was it not, made to several journalists?

A. It was not intended as that. I said at the end of the Lobby briefing on the afternoon of 9th [July] that I did not intend to demean or understate the role of the official who came forward. That was my view all the way through. What I, however, did think was legitimate was the issue of whether the source of Andrew Gilligan's story had been in the position to make the claim that Andrew Gilligan reported that person as having made, whether he did or did not. And that, I believe, was always a legitimate issue and I had expressed that view from 4th June right up to 7th July, and on seven different occasions during Lobby, because I thought that was a legitimate issue. It was that I was trying to examine in my conversations with journalists, without demeaning Dr Kelly in any way.

381. At the end of his cross-examination Mr Gompertz put the following question to Mr Kelly:

[23 September, page 40, line 21]

Q. So there was no Government campaign to belittle, demean or slur him?

A. I was not aware of any explicit or implicit strategy to do so and I was not part of any strategy to do so.

382. In the course of his examination by Mr Dingemans Mr Kelly said:

[23 September, page 48, line 9]

MR DINGEMANS: So once the statement had been issued, everyone knew that his name was going to come out from the professional press department side of things?

A. Well, that was my professional opinion and I believe that Dr Kelly had accepted the inevitability of that.

Q. We have heard evidence on that. Can I just press you, though, for an answer to my question, which was whether you wanted, on 9th July, the source out; and you have given us a long answer but I rather think it permits of a yes or no.

A. The short answer is: no.

Q. You did not want the source out?

A. I did not want any of this to be happening. I wanted to try and resolve this as a private matter; but I had to do my job and my job was to do the Lobby that day and address the discrepancies.

Q. So Mr Campbell got it wrong when he said: "… the biggest thing needed was the source out. We agreed we should not do it ourselves", and you were keeping going at the press briefings?

A. What I did not want to do was to say anything at Lobby which helped identify David Kelly; but what I did have to do was address the questions which the BBC statement made inevitable that I was going to have to address.

The evidence of Sir Kevin Tebbit, on 13 October

383. Sir Kevin Tebbit gave further evidence on 13 October 2003. In his minute to Mr Hatfield, the Personnel Director of the MoD, dated 8 July 2003, Sir Kevin had written that one of the key issues in deciding whether to recommend a public announcement was:

> Kelly's readiness to be associated with a public statement that names him and carries a clear and sustainable refutation of the core allegation on the '45 minute' intelligence.

Sir Kevin was asked by his own counsel about this point in his minute and his evidence was as follows:

[13 October, page 7, line 12]

Q…… Why did you give that instruction to ascertain Dr Kelly's readiness to be associated with a public statement that names him?

A. Well, there are a number of points here. Firstly, I felt from the outset that an allegation made based on a single anonymous source could only be countered credibly and authoritatively and finally if that single anonymous source is identified and clarifies the issue personally. It so happened that Dr Kelly came forward and seemed very likely to be that source. There have, I know, been explanations or arguments advanced as to other ways of correcting or clarifying the public record. None of them could have been as complete as this method.

The second reason is that I felt that once we were satisfied or could be satisfied this was indeed the explanation for Gilligan's story, there would be no reason whatsoever for Dr Kelly to feel that this was an undue piece of pressure placed on him. We expected this to come out at any moment. I expected to see in the press, you know, "Kelly responsible for [this allegation]". Had Dr Kelly really been responsible for saying the things that were in that article, had he really said that Alastair Campbell and the Government had intervened in the intelligence judgments overturning the advice of the intelligence community, using information which they knew indeed to be untrue or no longer valid, then that would have been a very, very grave charge indeed. Had he actually said that, Dr Kelly would have been guilty of a very serious disciplinary offence. So I believe that he himself would have an interest in correcting the record and thereby removing this slur on him, as a respected technical source but not somebody who got caught up in making such politically damaging allegations. So I thought this was again a perfectly reasonable thing to be putting to Dr Kelly, as well as a necessary thing in terms of clarifying and clearing up the record. When I say "clarifying and clearing up the record", right at the beginning when I spoke to Geoff Hoon about this, he put it to me, and I agreed, that it is very difficult for good Government to proceed on the basis of judgments made in the public mind as a result of allegations in the press and repeated in Parliament, judgments based on anonymous sources. Good Government can only proceed if the evidence is made available and the people, through Parliament and through the press, are able to actually judge for themselves. That is what I meant about clearing up the record.

Q. We know that –

A. I am sorry, I have probably said too much.

Q. Sorry, had you completed your answer?

A. The final point is that I had no particular view as to precisely when Mr Hatfield would actually put this point to Dr Kelly. I had assumed he would do it more or less straightaway. But it did need to be read in conjunction with the other point, that until we were satisfied or reasonably satisfied that it was Dr Kelly, clearly I understood that it would be very hard to expect him to put his name to this and wrong of us to do so.

384. On the evening of Monday 7 July Sir Kevin Tebbit had a conversation with Mr Jonathan Powell and his evidence was as follows:

[13 October, page 13, line 5]

Q. In the conversation which you had with Mr Powell that evening was anything said about the amount of detail which might be required in such a statement?

A. Yes, Jonathan Powell took the view that if we made a statement, we would need to be able to stand it up fully in public to explain why it was we were bringing forward this information and that we would need to explain that the status of the individual was such as to render it highly improbable that he could authoritatively have made the allegations that were central to Gilligan's broadcast, as well as the denial that he actually made those statements.

Q. As matters stood at close of play on Monday 7th July, how did you expect the handling of the matter to proceed?

A. I expected that during the course of Tuesday there would be a meeting, at which I had hoped to be present, in No.10 with the Cabinet Office where we would discuss this further and decide what to do. The next prominent event from the Liaison Committee meeting was the beginning of the Intelligence and Security Committee hearings into the use of intelligence surrounding the Iraq campaign; and we were already, as it were, sitting on what we felt was a ticking bomb from the Foreign Affairs Committee, it now being virtually 10 days since we had had the letter. They had already reported and in their report they had asked, recommended, that Gilligan's contacts should be further investigated. I felt – there was a collective feeling that we had a dual problem: 1. Bringing forward the information we had, because we believed it was at a state where it was justified to bring it forward, without naming Dr Kelly, while at the same time equally avoiding allegations of a cover-up or of misleading the Intelligence and Security Committee. That was a particular – the latter point was a particular concern in the Cabinet Office, because officials, beginning with John Scarlett, were due to start testifying before the Intelligence and Security Committee on the Wednesday; and it would have therefore been very difficult for them to do so holding to themselves, as it were, the information we had and not sharing that with the Committee.

385. Sir Kevin Tebbit was asked about a meeting in 10 Downing Street on 8 July. He said:

[13 October, page 18, line 15]

Q. So by the time you arrived the meeting was in fact over?

A. It was in fact over. I was in time to see the Prime Minister saying: Sorry, we have just finished but Jonathan Powell will brief you.

Q. On what did Mr Powell brief you as to what had been decided?

A. He said that we were back, as it were, to the idea of issuing a statement because Ann Taylor would not consider it without that; and that the statement material was there, and colleagues were beginning to draft on that basis; and he suggested, after briefing me on the approach that was being taken, that we went to the room where this was being done, which we subsequently did, and I –

Q. Do you know why that decision had been taken?

A. Well -

Q. The decision to publish the statement at that time?

A. Yes, as I say, because it was felt that we could not wait longer before we disclosed what we knew. Given the immediate pressure of the ISC meeting and the growing problem, the longer we failed to bring the information forward of, as it were, the risk of a cover-up from the Foreign Affairs Committee which was a real concern, as has been testified to subsequently by the Chairman of the FAC, had we sought not to tell them about this.

Q. Did you in fact concur with the decision which had been taken in your absence?

A. I did, as I say. I think had I been at the meeting I would have joined the consensus. The fact was I was not.

Q. What was to be your part in relation to the statement?

A. Well, my part was clearly to ensure that this was something that Dr Kelly would be prepared to put his name to, as it were, not on the statement but to defend in public, as and when it was necessary to do so, which had been made clear to Dr Kelly, in fact, by Mr Hatfield. I mean, I was not actually invited to challenge the judgment of a meeting that had been chaired by the Prime Minister but there was a concern, clearly, this should be something which was acceptable also to Dr Kelly. It was no good trying to issue a statement which he could not live with.

386. Sir Kevin was asked whether, with the benefit of hindsight, it would not have been better to have named Dr Kelly on 8 July. He replied:

[13 October, page 22, line 23]

A. I do not think so. I think, firstly, we had enough to justify making a statement. In other words, I think it was sufficiently clear that the meeting with Dr Kelly was likely to be the explanation for his story, to justify making a statement of that. I do not think, at that stage, we had enough to be able to say we were absolutely certain it was Dr Kelly, when Dr Kelly himself gave that as one option but not the one he believed to be the case.

The reason for making the statement was we did not feel we could hold on to this information any longer before we brought it into the public domain. As I say, the fear of being accused of a cover-up by the Foreign Affairs Committee, of putting our own Government witnesses in an untenable position really before the ISC. So the statement was made on that basis. There have been arguments, I know, that at least this gave Dr Kelly more time to prepare for the press interest that would be expressed in him. That happens to be true but it was not a driving consideration for us at the time, for me anyway, at the time. I am glad it did provide some time but that was not the overriding reason. The overriding reason was we felt that a statement did need to go out, preferably on Tuesday. Had Dr Kelly said, "I am not happy with it" or, "I want to discuss it further" or, "I am concerned about the implications of this statement", I think – I have no doubt whatsoever we would have discussed it with him and explained to him the reasons why it was necessary for the Government to come forward with a statement of this kind. As it happened, that was not necessary. But I think we could only have delayed it a matter of hours. The sense in No.10 was we really did need to come forward with a statement.

387. Sir Kevin Tebbit was asked about the Question and Answer material. His evidence was as follows:

[13 October, page 24, line 18]

Q.…. The first of those matters, Sir Kevin, is the Q and A brief. Can I ask you, what was your first involvement with the Q and A brief prepared in this case?

A. When it was shown to me, very briefly, at the end of the discussions about the statement with my staff on the late afternoon of the 8th.

Q. Did you approve it?

A. Yes.

Q. With which aspects of the Q and A brief did you concern yourself at that time?

A. Only with the proposition that if the press came forward with Dr Kelly's name we would have no option but to confirm that information; I am afraid I did not trouble – I should not use this phrase, but I did not go through the thing line by line to look at the detail of information. I regarded it partly as supporting information if Dr Kelly's name was brought forward by the press, and for the most part justificatory information for the statement.

In other words, you know, it is rather old fashioned and quaint to think that the press will simply publish a statement. They are very sceptical. They ask lots of questions on individuals parts of the statement. This is true of any policy issue or any major issue, as this was; and therefore Q and A material is routinely and regularly prepared to, in the modern parlance, stand up the statement, and this was no different from the others.

I never see Q and A briefs as a routine matter. It is done by the staff as subordinate supporting material. Their professional judgment is trusted. The factual basis is usually critical. And this was no different from the rest. I mean, one does not wander around with Q and A material in one's own pocket or talk to the Secretary of State about the details of a Q and A brief. I can understand why it has been focussed on, but it really was not right, that.

Q. Sir Kevin, can I ask you this: was it ever your intention that this Q and A brief should be used as a device or a strategy for covertly making Dr Kelly's name public?

A. Absolutely not. Absolutely categorically not.

Q. Why, then, was it necessary for the press office to confirm Dr Kelly's name, if the press already had it?

A. Well, what were the other options? The options were to deny, which would have been completely untrue and absurd, not just as a matter of credibility but, you know, what was the basic policy here? It was to actually bring this information forward. Denial would have been unacceptable both in principle and in terms of the process we were engaged in. No comment? My guess is "no comment" would have lasted a matter of hours while the press continued to beaver away assiduously to try to find out who it was.

There was a real reason here which was not completely Dr Kelly specific. I do not think there was really anything we could have done to prevent Dr Kelly's name coming into the public domain. We felt this was going to happen, right from the outset, from the moment we received his letter, through the article by Tom Baldwin, through that weekend. But we could prevent other people being the subject of press speculation and spotlight, people who had nothing whatsoever to do with this, but were often in sensitive positions. I mean, we do have some staff that are very sensitively placed and their identity is a matter of concern for us.

Indeed, this was not an abstract concern. One of these individuals did have, as I have testified before, the press round his house trying to get the attention of his children; somebody who did have a threat to his life; and we could protect those people and decided to do so.

So the idea of confirming, if the name was put, was not entirely dependent on Dr Kelly, it was also dependent on other considerations. Protecting other members of staff and the press office themselves, and the Director of News felt that this was also a way of increasing the probability that the press would talk to us before they published a name, which was quite important in trying to manage the issue.

LORD HUTTON: When you refer to someone being under a threat, was that a threat arising from quite separate matters?

273

A. Yes, totally different matters, my Lord.

LORD HUTTON: The threat was already in existence.

A. Yes, completely different issues.

LORD HUTTON: Your concern was what precisely, Sir Kevin?

A. Well, we have other scientists, other technical specialists who are working in other fields who had had threats against their lives whose names we were keenly anxious not to have in the public domain, or indeed have the press round their houses knowing their identity. If you wish for details, my Lord, I would be very happy to give them to you privately.

LORD HUTTON: No, I just wanted that point clarified. Thank you very much.

388. In relation to the question whether Dr Kelly was under intolerable pressure, Sir Kevin Tebbit's evidence was as follows:

[13 October, page 35, line 6]

Q. At this time, Sir Kevin, on the basis of what you were being told and the reports you were receiving, did you have any reason to believe that Dr Kelly might be under intolerable pressure?

A. No, I did not. As I say, all that he was being asked to do was to state before the Committee what he had said to us in his letter. He was put under no pressure to go further than that or to say less than that. Indeed, I was concerned that if he wanted to say that he did not believe he was the source, then he must be free to say that and not be put under the burden of assuming – having to accept our own judgment in the matter. With the benefit of hindsight, of course, I can now appreciate he had a lot more pressures on him than we recognised, but he gave no indication of those pressures whatsoever, and we accepted his account at face value. Of course, at that stage we had no idea of some of the further information that has come out from Andrew Gilligan, from Susan Watts, from Mr Beaumont, from Julie Flint, from Gavin Hewitt. We were unaware of those contacts and therefore had no reason to suppose he was under the pressure he may well in fact have been under.

389. In relation to Dr Kelly's security clearance and his pension, Sir Kevin Tebbit's evidence was as follows:

13 October, page 37, line 22]

A.......There was absolutely no question, as far as I was concerned, of his security clearance being withdrawn or his pension. I was aware that plans were going on for him to go to Iraq. I was content with those, and indeed confirmed it myself on the 17th in a conversation with Martin Howard in that: it is now time for Dr Kelly to go and do what he does best, which is inspect for weapons in Iraq.

390. Sir Kevin Tebbit was cross-examined by Mr Gompertz and Mr Gompertz asked him if Dr Kelly ever consented to the publication of his name:

[13 October, page 41, line 6]

Q..... But can I ask you this: did Dr Kelly ever consent to the publication of his name?

A. My understanding, which is very clear, is that there was an understanding between him and Mr Hatfield, as a result of two quite long interviews and the clearing of the statement, that Dr Kelly expected his name to come out and that this was understood, and that this was not something that was cleared with him because we were not, ourselves, in complete control as to when and in precisely what circumstances his name did come out. But I believe this to be part of the a qui that existed between Dr Kelly and the Department.

Q. Would you agree that there is a difference between a person accepting that inevitably his name may come out some time and accepting that the MoD should take positive steps which would lead to the publication of his name?

A. There is a difference but I do not believe that was the critical issue. The Department was taking positive steps to bring forward information which they believed was necessary and vital in the public interest. The Prime Minister himself has said how serious it would have been for him if that slur had remained unchallenged and unchecked and uncorrected. In the process of doing so, it became necessary to provide information about the source which gave credibility to the point that while this was a man who would have certainly been found very interesting by Andrew Gilligan, and who Gilligan may well have regarded as being an important source for information, his identity, his nature, his role was not such as to be able to say with any authority the sorts of things that were alleged by Andrew Gilligan in terms of the sexing up of the dossier by the Government, and by Campbell in particular, against the wishes of the intelligence community. It was in order to give credibility to that statement that the details were made available, not in order to release, as it were, Dr Kelly's name.

Q. And he was never asked that question, was he?

A. Which question?

Q. As to whether he consented to the publication of his name by whatever means.

A. We confirmed the name when it was put to us; and, as I have said before, my understanding was he had reached a point in his discussions with us where he expected his name to come out, and he said it to other people. It was not just a question of relying on what we said. He told Olivia Bosch that he accepted his name would come out. He was reconciled to it or was resigned to it. We know that we told Mrs Kelly that that was so, on the basis of the statement. I do not think he was even aware of the Q and A material.

391. Mr Gompertz put it to Sir Kevin that Dr Kelly was never asked the question whether the MoD could give out his name, and he replied:

[13 October, page 44, line 24]

A. No, he was never asked that question because that was not the question we were seeking to establish. As I have said to you before, the problem here is you are assuming, if I may put it like that, there was some process to reveal Dr Kelly's name. There was not a process to reveal Dr Kelly's name. There was a process to release the information which the Government believed it could not sit on any longer because of fear of cover-up, because of witnesses being in very difficult – I mean false positions in front of the ISC, which meant that a statement needed to be made. We hoped that the information could be evaluated further in confidence, in the ISC. We hoped that the BBC would help to resolve remaining doubts by being prepared to say, if only this: no, it is not this individual, it is somebody else; but they were not prepared to cooperate.

We believed on that Tuesday that we had enough justification and need to bring forward the information, without naming Dr Kelly, while not being sufficiently certain to be justified in actually naming Dr Kelly as some people felt would have been ideal. But the force of the requirement to come forward with the statement was what was determining this issue. There was no devious strategy involved, as you put it. We had no need to follow that sort of course.

392. In reply to questions from Mr Gompertz Sir Kevin Tebbit gave evidence as to the decision taken in 10 Downing Street on 8 July:

[13 October, page 55, line 3]

Q. Did you see the Q and A version 2 before you went to No.10, or not?

A. No, as I have already explained, the first time I saw any Q and A material was after I had returned from No.10, when it was shown to me very briefly at the end of my meeting in finalising the statement.

Q. Thank you. When you went to No.10, effectively what you found was a fait accompli, was it not?

A. No, I found that the meeting had ended. As I have already explained, had I been present at the meeting, I have no reason to suppose that I would have disagreed or differed or had a different judgment to offer the Prime Minister. So therefore I was content with the outcome.

Q. You were part of the drafting process which then took place in the afternoon?

A. Yes, I was in the room when the draft was worked up. We did not sit round a table and deliberate sentence by sentence because I think the material was taken from drafts which were already in existence.

Q. Because what took place on the 8th was a very considerable change of stance, was it not?

A. The issue had moved forward.

Q. Yes.

A. There had been several developments since before the weekend.

Q. The statement which was, in fact, approved and released eventually – it is on MoD/1/67 if you want to look at it, page 34 – contained considerably more information about Dr Kelly, did it not?

A. Yes, it did.

Q. I have in mind, in particular, the third paragraph, which we have looked at a number of times previously. But do you agree with that?

A. It does have more material, yes, about the nature of the source.

Q. When you eventually did look at the Q and A material, there had been, within the questions and answers proposed, a similar change of stance, had there not?

A. Well, on that I cannot help you because the only version of the Q and A material I saw was the version which I saw at the end of the day on Tuesday.

Q. Because in the first version – all right, you did not see it – the position adopted with regard to naming was that there was nothing to be gained by naming the individual and that the MoD were not prepared to name him. I expect you know that now, even if you did not know it at the time?

A. Yes, and I assume that was the press office interpretation of the position we had on the Friday evening, after Mr Hatfield's first conversation, which suggested that we would not be going forward with this information, because we were not able, at that stage, to be certain that this was the source.

Q. In version 2 the question asked was, "Is it X?", ie the correct name. And the response to be given was that: we need to tell the individual. You know that now?

A. Yes, because this was before the Government had decided on the statement which was then put to Dr Kelly, which he approved.

Q. So it is all based on the approval of that statement, is it, the change in stance?

A. The approval of that statement was part of the reflection of the – the change in stance, as you put it, was a decision taken by a meeting chaired by the Prime Minister.

Q. And version 3, of course, the answer was different, that if the correct name was put it was to be confirmed without consulting the individual. You know that now, do you not?

A. I knew that then because I had seen that press statement.

Q. Yes, it is the change that I am asking you about.

A. The change, I have to tell you, is irrelevant because a policy decision on the handling of this matter had not been taken until the Prime Minister's meeting on the Tuesday. And it was only after that that any of the press people had an authoritative basis on which to proceed.

Q. So are you saying this: that the decisions which led, in fact, to the naming of Dr Kelly were taken at No.10 Downing Street and not by the Ministry of Defence?

A. I was not trying to make that point. I was trying to contrast to you the difference between a formal decision on bringing forward the information into the public arena and the stage before any such decision had been taken.

Q. Whether you were making that point or not, what is the position? That the decision was taken at No.10 and not by the Ministry of Defence, or by the Ministry of Defence?

A. The decision was taken at a meeting in No.10 with which the Ministry of Defence concurred.

Q. You were not there but concurred when you returned; is that right?

A. Yes. But, I mean, it was in line with the sort of advice I was giving from the previous evening.

Q. Could you look, please, at CAB/39/1, which you will find on page 64 of the bundle? This is the extract that we have from Mr Campbell's diary. The entry towards the bottom of the page, last two lines: "Several chats with MoD, Pam Teare, then Geoff H re the source. Felt we should get it out through the papers, then have line to respond and let TB take it on at Liaison Committee." Do you recognise that – I hesitate to use the word "strategy", which you do not like – but do you recognise that as a possible cause of action? Never put to you?

A. No, it was not ever.

Q. Over the page: "TB felt we had to leave it to Omand/Tebbit judgment and they didn't want to do it." What do you understand about "they didn't want to do it"?

A. I understand that Alastair Campbell has a very racy diary style, but this was never to put to us as an option. Omand and Tebbit were unaware of any such suggestion; and I think had we been consulted we would still have been against it. But the Prime Minister was against it before we ever got informed, so there we are.

Q. So you simply do not recognise any suggestion that getting it out through the papers was a matter which was discussed?

A. No. I really am completely unaware of that. It would have been the easiest thing to do had anybody decided to do it, but they did not decide it to do it because it would have been wrong.

Q. It goes on: "Had to go for natural justice." Was that your view?

A. Really I do not think it is helpful for me to discuss Alastair Campbell's diaries because I recognise nothing here that I was aware of. I think, if I may say so, you are coming still at that we had a stratagem to reveal the name, we did not. We had a stratagem to put the information in the public arena without revealing the name, in the hope that it could have been discussed in the ISC, and in the hope we could have had dialogue with the BBC before we reached the stage where we came forward with the name.

Q. What I am investigating, Sir Kevin, is whether there was a difference of opinion between civil servants and politicians. Do you recognise that possible suggestion?

A. What I do recognise, because it was very clear from the meeting I did attend on the Monday morning that the Prime Minister was quite clear that he wanted this handled on the basis of advice from Sir David Omand and myself; and that seems to me to have been a consistent theme throughout. And I was unaware of any other activities that were underway.

Q. Let us go on to examine the position from Dr Kelly's perspective at this stage.

393. Mr Gompertz asked Sir Kevin Tebbit about the Welfare Department in the MoD:

[13 October, page 71, line 24]

Q. Was the Welfare Department involved at all in Dr Kelly's case?

A. I mean, we had no reason to suppose that the Welfare Department should have been involved in -

Q. So the answer to my question is "no".

A. The answer to your question is no, for good informed reasons as opposed to negligent aspects.

Q. I am not stopping you giving the reasons but I am keen you should answer the questions. If you want to give the reasons, please do. Do you want to give any further explanation?

A. There was absolutely no reason for us to suppose that Dr Kelly needed any welfare assistance. He had several conversations with members of my staff, his line manager and the media people, as well as others in his own Department, and there was no evidence that he felt under these pressures. Indeed, to the extent that there was any information, it was that he was rather, as it were, dismissive of the suggestions and help he was given, giving the impression that he was handling it and he knew how to deal with it.

I know Mrs Kelly said he could sometimes be a difficult person to help. There was certainly no impression coming from him to my staff that he was in difficulty. And on the basis of the information we were operating to, there was no real reason why he should have been.

394. In answer to counsel to the Inquiry Sir Kevin Tebbit said with reference to the decision to issue a statement on 8 July:

[13 October, page 110, line 25]

A... the decision to issue a statement, that a statement should be made, was one which was arrived at in No.10 which, as it happened, the Ministry of Defence was not present at but which had it been it would, I know, at that point, be fully associated with that decision. The timing of the statement was dictated primarily by the concern to get it out before the ISC began taking testimony the following day, although there was concern about the allegations of cover-up the longer it went on after the FAC had reported.

Q. You mentioned this morning, and I think you were touching on that when you said you have already given evidence about this, that there was a change in stance after the Prime Minister's meeting, is that right, on 8th July? That is what you said this morning.

A. I think the words were put to me in that form.

Q. Do you adopt them or not?

A. I think that there was a continuing process throughout this, as Ministers and officials were judging the situation. It just happened to be that that was the decisive meeting, yes.

Q. The decisive meeting?

A. I would not say there was a change in stance quite. I would not particularly use those words.

Q. What changed as a result of that meeting?

A. What changed was a decision to issue a statement.

Q. And a decision to issue the Q and A material with it or was that –

A. Yes. But as I keep insisting, the Q and A was simply the subordinate material supporting a statement, as it always does when you have a major statement on an issue of policy.

Consideration of the issue whether the Government behaved in a way which was dishonourable or underhand or duplicitous in revealing Dr Kelly's name to the media

395. Having set out some relevant parts of the evidence I turn to consider the issue whether the Government behaved in a way which was dishonourable or underhand or duplicitous in revealing Dr Kelly's name to the media. Stating the same issue in different words: did the Government devise and implement an underhand strategy to name Dr Kelly whereby his name was deliberately leaked to the press without the Government appearing to do so in order to strengthen its case in its battle with the BBC?

396. If the bare details of the MoD's statement dated 8 July 2003, the changing drafts of the Q and A material prepared in the MoD, and the lobby briefings by the Prime Minister's official spokesman on 9 July are looked at in isolation from the surrounding circumstances it would be possible to infer, as some commentators have done, that there was an underhand strategy by the Government to leak Dr Kelly's

name to the press in a covert way. For a time at the start of the Inquiry it appeared to me that a case of some strength could be made that there was such a strategy, and some of the questions I put to Government witnesses (in addition to questions put by counsel to the Inquiry) were directed to this issue. In particular I was concerned to find out why it would not have been possible for the Government "to batten down the hatches" and ride out the controversy fuelled by Mr Gilligan's broadcasts without revealing that a civil servant had come forward to admit that he had spoken to Mr Gilligan about WMD or, alternatively, to issue a statement that a civil servant had come forward but to decline to identify that civil servant to the press. However as the Inquiry proceeded and I heard more evidence about the surrounding circumstances and the considerations which influenced those in Government I came to the conclusion that the reality was that there was no such underhand strategy.

397. I enumerate the surrounding circumstances and considerations which led me to this conclusion as follows:

(1) I am satisfied that the reports contained in Mr Gilligan's broadcasts at 6.07am and 7.32am on 29 May that the Government probably knew that the 45 minutes claim was wrong or was questionable before it was written in the dossier was an allegation against the integrity of the Government of the greatest gravity which was unfounded and which created a major controversy.

(2) I am satisfied from the evidence of the Prime Minister, Mr Geoffrey Hoon, the Secretary of State for Defence, Sir David Omand, Sir David Manning, Sir Kevin Tebbit and a number of other witnesses that throughout the period from 4 July to 8 July the Government was becoming increasingly concerned that if it did not issue a statement that a civil servant had come forward to say that he had had a meeting with Mr Gilligan, it would be charged with a cover up and with concealing this fact from the FAC which on 7 July published its report into its inquiry into the decision to go to war in Iraq, Mr Gilligan's broadcasts on the Today programme being an important part of the context within which the FAC had decided to embark on this inquiry. I am further satisfied that this was the principal reason why it was decided to issue the MoD statement on Tuesday 8 July.

(3) I am satisfied that the Government's concern that it would be charged with a cover up if it did not issue a statement was justified and well founded. In his evidence Mr Donald Anderson MP, the Chairman of the FAC, stated that he and other members of the FAC learned of the MoD's statement on 8 or 9 July and decided to hold a meeting of the Committee on 10 July. At that meeting there was a difference of opinion as to whether the FAC should reopen its inquiry and call Dr Kelly to give evidence. Mr Anderson was not in favour of recalling Dr Kelly because he felt that the Committee would meet the difficulty that people would not be prepared to disclose things in respect of journalists, but the majority of the Committee voted to call Dr Kelly to give evidence.

In his evidence Mr Anderson said:

[21 August, page 22, line 15]

A. But I made clear my own view to the Committee. There were a number of colleagues who agreed with me. In a good tempered way other colleagues said: no, this really needs to be clarified, because fundamental to our report had been this question whether the politicians had overborne the intelligence community in respect of the information, and that we had come to certain views, and those views might well be fundamentally overturned as a result of meeting the person who may have been the source, and therefore it would look odd if we did not seek to clarify the position.

In my own judgment, my Lord, if we had known, for example, prior to concluding the report that the civil servant had volunteered himself, probably members of the Committee, because of the importance of that, would have deferred publishing the report and would have sought to clarify matters as best we could. But we had concluded our report, we had published it, and this was the difference of view; and those who thought that we would be open to criticism if we did not seek to clarify these matters were in the majority.

LORD HUTTON: Yes. So if you had known on the Friday, 4th July, when the report was in the process of being printed, that this civil servant had come forward, you might have delayed publication of your report?

A. I can only give my own opinion on this my Lord.

LORD HUTTON: Yes, quite.

A. That the Committee works in a wonderful way and I cannot always anticipate what my -

LORD HUTTON: But your own personal view would have been?

A. My own judgment would have been that it was such an important new development that it could well have persuaded the Committee to hear further witnesses because our conclusions could well have been fundamentally altered.

Mr Andrew Mackinlay, a member of the FAC, said in his evidence:

[26 August, page 2, line 19]

A. The conflict between Gilligan and Campbell, No.10 and the BBC is not my business. The important thing was there was somebody out there, amongst others probably, who we know was a senior public servant – or that is what was reported – who was repeatedly uttering that the Government had exaggerated the case. Mr Gilligan is the one who is continually reporting that. Clearly it is key to our inquiry to try to seek and to probe what Gilligan's source is and, if we can find a source, on what basis is he saying the Government exaggerated the case for war. That was our interest.

I could not give a damn about conflict as such between Gilligan and Campbell. It is the fact that the Gilligan man was reporting that there was somebody senior out there who was saying that the case had been exaggerated. Of course there were others printing it as well. I go back to this question of currency. In my view we would have been failing in our duty if we had not pursued it, but the Gilligan/Campbell thing is because of what Gilligan was saying and the fact that there was somebody out there who I think we needed to see.

....

[26 August, page 17, line 21]

LORD HUTTON: There has been evidence from a number of witnesses in the Government that the view which they took was that your Committee had been investigating Mr Gilligan's report, that this civil servant had come forward to say that he might be regarded as the source and that therefore the Government was under a duty to inform your Committee and to let your Committee examine him, if they so wished, and that if they had not done that, they might have been charged with conducting a cover-up. Now what is your view on that?

A. Yes, sir. A number of aspects there, sir.

LORD HUTTON: Yes.

A. May I just complete this one? Again those questions were against a backdrop, if you remember, of me saying: Dr Kelly, has there been any investigation you know of to find out the sources?

LORD HUTTON: If you would like to continue adding about your –

A. Sorry, counsel, I do apologise.

MR DINGEMANS: Do not worry. Answer his Lordship's question.

A. I do not buy this business of him coming forward voluntarily. I think by this time the heat was on. I also -

LORD HUTTON: I was asking you more about the Government's views that they were obliged to disclose to your Committee that this civil servant had come forward.

A. Lord Hutton, you are absolutely correct, they were obliged to disclose this to the Committee but they did not. They became aware of this I think on 30th June. They in my view deliberately stalled, hoping our report would come out. I saw on your website some note from – I forget who it was, one of the senior people, saying: I think they were already abroad. We were not already abroad. How he knows our discussions, our travel arrangements, et cetera.

The whole thing, in my view, was designed to hope that they could avoid him coming before the Foreign Affairs Select Committee. I noticed that Sir Kevin in his evidence to you argued he should not do so. Sir Kevin, in my view, is wrong on two counts. One, basic British constitution that we are entitled to scrutinise; I have already covered that. The second one, I think he is badly lacking in political antennae, which he is paid to have, because there is no way on God's earth in my view that the press would have allowed, once Dr Kelly became known, for him not to have been scrutinised in public, and I have to be candid with you: I for one would not have acquiesced in that by my silence. I think it is our duty to have Dr Kelly before the Foreign Affairs Select Committee.

LORD HUTTON: So therefore is your view that once it was known to the Ministry of Defence that he had come forward –

A. Yes.

LORD HUTTON: - and might have been the source, they were then under a duty to inform your Committee and also to – whether one says require or ask him to come forward?

A. As I said in my witness statement, my Lord, I think what they should have done immediately -

LORD HUTTON: Just on that direct question: is it your view that once Dr Kelly had come forward to the Ministry of Defence, that they were under a duty to inform your Committee and also were under a duty to ask him or to require him to appear before your Committee?

A. They are under a duty to inform us immediately and then give us the opportunity of deciding if we wanted to call him, which we would have done. All of this is against a backdrop. I do not believe they were really trying to find the source. That is why I go back to also the questions before. They did not want to discover Dr Kelly. They hoped the thing would burn out, fizzle out, in my view. That is why I asked him if there had been any investigations. There clearly had not been rigorous or vigorous investigations.

When Dr Kelly appeared before the FAC Sir John Stanley MP asked him:

Q171 Sir John Stanley: One final point on the timetable. What was the date on which you went to your line managers expressing the concern that Mr Gilligan might have drawn on his conversation with you?

Dr Kelly: I wrote a letter on Monday 30 June.

Q172 Sir John Stanley: How do you explain the reasons for the delay between the letter you wrote on 30 June and the release of the Ministry of Defence statement throwing you to the wolves?

Dr Kelly: I cannot explain the bureaucracy that went on in between. I think it went through the line management system and went through remarkably quickly.

Q173 Sir John Stanley: Did you get any impression that the statement was delayed by the Ministry of Defence in order to ensure that it went out only after our report was published?

Dr Kelly: I cannot answer that question. I really do not know.

398. Therefore I consider it to be clear that if the Government had not issued a statement that a civil servant had come forward and information of this leaked out later (as I consider it is very probable it would have done – see paragraph 399 below) the Government would have been faced with a serious charge of a cover up and of attempting to conceal an important piece of information from the FAC. Accordingly I consider that the Government acted reasonably in issuing the press statement on 8 July that a civil servant had come forward to volunteer that he had met Mr Gilligan on 22 May and that the issuing of the statement was not part of a dishonourable or underhand or duplicitous strategy to leak Dr Kelly's name covertly in order to assist the Government in its battle with the BBC.

399. I am satisfied that once Dr Kelly had informed the MoD that he had spoken to Mr Gilligan, the Government's view that Dr Kelly's name as a source for Mr Gilligan's reports was bound to become public whether the Government issued a statement or not was well founded. The question who was Mr Gilligan's source was one of intense interest to the press which the press would pursue with the greatest vigour and it is unrealistic to think that the name could have been kept secret indefinitely by the MoD. On this point the evidence of Mr Gavyn Davies, the Chairman of the Board of Governors of the BBC, is relevant because, when asked why the name of Mr Gilligan's source was not revealed to the Governors at their meeting on the evening of Sunday 6 July 2003 attended by senior BBC management, he said:

> **[24 September, page 15, line 19]**
>
> Q. Are you suggesting that these eminent Governors, whose qualifications you described a few minutes ago, were people who although they embodied the BBC cannot be trusted with that information?
>
> A. I am certainly not suggesting my Governors cannot be trusted. What I am saying is information given to 12 Governors with a lot of other people present is not likely to remain secret. That is not because the people cannot be trusted.
>
> Q. It must be because somebody cannot be trusted.
>
> A. No, I do not believe it is because anybody cannot be trusted. I think that making the name of a source known to such a wide circle of people or even the position of the source, Mr Sumption, in real life, despite the fact that you actively trust the people you are telling, greatly increases the likelihood that the name of the source will become public.
>
> If I believed that information could be held secret among such a large number of Governors and non-Governors, I think I would be flying in the face of a great deal of evidence of what happens in governments and in other organisations. I do not believe that you could have assumed that would be held secret by the most trustworthy group of people in the world, and these are trustworthy people.

400. Once the MoD had issued the statement on Tuesday 8 July it became even more probable that Dr Kelly's name would become public. In her evidence, referring to the evening of 8 July, Mrs Kelly said:

> **[1 September, page 19, line 7]**
>
> A. Well, we had a meal and then we went in to sit and watch the news. He seemed a little bit reluctant to come and watch the news. The main story was a source had identified itself. Immediately David said to me "it's me".

Q. The story, we have seen a press statement that was put out by the Ministry of Defence on 8ᵗʰ July, was that the story that was on the television?

A. That is right.

Q. And which channel were you watching, do you recall?

A. I am not sure. I think it was probably Channel 4, I am not sure.

Q. Dr Kelly said to you "it's me"?

A. "It's me". My reaction was total dismay. My heart sank. I was terribly worried because the fact that he had said that to me, I knew then he was aware his name would be in the public domain quite soon. He confirmed that feeling of course.

....

[1 September, page 20, line 19]

LORD HUTTON: Did he say, Mrs Kelly, why he thought his name might or would become public?

A. Yes. Because the MoD had revealed that a source had made itself known, he, in his own mind, said that he knew from that point that the press would soon put two and two together. We have an amazing press in this country who it does not take them long to find out details of this sort and he is well known of course in his field, so that would have been another easy job for them.

401. The evidence of Ms Olivia Bosch is also relevant. Her evidence was that on the evening of Monday 7 July before the statement was issued on 8 July Dr Kelly was somewhat resigned to his name coming out:

[4 September, page 51, line 12]

Q. And did you get the impression after the 10ᵗʰ July, which was when his name was out in the press, did you get any impression that there was a radical change in his behaviour or the way he spoke to you?

A. No. At some point, I think before his name actually came out, he mentioned that he had, in his meeting with the MoD, that they had told him that his name might come out. And that evening when I spoke to him he says: well, you know – he was somewhat resigned to the fact that his name would be coming out, at that time, yes.

LORD HUTTON: What date would it have been that you had this conversation that it seemed his mind was resigned to his name coming out?

A. Well, he seemed – accepted – this would have been around 9ᵗʰ – the meeting he – it was a meeting he had at the MoD where it was discussed.

LORD HUTTON: I see, yes.

A. This is backtracking now.

LORD HUTTON: I appreciate that, yes.

A. He understood that his name was likely to come out.

MR KNOX: You understood that from conversations you had with him on about 7ᵗʰ July or was that something –

A. Whenever it was the day that he had the meeting where I think in the previous testimony we heard discussions where he was at the MoD and there was -

LORD HUTTON: Yes, he had two meetings with the MoD.

A. Hmm.

LORD HUTTON: One was on –

A. The training course day?

LORD HUTTON: Yes, that was the second meeting. He came back for that second meeting. Do you think it was the-

A. The second one, I think.

LORD HUTTON: This was the second meeting, was it?

A. Yes. The first one I surmised that something was up, but he did not tell me anything about it. He did not mention anything, no.

Consideration of the evidence of the Prime Minister and Sir Kevin Tebbit

402. It has been suggested by a number of commentators that there was a conflict between the evidence given by the Prime Minister on 28 August and the evidence given by Sir Kevin Tebbit on the second occasion he was in the witness box on 13 October, and that the evidence which Sir Kevin gave on that occasion, if it was truthful, proved that the Prime Minister's evidence was untrue and further proved that the Prime Minister had made a policy decision at a meeting in 10 Downing Street on 8 July to make known Dr Kelly's name to the public.

403. I consider this suggestion is incorrect and is not supported by the evidence. When Sir Kevin Tebbit first gave evidence on 20 August he said that a decision was made at a meeting in 10 Downing Street on 8 July that a statement should be made that an unnamed civil servant had come forward and Sir Kevin made it clear that that decision was one in which the Prime Minister was directly involved. He said **[page 86, line 17]** "it was a collective view of Sir David Omand, John Scarlett, the Prime Minister" (this part of his evidence is set out in full in paragraph 315). When he gave evidence on 28 August the Prime Minister also made it clear that the decision to issue a statement that a civil servant had come forward but not to name him, was taken at a meeting in 10 Downing Street on 8 July which he chaired. In his evidence the Prime Minister referred **[page 74, line 12]** to "the decisions we were taking at that meeting" and "in the end it was decided that the MoD should put out a press statement; that they should give the fact openly that someone had come forward but not give the name." When Sir Kevin Tebbit gave evidence for the second time on 13 October he confirmed what he and the Prime Minister had previously said – that the decision to issue the statement was taken by the Prime Minister in a meeting at 10 Downing Street on 8 July. There was nothing new or dramatic in that evidence; he was stating what he and the Prime Minister had previously said in evidence.

404. Some commentators have directed particular attention to four answers which Sir Kevin Tebbit gave when he was cross-examined by Mr Gompertz on 13 October **[page 58, line 1]** (see paragraph 392):

Q. Yes, it is the change [in the Q and A material] that I am asking you about.

A. The change, I have to tell you, is irrelevant because a policy decision on the handling of this matter had not been taken until the Prime Minister's meeting on the Tuesday. And it was only after that that any of the press people had an authoritative basis on which to proceed.

Q. So are you saying this: that the decisions which led, in fact, to the naming of Dr Kelly were taken at No.10 Downing Street and not by the Ministry of Defence?

A. I was not trying to make that point. I was trying to contrast to you the difference between a formal decision on bringing forward the information into the public arena and the stage before any such decision had been taken.

Q. Whether you were making that point or not, what is the position? That the decision was taken at No. 10 and not by the Ministry of Defence, or by the Ministry of Defence?

A. The decision was taken at a meeting in No.10 with which the Ministry of Defence concurred.

Q. You were not there but concurred when you returned; is that right?

A. Yes. But, I mean, it was in line with the sort of advice I was giving from the previous evening.

405. Commentators have suggested that Sir Kevin Tebbit was stating that not only did the Prime Minister at a meeting in 10 Downing Street decide to issue a statement that an unnamed civil servant had come forward but that the Prime Minister had also decided that the Question and Answer material would be used by which, if Dr Kelly's name was put to the MoD by a journalist, it would be confirmed as the correct name. It is also relevant to have regard to answers which Sir Kevin Tebbit gave to counsel to the Inquiry on 13 October [page 111, line 25]:

Q. What changed as a result of that meeting [on 8 July]?

A. What changed was a decision to issue a statement.

Q. And a decision to issue the Q and A material with it or was that –

A. Yes. But as I keep insisting, the Q and A was simply the subordinate material supporting a statement, as it always does when you have a major statement on an issue of policy.

406. It would be possible (if they are read in isolation) to read Sir Kevin Tebbit's answers at page 58 and at pages 111 and 112 of the transcript as stating that a decision was taken in 10 Downing Street on 8 July not only to issue the statement but also to make use of the Question and Answer material which the MoD did use on 9 July, but I do not consider that this is what Sir Kevin Tebbit was saying. What Sir Kevin was saying was that the change which occurred after the meeting in 10 Downing Street on 8 July was brought about by the decision at the meeting, and that decision was one to issue the statement that an unnamed civil servant had come forward. He had already said this earlier in his evidence on 13 October when he described arriving at 10 Downing Street on 8 July after the meeting with the Prime Minister was over [page 17, line 25]:

A… By the time I got back to London there had been a further meeting involving the Prime Minister and there had also been the news that Ann Taylor was not prepared to take this into the Committee without a public statement being made first.

Q. Do you recall what time you got back from Portsmouth?

A. I think about 2.15.

Q. Did you go straight to No.10?

A. I did not go straight to No. 10, I went to my office. I think there was a misunderstanding. I thought the meeting was at 2.30; in fact, the meeting finished at 2.30 in No.10. I was in time only to be given some statement material that officials had been working on during my absence.

Q. So by the time you arrived the meeting was in fact over?

A. It was in fact over. I was in time to see the Prime Minister saying: Sorry, we have just finished but Jonathan Powell will brief you.

Q. On what did Mr Powell brief you as to what had been decided?

A. He said that we were back, as it were, to the idea of issuing a statement because Ann Taylor would not consider it without that; and that the statement material was there, and colleagues were beginning to draft on that basis; and he suggested, after briefing me on the approach that was being taken, that we went to the room where this was being done, which we subsequently did, and I –

Q. Do you know why that decision had been taken?

A. Well –

Q. The decision to publish the statement at that time?

A. Yes, as I say, because it was felt that we could not wait longer before we disclosed what we knew. Given the immediate pressure of the ISC meeting and the growing problem, the longer we failed to bring the information forward of, as it were, the risk of a cover-up from the Foreign Affairs Committee which was a real concern, as has been testified to subsequently by the Chairman of the FAC, had we sought not to tell them about this.

Q. Did you in fact concur with the decision which had been taken in your absence?

A. I did, as I say. I think had I been at the meeting I would have joined the consensus. The fact was I was not.

The Question and Answer material was ancillary material prepared in the MoD and there is nothing in the evidence to suggest that there was any consideration by the Prime Minister of the Question and Answer material in the meeting in 10 Downing Street, and I do not consider that Sir Kevin Tebbit's evidence conflicts with the evidence of the Prime Minister when he said on 28 August **[at page 77, line 18]** (see paragraph 339) that he was not aware of the existence of the Question and Answer material. In his evidence Mr Powell referred to Question and Answer material which he drafted on 8 July at 4.35pm (see paragraph 299) but in his draft he said that most of the answers were for the MoD and this Question and Answer material made no reference to the name of the civil servant.

407. The issuing of the statement authorised by the Prime Minister did give rise to the questions by the press as to the identity of the civil servant and these questions led on to the MoD confirming Dr Kelly's name, but I do not consider that there was any plan or strategy by the Prime Minister and the officials in 10 Downing Street to bring this about. Such a plan or strategy would appear to have involved the following line of thought by the Prime Minister and his officials:

(1) It is in the interests of the Government to name Dr Kelly as Mr Gilligan's source because this will help the Government to show that Dr Kelly did not have the knowledge about the dossier to justify Mr Gilligan's allegations.

(2) The Government is not prepared to name Dr Kelly directly because if this is done it will bring down criticism on the Government.

(3) Therefore, instead of naming Dr Kelly directly, the Government will issue a statement that an unnamed civil servant has come forward, and the Government will expect or hope that a journalist will suggest that the unnamed civil servant is Dr Kelly.

(4) This will enable the Government to confirm that Dr Kelly was the civil servant.

(5) In this way the Government will be able to identify Dr Kelly as Mr Gilligan's source without incurring the criticism which would arise from naming Dr Kelly directly.

408. Having considered a large volume of evidence I consider that there was no such dishonourable or underhand or duplicitous strategy devised by the Prime Minister and his officials. The surrounding circumstances confirm, in my opinion, that the purpose of the Prime Minister and his officials in deciding to issue the statement that an unnamed civil servant had come forward was to protect the Government from a charge of a cover-up and of withholding important and relevant information from the FAC.

409. Therefore I consider that the Question and Answer material used by the MoD press office on 9 July was not an underhand way of covertly making Dr Kelly's name public. I think that the decision not to name Dr Kelly in the MoD statement was influenced by the consideration that the officials concerned with the matter were not absolutely certain that he was Mr Gilligan's source and I satisfied that there was no deliberate plan or strategy to name him by the Question and Answer procedure rather than by naming him directly in the statement. Whatever may be the position in other cases, I think that in this case it was recognised by the MoD that because Dr Kelly's name was bound to come out and because the issue was one of great importance, it was better to be frank with the press and confirm the correct name if it was given. I think that the MoD was also concerned that the press should not publicise the name or names of other civil servants as being the source and that this was a consideration which influenced the decision to confirm the correct name if it was given.

410. The first Question and Answer brief prepared on 4 July stated that the name of the civil servant would not be given whereas the final Question and Answer brief stated that if the correct name was given it would be confirmed. But I do not think that this shows a change in approach by the MoD which evidences a deliberate strategy to name Dr Kelly. The reason for the first Question and Answer brief was that it was prepared to answer press inquiries before the Government had decided to issue a statement that a civil servant had come forward and in case the press learned of this through a leak, whereas the final Question and Answer brief was prepared to deal with the changed position after the decision had been taken to issue such a statement.

411. Some commentators have referred to answers by the Prime Minister to questions from members of the press travelling with him on an aeroplane to Hong Kong on 22 July and I have read the transcript of that press briefing. As I have stated, I am satisfied that there was not a dishonourable or underhand or duplicitous strategy on the part of the Prime Minister and officials to leak Dr Kelly's name covertly, and I am further satisfied that the decision which was taken by the Prime Minister and his officials in 10 Downing Street on 8 July was confined to issuing a statement that an unnamed civil servant had come forward and that the Question and Answer material was prepared and approved in the MoD and not in 10 Downing Street. The series of events and considerations which led to the decision in 10 Downing Street on 8 July to issue a statement was a complex one for the reasons which I have previously set out and I consider that the answers given by the Prime Minister to members of the press in the aeroplane cast no light on the issues about which I have heard a large volume of evidence.

412. The lobby briefings given by the Prime Minister's official spokesman, Mr Tom Kelly, on the morning and afternoon of Wednesday 9 July helped to identify Dr Kelly as Mr Gilligan's source, but I consider that Mr Kelly's intention was not to leak Dr Kelly's name covertly as Mr Gilligan's source but that his intention was to give answers which supported the MoD statement against the statement issued by the BBC on the evening of 8 July and helped to show that Mr Gilligan's source was not "one

of the senior officials in charge of drawing up that dossier" as stated by Mr Gilligan in his broadcast at 6.07am on 29 May and was not "a source within the intelligence service" as stated by Mr John Humphreys when he interviewed Mr Adam Ingram MP, the Armed Forces Minister, later in the Today programme, and was therefore not in the position to make the claims that Mr Gilligan reported him as having made. Therefore I consider that Mr Kelly's briefings were not part of a strategy to leak Dr Kelly's name covertly. It is regrettable that Dr Kelly was upset by these briefings and felt that they belittled his position in the Government service, but I consider that the briefings were for the purpose described above and were not for the purpose of belittling or demeaning him.

413. Evidence was given by Mr Peter Beaumont of the Observer that before 7 July he was receiving hints from sources that Dr Kelly was a strong candidate to be Mr Gilligan's source:

[21 August, page 122, line 20]

Q. We know that Dr Kelly's name was finally put in the press on 10th July as Gilligan's source. Did you begin to have your suspicions as to this before 10th July?

A. Yes.

Q. If so, could you explain when and why?

A. It first occurred to me that Dr Kelly could be the source about five days before he was named, and I recall –

Q. That would be, what, Saturday 5th July?

A. It may have been the Friday then, because I recall – I just recall it striking me that it could have been Dr Kelly.

Q. Can you give –

A. There was so much detail about him, you know – I was aware of who Dr Kelly was before I had actually spoken to him, and because of that it seemed patently obvious, from a lot of the hints that were being dropped, that he had to be a very strong candidate.

LORD HUTTON: There was so much detail about him, this was on 4th and 5th July. Where was this detail?

A. I suppose – yes, this is difficult. I would rather not answer that question.

LORD HUTTON: I see. You said hints were being dropped about him.

A. Yes.

MR KNOX: Was this hints you were receiving privately or hints you were receiving by reading the press?

A. I think both. I am sorry, I do not want to be drawn on this simply because of confidentiality of sources and because – yes.

Q. I am obviously not asking you about your sources now, but certainly so far as the press is concerned, the first time that any major development appears to have taken place is Saturday, 5th July when there is more information put out?

A. It must have been the Saturday then. It must have been the Saturday then because it struck me, I remember having a conversation with a colleague saying: I have an idea who this is. But I thought it was on the Friday, not the Saturday.

It is understandable that Mr Beaumont did not wish to reveal the identities and positions of his sources and what they said to him, but in the absence of more specific information from him it is not possible for me to draw any clear inferences from his evidence.

414. It is apparent from the evidence which I have heard that whilst all the Government Ministers and officials who were considering the situation which had arisen following Dr Kelly's letter to his line manager were concerned that the Government would be charged with a cover up if the Government concealed the fact that a civil servant had come forward who might have been Mr Gilligan's source, there were somewhat differing views as to the steps which should be taken and as to whether Dr Kelly's name should be made public.

415. Mr Campbell's evidence, stated in summary form, was that in his view it would assist the Government, subject to the qualification that not all of Dr Kelly's views supported the Government, if Dr Kelly's name came into the public domain as this would show that Mr Gilligan's reports were unworthy of belief. It was Mr Hoon's evidence, stated in summary form, that his view was that it would not be fair to name Dr Kelly unless there was certainty that he was Mr Gilligan's source and he, Mr Hoon, was never certain of this at any time up until Dr Kelly's death. Sir Kevin Tebbit said in his evidence that in his view the only way of clarifying reliably the public record was to name the civil servant who had stated that he had not said what Mr Gilligan reported.

416. However I am satisfied that the decision to issue the statement which said that a civil servant, who was not named, had come forward was taken by the Prime Minister at a meeting in 10 Downing Street on 8 July which was not attended by Mr Hoon, and that in coming to this decision the Prime Minister was largely guided by the advice of Sir David Omand and that the decision was taken for the reasons which I have set out.

417. Mr Hoon stated in his evidence that the decision to issue the statement was taken by 10 Downing Street and not by the MoD and that he regarded the interviewing of Dr Kelly as a personnel matter which fell within the area of responsibility of the Permanent Under-Secretary and not within his area of responsibility. Mr Campbell also stated in his evidence that the Prime Minister did not accept his view that Dr Kelly's name should be deliberately put into the public domain by the Government.

418. Therefore it is not necessary for me to resolve some differences and areas of uncertainty arising in the evidence of Mr Campbell and Mr Hoon. In his diary Mr Campbell wrote the term "plea bargain" in describing a telephone discussion with Mr Hoon on 4 July. One of those areas of uncertainty is whether in his discussion with Mr Campbell, Mr Hoon used the term "plea bargain" in relation to Dr Kelly and, if he did, what did he mean by that term. Whether or not Mr Hoon used that precise term and, if he did, what he meant by it, I am satisfied that in his two interviews with Dr Kelly Mr Hatfield suggested nothing and did nothing which could be regarded as a "plea bargain".

Consideration of the evidence of the Rt Hon Geoffrey Hoon MP

419. However, as there was a suggestion implicit in Mr Gompertz's cross-examination of Mr Hoon when he gave evidence on 26 September that he had been untruthful in his earlier evidence on 27 August in relation to the Question and Answer material, it is right that I should consider that suggestion in some detail and in order to do so I set out again the most relevant parts of the evidence. On 27 August Mr Hoon was asked:

[27 August, page 52, line 6]

Q. Do you know whether or not Dr Kelly was told about the draft Q and A material and the Q and A material as deployed?

A. I do not, no. But can I make clear that I did not see either of these documents. They were not submitted to my office. That would not be something that I would normally deal with.

....

[27 August, page 69, line 22]

A.... I did not see this Q and A and played no part in its preparation, so it is a little difficult for me to comment about any underlying purpose.

420. At the end of his evidence on 27 August it was put to Mr Hoon that his special adviser, Mr Richard Taylor, was aware of the Question and Answer material:

[27 August, page 100, line 6]

Q. Were you aware that there has been some evidence that Mr Taylor, who I think is your special adviser, is that right?

A. Yes.

Q. Had confirmed Dr Kelly's name to journalists?

A. Hmm.

Q. Were you aware of that?

A. I was not specifically aware at the time but I – excuse me. I have learned since that that happened, yes.

Q. And what is your view on that?

A. Well, I assume that that was consistent with the question and answer process that had been agreed within the department. I do not think it occurred in any earlier timeframe.

Q. The question and answers material that your special adviser knows about but you did not?

A. I did not see the question and answer, but I was obviously aware of the advice that I had received that if the right name was given to an MoD press officer they should confirm it. I am not suggesting – I am not suggesting, for a moment, that I was not aware of that; and obviously my special adviser would have been aware of it as well.

421. In his evidence on 22 September Mr Hoon said in answer to counsel for the Government:

[22 September, page 2, line 4]

Q. The Inquiry has heard that in the early evening of 9th July the MoD press office confirmed to a journalist the identity of the person who had come forward, Dr Kelly. Were you aware, on 9th July, that the MoD press office was adopting an approach under which it was proposing to confirm the identity of the individual if the correct name was put?

A. Yes, I was. I had had a conversation earlier that day with Sir Kevin Tebbit, the Permanent Secretary, in which he had set out to me the concerns that he had as far as the press office were concerned, in particular that individual press officers should not be seen to be lying to journalists, and that it was better that they should, if the right name was put to them, acknowledge the fact. He was also very concerned that there was a risk to other members of staff, other officials, and he did not want anything said by the press office to lead journalists in the direction of the wrong official.

Q. It has been suggested in certain quarters that your previous evidence to this Inquiry in relation to this matter may have been inaccurate, so perhaps we should take a moment to look at that. You gave oral evidence to the Inquiry on 27th August. Prior to that, had you provided to the Inquiry a written statement?

A. Yes, I had.

Q. Do you have a copy of that statement?

A. Yes, I do.

Q. When did you write that statement?

A. It was shortly before my previous appearance. I was required to submit it 24 hours in advance.

Q. Could I ask you, please, to read aloud paragraphs 25, 26 and 27 of that statement?

....

[22 September, page 4, line 5]

A.....26. During the course of Wednesday 9th July the Permanent Secretary told me how the Ministry of Defence press office would deal with press enquiries trying to identify the official referred to in the Ministry of Defence statement. The decision to confirm the name of Dr Kelly if it was put to the MoD directly was to avoid any suggestion that we were in any way misleading journalists. We did not want anyone to claim that we had been less than straightforward in our dealing with them, not least in the light of the FAC's conclusion that Andrew Gilligan's alleged contact should be thoroughly investigated.

27. I did not brief Dr Kelly's name to any journalists, neither was I aware of any strategy to do so. The defensive question and answer material prepared to help the MoD press office respond to possible press enquiries was not put to me for approval and I did not see it at the time.

422. In his evidence on 13 October Sir Kevin Tebbit said:

[13 October, page 29, line 14]

Q. Did you discuss with the Secretary of State at all the fact that the press office would confirm Dr Kelly's name if the press already had it?

A. Yes, I did.

Q. Do you recall when and on what occasion you discussed that with him?

A. Well, I think I probably mentioned it first on the early evening of the 8th. My recollection of that is not absolutely precise. Our offices are next to each other. There is a level of trust between myself and the Secretary of State which is quite strong and therefore we do talk to each other quite regularly. I could not recall whether I had directly said this to the Secretary of State or through my private secretary. I certainly had that conversation with him during the following day and recall, very specifically, confirming this approach in the late morning in the margins of the commemorative event for the Korean war victims. So, I mean, there is no doubt in my own mind that this was understood between us.

423. In her evidence on 18 September Ms Pamela Teare said:

[18 September, page 116, line 13]

Q. Moving on, then, to 9th July, was there a Secretary of State's briefing meeting that morning?

A. Yes, there was.

Q. Did you attend it?

A. Yes, I did.

Q. How clear is your recollection as to what was discussed at the meeting?

A. I mean, I recall there was a meeting. I can recall what the key topics of conversation were, but I do not recall exactly who said what.

Q. Do you recall who was there?

A. The Secretary of State, his principal private secretary, Richard Taylor, special adviser, myself. I think that was all.

Q. What is your recollection as to what was discussed?

A. Well, it was a fairly brief meeting, because I know we had another one that was about to start very shortly afterwards. But my recollection is that the bulk of the meeting was to do with discussions of how we might follow up with the correspondence with the BBC.

Q. Was anything said about the Q and A material?

A. I think it is likely that I might have run through the – an outline of the Q and A material and the approach that we were adopting.

Q. Would you have had any particular reason to do that?

A. No, other than at that meeting it has several purposes: one, I go through the press coverage of the morning and I would normally outline how we were handling sort of main issues of the day. And it would be in that line that I would have done so.

424. When cross-examined by Mr Gompertz on 18 September Ms Teare said:

[18 September, page 132, line 17]

Q. What about the routine press meeting on 9th July which you attended and which other people attended as well?

A. That was the day after the draft had been approved.

Q. Yes. Did the Secretary of State see that document at that meeting?

A. I do not recall.

Q. You see, we have heard some evidence to suggest that he did, and that there was some brief discussion about this document at that meeting.

A. Hmm, hmm.

Q. You know that, I expect. Do you agree or disagree with that evidence or do you not remember?

A. I do not recall there being a long discussion about the Q and A.

Q. Nobody said that there was a long discussion.

A. No.

Q. A brief discussion is what I put to you.

A. I cannot recall the detail, though I think it is highly likely that I would have outlined some of the material in the Q and A, but I cannot give you a verbatim account.

Q. To the Secretary of State?

A. Yes.

Q. And no doubt in order to outline the material you would have had the document with you.

A. Yes, I suspect I would have done.

Q. And no doubt you would have shown it to him?

A. He may have already had it. He may have already –

Q. Do you know or not know?

A. I do not know. I did not show him a document at that meeting, because, as I say, the bulk of that meeting was about how to follow up the correspondence with the BBC.

425. In his evidence on 4 September Mr Richard Taylor, a special adviser to Mr Hoon, said:

[4 September, page 76, line 14]

A. Yes. On the morning of Wednesday 9th July I attended the routine meeting in the Secretary of State's office to discuss media issues of the day.

Q. Is that a morning meeting every day?

A. Yes, it happens most days. It starts each morning with looking through press cuttings for the day and considering whether there is any follow up which may be required by the Ministry of Defence.

Q. Had there been a similar meeting on the 8th July?

A. To the best of my recollection, yes.

Q. But, at that, nothing had been said about the draft press statement?

A. No.

Q. And on 9th July, what is said at that meeting?

LORD HUTTON: Could I just ask you: who was at that meeting, Mr Taylor?

A. On that day, Wednesday 9th July, the routine press meeting was attended by the Secretary of State, by his principal private secretary, Mr Peter Watkins, by the Director of News, Pamela Teare, and me.

....

[4 September, page 81, line 8]

Q. Was anything mentioned about the Q and A material?

A. At the end of a discussion on how to follow up the letter to Mr Davies there was a brief discussion on what we should do if journalists were to ring and put the name directly to the Department of who the official was. I would not call it a discussion of the Q and A material. There was a discussion of one of the questions, which I have since learnt was in the Q and A material.

Q. Was there any discussion about the other questions in the Q and A material?

A. No, not –

Q. Was he a member of UNSCOM et cetera?

A. No, to the best of my recollection we only discussed the rationale for what to do if the name was put directly to the department.

....

[4 September, page 82, line 21]

Q... Do you know from the discussions that took place on 9th July whether Ms Teare had discussed this Q and A material with anyone else?

A. Not in that discussion. It was a brief discussion about the rationale for the approach of what to do if a journalist rang directly with Dr Kelly's name.

Q. Have you found out since whether or not Ms Teare discussed this Q and A material with anyone?

A. I have only learnt through the course of the Inquiry that she discussed it with the Permanent Secretary's office, but not at the time.

Q. Not from what the Inquiry has heard, from our own research at the Ministry of Defence. No-one has told you, as it were?

A. I did not see the question and answer brief until after Dr Kelly had died; and I did not therefore ask any questions about it in this timeframe.

426. Therefore I consider that Mr Hoon was not untruthful when he said in evidence on 27 August that he had not seen the Question and Answer material. But it is clear that he was told on 9 July that the press office of the MoD was going to take the approach that if Dr Kelly's name was put to it the name would be confirmed, and he did not dissent from this approach being taken. He only stated at a late stage in his evidence on 27 August that he was aware that this approach was going to be taken, but having regard to the fact that he had stated in paragraph 26 of the written statement which he provided to the Inquiry before he gave evidence on 27 August (and which he read out in evidence on 22 September) that he had been told that this approach was going to be taken, I do not consider that he was seeking in his evidence to conceal his knowledge of this approach.

Conclusion on the issue whether the Government behaved in a way which was dishonourable or underhand or duplicitous in revealing Dr Kelly's name to the media

427. My conclusion is that there was no dishonourable or underhand or duplicitous strategy by the Government covertly to leak Dr Kelly's name to the media. If the bare details of the MoD statement dated 8 July 2003, the changing drafts of the Q and A material prepared in the MoD, and the lobby briefings by the Prime Minister's official spokesman on 9 July are looked at in isolation from the surrounding circumstances it would be possible to infer, as some commentators have done, that there was an underhand strategy by the Government to leak Dr Kelly's name in a covert way. However having heard a large volume of evidence on this issue I have concluded that there was no such strategy on the part of the Government. I consider that in the midst of a major controversy relating to Mr Gilligan's broadcasts which had contained very grave allegations against the integrity of the Government and fearing that Dr Kelly's name as the source for those broadcasts would be disclosed by the media at any time, the Government's main concern was that it would be charged with a serious cover up if it did not reveal that a civil servant had come forward. I consider that the evidence of Mr Donald Anderson MP and Mr Andrew Mackinlay MP, the Chairman and a member respectively of the FAC, together with the questions put by Sir John Stanley MP to Dr Kelly when he appeared before the FAC, clearly show that the Government's concern was well founded. Therefore I consider that the Government did not behave in a dishonourable or underhand or duplicitous way in issuing on 8 July, after it had been read over to Dr Kelly and he had said that he was content with it, a statement which said that a civil servant, who was not named, had come forward to volunteer that he had met Mr Gilligan on 22 May.

428. I further consider that the decision by the MoD to confirm Dr Kelly's name if, after the statement had been issued, the correct name were put to the MoD by a reporter, was not part of a covert strategy to leak his name, but was based on the view that in a matter of such intense public and media interest it would not be sensible to try to conceal the name when the MoD thought that the press were bound to discover the correct name, and a further consideration in the mind of the MoD was that it did not think it right that media speculation should focus, wrongly, on other civil servants.

429. In addition I consider that it was reasonable for the Government to take the view that, even if it sought to keep confidential the fact that Dr Kelly had come forward, the controversy surrounding Mr Gilligan's broadcasts was so great and the level of media interest was so intense that Dr Kelly's name as Mr Gilligan's source was bound to become known to the public and that it was not a practical possibility to keep his name secret.

Consideration of the issue whether the Government failed to take proper steps to help and protect Dr Kelly in the difficult position in which he found himself

430. The evidence has satisfied me that officials in the MoD did give some consideration to Dr Kelly's welfare and did take some steps to help him.

(1) It is apparent from the evidence that Sir Kevin Tebbit gave thought to Dr Kelly's welfare. In his minute of 10 July 2003 to Mr Hoon he recommended that Mr Hoon should resist Dr Kelly appearing before the FAC when he was going to appear before the ISC, and he wrote:

> A further reason for avoiding two hearings, back to back, is to show some regard for the man himself. He has come forward voluntarily, is not used to being thrust into the public eye, and is not on trial. It does not seem unreasonable to ask the FAC to show restraint and accept the [ISC] hearing as being sufficient for their purposes (eg testing the validity of Gilligan's evidence).

However it would not have been possible for Mr Hoon to refuse to permit Dr Kelly to appear before the ISC as it is the Committee directly responsible for investigating intelligence matters. I also consider that the evidence of Mr Donald Anderson MP and Mr Andrew Mackinlay MP shows that there would have been a serious political storm if Mr Hoon had refused to permit Dr Kelly to appear before the FAC and that Mr Hoon's decision not to accept Sir Kevin Tebbit's advice and to agree to Dr Kelly appearing before the FAC is not a decision which can be subject to valid criticism.

(2) Sir Kevin Tebbit also enquired from other officials how Dr Kelly was bearing up under the stress and he was told that Dr Kelly was handling the pressure pretty well. There is a minute from Mr Colin Smith of the FCO to another official in the FCO dated 14 July 2003 referring to a meeting which he had attended that morning on Iraq's WMD and which also had been attended by Mr Martin Howard. In the minute Mr Smith stated "Kelly is apparently feeling the pressure, and does not appear to be handling it well". In his evidence Mr Howard said that he did not recall saying that, and if he did, it would purely have been passing on a second hand account of what might have been said to him because he had not seen Dr Kelly since his meeting with him and Mr Hatfield on 7 July. Mr Howard said that at the end of the meeting with Dr Kelly on the afternoon of 14 July Dr Kelly was composed, obviously nervous, which was to be expected, but he saw no evidence to show that he was not ready for the meeting. When Dr Wells was asked by Mr Gompertz whether he thought that some form of professional counselling would have been a good idea Dr Wells replied:

[24 September, page 138, line 2]

> A. David was an experienced civil servant; he had experience of stressful situations as a UN weapons inspector. In answer to repeated questions, he said he was tired but otherwise fine. And I have to say when someone of that seniority and experience repeatedly assures me that he is fine, then I am bound to take him at his word.

The assessment of how a person under stress is reacting can be a somewhat subjective one which depends to some extent on the person making it, and I think that different people may have formed different impressions as to how Dr Kelly was reacting to the strain. Dr Kelly's daughter, Rachel, who was very close to her father, knew that he was under great strain but her fiancé, Mr David Wilkins said that on Sunday night, 13 July, and on the morning and evening of Monday 14 July, he did not seem overly agitated or under stress and seemed "okay", although at supper on Tuesday evening, 15 July, after he had appeared before the FAC he seemed to be very withdrawn within himself and it was noticeable that he was going through some personal trauma. Therefore I think it was reasonable for Sir Kevin Tebbit to take the view, which he described in evidence, that Dr Kelly was an experienced and robust individual who had dealt well with stressful and difficult situations in Iraq.

(3) As I have stated, I am satisfied that Mr Hatfield was not engaged in any "plea bargain" strategy when he conducted his meetings with Dr Kelly on 4 and 7 July, and I think his notes dated 7 and 8 July of meetings (see paragraphs 49 and 64) show that he dealt with Dr Kelly in a way which was fair to him.

(4) On the afternoon of 8 July after Mr Hatfield had read over on the telephone to Dr Kelly the new draft of the MoD press statement, Mr Hatfield advised him that he should talk to the press office and to Dr Wells about support.

(5) On the evening of 8 July between 8pm and 9pm after the MoD statement had been issued Mrs Kate Wilson, the chief press officer in the MoD, having agreed to do so in a discussion with Ms Pamela Teare, the Director of News in the MoD, telephoned Dr Kelly and told him that the statement had been put out, that the press office had had a lot of follow up questions and that he needed to think about alternative accommodation. Mrs Wilson asked Dr Kelly if there was anything he wanted from her and he said there was not.

(6) I am satisfied that Dr Wells, who liked and admired Dr Kelly, tried to help and support him after the MoD statement was issued on 8 July. Dr Wells telephoned Dr Kelly when he was in the West Country from 10 to 13 July to arrange his appearances before the FAC and the ISC, but he also called him to check that he was bearing up under the stress of press interest. In addition Dr Wells had arranged to attend a meeting in New York during the first part of the week commencing Monday 14 July, but he cancelled his visit to New York in order to be in London to give support to Dr Kelly and he told Dr Kelly that he was doing this. Dr Wells also offered Dr Kelly hotel accommodation in London on the night of Monday 14 July to save him from travelling up and down to London from his home in Oxfordshire, but Dr Kelly said that he wished to stay with his daughter in Oxford.

(7) When Dr Kelly went to give evidence before the FAC on Tuesday 15 July Dr Wells and Wing Commander Clark, who was a friend and colleague of Dr Kelly in the MoD, accompanied him in order to give him moral support and sat behind him during the hearing. They were also accompanied by Mrs Wilson who was present to give Dr Kelly assistance if the press tried to interview him. Dr Wells and Wing Commander Clark also accompanied Dr Kelly when he gave evidence in private before the ISC on Wednesday 16 July.

(8) The issue was raised in the course of the Inquiry whether an official of the MoD should have sat, not behind, but beside Dr Kelly at the table to give him support when he was questioned by the FAC. Dr Wells gave evidence that when he was in the West Country Dr Kelly told him on the telephone that he would like a colleague to accompany him to the FAC because he was uncertain about procedures. Therefore when Mr Hoon wrote to the Chairman of the FAC, Mr Donald Anderson, on 11 July, he said in the course of the letter: "As he is not used to this degree of public exposure, Dr Kelly has asked if he could be accompanied by a colleague. MoD officials will discuss this further with the Clerk." However when Dr Wells discussed this point with the Clerk of the FAC on the morning of Monday 14 July the Clerk told him that if a colleague sat beside Dr Kelly at the table it would be open to the FAC to ask questions of the colleague. In his evidence Dr Wells said that when he and Mr Martin Howard met Dr Kelly in the afternoon of Monday 14 July he raised with him the matter of a colleague sitting beside him, and it was implicit in Dr Wells'

evidence that he told Dr Kelly about the point made by the Clerk of the FAC. At the end of the meeting after the discussion about the likely areas of questioning by the FAC and the ISC and about how the two Committees were differently constituted, Dr Wells asked Dr Kelly how he felt about having a colleague next to him at the table and Dr Kelly said that as he now had a good understanding of the procedures and the likely areas of questioning he no longer felt the need to have a colleague sitting beside him. I think it is probable that if a colleague had been sitting beside him this would have given Dr Kelly a feeling of support, particularly when he was questioned in a forceful way by one member of the Committee. But looking at the situation as it presented itself to the MoD before the hearing, I think it is understandable that the MoD decided not to have an official sitting beside Dr Kelly. First, because Dr Kelly was being called as a witness, not to state an official line, but to state his own personal involvement in having an unauthorised meeting with Mr Gilligan and, secondly, because a colleague sitting beside Dr Kelly might have been regarded as an official "minder" who was sitting beside Dr Kelly to inhibit him in the expression of his own views relating to WMD.

431. Therefore I am satisfied that some efforts were made by officials in the MoD to give help and support to Dr Kelly. Mrs Kelly and Miss Rachel Kelly's fiancé, Mr David Wilkins, gave evidence as to Dr Kelly's view of the support he was receiving. Mrs Kelly said:

> **[1 September, page 38, line 5]**
>
> Q. Did you speak to him at all on the Monday [14th July]?
>
> A. Yes, I did. After he had returned to Rachel's he rang me to say that the day had not been too tormenting. He was not worried about what had gone on by that day. I asked if he was being supported by the MoD and he said: I suppose so, yes. He always previously said yes when I asked this question on several occasions before, so he was a little bit less certain, I felt.
>
> I was a bit worried about the lack of support or the lack of apparent support. He was not an easy man to support in some ways, he would always try to give the impression that he was okay, and I think his immediate line manager was a much younger man than him and he would have tried, as he did with us, to protect him from his own feelings. He tried to keep his feelings to himself.

Mr David Wilkins said, referring to Wednesday 16 July:

> **[1 September, page 159, line 2]**
>
> Q. And did he comment about the support or absence of support he was getting?
>
> A. Yes, he did. He said that his colleagues – he said that colleagues had been "tremendously supportive", that is a direct quote. I remember him saying that, that they had been tremendously supportive. I did get the impression that it was not all colleagues. I cannot remember his exact wording, but the implication and the impression I was left with was that it was some but not all.

432. However, notwithstanding that steps were taken by a number of officials to give support to Dr Kelly and despite the fact that Dr Kelly was told expressly by Mrs Wilson, the chief press officer at the MoD, in a telephone conversation on the evening of 8 July that he needed to think about staying with friends, which would have conveyed to him that he could be the subject of intense press interest, and although it is clear from remarks which he made to Mrs Kelly (see paragraph 400) and to Ms Olivia Bosch (see paragraph 401) that Dr Kelly realised that his name would come out, I consider (without engaging in hindsight) that the MoD was at fault in the procedure which it adopted in relation to Dr Kelly after the decision had been taken to release the statement which was issued about 5.30pm on Tuesday 8 July. The principal fault lay in the failure of the MoD to inform Dr Kelly that the press office

was going to confirm his name if a journalist suggested it. It would have been a better course if (1) the MoD had decided to name Dr Kelly with his consent in the statement it issued; (2) the MoD had told Dr Kelly in a face to face meeting with an official or officials that this was its intention and had obtained his consent to this course; and (3) the MoD had delayed issuing a statement for a period of, perhaps, twenty-four hours, to give adequate time for the press office to give Dr Kelly advice about the intense press interest to which he would be subject and for him to consider whether he wished to move to alternative accommodation to avoid press intrusion or, if he did not, for the press office to have a press officer in position at his home to deal with members of the press. In his evidence Mr Campbell recognised that this would have been a better course to adopt and he said:

[19 August, page 151, line 7]

A.... But I think again, and I emphasise this is with an element of hindsight, that probably what I feel I maybe should have expressed more forcefully at that time is: look, if you are in this kind of situation you do have to have some element of control over the process here. You cannot just let this sort of dribble out in a way that you are not clear how it is then going to unfold. So I think the desired outcome, given that everybody, including it seems Dr Kelly, understood that it is likely because of the importance of this development he was likely to be identified, he was likely to have to appear at one or both Select Committees, far better it would have been for that to be announced properly, cleanly, straightforwardly and then you can actually put in place all the proper support that somebody who is not used to this kind of pressure can then maybe better deal with.

433. However because of its concern that the press might become aware of, and publish, Dr Kelly's name at any moment and it would then be charged with a cover up, the Government did not follow this course but decided on Tuesday 8 July that a statement should be issued without delay that a civil servant had come forward without naming the civil servant. For the reasons which I have given, I consider that the Government's concern was justifiable and that it should not be criticised for underhand or dishonourable or duplicitous conduct in issuing the statement without naming Dr Kelly once it was reasonably satisfied, without being certain, that he was Mr Gilligan's source.

434. But once the decision had been taken to issue the statement I consider that the MoD was at fault in two respects. The principal fault lay, as I have stated, in not telling Dr Kelly that the press office would confirm his name if a journalist suggested it. Although I am satisfied that Dr Kelly realised, once the statement had been issued, that his name would come out, and although he had been told by Mrs Wilson on the previous evening that he should consider staying with friends, it must have been a great shock for him to learn in a brief telephone call from Dr Wells that the press office of his own department had confirmed his name to the press, and to discover this at about the same time as Mr Rufford told him that the press were on their way in droves, and in consequence he made a very hurried departure from his home.

435. In her evidence Mrs Kelly said that Dr Kelly felt betrayed by the MoD because he told her that he had received assurances from it that his name would not go into the public domain:

[1 September, page 23, line 8]

Q. Had you spoken with Dr Kelly at all during the day [Wednesday 9th July] about his reaction to the news the night before?

A. Yes, I had. He said several times over coffee, over lunch, over afternoon tea that he felt totally let down and betrayed. It seemed to me that this was all part of what might have happened anyway because it seemed to have been a very loose arrangement with the MoD, they did not seem to take a lot of account of his time. There was a lot of wasting of his time. I just felt that this must have been very frustrating for him. David often said: they are not using me properly. He felt that the MoD were not quite sure how to use his expertise at times, although I have later seen his manager's reports on his staff appraisals where he obviously did warrant his or respect his expertise. But that is not the impression that I got.

Q. You say, I think, that he had felt totally let down and betrayed. Who did he say that of?

A. He did not say in so many terms but I believed he meant the MoD because they were the ones that had effectively let his name be known in the public domain.

Q. And did you get the impression that he was happy or unhappy that this press statement had been made?

A. Well, he did not know about it until after it had happened. So he was – I think initially he had been led to believe that it would not go into the public domain. He had received assurances and that is why he was so very upset about it.

Q. What, he did not know that the press statement saying an unnamed source had come forward would be made?

A. Not until after the event.

LORD HUTTON: Did he say from whom he had received assurances Mrs Kelly?

A. From his line manager, from all their seniors and from the people he had been interviewed by.

MR DINGEMANS: And his reaction on hearing the news, you said he had seemed slightly reluctant to watch the news that night.

A. Yes, indeed.

Q. Was that because he had seen an earlier news, do you think, or because he knew something might be coming up?

A. I think it was probably trepidation that this was the moment. He was not quite sure when it would actually happen but since Nick had come it was going to be a big problem. He knew that.

I am satisfied that Dr Kelly had been told by the MoD that his name would probably come out and that he realised this himself, as is shown by his telephone conversation with Ms Olivia Bosch (see para 401), and I am also satisfied that he knew that the MoD was going to issue a statement that a civil servant had come forward and that the text of the statement was read over to him on the telephone by Mr Hatfield on the afternoon of 8 July and that he said that he was content with it. However the sudden information from Dr Wells that his name had been confirmed to the press by the MoD's own press office without any explanation as to why this had been done must have been very upsetting for him and must have given rise to a feeling that he had been badly let down by his employer.

436. In addition I think that the MoD, having taken no steps to inform Dr Kelly that the press office would confirm his name if put to it by a journalist, was at fault in not having set up a procedure whereby Dr Kelly would be informed immediately his name had been confirmed to the press. The period of one and a half hours between 5.30pm (when the name was confirmed) and 7pm (when Dr Wells spoke to Dr Kelly) was too long a period to permit to elapse. The press officers' view that Dr Wells, as his line manager, should break the news to Dr Kelly was understandable, and it was not unreasonable to think that the press would take a little time to find out where Dr Kelly lived, but it should have been foreseen that the confirmation of the name might take place at a time when (as happened) Dr Wells was not easily contactable and the possibility that the press might arrive quickly at Dr Kelly's house should have been taken into account.

437. However, whilst the MoD is subject to these criticisms I consider that the criticisms are subject to the mitigating circumstances that (1) for the reasons which I set out later in paragraphs 444, 445 and 446 his exposure to press attention and intrusion, whilst obviously very stressful, was only one of the factors placing Dr Kelly under great stress; (2) individual officials did try to help and support Dr Kelly in the ways which I have described in paragraphs 430 and 431 above; and (3) because of his intensely private nature, Dr Kelly was not an easy man to help or to whom to give advice. It is also right to emphasise, as I have already stated, that no-one, including the officials in the MoD could have contemplated that Dr Kelly might take his own life. In her evidence Dr Kelly's sister, Dr Pape said:

[1 September, page 87, line 11]

Q. How did he seem generally to be in this conversation [on Tuesday 15th July]?

A. Tired, but otherwise it really was a very normal conversation. Believe me, I have lain awake many nights since, going over in my mind whether I missed anything significant. In my line of work I do deal with people who may have suicidal thoughts and I ought to be able to spot those, even on a telephone conversation. But I have gone over and over in my mind the two conversations we had and he certainly did not betray to me any impression that he was anything other than tired. He certainly did not convey to me that he was feeling depressed; and absolutely nothing that would have alerted me to the fact that he might have been considering suicide.

438. In her evidence Mrs Kelly said:

[1 September, page 47, line 4]

Q. How would you describe him at this time [lunchtime on Thursday 17th July]?

A. Oh, I just thought he had a broken heart. He really was very, very – he had shrunk into himself. He looked as though he had shrunk, but I had no idea at that stage of what he might do later, absolutely no idea at all.

Conclusion on the issue whether the Government failed to take proper steps to help and protect Dr Kelly in the difficult position in which he found himself

439. I consider that once the decision had been taken on 8 July to issue the statement, the MoD was at fault and is to be criticised for not informing Dr Kelly that its press office would confirm his name if a journalist suggested it. Although I am satisfied that Dr Kelly realised, once the MoD statement had been issued on Tuesday 8 July, that his name would come out, it must have been a great shock and very upsetting for him to have been told in a brief telephone call from his line manager, Dr Wells, on the evening of 9 July that the press office of his own department had confirmed his name to the press and must have given rise to a feeling that he had been badly let down by his employer. I further consider that the MoD was at fault in not having set up a procedure whereby Dr Kelly would be informed immediately his name had been confirmed to the press and in permitting a period of one and a half hours to elapse between the confirmation of his name to the press and information being given to Dr Kelly that his name had been confirmed to the press. However these criticisms are subject to the mitigating circumstances that (1) Dr Kelly's exposure to press attention and intrusion, whilst obviously very stressful, was only one of the factors placing him under great stress (see paragraphs 433, 434 and 435); (2) individual officials in the MoD did try to help and support him in the ways which I have described in paragraphs 430, 431; and (3) because of his intensely private nature, Dr Kelly was not an easy man to help or to whom to give advice.

CHAPTER 10

The factors which may have led Dr Kelly to take his own life

440. In his evidence on 2 September Professor Hawton, an eminent expert on the subject of suicide, stated the factors which, in his opinion, contributed to Dr Kelly taking his own life. The parts of his evidence which I consider to be of particular relevance are the following:

[2 September, page 98, line 10]

Q.... what styles of thinking are most associated with suicide?

A. Well, the one for which there is most evidence is the tendency to feel hopeless when faced with a difficult circumstance.

Q. Are there any other relevant feelings?

A. Yes, certainly a sense of feeling trapped, being unable to escape from an unbearable situation. Isolation may be another factor, either actual isolation in the sense of not having people around or relative isolation where a person is unable to communicate with those around them because of their particular personality style.

Q. Are there any other additional factors that one might consider here?

A. Well, another important factor is where a person has suffered a severe blow to their self esteem, that is their sense of self worth. Shame can be another factor. Sometimes people appear to engage in a suicidal act, and I am here including attempting suicide to show other people how bad they are feeling, and occasionally there seems to be a desire for revenge, that revenge is a part of the motivation.

....

[2 September, page 112, line 21]

Q. We have also heard some of Dr Kelly's reaction reported by Mrs Kelly yesterday. Was there anything in that that is relevant?

A. This is his reaction to -

Q. The fact that his name is coming out.

A. It seemed to be extremely painful for him. Being a very private person, I think the idea that he would not only be questioned but this would be in public and televised – this would be on television, was extremely difficult for him.

Q. And the circumstances of his appearance itself before the Foreign Affairs Committee, you have seen the video. Is there anything that you can, from an expert perspective, help us with?

A. Well, I watched part of it before I got involved at all in the Inquiry; and I remember thinking at the time that I was surprised that – not about the questions he was asked but about the style of some of the questions, the questioning of someone who was obviously such a senior and important person in his field; and having watched the full video, I would confirm my – you know, I would agree, if you like, with the impression that I had beforehand.

There were clearly times during the interview when he became uncomfortable and almost seemed a little bit confused, I do not mean in a pathological sense, but he seemed quite uncertain.

Q. What were the indications that you, from an expert point of view, would look at for that?

A. Well, in terms of his – the way he looked, when he looked down and moved in a slightly uncomfortable way and he looked, at times, rather sort of hot and flustered, but there were also, I understand, environmental circumstances which did not help.

Q. Yes, we have heard it was a hot day; and we have heard that the fans were turned off.

A. Hmm.

Q. We have also heard Rachel's description of her father as he returned from that. Was there anything in that description which has assisted you?

A. Yes. I think, again, I am relying, obviously, on the information – the information you heard was very similar to the information I was given. There were no major discrepancies. He seemed to have been very disturbed – distressed, rather, by that hearing. He gave the impression of having felt belittled by some of the questioning; and I gather he expressed, unusually for him, a certain degree of anger about a particular style of particular questioning that he received. She told me that when he came to her house in Oxford where he was staying, he, using her words, appeared to be "shocked, broken and humiliated". This was obviously a very, very, very stressful experience for him.

....

441. Professor Hawton referred to the fact that when Dr Kelly left his daughter Rachel's house in Oxford on the evening of Wednesday 16 July he arranged to meet her the following evening, 17 July, to go for a walk:

[2 September, page 115, line 15]

Q. What significance does that have?

A. Well it suggests to me that it was probably unlikely he was thinking of suicide at that point in time.

Q. Because?

A. I think having become more aware about the nature of the relationship with his daughter, I doubt very much whether he would have arranged to meet her to go for a walk knowing that he was likely not to have been alive when it came to the point.

442. Professor Hawton referred to a series of e-mails which Dr Kelly had sent to friends and colleagues around 11.18am on the morning of Thursday 17 July [paragraph 123]:

[2 September, page 116, line 20]

A. Well, I understand that around 11.18 he sent a series of e-mails to friends and colleagues who had sent him messages during the days beforehand. He obviously had not seen these because he had not been at home and he had only gone to his computer that morning. I got the impression he had written a series of e-mails offline and then sent them off all at the same time.

Q. At 11.18.

A. Yes. And these were to colleagues, ex colleagues and professional acquaintances; and the striking thing in those messages is that he talked, briefly – he mentioned, briefly, the difficulties that he was facing, but he also talked about how he hoped to get back to Iraq and continue his work there. So there was also a sense of optimism at the same time.

Q. Can I take you to an illustration of that, at COM/1/10? If you look towards the bottom of the screen you can see:

"Dear David

"Sorry about your latest run in with the media. I hope you are not getting too much flack. As we both know only too well dealing with the media is always a balancing act and its always impossible to predict which way it will go. When you get it right everybody is in favour but when you get it wrong you don't see their feet for dust."

We can see the response: "Many thanks for your thoughts. It has been difficult. Hopefully it will all blow over by the end of the week and I can travel to Baghdad and get on with the real work."

Is that the type of e-mail you are referring to?

A. Absolutely.

Q. What does that illustrate for you?

A. Well, it would suggest – one cannot be definite about this – that at that stage he still had optimism for the future and that it was probably unlikely that he had ideas or certainly definite ideas of suicide at that point in time. Obviously it is conceivable that he was presenting a different light in those e-mails but I think a logical conclusion would be that he was not thinking of suicide at that time.

....

443. Professor Hawton was then asked about the e-mails which Dr Kelly received on the morning of Thursday 17 July which set out Parliamentary Questions including the Question:

> To ask the Secretary of State for Defence, what (a) Civil Service and (b) MoD rules and regulations may have been infringed by Dr David Kelly in talking to BBC Radio 4 Defence Correspondent Andrew Gilligan.

and the Question:

> To ask the Secretary of State for Defence, what disciplinary measures his department will take against Dr David Kelly.

Professor Hawton was asked:

[2 September, page 120, line 15]

Do you think any of those might have been relevant?

A. Well, I think it is likely that he would have begun to perceive that the problem was escalating, the difficulties for him were escalating and that the prospects for an early resolution of his difficulties were diminishing.

....

[2 September, page 122, line 15]

Q. So when do you believe that Dr Kelly is likely to have formed the intention?

A. Well, it is my opinion that it is likely that he formed the opinion either during the morning, probably later in the morning or during the early part of the afternoon, before he went on that walk.

444. I think it probable that one of the concerns which must have been weighing heavily on Dr Kelly's mind during the last few days of his life was the knowledge that there appeared to be in existence, known to members of the FAC, a full note of his conversation with Ms Susan Watts on 30 May. This concern would have included the knowledge that he had denied (question 132 in his evidence to the FAC) that the words which he had spoken to Ms Watts in his telephone conversation with her on 30 May and which she had quoted on the Newsnight programme were his words. Dr Kelly had told the MoD at the meeting on 14 July that he had not spoken to Ms Watts about the September dossier (see paragraph 97) and he must also have been worried that it would emerge and would become known to the MoD that he had had a lengthy discussion with Ms Watts about intelligence matters in relation to the 45 minutes claim and that he had had a similar but shorter conversation with Mr Gavin Hewitt.

445. In their evidence both Ms Rachel Kelly and Dr Pape suggested that when giving evidence to the FAC Dr Kelly was probably misled because Mr Chidgey suggested that the words which he quoted to Dr Kelly were said by him in a meeting with Ms Watts, whereas they were said in a telephone conversation. This may be so, but after the hearing before the FAC I think that Dr Kelly must have been concerned by his express denial that the words quoted on the Newsnight programme by Ms Watts came from him.

446. The Parliamentary Question, which was an entirely proper one, sent to him on the morning of 17 July asking what Civil Service and MoD rules and regulations had been infringed by him talking to Mr Gilligan and the Parliamentary Question, which was also an entirely proper one, asking the Secretary of State for Defence what disciplinary measures his Department would take against him, would have made it appear likely to him that his discussions with journalists were going to come under investigation. As Professor Hawton stated, the difficulties for him were escalating and the prospect for an early resolution of his difficulties were diminishing.

447. Later in his evidence Professor Hawton gave the following evidence:

[2 September, page 124, line 6]

MR DINGEMANS: Do you consider Dr Kelly had developed any sort of psychiatric disorder before his death?

A. I have thought very carefully about this; and my conclusion is that he was not suffering from a severe psychiatric disorder.

Q. We have heard of his weight loss; and we have also heard about some of the sparkle going out of his eyes. Are those features relevant?

A. Those are certainly relevant; but other features which suggest that he did not have a psychiatric disorder, and I am particularly thinking here of depression, is that his mood was predominantly reported as being quite upbeat in spite of all his difficulties, except at certain times. There was not a sense of a persistent depressive mood. His sleep, as far as we can gather from the family accounts, was not disturbed and his appetite was good.

Q. And those are contra-indicators are they?

A. They are.

....

[2 September, page 126, line 10]

Q. We have heard that he was a weapons inspector, it must have put him in all sorts of difficult situations. Was that similar to the situation that he found himself in towards the end of his life?

A. No, I think there was an important difference. One has heard about the situations he faced, for example, in Iraq, while cross-examining people, which sounded to me quite terrifying situations. I gather he could cope with those extremely well. I think the importance about the problems he was facing shortly before his death was that these really challenged his identity of himself, his self esteem, his self worth, his image of himself as a valued and loyal employee and as a significant scientist.

Q. And in that respect some of the comments reported of him being middle level, et cetera, how are they likely to have affected him?

A. Well, I can only really go on particularly his wife's account that these were really very upsetting for him.

....

448. At the conclusion of his evidence on 2 September Professor Hawton was asked:

[2 September, page 132, line 2]

Q. Have you considered, now, with the benefit of hindsight that we all have, what factors did contribute to Dr Kelly's death?

A. I think that as far as one can deduce, the major factor was the severe loss of self esteem, resulting from his feeling that people had lost trust in him and from his dismay at being exposed to the media.

Q. And why have you singled that out as a major factor?

A. Well, he talked a lot about it; and I think being such a private man, I think this was anathema to him to be exposed, you know, publicly in this way. In a sense, I think he would have seen it as being publicly disgraced.

Q. What other factors do you think were relevant?

A. Well, I think that carrying on that theme, I think he must have begun – he is likely to have begun to think that, first of all, the prospects for continuing in his previous work role were diminishing very markedly and, indeed, my conjecture that he had begun to fear he would lose his job altogether.

Q. What effect is that likely to have had on him?

A. Well, I think that would have filled him with a profound sense of hopelessness; and that, in a sense, his life's work had been not wasted but that had been totally undermined.

LORD HUTTON: Could you just elaborate a little on that, Professor, again? As sometimes is the case in this Inquiry, witnesses give answers and further explanation is obvious, but nonetheless I think it is helpful just to have matters fully spelt out. What do you think would have caused Dr Kelly to think that the prospects of continuing in his work were becoming uncertain?

A. Well, I think, my Lord, that first of all, there had been the letter from Mr Hatfield which had laid out the difficulties that Dr Kelly, you know, is alleged to have got into.

LORD HUTTON: Yes.

A. And in that letter there was also talk that should further matters come to light then disciplinary proceedings would need to be instigated.

LORD HUTTON: Yes.

A. And then of course there were the Parliamentary Questions which we have heard about, which suggested that questions were going to be asked about discipline in Parliament.

LORD HUTTON: Yes. Thank you.

MR DINGEMANS: Were there any other relevant factors?

A. I think the fact that he could not share his problems and feelings with other people, and the fact that he, according to the accounts I have been given, actually increasingly withdrew into himself. So in a sense he was getting further and further from being able to share the problems with other people, that is extremely important.

Q. Were there any other factors which you considered relevant?

A. Those are the main factors that I consider relevant.

....

[2 September, page 134, line 23]

Q. ...you have had the benefit of judging everything with hindsight. You have had the benefit of exploring Dr Kelly's psychology and his make up in a way that no-one could have done at the time.

A. Hmm.

Q. If I was a lay person before Dr Kelly's death, would I have had any chance of knowing the possible outcomes?

A. I think for a lay person then certainly not. I think it would not have been an outcome one would have predicted.

In those answers Professor Hawton referred to the letter which Mr Hatfield had sent to Dr Kelly dated 9 July 2003. It appears from the evidence of the police that Dr Kelly had not opened the letter, but Mr Hatfield had already told Dr Kelly of the matters set out in the letter at the conclusion of the interview on 7 July.

449. Professor Hawton gave further evidence on 24 September in relation to information that the death certificate of Dr Kelly's mother, who had died on 13 May 1964, stated the cause of death as a chest infection due to barbiturate poison and that a coroner had returned an open verdict, and that Dr Kelly believed that his mother had taken her own life after suffering from depression for many years. Professor Hawton stated that there was no evidence that Dr Kelly had suffered significant mental illness before or at the time of his death and Professor Hawton further stated that the fact that his mother appeared to have committed suicide was of no relevance in determining the factors which contributed to Dr Kelly's death. Referring to the facts relating to the death of Dr Kelly's mother, counsel to the Inquiry asked Professor Hawton:

[24 September, page 166, line 22]

Q. So in the light of those matters, can I relate those back to your previous conclusions and ask you now, in the light of all the evidence, to state your conclusions or the summary of factors that you believe may have contributed to Dr Kelly's death?

A. Well, I stick with the conclusions that I presented when I appeared before. Firstly, that I think one major factor was the severe loss of self esteem that he had from feeling that people had lost trust in him and from his "dismay" was the word I used before, maybe that was an understatement, at being exposed in the media. And I think the fact, as I think has now been generally acknowledged, that he was a very private person made his being in the media all the more stressful for him.

The second factor, I believe, was that he probably was coming to fear that the prospects for continuing his previous work were diminishing and it is possible that he feared he would lose his job altogether, perhaps particularly when he saw some of the communications that he had received on the morning of his death.

And thirdly I think the effect of this on him would have been to have filled him with a profound sense of hopelessness. I think another very relevant factor, as I said when I appeared before, was his private nature, his dislike of sharing personal problems and feelings with other people; and according to several accounts, he had become increasingly withdrawn during the – into himself during the period shortly before his death which meant that I think he became even less accessible or less able to discuss his problems with other people.

Q. And those remain your conclusions?

A. They do.

450. It is not possible to be certain as to the factors which drove Dr Kelly to commit suicide but in the light of the evidence which I have heard I consider that it is very probable that Professor Hawton's opinion as to the factors which contributed to Dr Kelly taking his own life is correct.

Conclusion on the factors which may have led Dr Kelly to take his own life

451. I consider that it is very probable that Professor Hawton's opinion is correct when he stated:

> **[2 September, page 132, line 2]**
>
> Q. Have you considered, now, with the benefit of hindsight that we all have, what factors did contribute to Dr Kelly's death?
>
> A. I think that as far as one can deduce, the major factor was the severe loss of self esteem, resulting from his feeling that people had lost trust in him and from his dismay at being exposed to the media.
>
> Q. And why have you singled that out as a major factor?
>
> A. Well, he talked a lot about it; and I think being such a private man, I think this was anathema to him to be exposed, you know, publicly in this way. In a sense, I think he would have seen it as being publicly disgraced.
>
> Q. What other factors do you think were relevant?
>
> A. Well, I think that carrying on that theme, I think he must have begun – he is likely to have begun to think that, first of all, the prospects for continuing in his previous work role were diminishing very markedly and, indeed, my conjecture that he had begun to fear he would lose his job altogether.
>
> Q. What effect is that likely to have had on him?
>
> A. Well, I think that would have filled him with a profound sense of hopelessness; and that, in a sense, his life's work had been not wasted but that had been totally undermined.
>
> LORD HUTTON: Could you just elaborate a little on that, Professor, again? As sometimes is the case in this Inquiry, witnesses give answers and further explanation is obvious, but nonetheless I think it is helpful just to have matters fully spelt out. What do you think would have caused Dr Kelly to think that the prospects of continuing in his work were becoming uncertain?
>
> A. Well, I think, my Lord, that first of all, there had been the letter from Mr Hatfield which had laid out the difficulties that Dr Kelly, you know, is alleged to have got into.
>
> LORD HUTTON: Yes.
>
> A. And in that letter there was also talk that should further matters come to light then disciplinary proceedings would need to be instigated.
>
> LORD HUTTON: Yes.
>
> A. And then of course there were the Parliamentary Questions which we have heard about, which suggested that questions were going to be asked about discipline in Parliament.
>
> LORD HUTTON: Yes. Thank you.
>
> MR DINGEMANS: Were there any other relevant factors?
>
> A. I think the fact that he could not share his problems and feelings with other people, and the fact that he, according to the accounts I have been given, actually increasingly withdrew into himself. So in a sense he was getting further and further from being able to share the problems with other people, that is extremely important.
>
> Q. Were there any other factors which you considered relevant?
>
> A. Those are the main factors that I consider relevant.

CHAPTER 11

Other Matters

Did Mr Gilligan give adequate notice to the Government on 28 May 2003 of the allegations to be reported in his broadcasts on WMD on the Today programme on 29 May?

452. On this issue there was a conflict between the evidence of Mr Gilligan and the evidence of Mrs Wilson, the chief press officer of the MoD. When he gave evidence on 12 August Mr Gilligan said:

[12 August, page 55, line 22]

Q. So who was the person who had contacted someone to talk from the Government side about this story?

A. Well, the contact with – deciding how the programme should get a Government response is the responsibility of the office team. They said they would speak to the MoD about Ingram. Now I think one of the producers on the team – each item is assigned a producer and the assigned producer spoke to the Ministry of Defence and told them about the story. As I say, I also spoke to the MoD. I spoke to Kate Wilson, who is the chief press officer at the MoD, on my mobile phone about 7.30 and I told her.

Q. And what did you tell her?

A. I cannot remember exactly what I told her because it was a mobile phone and I did not take notes of my conversation.

Q. You have no notes of that conversation?

A. No, but I took her through the story in outline.

Q. And what was the gist of the outline that you gave to her?

A. I cannot remember the exact words I used, to be absolutely honest, because so much has happened since then and it was one of the dozens and dozens of calls I made that day to MoD press officers. I know I took her through the outline of the story. I said that Ingram would be asked about it the next day.

....

[12 August, page 61, line 22]

A... I would not have spent seven and a half minutes discussing another reporter's story. I did not know what the cluster bomb story was; and I would not have done it anyway. You know, it would have been a breach of protocol to talk to a Government press officer about another reporter's story. I think it is correct to say – I did not ask the MoD press office to go away and seek specific responses to these specific points. I simply wanted to forewarn them about what was going to be in the broadcast so that Adam Ingram was equipped to discuss it the following day. But I certainly did not spend the whole time talking about cluster bombs.

Q. Did you put some of the specific allegations that you made in the broadcast? In the early morning broadcast, the 6 o'clock broadcast, you have referred to the Government knowing that the 45 minute claim was wrong before it was put in. Did you put that allegation to the Ministry of Defence press officer?

A. I do not believe I did put those specific words, no. As I say, I cannot remember exactly what I said. I gave them an outline of the story, a summary of the story. But I cannot remember exactly what I said to them.

Q. Did you put the other perhaps major allegation, that Downing Street had ordered the dossier to be sexed up and more facts to be discovered as broadcast; did you put that to the MoD press officer?

A. Yes, again I may not have used those exact words because I cannot remember which words I used. But I put the gist of the story, which was that the dossier had been exaggerated at Downing Street's behest.

453. When she gave evidence on 16 September Mrs Wilson said:

[16 September, page 130, line 10]

Q. Did you have any contact with Mr Gilligan on that day [28th May]?

A. Yes. I spoke to him at about 7.30.

Q. Did you know Mr Gilligan beforehand?

A. Yes. I have known him since I first started doing press office work in 1996.

Q. At 7.30 what was said?

A. He called me to say that they were looking for an interview with Adam Ingram the next morning which was about cluster bombs, which was quite a topical issue. We talked through various issues around the subject of cluster bombs, things like the detonation rates of different weapon systems and things like that. At the end of the conversation I asked him whether there was anything else running on the programme and he said he had something he was working on on WMD and a dodgy dossier. He said that was not a matter for the MoD, so I did not pursue it.

Q. How long do you think this conversation lasted?

A. I have heard since that it was about 7 minutes. That sounds about right.

Q. It accords with your recollection?

A. Yes.

Q. How many minutes, estimating, do you think you were talking about the cluster bombs for?

A. At a guess – it was most of the conversation, 6 minutes or so. It was only when I asked him at the end of the conversation whether he was working on anything else, which is standard practice, so that I could brief the Minister if there was anything else he needed to know about, he mentioned the WMD story.

Q. So far as you can recollect, what exactly did he say about the WMD story?

A. He said he had – he was working on a story about WMD and the dodgy dossier, which I took at the time to be the February dossier.

Q. Did you make any notes of that conversation?

A. I did not make any notes of the conversation. The reason I did not is because I was working from a Q and A document on cluster bombs. I tend to make notes if I have something new or different that I need to go away and look into or research. There was not anything new or different in what he was talking about so I did not make any notes.

....

[16 September, page 215, line 11]

Q. But Mr Gilligan's recollection is that he rings you, not about somebody else's story but about his own story, and that he outlines that he has a source who says the dossier is exaggerated.

A. Well, when we first complained to Richard Sambrook, Richard Sambrook's response said that Andrew Gilligan acknowledged that he had spoken to me about cluster bombs but felt he had added something on the end. I am very clear that he spoke to me about cluster bombs; and I am very clear that he only asked me about the WMD accusation when I asked him if he had anything running. He did not tell me what the accusation was.

Q. He does mention that there is a WMD story?

A. Yes. I have always been clear. He said he was working on something on WMD and the dodgy dossier.

Q. And you do not ask him any questions about it?

A. He said specifically it was not a matter for the MoD, and I agreed with him.

Q. In terms of referring to a dossier, I think you accept that there is a reference to a dossier which you took to be a reference to the February dossier?

A. Yes.

Q. There is certainly a reference to a dossier.

A. Hmm, hmm.

Q. And to a dossier being exaggerated?

A. No, just to the dodgy dossier.

LORD HUTTON: You think Mr Gilligan referred to the dodgy dossier? Did he use the word "dodgy"?

A. Yes, I think he did.

MS ROGERS: You think he did?

A. No, I am clear he did.

Q. In terms of the intelligence community being unhappy with the dossier, you think he did not mention that at all?

A. No, I am clear. You have seen the briefing that we did get. If Andrew had mentioned exactly what the allegations were, when we spoke to No.10 we would have told them. We would have had the denial the night before and it would all have been perfectly straightforward. The only reason why I would not have mentioned it to No.10 is because I would not have known about it.

Q. You are, in a sense, working backwards that No.10 was not told, therefore you cannot have been told because if you had been told you would have mentioned it?

A. No, I am working forwards. I am very clear that when I spoke to Andrew Gilligan the conversation was about cluster bombs. At the end of the conversation I asked him, he did not volunteer to me, that he was working on something on WMD and the dodgy dossier but he said it was not a matter for the MoD. So I do not see how that can be classified as checking the story with MoD.

Q. Leaving aside whether it is checking the story with MoD. Speaking about a dossier being exaggerated and referring to the 45 minutes intelligence –

A. He did not mention that.

Q. And he did not mention any unhappiness with the intelligence community, so far as you recall?

A. No. He said WMD and the dodgy dossier. He mentioned it in passing, because that was not what the conversation was all about.

Q. Do you think that it would have been better to have made a note of this conversation at the time?

311

A. No. I wish I had, but it is not my normal practice. If I had known that it would be claimed that he had checked the story then obviously I wish I had, and I wish I had recorded the conversation, but it was not my normal practice to do that.

454. When he gave evidence again on 17 September Mr Gilligan said:

[17 September, page 13, line 3]

LORD HUTTON: Did you give any details of the story you were going to run?

A. Yes, I gave the gist of the allegations, which is that the dossier had been exaggerated and that there was concern in the Intelligence Services about the inclusion of the 45 minutes claim or the ready in 45 minutes claim, and that people in intelligence did not think it reflected the considered views they were putting forward.

MS ROGERS: It is right that you have no notes of that conversation?

A. No. Indeed, I do not think Ms Wilson has either.

Q. All we know is it lasted 7 minutes 24 seconds.

A. Yes, 7 and a half minutes. I understand Ms Wilson has said I spoke about cluster bombs. I may have spoken briefly about cluster bombs but the cluster bombs story was not my story. I did not know what it was.

Q. Had you spoken to Ms Wilson about cluster bombs on previous occasions?

A. I may have done, certainly. But on this occasion the cluster bombs story was another reporter's story. I did not know what the story was.

Q. It is Ian Watson who is the cluster bombs story.

A. Yes.

Q. Had you done any work on Ian Watson's story?

A. No, I do not think I would have spent 7 and a half minutes talking about another reporter's story.

....

[17 September, page 47, line 19]

MR SUMPTION: Mr Gilligan, you accept that the department concerned was No.10. You accept, as I understand it, that you never gave advance notice to No.10?

A. Yes.

Q. Could you look, please, at BBC/5/153. This is a letter from Richard Sambrook to Ben Bradshaw shortly after the interview which was referred to in your evidence-in-chief a few minutes ago. One of the things that Mr Sambrook says when he recites the facts about this advance notice to the Ministry of Defence is: "At 6.30pm Andrew Gilligan spoke to Kate O'Connor [that is the same as Kate Wilson], the MoD press officer, about the cluster bomb interview and added there would be another story running on WMD." Was that an accurate statement?

A. Certainly the cluster bomb issue came up, because that was the reason that Adam Ingram had been booked to talk on the programme the next day. So I began by saying: Adam Ingram, you know, is booked to talk on the cluster bomb subject but I want to put another subject to him as well, and I described the story, as the letter says.

Q. This statement was based on what you told Mr Sambrook, was it not?

A. I am not sure it was, in fact, because the time is wrong here, 6.30. It should have been 7.30. I am not quite sure where this comes from.

Q. Mr Gilligan, there was no written record of this conversation, so the only place where Mr Sambrook could possibly have got it from was you.

A. I think I had spoken to the Controller of Editorial Policy, Stephen Whittle, about this. I think Mr Whittle had conveyed some of it to Mr Sambrook. Sometimes some of these things get a bit lost in the telling.

Q. What is being said here and what I suggest what you had told your superiors within the BBC is that you spoke to Ms Wilson about the cluster bomb interview and added that there would be another story on WMD.

A. Well, I certainly began by speaking about the cluster bomb interview because that was the starting point for Mr Ingram's appearance on the Today Programme the following morning. I really had very little to say about the subject of cluster bombs because I did not know what the story was, it was another reporter's story. As I said earlier, I simply would not discuss another reporter's story with the Ministry of Defence, even if I had been able to. It is a breach of protocol.

LORD HUTTON: Mr Gilligan, can I ask you: what was your purpose, then, for ringing Ms Wilson?

A. It was to give her an outline of the WMD story so that Adam Ingram could be briefed to answer questions on it.

LORD HUTTON: Why did you refer to the cluster bombs story? Was it just, as it were, as an introduction?

A. Yes.

LORD HUTTON: Because you knew Adam Ingram was coming on for that purpose.

A. Yes. And I said: you know Adam Ingram is booked to talk about cluster bombs, we want to broaden the bid to talk about the dossier; and I gave her an outline of the story.

LORD HUTTON: Yes.

MR SUMPTION: You also said to your superiors within the BBC, did you not, that what you had said about WMD was that it was not a matter for the MoD but for another Government department. Do you remember that?

A. What I said to the MoD was that I was not seeking a point by point response from the press office, I did not want them to go away and come back with a point by point response to the allegations that were made. I wanted them to notify Mr Ingram so he would be prepared to answer on the subject the following morning; and that was how both I and the programme team, which included the day editor, Miranda Holt, and the overall editor of the programme, Kevin Marsh, had decided how this story would be handled. Similar calls were made by two others on the Today Programme team on that evening, by Martha Findlay and by Chris Howard.

Q. Let me remind you of my question: I did not ask you what you had told the MoD, I asked you what you had told your superiors within the BBC, which was rather different.

A. Well, my answer is the same because that – you know, that is – as I have just said, that is what we had agreed, what my superiors, in other words Miranda Holt and Kevin Marsh, had agreed with me.

Q. Did you say to Mr Sambrook that you said something to the MoD to indicate that the WMD story was not an MoD story? Do you follow me?

A. Well, as I said, I told the press officer, I told Kate Wilson that it was not – I did not seek a point by point response from the MoD press office but I did hope that Adam Ingram would be able to answer questions on it.

Q. Just focus on my question, please, Mr Gilligan. Did you say to Mr Sambrook: I told the MoD that I was working on a WMD story, but it was not a matter for the MoD? Did you say that to him or words to that effect?

A. I cannot remember what I said to him, but what I – if I indeed said that, and I am not sure I did, but what I meant from that was that I had told them that it was not a matter on which I was expecting a point by point response from the MoD but one which I expected them to brief Adam Ingram on for his appearance on the programme the next morning.

455. Neither Mr Gilligan nor Mrs Wilson made notes of the conversation between them and it is not possible to reach a clear conclusion as to what was said. A point which supports Mr Gilligan's account is that it is unlikely that the conversation which lasted for 7 minutes 24 seconds would have been confined only to cluster bombs, which was not Mr Gilligan's story. But, on balance, I think it is more probable than not that Mr Gilligan failed to give Mrs Wilson a clear indication of the allegations which he was going to make that the dossier was exaggerated and that there was concern in the Intelligence Services about the inclusion of the 45 minutes claim, because if he had done so I think that Mrs Wilson would almost certainly have alerted 10 Downing Street to those allegations.

Mr Campbell's evidence to the FAC on 25 June 2003 about his involvement in September 2002 in the preparation of the draft dossiers

456. The BBC has criticised parts of Mr Campbell's evidence to the FAC on this subject. I have considered in detail in this report, with reference to relevant documents, the part which Mr Campbell played in the preparation of the draft dossiers and therefore I consider that it is unnecessary for me to express an opinion on this criticism.

Mr Gilligan's e-mail of 14 July 2003 intended for some members of the FAC

457. In his evidence Mr Gilligan acknowledged that it had been quite wrong for him to have sent this e-mail suggesting that Dr Kelly was Ms Watts' source and he apologised for doing so:

[17 September, page 14, line 5]

Q. One final matter before I leave you to Mr Sumption. We have heard, since you gave your evidence last time, about an e-mail that you sent on 14th July to some members of the Foreign Affairs Committee Select Committee. I hesitate to have it called up, but it is BBC/12/22. Is there anything you want to say about that e-mail to this Inquiry?

A. Yes. It was quite wrong to send it and I can only apologise. I did not even know for sure that David Kelly was Susan Watts' source. I was under an enormous amount of pressure at the time and I simply was not thinking straight, so I really do want to apologise for that.

Dr Kelly's meeting with the MoD on 14 July 2003

458. As stated in paragraph 98 the handwritten notes made by Dr Wells, Dr Kelly and Ms Heather Smith of the meeting on 14 July 2003 contained the words "tricky areas" which appeared to relate to:

(a) What Dr Kelly thought of Government Policy on Iraq;

(b) Whether Dr Kelly thought he was Mr Gilligan's source; and

(c) What disciplinary action was being taken against Dr Kelly.

Mr Hoon had written to Mr Donald Anderson MP, the Chairman of the FAC, on 11 July stating:

I am prepared to agree [to Dr Kelly appearing before the FAC] on the clear understanding that Dr Kelly will be questioned only on those matters which are directly relevant to the evidence that you were given by Andrew Gilligan, and not on the wider issue of Iraqi WMD and the preparation of the Dossier.

On 11 July Mr Hoon had also written to Mrs Ann Taylor MP, the Chairman of the ISC, in somewhat similar terms.

459. Therefore having regard to the boundaries laid down by Mr Hoon (which Mr Anderson agreed to) I consider that it was not impermissible for Mr Howard to tell Dr Kelly that the three areas were "tricky" ones. I consider that Mr Howard also told Dr Kelly that he was free to tell his own story to the FAC and the ISC, but it is apparent from Mr Hoon's letters that the MoD wished to confine Dr Kelly's evidence to the matters referred to by Mr Hoon.

The manner in which Dr Kelly was questioned when he gave evidence to the FAC on 15 July 2003

460. Some questions which Mr Andrew Mackinlay MP put to Dr Kelly when he appeared before the FAC gave rise to criticism from some members of the public. When he gave evidence to the Inquiry Mr Mackinlay explained that some of his questioning was prompted by his conclusion that Dr Kelly was not Mr Gilligan's source:

> [26 August, page 13, line 17]
>
> MR DINGEMANS: Can I ask you some questions about your other questioning towards the end of the session? FAC/4/24: "Andrew Mackinlay: Since you wrote to your superiors in the way you have done, have you met Geoff Hoon?
>
> "Mr Kelly: No.
>
> "Andrew Mackinlay: Any ministers?
>
> "Mr Kelly: No.
>
> "Mr Pope: Any special advisers?"
>
> You pick up the question: "Any special advisers?
>
> "Dr Kelly: No.
>
> "Andrew Mackinlay: Do you know of any other inquiries which have gone on in the department to seek the source – to clarify in addition to you or instead of you or apart from you? None whatsoever?
>
> Dr Kelly: No."
>
> Perhaps you can read out your next question?
>
> A. That is question?
>
> Q. 167.
>
> A. "I reckon you are chaff; you have been thrown up to divert our probing. Have you ever felt like a fall guy? You have been set up, have you not?"
>
> Q. Did you consider that to be a fair question?
>
> A. Yes, I do think it is; and because it is against a backdrop of where the Government had indicated they think that Dr Kelly is the sole source. He then comes along to us. He has convinced me and everybody else at this stage, because we have made a quantum leap, he has convinced me that he is not the source – the Gilligan source, very impressively, very impressively indeed. I could take you through that if you like. I hope you will just take from me by this stage I am, along with others, absolutely convinced that he is not the source. I feel very angry for him and for Parliament against the backdrop of what I just said, you know, about misleading Parliament and so on.

461. The Bill of Rights provides that the affairs of Parliament (which include the proceedings of a Select Committee of the House of Commons, such as the FAC) should not be commented on other than in Parliament. Therefore it would not be proper for me to express an opinion on the way in which Dr Kelly was questioned

before the FAC, but it is relevant to record that on 16 October 2003 the Liaison Committee of the House of Commons decided to review the working of Select Committees in the light of this Inquiry.

The Walter Mitty remark by Mr Thomas Kelly

462. In a conversation with journalists about the start of August 2003 Mr Tom Kelly made a remark to the effect that Dr Kelly was a "Walter Mitty" character. On 5 August Mr Kelly issued a press statement in which he apologised unreservedly to Mrs Kelly and her daughters for this remark. In the course of his evidence to the Inquiry Mr Kelly twice repeated his apology. On 20 August he said:

[20 August, page 204, line 18]

... as I said on the day after this article appeared, I unreservedly apologise to the Kelly family that words of mine intrude into their grief at that time. Whatever my motives, it was a mistake that led to that intrusion and I have to take responsibility for that mistake.

On 23 September he said:

[23 September, page 35, line 3]

... I fully accept that I should not have used what was a too colourful phrase. I fully accept that in doing so I ran the risk of misunderstanding; and I fully accept that that must have caused the family much distress. It was not what I intended and that is why I gave my unreserved apology at the time, why I repeated it when I appeared at this Inquiry the first time and why I repeat it again today.

463. The remark was a wholly improper one for Mr Kelly to make and he has apologised for it unreservedly. However I consider that it casts no light on the issue whether there was an underhand strategy on the part of the Government to leak Dr Kelly's name covertly.

Dr Brian Jones' letter to the Deputy Chief of Defence Intelligence dated 8 July 2003

464. On 8 July 2003 Dr Jones wrote to the DCDI, who was Mr Martin Howard the successor to Mr Anthony Cragg who had retired. In his letter Dr Jones stated:

The Foreign Affairs Committee appears to consider it important that the Foreign Secretary told them, "... that there had been no formal complaint from members of the security and intelligence services about the content of the [September 2002] dossier." I believe his evidence was, in fact, that he was not *aware* of any such complaint, and there is no reason to suppose he should have become aware of mine. Nonetheless, it is now a matter of record, and I feel very uneasy that my minute could be uncovered at some future date, and that I might be judged culpable for not having drawn attention to it.

Mr Howard replied on 23 July and stated:

I am grateful to you for drawing my attention to this. I assume you are referring to the minute you wrote on 19 September to DIST, copy to Tony Cragg, my predecessor. I was aware of this and regard it as an entirely proper expression of your views at the time. The Defence Secretary and the former CDI have also been briefed on your note as part of the preparations for the evidence they gave this week to the Intelligence & Security Committee. There is, therefore, no question of your being found culpable in any way for what was, as I say, a perfectly legitimate action.

These letters are set out in appendix 18.

465. This matter was considered by the ISC and in the conclusions to its report of September 2003 it stated at page 44:

R. The Agencies and the JIC reported that none of their staff had concerns about the 24 September dossier. Two individuals in the DIS wrote to their line managers to register their concerns. We were told that these concerns were discussed within the DIS in the normal way. CDI agreed the text of the draft dossier, which was informed by intelligence that he, but not the two individuals, had seen. We have seen that intelligence and understand the basis on which CDI and JIC took the view they did. The concerns were not brought to the attention of the Defence Secretary or the JIC Chairman. (Paragraph 114)

S. We regard the initial failure by the MoD to disclose that some staff had put their concerns in writing to their line managers as unhelpful and potentially misleading. This is not excused by the genuine belief within the DIS that the concerns had been expressed as part of the normal lively debate that often surrounds draft JIC Assessments within the DIS. We are disturbed that after the first evidence session, which did not cover all the concerns raised by the DIS staff, the Defence Secretary decided against giving instructions for a letter to be written to us outlining the concerns. (Paragraph 104 and 115).

T. It is important that all DIS staff should be made aware of the current procedures for recording formal concerns on draft JIC Assessments. We recommend that if individuals in the intelligence community formally write to their line managers with concerns about JIC Assessments the concerns are brought to the attention of the JIC Chairman. (Paragraph 105 and 116)

As I have set out Dr Jones' evidence at some length and as this matter has been considered by the ISC I consider that it is unnecessary for me to express an opinion on it.

CHAPTER 12

Summary of conclusions

466. In this chapter I set out the conclusions which I have reached on the question how Dr Kelly came to his death and on the five groups of issues which arise from the evidence which I have heard.

467. I am satisfied that Dr Kelly took his own life and that the principal cause of death was bleeding from incised wounds to his left wrist which Dr Kelly had inflicted on himself with the knife found beside his body. It is probable that the ingestion of an excess amount of Coproxamol tablets coupled with apparently clinically silent coronary artery disease would have played a part in bringing about death more certainly and more rapidly than it would have otherwise been the case. I am further satisfied that no other person was involved in the death of Dr Kelly and that Dr Kelly was not suffering from any significant mental illness at the time he took his own life.

(1) On the issues relating to the preparation of the Government's dossier of 24 September 2002 entitled IRAQ'S WEAPONS OF MASS DESTRUCTION, my conclusions are as follows:

(i) The dossier was prepared and drafted by a small team of the assessment staff of the JIC. Mr John Scarlett, the Chairman of the JIC, had the overall responsibility for the drafting of the dossier. The dossier, which included the 45 minutes claim, was issued by the Government on 24 September 2002 with the full approval of the JIC.

(ii) The 45 minutes claim was based on a report which was received by the SIS from a source which that Service regarded as reliable. Therefore, whether or not at some time in the future the report on which the 45 minutes claim was based is shown to be unreliable, the allegation reported by Mr Gilligan on 29 May 2003 that the Government probably knew that the 45 minutes claim was wrong before the Government decided to put it in the dossier, was an allegation which was unfounded.

(iii) The allegation was also unfounded that the reason why the 45 minutes claim was not in the original draft of the dossier was because it only came from one source and the intelligence agencies did not really believe it was necessarily true. The reason why the 45 minutes claim did not appear in draft assessments or draft dossiers until 5 September 2002 was because the intelligence report on which it was based was not received by the SIS until 29 August 2002 and the JIC assessment staff did not have time to insert it in a draft until the draft of the assessment of 5 September 2002.

(iv) The true position in relation to the attitude of "the Intelligence Services" to the 45 minutes claim being inserted in the dossier was that the concerns expressed by Dr Jones were considered by higher echelons in the Intelligence Services and were not acted upon, and the JIC, the most senior body in the Intelligence Services charged with the assessment of intelligence, approved the wording in the dossier. Moreover, the nuclear, chemical and biological weapons section of the Defence Intelligence Staff, headed by Dr Brian Jones, did not argue that the intelligence relating to the 45 minutes claim should not have been included in the dossier but they did suggest that the wording in which the claim was stated in the dossier was too strong and that instead of the dossier stating "we judge" that "Iraq has:- military plans for the use of chemical and biological weapons, including against its own Shia population. Some of these weapons are deployable within 45 minutes of an order to use them", the wording should state "intelligence suggests".

(v) Mr Alastair Campbell made it clear to Mr Scarlett on behalf of the Prime Minister that 10 Downing Street wanted the dossier to be worded to make as strong a case as possible in relation to the threat posed by Saddam Hussein's WMD, and 10 Downing Street made written suggestions to Mr Scarlett as to changes in the wording of the draft dossier which would strengthen it. But Mr Campbell recognised, and told Mr Scarlett that 10 Downing Street recognised, that nothing should be stated in the dossier with which the intelligence community were not entirely happy.

(vi) Mr Scarlett accepted some of the drafting suggestions made to him by 10 Downing Street but he only accepted those suggestions which were consistent with the intelligence known to the JIC and he rejected those suggestions which were not consistent with such intelligence and the dossier issued by the Government was approved by the JIC.

(vii) As the dossier was one to be presented to, and read by, Parliament and the public, and was not an intelligence assessment to be considered only by the Government, I do not consider that it was improper for Mr Scarlett and the JIC to take into account suggestions as to drafting made by 10 Downing Street and to adopt those suggestions if they were consistent with the intelligence available to the JIC. However I consider that the possibility cannot be completely ruled out that the desire of the Prime Minister to have a dossier which, whilst consistent with the available intelligence, was as strong as possible in relation to the threat posed by Saddam Hussein's WMD, may have subconsciously influenced Mr Scarlett and the other members of the JIC to make the wording of the dossier somewhat stronger than it would have been if it had been contained in a normal JIC assessment. Although this possibility cannot be completely ruled out, I am satisfied that Mr Scarlett, the other members of the JIC, and the members of the assessment staff engaged in the drafting of the dossier were concerned to ensure that the contents of the dossier were consistent with the intelligence available to the JIC.

(viii) The term "sexed-up" is a slang expression, the meaning of which lacks clarity in the context of the discussion of the dossier. It is capable of two different meanings. It could mean that the dossier was embellished with items of intelligence known or believed to be false or unreliable to make the case against Saddam Hussein stronger, or it could mean that whilst the intelligence contained in the dossier was believed to be reliable, the dossier was drafted in such a way as to make the case against Saddam Hussein as strong as the intelligence contained in it permitted. If the term is used in this latter sense, then because of the drafting suggestions made by 10 Downing Street for the purpose of making a strong case against Saddam Hussein, it could be said that the Government "sexed-up" the dossier. However in the context of the broadcasts in which the "sexing-up" allegation was reported and having regard to the other allegations reported in those broadcasts, I consider that the allegation was unfounded as it would have been understood by those who heard the broadcasts to mean that the dossier had been embellished with intelligence known or believed to be false or unreliable, which was not the case.

(2) On the issues relating to Dr Kelly's meeting with Mr Andrew Gilligan in the Charing Cross Hotel on 22 May 2003 my conclusions are as follows:

(i) In the light of the uncertainties arising from Mr Gilligan's evidence and the existence of two versions of his notes made on his personal organiser of his discussion with Dr Kelly on 22 May it is not possible to reach a definite conclusion as to what Dr Kelly said to Mr Gilligan. It may be that Dr Kelly said to Mr Gilligan that Mr Campbell was responsible for transforming the dossier, and it may be that when Mr Gilligan suggested to Dr Kelly that the dossier was transformed to make it "sexier", Dr Kelly agreed with this suggestion. However I am satisfied that Dr Kelly did not say to Mr Gilligan that the Government probably knew or suspected that the 45 minutes claim was wrong before that claim was inserted in the dossier. I am further satisfied that Dr Kelly did not say to Mr Gilligan that the reason why the 45 minutes claim was not included in the original draft of the dossier was because it only came from one source and the intelligence agencies did not really believe it was necessarily true. In the course of his evidence, which I have set out in paragraphs 244, 245 and 246, Mr Gilligan accepted that he had made errors in his broadcasts in the Today programme on 29 May 2003. The reality was that the 45 minutes claim was based on an intelligence report which the SIS believed to be reliable and the 45 minutes claim was inserted in the dossier with the approval of the JIC, the most senior body in the United Kingdom responsible for the assessment of intelligence. In addition the reason why the 45 minutes claim was not inserted in the first draft of the dossier was because the intelligence on which it was based was not received by the SIS in London until 29 August 2002. Therefore the allegations reported by Mr Gilligan that the Government probably knew that the 45 minutes claim was wrong or questionable and that it was not inserted in the first draft of the dossier because it only came from one source and the intelligence agencies did not really believe it was necessarily true, were unfounded.

(ii) Dr Kelly's meeting with Mr Gilligan was unauthorised and in meeting Mr Gilligan and discussing intelligence matters with him, Dr Kelly was acting in breach of the Civil Service code of procedure which applied to him.

(iii) It may be that when he met Mr Gilligan, Dr Kelly said more to him than he had intended to say and that at the time of the meeting he did not realise the gravity of the situation which he was helping to create by discussing intelligence matters with Mr Gilligan. But whatever Dr Kelly thought at the time of his meeting with Mr Gilligan, it is clear that after Mr Gilligan's broadcasts on 29 May Dr Kelly must have come to realise the gravity of the situation for which he was partly responsible by commenting on intelligence matters to him and he accepted that the meeting was unauthorised, as he acknowledged in a telephone conversation with his friend and colleague Ms Olivia Bosch after his meeting with Mr Gilligan.

(3) On the issues relating to the BBC arising from Mr Gilligan's broadcasts on the BBC Today programme on 29 May 2003 my conclusions are as follows:

(i) The allegations reported by Mr Gilligan on the BBC Today programme on 29 May 2003 that the Government probably knew that the 45 minutes claim was wrong or questionable before the dossier was published and that it was not inserted in the first draft of the dossier because it only came from one source and the intelligence agencies did not really believe it was necessarily true, were unfounded.

(ii) The communication by the media of information (including information obtained by investigative reporters) on matters of public interest and importance is a vital part of life in a democratic society. However the right to communicate such information is subject to the qualification (which itself exists for the benefit of a democratic society) that false accusations of fact impugning the integrity of others, including politicians, should not be made by the media. Where a reporter is intending to broadcast or publish information impugning the integrity of others the management of his broadcasting company or newspaper should ensure that a system is in place whereby his editor or editors give careful consideration to the wording of the report and to whether it is right in all the circumstances to broadcast or publish it. The allegations that Mr Gilligan was intending to broadcast in respect of the Government and the preparation of the dossier were very grave allegations in relation to a subject of great importance and I consider that the editorial system which the BBC permitted was defective in that Mr Gilligan was allowed to broadcast his report at 6.07am without editors having seen a script of what he was going to say and having considered whether it should be approved.

(iii) The BBC management was at fault in the following respects in failing to investigate properly the Government's complaints that the report in the 6.07am broadcast was false that the Government probably knew that the 45 minutes claim was wrong even before it decided to put it in the dossier. The BBC management failed, before Mr Sambrook wrote his letter of 27 June 2003 to Mr Campbell, to make an examination of Mr Gilligan's notes on his personal organiser of his meeting with Dr Kelly to see if they supported the allegations which he had made in his broadcast at 6.07am. When the BBC management did look at Mr Gilligan's notes after 27 June it failed to appreciate that the notes did not fully support the most serious of the allegations which he had reported in the 6.07am broadcast, and it therefore failed to draw the attention of the Governors to the lack of support in the notes for the most serious of the allegations.

(iv) The e-mail sent by Mr Kevin Marsh, the editor of the Today programme on 27 June 2003 to Mr Stephen Mitchell, the Head of Radio News, which was critical of Mr Gilligan's method of reporting, and which referred to Mr Gilligan's "loose use of language and lack of judgment in some of his phraseology" and referred also to "the loose and in some ways distant relationship he's been allowed to have with Today," was clearly relevant to the complaints which the Government was making about his broadcasts on 29 May, and the lack of knowledge on the part of Mr Sambrook, the Director of News, and the Governors of this critical e-mail shows a defect in the operation of the BBC's management system for the consideration of complaints in respect of broadcasts.

(v) The Governors were right to take the view that it was their duty to protect the independence of the BBC against attacks by the Government and Mr Campbell's complaints were being expressed in exceptionally strong terms which raised very considerably the temperature of the dispute between the Government and the BBC. However Mr Campbell's allegation that the BBC had an anti-war agenda in his evidence to the FAC was only one part of his evidence. The Government's concern about Mr Gilligan's broadcasts on 29 May was a separate issue about which specific complaints had been made by the Government. Therefore the Governors should have recognised more fully than they did that their duty to protect the independence of the BBC was not incompatible with giving proper consideration to whether there was validity in the Government's complaints, no matter how strongly worded by Mr Campbell, that the allegations against its integrity reported in Mr Gilligan's broadcasts were unfounded and the Governors failed to give this issue proper consideration. The view taken by the Governors, as explained in evidence by Mr Gavyn Davies, the Chairman of the Board of Governors, that they had to rely on the BBC management to investigate and assess whether Mr Gilligan's source was reliable and credible and that it was not for them as Governors to investigate whether the allegations reported were themselves accurate, is a view which is understandable. However this was not the correct view for the Governors to take because the Government had stated to the BBC in clear terms, as had Mr Campbell to the FAC, that the report that the Government probably knew that the 45 minutes claim was wrong was untruthful, and this denial was made with the authority of the Prime Minister and the Chairman of the JIC. In those circumstances, rather than relying on the assurances of BBC management, I consider that the Governors themselves should have made more detailed investigations into the extent to which Mr Gilligan's notes supported his report. If they had done this they would probably have discovered that the notes did not support the allegation that the Government knew that the 45 minutes claim was probably wrong, and the Governors should then have questioned whether it was right for the BBC to maintain that it was in the public interest to broadcast that allegation in Mr Gilligan's report and to rely on Mr Gilligan's assurances that his report was accurate. Therefore in the very unusual and specific circumstances relating to Mr Gilligan's broadcasts, the Governors are to be criticised for themselves failing to make more detailed investigations into whether this allegation reported by Mr Gilligan was properly supported by his notes and for failing to give proper and adequate consideration to whether the BBC should publicly acknowledge that this very grave allegation should not have been broadcast.

(4)(A) On the issue whether the Government behaved in a way which was dishonourable or underhand or duplicitous in revealing Dr Kelly's name to the media my conclusions are as follows:

(i) There was no dishonourable or underhand or duplicitous strategy by the Government covertly to leak Dr Kelly's name to the media. If the bare details of the MoD statement dated 8 July 2003, the changing drafts of the Q and A material prepared in the MoD, and the lobby briefings by the Prime Minister's official spokesman on 9 July are looked at in isolation from the surrounding circumstances it would be possible to infer, as some commentators have done, that there was an underhand strategy by the Government to leak Dr Kelly's name in a covert way. However having heard a large volume of evidence on this issue I have concluded that there was no such strategy on the part of the Government. I consider that in the midst of a major controversy relating to Mr Gilligan's broadcasts which had contained very grave allegations against the integrity of the Government and fearing that Dr Kelly's name as the source for those broadcasts would be disclosed by the media at any time, the Government's main concern was that it would be charged with a serious cover up if it did not reveal that a civil servant had come forward. I consider that the evidence of Mr Donald Anderson MP and Mr Andrew Mackinlay MP, the Chairman and a member respectively of the FAC, together with the questions put by Sir John Stanley MP to Dr Kelly when he appeared before the FAC, clearly show that the Government's concern was well founded. Therefore I consider that the Government did not behave in a dishonourable or underhand or duplicitous way in issuing on 8 July 2003, after it had been read over to Dr Kelly and he had said that he was content with it, a statement which said that a civil servant, who was not named, had come forward to volunteer that he had met Mr Gilligan on 22 May.

(ii) The decision by the MoD to confirm Dr Kelly's name if, after the statement had been issued, the correct name were put to the MoD by a reporter, was not part of a covert strategy to leak his name, but was based on the view that in a matter of such intense public and media interest it would not be sensible to try to conceal the name when the MoD thought that the press were bound to discover the correct name, and a further consideration in the mind of the MoD was that it did not think it right that media speculation should focus, wrongly, on other civil servants.

(iii) It was reasonable for the Government to take the view that, even if it sought to keep confidential the fact that Dr Kelly had come forward, the controversy surrounding Mr Gilligan's broadcasts was so great and the level of media interest was so intense that Dr Kelly's name as Mr Gilligan's source was bound to become known to the public and that it was not a practical possibility to keep his name secret.

(4)(B) On the issue whether the Government failed to take proper steps to help and protect Dr Kelly in the difficult position in which he found himself my conclusion is as follows:

(i) Once the decision had been taken on 8 July to issue the statement, the MoD was at fault and is to be criticised for not informing Dr Kelly that its press office would confirm his name if a journalist suggested it. Although I am satisfied that Dr Kelly realised, once the MoD statement had been issued on Tuesday 8 July, that his name would come out, it must have been a great shock and very upsetting for him to have been told in a brief telephone call from his line manager, Dr Wells, on the evening of 9 July that the press office of his own department had confirmed his name to the press and must have given rise to a feeling that he had been badly let down by his employer. I further consider that the MoD was at fault in not having set up a procedure whereby Dr Kelly would be informed immediately his name had been confirmed to the press and in permitting a period of one and a half hours to elapse between the confirmation of his name to the press and information being given to Dr Kelly that his name had been confirmed to the press. However these criticisms are subject to the mitigating circumstances that (1) Dr Kelly's exposure to press attention and intrusion, whilst obviously very stressful, was only one of the factors placing him under great stress; (2) individual officials in the MoD did try to help and support him in the ways which I have described in paragraphs 430 and 431; and (3) because of his intensely private nature, Dr Kelly was not an easy man to help or to whom to give advice.

(5) On the issue of the factors which may have led Dr Kelly to take his own life I adopt as my own conclusion the opinion which Professor Hawton, the Professor of Psychiatry at Oxford University, expressed in the course of his evidence:

Q. Have you considered, now, with the benefit of hindsight that we all have, what factors did contribute to Dr Kelly's death?

A. I think that as far as one can deduce, the major factor was the severe loss of self esteem, resulting from his feeling that people had lost trust in him and from his dismay at being exposed to the media.

Q. And why have you singled that out as a major factor?

A. Well, he talked a lot about it; and I think being such a private man, I think this was anathema to him to be exposed, you know, publicly in this way. In a sense, I think he would have seen it as being publicly disgraced.

Q. What other factors do you think were relevant?

A. Well, I think that carrying on that theme, I think that he must have begun – he is likely to have begun to think that, first of all, the prospects for continuing in his previous work role were diminishing very markedly and, indeed, my conjecture that he had begun to fear he would lose his job altogether.

Q. What effect is that likely to have had on him?

A. Well, I think that would have filled him with a profound sense of hopelessness; and that, in a sense, his life's work had been not wasted but that had been totally undermined.

LORD HUTTON: Could you just elaborate a little on that, Professor, again? As sometimes is the case in this Inquiry, witnesses give answers and further explanation is obvious, but nonetheless I think it is helpful just to have matters fully spelt out. What do you think would have caused Dr Kelly to think that the prospects of continuing in his work were becoming uncertain?

A. Well, I think, my Lord, that first of all, there had been the letter from Mr Hatfield which had laid out the difficulties that Dr Kelly, you know, is alleged to have got into.

LORD HUTTON: Yes.

A. And in that letter there was also talk that should further matters come to light then disciplinary proceedings would need to be instigated.

LORD HUTTON: Yes.

A. And then of course there were the Parliamentary Questions which we have heard about, which suggested that questions were going to be asked about discipline in Parliament.

LORD HUTTON: Yes. Thank you.

MR DINGEMANS: Were there any other relevant factors?

A. I think the fact that he could not share his problems and feelings with other people, and the fact that he, according to the accounts I have been given, actually increasingly withdrew into himself. So in a sense he was getting further and further from being able to share the problems with other people, that is extremely important.

Q. Were there any other factors which you considered relevant?

A. Those are the main factors that I consider relevant.

CHAPTER 13

Final observations

468. I wish to record my gratitude and thanks to Mrs Kelly and her daughters for the great assistance which they have given to the Inquiry in a time of great sorrow and stress for them.

469. The work of the Inquiry was greatly assisted by its counsel, Mr James Dingemans QC and Mr Peter Knox, and by its solicitor, Mr Martin Smith, and I am very indebted to them. It is a tribute to their skill and industry that after the announcement of the establishment of the Inquiry on 18 July 2003 their preparation and analysis of the very large volume of written material received by the Inquiry enabled 74 witnesses to be examined between 11 August and 24 September (evidence being taken from one witness, who had been ill, on 13 October). I am also very indebted to counsel and solicitors who appeared for those parties to whom leave was given to be represented; their well prepared examination and cross-examination of witnesses and their final statements were of great assistance to me in coming to my conclusions. I also wish to thank the Government and the BBC and the other parties and their legal advisers for the very large volume of documents which were provided to the Inquiry and which cast much light on the decisions and actions taken during the relevant periods.

470. I was greatly assisted in conducting the Inquiry by the very thorough investigations which had been carried out by the Thames Valley Police into the circumstances surrounding Dr Kelly's death and I was very fortunate to have had the benefit of the assistance of Assistant Chief Constable Michael Page and Detective Chief Inspector Alan Young.

471. I also wish to record the admiration and appreciation I feel for the excellent and dedicated work of Mr Lee Hughes, the Secretary to the Inquiry, and the two other members of the administrative staff, Miss Helen Smith and Miss Vanessa Watling. The unfailing assistance which they have given me has been of inestimable value and I am most grateful to them. I also wish to express my admiration and appreciation for the immensely skilful work of Mrs Kathy Knox who has typed, with great care, the entirety of this lengthy report.

472. The circumstances leading up to Dr Kelly's death were wholly exceptional and I have decided that it is unnecessary for me to make any express recommendations because I have no doubt that the BBC and the Government will take note of the criticisms which I have made in this report.

473. Dr Kelly was a devoted husband and father and a public servant who served his country and the international community with great distinction both in the United Kingdom and in very difficult and testing conditions in Russia and Iraq. The evidence at this Inquiry has concentrated largely on the last two months of Dr Kelly's life, and therefore it is fitting that I should end this report with some words written in

Dr Kelly's obituary in The Independent on 31 July by Mr Terence Taylor, the President and Executive Director of the International Institute of Strategic Studies, Washington DC and a former colleague of Dr Kelly:

> "It is most important that the extraordinary public attention and political fallout arising from the events of the past month do not mask the extraordinary achievements of a scientist who loyally served not only his Government but also the international community at large."

Brian Hutton

28 January 2004

APPENDICES

APPENDIX 1

The Kelly Family

Jeremy Gompertz QC and Jason Beer, instructed by Bircham Dyson Bell

The Government

Jonathan Sumption QC, David Lloyd-Jones QC, Philip Sales, Robin Tam, James Maxwell-Scott and Kristina Stern instructed by the Treasury Solicitor

The BBC

Andrew Caldecott QC, Rupert Elliott, and Sarah Palin instructed by Sarah Jones, Head of Litigation at the BBC

Mr Andrew Gilligan

Heather Rogers instructed by Farrer & Co

The Authorities of the House of Commons

Nigel Pleming QC and Eleanor Grey, instructed by Mr John Vaux, Speaker's Counsel

Ms Susan Watts

Fiona Campbell, Solicitor Advocate of Finers Stephens Innocent

APPENDIX 2

NEWSREADER FIONA BRUCE

FB.   Tony Blair In Iraq pays tribute to British troops and defies critics of the war.

(CLIP OF TB SPEAKING IN IRAQ)

Here questions are asked about whether the government distorted intelligence reports to justify the war. Also tonight ...(HEADLINES)

(REPORT ON TB'S VISIT TO IRAQ)

FB.   Here, MPs are calling for an enquiry after accusations that the government's dossier on Iraq's weapons was distorted by Downing Street. Security sources have told the BBC they believe parts of the report overstated the threat posed by Saddam Hussein. Downing Street though has dismissed the claims. Our special correspondent Gavin Hewitt investigates.

GH   This is really a story about trust. it begins here at MI6, the headquarters of the intelligence service. Some of those who work here are said to be uneasy about what the government did with information they passed on about Iraq. There were claims today that when Downing Street received the dossier it wanted

BBC/1/0020

333

it toughened up. When it was eventually published it did contain some dramatic warnings.

TONY BLAIR

That he has existing and active military plans for the use of chemical and biological weapons, which could be activated within forty five minutes.

GH   The government acknowledged today that the forty five minute threat was based on a single source, it wasn't corroborated. This has rattled some MPs who are calling for an investigation.

MENZIES CAMPBELL MP

If you take intelligence and you massage it for political purposes, then essentially you turn it into propaganda. If these allegations are true, then there will be very considerable anxiety in all branches of the security services.

GH   The government said today that every word within the dossier was the work of the security services. There had been no pressure from Number 10.

BBC/1/0021

ADAM INGRAM

All of the information which the prime
minister, and others, including myself,
presented in the build up to this conflict was
based upon well informed information.

GH   But others with experience in the intelligence
community say there were some murmurings about
the final wording of a dossier. This is what
they think happened:

PAULINE NEVILLE-JONES

Professionals are cautious. They will only
have put things into it which they were really
confident about. I think probably that when it
got into the political part of the machine,
into the government information services, they
probably said to themselves, this won't
convince anybody because it doesn't come across
clearly enough, you know, we need actually to
beef up the language in a way so it carries
conviction.

GH   I have spoken to one of those who was consulted
on the dossier. Six months work was apparently
involved. But in the final week before
publication, some material was taken out, some
material put in. His judgement, some spin from

BBC/1/0022

Number Ten did come into play.   Even so the intelligence   community   remains   convinced weapons of mass destruction will be found in Iraq.   Only then will all the doubts go away. Gavin Hewitt, BBC News.

FB   Our political correspondent John Pienaar has been travelling with the prime minister. He's now in Poland's capital Warsaw for the start of a round of discussions with world leaders. John, Mr Blair we saw there in a very upbeat mood in Iraq. Is there any sign of concern about the fact that the weapons of mass destruction have still not been found, and now these allegations about overstating the threat posed by Iraq in the first place?

JP   I think it must be embarrassing to have such a fundamental justification for the war in Iraq called into question continually like this. And there's no denying that that case, that justification, has been rather rescripted by Mr Blair, just as it has been by political leaders in Washington. Now all the emphasis as we saw in Jeremy's report today, was on the liberation of an oppressed people, was on bringing stability to the region. The absence of those

BBC/1/0023

weapons of mass destruction in the speech was a glaring omission. And meanwhile politically those who are most critical of the war in the first place, and plenty of others besides are now beginning to find their voices again.

FB   And John, that statement were saw from Mr Blair there about the war being seen as one of the defining moments of the century, it's quite ambitious given it's only 2003. What did he mean by that?

JP   Well it was quite, quite a statement, not the sort of thing you just casually drop into, into conversation. And what Tony Blair meant by that was that the war had shown that it was possible for armed intervention to, to end in good. That it was possible to give some stimulus to the Middle East peace process, but the diplomatic wounds are still fresh, and all the diplomacy of which this is a part, he goes onto Russia and then France can only just make a start in healing those wounds at best.

FB   John, thanks very much.

OTHER NEWS

APPENDIX 3

Telephone rings...
DK: "David Kelly"

SW: Hi David It's susan here

DK: Oh hi! I've just left you a voicemail

SW: Yes I just picked that up...just relaxing after a week of doing GM crops
(laugh)

I was hoping I wouldn't have to cover that story much again after the previous round ...but it's all come up again with the national debate stuff next week - so there we are...ummm...so you've been in New York?

DK: Yes it was the UNMOVIC's commissioners meeting – it was Blix' farewell one so ...(SW: oh of course) xxx (make sure) no one said anything controversial, I think

DK: Of course he gives his presentation to the security council next week on his report

SW: aah right which day is that?

DK: err it's not yet been fixed – but it'll be one day next week

SW: right, and what's that likely to contain - anything interesting or...?

DK : it's actually a factual account of the inspections that they undertook, it's padded out with all sorts of discussions,...well I shouldn't say padded out, with all sorts of statistical stuff that is in there ...it's pretty comp ..it's not controversial – at least in my eyes it's not controversial...but it does comment on the mobile labs, it does comment on some of the finds that they have and the destruction of the arms xx)

SW: OK, um While I'm sure since you've been in New York I don't know whether you've been following the kind of the rumpus that's erupted over here over the ...spat between the intelligence service and the umm..

DK: I guessed something was up – I read the Times this am and I could see there was something there and I think this follows on from what was happening in the states with Rumsfeld's comments

SW: yes it's partly prompted by Rumsfeld – two statements by Rumsfeld – the first one saying that it was "possible" the weapons were destroyed before the war started and then he went on I think in another speech yesterday to say that the use of the argument on the position on WMD was for bureaucratic reasons rather than being the prime motive for the war, which is a rather vague statement

DK: yes

SW: But what intrigued me and which made, prompted me to ring you, (huh) was the quotes yesterday on the Today programme about the 45 minutes part of the dossier

DK: yep. We spoke about this before of course...

SW: We have

DK: I think you know my views on that.

SW: Yes, I've looked back at my notes and you were actually quite specific at that time – I may have missed a trick on that one, but err

(both laugh)

SW: you were more specific than the source on the Today programme – not that that necessarily means that it's not one and the same person…but, um in fact you actually referred to Alastair Campbell in that conversation…

DK: err yep yep …with you?…
SW: yes

DK: I mean I did talk to Gavin Hewitt yesterday – he phoned me in New York, so he may have picked up on what I said…because I would have said exactly the same as I said to you…

SW: Yes, so he presumably decided not to name Alastair Campbell himself but just to label this as Number 10…

DK: yep yep

SW: are you getting much flak over that?

DK: me? No, not yet anyway I was in New York..(laughs)

SW: yes good timing I suppose

DK: I mean they wouldn't think it was me, I don't think. Maybe they would, maybe they wouldn't. I don't know.

SW: um so is that the only item in the report that you had concerns over being single-sourced rather than double -sourced? .

DK: You have to remember I'm not part of the intelligence community – I'm a user of intelligence…of course I'm very familiar with a lot of it, that's why I'm asked to comment on it…but I'm not deeply embedded into that …xxx…So some of it I really can't comment because I don't know whether it's single-sourced or not

SW: but on the 45 minutes

DK: oh that I knew because I knew the concern about the statement …it was a statement that was made and it just got out of all proportion …you know someone…They were desperate for information. ..they were pushing hard for information which could be released …that was one that popped up and it was seized on…and it was unfortunate that it was…which is why there is the argument between the intelligence services and cabinet office/number ten, because things were picked up on, and once they've picked up on it you can't pull it back, that's the problem…

SW: but it was against your advice that they should publish it?

DK: I wouldn't go as strongly as to say …that particular bit , because I was not involved in the assessment of it…no…I can't say that it was against MY advice…I was uneasy with it…I mean my problem was I could give other explanations…which I've indicated to you…that it was the time to erect something like a scud missile or it was the time to fill a 40 barrel, multi-barrel rocket launcher

…(Next 5 words physically removed from tape…not present on Monday 14/7/03…assume due to rubbing as tape constantly re-wound)

…("all sorts of reasons why") 45 minutes might well be important and… I mean I have no idea who de-briefed this guy quite often it's someone who has no idea of the topic and the information comes through and people then use it as they see fit…

SJW|1|0039

340

SW: so it wasn't as if there were lots of people saying don't put it in don't put it in...it's just it was in there and was seized upon ...rather than number ten specifically going against...?

DK: ...there were lots of people saying that – I mean it was an interesting week before the dossier was put out because there were so many things in there that people were saying well...we're not so sure about that, or in fact they were happy with it being in but not expressed the way that it was, because you know the word-smithing is actually quite important, and the intelligence community are a pretty cautious lot on the whole but once you get people putting it/presenting it for public consumption then of course they use different words. I don't think they're being wilfully dishonest I think they just think that that's the way the public will appreciate it best. I'm sure you have the same problem as a journalist don't you, sometimes you've got to put things into words that the public will understand.

SW: simple

DK: in your heart of hearts you must realise sometimes that's not actually the right thing to say...but it's the only way you can put it over if you've got to get it over in two minutes or three minutes

SW: did you actually write that section which refers to the 45 minutes Or was it somebody else?

DK: errr. I didn't write THAT section, no. I mean I reviewed the whole thing, I was involved with the whole process... In the end it was just a flurry of activity and it was very difficult to get comments in because people at the top of the ladder didn't want to hear some of the things

SW: so you expressed your unease about it? Put it that way

DK: errr well...yes yep yes

SW: so how do you feel now number ten is furiously denying it and Alastair Campbell specifically saying it's all nonsense it was all in the intelligence material?

DK: well I think it's matter of perception isn't it. I think people will perceive things and they'll be, how shall I put it, they'll see it from their own standpoint and they may not even appreciate quite what they were doing

SW: do you think there ought to be a security and intelligence committee inquiry?

DK: yes but not now. I think that has to be done in about six months time when we actually have come to the end of the evaluation of Iraq and the information that is going to come out of it . I still think it's far too early to be talking about the intelligence that is there... a lot of intelligence that would appear to be good quality intelligence , some of which is not and it take a long long time to get the information that's required from Iraq. The process has only just started. I think one of the problems with the dossier – and again I think you and I have talked about it in the past is that it was presented in a very black and white way without any sort of quantitative aspects of it. The only quantitative aspects were the figures derived essentially from UNSCOM figures, which in turn are Iraq's figures presented to UNSCOM – you know the xxx litres anthrax, the 4 tonnes VX – all of that actually is Iraqi figures – but there was nothing else in there that was quantitative or even remotely qualitative – I mean it was just a black and white thing – they have weapons or they don't have weapons. That in turn has been interpreted as being a vast arsenal and I'm not sure any of us ever said that ...people have said to me that that was what was implied, Again we discussed it...and I discussed it with many people, that my own perception is that yes they have weapons but actually not xzxxx (xxx not problem) at this point in time. The PROBLEM was that one could anticipate that without any form of inspection, and that forms a real deterrence, other than the sanctions side of things, then that that would develop. I think that was the real concern that everyone had, it was not so much what they have now but what they would have in the future. But that unfortunately wasn't expressed strongly in the dossier because that takes away the case for war...(I cough) to a certain extent

SW: a clear and present, imminent threat?
DK: yes

SJW/1/0040

SW: yes...so did you pick up anything in NY last week as to whether you'll be going back in or the chances of UNMOVIC going back in?

DK: yes...remember I don't wear a blue hat anymore...I mean I go out to advise them, but I don't wear a blue hat..

SW: you were hoping you might get involved in some of the interviewing process

DK: yes hopeful but it hasn't happened yet...and the reason for that is of course these guys aren't talking and there's actually not a lot of point in me discussing things if they are actually saying no. Once they start opening up, that's the time (to go back)

SW: what's likely to make them start opening up though – do we need to get to the stage of talking about war trials? Or is that only going to make things worse

DK: well I think there has to be a whole selection of tools so to speak, depending on who the individual is... there will be some individuals where I suspect there's no option but for them to face up to the fact that they are going to be tried...one hopes it's going to be an Iraqi court eventually , but it may be another court and there will be others who will naturally hope that that's not going to happen to them and they get reassurances that won't happen...some form of custody. Who can actually provide that custody ...I don't know – can't be just the US or the UK. So I really don't know, and then of course there are all sorts of other incentives...I mean financial incentives. I gather US has said the arrangement that they have that they will give financial support to people who come forward which is fine, but if no security for those guys...(because there's no govt) ...there are forces that are against the US who are Saddam loyalists – they maybe , maybe not ...and they face retribution afterwards ...it's actually quite a complex situation... sorry I'm really talking about those who haven't surrendered or they're just talking and want to surrender...

SW: ok..just back momentarily on the 45 minute issue...I'm feeling like I ought to just explore that a little bit more with you...the um..err So would it be accurate then, as you did in that earlier conversation, to say that it was Alastair Campbell himself who...?

DK: No I can't. All I can say is the Number Ten press office. I've never met Alastair Campbell so I cant...(SW interrupts: they seized on that ?) But... I think Alastair Campbell is synonymous with that press office because he's responsible for it.

SW: yeah..hmmm..right ok, and now that we know that the IAEA inspectors are going back in do you feel any more optimistic that the replacement for Blix will lead a team back in?

DK: well the IAEA inspectors are going to do one thing...not going back in to do
SW: a proper job?

DK: yep – they're can't do the job that they did before – they'll go in – they'll check on the distribution of looted radioactive materials - evaluate the hazards associated with that. And make recommendations about how that can be dealt with – they may have a role in supervising that but I don't think much beyond that

SW right, so you don't feel optimistic then?

DK: well I think that eventually the UN is going to have a role to play in this, but I think the difficulty is how does the UN engage with the coalition forces – there has to be a process – they can't both do the same job. I think it's going to be very difficult for them to work in harmony together, because of the anymosity between the UN and the US, both as institutions, and between people who are involved. There's tremendous....in UNSCOM possibly UNMOVIC - there's tremendous anti-US feeling. That they were pulled out and they were doing their job and that if they had continued to do their job they would have solved the problem. That may not be the case but they actually think that. And so they are very resentful of the US. ....xxxx I think you know...

SJW|1|0041

...we've seen on the mobile labs the POLITICS of that is so STRONG that it deflects all practical objectivity .

SW: Has your assessment of whether that, of how important that is changed - I think was 90 and went down to 45% ?

DK: In terms of its likelihood of being a fermentor?...it's still down in 40s

SW: Really? It's still that low?

DK: oh yes

SW: Is that still because you don't have the right information

DK: Well I have more than I did before, but I still don't have the right information so until this team reports back and I'm unsighted as to whether they've actually finished their job because I've been in NY ... as you know there's team in at the moment - .until they come back and actually give their data I think it's actually quite difficult to make that determination ...but whatever it is it's certainly a very unusual fermentor.

SW: so where do you stand on the Rumsfeld point about the possibility of the weapons having been destroyed before the war started?

DK: Well it is a possibility. I find it difficult to comment I mean it is a possibility that that's the case...ummm...It may be that they had such a small arsenal that they determined that it wouldn't be militarily effective and therefore it would provide the embarrassment that's required to embarrass the coalition – I'm not sure, I mean it's such a trivial thing, that I can't see that being the case, but it's very difficult to rationalise why they would be destroyed when they worked so hard for years to conceal xxx capable

SW: Although I suppose there's some evidence that Saddam was a fairly strategic thinker so if he decided that this was IT. That he'd rather history record that he had nothing....

DK: yes yes

SW: that's the only way you can make any sense out of it...

DK: I think a lot is going to come out . it's one thing to be talking about hardware – which is what people are concerned about. But I think it's actually going to either come out of individuals, if they choose to talk, or it will come out of documentation...xxx might lead to incriminating evidence – there will be something somewhere in Saddam's documents that indicate (interrupt) ...destroyed

SW: Sorry that indicate it WAS destroyed?

DK: No unless those documents have been destroyed (SW: oh themselves) I'm not sure at the highest level what they did in terms of keeping multiple copies of things ...but certainly lower down the chain Iraq was so bureaucratic you could virtually guarantee there would be 6 copies of something. But at the highest level I just have no idea.

SW: good ok...well un. So are you around next week or are you off?

DK: am I around next week? I'm going back to the states ...I'm around but I expect to be more away than I am in the country, put it that way, but my days seem to change/ my plans seem to change daily

SW: ok, well if we suddenly have a surprise in the Blix document I'll perhaps ring you, but you're not anticipating that?

DK: I'm not, but you think differently to me so you might find there's a surprise there, I don't know ...(laughs) I'm certainly around Mon, Tues, Weds that's for sure...

SJW/1/0042

SW: right ok

DK: I'm in London Mon /Tues – probably my mobile will be on

SW: ok I'll pester you if I need to but I'll avoid doing that if I don't

DK: Call me in the evenings that's no problem if you have to do that ...in the day – because I tend to be in the MoD or the Foreign Office that's not convenient

SW: no, ok , good ok well many thanks again and I'll talk to you soon

DK: Are you doing anything for NN?

SW: at the moment I've been mainly concentrating on GM crops...but NN has been doing pieces that last 2 or 3 nights on the Rumsfeld situation and I've been feeding things in or pointing people in...the CIA report on the mobile labs came out yesterday and I made sure that was fed into the process..

DK: That was a funny report to me it looked like it had just been pushed out at a whim...overnight

SW: well yes that would be interesting to coincide with what Rumsfeld said

DK: Well if you look at it it's not well edited ...the same thing is said in different paragraphs – there's been some cutting and pasting going on and things have got left around the place.

SW: It was odd because was put on the site – wasn't announced was put on the site CIA site for 7 hours which is kind of weird if you want to draw peoples attention to it...I don't know. It was all very odd...but it might be that come Tues when the commons is back, and Blair is going to be under pressure to make a statement or hold a debate or something on this whole question I may be put back onto it again...so we'll see

DK: yep, ok

SW: it kind of varies between me and the general reporters (DK laughs) depending on what I'm up to.

SW: Ok well thanks again – thanks for calling back David...and I'll keep in touch...ok cheers...

DK: OK, thanks bye

ringing tone

APPENDIX 4

PRESS STATEMENT

An individual working in the MOD has volunteered that he met with Andrew Gilligan on 22 May to discuss Iraq in general. This was one week before Gilligan's story claiming that the Iraq dossier was "sexed up". The account of the meeting given by this official does not match the account given by Gilligan of his "single source".

This was an unauthorised contact which is being dealt with appropriately by line management.

There is no reason to suspect that a breach of security is involved.

CAB/1/0013

APPENDIX 5

PRODUCED ON BEHALF OF T.T.US

Q&A

Who is the official?
We are not prepared to name the individual involved.

Why not?
We have released all the relevant details. There is nothing to gain by revealing the name of the individual who has come forward voluntarily.

Can we interview the individual?
No.

Is it a senior figure?
It is not a member of the SCS
(steer – a middle-ranking official)

Where did they meet?
The meeting was in London. I do not have details of the specific location.

Why has the official come forward now?
Only when the official read Mr Gilligan's evidence to the FAC did it occur to him that his conversation with Mr Gilligan might be relevant.

In what form did this official 'confess'?
The official approached his line manager which is standard procedure for raising concerns.

What in Mr Gilligan's evidence made the official think this conversation relevant?
As we have said, Mr Gilligan's account does not match the account given my Mr Gilligan of his 'single source.' But the official felt that some elements of the conversation with Mr Gilligan's evidence may have been linked to his conversation which was why he came forward.

If the story does get legs we will get pushed very hard on the detail of the conversation and the discrepancies.

Do you believe that your official is the 'single source?'
At this stage, we are not in a position to judge. This is a question only Mr Gilligan can answer.

Are you suggesting that Andrew Gilligan has deliberately 'sexed up' his story and twisted/exaggerated the information he received?
The MoD has drawn no conclusions and is not making any suggestions. We have simply given the facts. Only Mr Gilligan can know how he handled the information he received.

This is just spin – you've releasing this information in order to help clear the Government's name?
MoD did not break this story. We have today put out a statement in response to clarify speculation.

If/when the existence of the letter is leaked: Have you published the whole letter and if not, will you?
No. The substance of the issue is contained in our statement. We have nothing to add.
If pushed: a further consideration is that the account names of various people who have nothing to do with the story but our involved in the work of the individual including other journalists with whom the individual has had contact.

The letter was written on 30 June. Why did it take a week to deal with?
The letter was put in the in-tray (true?) of the individual's line manager which is standard procedure for raising concerns. When the line manager had read the letter he informed the Personnel Director who immediately organised an interview with the individual to establish the facts and informed the PUS.

CAB/10/0003

If needed:

The Personnel Director was informed on ?? PUS was informed on Thursday afternoon and the interview conducted on Friday morning.

When was SofS informed?

PUS informed SofS of the issue on Thursday evening and told him that the individual would be interviewed the following day to establish the facts.

Did SofS see the letter?

No. SofS was informed of the substance of the letter and told that an interview had been organised to check the facts.   He was then briefed on the outcome of the interview.

If pressed for detail of exactly who knew what and when:
Chronology?

Has Alastair Campbell/No10 seen the letter?

The relevant Government departments have been informed, including No10.

When were No10 informed?

Why are you not taking disciplinary action?
??

How can you be sure that there has been no breach of the Official Secrets ACt?

There is no evidence to suggest that a breach of the OSA has occurred -- the individual did come forward voluntarily.

21

CAB/~~240~~/0004

SENT TO RUS OFFICE AT 08.07 ON TUESDAY 8 JULY SUBJECT TO DISCUSSION AND APPROVAL.

Q&A

Who is the official?
The official works within the MOD

What is the official's name and what post is currently held?

Why not?
We have released all the relevant details. There is nothing to gain
by revealing the name of the individual who has come forward
voluntarily.

Is it x (i.e. the wrong name)?
No

Is it x (i.e the correct name)?
If the correct name is put to us from a number of callers, we will
need to tell the individual we are going to confirm his name before
doing sp.

**It is most unusual for a Government Department to make a
statement of this sort. Why have you done this?**

Can we interview the individual?
No.

Did the official play any role in drawing up the dossier?

Is it a senior figure?
It is not a member of the SCS
(steer – a middle-ranking official)

Where did they meet?
The meeting was in a London hotel. I do not have details of the
specific location.

In what form did this official 'confess'?
The official approached the line manager which is standard
procedure for raising concerns.

21
CAB/260/0005

Why has the official come forward now?
The official has indicated that it follows from recently reading Mr
Gilligan's FAC evidence.

**What in Mr Gilligan's evidence made the official think this
conversation relevant?**
The official felt that a number of elements of the conversation had
with Mr Gilligan were consistent with Mr Gilligan's evidence to the
FAC when describing his conversation with his single source.

Do you believe that your official is the 'single source?'
See statement

**Are you suggesting that Andrew Gilligan has deliberately
'sexed up' his story and twisted/exaggerated the information
he received?**
See statement

**This is just spin – you've releasing this information in order to
help clear the Government's name?**
The official volunteered this information

**If/when the existence of the memo (official to line manager) is
leaked: Have you published the whole memo and if not, will
you?**
No. The substance of the issue is contained in our statement. We
have nothing to add.
If pushed: a further consideration is that the account names
various people who have nothing to do with the story.

**The memo was written on 30 June. Why did it take a week to
deal with?**
The memo was put in the in-tray (true?) of the individual's line
manager which is standard procedure for raising concerns. When
the line manager had read the memo, senior personnel were
informed, including the PUS.
If needed:
The PUS was informed on Thursday afternoon.

When was SofS informed?
PUS informed SofS of the issue on Thursday evening and told him
that the individual would be interviewed the following day to
establish the facts.

CAB | 21 | 0006

350

Did SofS see the memo?
No. SofS was informed of the substance of the memo and told
that an interview had been organised to check the facts.   He was
then briefed on the outcome of the interview.

If pressed for detail of exactly who knew what and when:
Chronology?

Has Alastair Campbell/No10 seen the memo?
The relevant Government departments, (i.e. Cabinet office, FCO)
including No10, were made aware of the substance.

When were No10 informed?

Why are you not taking disciplinary action?
??

**How can you be sure that there has been no breach of the
Official Secrets ACt?**
There is no evidence to suggest that a breach of the OSA has
occurred.

Have the FAC/ISC been informed?
?

Can they interview him?
?

Is the official still at work in MoD?

Yes

Is the official a career diplomat?

?

CAB/21/0007

Q & A

Who is the official?

The official works in MoD.

What is his name and current post?

We wouldn't normally volunteer a name

If the correct name is given, we can confirm it and say that he is senior advisor to the Proliferation and Arms Control Secretariat.

How long has he been in MOD?
He has been in his current position for 3 to 4 years. Before that he was a member of UNSCOM.

Did the official play any part in drawing up the dossier?

He was involved in providing historical details of UNSCOM's activities prior to 1998.

Is he a senior figure?

He is not a member of the SCS – he is a middle - ranking official.

Is he still working for MOD?

Yes

Is he in Iraq?

No, though he visited Iraq recently for a week.

Is he a member of the ISG?

No

Do you believe he is the single source?

It is not for us to say – only the BBC can confirm that.

MOD/1/0062

So he hasn't volunteered to being the source?

No. He volunteered that he met Mr Gilligan and discussed the
September dossier.

**It is unprecedented for a Government Department to make a
statement of this sort. Why have you done it?**

There is no comparable situation that springs to mind.
We have set out the facts as they have been put to us, on an issue
of considerable public concern. The official involved volunteered
the information to us.

Can we interview the individual?

No – this is not appropriate as the consequences will be dealt with
by MoD internally.

Will he be disciplined/sacked?

Appropriate management steps will be taken. On the basis of our
current understanding of the situation, he will not be sacked.

Where did he meet Mr Gilligan?

He says they met in the Charing Cross Hotel, central London.

In what form did this official come forward?

The official approached his line manager, which is the standard
procedure for raising concerns. He has also been interviewed by
the relevant members of senior staff.

Why has the official come forward now?

It followed his reading of the detailed evidence Mr Gilligan gave to
the FAC

**What was it in that evidence that made the official consider
that his conversation might be relevant?**

The official felt that a number of elements of the conversation he
had with Mr Gilligan were consistent with Mr Gilligan's evidence to

the FAC when describing his single source. Though a number were not. For details – see the statement.

Are you suggesting Mr Gilligan deliberately "sexed up" his story?

We are making no accusations. We are merely setting the information that has been put to us.

When did he come forward?

At the beginning of last week.

Why has it taken you a week to produce the information?

It was necessary to arrange for the official to be interviewed to establish, as far as we can, the details of his meeting with Gilligan.

When was he interviewed?

On Friday and Monday.

Which senior staff were informed?

The PUS was informed on Thursday. He informed the Secretary of State that evening.

When were No 10 told and if they were, why?

No 10 were told on Friday. It is only natural that they would be informed of a development on an issue of major concern.

Which other government departments were told?

As you would expect, Cabinet office and FCO.

Why did you not tell the FAC over the weekend?

A further interview was required and that took place on Monday afternoon.

What if the BBC deny he is the source?

We have not claimed he is – I refer you back to our statement

Can the FAC/ISC interview him?

We will be willing to consider any such request.

Were No 10 involved in this announcement?

The decision to issue a statement was made by the MoD.

How can you be sure that there has been no breach of the OSA?

On the basis of the information we have been given, there is no evidence to suggest a breach.

MOD/1/0065

APPENDIX 6

Gavin Hewitt

- Press Handling.   Para 70
- Colleagues.

M H / D K / C M + B W   14/vii

Purpose talk through. Not give CTI.

MH : / Explained FAC : by to Parliament. Public
ISC : Set up by PM. Rep to PM. si2.

DK : FAC. Clear up under H'com instruct^s cause free to ans.
ISC : interests : topic. ISC. Pass CV.
BW   - give statement - role
                                      + exp in Iraq.

MH: Colleagues.

MH: Role. Relationship with OCD / media. (eg)
Role on Dossier (DK - 1155. MH - S us expert) - (eg)
(ISC), Access to int. (eg)
(ISC) Access to 45 (eg)   why/the
Meeting with G. who when etc / Expand BW

BW : Possible.

MH : Factual / straight fd.
Tricky areas : Yr own views. Give own personal pt. (margins
                                          of (eg, but link to reports).

: What think of Gvt : Matter for Mins.
: RO Gilligan scene : Matter for BBC. Reply what I said.
  (can I say "I don't believe" MH : what you say is for you).
: Disapply act^ . "2 interviews, what effect is for MoD.

MOD/S/0031

JK: Nige MH: Can't count of GIJ.

MH: Contact with Sen W (Son of Newright). Do not sph about Dossier.

DK: Nil F.

MH/SW: Colley / News.

MOD/5/0032

DCDI.

areas to be covered

Foreign Affairs poli... ...ing committee → House.

IC   qos.   not parliamentary committee → PM   ... to ...

          access to intelligence

---

role + jobs sp

relationship to MOD FCO Dstl

relationship to Media.

Dossier   IISS Dossier

CSC   intelligence.

45 minute   did not see

Gilligan

Letter to Bryan

Tricky areas

1) views on Iraqi WMD

2) handling by Gov. matter [o minister]

3) Gilligan's source.   matter fo ... did not say... ...

4) disciplinary   ... interview... with senior intelligence

          ... consequences for MoD.

5) Nigo'

6) Susan Watts

TVP/2/0036

29th article

19th Gill ... FAC

26th possibly ...

30th Gill

TVP/2/0037

David Kelly

Senior Adviser PACS on CBW - Iraq

Background   Once head of microbiology Porton Down

                   ...led investigat... BW in Russia + Iraq

Iraq   Special Adviser to UNSCOM on bio weapons
               participated in many inspection - technical neutral

Contact... in contact with press this week.

Contact with Andrew Gilligan   3x

            answered questions

TVP/2/0038

361

Margaret

Sarah Parry.

~~Steve J~~ - PRD, David Bate
@dpa.mod.ok.

Sarah ~~~~

(SA?) April

Quarterly Performance Report

FAC — public session
— resp to Hse (rett to Minister)
ISC — Intelligence Cttee — appointed by PM
+ report to PM.
May base ? on — sessions in private
Government Statement.
FAC do not give guidance on questions

ISC — 1 minute statement — nk
— confers with purchase

FAC — don't want statement,
— asked for CV

role
Job spec
relationship with HCDC
~~~~ ~~~~ meetings — Moolatoonz

362

role with drawing up dossier

IISS dossier — first have met Gilligan's

day to day access to intelligence

access to 45 min intell. (—did w

acc of mtg with JG   — whon
                       — whent
                       — who set i

has long know JG   — nature of relat

circumstances of how twofold CM Rtns
                              — will
                              have
                              whon.

Status of DK.

Thday Areas   — ?s & answers only j wrd
                 what do you think Gilligan
                 cert for wear — [matter for
                                  Minister]

                 cert you sare? [Don't kn

Susan writes

BRITISH GOVERNMENT
BRIEFING PAPERS
ON
IRAQ

CAB/33/0005

CONTENTS

2

IRAQ

The Government has made clear its concern that Saddam Hussain previously developed and is still developing weapons of mass destruction and is ignoring UN Security Council Resolutions. We are also concerned at Saddam's continuing abuse of the human rights of the people of Iraq.

Saddam Hussain continues to claim that he has no chemical, biological or nuclear weapons, that the people of Iraq do not directly suffer under his leadership and he has not agreed to the return of UN weapons inspectors on UN terms. We are therefore taking this step of publishing this set of papers.

These papers show that Saddam Hussain has dangerous chemical and biological weapons and is still seeking to acquire nuclear weapons. These also shows the appalling human rights abuses the Iraqi people continue to suffer directly from Saddam Hussain.

Our concern is heightened by the knowledge that he may use these weapons – he has already used them against his own people and neighbours. This makes him unique among modern dictators: his threat is unique.

We are convinced that he will be prepared to use these weapons again against his neighbours and our friends and allies

Doing nothing is not an option.

The world is urging Saddam Hussain to comply with UN Security Council Resolutions (UNSCR) of which he is in breach, in line with UNSRC 1284 which demands that he agree to the return of UN weapons inspectors with full access to Iraq – **any time, any place, any where**.

No decision has been taken to launch military action. It is up to Saddam Hussain to show the world that he is serious about fulfilling Iraq's international and humanitarian obligations.

[Ministers to sign]

X.X. 2002

CAB/33/0007

EXECUTIVE SUMMARY

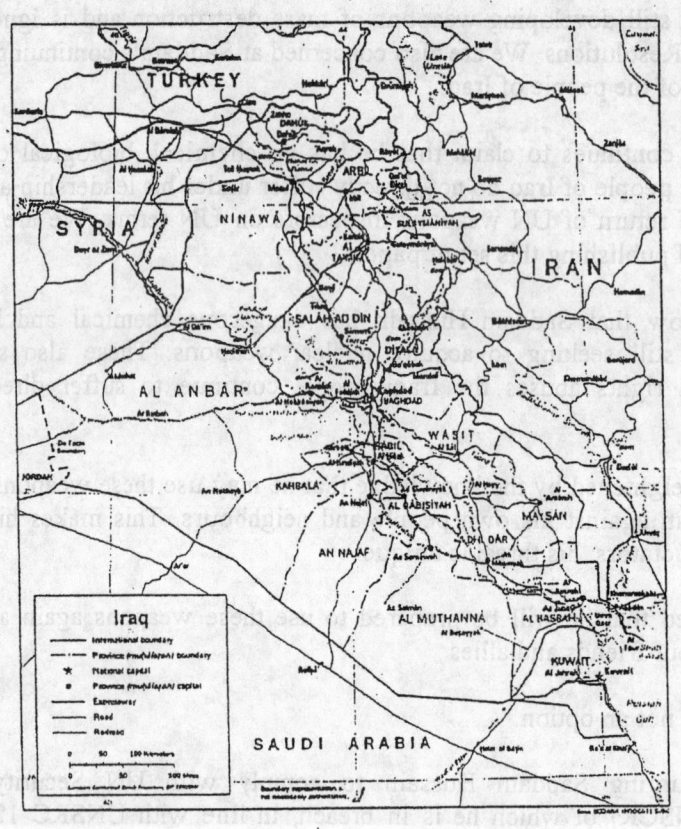

CAB/33/0008

IRAQI WMD PROGRAMMES

NUCLEAR WEAPONS:

Iraq has a nuclear weapons programme, **in breach of its NPT and IAEA obligations and of UNSCR 687**, but will find it difficult to produce fissile material while sanctions remain in place.

- Comprehensive programme prior to the Gulf War;
- Recalled scientists to work on a nuclear weapons programme;
- Covert efforts to procure nuclear related materials and technology.

CHEMICAL AND BIOLOGICAL WEAPONS:

Iraq has a capability to produce chemical and biological weapons **in breach of UNSCR 687.**

- The amount of chemical and biological material, including weapons and agents, left unaccounted for when the UNSCOM inspections terminated would provide a significant offensive capability;
- Produced and used proficiently a variety of chemical weapons in 1980s against Iran and its own citizens;
- Concealed large scale production of the nerve agent VX until discovered by UNSCOM;
- Produced and weaponised at least three BW agents but concealed this capability until forced to declare it in 1995;
- Failed to convince UNSCOM of the accuracy of its declarations.

BALLISTIC MISSILES:

Retains more than a dozen prohibited Al Hussain missiles (650km) **in breach of UNSCR 687**; working on designs for longer-range missiles **in breach of UNSCR 687**;

- Infrastructure damaged in the Gulf War and Operation Desert Fox has now largely been reconstituted;
- Infrastructure for longer-range missiles is under construction;
- UNSCOM unable to account for all imported missiles; others could have been built using hidden retained components.

CAB/33/0009

UN WEAPONS INSPECTIONS IN IRAQ

- UNSCR 687 fixed the terms of the cease-fire in the Gulf conflict following the illegal invasion and occupation of Kuwait by Iraq under Saddam Hussain.

- The history of UN weapons inspections in Iraq has been characterised by persistent Iraqi efforts to frustrate, deceive and intimidate inspectors.

- One of the greatest threats to Allied forces during Operation Desert Storm in 1991 was Iraq's stockpile of chemical and biological weapons and long-range ballistic missiles.

- UNSCOM and the IAEA were given the remit to designate **any locations** for inspection at **any time**, review **any document** and interview **any scientist,** technician or other individual and seize **any prohibited items for destruction**.

- UNSCR 707 demanded that Iraq should allow inspection teams "immediate, unconditional and unrestricted access to any and all areas". For over a decade **Iraq has consistently failed** to meet this standard.

- Iraq has **admitted** having had a large, effective, system for hiding proscribed material including documentation, components, production equipment and, possibly, biological and chemical agents and weapons from the UN.

- In July 1995, Iraq **acknowledged that biological agents had been produced** on an industrial scale at Al-Hakam.

- Iraq acknowledged that it had pursued a biological programme that led to the deployment of actual weapons. Iraq admitted producing in excess of **200 biological weapons** with a reserve stock of agent to fill considerably more.

- Saddam has refused to admit UN-mandated weapons inspectors to Iraq since 1998.

- The IAEA has pointed out that their annual inspection does "not serve as a substitute for the verification activities required by the relevant resolutions of the UN Security Council."

- In April 1999, an independent UN panel of experts endorsed the Butler report and noted that "the longer inspection and monitoring activities remain suspended, the more difficult the comprehensive implementation of Security Council resolutions becomes, increasing the risk that **Iraq might reconstitute its proscribed weapons programmes**."

CAB/33/0010

IRAQI REGIME: CRIMES AND HUMAN RIGHTS ABUSES

- Saddam Hussain seized control of Iraq in 1979. Five of his close friends were subsequently executed after they opposed his take-over.

- In 1983, 8,000 male Kurds aged 13 and upwards were taken prisoner and later executed – for no reason, except that they were Kurds.

- Amnesty International in 1985 told of 300 KURDISH CHILDREN who were arrested in Sulaimaniya – some were tortured and three were killed.

- At least 100,000 Kurds were killed or disappeared during the Anfal campaign.

- According to Human Rights Watch, a single CHEMICAL WEAPONS attack on the town of Halabja killed up to 5,000 civilians and injured some 10,000 more.

- The Iraqi regime used chemical weapons – MUSTARD GAS and the nerve agents TABUN and SARIN – extensively from 1984, resulting in over 20,000 Iranian casualties.

- Iraq invaded Kuwait on 2 August 1990. Abuses committed by its forces included ROBBERY, RAPE of Kuwaitis and expatriates, and summary EXECUTIONS.

- More than 600 Kuwaitis taken by the Iraq regime ARE STILL MISSING and unaccounted for over TEN YEARS after the Gulf War.

- More than 100 MUSLIM CLERICS have disappeared since 1991.

- An estimated 2,500 PRISONERS WERE EXECUTED between 1997 and 1999 in a "prison cleansing" campaign.

- In October 2000, dozens of women accused of prostitution were BEHEADED WITHOUT ANY JUDICIAL PROCESS, together with men accused of pimping. Some were accused for political reasons.

- Men, women and CHILDREN continue to be ARRESTED, DETAINED, TORTURED AND MURDERED on suspicion of political or religious activities, or because they are related to members of the opposition.

CAB/33/0011

IRAQI WMD PROGRAMMES

This document draws on information from a range of sources, including intelligence. Because of the need to protect the safety of sources, details underpinning intelligence judgements cannot be made public. But the Government is confident of the judgements set out in this paper.

Introduction

- Nuclear, chemical and biological weapons are collectively known as Weapons of Mass Destruction (WMD). Several countries have WMD programmes and missile systems capable of delivering nuclear, chemical or biological warheads. They are working to develop more accurate and longer-range missiles that will allow them to threaten more than just their immediate neighbours.

- Most countries have promised not to acquire these weapons. They have signed relevant international agreements including the Treaty on the Non Proliferation of Nuclear Weapons (NPT), the Chemical Weapons Convention (CWC), and the Biological and Toxins Weapons Conventions (BTWC).

- A few countries have either failed to sign these agreements or have decided to break them. The position of Iraq is a particular concern. Iraq is a signatory to the NPT, but since the late 1980s it has not abided by its obligations. Since the Gulf War Iraq has been bound by five UN Security Council Resolutions (UNSCRs) relating to its WMD programmes. It remains in breach of all of them. In 1980 and 1990 Saddam Hussain used his conventional forces to mount unprovoked attacks against his neighbours, Iran and Kuwait respectively. He has used chemical weapons both against Iran and against his own Kurdish people.

- The International Community has repeatedly sought to disrupt Iraq's efforts to acquire WMD. On each occasion Saddam has sought to rebuild his capabilities. His efforts are making progress. The Government monitors these efforts very closely. This paper sets out what the Government is able to say about them.

CAB/33/0012

Background

Before the Gulf War, Saddam Hussain demonstrated his readiness to deploy extensively WMD in the form of chemical weapons both against his neighbours and his own population. Since the Gulf War, he has **failed to comply with UN Security Council Resolutions**, which his government accepted.

While the successful enforcement of the sanctions regimes and the UN arms embargo have impeded Iraq's efforts to reconstitute its weapons of mass destruction, they have not halted them. Much of Iraq's missile infrastructure has been rebuilt; the nuclear weapons programme is being reconstituted; and Iraq continues to have the capability to produce chemical and biological weapons, and may already have done so.

Since the withdrawal of inspectors in 1998, monitoring of Iraqi attempts to restore a WMD capability has become more difficult.

UN Security Council Resolutions (UNSCR) relating to WMD

UNSCR 687, April 1991 created the UN Special Commission (UNSCOM) and required Iraq to accept, unconditionally, "the destruction, removal or rendering harmless, under international supervision" of its chemical and biological weapons, ballistic missiles with a range greater than 150km, and their associated programmes, stocks, components, research and facilities. The International Atomic Energy Agency (IAEA) was charged with abolition of Iraq's nuclear weapons programme. UNSCOM and the IAEA must report that their mission has been achieved before the Security Council can end sanctions. They have not yet done so.

UNSCR 707, August 1991, stated that Iraq must provide full, final and complete disclosure of all its WMD programmes and provide unconditional and unrestricted access to UN inspectors. Iraq must also cease all nuclear activities of any kind other than civil use of isotopes.

UNSCR 715, October 1991 approved plans prepared by UNSCOM and IAEA for the monitoring and verification arrangements to implement UNSCR 687.

UNSCR 1051, March 1996 stated that Iraq must declare the shipment of dual-use WMD goods.

UNSCR 1284, December 1999, established UNMOVIC (United Nations Monitoring, Verification and Inspection Commission) as a successor to UNSCOM and calls on Iraq to give UNMOVIC inspectors "immediate, unconditional and unrestricted access to any and all areas, facilities, equipment, records and means of transport"

CAB/33/0013

Saddam's Weapons

Nuclear Weapons

Before the Gulf War, Iraqi plans for the development of a nuclear weapon were well advanced. Iraq was planning and constructing fissile material production facilities and work on a weapon design was underway. Their declared aim was to produce a weapon with a 20 kiloton yield, which would ultimately be delivered in a ballistic missile warhead.

We assessed in 1991 that Iraq was less than three years away from possessing a nuclear weapon.

After the Gulf War, Iraq's nuclear weapons infrastructure was dismantled by the IAEA. But we judge that Iraq is still working to achieve a nuclear weapons capability, **in breach of its NPT and IAEA obligations and UN Security Council Resolution 687**. Much of its former expertise has been retained.

Effect of a 20 kiloton nuclear device in a built up area

A detonation occurring over a city might flatten an area of approximately 3 square miles.

Within 1.6 miles of detonation, blast damage and radiation would cause 80% casualties, three-quarters of which would be fatal. Between 1.6 and 3.1 miles from the detonation, there would still be 10% casualties, 10% of which would be fatal injuries.

In the last year intelligence has indicated that specialists were recalled to work on a nuclear weapons programme in the autumn of 1998. But Iraq needs certain key equipment and materials for the production of the fissile material necessary before a nuclear bomb could be developed. We judge that the Iraqi programme is based on gas centrifuge uranium enrichment, which was the route Iraq was following for producing fissile material before the Gulf War.

Iraq is covertly attempting to acquire technology and materials with nuclear applications. This includes specialised aluminium, which is subject to international export controls because of its potential application in gas centrifuges used to enrich uranium. Although this material has applications in a range of other weapon systems.

So long as sanctions continue to hinder the import of such crucial goods, Iraq would find it difficult to produce a nuclear weapon. After the lifting of sanctions we assess that Iraq would need at least five years to produce a weapon.

Progress would be much quicker if Iraq was able to buy suitable fissile material.

CAB/33/0014

Chemical And Biological Weapons

Iraq made frequent use of a variety of **chemical weapons** during the Iran-Iraq War. Iraq used significant quantities of mustard, tabun and sarin resulting in over 20,000 Iranian casualties. In 1988 Saddam also used mustard and nerve agents against the Kurds in northern Iraq. Estimates vary, but according to Human Rights Watch up to 5,000 people were killed. Iraq's military maintains the capability to use these weapons, with command, control and logistical arrangements in place.

Iraq admitted in 1991 to the production of blister agent (mustard) and nerve agents (tabun, sarin, and cyclosarin).

Effects of chemical agents

Mustard is a liquid agent that causes burns and blisters to exposed skin. It attacks and damages the eyes, mucous membranes, lungs, skin, and blood-forming organs. When inhaled, mustard damages the respiratory tract; when ingested, it causes vomiting and diarrhoea.

Tabun, sarin and VX are all nerve agents of which VX is the most toxic. They all damage the nervous system, producing muscular spasms and paralysis. As little as 10 milligrammes of VX on the skin can cause death.

A chemical weapon is the agent combined with a means of dispersing it.

After years of denial Iraq admitted to producing about 4 tons of VX nerve agent, but only after the defection of Saddam's son-in-law, Hussain Kamil in 1995. Iraq maintains that the chemical weapons programme was halted in January 1991 and all agents under its control were destroyed by the summer of 1991. However, there are inconsistencies in Iraqi documentation on destruction.

Analysis of figures provided by UN weapons inspectors indicate that they have been unable to account for:

- up to 360 tonnes of bulk chemical warfare agent, including 1.5 tonnes of VX nerve agent;
- up to 3000 tonnes of precursor chemicals including approximately 300 tonnes which, in the Iraqi CW programme, were unique to the production of VX;
- over 30,000 special munitions for delivery of chemical and biological agents.

11

CAB/33/0015

We cannot be sure whether these have been destroyed or remain at the disposal of the Iraqi government. But we judge that Iraq retains some production equipment and at least small amounts of chemical agent precursors.

Following four years of pressure from weapons inspectors and the information provided by Hussein Kamil, Iraq finally admitted to the existence of a **biological weapons** programme in 1995.

Iraq admitted to:
- producing anthrax spores, botulinum toxin and aflatoxin and to working on a number of other agents;
- weaponising some agents, which included the filling of warheads for its Al Hussain ballistic missiles;
- testing spraying devices for agents.

Iraq has claimed that all its biological agents and weapons have been destroyed, although no convincing proof of this has been offered. UN inspectors could not account for large quantities of growth media procured for biological agent production, enough to produce over three times the amount of anthrax Iraq admits to having manufactured. Reports that Iraq has conducted research on smallpox and a number of toxins cannot be corroborated. Iraq is assessed to be self-sufficient in the technology required to produce biological weapons.

We assess that Iraq has a covert chemical and biological weapons programme, **in breach of UN Security Council Resolution 687.**

All the necessary expertise has been retained. Iraq appears to be refurbishing sites formally associated with its chemical and biological weapons programmes. This includes a facility near Habbaniyah, previously associated with the production of precursors. Iraq is assessed to have some chemical and biological agents available, either from pre-Gulf War stocks or more recent production.

We judge Iraq has the capability to produce the chemical agents:
- **sulphur mustard, tabun, sarin, cyclosarin, and VX.**

and the biological agents:
- **anthrax, botulinum toxin, aflatoxin and ricin.**

12

CAB/33/0016

Iraq retains conventional delivery means for chemical and biological weapons such as free fall bombs and missile warheads. But given Iraq's admission of testing spray devices, we judge that the modification of the L-29 jet trainer could allow it to be used for the delivery of chemical and biological agents. The L-29 was subject to UNSCOM inspection for this reason.

Effects of biological agents

Anthrax

Anthrax is a disease caused by the bacterium Bacillus anthracis. Inhalation anthrax is the manifestation of the disease likely to be expected in biological warfare. The symptoms may vary. If the dose is large (8,000 to 10,000 spores) death is common. The incubation period for anthrax is 1 to 7 days, with most cases occurring within 2 days of exposure.

Botulinum toxin

Botulinum toxin is a neurotoxin produced by the bacterium Clostridium botulinum and is one of the most toxic substances known to man. The first symptoms of botulinum toxin A poisoning may appear as early as 1 hour post exposure or as long as 8 days after exposure, with the incubation period between 12 and 22 hours. Paralysis leads to death by suffocation.

Aflatoxin

Aflatoxins are fungal toxins, which are potent carcinogens. Aflatoxin contaminated food products can cause liver inflammation and cancer.

Ricin

Ricin is derived from castor beans and can cause multiple organ failure within one or two days of inhalation. A lethal does is estimated to be about 1 milligram

A biological weapon is the agent combined with a means of dispersing it.

CAB/33/0017

Saddam's Missiles

Ballistic Missiles

Prior to the Gulf War, Iraq had a well-developed missile industry. Iraq fired over 500 SCUD-type missiles at Iran during the Iran-Iraq War and 93 SCUD type-missiles during the Gulf War. The latter were targeted at Coalition forces stationed in the Gulf region and Israel .Armed with conventional warheads they did limited damage. Iraq had chemical and biological warheads available but did not use them.

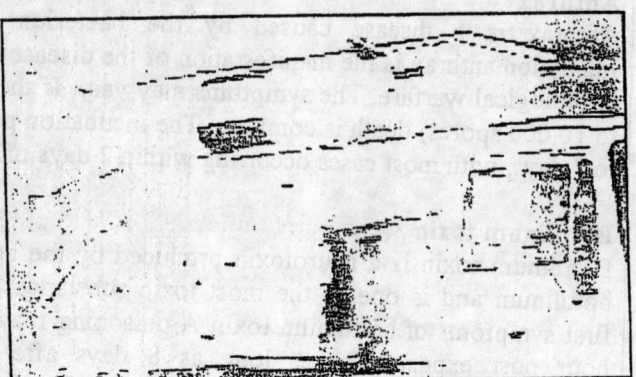

ABABIL-100

Most of the missiles fired in the Gulf War were an Iraqi produced stretched version of the SCUD missile, the Al Hussain, with an extended range of 650 km. Iraq was working on other longer-range stretched SCUD variants, such as the Al Abbas, which had a range of 900km. Iraq was also seeking to reverse engineer the SCUD engine with a view to producing new missiles; recent evidence indicates they may have succeeded at that time. In particular Iraq had plans for a new SCUD-derived missile with a range of 1200km. Iraq also conducted a partial flight test of a multi-stage satellite launch vehicle based on SCUD technology, known as the Al Abid.

SCUD missiles

The short-range mobile SCUD ballistic missile was developed by the Soviet Union in the 1950s, drawing from the technology of the German liquid-propellant V-2 which saw operational service towards the end of World War II.

For many years it was the mainstay of Soviet and Warsaw Pact tactical missile forces, and it was also widely exported. Recipients of Soviet-manufactured SCUDs included Iraq, North Korea, Iran, and Libya, although not all were sold directly by the Soviet Union.

Also during this period, Iraq was developing the BADR-2000, a 700-1000km range two-stage solid propellant missile (based on the Iraqi part of the 1980s CONDOR-2 programme run in co-operation with Argentina and Egypt). There were plans for 1200-1500km range solid propellant follow-on systems.

14

Since the Gulf War, Iraq has been openly developing two short-range missiles up to a range of 150km, which are permitted under UN Security Council Resolution 687. The Al-Samoud liquid propellant missile has been extensively tested, has appeared on public parade in Baghdad and is judged to be nearing deployment. In the absence of UN inspectors, Iraq has also worked on extending its range to at least 200km. Testing of the solid propellant Ababil-100 is also underway, with plans to extend its range to at least 200km.

AL HUSSEIN

Any extension of a missile's range to beyond 150km would be in breach of UN Security Resolution 687.

Compared to liquid propellant missiles, those powered by solid propellant offer greater ease of storage, handling and mobility. They are also quicker to take into and out of action and can stay at a high state of readiness for longer periods. We judge that Iraq has retained more than a dozen Al Hussain missiles, in breach of UN Security Council Resolution 687.

These missiles were either hidden from the UN as complete systems, or could have been re-assembled using illegally retained engines and other components. We judge that the engineering expertise available would allow these missiles to be effectively maintained. We assess that some of these missiles could be available for use.

Although not very accurate when used against *other countries*, they are still an effective system, which could be used with a conventional, chemical or biological warhead.

15

CAB/33/0019

Reporting has recently confirmed that Iraq's priority is to develop longer-range missile systems, which we judge are likely to have ranges over 1000km, enabling it to threaten regional neighbours, Israel and some NATO members. These programmes employ hundreds of people. Imagery below has shown a new engine test stand being constructed (A), which is larger than the current one used for Al Samoud (B), and that formerly used for testing SCUD engines (C) which was dismantled under UNSCOM supervision.

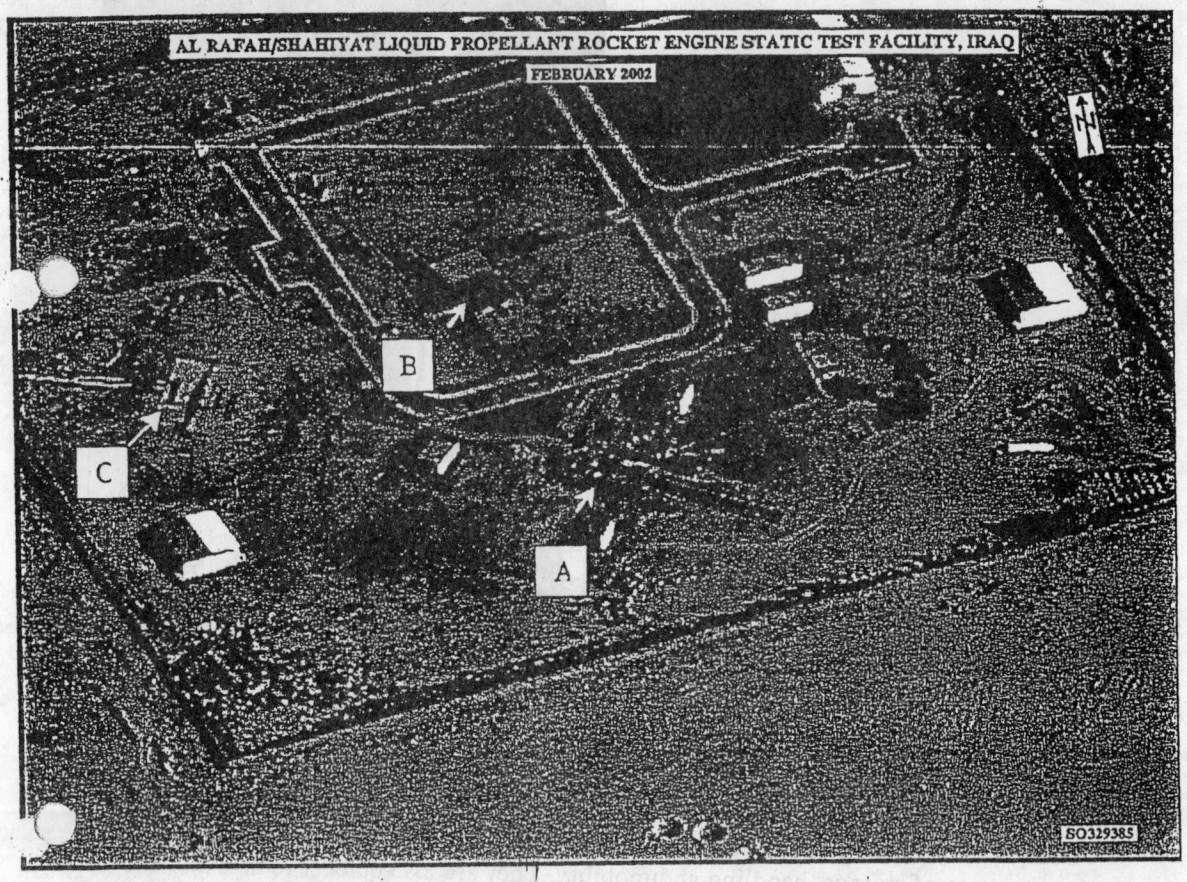

AL RAFAH/SHAHIYAT LIQUID PROPELLANT ROCKET ENGINE STATIC TEST FACILITY, IRAQ

FEBRUARY 2002

SO329385

We judge that this new stand will be capable of testing engines for missiles with ranges over 1000km, which are not permitted under UN Security Council Resolution 687.

Iraq is also working to obtain improved guidance technology to increase missile accuracy. The success of UN restrictions means the development of new longer-range missiles is likely to be a slow process.

16

These restrictions impact particularly on the:

- availability of foreign expertise;
- conduct of test flights to ranges above 150km;
- acquisition of guidance and control technology.

Saddam remains committed to developing longer-range missiles. We assess that, if sanctions remain in place, the earliest Iraq could achieve a limited missile capability of over 1000km is 2007, but it is more likely to be towards the end of the decade (Figure 4 shows the range of Iraq's various missiles).

To be confident that it has successfully developed a longer-range missile Iraq would need to conduct a flight-test. Current UN Security Council Resolutions do not permit tests of over 150km.

Iraq has managed to rebuild much of the missile production infrastructure destroyed in the Gulf War and in Operation Desert Fox in 1998. New missile-related infrastructure is currently under construction, including a plant for indigenously producing ammonium perchlorate, which is a key ingredient in the production of solid propellant rocket motors. This was obtained through an Indian chemical engineering firm with extensive links in Iraq.

Despite a UN embargo, Iraq has also made concerted efforts to acquire additional production technology, including machine tools and raw materials, **in breach of UN Security Council Resolution 1051.**

The embargo has succeeded in blocking many of these attempts, but, despite the dual use nature of some of the items, we know some items have found their way to the Iraqi ballistic missile programme and will inevitably continue to do so.

Concealment

Strategies to conceal and protect key parts of Iraq's WMD and ballistic missile programmes from a military attack or a UN inspection have been developed. These include the:

- use of transportable laboratories in their chemical and biological weapons programmes;
- use of covert facilities;
- dispersal of equipment when a threat is perceived.

In particular we know that the Iraqi leadership has recently ordered the dispersal of its most sensitive WMD equipment and material. This order is being carried out.

17

CAB/33/0021

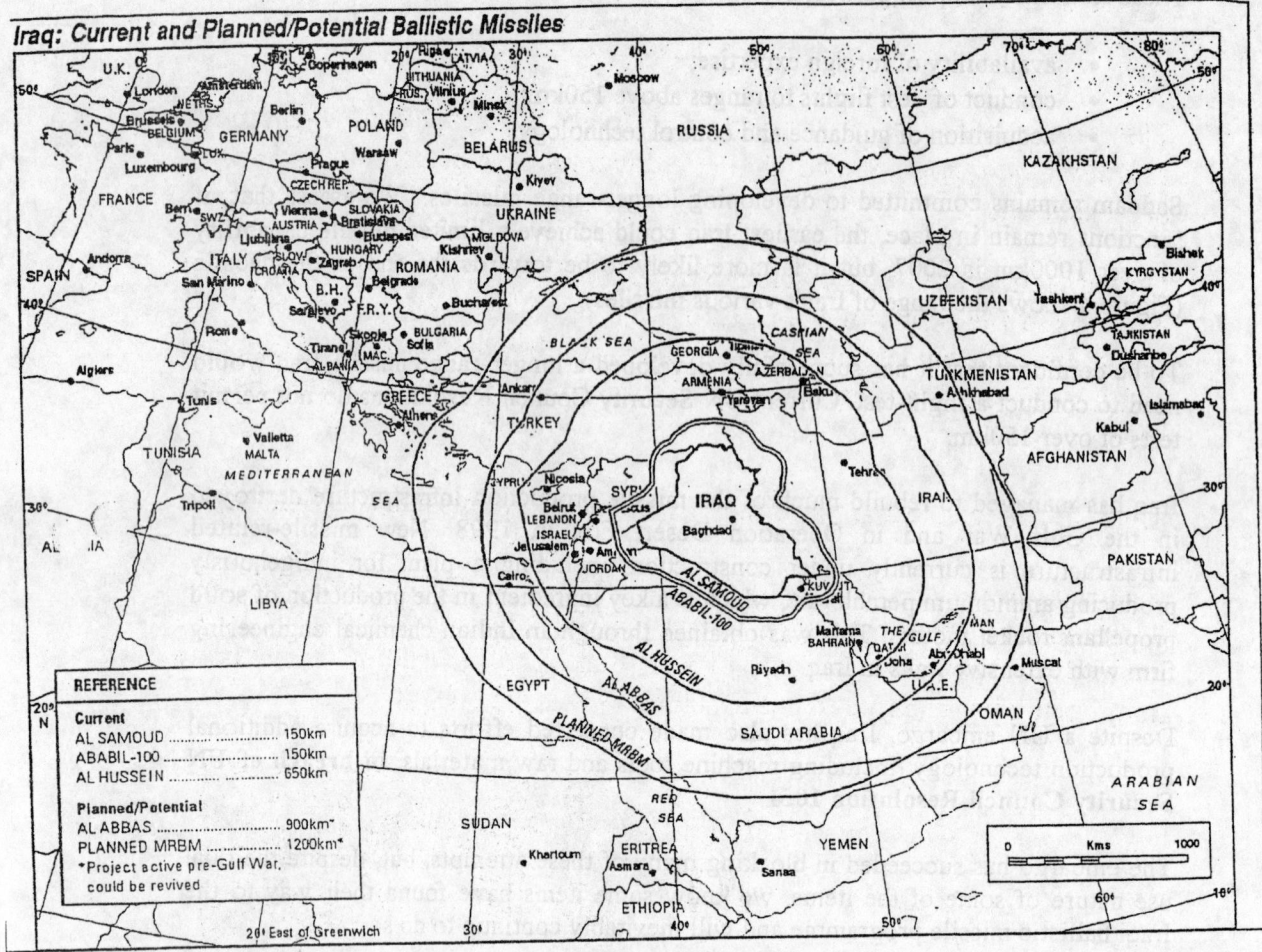

CURRENT AND PLANNED/POTENTIAL BALLISTIC MISSILES

CONCLUSION

- Iraq retains some prohibited missile systems.

- Iraq is developing longer-range ballistic missiles capable of delivering weapons of mass destruction throughout the Middle East and Gulf Region.

- Iraq is seeking a nuclear weapons capability.

- Iraq has a chemical weapons capability, and has used it. It also has a biological weapons capability.

18

CAB/33/0022

)

HISTORY OF UN WEAPONS INSPECTIONS IN IRAQ

This paper draws on a number of different published and intelligence sources, including reports by UN personnel and non-Governmental organisations.

United Nations Security Council Resolution 687 (UNSCR 687) of 3 April 1991 fixed the terms of the cease-fire in the Gulf conflict following the illegal invasion and occupation of Kuwait by Iraq under Saddam Hussain and his defeat by an international coalition of forces in Operation Desert Storm.

UNSCR 687 also established the UN Special Commission (UNSCOM).

The purpose of this body was to oversee, in conjunction with the International Atomic Energy Agency (IAEA), the dismantling of Iraq's arsenal of weapons of mass destruction (WMD) and to maintain a monitoring programme to ensure that it was never rebuilt.

Saddam Hussain

The history of UN weapons inspections in Iraq has been characterised by persistent Iraqi efforts to frustrate, deceive and intimidate inspectors. Despite the conduct of the Iraqi authorities towards them, both UNSCOM and the IAEA Action Team have valuable records of achievement in discovering and destroying biological and chemical weapons stocks, missiles and the infrastructure for Iraq's nuclear weapons programme.

By the end of 1998 there nevertheless remained significant uncertainties about the disposition of Iraq's prohibited WMD programmes. A series of confrontations and the systematic refusal by Iraq to co-operate, left UNSCOM unable to perform its disarmament mandate and the inspectors withdrew on 13 December 1998.

The US and the UK had made clear that anything short of full co-operation would make military action unavoidable. Operation Desert Fox (16-19 December 1998) was designed to degrade Saddam's ability to regenerate and deploy biological and chemical weapons and prevent him from threatening his neighbours with these or other weapons.

Since December 1998, Iraq has refused absolutely to comply with its UN disarmament and monitoring obligations and allow access to weapons inspectors. We judge that Iraq has used the intervening 40-month period to rebuild significant aspects of its chemical, biological, nuclear and ballistic missile programmes.

These actions not only present a direct challenge to the authority of the United Nations. They also breach Iraq's commitments under two key international arms control agreements:

- the Biological and Toxin Weapons Convention – which bans the development, production, stockpiling, acquisition or retention of biological weapons; and,

- the Nuclear Non-Proliferation Treaty (NPT) – which prohibits Iraq from manufacturing or otherwise acquiring nuclear weapons.

This note clarifies the UN's inspection mandate in Iraq, records just some instances of Iraqi obstruction over the past decade and focuses on one of the most egregious examples of non-compliance with UN resolutions: Iraq's consistent denial of a biological weapons programme. The note ends with a summary of developments since the last inspection in December 1998, and the steps we think Iraq now needs to take if the international community is ever to have any assurance that Saddam Hussain's ambitions to develop weapons of mass destruction (WMD) have finally been thwarted.

UNSCR 687 and the Formation of the UN Special Commission (UNSCOM)

One of the greatest threats to Allied forces during Operation Desert Storm in 1991 was Iraq's stockpile of chemical and biological weapons and long-range ballistic missiles. At the time, there were genuine concerns that Saddam Hussain would authorise the use of such weapons against Allied troops and his neighbours. In the mid-late 1980s Iraq had shown no compunction about using chemical weapons in its war with Iran and against the Kurdish people of Halabja. According to the non-governmental organisation (NGO), Human Rights Watch, the latter resulted in up to 5,000 deaths.

20

CAB/33/0024

But the true scale of Iraq's programme to acquire WMD and their means of delivery only became apparent with the establishment of a UN weapons inspection regime in the aftermath of Desert Storm. UN Security Council Resolution (UNSCR) 687 was adopted in April 1991. It obliged Iraq to provide declarations on all aspects of its WMD programmes within 15 days and accept the destruction, removal or rendering harmless under international supervision of its chemical, biological and nuclear programmes, and all ballistic missiles with a range beyond 150km.

UNSCR 687 mandated two inspection teams to handle Iraqi disarmament and establish long term monitoring regimes: the UN Special Commission (UNSCOM) would tackle the chemical, biological and missile programmes; and the Action Team within the International Atomic Energy Agency (IAEA) would be responsible for tracking down and dismantling Iraq's illicit nuclear weapons programme.

UNSCOM and the IAEA were given the remit to designate **any locations** for inspection at **any time**, review **any document** and interview **any scientist**, technician or other individual and seize **any prohibited items for destruction**.

Iraqi Non-Co-operation with UN Weapons Inspectors

The UN passed a further Resolution in 1991 that set out in clear and specific terms the standard of co-operation the international community expected of Iraq. UNSCR 707 (August 1991) demanded that Iraq should allow inspection teams "immediate, unconditional and unrestricted access to any and all areas". For over a decade Iraq has consistently failed to meet this standard.

Prior to the first inspection, the Iraqi regime did its utmost to hide stocks of WMD. The former Chairman of UNSCOM, Richard Butler, reported to the UN Security Council that in 1991 a decision was taken by a high-level Government committee to provide inspectors with only a portion of its proscribed weapons, components, production capabilities and stocks. UNSCOM concluded that Iraqi policy was based on the following actions:

- to provide only a portion of extant weapons stocks, releasing for destruction only those that were least modern;

- to retain the production capability and documentation necessary to revive programmes when possible;

- to conceal the full extent of its chemical weapons programme, including the VX nerve agent project;

- to conceal the number and type of chemical and biological warheads for proscribed long –range missiles;

21

CAB/33/0025

- and to conceal the very existence of its massive biological weapons programme.

At the same time, Iraq tried to maintain its nuclear weapons programme via a concerted campaign to deceive IAEA inspectors. In 1997 the Agency's Director General stated that the IAEA was "severely hampered by Iraq's persistence in a policy of concealment and understatement of the programme's scope."

Harassment of Inspectors by Iraq

Once inspectors had arrived in-country, it quickly became apparent that Iraq would resort to any measures (including physical threats and psychological intimidation of inspectors) to prevent UNSCOM and the IAEA from fulfilling their mandate. Examples of Iraqi obstruction are too numerous to list in full. But some of the more infamous examples include:

- firing warning shots in the air to prevent IAEA inspectors from intercepting nuclear related equipment (June 1991);

- keeping IAEA inspectors in a car park for 4 days and refusing to allow them to leave with incriminating documents on Iraq's nuclear weapons programme (September 1991);

- announcing that UN monitoring and verification plans were "unlawful" (October 1991);

- refusing UNSCOM inspectors access to the Ministry of Agriculture. Threats were made to inspectors who remained on watch outside the building. The inspection team had reliable evidence that the site contained archives related to proscribed activities;

- refusing to allow UNSCOM the use of its own aircraft to fly into Iraq (January 1993). In 1991-2 Iraq objected to UNSCOM using its own helicopters and choosing its own flight plans;

- refusing to allow UNSCOM to install remote-controlled monitoring cameras at two key missile sites (June-July 1993);

- repeatedly denying access to inspection teams (1991- December 1998);

- interfering with UNSCOM's helicopter operations, threatening the safety of the aircraft and their crews (June 1997);

- demanding end of U2 overflights and the withdrawal of US UNSCOM staff (October 1997);

- destroying documentary evidence of WMD programmes (September 1997);

- and refusing access to inspection teams on the grounds that certain areas and even roads were deemed "Presidential Sites" (1997-98).

In response to these incidents, the President of the Security Council issued frequent statements calling on Iraq to comply with its disarmament and monitoring obligations.

In December 1997 Richard Butler reported to the UN Security Council that Iraq had created a new category of sites – presidential and sovereign – from which it claimed that UNSCOM inspectors were henceforth barred.

The terms of the cease-fire in 1991 foresaw no such limitation.

22

CAB/33/0026

Iraq consistently refused to allow inspections access to the eight Presidential sites until the invention of the UN Secretary General in February 1998, which enabled special access to UNSCOM/IAEA teams observed by diplomatic representatives. These sites are in fact massive compounds containing many buildings, some of which house security units that have in the past been assosiated with concealing Iraqs WMD programme.

A photograph of a presidential site or what have been called "palaces".

Buckingham palace has been super-imposed to demonstrate their comparative size

23

CAB/33/0027

Buckingham Palace and grounds

Iraq's Chemical and Biological Weapon sites

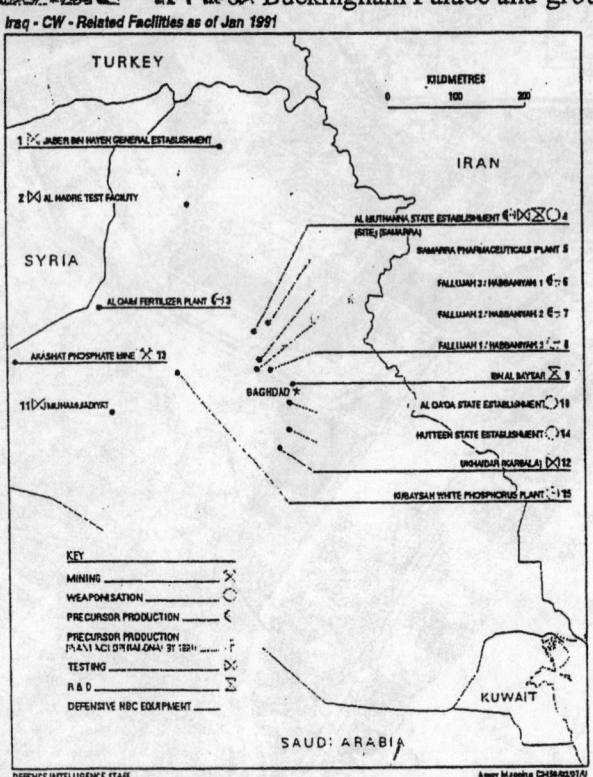

Iraq - CW - Related Facilities as of Jan 1991

DEFENCE INTELLIGENCE STAFF

24

CAB/33/0028

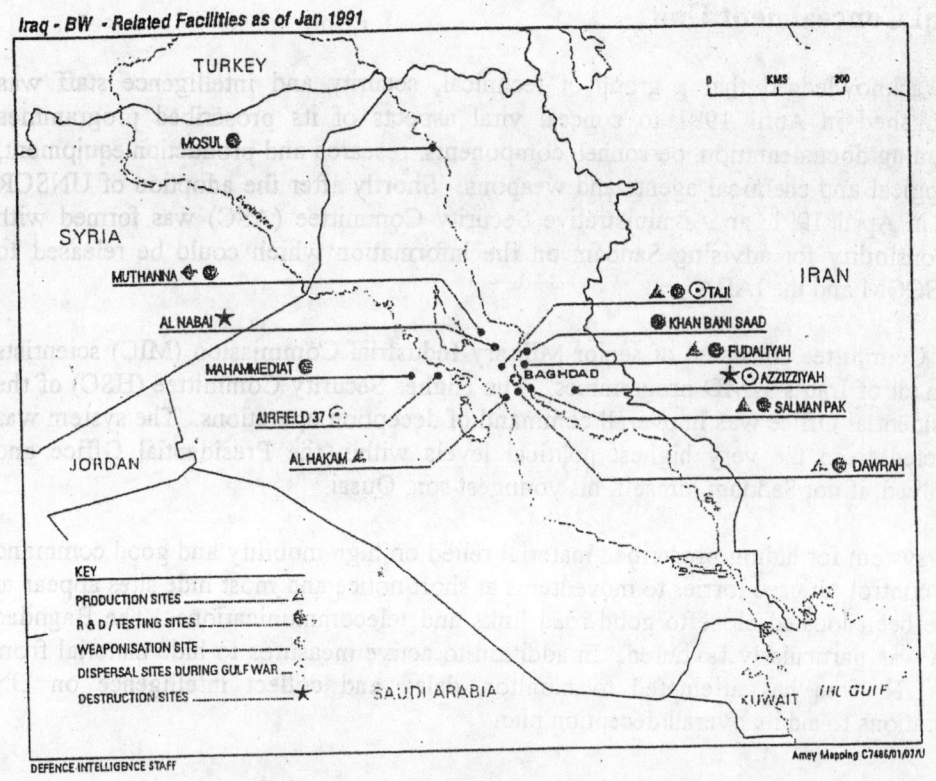

Iraq - BW - Related Facilities as of Jan 1991

KEY

PRODUCTION SITES

R & D / TESTING SITES

WEAPONISATION SITE

DISPERSAL SITES DURING GULF WAR

DESTRUCTION SITES

DEFENCE INTELLIGENCE STAFF

Amey Mapping C7486/01/07/U

CAB/33/0029

Iraqi Concealment Unit

Iraq acknowledged that a group of technical, security and intelligence staff was established in April 1991 to conceal vital aspects of its proscribed programmes including documentation, personnel, components, research and production equipment, biological and chemical agents and weapons. Shortly after the adoption of UNSCR 687 in April 1991, an Administrative Security Committee (ASC) was formed with responsibility for advising Saddam on the information which could be released to UNSCOM and the IAEA.

The Committee consisted of senior Military Industrial Commission (MIC) scientists from all of Iraq's WMD programmes. The Higher Security Committee (HSC) of the Presidential Office was in overall command of deception operations. The system was directed from the very highest political levels within the Presidential Office and involved, if not Saddam himself, his youngest son, Qusai.

The system for hiding proscribed material relied on high mobility and good command and control. It used lorries to move items at short notice and most hide sites appear to have been located close to good road links and telecommunications. The Baghdad area was particularly favoured. In addition to active measures to hide material from the UN, Iraq has attempted to monitor, delay and collect intelligence on UN operations to aid its overall deception plan.

Iraq's Biological Weapons Programme

Nowhere was Iraqi obstruction of UN inspectors more blatant than in the field of biological weapons. Iraq denied that it had pursued a biological weapons programme until July 1995. Between 1991 and 1995, Iraq refused to disclose any details of its past programme.

In the course of the first biological weapons inspection in August 1991, Iraq indicated that it had merely conducted a military biological research programme. At the site visited, Al-Salman, Iraq had removed equipment, documents and even entire buildings. Later in the year, during a visit to the Al-Hakam site, Iraq declared to UNSCOM inspectors that the facility was used as a factory to produce proteins derived from yeast to feed animals. Inspectors subsequently discovered that the plant was a central site for the production of anthrax spores and botulinum toxin for weapons. Iraqi officials had also systematically cleaned up the factory in order to deceive inspectors.

Another key site, the Foot and Mouth Disease Vaccine Institute at Daura which produced botulinum toxin and probably anthrax, was not divulged as part of the programme. Five years later, after intense pressure, Iraq acknowledged that tens of tonnes of bacteriological warfare agent had been produced there and at Al-Hakam.

26

CAB|33|0030

Iraq's Nuclear
Weapon sites

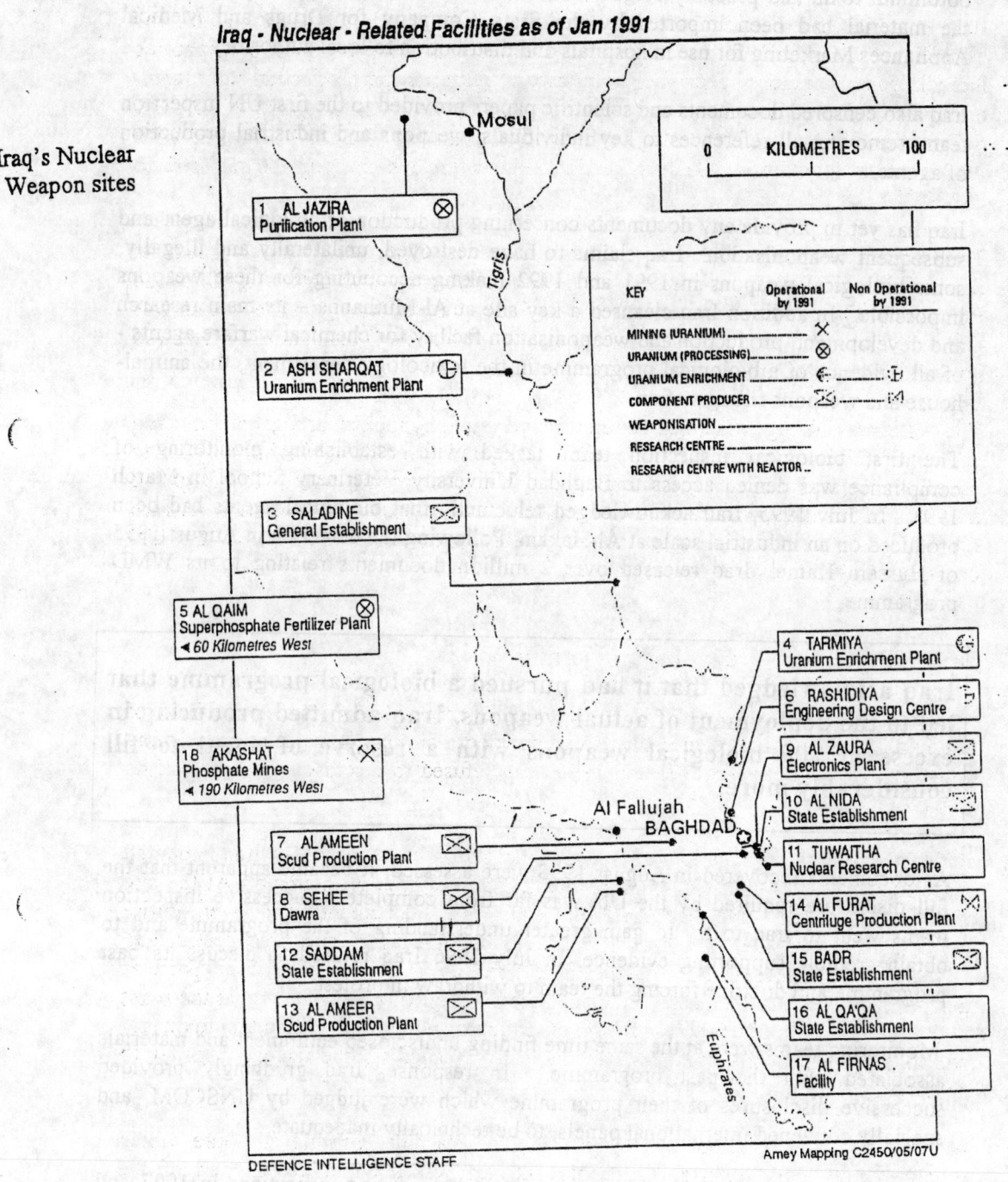

Iraq - Nuclear - Related Facilities as of Jan 1991

Mosul

KEY	Operational by 1991	Non Operational by 1991
MINING (URANIUM)	✕	
URANIUM (PROCESSING)	⊗	
URANIUM ENRICHMENT		
COMPONENT PRODUCER	⊠	⊠
WEAPONISATION		
RESEARCH CENTRE		
RESEARCH CENTRE WITH REACTOR		

1 AL JAZIRA
Purification Plant ⊗

2 ASH SHARQAT
Uranium Enrichment Plant

3 SALADINE
General Establishment ⊠

5 AL QAIM
Superphosphate Fertilizer Plant ⊗
◄ 60 Kilometres West

18 AKASHAT
Phosphate Mines ✕
◄ 190 Kilometres West

7 AL AMEEN
Scud Production Plant ⊠

8 SEHEE
Dawra ⊠

12 SADDAM
State Establishment ⊠

13 AL AMEER
Scud Production Plant ⊠

4 TARMIYA
Uranium Enrichment Plant

6 RASHIDIYA
Engineering Design Centre

9 AL ZAURA
Electronics Plant ⊠

10 AL NIDA
State Establishment ⊠

11 TUWAITHA
Nuclear Research Centre

14 AL FURAT
Centrifuge Production Plant ⊠

15 BADR
State Establishment ⊠

16 AL QA'QA
State Establishment

17 AL FIRNAS
Facility

Al Fallujah
BAGHDAD

Tigris

Euphrates

0   KILOMETRES   100

DEFENCE INTELLIGENCE STAFF

Amey Mapping C2450/05/07U

Iraq consistently tried to obstruct UNSCOM's efforts to investigate the scale of its biological weapons programme. It created forged documents to account for bacterial

27

CAB/33/0031

growth media, imported in the late 1980s, specifically for the production of anthrax, botulinum toxin and probably plague. The documents were created to indicate that the material had been imported by the State Company for Drugs and Medical Appliances Marketing for use in hospitals and distribution to local authorities.

Iraq also censored documents and scientific papers provided to the first UN inspection team, removing all references to key individuals, weapons and industrial production of agents.

Iraq has yet to provide any documents concerning production of biological agent and subsequent weaponisation. Iraq claims to have destroyed, unilaterally and illegally, some biological weapons in 1991 and 1992 making accounting for these weapons impossible. In addition Iraq cleansed a key site at Al-Muthanna – its main research and development, production and weaponisation facility for chemical warfare agents - of all evidence of a biological programme in the toxicology department, the animal-house and weapons filling station.

The first biological inspection team tasked with establishing monitoring of compliance was denied access to Baghdad University Veterinary School in March 1993. In July 1995, Iraq acknowledged reluctantly that biological agents had been produced on an industrial scale at Al-Hakam. Following the defection in August 1995 of Hussain Kamel, Iraq released over 2 million documents relating to its WMD programme.

> **Iraq acknowledged that it had pursued a biological programme that led to the deployment of actual weapons. Iraq admitted producing in excess of 200 biological weapons with a reserve of agent to fill considerably more.**

As documents recovered in August 1995 were assessed, it became apparent that the full disclosure required by the UN was far from complete. Successive inspection teams went to Iraq to try to gain greater understanding of the programme and to obtain credible supporting evidence. In July 1996 Iraq refused to discuss its past programme and doctrine forcing the team to withdraw in protest.

Monitoring teams were at the same time finding undisclosed equipment and materials associated with the past programme. In response, Iraq grudgingly provided successive disclosures of their programme which were judged by UNSCOM, and specially convened international panels, to be technically inadequate.

Iraq refused to elaborate further on the programme during inspections in 1997 and 1998, confining discussion to previous topics. In July 1998, Tariq Aziz personally intervened in the inspection process stating that the biological programme had been more secret and more closed than other WMD programmes. He also played down the significance of the programme. This is consistent with Iraq's policy of trivialising the

28

CAB/33/0032

biological weapons programme as the personal adventure of a few misguided scientists.

In late 1995, Iraq acknowledged weapons testing the biological agent ricin, but did not provide production information. Two years later – in early 1997 – UNSCOM discovered evidence that Iraq had produced ricin. Ricin is a highly dangerous toxin derived from castor bean pulp which can cause multiple organ failure and death within one or two days of inhalation

UNSCOM and IAEA Achievements

UNSCOM surveyed 1015 sites in Iraq, carrying out 272 separate inspections. Despite Iraqi obstruction and intimidation, UN inspectors uncovered details of chemical, biological, nuclear and ballistic missile programmes the scale of which surprised the world.

One of the most sobering discoveries was that at the time of the Gulf War, Iraq had been within less than three years of acquiring a nuclear weapon. Other major UNSCOM/IAEA achievements included:

- the destruction of 40,000 munitions for chemical weapons, 2,610 tonnes of chemical precursors and 411 tonnes of chemical warfare agent;

- the dismantling of Iraq's prime chemical weapons development and production complex at Al-Muthanna, and a range of key production equipment;

- the destruction of 48-SCUD type missiles, 11 mobile launchers and 56 static sites, 30 warheads filled with chemical or biological agents, and 20 conventional warheads;

- the destruction of the Al-Hakam biological weapons facility and a range of production equipment, seed stocks and growth media for biological weapons;

- and the removal and destruction of the infrastructure for the nuclear weapons programme, including the Al-Athir weaponisation/testing facility.

Operation Desert Fox

The US and The UK had made clear, when calling off airstrikes in November 1998, that anything short of full co-operation would lead to immediate military action against Iraq.

Richard Butler was requested to report to the UN Security Council in December 1998 and made clear that, following a series of direct confrontations, coupled with the systematic refusal by Iraq to co-operate, UNSCOM was no longer able to perform its disarmament mandate.

29

CAB/33/0033

As a direct result, on December 13 the weapons inspectors withdrew and Operation Desert Fox was launched by the US and the UK three days later.

During Operation Desert Fox (16-19 December 1998):

- Iraq's ability to deliver biological or chemical agents by ballistic missile was weakened.

- There were attacks against missile production and research facilities and the destruction of infrastructure associated with the concealment of material and documents associated with the biological, chemical, nuclear and long-range missile programmes;

- Key facilities associated with Saddam's Ballistic Missile programme were significantly degraded, setting this back between one and two years.

The Situation Since 1998

Despite UNSCOM's efforts, a series of significant disarmament issues nevertheless remained to be resolved. In summarising the situation in a report to the Security Council in February 1999, the UNSCOM Chairman, Richard Butler, set out a damning account of Iraqi deceit. For example:

- Butler declared that obstructive Iraqi activity had had "a significant impact upon the Commission's disarmament work;"

- contrary to the requirement that destruction be conducted under international supervision, "Iraq undertook extensive, unilateral and secret destruction of large quantities of proscribed weapons and items";

- and Iraq "also pursued a practice of concealment of proscribed items, including weapons, and a cover up of its activities in contravention of Council resolutions."

There have been no UN-mandated weapons inspections in Iraq since 1998. In an effort to enforce Iraqi compliance with its disarmament and monitoring obligations, the Security Council passed resolution 1284 in December 1999. This established the United Nations Monitoring, Verification and Inspection Commission (UNMOVIC) as a successor organisation to UNSCOM. It also set out the steps Iraq needed to take to in return for the eventual suspension and lifting of sanctions.

A key measure of Iraqi compliance will be full co-operation with UN inspectors, including unconditional, immediate and unrestricted access to any and all sites.

CAB/33/0034

Iraq - Missile - Related Facilities

Iraq's
Missile sites

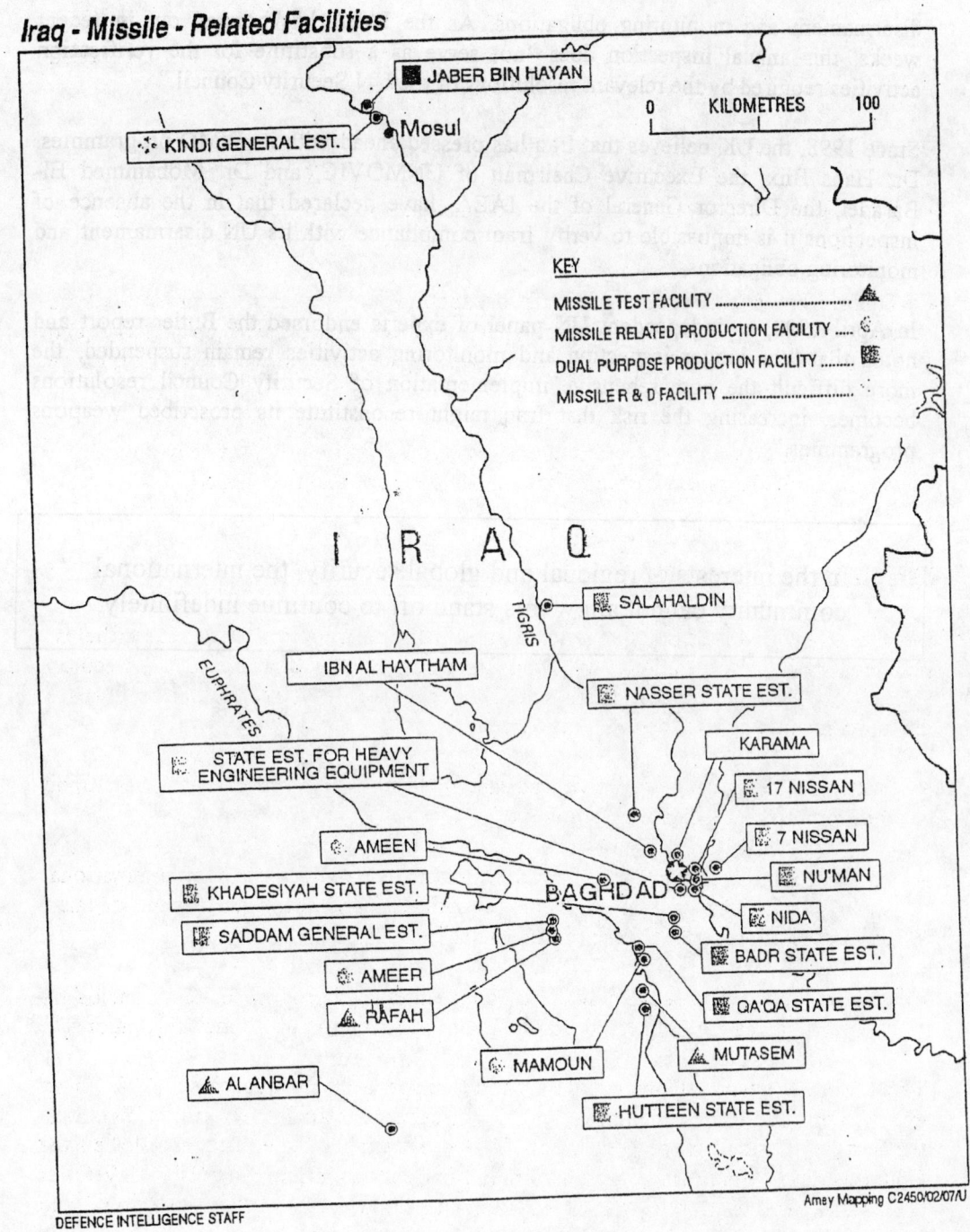

DEFENCE INTELLIGENCE STAFF

Amey Mapping C2450/02/07/U

KEY

MISSILE TEST FACILITY .... △
MISSILE RELATED PRODUCTION FACILITY ..... ⌂
DUAL PURPOSE PRODUCTION FACILITY .... ▦
MISSILE R & D FACILITY ....

For the past three years, Iraq has allowed the IAEA to carry out an annual inspection
of a stockpile of low-enriched uranium. This has led some countries and western
commentators to conclude – erroneously – that Iraq is meeting its nuclear

31

CAB/33/0035

disarmament and monitoring obligations. As the IAEA has pointed out in recent weeks, this annual inspection does "not serve as a substitute for the verification activities required by the relevant resolutions of the UN Security Council."

Since 1998, the UK believes that Iraq has pressed ahead with its WMD programmes. Dr. Hans Blix, the Executive Chairman of UNMOVIC, and Dr. Mohammed El-Baradei, the Director General of the IAEA, have declared that in the absence of inspections it is impossible to verify Iraqi compliance with its UN disarmament and monitoring obligations.

In April 1999, an independent UN panel of experts endorsed the Butler report and noted that "the longer inspection and monitoring activities remain suspended, the more difficult the comprehensive implementation of Security Council resolutions becomes, increasing the risk that Iraq might reconstitute its proscribed weapons programmes."

> In the interests of regional and global security, the international community cannot allow this stand off to continue indefinitely.

32

CAB/33/0036

IRAQI REGIME: CRIMES AND HUMAN RIGHTS ABUSES

Not only does Saddam Hussain's regime represent a threat to international security because of its continuing development of weapons of mass destruction, its aggression, violation of the laws of armed conflict and its record of systematic abuse of human rights is chilling.

This paper draws on a number of different published and intelligence sources, including reports by UN personnel and non-Governmental organisations.

Saddam Hussain

Pre-Gulf War Record

Saddam's rise to power was marked by the brutality that now characterises his regime. Five of his close friends, members of the ruling Revolutionary Command Council, were executed for opposing his takeover of the Presidency in 1979. His uncle, General Ahmad Hassan al-Bakr, who stepped down from the Presidency in Saddam's favour, was also killed. Saddam is also widely believed to have been behind the helicopter "accident" that killed his wife's brother, Adnan Khairallah, in June 1989.

Saddam quickly established all-pervasive control of Iraq. Right from the start, he committed numerous atrocities. Iraq's Shi'a Muslim and Kurdish communities in particular have suffered at his hands.

In April 1980, a leading Iraqi Shi'a cleric, Ayatollah Mohammed Baqir al-Sadr, was executed. Many members of another leading clerical family, the Hakims, were arrested in May 1983 and executed. Another member of the same clerical family, Sayed Mahdi al-Hakim, was murdered in Khartoum in January 1988.

CAB/33/0037

Documents captured by the Kurds during the Gulf War and handed over to the non-governmental organisation Human Rights Watch indicated that Saddam's persecution of the Kurds amounts to a policy of genocide. 8,000 Kurds, males aged 13 and upwards, were taken prisoner in 1983 and later put to death.

Amnesty International in 1985 drew attention to reports of hundreds more dead and missing, including the disappearance of 300 Kurdish children arrested in Sulaimaniya, of whom some were tortured and three died in custody.

In 1988, Iraqi government forces systematically razed Kurdish villages and killed civilians.

Amnesty International estimates that over 100,000 Kurds were killed or disappeared during the 1987-1988 campaign, known as the Anfal campaigns, to quell Kurdish insurgency and activities.

The campaign included the use of chemical weapons. According to the non-governmental organisation Human Rights Watch, a single attack on the Kurdish town of Halabja killed up to 5,000 civilians and injured some 10,000 more.

Chemical Massacre at Halabja, March 1988

The brutal massacre of the oppressed and innocent people of Halabja began before the sunrise of Friday, 17th of March 1988. The Iraqi regime committed one of its most tragic and horrible crimes against the civilian people on Friday, 17th of March. On that day, Halabja was bombarded more than twenty times by Iraqi regime's warplanes with chemical and cluster bomb.

That Friday afternoon, the magnitude of Iraqi crimes became evident. In the streets and alleys of Halabja, corpses piled up over one another. Children playing in front of their houses were killed instantly. The children did not even have time to run back home. Some children fell down at the threshold of the door of their houses.

Early in the Iran-Iraq war, Saddam shot a Minister who argued for peace during a Cabinet meeting. Saddam started the war because he disputed the Iran-Iraq border, despite having himself negotiated that border before he became President.

34

CAB/33/003&

The war claimed a million casualties. The Iraqi regime used chemical weapons –
mustard gas and the nerve agents tabun and sarin – extensively from 1984, resulting
in over 20,000 Iranian casualties.

Ali Hasan al-Majid

"Chemical Ali"
As commander for the northern region, he bears direct
command responsibility for the chemical weapons attack on
the town of Halabja in northern Iraq which resulted in the
death of up to 5,000 people.

He also took a leading role in the brutal repression of the
uprising that followed the Gulf War in 1991, which included
mass executions, torture and widespread destruction.

The UN Security Council considered the report prepared by a team of three specialists
appointed by the UN Secretary General in March 1986, following which the President
made a statement condemning Iraqi use of chemical weapons. This marked the first
time a country had been named for violating the 1925 Geneva Convention banning
the use of chemical weapons.

Non-Judicial Beheading and Torture

This document follows the Iraqi Revolutionary Command Council's appointment of **Hasan al-Majid** as the one in
charge of all security, military and civil affairs in northern Iraq in March 1987. Immediately after his appointment,
the Anfal campaign was launched. Indiscriminate deadly methods, ranging from chemical attacks against Kurdish
civilians to destruction of Kurdish villages to beheading of Kurds, were used by the regime to follow through on its
campaign.

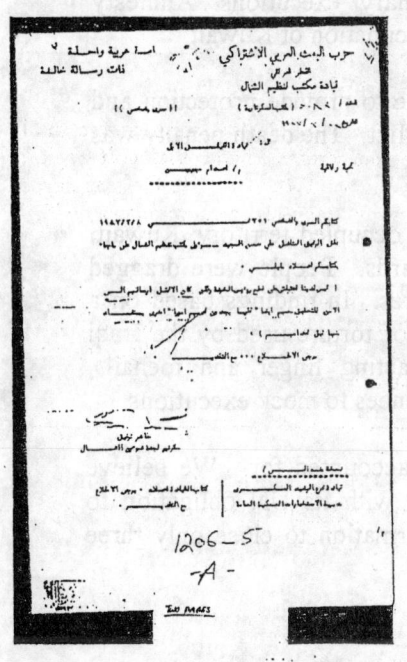

One Arab Nation With an Eternal Message
The Ba'ath Arab Socialist Party
The Qutr of Iraq
Northern Organisation Bureau Command
Number: 5083 (Secretariat Office)
Date 22 Aug 1987
-Confidential and Personal-
To: First Corps Command
Subject: Execution of Criminals
Comradely Salute,
[Re:] your personal and confidential letter [No.] 352 on 8 Aug
1987.
The valiant comrade, Ali Hasan al-Majid, Commander of the
Northern Organisation Bureau, has commented as follows on your
aforementioned letter:
"We do not object to the decapitation of traitors. But it would have
been preferable had you also sent them to Security for the purpose
of interrogating them. [Security personnel] could have found with
them other significant information that could have been useful,
prior to their execution."
Kindly review...Respectfully
[Signature]
Tahir Tawfiq
Secretary of Northern Affairs Committee

35

Iraq also started the "war of the cities", involving the indiscriminate bombing of civilian targets, with its attack on Ahwaz in March 1985.   And it consistently mistreated POWs, including by brainwashing.

Farzad Bazoft

Farzad Bazoft was a young journalist working for the Observer when he was arrested by the Iraqi authorities in September 1989. The 31-year old Iranian exile, who was travelling on British travel documents, had visited Iraq at the invitation of the Iraqi authorities on several occasions previously. He was researching a story on a large explosion at the rocket-testing complex at Qaqa, south of Baghdad when he was arrested. Detained with him was Mrs Daphne Parish, a British nurse who worked at one of Baghdad's major hospitals, who had driven him to the site. They were accused of spying for Britain and Israel. Mrs Parish was sentenced to 15 years imprisonment, spent six months in solitary confinement before being moved to a women's prison, and was eventually released in 1990.

Bazoft was less fortunate. He was forced to make a confession (allegedly after being drugged) and sentenced to death by hanging after a cursory trial. Despite widespread international protest and condemnation, the Iraqi regime carried out the death sentence on 15 March 1990. In a callous snub, Mr Latif Nassif Jassem, the Iraqi Information Minister and confidant of President Saddam, said "Mrs Thatcher wanted him alive. We gave her the body", after Mr Bazoft's corpse was handed over to the British embassy in Baghdad.

Invasion of Kuwait

Iraq invaded Kuwait on 2 August 1990.   Abuses committed by its forces included robbery, rape of Kuwaitis and expatriates, and summary executions. Amnesty International documented many other abuses during the occupation of Kuwait.

Iraq denied access to the Red Cross, which has a mandate to provide protection and assistance to civilians affected by international armed conflict. The death penalty was extended to looting and hoarding of food.

As Iraq tried to implement a policy of Iraqisation of the occupied territory, Kuwaiti civilians were arrested for "crimes" such as wearing beards. People were dragged from their homes and held in improvised detention centres. In findings based on a large number of interviews, Amnesty listed 38 methods of torture used by the Iraqi occupiers, including beatings, breaking of limbs, extracting finger and toenails, inserting bottle necks into the rectum, and subjecting detainees to mock executions.

More than 600 Kuwaiti POWs and missing are still unaccounted for. We believe some were still alive in 1998. Iraq refuses to comply with its UN obligation to account for the missing. It has provided sufficient information to close only three files.

36

CAB/33/0040

Aziz Salih Numan

Aziz Salih al-Nu'man

As Governor of Kuwait during the latter part of the occupation, November 1990 – February 1991, he bears responsibility for grave breaches of Geneva Convention IV Relative to the Protection of Civilian Persons in Time Of War committed by Iraqi forces during that period, including murder, torture, rape and deportation.

In an attempt to deter military action to expel it from Kuwait, the Iraqi regime took several hundred foreign nationals (including children) in Iraq and Kuwait hostage, and prevented thousands more from leaving. Worse still, hostages were held as human shields at a number of strategic military and civilian sites, many in inhumane conditions. These acts constituted a flagrant violation of international law – the Fourth Geneva Convention, to which Iraq is a party – as was confirmed in United Nations Security Council resolutions 670 and 674.

At the end of the Gulf War, the Iraqi army fleeing Kuwait set fire to over 1,160 Kuwaiti oil wells, with serious environmental consequences. And inside Iraq, an uprising by Iraqi Kurds and Shi'a Muslims was brutally suppressed, with the loss of tens of thousands of lives.

Continuing abuses

Since the Gulf War, the Iraqi regime's systematic repression of the Iraqi people has continued unabated.

Persecution of the Kurds

Persecution of Iraq's Kurds continues, although the protection provided by the northern No-Fly Zone has curbed the worst excesses. The Baghdad regime has continued a policy of Arabisation in northern Iraq to remove Kurdish claims to the oil-rich area around the city of Kirkuk. Kurds and other non-Arabs are forcibly relocated to the three northern Iraqi governorates – Dohuk, Arbil and Sulaimaniyah – which are under de facto Kurdish control.

The United Nations Commission on Human Rights (UNCHR) Special Rapporteur for Iraq reports that 94,000 individuals have been expelled since 1991. Kurdish reports indicate that four million square metres of agricultural land owned by Kurds has been

37

CAB/33/0041

confiscated and redistributed to Iraqi Arabs. Arabs from southern Iraq have been offered incentives to move into the Kirkuk area and, in disputes with their Kurdish neighbours, are always favoured by the authorities.

'B'

B (name withheld), a Kurdish businessman from Baghdad, married with children, was arrested in December 1996 outside his house by plainclothes security men. Initially his family did not know his whereabouts and went from one police station to another inquiring about him. Then through friends they found out that he was being held in the headquarters of the General Security Directorate in Baghdad. The family was not allowed to visit him.

Eleven months later in November 1997 the family was told by the authorities that he had been executed and that they should go and collect his body. His body bore evident signs of torture. His eyes were gouged out and the empty eye sockets were filled with paper. His right wrist and left leg were broken. The family was not given any reason for his arrest and subsequent execution. However, they suspected that he was executed because of his friendship with a retired army general who had links with the Iraqi opposition outside the country and who was arrested just before B's arrest and also executed.

In addition, ethnic Kurds and Turcomans have been prevented from buying property and those who own property and wish to sell have to do so to an Arab. Kurds have also been encouraged to change the ethnicity on their identity cards to Arab as part of this process.

Persecution of the Shi'a community, including murder of Shi'a religious leaders

More than 100 Shi'a clerics have disappeared since the 1991 uprising. Sayyed Muhammed Taghi al-Khoie was killed in a staged car accident in July 1994. Following the assassination in 1998 of two leading Shi'a clerics, Grand Ayatollah Shaykh Mirza Ali al-Gharawi and Ayatollah Shaykh Murtadaal-Burujerdi, the UN Special Rapporteur on Human Rights reported his fears that this formed part of a systematic attack on the independent leadership of Shi'a Muslims in Iraq.

Barzan al-Tikriti

Saddam's half brother. Personally responsible for the detention and/or murder of several thousand male members of the Barzani tribe in 1983. While head of Iraqi Intelligence (the Mukhabarat) 1979-1983, he was responsible for the repression of religious and ethnic minorities, including forced deportation, disappearances and murder.

Linked to the arrest of 90 members of the al-Hakim family and the murder of at least six of them

CAB/33/0042

In early 1999, during a peaceful demonstration in response to the Iraqi regime's murder of the most senior Shi'a cleric in Iraq, Grand Ayatollah Sayyed Mohammed Sadiq al-Sadr, security forces fired into the crowd of protestors, killing hundreds of civilians, including women and children. Security forces were also involved in efforts to break-up Shi'a Friday prayers in Baghdad and other cities. Large numbers of Shi'a were rounded up, imprisoned without trial and tortured. In May 2001, two more Shi'a clerics were executed in Baghdad for publicly accusing the regime of the Grand Ayatollah's murder.

Al-Shaikh Yahya Muhsin Ja'far al-Zeini

Al-Shaikh Yahya Muhsin Ja'far al-Zeini, from Saddam City, is a 29-year-old former theology student in *al-Hawza al-'Ilmiya* in al-Najaf. On 2 July 1999 he was arrested in his parents' house following his arrival from al-Najaf. His father and two brothers had been detained as substitute prisoners until his arrest. Security men blindfolded him and took him to a Security Directorate building. Once there, he was taken to a room and his blindfold was removed. He told Amnesty International:

" ... I saw a friend of mine, al-Shaikh Nasser Taresh al-Sa'idi, naked. He was handcuffed and a piece of wood was placed between his elbows and his knees. The two ends of the wood were placed on two high chairs and al-Shaikh Nasser was being suspended like a chicken. This method of torture is known as *al-Khaygania* (a reference to a former security director known as al-Khaygani). An electric wire was attached to al-Shaikh Nasser's penis and another one attached to one of his toes. He was asked if he could identify me and he said "this is al-Shaikh Yahya". They took me to another room and then after about 10 minutes they stripped me of my clothes and a security officer said "the person you saw has confessed against you". He said to me "You followers of [Ayatollah] al-Sadr have carried out acts harmful to the security of the country and have been distributing anti-government statements coming from abroad". He asked if I have any contact with an Iraqi religious scholar based in Iran who has been signing these statements. I said "I do not have any contacts with him"... I was then left suspended in the same manner as al-Shaikh al-Sa'idi. My face was looking upward. They attached an electric wire on my penis and the other end of the wire is attached to an electric motor. One security man was hitting my feet with a cable. Electric shocks were applied every few minutes and were increased. I must have been suspended for more than an hour. I lost consciousness. They took me to another room and made me walk even though my feet were swollen from beating.... They repeated this method a few times."

In response to on-going attacks on government buildings and officials in southern Iraq during 1999, the Iraqi army and militia forces destroyed entire Shi'a villages in the south. This was a continuation of the regime's policy, pursued throughout the 1990s, of draining the marshes area of southern Iraq, so forcing the population to relocate to urban areas where it was unable to offer assistance to anti-regime elements and could be controlled more effectively by the regime's security forces.

Harassment of the Opposition

The UNCHR Special Rapporteur on Iraq has received numerous reports of harassment, intimidation and threats against the families of opposition members living abroad.

In mid February 1999 the brother of a senior London-based member of the Iraqi National Accord (INA) was arrested by Iraqi Intelligence (the Mukhabarat) in Basra and forced to phone his brother in the UK and explain his predicament. A

CAB/33/0043

Mukhabarat officer subsequently spoke to the INA member and demanded that he co-operate with the Mukhabarat.

In January 1999 the Mukhabarat phoned another INA official, who was told that his children and brother were under arrest and would face punishment if he did not co-operate with the Mukhabarat. The Mukhabarat demanded details of the home, car and routines of INA head Dr Ayed Allawi.

A Professional Rapist

Government personnel card of Aziz Saleh Ahmed, identified as a "fighter in the popular army" whose "activity" is "violation of women's honour" (i.e. a professional rapist).

The family of General Nahib al-Salehi, a political opponent living in Jordan, have been subjected to arrests, questioning and other forms of harassment. In June 2000, he received a videotape showing the rape of a female relative. Ten days later, he was contacted by the Iraqi Intelligence Service, who told him that they were holding another female relation and urged him to stop his activities.

Special Operations

"Special Operations" refers to regime-sanctioned sabotage, kidnapping and assassination missions. Since the early 1970s the Intelligence Services have planned and carried out assassinations of prominent Iraqi oppositionists and other political targets. Since 1991, these include:

- MUAYAD HASAN NAJI AL-JANABI, a scientist formerly engaged in Iraq's nuclear programme, who was murdered in Jordan in late 1992.
- SHAYKH TALIB AL-SUHAYL, an Iraqi dissident, murdered in Lebanon in 1994.
- The attempted assassination of former US President GEORGE BUSH in Kuwait in early 1993.

Arbitrary killings

Executions are carried out without due process of law. Relatives are often prevented from burying the victims in accordance with Islamic practice, and have even been charged for the bullets used. An estimated 2,500 prisoners were executed between 1997 and 1999 in a "prison cleansing" campaign (not the first – in 1984, 4,000 political prisoners were executed at a single prison, the Abu Ghraib). In February 2000, 64 male prisoners were executed at Abu Ghraib, followed in March by a further 58, all of whom had previously been held in solitary confinement. In October 2001, 23 political prisoners, mainly Shi'a Muslims, were executed at Abu Ghraib.

40

CAB/33/0044

Between 1993 and 1998 around 3,000 prisoners from the "Mahjar" prison (see below) were executed in an execution area called the "Hadiqa" (garden) near to the prison. The "Hadiqa" consisted of an open area and sand bank which was covered by a steel awning. Prisoners from the "Mahjar" were executed in the "Hadiqa" by machine gun. A Special Oversight Committee at the prison decided on the executions.

Udayy Saddam Hussain

Saddam's elder son. Has been frequently accused of serial rape and murder of young women.

Personally executed dissidents in Basra during the uprising which followed the Gulf War in March 1991.

As a member of the National Security Council, he bears command responsibility for all crimes committed with the authority or acquiescence of that body.

In October 2000, dozens of women accused of prostitution were beheaded without any judicial process, together with men accused of pimping. Some were accused for political reasons. Members of the Feda'iyye Saddam (the militia created in 1994 by Saddam's elder son, Udayy Hussain) used swords to execute victims in front of their homes.

'Ala 'Abd Al-Qadir Al-Majid

In mid 2001, 'Ala 'Abd Al-Qadir Al-Majid fled to Jordan from Iraq, citing disagreements with the regime over business matters. 'Ala was a cousin of Saddam Hussain, a former intelligence officer and, latterly, a businessman. He returned to Iraq after the Iraqi Ambassador in Jordan declared publicly that his life was not in danger. He was met at the border by Tahir Habbush, Head of the Iraqi Intelligence Service (the Mukhabarat), and taken to a farm owned by 'Ali Hasan Al-Majid. At the farm 'Ala was tied to a tree and executed by members of his immediate family who, following orders from Saddam, took it in turns to shoot him.

Saddam has a history of dealing with disloyalty by arranging for traitors, as Saddam sees them, to be killed by their family or tribal associates. This helps to prevent blood feuds between different family/tribal groups and to distance his involvement.

'Ala is just the latest of some 40 of Saddam's relatives, including women and children, that he has had killed. In February 1996, his sons-in-law Hussain Kamal and Saddam Kamal were executed. They had defected in 1995 and returned to Iraq from Jordan after the government had announced amnesties for them.

41

Arbitrary arrest, detention under inhumane conditions, inhumane punishments, and torture

Men, women and children continue to be arrested and detained on suspicion of political or religious activities, or simply because they are related to members of the opposition. Political prisoners are held in inhumane and degrading conditions throughout Iraq.

The "Mahjar" prison located on the Police Training College site in central Baghdad formerly housed the Police Dog Training Centre. The normal occupancy of the "Mahjar" is 600-700 people. Thirty of the cells are underground and thirty other cells used to be dog kennels. Prisoners are beaten twice a day and the women regularly raped by their guards. They receive no medical treatment, but some prisoners have survived up to a year in the "Mahjar". Two large oil storage tanks each with a capacity of 36,000 litres have been built close to the "Mahjar". The tanks are full of petrol and are connected by pipes to the prison buildings in the "Mahjar". The prison authorities have instructions to set light to the petrol and destroy the "Mahjar" in an emergency.

Torture and Mistreatment in Abu Ghraib Prison

Abdallah, a member of the Ba'ath Party whose loyalty became suspect has still-vivid personal memories from his four years of imprisonment at Abu Ghraib in the 1980s, where he was held naked the entire time and frequently tortured.

On the second day of his imprisonment, the men were forced to walk between two rows of five guards each, to receive their containers of food. While walking to get the food, they were beaten by the guards with plastic telephone cables. They had to return to their cells the same way, so that a walk to get breakfast resulted in twenty lashes. "It wasn't that bad going to get the food", Abdallah said, "but coming back the food was spilled when we were beaten." The same procedure was used when the men went to the bathroom.

On the third day, the torture began. "We were removed from our cells and beaten with plastic pipes. This surprised us, because we were asked no questions. Possibly it was being done to break our morale", Abdallah speculated. The torture escalated to sixteen sessions daily. The treatment was organised and systematic. Abdallah was held alone in a 3x2-meter room that opened onto a corridor. "We were allowed to go to the toilet three times a day, then they reduced the toilet to once a day for only one minute. I went for four years without a shower or a wash", Abdallah said. He also learned to cope with the deprivation and the hunger that accompanied his detention:

"I taught myself to drink a minimum amount of water because there was no place to urinate. They used wooden sticks to beat us and sometimes the sticks would break. I found a piece of a stick, covered with blood, and managed to bring it back to my room. I ate it for three days. A person who is hungry can eat anything. Pieces of our bodies started falling off from the beatings and our skin was so dry that it began to fall off. I ate pieces of my own body.

"No one, not Pushkin, not Mahfouz, can describe what happened to us. It is impossible to describe what living this day to day was like. I was totally naked the entire time. Half of the original group [of about thirty men] died. It was a slow type of continuous physical and psychological torture. Sometimes, it seemed that orders came to kill one of us, and he would be beaten to death."

The "Sijn Al-Tarbut" (the casket prison) is located on the third underground level of the new Directorate of General Security (DGS) building in Baghdad. The prisoners here are kept in rows of rectangular steel boxes, as found in mortuaries, until they either confess to their crimes or die. There are around 100-150 boxes which are

42

CAB/33/0046

opened for half an hour a day to allow the prisoners some light and air. The prisoners receive only liquids.

Qusayy Saddam Hussain

Saddam's younger son. As head of the Iraqi internal security agencies, he has permitted and encouraged the endemic use of torture, including rape and the threat of rape, in Iraq.

The "Qurtiyya" (the can) prison is located in a DGS compound in the Talbiyyah area of the Saddam City district of Baghdad. This consists of 50-60 metal boxes the size of old tea chests in which detainees are locked under the same conditions as the "Sijn Al-Tarbut". Each box has a tap for water and a floor made of mesh to allow the detainees to defecate.

A Tortured Family

A particularly nasty example of torture involved a family which was arrested in late 2000 and taken to two separate interrogation centres within Republican Guard facilities located along the road to Abu Ghraib. The husband was held in one centre whilst the wife and children were held at a women's facility. The husband and wife were interrogated under torture about the husband's sale of a vehicle which, the interrogators said, had been captured by Iraqi security forces during a raid on Iraqi oppositionists.

The interrogators said separately to both husband and wife that they would cease the torture if they signed confessions admitting to be collaborating with the oppositionists. They refused. The wife was stripped naked and cigarettes stubbed out on all parts of her body whenever she refused to implicate her husband. She was beaten and thrown around the interrogation room. Her children were forced to watch the torture. She was eventually released, having been told that her husband would continue being tortured until she returned to confess. She was arrested again two weeks later and the same pattern of torture was repeated, leaving her a psychological wreck.

During his interrogation, the husband's arms were tied behind his back and he was then suspended in the air using a hook hung from the ceiling. This caused intense pain as his shoulder muscles and ligaments were torn. After a period, the interrogators entered the room and the husband was unhooked and placed in a chair in the middle of the room. From close range, he was then shot at with a pistol whenever he refused to agree to sign his confession. Sometimes shots were fired which missed his body, at other times the pistol muzzle was placed against his fingers, toes or arms and fired so as to mutilate these areas.

Over the following two weeks further interrogations occurred at intervals, following periods of food and water deprivation. Eventually a bribe was paid to an Iraqi Intelligence officer by the husband's and wife's wider family and both the husband and wife were released. They subsequently escaped Iraq.

CAB/33/0047

Prisoners are also subjected to brutal torture. Methods include knife cuts, sexual attacks, electric shocks, eye gouging, cigarette burns, pulling out of fingernails and mutilation of hands with electric drills. "Official" rape is also systematically used against Iraqi women.

In early 1998, the Iraqi regime obstructed a UN weapons inspection team which was trying to investigate claims that Iraq had conducted biological weapons experiments on prisoners during the mid-1990s.

Saddam has issued a series of decrees establishing severe penalties (amputation, branding, cutting off of ears, or other forms of mutilation) for criminal offences. Anyone found guilty of slandering the President has their tongue removed. These punishments are practised mainly on political dissenters. Iraqi TV has broadcast pictures of these punishments as a warning to others.

Senior regime figures have been personally involved in these abuses. General 'Abd Hamud, the head of Saddam's private office, has played a direct role in supervising all of these prisons and their security. Both he and Saddam have signed death warrants for prisoners. The archive files holding these death warrants were kept hidden within the cafeteria area on the eighth floor of the main Ministry of Interior building in Baghdad.

Udayy Hussain maintained a private torture chamber, known as the "Ghurfa Hamra" (Red Room) in a building on the banks of the Tigris disguised as an electricity installation. In one infamous incident of mass torture, Udayy Hussain ordered the national football team to be caned on the soles of their feet after losing a World Cup qualifying match.

Saddam's chemical gifts to the Marsh Arabs

44

CAB/33/0048

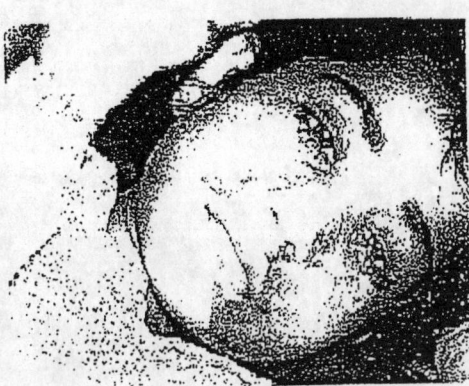

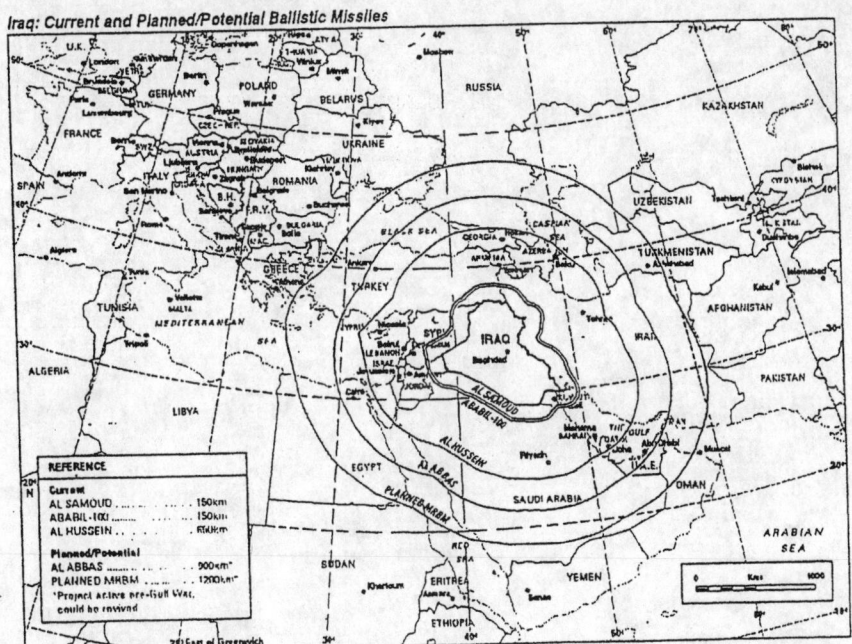

Iraq: Current and Planned/Potential Ballistic Missiles

CAB/33/004

APPENDIX 8

From:	Alastair Campbell
Date:	9 September 2002

JOHN SCARLETT

Cc: Jonathan Powell
David Manning
PMOS
Jim Poston
PS/Foreign Secretary
PS/Defence Secretary
PS/"C"
PS/DG of Security Servi
██████████ (GCHC
John Williams (FCO)
Peter Ricketts
Stephen Wright (FCO)
████████ (SIS)
████████ (SIS)
Martin Howard (MOD)
David Omand (CO)

At our discussion this morning, we agreed it would be helpful if I set out for colleagues the process by which the Iraq dossier will be produced.

The first point is that this must be, and be seen to be, the work of you and your team, and that its credibility depends fundamentally upon that.

The second is that you are working on a new dossier, according to the structure we agreed at the meeting last week, to meet the new circumstances which have developed over recent weeks and months. Therefore, the rush of comments on the old dossier are not necessary or totally relevant. People should wait for the new one, which will be more detailed and substantial.

The structure we agreed last week was roughly as follows:

- why the issue arose in the first place
- why the inspection process was necessary
- the history of concealment and deception
- the story of inspectors, leading to their departure
- the story of weapons unaccounted for, and what they could do
- a section on ballistic missile technology
- CW/BW
- nuclear
- the sanctions regime, and how the policy of containment has worked only up to a point
- illicit money
- the repressive nature of the regime
- why the history of the man and the regime (Iraq/Iran; chemical weapons on his own people; Kuwait; human

CAB| 6|0002

rights) makes us worried he cannot be allowed further to develop these weapons.

Much of this is obviously historical, but the history is a vital part of the overall story. This is something the IISS Report deals with very well.

The media/political judgement will inevitably focus on "what's new?" and I was pleased to hear from you and your SIS colleagues that, contrary to media reports today, the intelligence community are taking such a helpful approach to this in going through all the material they have. It goes without saying that there should be nothing published that you and they are not 100% happy with.

It is of course inevitable that the media and political speculation surrounding the dossier will grow prior to publication. But it is important that nobody in government feeds it. Partial leaks, or running commentaries on an out of date document help nobody.

Our public line is that the dossier will set out the facts which make HMG judge Iraq/WMD to represent a real threat. It will be detailed and comprehensive. As to why we can't publish it now, it has to be cleared by all those who have helped to build the case. This involves important judgements, and we will take our time.

In the meantime, we should encourage the fullest possible coverage of the IISS Report, and other publicly available material. But we should not talk up the dossier. We should be making clear that even with the intelligence material, the picture can never be a complete one because the inspectors have been out for so long. We have to be disciplined in holding the line until publication.

We agreed that by the end of today, you should have most of the draft material together, with the Agencies providing the sections relevant to the middle part of our structure, and the FCO providing the more historical material.

You will want to go through this material before submitting a consolidated draft to No. 10 and others. You will also take this to the US on your visit at the end of the week.

In the meantime, I will chair a team that will go through the document from a presentational point of view, and make recommendations to you. This team, I suggest, will include John Williams (FCO) Paul Hamill (CIC) and Phil Bassett and David Bradshaw from here. Writing by committee does not work but we will make recommendations and suggestions, and you can decide what you want to incorporate. Once they are incorporated, we need to take a judgement as to whether a single person should be appointed to write the final version.

CAB/6/0003

INVESTOR IN PEOPLE

It would be helpful to me and my colleagues if I could have something to look at by the time we get back from the TUC tomorrow.

We also discussed the importance of translating the dossier into other languages. Perhaps the FCO could look at the feasibility and timescale questions involved on this, but the Al Qaida evidence document benefited greatly in its impact through the various translations and their use diplomatically and on websites, etc.

We also need to consider whether to do a shorter version more aimed at the general public than the media.

So our current thinking and planning points to sometime in the middle of next week as the earliest possible time to do this. Once we have an advanced draft, we can address the questions of exact timing, launch details, Prime Ministerial and other ministerial involvement. The Prime Minister has expressed an interest in seeing an advanced draft.

I also briefed you on our discussions with US officials at Camp David, recorded separately. They intend to produce a series of dossiers, starting with one of Saddam's record of defiance of the UN, to be published alongside President Bush's speech on Thursday. They will then roll out several reports in the coming weeks. I am confident we can make yours one that complements rather than conflicts with them.

Dictated by ALASTAIR CAMPBELL and signed in his absence.
Director of Communications and Strategy

CAB/6/0004

INVESTOR IN PEOPLE

APPENDIX 9

FOREWORD

- The threat posed to international peace and security by the spread of weapons of mass destruction cannot be ignored. Unless members of the international community face up to the challenge represented by this threat, they will place at risk the lives of their own citizens.

- Saddam Hussein's Iraqi regime is a uniquely dangerous example of the general threat, both because of his record and his persistent flouting of international norms of behaviour.

- Saddam Hussein is the only modern leader to have used chemical weapons, against Iran in the war which he initiated in the 1980s, causing 20,000 casualties, and against Iraqi citizens at Halabja, resulting in several thousand deaths.

- He has shown his capacity for aggression, by invading Kuwait, terrorising its people and ransacking the country. [Many thousand] Kuwaiti civilians have never been accounted for and must be presumed to have been killed by forces loyal to Saddam.

- It was only because of firm action by the international community that Kuwait was freed. And it was only because of the international community's resolve, through the United Nations, that Saddam Hussein was forced to dismantle some of his weapons of mass destruction.

- In the 1990s UN Weapons Inspectors worked to implement UN Security Council Resolutions passed following the end of the Gulf conflict, which called for the elimination of Iraqi nuclear, biological and chemical weapons. Saddam Hussein worked throughout this period to thwart the efforts of the

DOS/2/0002

UN personnel. And even after the US and British Air Forces were deployed in 1998 in operations designed to degrade Iraq's capability to use chemical, biological and nuclear weapons, it was assessed that he retained sufficient materials and technical capacity to rebuild his arsenal.

- Since then the UN has tried repeatedly to achieve compliance with UN Resolutions and accept the return of weapons inspectors able to go anywhere at any time to track down and destroy his nuclear, biological and chemical weapons and supporting infrastructure.

- At every turn Saddam has played games with the UN, flouting its authority. He has consistently sought to divert attention from his failure to comply with the will of the international community. The only reasonable explanation for his prevarication is that he has something to hide, something he is unwilling to give up.

- Containment of Saddam's ambitions through sanctions was intended to ensure Iraqi disarmament, as demanded by the United Nations. This policy had significant success when UN inspectors were able to operate. And it continues to slow Saddam's efforts to build weapons of mass destruction. But without effective enforcement of UN resolutions, he will achieve his ambitions.

- We cannot wait forever for the right answer from Saddam, when all the time he is engaged in work on weapons which could threaten the whole Gulf region and the Eastern Mediterranean. The UK's own vital interests and security could be directly threatened. If we were to do so, particularly after 11 September, and our patience were to be rewarded with another devastating attack, we would rightly be castigated for our inaction.

CONFIDENTIAL UNTIL RELEASED

2

DOS/2/0003

416

- The time has come for Saddam to comply with international law as set out most recently in [UNSCR....] and accept the deployment of UN Weapons Inspectors or face the consequences.

- This dossier sets out in detail our best assessment of the facts about Saddam Hussein's nuclear, biological and chemical weapons capabilities, his ballistic missile programmes, the history of UN weapons inspections in Iraq and Saddam's record of human rights abuses and aggression towards his neighbours. Taken individually each chapter is damning enough. As a whole they present a picture of a regime which is so opposed to international norms of behaviour that the threat it poses cannot be ignored.

3

DOS/2/0004

EXECUTIVE SUMMARY

1.   Under Saddam Hussein, Iraq has developed chemical and biological weapons, acquired missiles able to attack neighbouring countries with these weapons, and tried hard to develop a nuclear bomb. Iraq has admitted to all of these programmes to acquire weapons of mass destruction. And Saddam has used chemical weapons, both against Iran and against his own people.

2.   This paper sets out the British Government's knowledge of these weapons programmes. It traces their history from the first use of chemical weapons against Iraq's own Kurdish population in 1987, through their further use against Iran and the details uncovered by UN inspectors after the Gulf War. Drawing on very sensitive intelligence, the paper also sets out our assessment of Iraq's current capabilities, and shows how the picture is continuing to develop as new information becomes available.

3.   But the threat from Iraq does not depend solely on these capabilities. It arises also because of the violent and aggressive nature of Saddam's regime. His record of international repression and external aggression gives rise to unique concerns about the threat he poses. The paper briefly outlines his rise to power, the nature of his regime and his history of regional aggression. Vivid and horrifying accounts of Saddam's human rights abuses are also catalogued.

4.   The importance of denying Saddam access to weapons of mass destruction was recognised by the United Nations in 1991. The paper sets out the key UN Security Council Resolutions, accepted by Iraq, which required the destruction of these weapons. It also summaries the history of the UN inspections regime. This includes both the extent of Saddam's capabilities uncovered by the inspectors and Iraq's history of dishonesty, deception, intimidation and concealment in its dealings with the UN

DOS/2/0005

inspectors. It also describes the extent of Saddam's weapons programmes left unaccounted for at the end of the inspections process.

5.   At the heart of the paper is an account, confirmed by secret intelligence as well as evidence from the UN inspections, of Iraq's current capabilities in the fields of chemical, biological and nuclear weapons and of the ballistic missiles to deliver them. Our judgement, based on all the available sources is that Iraq:

- has stocks of chemical and biological agents and weapons available, both retained from before the Gulf War, and probably from more recent production;

- is self-sufficient in the technology and expertise required to produce chemical and biological weapons, specifically: sulphur mustard, tabun, sarin, GF, VX; and anthrax, botulinum toxin, and aflatoxin;

- is refurbishing sites formerly associated with its chemical, biological and nuclear weapons programmes;

- retains a range of delivery means for chemical and biological weapons;

- has modified the L-29 jet trainer to make it capable of delivering chemical and biological agents;

- has assembled specialists to work on its nuclear programme, which was aimed at producing a 20-kiloton weapon, capable of causing 80 per cent casualties within 1.6 miles of the detonation;

- is covertly attempting to acquire technology and materials for use in nuclear weapons, including specialised aluminium controlled because of its potential use in enriching uranium;

- has retained up to 20 Al Hussein missiles, capable of carrying chemical or biological warheads;

- is deploying its Al-Samoud liquid propellant missile, and has used the absence of weapons inspectors to work on extending its range;

DOS/2/0006 5

- is testing the solid-propellant missile Ababil-100, and is making efforts to extend its range;

- has constructed a new engine test stand bigger than the one used for its current missile systems, to test missiles with a range longer than permitted under Security Council resolution 687 and capable of threatening the UK Sovereign Bases in Cyprus, NATO members (e.g. Greece or Turkey), Israel and all Iraq's Gulf neighbours;

- is working to obtain improved guidance technology to increase missile accuracy;

6.   Recent intelligence adds to this picture. It indicates that Iraq:

- attaches great importance to the possession of weapons of mass destruction and that Saddam Hussein is committed to using them if necessary;

- envisages the use of weapons of mass destruction in its current military planning, and could deploy such weapons within 45 minutes of the order being given for their use;

- has begun dispersing its most sensitive weapons, equipment and material, because Saddam is determined not to lose the capabilities developed in the last four years;

- is preparing plans to conceal evidence of its weapons of mass destruction from any renewed inspection, including by dispersing incriminating documents;

- has acquired mobile laboratories for military use, corroborating earlier report about the mobile production of biological warfare agents;

- has purchased large quantities of uranium ore, despite having no civil nuclear programme that could require it.

7.   The paper also briefly sets out how Iraq is able to finance its weapons programme. Drawing on illicit earnings generated outside UN control, Iraq generated income of some

$3 billion in 2001. Further substantial earnings may have been generated though abuse of the UN oil for food programmes.

[8.   Finally, this paper includes an account of the recent history of intelligence assessment on Iraq's weapons of mass destruction. Reflecting the great importance of the risk posed by Saddam, we summarise key judgements reached by the Joint Intelligence Committee and briefed to the Prime Minister each year since the withdrawal of UN inspectors in 1998. Together with the even more recent intelligence referred to in this paper, these assessments demonstrate the continuing and growing grounds for concern about the Iraqi programmes and help explain the government's view that the time has now come to see decisive action taken to tackle them.]

SECTION 1

SADDAM'S REGIME AND HIS RISE TO POWER

Origins and early years

1. Saddam Hussein was born in the district of Tikrit in 1937. In 1955 he moved to Baghdad, where he joined the Ba'ath Party. After a bungled attempt at a political assassination in 1959, Saddam escaped, first to Syria and then to Egypt. He was sentenced to 15 years imprisonment in absentia.

2. Saddam returned to Baghdad in 1963. When the Ba'ath Party fell from power, he went into hiding. Captured and imprisoned, he eventually escaped in 1967 with the co-operation of his guards, and became a bodyguard responsible for Ba'ath Party security. In this capacity, he set about establishing himself at the centre of power, rapidly increasing his influence with the Party. [Brief details about his progress in the 1970s]

3. Following the Ba'ath Party's return to power, Saddam took over the Presidency of Iraq in July 1979. Within days, five fellow members of Iraq's Revolutionary Command Council were arrested and accused of involvement in a coup attempt. They and 17 others were summarily sentenced to death and executed.

4. After the revolution that ousted the Shah in Iran, Saddam started a campaign against the Shia majority of Iraq, fearing that they might be encouraged by the new Islamic regime. A campaign of mass arrests and executions of Islamic activists led to the execution of the Ayatollah Baqir al-Sadr and his sister in April 1980. In 1983, 80 members of another leading Shia family were arrested and six of them, all religious leaders, executed. A fuller account of Saddam's record on human rights is at Annex A.

CONFIDENTIAL UNTIL RELEASED

Dos/2/0009

5. Saddam attacked Iran in 1980, in an attempt to reverse earlier territorial concessions to the Shah. But the war went badly, and when the Iraqi army was driven back to the Iraqi frontier in 1982 he faced a serious crisis of confidence. The murmurers were purged, and Saddam's only potential rival conveniently died. In 1983 the army was cowed by the elimination of unsuccessful officers, and the Shia by the arrest of the family of their dead leader.

6. After the end of the conflict Saddam resumed his previous pursuit of primacy in the Gulf. When these efforts evoked international criticism, he challenged the presence of the US navy in the Gulf and threatened CW retaliation against the Israelis should they dare to attack Iraq. But his policies were expensive, and in a period of low oil prices left Iraq in severe financial difficulties.

7. By 1990, a number of factors, including his financial problems and resentment at Kuwait's oil production policies, prompted the invasion that led to the Gulf War (see section 2).

[The above section needs amendment]

Saddam's Iraq

8. Saddam now depends on a narrow inner circle of his relatives to convey his requirements to others, even members of the government. He has created a larger circle of trusted cronies from his home region of Tikrit at the centre of his Government.

9. Saddam keeps the various groupings in check by balancing the advantages he can offer and the fearful consequences of crossing him. His ruthlessness is demonstrated not only against those who have offended him, but also their families, friends or colleagues. For example a large number of officers from the Jabbur tribe were executed for the alleged disloyalty of a few of them. Saddam used the same system of

DOS/2/0010

rewards, promises and punishment with the nations whose hostages he took during the war against Iran and the occupation of Kuwait.

10. To control the flow of rewards, inducements and penalties Saddam has to be the exclusive and individual source of all power in Iraq. To this end he has acted ruthlessly to ensure that there should be no other centres of power. The many security services report on the population and their colleagues upwards to him. Parties and tribes which might try to assert themselves, eg the Kurds and the communists have been crushed.

11. Army officers have been enmeshed in the government's web of informers. Suspicion that they have ambitions other than the service of the President leads to immediate execution. Even the war hero (and Saddam's erstwhile son in law) General Maher al Rashid was placed under house arrest, and his popular brother, General Taher al Rashid disposed of in a helicopter "accident".

12. It is routine for Saddam to pre-empt those who might conspire against him. He has said he knows who will conspire before they know it themselves. He constantly devises tests of his inner circle's reliability; and ostentatious enthusiasm for him or for his cause of the moment arouse his suspicions. He is perpetually aware that if he fails to deliver the benefits his supporters expect; or looks indecisive; or gives the impression of flagging, some of his supporters could be emboldened to dispose of him. So his need to retain their confidence, or to pre-empt them if they begin to doubt, constantly drives him to new adventures.

13. His experience has made Saddam a wily and sophisticated manipulator. He does not allow himself to be trammelled by friendships or loyalties, and these are always subject to his suspicions. And he never forgives those he believes have betrayed or opposed him; several have been assassinated abroad long after they have lost any significance at home.

10

DOS|2|0011

14. Saddam sees himself as the personification of the new Iraq. His ubiquitous pictures portray him in a variety of guises – Saddam the peasant, Bedouin, townsman, Kurd, Shiite, family man and embattled warrior. As his personality cult has developed, he has come to thinks that he is creating an Iraq to dominate the Gulf. At the same time, he has become hypersensitive to criticism, regarding it not only as a personal slight, but also derogatory to his mission.

15. Behind everything is Saddam's own ambitious hunger for the power which he manipulates with such skill. Throughout his career he has sought power and control, and now he will do everything to preserve the domination over Iraq which he has achieved.

[The above section needs further amendment]

11

DOS12|0012

14. Saddam sees himself as the per... the new Iraq. His ubiquitous portraits portray him in a variety of... ... ... Bedouin, townsman, Kurd, Shiite, family man and embattled warrior. As his personality cult has developed, he has come to think that he is creating an Iraq to dominate the Gulf. At pres...

15. Behind everything is Saddam's own ambitious hunger for the power wh...

SECTION 2

SADDAM'S WARS

1. Saddam Hussein has fought two wars of aggression; the Iran-Iraq war and the invasion of Kuwait. He has also pursued a long-term programme of persecution against Iraqi Kurds.

War on Iran

2. The Iran-Iraq war broke out when Saddam decided to take advantage of the state of weakness, isolation and disorganisation that he perceived in post-revolutionary Iran. He wanted to assert Iraq's position as a leader of the Arab world and to recover frontier territory ceded to Iran a few years earlier. In September 1980 he publicly abrogated the border treaty reached with Iran in 1975 and launched attacks on Iranian targets a few days later. Saddam expected it to be a short, sharp campaign. But the Iranians fought back and the bloody conflict lasted for eight years.

3. There were a million casualties in the conflict with Iran. Twenty thousand Iranians were killed by chemical weapons: mustard gas and the nerve agents tabun and sarin: all of which Iraq still possesses.

Persecution of the Kurds

4. In the early years of the war against Iran, Saddam had encouraged rivalry between the KDP (Kurdish Democratic Party, who supported Iran) and the PUK (Patriotic Union of Kurdistan). But the PUK started to move towards the KDP and Iran in the mid 1980s and Saddam, under pressure elsewhere, felt the need to reassert control over the Kurdish areas. Saddam appointed his cousin, Ali Hassan al'Majid, as his deputy in the north and a campaign of attacks on Kurdish villages – the notorious Anfal campaign – began. Chemical weapons were used from April 1987 and the countryside was progressively devastated by Saddam's forces. The most horrific attack was on Halabja in 1988, although it was far from unique.

5. Amnesty International estimates that more than 100,000 Kurds were killed or disappeared during Saddam's 1987-88 campaign to crush Kurdish insurgency. Kurdish villages were systematically razed. This was a policy of genocide.

Invasion of Kuwait

6. The invasion of Kuwait was the only case in recent times of one member of the United Nations taking over another.

7. Iraq invaded Kuwait on 2 August 1990. Abuses committed by its forces included robbery, rape of Kuwaitis and expatriates, and summary executions. Amnesty International documented many other abuses during the occupation of Kuwait.

8. Iraq denied access to the Red Cross, which has a mandate to provide protection and assistance to civilians affected by international armed conflict. The death penalty was extended to looting and hoarding of food.

9. As Iraq tried to implement a policy of Iraqisation of the occupied territory, Kuwaiti civilians were arrested for "crimes" such as wearing beards. People were dragged from their homes and held in improvised detention centres. In findings based on large number of interviews, Amnesty listed 38 methods of torture used by the Iraqi occupiers, including beatings, breaking of limbs, extracting finger and toenails, inserting bottle necks into the rectum, and subjecting detainees to mock executions.

10. More than 600 Kuwaiti POWs and missing are still unaccounted for. We believe some were still alive in 1998. Iraq refuses to comply with its UN obligation to account for the missing. It has provided sufficient information to close only three files.

11. In an attempt to deter military action to expel it from Kuwait, the Iraqi regime took several hundred foreign nationals (including children) in Iraq and Kuwait hostage, and prevented thousands more from leaving. Worse still, hostages were held as human shields at a number of strategic military and civilian sites, many in inhumane conditions. These acts constituted a flagrant violation of international law – the Fourth Geneva Convention, to which Iraq is a party – as was confirmed in United Nations Security Council resolutions 670 and 674.

12. At the end of the Gulf War, the Iraqi army fleeing Kuwait set fire to over 1,160 Kuwaiti oil wells, with serious environmental consequences. And inside Iraq, an uprising by Iraqi Kurds and Shi'a Muslims was brutally suppressed, with the loss of tens of thousands of lives.

Continuing abuses

13. Persecution of Iraq's Kurds continues, although the protection provided by the northern No-Fly Zone has curbed the worst excesses. The Baghdad regime has continued a policy of Arabisation in northern Iraq to remove Kurdish claims to the oil-rich area around the city of Kirkuk. Kurds and other non-Arabs are forcibly relocated to the three northern Iraqi governorates – Dohuk, Arbil and Sulaimaniyah – which are under de facto Kurdish control.

14. The United Nations Commission on Human Rights (UNCHR) Special Rapporteur for Iraq reports that 94,000 individuals have been expelled since 1991. Kurdish reports indicate that four million square metres of agricultural land owned by Kurds has been confiscated and redistributed to Iraqi Arabs. Arabs from southern Iraq have been offered incentives to move into the Kirkuk area and, in disputes with their Kurdish neighbours, are always favoured by the authorities.

15. In the wake of Operation Desert Storm, riots broke out in Basra on 1 March 1991, which spread quickly to other cities in Shia - dominated southern Iraq. A similar uprising against Baghdad's rule occurred in the Kurdish north. The Iraqi regime responded ruthlessly, killing or imprisoning thousands and prompting a humanitarian crisis as over a million Kurds fled into the mountains and tried to escape Iraq.

SECTION 3

IRAQ'S WMD PROGRAMMES - THE THREAT IN 1991

1. By the beginning of the Gulf War in 1991 Iraq had developed a wide range of chemical and biological weapons and had equipped a significant number of missiles to deliver them. Iraq also had an ambitious programme for the development of nuclear weapons.

2. The threat from **chemical weapons** was already well known. Iraq had made frequent use of a variety of chemical weapons during the Iran-Iraq War. (Many of the casualties are still alive in Iranian hospitals suffering from the long-term effects of numerous types of cancer and lung diseases.) In 1988 Saddam also used mustard and

---

The Attack on Halagbja

Shortly before sunrise on Friday, 17th March 1988, the village of Halabja was bombarded by Iraqi warplanes. The raid was over in minutes (?). In that short time, Saddam Hussein had committed a crime that no other dictator in recent times has carried out. A Kurd described the effects of a chemical attack on another village:

"My brothers and my wife had blood and vomit running from their noses and their mouths. Their heads were tilted to one side. They were groaning. I couldn't do much, just clean up the blood and vomit from their mouths and try in every way to make them breathe again. I did artificial respiration on them and then I gave them two injections each. I also rubbed creams on my wife and two brothers."

(From "Crimes Against Humanity," Iraqi National Congress.)

Among the corpses at Halabja, children were found dead where they had been playing outside their homes. In places, streets were piled with bodies. Five thousand villagers died.

nerve agents against Iraqi Kurds at Halabja in northern Iraq (see photo). Estimates vary, but according to Human Rights Watch up to 5,000 people were killed.

3.   A month after the attack on Halabja, Iraqi troops used over 100 tons of sarin nerve agent against Iranian troops on the Al Fao peninsula. Over the next three months Iraqi troops used sarin and other nerve agents on Iranian troops causing extensive casualties.

4.   In 1988 Saddam Hussein also ordered the use of nerve agents against Iraqi Kurds in northern Iraq.   And in 1991 Iraq used the biological warfare agent aflatoxin against the Shia population of Karbala [casualties].

5.   We now know that Iraq had the following range of agents available at this time:

- **Mustard** is a liquid agent that causes burns and blisters to exposed skin. When inhaled, mustard damages the respiratory tract; when ingested, it causes vomiting and diarrhoea.   It attacks and damages the eyes, mucous membranes, lungs, skin, and blood-forming organs.   It can kill in [] minutes.

- **Tabun, sarin and VX** are all nerve agents of which VX is the most toxic. They all damage the nervous system, producing muscular spasms and paralysis. As little as 10 milligrammes of VX on the skin can cause rapid death.

- **Anthrax** is a disease caused by the bacterium Bacillus anthracis.   Inhalation anthrax is the manifestation of the disease likely to be expected in biological warfare. The symptoms may vary [which are?]. If the dose is large (8,000 to 10,000 spores) death is common. The incubation period for anthrax is 1 to 7 days, with most cases occurring within 2 days of exposure.

CONFIDENTIAL UNTIL RELEASED

16

DOS/2/0017

430

- **Botulinum toxin** is a neurotoxin produced by the bacterium Clostridium botulinum and is one of the most toxic substances known to man. The first symptoms of botulinum toxin A poisoning may appear as early as 1 hour post exposure or as long as 8 days after exposure, with the incubation period between 12 and 22 hours. Paralysis leads to death by suffocation.

- **Aflatoxins** are fungal toxins, which are potent carcinogens. Most symptoms take a long time to show. Food products contaminated by aflatoxin can cause liver inflammation and cancer. It can also affect pregnant women, leading to stillborn babies and children born with mutations.

- **Ricin** is derived from the castor bean and can cause multiple organ failure leading to death within one or two days of inhalation.

6. Iraq also had the ability to deliver chemical and biological agents through a wide variety of means from artillery shells to ballistic missiles.

7. Iraqi plans for the development of a **nuclear weapon** were well advanced before the Gulf War. Iraq was planning and constructing fissile material production facilities and work on a weapon design was underway. Its declared aim was to produce a weapon with a 20-kiloton yield. A detonation of a 20-kiloton nuclear warhead over a city might flatten an area of approximately 3 square miles. Within 1.6 miles of detonation, blast damage and radiation would cause 80% casualties, three-quarters of which would be fatal. Between 1.6 and 3.1 miles from the detonation, there would still be 10% casualties, 10% of which would be fatal injuries.

8. Iraq's ultimate aim was to deliver nuclear devices in a **ballistic missile** warhead. Prior to the Gulf War, Iraq had a well-developed missile industry. Iraq fired over 500 SCUD-type missiles at Iran during the Iran-Iraq War at both civilian and military targets, and 93 SCUD type-missiles during the Gulf War. The latter were targeted at

CONFIDENTIAL UNTIL RELEASED

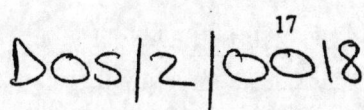

17

DOS/2/0018

Israel and at Coalition forces stationed in the Gulf region. Armed with conventional warheads they did only limited damage. Iraq admitted to UNSCOM that it had 50 chemical and 25 biological warheads available for these missiles, but did not use them. Annex B gives a brief history of the Iraqi WMD programmes prior to 1991

Iraqi Declarations

9. From subsequent UN investigations, evidence from defectors and Iraqi admissions, we know that by the time of the Gulf War Iraq had produced:

- 19,000 litres of botulinum toxin, 8,500 litres of anthrax and 2,200 litres of aflatoxin, and to working on a number of other agents;

- 2,850 tonnes of mustard gas, 210 tonnes of tabun, 795 tonnes of sarin, 795 tonnes of cyclosarin; 3.9 tonnes of VX;

- 260 missile warheads including 75 "special" warheads for delivery of CBW;

- over 16,000 free-fall bombs for delivery of CBW;

- over 110,000 artillery rockets and shells for delivery of CBW;

- or purchased 819 missiles.

10. This was the substantial arsenal which the International Community set itself to dismantle once the war was over.

DOS/2/0019

SECTION 4

THE RESPONSE OF THE INTERNATIONAL COMMUNITY

1. At the end of the Gulf War Iraq's conventional forces had been substantially reduced and weakened. But the International Community was determined that Saddam should be denied the ability to threaten the region and wider world through his possession of weapons of mass destruction.

2. The method chosen to achieve this aim was the establishment of the UN Special Commission (UNSCOM) to carry out intrusive inspections within Iraq, to ensure compliance with the requirements of the UN Security Council. The Security Council passed [unaminously?] a series of resolutions establishing the authority of UNSCOM to carry out its work in Iraq. [see box]

UN Security Council Resolutions (UNSCR) relating to WMD

UNSCR 687, April 1991 created the UN Special Commission (UNSCOM) and required Iraq to accept, unconditionally, "the destruction, removal or rendering harmless, under international supervision" of its chemical and biological weapons, ballistic missiles with a range greater than 150km, and their associated programmes, stocks, components, research and facilities. The International Atomic Energy Agency (IAEA) was charged with abolition of Iraq's nuclear weapons programme. UNSCOM and the IAEA must report that their mission has been achieved before the Security Council can end sanctions. They have not yet done so.

UNSCR 707, August 1991, stated that Iraq must provide full, final and complete disclosure of all its WMD programmes and provide unconditional and unrestricted access to UN inspectors. Iraq must also cease all nuclear activities of any kind other than civil use of isotopes.

UNSCR 715, October 1991 approved plans prepared by UNSCOM and IAEA for the ongoing monitoring and verification (OMV) arrangements to implement UNSCR 687. Iraq did not accede to this to November 1993. OMV was conducted from April 1995 to 15 December 1998, when the UN left Iraq.

UNSCR 1051, March 1996 stated that Iraq must declare the shipment of dual-use WMD goods.

19

DOS/2/0020

3. Iraq accepted the UNSCRs and agreed to co-operate with UNSCOM. In reality, as subsequently became clear, Iraq immediately mounted a major effort to conceal weaponry, related equipment and information from the inspectors and to deceive the UN about the extent of their programmes for mass destruction weaponry.

SECTION 5

THE HISTORY OF UN WEAPONS INSPECTORS

1. The UN Special Commission (UNSCOM) was established by United Nations Security Council Resolution 687 (UNSCR 687) of 3 April. Its purpose was to oversee, in conjunction with the International Atomic Energy Agency (IAEA), the dismantling of Iraq's arsenal of weapons of mass destruction and to maintain a monitoring programme to ensure that it was never rebuilt.

2. The subsequent history of the UN weapons inspections was characterised by persistent Iraqi efforts to frustrate, deceive and intimidate inspectors. Despite the conduct of the Iraqi authorities towards them, both UNSCOM and the IAEA Action Team have valuable records of achievement in discovering and destroying biological and chemical weapons stocks, missiles and the infrastructure for Iraq's nuclear weapons programme.

3. By the end of 1998 there nevertheless remained significant uncertainties about the state of Iraq's prohibited programmes. A series of confrontations and the systematic refusal by Iraq to co-operate left UNSCOM unable to perform its disarmament mandate and the inspectors were consequently withdrawn on 13 December 1998. The US and the UK had made clear that anything short of full co-operation would make military action unavoidable. Operation Desert Fox (16-19 December 1998) was designed to degrade Saddam's ability to regenerate and deploy biological and chemical weapons and prevent him from threatening his neighbours with these or other weapons.

4. Since Operation Desert Fox in December 1998, Iraq has refused to comply with its UN disarmament and monitoring obligations and allow access to weapons inspectors. We judge that Iraq has used the intervening period to rebuild significant

21

DOS/2/0022

aspects of its chemical, biological, nuclear and ballistic missile programmes. These actions not only present a direct challenge to the authority of the United Nations. They also breach Iraq's commitments under two key international arms control agreements:

- the Biological and Toxin Weapons Convention – which bans the development, production, stockpiling, acquisition or retention of biological weapons;

- and the Nuclear Non-Proliferation Treaty (NPT) – which prohibits Iraq from manufacturing or otherwise acquiring nuclear weapons

The Establishment of UNSCOM

5. One of the greatest threats to Allied forces during Operation Desert Storm in 1991 was Iraq's stockpile of chemical and biological weapons and long-range ballistic missiles. At the time, there were genuine concerns that Saddam Hussein would authorise the use of such weapons against Allied troops or Israeli civilians.

6. But the true scale of Iraq's programme to acquire WMD and their means of delivery only became apparent with the establishment of a UN weapons inspection regime in the aftermath of Desert Storm. UN Security Council Resolution (UNSCR) 687 obliged Iraq to provide declarations on all aspects of its WMD programmes within 15 days and accept the destruction, removal or rendering harmless under international supervision of its chemical, biological and nuclear programmes, and all ballistic missiles with a range beyond 150 km. UNSCR 687 mandated two inspection teams to handle Iraqi disarmament and establish long term monitoring regimes: the UN Special Commission (UNSCOM) would tackle the chemical, biological and missile programmes; and the Action Team within the International Atomic Energy Agency (IAEA) would be responsible for tracking down and dismantling Iraq's illicit nuclear weapons programme. UNSCOM and the IAEA were given the remit to designate any locations for inspection at any time, review any document and interview any scientist, technician or other individual and seize any prohibited items for destruction.

DOS/2/0023

Iraqi Non-Co-operation with UN Weapons Inspectors

7. The UN passed a further Resolution in 1991 that set out in clear and specific terms the standard of co-operation the international community expected of Iraq. UNSCR 707 (August 1991) demanded that Iraq should allow inspection teams "immediate, unconditional and unrestricted access to any and all areas". For over a decade Iraq has consistently failed to meet this standard.

8. Prior to the first inspection, the Iraqi regime decided to do its utmost to hide its stocks of WMD. The former Chairman of UNSCOM, Richard Butler, reported to the UN Security Council that in 1991 a decision was taken by a high-level Government committee to provide inspectors with only a portion of its proscribed weapons, components, production capabilities and stocks. UNSCOM concluded that Iraqi policy was based on the following actions:

- to provide only a portion of extant weapons stocks, releasing for destruction only those that were least modern;

- to retain the production capability and documentation necessary to revive programmes when possible;

- to conceal the full extent of its chemical weapons programme, including the VX nerve agent project;

- to conceal the number and type of chemical and biological warheads for proscribed long –range missiles;

- and to conceal the very existence of its massive biological weapons programme.

9. At the same time, Iraq tried to maintain its nuclear weapons programme via a concerted campaign to deceive IAEA inspectors. In 1997 the Agency's Director General stated that the IAEA was "severely hampered by Iraq's persistence in a policy of concealment and understatement of the programme's scope."

CONFIDENTIAL UNTIL RELEASED

10. Iraq's mistake was to underestimate the persistence and technical ability of the UN inspection teams and the will of the Security Council. Once inspectors had arrived in-country, it quickly became apparent that Iraq would resort to any measures (including physical threats and psychological intimidation of inspectors) to prevent UNSCOM and the IAEA from fulfilling their mandate. Examples of Iraqi obstruction are too numerous to list in full. But some of the more infamous examples include:

- firing warning shots in the air to prevent IAEA inspectors from intercepting nuclear related equipment (June 1991);

- keeping IAEA inspectors in a car park for 4 days and refusing to allow them to leave with incriminating documents on Iraq's nuclear weapons programme (September 1991). See Annex C for more details.

11. In response to such incidents, the President of the Security Council issued frequent statements calling on Iraq to comply with its disarmament and monitoring obligations.

12. In December 1997 Richard Butler reported to the UN Security Council that Iraq had created a new category of sites – "Presidential" and "sovereign" – from which it claimed that UNSCOM inspectors would henceforth be barred. The terms of the ceasefire in 1991 foresaw no such limitation. However, Iraq consistently refused to allow UNSCOM inspectors access to any of these 8 Presidential sites. Many of these so-called "palaces" are in fact massive compounds which are an integral part of Iraqi counter-measures expressly designed to hide weapons material.

13. Despite UNSCOM's efforts, following the effective ejection of UN inspectors in December 1998, there remained a series of significant unresolved disarmament issues. In summarising the situation in a report to the Security Council, the UNSCOM Chairman, Richard Butler, set out a damning account of Iraqi deceit. For example:

24

DOS|2|0025

- contrary to the requirement that destruction be conducted under international supervision, "Iraq undertook extensive, unilateral and secret destruction of large quantities of proscribed weapons and items";

- and Iraq "also pursued a practice of concealment of proscribed items, including weapons, and a cover up of its activities in contravention of Council resolutions."

Overall, Butler declared that obstructive Iraqi activity had had "a significant impact upon the Commission's disarmament work."

Operation Desert Fox

14. The US and the UK made clear, when suspending air strikes in November 1998, that anything short of full co-operation would lead to immediate military action against Iraq.

15. Richard Butler was requested to report to the UN Security Council in December 1998 and made clear that, following a series of direct confrontations, coupled with the systematic refusal by Iraq to co-operate, UNSCOM was no longer able to perform its disarmament mandate. As a direct result, on December 13 the weapons inspectors were withdrawn and Operation Desert Fox was launched by the US and the UK three days later.

16. During Operation Desert Fox (16-19 December 1998):

- Almost 80 per cent of the 100 targets identified were damaged or destroyed;

- There were attacks against missile production and research facilities and the destruction of infrastructure associated with the concealment of material and documents associated with the biological, chemical, nuclear and long-range missile programmes;

- The Iraqi Directorate of General Security, in particular, lost some of its most important buildings. We believe that these contained key equipment and documents;

CONFIDENTIAL UNTIL RELEASED

25

DOS/2/0026

- Key facilities associated with Saddam's Ballistic Missile programme were significantly degraded, setting this back between one and two years;

- Iraq's ability to deliver biological or chemical agents by ballistic missile was seriously weakened.

UNSCOM and IAEA Achievements

UNSCOM surveyed 1015 sites in Iraq, carrying out 272 separate inspections. Despite Iraqi obstruction and intimidation, UN inspectors uncovered details of chemical, biological, nuclear and ballistic missile programmes (see maps) the scale of which stunned the world. One of the most sobering discoveries was that at the time of the Gulf War, Iraq had been within 1-2 years of acquiring a nuclear weapon. Other major UNSCOM/IAEA achievements included:

- the destruction of 40,000 munitions for chemical weapons, 2,610 tonnes of chemical precursors and 411 tonnes of chemical warfare agent;

- the dismantling of Iraq's prime chemical weapons development and production complex at Al-Muthanna, and a range of key production equipment;

- the destruction of 48-SCUD type missiles, 11 mobile launchers and 56 sites, 30 warheads filled with chemical or biological agents, and 20 conventional warheads;

- the destruction of the Al-Hakam biological weapons facility and a range of production equipment, seed stocks and growth media for biological weapons;

- the discovery in 1991 of 15 kg of highly enriched uranium, forcing Iraq's acknowledgement of uranium enrichment programmes and attempts to preserve key components of its prohibited nuclear weapons programme; and

the removal and destruction of the infrastructure for the nuclear weapons programme, including the Al-Athir weaponisation/testing facility.

The Situation Since 1998

17. There have been no UN-mandated weapons inspections in Iraq since 1998. In an effort to enforce Iraqi compliance with its disarmament and monitoring obligations,

DOS/2/0027

the Security Council passed resolution 1284 in December 1999. This established the United Nations Monitoring, Verification and Inspection Commission (UNMOVIC) as a successor organisation to UNSCOM and calls on Iraq to give UNMOVIC inspectors "immediate, unconditional and unrestricted access to any and all areas, facilities, equipment, records and means of transport.". It also set out the steps Iraq needed to take to in return for the eventual suspension and lifting of sanctions. A key measure of Iraqi compliance will be full co-operation with UN inspectors, including unconditional, immediate and unrestricted access to any and all sites. Given Iraq's track record of co-operation with UNSCOM and the IAEA between 1991-98, the prospects of Iraq meeting this standard are dim.

18. For the past three years, Iraq has allowed the IAEA to carry out an annual inspection of a stockpile of low-enriched uranium. This has led some countries and western commentators to conclude – erroneously – that Iraq is meeting its nuclear disarmament and monitoring obligations. As the IAEA has pointed out in recent weeks, this annual inspection does "not serve as a substitute for the verification activities required by the relevant resolutions of the UN Security Council."

19. Dr. Hans Blix, the Executive Chairman of UNMOVIC, and Dr. Mohammed El-Baradei, the Director General of the IAEA, have declared that in the absence of inspections it is impossible to verify Iraqi compliance with its UN disarmament and monitoring obligations. In April 1999, an independent UN panel of experts noted that "the longer inspection and monitoring activities remain suspended, the more difficult the comprehensive implementation of Security Council resolutions becomes, increasing the risk that Iraq might reconstitute its proscribed weapons programmes."

What Remains Unaccounted For?

20. The so-called "Butler Report" remains the single most authoritative document on the activities of UNSCOM inspectors in Iraq between 1991-98.

21. Based on the Butler Report and earlier UNSCOM reports, we assess that UN inspectors were unable to account for:

DOS/2/0028

- up to 360 tonnes of bulk chemical warfare (CW) agent, including 1.5 tonnes of VX nerve agent;

- up to 3,000 tonnes of precursor chemicals, including approximately 300 tonnes which, in the Iraqi CW programme, were unique to the production of VX;

- growth media procured for biological agent production (enough to produce over three times the 8,500 litres of anthrax spores Iraq admits to having manufactured);

- over 30,000 special munitions for delivery of chemical and biological agents; and

- up to 20 650 km-range Al Hussein ballistic missiles.

CONFIDENTIAL UNTIL RELEASED

DOS/2/0029

IRAQI CHEMICAL, BIOLOGICAL, NUCLEAR AND BALLISTIC MISSILE PROGRAMMES: THE CURRENT POSITION

1. Intelligence plays a central role in informing government policy towards Iraq's weapons of mass destruction and ballistic missile programmes. The reports are often very sensitive. Much of the detail cannot be made public since great care has to be taken to protect our sources. But, taken with Saddam's record of using chemical weapons and the evidence from UN weapons inspections, the intelligence builds a compelling picture of Saddam's capabilities.

2. This section sets out what we now know of Saddam's chemical, biological, nuclear and ballistic missile programmes, drawing on all the available evidence. The **main conclusions** are that:

- Iraq has a useable chemical and biological weapons capability, in breach of UNSCR 687. And it is able to add to this capability despite sanctions;

- Iraq can deliver chemical and biological agents using an extensive range of artillery shells, free-fall bombs, sprayers and ballistic missiles;

- Iraq continues to work on developing nuclear weapons, in breach of its obligations under the Non-Proliferation Treaty, and in breach of UNSCR 687. Uranium to be used in the production of suitable fissile material has been purchased from Africa. But sanctions continue to hinder development of a nuclear weapon;

- Iraq possesses extended-range versions of the SCUD ballistic missile, capable of reaching Israel and Gulf States in breach of UNSCR 687. It is also developing longer range ballistic missiles to improve its capability to target neighbouring countries;

- Iraq's current military planning specifically envisages the use of chemical and biological weapons;

DOS/2/0030 29

- Iraq's military forces maintain the capability to use chemical and biological weapons, with command, control and logistical arrangements in place;

- Iraq's WMD and ballistic missiles programmes are not short of funds, despite the parlous state of the Iraqi economy.

WHY ARE WE CONCERNED?

3. While the successful enforcement of the sanctions regimes and the UN arms embargo have impeded Iraq's efforts to reconstitute its weapons of mass destruction, they have not halted them. Much of Iraq's missile infrastructure has been rebuilt; the nuclear weapons programme is being reconstituted; and Iraq continues to have the capability to produce chemical and biological weapons, and has probably already done so. Since the withdrawal of inspectors in 1998, monitoring of Iraqi attempts to restore a WMD capability has become more difficult.

4. **Intelligence** from reliable and well-informed sources has become available in the last few weeks. This has confirmed that Iraq has chemical and biological weapons and the Iraqi leadership has been discussing a number of issues related to them. These include:

- **The important role of chemical and biological weapons in Iraq's military thinking**: Saddam attaches great importance to the possession of weapons of mass destruction which he regards as being the basis for Iraq's regional power. Respect for Iraq rests on its possession of chemical and biological weapons and the missiles capable of delivering them. Saddam is determined to retain this capability and recognises that Iraq's political weight would be diminished if Iraq's military power rested solely on its weakened conventional military forces.

- Iraqi attempts to retain its existing banned weapons systems: **Iraq is already taking steps to undermine the return of any UN weapons inspectors: We know from intelligence that Iraq has begun removing sensitive equipment and papers relating to its chemical and biological programmes and dispersing them beyond the gaze of inspectors, for example by hiding sensitive documents in the homes of his trusted officials. Saddam is determined not to lose the capabilities that he has been able to develop in the four years since inspectors left.**

Dos/2/0031

30

- **Saddam's willingness to use chemical and biological weapons**: intelligence indicates that Saddam is prepared to use chemical and biological weapons. Saddam would not hesitate to use chemical and biological weapons against any internal uprising by the Shia population.

This intelligence confirms Saddam's readiness to use these weapons, even against his own people, and his disregard for the terrible consequences of using chemical and biological weapons.

CHEMICAL AND BIOLOGICAL WEAPONS

Existing chemical warfare stocks

5. We do not know precisely how many **chemical** agent-filled munitions from before the Gulf War have been destroyed, degraded or remain at the disposal of the Iraqi government. Declarations to UNSCOM deliberately obscure the picture. But, whatever the fate of these stocks, we judge that Iraq has retained production equipment and at least small amounts of chemical agent and precursors. There is intelligence that Iraqi firms are currently trying to procure precursors for mustard, Tabun and VX. Unaccounted for at the time of UNSCOM withdrawal were:

- up to 360 tonnes of bulk chemical warfare (CW) agent, including 1.5 tonnes of VX nerve agent;

- up to 3,000 tonnes of precursor chemicals, including approximately 300 tonnes which, in the Iraqi CW programme, were unique to the production of VX.

6. Iraq repeatedly claims that if it had retained any chemical agents they would have deteriorated sufficiently to render them harmless. Iraq has admitted having the knowledge and capability to add stabilisers to nerve agent, which would prevent such decomposition. In 1997 UNSCOM examined some munitions which had been filled with mustard gas prior to 1991 and found that they remained very toxic and showed little sign of deterioration.

Chemical agent production capabilities

7. During the Gulf War a number of facilities which intelligence reporting indicated were directly or indirectly associated with Iraq's CW effort were attacked and damaged. Following

the ceasefire UNSCOM destroyed or rendered harmless facilities and equipment used in Iraq's CW programme. Other equipment was released for civilian use either in industry or academic institutes, where it was tagged and regularly inspected and monitored, or else placed under camera monitoring, to ensure that it was not being misused. This monitoring ceased when UNSCOM withdrew from Iraq in 1998. However, capabilities remain and, although the main chemical weapon production facility at al-Muthanna was completely destroyed by UNSCOM and has not been rebuilt, other plants formerly associated with the chemical warfare programme have been rebuilt. This includes the chlorine plant at Fallujah 2.

8. Other dual use facilities, which could be used to support the production of CW agent and precursors, have been rebuilt and re-equipped. New chemical facilities have been built, some with illegal foreign assistance, and are probably fully operational or ready for production. These include the al-Daura State Establishment for Heavy Equipment Engineering and the Ibn Sina Company at Tarmiya (imagery requested). Parts of the al-Qa'Qaa chemical complex damaged in the Gulf War have also been repaired and are operational. Of particular concern, elements of the phosgene production plant at Al Qa'Qaa which were severely damaged during the Gulf War, and dismantled under UNSCOM supervision, have since been rebuilt. While phosgene does have industrial uses it can be used by itself as a chemical agent or as a precursor for nerve agents.

The Problem of Dual Use Facilities

Almost all components and supplies used in chemical and biological agent production are dual-use. Any major petrochemical or biotech industry, as well as public health organisations, will have legitimate need for most materials and equipment required to manufacture chemical and biological weapons. Without UN weapons inspectors it is very difficult therefore to be sure about the true nature of many of Iraq's facilities.

For example, Iraq has built a large new chemical complex, Project Baiji, in the desert in north west Iraq at Ash Sharqat. This site is a former uranium enrichment facility, which was damaged during the Gulf War, and rendered harmless under supervision of the IAEA. Part of the site has been rebuilt, with work starting in 1992, as a chemical production complex. Intelligence indicates the site will be a carbon copy of, and under the control of, al-Qa'Qaa State Company, Iraq's foremost chemical establishment. Despite the site being far away from populated areas it is surrounded by a high wall with watch towers and guarded by armed guards. Intelligence reports indicate that it will produce nitric acid, which can be used in explosives, missile fuel, and in the purification of uranium.

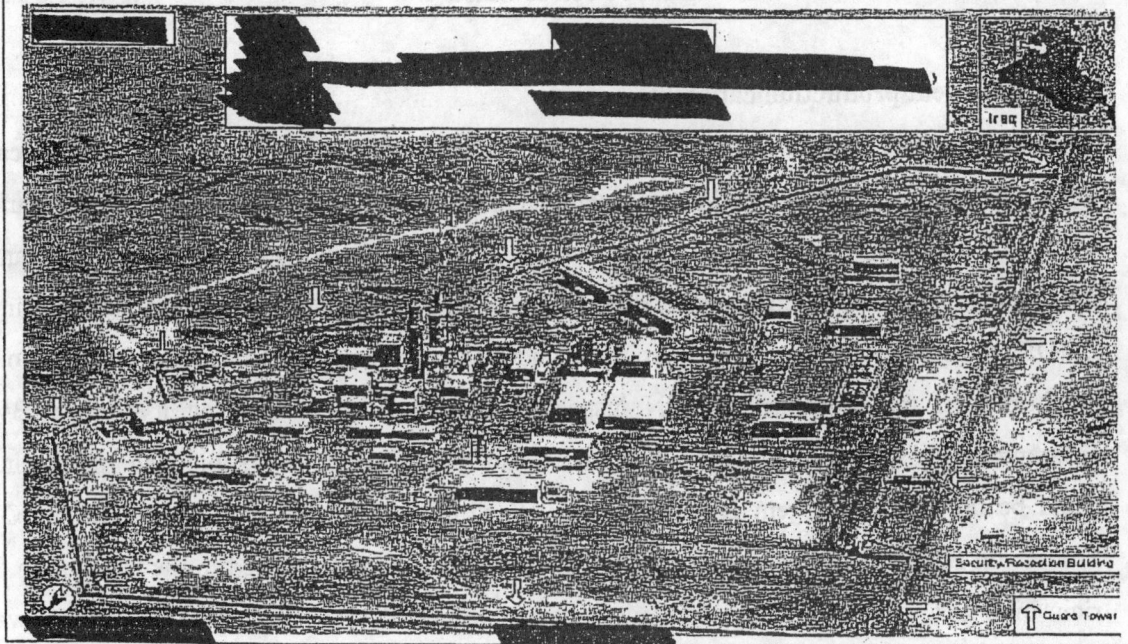

9. Iraq also retained the expertise for chemical research, agent production and weaponisation. The bulk of the personnel previously involved in the programme remain in country. Indeed, intelligence indicates that Haidar Husain Taha, recently reported in the media as being the factory manager of the Fallujah 2 plant, is almost certainly the same individual who from 1984 until the end of the Gulf war worked at Iraq's CW programme at the Muthanna State Establishment researching mustard gas. While UNSCOM found a number of technical manuals (so called "cook books") for the production of chemical agents and critical precursors, Iraq's claim to have unilaterally destroyed the bulk of the documentation cannot be confirmed and is almost certainly untrue. Recent intelligence indicates that Iraq is still discussing methods of

DOS/2/0034

concealing such documentation in order to ensure that it is not discovered by any future UN inspections.

Existing biological warfare stocks

10. Iraq has claimed that all its **biological agents and weapons** have been destroyed, although no convincing proof of any kind has been offered to support the claim. UN inspectors could not account for up to 20 tonnes of growth media (nutrients required for the specialised growth of agent) procured for biological agent production, enough to produce over three times the amount of anthrax Iraq admits to having manufactured. Reports that Iraq has conducted research on smallpox and a number of toxins cannot be corroborated.

Biological agent production capabilities

11. **We know that Iraq is self-sufficient in the technology required to produce biological weapons (BW).** As with some CW equipment, UNSCOM only destroyed equipment that could be directly linked to BW production. Iraq also has its own engineering capability to design and construct BW associated fermenters and other equipment. Some dual-use equipment, including ….(DIS to provide) has also been purchased under the Oil for Food programme, but without monitoring of the equipment by UN inspectors Iraq could have diverted it to their BW programme. This newly purchased equipment and others previously subject to monitoring could be used in a resurgent BW programme. Facilities of concern include: the Castor Oil Production Plant at Fallujah, the residue from the castor bean pulp is used in the production of ricin biological agent; and the Al-Daura Foot and Mouth Disease Vaccine Plant, which was involved in BW agent production and research before the 1991 Gulf War. Evidence has emerged from defectors over the last two years that Iraq has sought to develop mobile facilities to produce biological agents. Other intelligence confirms that the Iraqi military have acquired such facilities, which Iraq hopes will conceal and protect biological agent production from military attack or UN inspection.

Chemical and biological agent delivery means

12. Iraq has a variety of **delivery means** available for both chemical and biological agents, some of which are very basic. These include:

CONFIDENTIAL UNTIL RELEASED DOS/2/0035

34

448

- free fall bombs - Iraq acknowledged to UNSCOM the deployment to four sites of free fall bombs filled with biological agent during 1990-91. These bombs were filled with anthrax, botulinum toxin and aflatoxin. Iraq also acknowledged possession of four types of aerial bomb with various fills including sulphur mustard, tabun, sarin, cyclosarin, and VX

- artillery shells and rockets - Iraq made extensive use of artillery munitions filled with chemical agents during the Iran-Iraq War. Mortars can also be used for chemical agent delivery. Iraq also claimed to have tested the use of shells and rockets filled with biological agents. Over 20,000 artillery munitions remain unaccounted for by UNSCOM;

- helicopter and aircraft borne sprayers - Iraq carried out studies into aerosol dissemination of biological agent using these platforms prior to 1991. UNSCOM was unable to account for many of these devices and we judge that it is probable that Iraq retains a capability for aerosol dispersal of both chemical and biological agent;

- Al Hussein ballistic missiles (range 650km) - Iraq told UNSCOM that it filled 25 warheads with anthrax, botulinum toxin and aflatoxin. Iraq also developed chemical agent warheads for Al Hussein. Iraq also admitted to producing 50 CW warheads for Al Hussein which were intended for the delivery of a mixture of sarin and cyclosarin. Intelligence indicates Iraq retains up to 20 Al Husseins;

- Al Samoud/Ababil 100 ballistic missiles (range 150km plus) - It is unclear if chemical and biological warheads have been developed for these systems, but given their experience on other missile systems, Iraq probably has the technical expertise for doing so;

- L-29 remotely piloted vehicle programme - we judge that the modification of the L-29 jet trainer could allow it to be used as a pilot-less aircraft for the delivery of chemical and biological agents. The L-29 was subject to UNSCOM inspection for this reason;

Chemical and biological warfare: command and control

13. Special Security Organisation (SSO) and Special Republican Guard (SRG) units would be involved in the movement of any chemical and biological weapons to military units. The Iraqi

DOS|2|0036

35

military holds artillery and missile systems at Corps level throughout the Armed Forces and conducts regular training with them. The Directorate of Rocket Forces has operational control of strategic missile systems and some Multiple Rocket Launcher Systems. Within the last month intelligence has suggested that the Iraqi military would be able to use their chemical and biological weapons within 45 minutes of an order to do so.

Conclusion

14. Intelligence confirms that Iraq has covert **chemical and biological weapons** programmes, in breach of UN Security Council Resolution 687. We also judge that:

- Iraq has chemical and biological agents and weapons available, either from pre-Gulf War stocks or more recent production;

- Iraq has the capability to produce the chemical agents sulphur mustard, tabun, sarin, cyclosarin, and VX within weeks of an order to do so;

- Iraq has a biological agent production capability and can produce at least anthrax, botulinum toxin, aflatoxin and ricin within days of an order to do so. Iraq has also developed mobile facilities to produce biological agents.

- the order to produce to chemical and biological agents has been given;

- Iraq has a variety of delivery means available;

- Iraq's military forces maintain the capability to use these weapons, with command, control and logistical arrangements in place.

NUCLEAR WEAPONS

15. In 1991 we assessed that Iraq was less than three years away from possessing a nuclear weapon. After the Gulf War, Iraq's nuclear weapons infrastructure was dismantled by the IAEA. But we judge that Iraq is still working to achieve a nuclear weapons capability, **in breach of its NPT obligations and UN Security Council Resolution 687**. Much of its former

DOS/2/0037

36

expertise in fissile material production and weapons design has been retained. In 1991 Iraqi nuclear weapons programme had gone some way to developing a workable nuclear weapon design and were researching some more advanced concepts. **Intelligence has indicated that scientific specialists were recalled to work on a nuclear weapons programme in the autumn of 1998.**

16. Judging on the basis of the available intelligence it is almost certain that the present Iraqi programme is based on gas centrifuge uranium enrichment, which was one of the routes Iraq was following for producing fissile material before the Gulf War. But Iraq needs certain key equipment, such as gas centrifuge components, and materials for the production of the fissile material necessary before a nuclear bomb could be developed.

> **Gas Centrifuge Uranium Enrichment**
> Uranium in the form of uranium hexafluoride is separated into its different isotopes in rapidly spinning rotor tubes of special centrifuges. Many hundreds or thousands of centrifuges are connected in cascades to enrich uranium. If the lighter U235 isotope is enriched to more than 90% it can be used in the core of a nuclear weapon.

17. Following the expulsion of weapons inspectors in 1998 there has been an accumulation of intelligence indicating that Iraq is making concerted covert efforts to acquire technology and materials with nuclear applications. Iraq's existing holdings of processed uranium are under IAEA supervision. But **there is compelling evidence that Iraq has sought the supply of significant quantities of uranium from Africa.** Iraqi has no known civil nuclear programme or nuclear power plants, therefore it has no legitimate reason to acquire uranium. It also has sufficient indigenous uranium deposits for any small needs it has.

18. Other suspicious procurement since 1998 includes vacuum pumps, magnets, filament winding machines, and balancing machines. All are needed to manufacture gas centrifuges. Since 2001 Iraq has made a particularly determined effort illicitly to acquire specialised aluminium, which is subject to international export controls because of its potential application in gas centrifuges used to enrich uranium.

19. So long as sanctions continue to hinder the import of crucial goods for the production of fissile material..., Iraq would find it difficult to

> **Improvised nuclear device**

DOS/2/0038 37

produce a nuclear weapon. After the lifting of sanctions we assess that Iraq would need at least five years to produce a weapon. If Iraq acquired sufficient fissile material from abroad we judge it would take at least two years to make a working nuclear device. However, Iraq could produce an improvised nuclear device within a few months but this would be unreliable.

BALLISTIC MISSILES

20. Since the Gulf War, Iraq has been openly developing two short-range missiles up to a range of 150km, which are permitted under UN Security Council Resolution 687. The Al-Samoud liquid propellant missile has been extensively tested and is being deployed to military units. **Intelligence indicates that Iraq has also worked on extending its range to at least 200km in**

FIGURE 1: ABABIL-100

breach of UN Security Resolution 687. Testing of the solid propellant Ababil-100 (Figure 1) is also underway, with plans to extend its range to at least 200km. Compared to liquid propellant missiles, those powered by solid propellant offer greater ease of storage, handling and mobility. They are also quicker to take into and out of action and can stay at a high state of readiness for longer periods.

21. **According to intelligence, Iraq has retained up to 20 Al Hussein missiles (Figure 2), in breach of UN Security Council Resolution 687.** These missiles were either hidden from the UN as complete systems, or re-assembled using illegally retained engines and other components. Intelligence indicates that the engineering expertise available would allow these missiles to be maintained effectively. We assess that some of these missiles could be available for use. They could be used with a conventional, chemical or

FIGURE 2: AL HUSSEIN

DOS/2/0039

38

biological warheads and are capable of reaching a number of countries in the region including Israel, Iran, Saudi Arabia, and Turkey.

22. Intelligence has confirmed that Iraq's priority is to extend the range of its missile systems to over 1000km, enabling it to threaten other regional neighbours. These programmes employ hundreds of people. Satellite imagery (Figure 3) has shown a new engine test stand being constructed (A), which is larger than the current one used for Al Samoud (B), and that formerly used for testing SCUD engines (C) which was dismantled under UNSCOM supervision. This new stand will be capable of testing engines for **missiles with ranges over 1000km, which are not permitted under UN Security Council Resolution 687.** Such a facility would not be needed for systems that fall within the UN permitted range of 150km. The Iraqis have recently taken measures to conceal activities at this site.

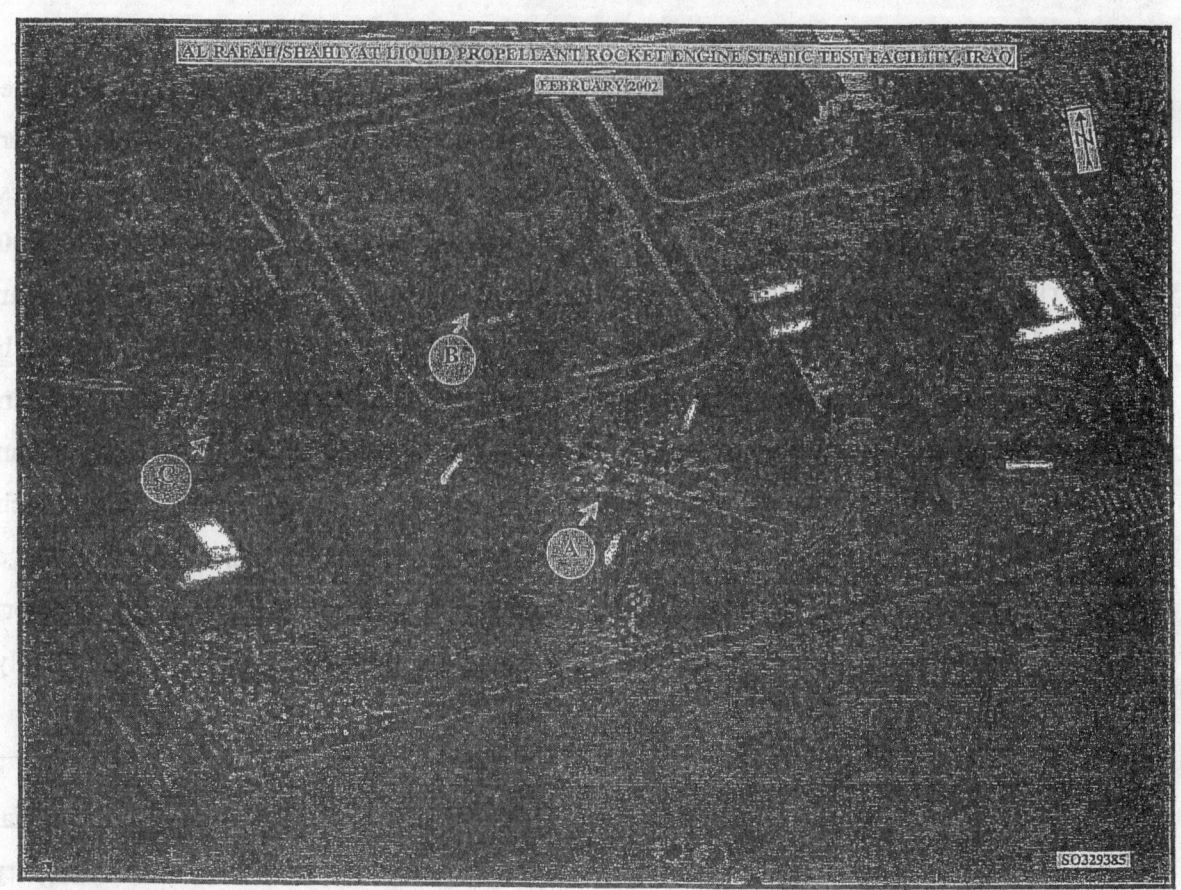

FIGURE 3: AL RAFAH/SHAHIYAT LIQUID PROPELLANT ENGINE STATIC TEST STAND

24. Iraq is also working to obtain improved guidance technology to increase missile accuracy. The success of UN restrictions means the development of new longer-range missiles is likely to be a slow process. These restrictions impact particularly on the:

- availability of foreign expertise;

- conduct of test flights to ranges above 150km;

- acquisition of guidance and control technology.

Saddam remains committed to developing longer-range missiles. We assess that, if sanctions remain effective, Iraq might achieve a missile capability of over 1000km within 5 years (Figure 4 shows the range of Iraq's various missiles).

25. Iraq has managed to rebuild much of the missile production infrastructure destroyed in the Gulf War and in Operation Desert Fox in 1998. New missile-related infrastructure is also under construction. **Some aspects of this, including rocket propellant mixing and casting facilities at the Al Mamoun Plant, appear to replicate those linked to the prohibited BADR-2000 programme (with a planned range of 700-1000km) that were destroyed in the Gulf War or by UNSCOM. A new plant for indigenously producing ammonium perchlorate, which is a key ingredient in the production of solid propellant rocket motors, has been constructed.** This has been provided illicitly by NEC Engineers Private Limited, an Indian chemical engineering firm with extensive links in Iraq, including to other suspect facilities such as the Fallujah 2 chlorine plant. After an extensive investigation, the Indian authorities have recently arrested NEC's General Manager for export control violations and suspended its export licence, although affiliated individuals and companies in the Middle East are still illicitly procuring for Iraq.

26. Despite a UN embargo, Iraq has also made concerted efforts to acquire additional production technology, including machine tools and raw materials, **in breach of UN Security Council Resolution 1051**. The embargo has succeeded in blocking many of these attempts, such as requests to buy magnesium powder and ammonium chloride. But, despite the dual use

nature of some of the items, we know from intelligence that some items have found their way to the Iraqi ballistic missile programme. More will inevitably continue to do so. Intelligence makes clear that Iraqi procurement agents and front companies in third countries are undertaking a global drive illicitly to acquire propellant chemicals for Iraq's ballistic missiles. This includes production level quantities of near complete sets of solid propellant motor ingredients such as aluminium powder and ammonium perchlorate. There have also been attempts to acquire large quantities of liquid propellant chemicals such as unsymmetrical dimethylhydrazine (UDMH) and hydrogen peroxide. We judge this is intended to support production and deployment of the Al Samoud and Ababil-100 and development of longer range systems.

Iraq: Current and Planned/Potential Ballistic Missiles

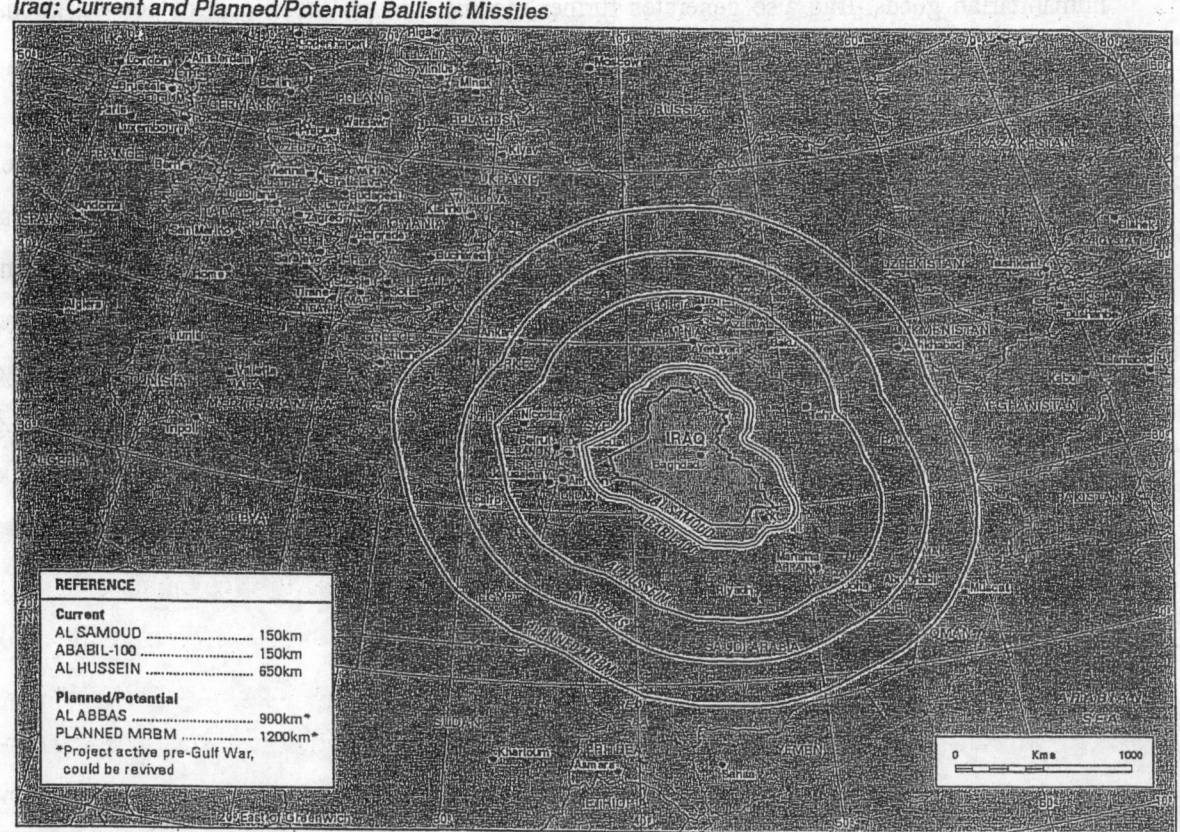

FIGURE 4: CURRENT AND PLANNED/POTENTIAL BALLISTIC MISSILES

FUNDING FOR THE WMD PROGRAMME

27. The UN has sought to restrict to generate funds for its military and WMD programmes. For example, Iraq earns money legally under the UN Oil For Food Programme (OFF) established

CONFIDENTIAL UNTIL RELEASED DOS/2/0042

by UNSCR 986, whereby the proceeds of oil sold through the UN is used to buy humanitarian supplies for Iraq. This money remains under UN control, and cannot be used for military/WMD procurement.

28. However, the Iraqi regime continues to generate income outside UN control, either in the form of hard currency, or barter goods (which in turn means existing Iraqi funds are freed up to be spent on other things). Iraq's illicit earnings amounted to around USD 3 billion during 2001. Of this, illegal oil exports may have been worth around USD 2 billion. A further USD 1 billion may have been generated through abuses of OFF, including placing a surcharge on every barrel of oil sold, and charging commissions for contracts either to lift Iraqi oil or supply Iraq with humanitarian goods. Iraq also generates further income through the export of non-oil goods. We assess that Iraq will generate up to a further USD 3 billion during 2002.

29. These illicit earnings go to the Iraqi regime. They are used for building new palaces, as well as purchasing luxury goods and other civilian goods outside OFF. Some of these funds are also used by Saddam to maintain his armed forces, and to develop or acquire military equipment, including for chemical, biological and nuclear programmes. There is no indication as to what proportion of these funds may be used in this fashion but we have seen no evidence that Iraqi attempts to develop its weapons of mass destruction and its ballistic missile programme, e.g. through covert procurement of equipment from abroad has been inhibited in any way by lack of funds.

ANNEX A

HUMAN RIGHT ABUSES IN IRAQ

1. In a centralised tyranny, human rights abuse is something for which the leadership must take responsibility. Saddam's younger son, Qusai, is head of the internal security agencies. He has encouraged a policy of systematic torture and rape, and the threat of rape to coerce.

2. You do not have to be a criminal, or even a political opponent of the regime, to be held in an Iraqi jail. You can go to jail for being related to members of the opposition. Sometimes relatives are held as 'substitute prisoners' until the person wanted for arrest if found.

3. This happened to the father and two brothers of Al-Shaik Yahya Muhsin Ja'far al-Zeini, a theology student from Saddam City. When he was finally arrested, this is what happened (source: testimony to Amnesty International):

4. "...I saw a friend of mine, al-Shaikh Nasser Taresh al-Sa'idi, naked. He was handcuffed and a piece of wood was placed between his elbows and his knees. Two ends of the wood were placed on two high chairs and al-Shaikh Nasser was being suspended like a chicken. This method of torture is know as *al-Khaygania* (a reference to a former security director known as al-Khaygani). An electric wire was attached to al-Shaikh Nasser's penis and another one attached to one of his toes. He was asked if he could identify me and he said "this is al-Shaikh Yahya". They took me to another room and then after about 10 minutes they stripped me of my clothes and a security officer said "the person you saw has confessed against you". He said to me "You followers of [Ayatollah] al-Sadr have carried out acts harmful to the security of the country and have been distributing anti-government statements coming from abroad". He asked if I have any contact with an Iraqis religious scholar based in Iran who has been signing these statements. I said "I do not have any contacts with him".... I was then left suspended in the same manner as al-Shaikh al-Sa'idi. My face was looking upward. They attached an electric wire on my pe3nis and the other end of the wire is attached to an electric motor. One security man was hitting my feet with a cable. Electric shocks were applied every few minutes and were increased. I must have been suspended for more than an hour. I lost consciousness.

DOS|2|0044₄₃

They took me to another room and made me walk even though my feet were swollen from beating… They repeated this method a few times."

5. Here is another personal testimony of Iraqi jail conditions:

6. Abdallah, a member of the Ba'ath Party whose loyalty became suspect has still-vivid personal memories from his four years of imprisonment at Abu Ghraib in the 1980s, where he was held naked the entire time and frequently tortured.

7. On the second day of his imprisonment, the men were forced to walk between two rows of five guards each, to receive their containers of food. While walking to get the food, they were beaten by the guards with plastic telephone cables. They had to return to their cells the same way, so that a walk to get breakfast resulted in twenty lashes. "It wasn't that bad going to get the food", Abdallah said, "but coming back the food was spilled when we were beaten." The same procedure was used when the men went to the bathroom.

8. On the third day, the torture began. "We were removed from our cells and beaten with plastic pipes. This surprised us, because we were asked no question. Possibly it was being done to bream our morale", Abdallah speculated. The torture escalated to sixteen sessions daily. The treatment was organised and systematic. Abdallah was held alone in a 3x2-meter room that opened onto a corridor.

9. "We were allowed to go to the toilet three times a day, then they reduced the toilet to once a day for only one minute. I went for four years without a shower or a wash", Abdallah said. He also learned to cope with the deprivation and the hunger that accompanied his detention:

10. "I taught myself to drink a minimum amount of water because there was no placed to urinate. They used wooden sticks to beat us and sometimes the sticks would break. I found a piece of a stick, covered with blood, and managed to bring it back to my room. I ate it for three days. A person who is hungry can eat anything. Pieces of our bodies started falling off from the beatings and our skin was so dry that it began to fall off. I ate pieces of my own body.

DOS/2/0045 [44]

11. "No one, not Pushkin, not Mahfouz, can describe what happened to us. It is impossible to describe what living this day to day was like. I was totally naked the entire time. Half of the original groups [of about thirty men] died. It was a slow type of continuous physical and psychological torture. Sometimes, it seemed that orders came to kill one of us, and he would be beaten to death".

12. In December 1996, **B** (name withheld), a Kurdish businessman from Baghdad, married with children, was arrested outside his house by plainclothes security men. Initially his family did not know his whereabouts and went from one police station to another inquiring about him. Then through friends they found out that he was being held in the headquarters of the General Security Directorate in Baghdad. The family was not allowed to visit him.

13. Eleven months later in November 1997 the family was told by the authorities that he had been executed and that they should go and collect his body. His body bore evident signs of torture. His eyes were gouged out and the empty eye sockets were filled with paper. His right wrist and left leg were broken. The family was not given any reason for his arrest and subsequent execution. However, they suspected that he was executed because of his friendship with a retired army general who had links with the Iraqi opposition outside the country and who was arrested just before **B's** arrest and also executed.

14. Executions are carried out with no judicial process. We know that in February 2000, 64 male prisoners were executed at Abu Ghraib, followed in March by a further 58. In October 2001, 23 political prisoners were executed there. The worst known case is the execution of 4,000 prisoners at Abu Ghraib in 1984. Prisoners at the Mahjar jail have been executed by machine gun. Mahjar has an execution area called 'Hadiqa' (garden) where 3,000 prisoners were executed between 1993 and 1998.

15. Between 1997 and 1999, an estimated 2,500 prisoners were executed in what was called a 'prison cleansing' campaign: they were killed in order to reduce prison overcrowding(?).

DOS/2/0046 45

16. No judicial process was evident when dozens of women accused of prostitution were beheaded in October 200, along with men accused of pimping. Some, at least, were accused for political reasons.

17. At the Mahjar prison in central Baghdad, which is part of the Police Training College(?), women prisoners are routinely raped by their guards. All prisoners are beaten twice a day. They receive no medical treatment. The normal occupancy is between 600 and 7800 prisoners in 30 cells underground and a further 30 cells which used to be dog kennels.

18. At the Sijn Al-Tarbut jail, three floors underground (?) at the Directorate of General Security building in Baghdad, prisoners are kept in rows of rectangular steel boxes, similar to the boxes in which bodies are stored in mortuaries. There are between 100 and 150 boxes. They are opened for half an hour a day, to allow the prisoner light and air. Prisoners have no food, only liquids. They remain in their boxes until they confess or die.

19. The Qurtiyya prison in the Talbiyyah area of the Saddam City district, Baghdad, consists of 50 to 60 metal boxes the size of tea chests in which prisoners are kept on the same confess-or-die basis. Each box has floor made of mesh to allow detainees to defecate.

20. Saddam favours such barbaric punishments. He has issued a series of decrees authorising amputation, branding, cutting off prisoners' ears. Methods of torture used in Iraqi jails include using electric drills to mutilate hands, pulling out fingernails, knife cuts, sexual attacks and 'official rape'.

21. He believes in the punishment fitting the crime. The penalty for slandering the President is to have your tongue cut out. Iraqi television has broadcast this form of political punishment as a warning.

22. Saddam and the head of his private office, General 'Abd Hamud, have both signed death warrants. The archives holding these warrants are held in the cafeteria on the eighth floor of the main Ministry of the Interior building in Baghdad.

DOS/2/0047 [46]

23. Saddam's sons take after their father. Udayy once maintained a private torture chamber known as the Red Room in a building on the banks of the Tigris disguised as an electricity installation. It was Udayy who ordered the Iraq football team to be caned on the soles of the feet for losing a World Cup match.

24. He created a militia in 1994 which has used swords to execute victims outside their own homes. He has personally executed dissidents, for instance in the uprising at Basra which followed the Gulf War.

25. But members of Saddam's family are far from being safe from persecution. A cousin of Saddam called Ala Abd Al-Qadir Al-Majid fled to Jordan … [tell the story on page 49].

26. In mid 2001, 'Ala 'Abd Al-Qadir Al-Majid fled to Jordan from Iraq, citing disagreements with the regime over business matters. 'Ala was a cousin of Saddam Hussein, a former intelligence officer and, latterly, a businessman. He returned to Iraq after the Iraqi Ambassador in Jordan declared publicly that his life was not in danger. He was met at the border by Tahir Habbush, Head of the Iraqi Intelligence Service (the Mukhabarat), and taken to a farm owned by 'Ali Hasan Al-Majid. At the farm 'Ala was tied to a tree and executed by members of his immediate family who, following orders from Saddam, took it in turns to shoot him.

27. Saddam has a history of dealing with disloyalty by arranging for traitors, as Saddam see them, to be killed by their family or tribal associates. This helps to prevent blood feuds between different family/tribal groups and to distance his involvement.

28. 'Ala is just the latest of some 40 of Saddam's relatives, including women and children, that he has had killed. In February 1996, his sons-in-law Hussein Kamal and Saddam Kamal were executed. They had defected in 1995 and returned to Iraq from Jordan after the government had announced amnesties for them.

DOS/2/0048 47

ANNEX B

A SHORT HISTORY OF IRAQI WMD PROGRAMMES PRIOR TO 1991

1. Iraq has been involved in Chemical and Biological Warfare (CBW) research for over 30 years. Its **Chemical Warfare** (CW) research commenced in 1971 at a small, well guarded site at Rashad to the Northeast of Baghdad. Here research was conducted on a number of CW agents including Mustard Gas, CS and Tabun. Later, in 1974 a dedicated organisation called Al-Hassan Ibn Al-Haitham was established. At the same time plans were made to build a large research and commercial-scale production facility in the desert some 70km Northwest of Baghdad under the Project cover of No 922. This was to become Muthanna State Establishment, also known as al-Muthanna, and operated under the front name of Iraq's State Establishment for Pesticide Production. It became partially operational in 1982-83. It had five research and development sections each tasked to pursue different programmes. In addition, the al-Muthanna site was the main CW agent production facility, and it also took the lead in weaponising CBW agents including all aspects of weapon development and testing, in association with the military. According to information supplied by the Iraqis, the total production capacity in 1991 was 4,000 tonnes of agent per annum, but we assess it could have been higher. Al-Muthanna was supported by three separate storage and precursor production facilities known as Fallujah 1, 2 and 3 near Habbaniyah, some of which were not completed before they were heavily bombed in the 1991 Gulf War.

2. Iraq started **Biological Warfare** (BW) research in the mid-1970s. The work started as small-scale research but Iraq believed in its utility, and authorised a purpose-built research and development facility at al-Salman, also known as Salman Pak, which is surrounded on 3 sides by the Tigris river and situated some 35km South of Baghdad. Intelligence suggests that although some progress was made in BW research, some staff were accused of mismanagement and fraud; also it appears that

DOS/2/0049 [48]

Iraq decided to concentrate on developing CW agents and their delivery systems at al-Muthanna. However, the BW programme was revived with the outbreak of the Iraq/Iraq war in the early 80s. But it was Dr Rihab Taha's appointment in 1985, to head a small BW research team at al-Muthanna, which revived and developed the programme. At about the same time plans were made to develop the Salman Pak site into a secure BW research facility. Dr Taha continued to work with her team at Muthanna until 1987 when it moved to Salman Pak which were under the control of the Directorate of General Intelligence. Significant resources were poured into the programme, including the construction of a dedicated production facility, (Project 324) at al-Hakam. Agent production began in 1988 and weaponisation testing and later filling of munitions was conducted in association with the staff at Muthanna State Establishment. Even after the Gulf War, Iraq denied it had an offensive BW programme and the al-Hakam production facility was passed off as a facility for producing animal feed and bio-pesticides research. From mid-1990, other civilian facilities were taken over and some adapted for use in the production and research and development of BW agents. These included:

- Daura Foot and Mouth Vaccination Plant where it produced botulinum toxin and conducted virus research. But there is some intelligence which suggests that work was also conducted on anthrax

- al-Fudaliyah Agriculture and Water Research centre where Iraq admitted it undertook Aflatoxin production and genetic engineering:

- Amariyah Sera and Vaccine institute was used for the storage of BW seed stocks, and involved in genetic engineering

3. Iraq's nuclear programme was established under the Iraqi Atomic Energy Commission in the 1950s. Under a nuclear co-operation agreement signed with the Soviet Union in 1959, a nuclear research centre, equipped with a research reactor, was

49

DOS/2/0050

built at Tuwaitha, the main Iraqi nuclear research centre. The surge in Iraqi oil revenues in the early 1970s supported an expansion of the research programme. This was bolstered by the signing of co-operation agreements with France and Italy in the mid-1970s. France agreed to supply two research reactors powered by highly enriched uranium fuel, and Italy supplied equipment for fuel fabrication and handling. By the end of 1984 Iraq was self-sufficient in uranium ore. One of the reactors was destroyed in an Israeli air attack in June 1981 shortly before it was to become operational the other was never completed.

4. By the mid-1980s Iraq's deteriorating situation in the Iran-Iraq War prompted renewed interest in the military use of nuclear technology, and additional resources were put in developing technologies to enrich uranium for use in nuclear weapons. Enriched uranium was preferred because it could be produced more covertly than plutonium. Iraq followed parallel programmes to produce highly enriched uranium - electromagnetic isotope separation (EMIS) and gas centrifuge enrichment. By 1991 one EMIS enrichment facility was nearing completion and another was under construction. Centrifuge facilities were also under construction, but the centrifuge design was still being developed. In August 1990 Iraq instigated a crash programme to develop a single nuclear weapon within a year, and considered the rapid development of a small 50 machine gas centrifuge cascade to produce the highly enriched uranium required. By the time of the Gulf War, the programme had made little progress. But it appears Iraq had probably decided to concentrate on gas centrifuges as a means for producing the necessary fissile material.

5. Prior to the Gulf War, Iraq had a well-developed **ballistic missile** industry. Iraq fired over 500 SCUD-type missiles at Iran during the Iran-Iraq War. 93 SCUD type-missiles were fired during the Gulf War. The latter were targeted at Israel and Coalition forces stationed in the Gulf region. Armed with conventional warheads they did limited damage. Iraq admitted to UNSCOM that it had 50 chemical and 25 biological warheads available but did not use them. Most of the missiles fired in the

50

DOS/2/0051

Gulf War were an Iraqi produced version of the SCUD missile, the Al Hussein, with an extended range of 650 km. Iraq was working on other stretched SCUD variants, such as the Al Abbas, which had a range of 900km. Iraq was also seeking to reverse engineer the SCUD engine with a view to producing new missiles; recent evidence indicates that they may have succeeded at that time. In particular Iraq had plans for a new SCUD-derived missile with a range of 1200km. Iraq also conducted a partial flight test of a multi-stage satellite launch vehicle based on SCUD technology, known as the Al Abid. Also during this period, Iraq was developing the BADR-2000, a 700-1000km range two-stage solid propellant missile (based on the Iraqi part of the 1980s CONDOR-2 programme run in co-operation with Argentina and Egypt). There were plans for 1200-1500km range solid propellant follow-on systems.

SCUD missiles

The short-range mobile SCUD ballistic missile was developed by the Soviet Union in the 1950s, drawing on the technology of the German liquid-propellant V-2.

For many years it was the mainstay of Soviet and Warsaw Pact tactical missile forces, and it was also widely exported. Recipients of Soviet-manufactured SCUDs included Iraq, North Korea, Iran, and Libya, although not all were sold directly by the Soviet Union.

ANNEX C

WEAPONS INSPECTIONS: OBSTRUCTION AND CONCEALMENT

Obstruction

1. In addition to the examples given in the body of the paper, Iraqi steps to obstruct the UN weapons inspectors included:

- announcing that UN monitoring and verification plans were "unlawful" (October 1991);

- refusing UNSCOM inspectors access to the Ministry of Agriculture. Threats were made to inspectors who remained on watch outside the building. The inspection team had reliable evidence that the site contained archives related to proscribed activities;

- refusing to allow UNSCOM the use of its own aircraft to fly into Iraq (January 1993). In 1991-2 Iraq objected to UNSCOM using its own helicopters and choosing its own flight plans;

- refusing to allow UNSCOM to install remote-controlled monitoring cameras at two key missile sites (June-July 1993);

- repeatedly denying access to inspection teams (1991- December 1998);

- interfering with UNSCOM's helicopter operations, threatening the safety of the aircraft and their crews (June 1997);

- demanding end of U2 overflights and the withdrawal of US UNSCOM staff (October 1997);

- destroying documentary evidence of WMD programmes (September 1997); and

- refusing access to inspection teams on the grounds that certain areas and even roads were deemed "Presidential Sites" (1997-98)

52

DOS/2/0053

A photograph of a presidential site or what have been called ~~~~~~ ~~~~~~ "palaces".

Buckingham palace has been super-imposed to demonstrate their comparative size

Buckingham Palace and grounds

53

DOS/2/0054

Concealment

2. Iraq has admitted having a large, effective, system for hiding proscribed material including documentation, components, production equipment and, possibly, biological and chemical agents and weapons from the UN. Shortly after the adoption of UNSCR 687 in April 1991, an Administrative Security Committee (ASC) was formed with responsibility for advising Saddam on the information which could be released to UNSCOM and the IAEA. The Committee consisted of senior Military Industrial Commission (MIC) scientists from all of Iraq's WMD programmes. The Higher Security Committee (HSC) of the Presidential Office was in overall command of deception operations. The system was directed from the very highest political levels within the Presidential Office and involved, if not Saddam himself, his youngest son, Qusai. The system for hiding proscribed material relies on high mobility and good command and control. It uses lorries to move items at short notice and most hide sites appear to be located close to good road links and telecommunications. The Baghdad area was particularly favoured. In addition to active measures to hide material from the UN, Iraq has attempted to monitor, delay and collect intelligence on UN operations to aid its overall deception plan.

3. Nowhere was Iraqi obstruction of UN inspectors more blatant than in the field of biological weapons. Iraq denied that it had pursued a biological weapons programme until July 1995. Between 1991 and 1995, Iraq refused to disclose any details of its past programme.

4. In the course of the first biological weapons inspection in August 1991, Iraq claimed that it had merely conducted a military biological research programme. At the site visited, Al-Salman, Iraq had removed equipment, documents and even entire buildings. Later in the year, during a visit to the Al-Hakam site, Iraq declared to UNSCOM inspectors that the facility was used as a factory to produce proteins derived from yeast to feed animals. Inspectors subsequently discovered that the plant was a central site for the production of anthrax spores and botulinum toxin for weapons. The factory had also been sanitised by Iraqi officials to deceive inspectors.

54

DOS/2/0055

5. Another key site, the Foot and Mouth Disease Vaccine Institute at Daura which produced botulinum toxin and probably anthrax, was not divulged as part of the programme. Five years later, after intense pressure, Iraq acknowledged that tens of tonnes of bacteriological warfare agent had been produced there and at Al-Hakam. Amazingly, Iraq *continued to develop* the Al-Hakam site into the 1990s, misleading UNSCOM about its true purpose.

6. Iraq consistently tried to obstruct UNSCOM's efforts to investigate the scale of its biological weapons programme. It created forged documents to account for bacterial growth media, imported in the late 1980s, specifically for the production of anthrax, botulinum toxin and probably plague. The documents were created to indicate that the material had been imported by the State Company for Drugs and Medical Appliances Marketing for use in hospitals and distribution to local authorities. Iraq also censored documents and scientific papers provided to the first UN inspection team, removing all references to key individuals, weapons and industrial production of agents.

7. Iraq has yet to provide any documents concerning production of agent and subsequent weaponisation. Iraq destroyed, unilaterally and illegally, biological weapons in 1991 and 1992 making accounting for these weapons impossible. In addition Iraq cleansed a key site at Al-Muthanna – its main research and development, production and weaponisation facility for chemical warfare agents - of all evidence of a biological programme in the toxicology department, the animal-house and weapons filling station.

8. The first biological inspection team tasked with establishing monitoring of compliance was denied access in March 1993. In July 1995, Iraq acknowledged reluctantly that biological agents had been produced on an industrial scale at Al-Hakam. Following the defection in August 1995 of Hussein Kamel, Iraq released over 2 million documents relating to its WMD programmes and acknowledged that it had pursued a biological programme that led to the deployment of actual weapons.

55

DOS/2/0056

Iraq admitted producing in excess of 200 biological weapons with a reserve of agent to fill considerably more.

9. As documents recovered in August 1995 were assessed, it became apparent that the full disclosure required by the UN was far from complete. Successive inspection teams went to Iraq to try to gain greater understanding of the programme and to obtain credible supporting evidence. In July 1996 Iraq refused to discuss its past programme and doctrine forcing the team to withdraw in protest. Monitoring teams were at the same time finding undisclosed equipment and materials associated with the past programme. In response, Iraq grudgingly provided successive disclosures of their programme which were judged by UNSCOM, and specially convened international panels, to be technically inadequate.

10. Iraq refused to elaborate further on the programme during inspections in 1997 and 1998, confining discussion to previous topics. In July 1998, Tariq Aziz personally intervened in the inspection process stating that the biological programme was more secret and more closed than other WMD programmes. He also played down the significance of the programme. This is consistent with Iraq's policy of trivialising the biological weapons programme as the personal adventure of a few misguided scientists.

11. In late 1995, Iraq acknowledged weapons testing the biological agent ricin, but did not provide production information. Two years later – in early 1997 – UNSCOM discovered evidence that Iraq had produced ricin.

12. Iraq has used the biological agent, aflatoxin, against the Shia population in Karbala in 1991 and there is substantial evidence that biological weapons were deployed ready for use during the Gulf War. Defectors' reports also indicate that Iraq also carried out biological experiments on human beings.

DOS/2/0057 56

APPENDIX 10

16 September 2002

IRAQ'S PROGRAMME FOR
WEAPONS OF MASS DESTRUCTION:

THE BRITISH GOVERNMENT ASSESSMENT

DOS/2/0058

471

CONTENTS

DOS/2/0059

CONFIDENTIAL UNTIL RELEASED

EXECUTIVE SUMMARY

1. Under Saddam Hussein, Iraq has developed chemical and biological weapons, acquired missiles allowing it to attack neighbouring countries with these weapons, and tried hard to develop a nuclear bomb. Iraq has admitted to all these programmes to acquire weapons of mass destruction. And Saddam has used chemical weapons, both against Iran and against his own people.

2. Information about Iraq's weapons of mass destruction is already in the public domain from UN reports and from Iraqi defectors. A valuable assessment was provided by the International Institute for Strategic Studies (IISS) on 9 September. The publicly available evidence points clearly to Iraq's continued possession of chemical and biological agents and weapons from before the Gulf War. It shows that Iraq has refurbished sites formerly associated with the production of chemical and biological agents. And it indicates a continuing Iraqi ability to manufacture these agents, and to use bombs, shells, artillery rockets and ballistic missiles to deliver them. The IISS report also judges that Iraq could assemble nuclear weapons within months of obtaining fissile material from foreign sources.

3. We endorse much of this analysis, which is largely based on information available prior to the de facto expulsion of UN inspectors in 1998. But significant additional information is available to the government from secret intelligence sources, described in more detail in this paper. This intelligence cannot tell us about everything. But it provides a fuller picture of Iraqi plans and capabilities. It shows that Saddam Hussein attaches great importance to possessing weapons of mass destruction which he regards as the basis for Iraq's regional power. It shows that he is does not regard them only as weapons of last resort. He is ready to use them, including against his own population, and is determined to retain them. Intelligence also shows that Iraq is preparing plans to conceal evidence of these weapons from any renewed inspection, including by dispersing incriminating documents. And it allows us to judge that Iraq

CAB/11/0141

- has continued to produce chemical and biological agents;

- has military plans for the use of chemical and biological weapons, some of which could be ready within 45 minutes of an order to use them. Saddam and his son Qusay have the political authority to authorise the use of these weapons;

- has developed mobile laboratories for military use, corroborating earlier reports about the mobile production of biological warfare agents;

- has assembled specialists to work on its nuclear programme;

- has pursued illegal programmes to procure controlled materials of potential use in the production of chemical and biological weapons programmes;

- has sought significant quantities of uranium from Africa, despite having no civil nuclear programme that could require it;

- is covertly trying to acquire technology and materials which could be used in the production of nuclear weapons, including specialised aluminium controlled because of its potential use in enriching uranium;

- has retained up to 20 Al Hussein missiles, capable of carrying chemical or biological warheads;

- is deploying its Al-Samoud liquid propellant missile, and has used the absence of weapons inspectors to work on extending its range beyond the limit of 150km imposed by the United Nations;

- is producing the solid-propellant missile Ababil-100, and is making efforts to extend its range;

- has constructed a new engine test stand for missiles capable of threatening Israel and all Iraq's Gulf neighbours as well as the UK Sovereign Bases in Cyprus and NATO members (Greece and Turkey);

- has pursued illegal programmes to procure materials for use in its illegal devevlopment of long range missiles;

- has begun dispersing its most sensitive weapons, equipment and material.

4. These judgements have been endorsed by the Joint Intelligence Committee (JIC). More details on the judgements, and on the development of the JIC's assessments since 1998, are set out later in this paper.

CAB|11|0142

5. The importance of denying Saddam access to weapons of mass destruction was recognised by the United Nations in a series of Resolution between 1991 and 1998. The paper sets out the key UN Security Council Resolutions, accepted by Iraq, which required the destruction of these weapons. It also summarises the history of the UN inspections regime. This includes both the extent of Saddam's capabilities uncovered by the inspectors and Iraq's history of dishonesty, deception, intimidation and concealment in its dealings with the UN inspectors.

6. But the threat from Iraq does not depend solely on the capabilities we have described. It arises also because of the violent and aggressive nature of Saddam's regime. His record of internal repression and external aggression gives rise to unique concerns about the threat he poses. The paper briefly outlines his rise to power, the nature of his regime and his history of regional aggression. Vivid and horrifying accounts of Saddam's human rights abuses are also catalogued.

7. The paper briefly sets out how Iraq is able to finance its weapons programme. Drawing on illicit earnings generated outside UN control, Iraq generated income of some $3 billion in 2001.

8. The paper concludes with a summary table setting out key points on Iraq's capabilities.

CAB/11/0143

PART 1

IRAQ'S CHEMICAL, BIOLOGICAL, NUCLEAR AND BALLISTIC MISSILE PROGRAMMES

CHAPTER 1: THE ROLE OF INTELLIGENCE

1. Since UN Inspectors were, in effect, expelled by Iraq in 1998, there has been little overt information on Iraq's chemical, biological, nuclear and ballistic missile programmes. Much of the publicly available information about Iraqi capabilities and intentions is necessarily dated. But we also have available a range of secret intelligence about these programmes and Saddam's intentions. This comes principally from the United Kingdom's intelligence and analysis agencies – the Secret Intelligence Service (SIS), the Government Communications Headquarters (GCHQ) and the Defence Intelligence Staff (DIS). We also have access to intelligence from close allies.

2. Intelligence rarely offers a complete account of activities which are designed to remain concealed. And the nature of Saddam's regime makes Iraq a difficult target for the intelligence services. Nonetheless, we have been able to develop a range of well positioned sources. The need to protect and preserve these sources inevitably limits the detail that can be made available. But intelligence has provided important insights into Iraqi programmes, and into Iraqi military thinking. Taken together with what is already known from other sources, this builds our understanding of Iraq's capabilities, and adds significantly to the analysis already in the public domain.

3. Iraq's capabilities have been regularly reviewed by the Joint Intelligence Committee (JIC), which has provided advice to the Prime Minister on the developing assessment on the basis of all available sources. Part 1 of this paper includes some of the most significant views reached by the JIC between 1999 and 2002.

DOS/2/0060

476

Joint Intelligence Committee (JIC)
The JIC is a Cabinet Committee with a history dating back to 1936. It brings together the Heads of the three Intelligence and Security Agencies (Secret Intelligence Service, Government Communications Headquarters and the Security Service), the Chief of Defence Intelligence and senior policy makers from the Foreign Office, the Ministry of Defence, the Home Office, the Treasury and the Department of Trade and Industry. It provides regular intelligence assessments to the Prime Minister, other Ministers and senior officials on a wide range of foreign policy and international security issues. The JIC meets each week in the Cabinet Office. Its current chairman is John Scarlett.

DOS/2/0061

CHAPTER 2: IRAQ'S PROGRAMMES: 1971-1998

1. Iraq has been involved in chemical and biological warfare research for over 30 years. Its **chemical warfare** research commenced in 1971 at a small, well guarded site at Rashad to the Northeast of Baghdad. Research was conducted here on a number of chemical agents including Mustard Gas, CS and Tabun. Later, in 1974 a dedicated organisation called Al-Hassan Ibn Al-Haitham was established. At the

---

Effects of Chemical Weapons

Mustard is a liquid agent, which gives also gives off a hazardous vapour, causing burns and blisters to exposed skin. When inhaled, mustard damages the respiratory tract; when ingested, it causes vomiting and diarrhoea. It attacks and damages the eyes, mucous membranes, lungs, skin, and blood-forming organs.

Tabun, sarin and VX are all nerve agents of which VX is the most toxic. They all damage the nervous system, producing muscular spasms and paralysis. As little as 10 milligrammes of VX on the skin can cause rapid death. ...grammes kills...people

---

same time plans were made to build a large research and commercial-scale production facility in the desert some 70km Northwest of Baghdad under the Project cover of No 922. This was to become Muthanna State Establishment, also known as al-Muthanna, and operated under the front name of Iraq's State Establishment for Pesticide Production. It became partially operational in 1982-83. It had five research and development sections each tasked to pursue different programmes. In addition, the al-Muthanna site was the main chemical agent production facility, and it also took the lead in weaponising chemical and biological agents including all aspects of weapon development and testing, in association with the military. According to information, subsequently supplied by the Iraqis, the total production capacity in 1991 was 4,000 tonnes of agent per annum, but we assess it could have been higher. Al-Muthanna was supported by three separate storage and precursor production facilities known as Fallujah 1, 2 and 3 near Habbaniyah, north-west of Baghdad, parts of which were not completed before they were heavily bombed in the 1991 Gulf War.

2. Iraq started **biological warfare** research in the mid-1970s. After small-scale research, a purpose-built research and development facility was authorised at al-

Salman, also known as Salman Pak. This is surrounded on three sides by the Tigris river and situated some 35km South of Baghdad. Although some progress was made in biological weapons research at this early stage, Iraq decided to concentrate on

---

The effects of biological agents

Anthrax is a disease caused by the bacterium Bacillus anthracis. Inhalation anthrax is the manifestation of the disease likely to be expected in biological warfare. The symptoms may vary, but can include fever and internal bleeding. The incubation period for anthrax is 1 to 7 days, with most cases occurring within 2 days of exposure.

Botulinum toxin is one of the most toxic substances known to man. The first symptoms of poisoning may appear as early as 1 hour post exposure or as long as 8 days after exposure, with the incubation period between 12 and 22 hours. Paralysis leads to death by suffocation.

Aflatoxins are fungal toxins, which are potent *carcinogens*. Most symptoms take a long time to show. Food products contaminated by aflatoxin can cause liver inflammation and cancer. It can also affect pregnant women, leading to stillborn babies and children born with mutations.

Ricin is derived from the castor bean and can cause multiple organ failure leading to death within one or two days of inhalation.

---

developing chemical agents and their delivery systems at al-Muthanna. With the outbreak of the Iran-Iraq War, in the early 1980s, the biological weapons programme was revived. The appointment of Dr Rihab Taha in 1985, to head a small biological weapons research team at al-Muthanna, helped to develop the programme. At about the same time plans were made to develop the Salman Pak site into a secure biological warfare research facility. Dr Taha continued to work with her team at Muthanna until 1987 when it moved to Salman Pak, which was under the control of the Directorate of General Intelligence. Significant resources were provided for the programme, including the construction of a dedicated production facility, (Project 324) at al-Hakam. Agent production began in 1988 and weaponisation testing and later filling of munitions was conducted in association with the staff at Muthanna State Establishment. From mid-1990, other civilian facilities were taken over and some adapted for use in the production and research and development of biological agents. These included:

DOS/2/0063

- Daura Foot and Mouth Vaccination Plant which produced botulinum toxin and conducted virus research. There is some intelligence to suggest that work was also conducted on anthrax;

- al-Fudaliyah Agriculture and Water Research centre where Iraq admitted it undertook Aflatoxin production and genetic engineering:

- Amariyah Sera and Vaccine institute which was used for the storage of biological agent seed stocks, and was involved in genetic engineering

3. By the time of the Gulf War Iraq was producing very large quantities of chemical and biological agents. From a series of Iraqi declarations to the UN during the 1990s we know that by 1991 they had produced at least:

- 19,000 litres of botulinum toxin, 8,500 litres of anthrax, 2,200 litres of aflatoxin, and were working on a number of other agents;

- 2,850 tonnes of mustard gas, 210 tonnes of tabun, 795 tonnes of sarin and cyclosarin, and 3.9 tonnes of VX.

4. Iraq's **nuclear programme** was established under the Iraqi Atomic Energy Commission in the 1950s. Under a nuclear co-operation agreement signed with the Soviet Union in 1959, a nuclear research centre, equipped with a research reactor, was built at Tuwaitha, the main Iraqi nuclear research centre. The surge in Iraqi oil revenues in the early 1970s supported an expansion of the research programme. This was bolstered by the signing of co-operation agreements with France and Italy in the mid-1970s. France agreed to supply two research reactors powered by highly enriched uranium fuel, and Italy supplied equipment for fuel fabrication and handling. By the end of 1984 Iraq was self-sufficient in uranium ore. One of the reactors was destroyed in an Israeli air attack in June 1981 shortly before it was to become operational, the other was never completed.

DOS/2/0064

5. By the mid-1980s the deterioration of Iraq's position in the war with Iran prompted renewed interest in the military use of nuclear technology, and additional resources were put into developing technologies to enrich uranium as fissile material for use in nuclear weapons. Enriched uranium was preferred because it could be produced more covertly than the alternative, plutonium. Iraq followed parallel programmes to produce highly enriched uranium: electromagnetic isotope separation (EMIS) and gas centrifuge enrichment. By 1991 one EMIS enrichment facility was nearing completion and another was under

> **Effect of a 20-kiloton nuclear detonation**
> A detonation of a 20-kiloton nuclear warhead over a city might flatten an area of approximately 3 square miles. Within 1.6 miles of detonation, blast damage and radiation would cause 80% casualties, three-quarters of which would be fatal. Between 1.6 and 3.1 miles from the detonation, there would still be 10% casualties. Centred on St Paul's three square miles cover....., centred on Edinburg Castle....

construction. Centrifuge facilities were also under construction, but the centrifuge design was still being developed. In August 1990 Iraq instigated a crash programme to develop a single nuclear weapon within a year, and envisaged the rapid development of a small 50 machine gas centrifuge cascade to produce the highly enriched uranium required. By the time of the Gulf War, the programme had made little progress. But, by that stage, Iraq decided to concentrate on gas centrifuges as the means for producing the necessary fissile material.

6. Iraq's declared aim was to produce a weapon with a 20-kiloton yield and weapons designs were produced for both a simple gun-type device and for more complex implosion weapons. The latter were similar to the device used at Hiroshima in 1945. Iraq was also working on more advanced concepts. By 1991 the Iraqi programme was supported by large body of Iraqi nuclear expertise, programme documentation and databases and manufacturing infrastructure. On the basis of reports from UN inspections after the Gulf War it was eventually concluded that in 1991 Iraq was .....away from producing a nuclear weapon.

7. Prior to the Gulf War, Iraq had a well-developed **ballistic missile** industry. Most of the missiles fired in the Gulf War were an Iraqi produced version of the SCUD

DOS/2/0065

> **SCUD missiles**
> The short-range mobile SCUD ballistic missile was developed by the Soviet Union in the 1950s, drawing on the technology of the German V-2 developed in World War II.
>
> For many years it was the mainstay of Soviet and Warsaw Pact tactical missile forces, and it was also widely exported. Recipients of Soviet-manufactured SCUDs included Iraq, North Korea, Iran, and Libya, although not all were sold directly by the Soviet Union.

missile, the Al Hussein, with an extended range of 650 km. Numbers before war…. Iraq was working on other stretched SCUD variants, such as the Al Abbas, which had a range of 900km. Iraq was also seeking to reverse engineer the SCUD engine with a view to producing new missiles; recent evidence indicates that they may have succeeded at that time. In particular Iraq had plans for a new SCUD-derived missile with a range of 1200km. Iraq also conducted a partial flight test of a multi-stage satellite launch vehicle based on SCUD technology, known as the Al Abid. Also during this period, Iraq was developing the BADR-2000, a 700-1000km range two-stage solid propellant missile (based on the Iraqi part of the 1980s CONDOR-2 programme run in co-operation with Argentina and Egypt). There were plans for 1200-1500km range solid propellant follow-on systems.

The use of chemical and biological weapons

8. Iraq had made frequent use of a variety of chemical weapons during the Iran-Iraq War. (Many of the casualties are still alive in Iranian hospitals suffering from the long-term effects of numerous types of cancer and lung diseases.) In 1988 Saddam also used mustard and nerve agents against Iraqi Kurds at Halabja in northern Iraq (see photograph). Estimates vary, but according to Human Rights Watch up to 5,000 people were killed.

9. A month after the attack on Halabja, Iraqi troops used over 100 tons of sarin nerve agent against Iranian troops on the Al Fao peninsula. Over the next three months Iraqi troops used sarin and other nerve agents on Iranian troops causing extensive casualties.

DOS/2/0066

The Attack on Halabja

Shortly before sunrise on Friday, 17th March 1988, the village of Halabja was bombarded by Iraqi warplanes. The raid was over in minutes. Saddam Hussein used chemical weapons against his own people. A Kurd described the effects of a chemical attack on another village:

"My brothers and my wife had blood and vomit running from their noses and their mouths. Their heads were tilted to one side. They were groaning. I couldn't do much, just clean up the blood and vomit from their mouths and try in every way to make them breathe again. I did artificial respiration on them and then I gave them two injections each. I also rubbed creams on my wife and two brothers."

(From "Crimes Against Humanity," Iraqi National Congress.)

Among the corpses at Halabja, children were found dead where they had been playing outside their homes. In places, streets were piled with corpses.

10. Intelligence indicates that in 1991 Iraq used the biological warfare agent aflatoxin against the Shia population of Karbala.

11. From Iraqi declarations to the UN after the Gulf War we know that by 1991 Iraq had produced a variety of delivery mean for chemical and biological agents including 75 ballistic missile warheads, over 16,000 free fall bombs and over 110,000 artillery rockets and shells

The use of ballistic missiles

12. Iraq fired over 500 SCUD-type missiles at Iran during the Iran-Iraq War at both civilian and military targets, and 93 SCUD-type missiles during the Gulf War. The

DOS|2|0067

latter were targeted at Israel and at Coalition forces stationed in the Gulf region. Armed with conventional warheads they did only limited damage. Iraq subsequently admitted to UNSCOM that it had 50 chemical and 25 biological warheads available for these missiles. It is not clear if the warheads were ever mated to the missiles. In any event they were not used.

13. At the end of the Gulf War the international community was determined that Iraq's arsenal of chemical and biological and ballistic missiles should be dismantled. The method chosen to achieve this aim was the establishment of the UN Special Commission (UNSCOM) to carry out intrusive inspections within Iraq and to eliminate its chemical and biological weapons and ballistic missiles with a range over 150km. The International Atomic Energy Agency (IAEA) was charged with the abolition of Iraq's nuclear weapons programme. Between 1991 and 1998 UNSCOM and the IAEA succeeded in identifying and destroying very large quantities of chemical and biological weapons and ballistic missiles as well as associated production facilities. They also destroyed the infrastructure for Iraq's nuclear weapons programme. This was achieved despite a continuous and sophisticated programme of harassment, obstruction and deception and denial (see Part 2). By 1998 UNSCOM concluded that they were unable to fulfil their mandate. The inspectors were withdrawn in December 1998.

14. Based on the UNSCOM report to the UN Security Council in January 1999 and earlier UNSCOM reports, we assess that when the UN inspectors left Iraq they were unable to account for:

- up to 360 tonnes of bulk chemical warfare agent, including 1.5 tonnes of VX nerve agent;

- up to 3,000 tonnes of precursor chemicals, including approximately 300 tonnes which, in the Iraqi CW programme, were unique to the production of VX;

DOS/2/0068

- growth media procured for biological agent production (enough to produce over three times the 8,500 litres of anthrax spores Iraq admits to having manufactured);

- over 30,000 special munitions for delivery of chemical and biological agents.

15. The departure of the Inspectors meant that the International Community was unable to establish the truth behind these large discrepancies. It also greatly diminished our ability to monitor and assess Iraq's continuing attempts to reconstitute its programmes.

16. While the enforcement of the sanctions regimes and the UN arms embargo and US/UK air operations in 1998 have impeded Iraq's efforts to reconstitute its weapons of mass destruction, they have not halted them. Much of Iraq's missile infrastructure has been rebuilt; the nuclear weapons programme is being reconstituted, albeit with difficulty; and Iraq continues to produce chemical and biological agents.

DOS/2/0069

CHAPTER 3: THE CURRENT POSITION: 1998-2002

1. This chapter sets out what we now know of Saddam's chemical, biological, nuclear and ballistic missile programmes, drawing on all the available evidence. While it takes account of the results from UN inspections and other publicly available information, it also draws heavily on intelligence about Iraqi efforts to develop their programmes and capabilities since 1998. The **main conclusions** are that:

- Iraq has a useable chemical and biological weapons capability, in breach of UNSCR 687, which has included recent production of chemical and biological agents;

- Saddam continues to attach great importance to the possession of weapons of mass destruction and ballistic missiles, which he regards as being the basis for Iraq's regional power. He is not prepared to lose capabilities he has developed over the last four years;

- Iraq can deliver chemical and biological agents using an extensive range of artillery shells, free-fall bombs, sprayers and ballistic missiles;

- Iraq continues to work on developing nuclear weapons, in breach of its obligations under the Non-Proliferation Treaty, and in breach of UNSCR 687. Uranium has been sought from Africa that has no known civil nuclear application in Iraq;

- Iraq possesses extended-range versions of the SCUD ballistic missile, capable of reaching Tehran, Eastern Turkey and Cyprus in breach of UNSCR 687. It is also developing longer range ballistic missiles;

- Iraq's current military planning specifically envisages the use of chemical and biological weapons;

- Iraq's military forces maintain the capability to use chemical and biological weapons, with command, control and logistical arrangements in place. The Iraqi military may be able to deploy these weapons within forty five minutes of a decision to do so;

DOS/2/0070

- Iraq is already taking steps to undermine the return of any UN weapons inspectors through concealment and dispersal of sensitive equipment and documentation;

- Iraq's chemical, biological, nuclear and ballistic missiles programmes are not short of funds, despite the parlous state of the Iraqi economy.

CHEMICAL AND BIOLOGICAL WEAPONS

JIC Assessment: 1999-2002

2. Since the withdrawal of the inspectors the Joint Intelligence Committee (JIC) has monitored evidence, including from secret intelligence, of continuing work on Iraqi offensive chemical and biological warfare capabilities. In the first half of 2000 the JIC noted intelligence on Iraqi attempts to procure dual-use chemicals and the reconstruction of civil chemical production at sites formerly associated with the chemical warfare programme. Iraq had also been trying to procure dual-use materials and equipment which could be used for a biological warfare programme. Personnel known to have been connected to the biological warfare programme up to the Gulf War had been conducting research into pathogens. There was intelligence that Iraq was starting to produce biological warfare agents in mobile production centres. Planning for the project had begun in 1995 under Dr Rihab Taha, known to have been a central player in the pre-1995 programme. The JIC concluded that Iraq had sufficient expertise, equipment and material to produce biological weapons agents within weeks using its legitimate biotechnology facilities.

3. A JIC assessment in mid-2001 concluded that intelligence on Iraqi former chemical and biological warfare facilities, their limited reconstruction and civil production pointed to a continuing research and development programme. Since 1998 Iraqi development of mass destruction weaponry had been helped by the absence of inspectors and the increase in illegal border trade, which provided available hard currency.

4. In early 2002 the JIC assessed that Iraq retained production equipment, stocks of chemical agents and at least small amounts of precursors from before the Gulf War. Iraq could produce quantities of mustard gas within weeks and of Sarin and VX within months. In the case of VX it might already have done so. Iraq held stocks of biological agents from either before the Gulf

War or from more recent production. The JIC judged Iraq to be self-sufficient in the production of biological weapons. It also judged that Iraq had the means to deliver chemical and biological weapons.

Recent Intelligence

5. Subsequently, intelligence has become available from reliable sources which complements and adds to previous intelligence and confirms the JIC assessment that Iraq has chemical and biological weapons. The intelligence also shows that the Iraqi leadership has been discussing a number of issues related to these weapons. This intelligence covers:

- **Confirmation that chemical and biological weapons play an important role in Iraqi military thinking.** Intelligence shows that Saddam attaches great importance to the possession of weapons of mass destruction which he regards as being the basis for Iraqi regional powers. He believes that respect for Iraq rests on its possession of chemical and biological weapons and the missiles capable of delivering them. Intelligence indicates that Saddam is determined to retain this capability and recognises that Iraqi political weight would be diminished if Iraq's military power rested solely on its weakened conventional military forces.

- **Iraqi attempts to retain its existing banned weapons systems:** Iraq is already taking steps to undermine the possible return of any UN weapons inspectors: Iraq has begun removing sensitive equipment and papers relating to its chemical and biological programmes and dispersing them beyond the gaze of inspectors, for example by hiding sensitive documents in the homes of his trusted officials. Saddam is determined not to lose the capabilities that he has been able to develop in the four years since inspectors left.

- **Saddam's willingness to use chemical and biological weapons:** intelligence indicates that Saddam is prepared to use chemical and biological weapons if he believes his regime is under threat. We also know from intelligence that as part of Iraq's military planning, Saddam is willing to use chemical and biological weapons against any internal uprising by the Shia population. The Iraqi military may be able to deploy chemical or biological weapons within forty five minutes of an order to do so.

Chemical and biological agents: surviving stocks

6. When confronted with questions about the unaccounted stocks, Iraq has claimed, repeatedly, that if it had retained any chemical agents from before the Gulf War they would have deteriorated sufficiently to render them harmless. But Iraq has admitted to having the knowledge and capability to add stabiliser to nerve agent which would prevent such decomposition.

7. Iraq has claimed that all its biological agents and weapons have been destroyed. No convincing proof of any kind has been produced to support this claim. In particular, Iraq could not explain large discrepancies between the amount of growth media (nutrients required for the specialised growth of agent) it procured before 1991 and the amounts of agent it admits to having manufactured. The discrepancy is enough to produce more than three times the amount of anthrax allegedly manufactured.

Chemical agent: production capabilities

8. Intelligence confirms that Iraq has continued to produce chemical agent. During the Gulf War a number of facilities which intelligence reporting indicated were directly or indirectly associated with Iraq's chemical weapons effort were attacked and damaged. Following the ceasefire UNSCOM destroyed or rendered harmless facilities and equipment used in Iraq's chemical weapons programme. Other equipment was released for civilian use either in industry or academic institutes, where it was tagged and regularly inspected and monitored, or else placed under camera monitoring, to ensure that it was not being misused. This monitoring ceased when UNSCOM withdrew from Iraq in 1998. However, capabilities remain and, although the main chemical weapon production facility at al-Muthanna was completely destroyed by UNSCOM and has not been rebuilt, other plants formerly associated with the chemical warfare programme have been rebuilt. This includes the chlorine and phenol plant at Fallujah 2 near Habbaniyah. In addition to their civilian uses, chlorine and phenol are used for precursor chemicals which contribute to the production of chemical agents.

9. The expansion of chlorine production facilities at Fallujah 2 gives Iraq a capacity well beyond that required for Iraq's civilian needs.

DOS/2/0073

10. Other dual use facilities, which could be used to support the production of chemical agent and precursors, have been rebuilt and re-equipped. New chemical facilities have been built, some with illegal foreign assistance, and are probably fully operational or ready for production. These include the Ibn Sina Company at Tarmiya (see figure 1), which is a chemical research centre. It undertakes research, development and production of chemicals previously imported but not now available and which are needed for Iraq's civil industry. But it is known to be supporting the missile programme and could also be involved in the chemical weapons programme. The Director General ...of what is Hickmat Na'im al-Jalu who, prior to the Gulf War worked in Iraq's nuclear weapons programme and after the war was responsible for preserving Iraq's chemical expertise.

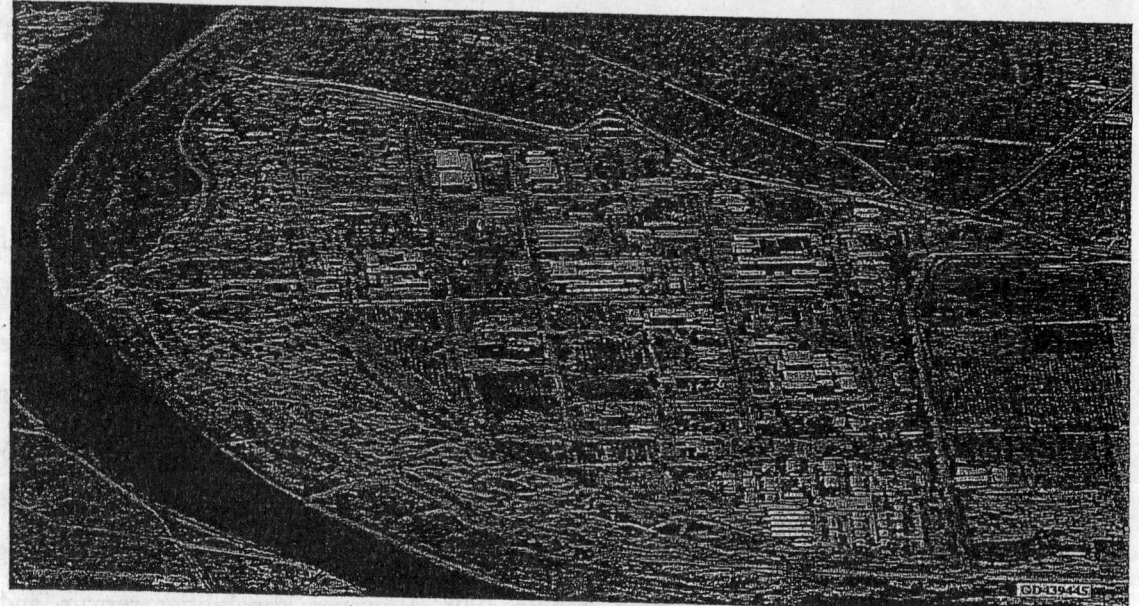

FIGURE 1: THE IBN SINA COMPANY AT TARMIYA

Parts of the al-Qa'Qaa chemical complex damaged in the Gulf War have also been repaired and are operational. Of particular concern are elements of the phosgene production plant at Al Qa'Qaa. These were severely damaged during the Gulf War, and dismantled under UNSCOM supervision, but have since been rebuilt. While phosgene does have industrial uses it can also be used by itself as a chemical agent or as a precursor for nerve agents.

11. Iraq has retained the expertise for chemical warfare research, agent production and weaponisation. Most of the personnel previously involved in the programme remain in country. Indeed, intelligence indicates that Haidar Husain Taha, recently reported in the media as being the factory manager of the Fallujah 2 plant, is almost certainly the same individual

DOS/2/0074

who from 1984 until the end of the Gulf war worked at Iraq's CW programme at the Muthanna State Establishment researching mustard gas. While UNSCOM found a number of technical manuals (so called "cook books") for the production of chemical agents and critical precursors, Iraq's claim to have unilaterally destroyed the bulk of the documentation cannot be confirmed and is almost certainly untrue. Recent intelligence indicates that Iraq is still discussing methods of concealing such documentation in order to ensure that it is not discovered by any future UN inspections.

The Problem of Dual Use Facilities

Almost all components and supplies used in weapons of mass destruction and ballistic missile programmes are dual-use. For example, any major petrochemical or biotech industry, as well as public health organisations, will have legitimate need for most materials and equipment required to manufacture chemical and biological weapons. Without UN weapons inspectors it is very difficult therefore to be sure about the true nature of many of Iraq's facilities.

For example, Iraq has built a large new chemical complex, Project Baiji, in the desert in north west Iraq at Ash Sharqat (see figure 2). This site is a former uranium enrichment facility, which was damaged during the Gulf War, and rendered harmless under supervision of the IAEA. Part of the site has been rebuilt, with work starting in 1992, as a chemical production complex. Despite the site being far away from populated areas it is surrounded by a high wall with watch towers and guarded by armed guards. Intelligence reports indicate that it will produce nitric acid, which can be used in explosives, missile fuel, and in the purification of uranium.

DOS/2/0075

Biological agent: production capabilities

12. We know from intelligence that Iraq has continued to produce biological warfare agents. As with some chemical equipment, UNSCOM only destroyed equipment that could be directly linked to biological weapons production. Iraq also has its own engineering capability to design and construct biological agent associated fermenters, centrifuges, sprayer dryers and other equipment and is judged to be self-sufficient in the technology required to produce biological weapons. The experienced personnel who were active in the programme have largely remained in the country. They include.........Some dual-use equipment, including growth media, has also been purchased under the Oil for Food programme, but without monitoring of the equipment by UN inspectors Iraq could have diverted it to their biological weapons programme. This newly purchased equipment and others previously subject to monitoring could be used in a resurgent BW programme. Facilities of concern include:

- the Castor Oil Production Plant at Fallujah: this was damaged in UK?US air attacks in 1998 (Operations Desert Fox) but has rebuilt. The residue from the castor bean pulp can be used in the production of ricin biological agent;

- the Al-Daura Foot and Mouth Disease Vaccine Plant, which was involved in biological agent production and research before the Gulf War. This has probably been renovated;

- The Amariyah Sera and Vaccine plant at....UNSCOM established that this was used to produce biological agents prior to the Gulf War. It has now expanded its storage capacity.

13. UNSCOM established that Iraq was planning to conceal from the inspectors the capability to produce biological warfare agents by developing mobile facilities. In the past two years evidence from defectors has indicated the existence of such facilities. **Recent intelligence** confirms that the Iraqi military have developed mobile facilities. These would help Iraq conceal and protect biological agent production from military attack or UN inspection.

Chemical and biological agents: delivery means

14. Iraq has a variety of delivery means available for both chemical and biological agents. These include:

DOS/21 0076.

- free fall bombs - Iraq acknowledged to UNSCOM the deployment to four sites of free fall bombs filled with biological agent during 1990-91. These bombs were filled with anthrax, botulinum toxin and aflatoxin. Iraq also acknowledged possession of four types of aerial bomb with various chemical agent fills including sulphur mustard, tabun, sarin, cyclosarin, and VX;

- artillery shells and rockets - Iraq made extensive use of artillery munitions filled with chemical agents during the Iran-Iraq War. Mortars can also be used for chemical agent delivery. Iraq also claimed to have tested the use of shells and rockets filled with biological agents. Over 20,000 artillery munitions remain unaccounted for by UNSCOM;

- helicopter and aircraft borne sprayers - Iraq carried out studies into aerosol dissemination of biological agent using these platforms prior to 1991. UNSCOM was unable to account for many of these devices. It is probable that Iraq retains a capability for aerosol dispersal of both chemical and biological agent; Any more on range and vulnerability

- Al Hussein ballistic missiles (range 650km) - Iraq told UNSCOM that it filled 25 warheads with anthrax, botulinum toxin and aflatoxin. Iraq also developed chemical agent warheads for Al Hussein. Iraq admitted to producing 50 chemical warheads for Al Hussein which were intended for the delivery of a mixture of sarin and cyclosarin. However, technical analysis of warhead remnants has shown traces of VX degradation product which indicate that some additional warheads were made and filled with VX;

- Al Samoud/Ababil 100 ballistic missiles (range 150km plus) - It is unclear if chemical and biological warheads have been developed for these systems, but given their experience on other missile systems, we judge that Iraq has the technical expertise for doing so;

- L-29 remotely piloted vehicle programme (see figure 3) - we know from intelligence that Iraq has attempted to modify the L-29 jet trainer to allow it to be used as a pilot-less aircraft (unmanned aerial vehicle - UAV) for the delivery of chemical and biological agents over a large area. This modification programme has had problems and Iraq is now focusing on developing smaller UAVs.

DOS121OO77

Chemical and biological warfare: command and control

15. The authority to use chemical and biological weapons ultimately resides with Saddam, but **intelligence indicates** that he may have also delegated this authority to his son Qusai. Special Security Organisation (SSO) and Special Republican Guard (SRG) units would be involved in the movement of any chemical and biological weapons to military units. The Iraqi military holds artillery and missile systems at Corps level throughout the Armed Forces and conducts regular training with them. The Directorate of Rocket Forces has operational control of strategic missile systems and some Multiple Rocket Launcher Systems.

Chemical and biological weapons: summary

16. Intelligence confirms that Iraq has covert chemical and biological weapons programmes, in breach of UN Security Council Resolution 687 and has continued to produce chemical and biological agents. Iraq has:

- chemical and biological agents and weapons available, both from pre-Gulf War stocks and more recent production;

- the capability to produce the chemical agents sulphur mustard, tabun, sarin, cyclosarin, and VX capable of producing mass casualties;

- a biological agent production capability and can produce at least anthrax, botulinum toxin, aflatoxin and ricin. Iraq has also developed mobile facilities to produce biological agents.

- a variety of delivery means available;

- military forces, which maintain the capability to use these weapons, with command, control and logistical arrangements in place.

NUCLEAR WEAPONS
JIC Assessments: 1999-2002

DOS/2/0078

17. Since 1998 the JIC has monitored Iraq's attempts to reconstitute its nuclear weapons programme. In mid-2001 the JIC assessed that Iraq had continued its nuclear research after 1991. The JIC drew attention to intelligence that Iraq had recalled its nuclear scientists to the programme in 1998. Since 1998 Iraq had been trying to procure items that could be for use in the construction of centrifuges for the enrichment of uranium.

18. In early 2002, the JIC assessed that sanctions were hindering the import of crucial goods for the production of fissile material. If sanctions continued, **Iraq would not be able to** indigenously to produce a nuclear weapon. If they were removed or became ineffective, it would take Iraq at least five years to produce a weapon. This time-scale would shorten if Iraq succeeded in obtaining fissile material from abroad.

> **Nuclear weapons - why are they difficult to make?**
> A nuclear warhead requires sophisticated science and engineering, complex calculations and meticulous experimentation to convert the simplistic concepts seen in text books into a reliable bomb or missile warhead. Many of the hundreds of finely-engineered, specialised components are unique and have to be individually developed, made and tested rigorously. The warhead needs to be designed and tested to withstand accelerations, temperatures, vibrations and weather, and finally fired, using inert materials in place of the nuclear core, to prove that it works. All this involves many dangerous nuclear and explosive materials which need specialised facilities and techniques to ensure safe handling and production.

Iraqi Nuclear Weapons Expertise

19. Although the IAEA dismantled the physical infrastructure (such as....) of Iraqi nuclear weapons programme. Iraq retained, and retains, its experienced nuclear scientists and technicians, specialised in the production of fissile material and weapons design. They include .... It also retains the accompanying programme documentation and data, which was withheld from the inspectors.

> **Gas Centrifuge Uranium Enrichment**
> Uranium in the form of uranium hexafluoride is separated into its different isotopes in rapidly spinning rotor tubes of special centrifuges. Many hundreds or thousands of centrifuges are connected in cascades to enrich uranium. If the lighter U235 isotope is enriched to more than 90% it can be used in the core of a nuclear weapon.

20. **Intelligence shows** that the present Iraqi programme is almost certainly based on gas centrifuge uranium enrichment, one of the routes Iraq was following for producing fissile material before the Gulf War. But Iraq needs certain key equipment, such as gas centrifuge components, and materials for the production of the fissile material necessary before a nuclear bomb could be developed.

OOS|2|0079

21. Following the expulsion of weapons inspectors in 1998 there has been **an accumulation of intelligence** indicating that Iraq is making concerted covert efforts to acquire dual-use technology and materials with nuclear applications. Iraq's existing holdings of processed uranium are under IAEA supervision. But there is compelling evidence that Iraq has sought the supply of significant quantities of uranium from Africa. Iraqi has no known civil nuclear programme or nuclear power plants, therefore it has no legitimate reason to acquire uranium.

22. Other important procurement since 1998 includes attempts to purchase vacuum pumps, which could be used.....an entire magnet production line of the correct specification for use in gas centrifuges, one large filament winding machine, which.....and a large balancing machine which could be used in initial centrifuge balancing work. Of particular concern are the repeated attempts by Iraq covertly to acquire a very large quantity (60,000 pieces) of specialised aluminium tubes. The specialised aluminium in question is subject to international export controls because of its potential application in the construction of gas centrifuges used to enrich uranium. In the case of aluminium and magnets it appears **from intelligence** that Iraq is attempting to acquire a capability to produce these components on its own rather than rely on foreign procurement.

Nuclear weapons: timelines

23. The projected timeline contained in the JIC assessment of early 2002 (see paragraph...) for Iraq to acquire a nuclear weapon through indigenous production of fissile material depend on a number of variables including the effectiveness of sanctions and other export controls and Iraqi success (or otherwise) to date in procuring items such as those listed above.

24. The continuing existence of the specialist teams and back-up data means that, were Iraq to obtain fissile material from abroad, the timeline would be much shorter. In those circumstances, and depending on the effectiveness of Iraqi weapons designs, we judge that Iraq could produce a nuclear weapon in between one and two years.

Radiological dispersal device
A Radiological Dispersal Device (RDD) is designed to cause injury, or to deny, access to an area through the dissemination of radioactive material. An RDD can be made using material from medical or industrial facilities, but makes an ineffective weapon. Very large amounts of highly radioactive material are required before an RDD will cause many fatalities or significant injuries.

DOS12|0077
0104

Iraq experimented with radiological dispersal devices (RDDs) during 1987, using Zirconium-95 as a dispersal material for area denial. This programme never progressed beyond the research stage, and was dropped.

BALLISTIC MISSILES

JIC Assessment: 1999-2002

25. In mid-2001 the JIC drew attention to what it described as a "step-change" in progress on Iraqi missile programme over the previous two years. It was clear from intelligence that the range of Iraqi missiles which was permitted by the UN and supposedly limited to 150 kilometres was being extended and that work was under way on larger engines for longer-range missiles.

26. In early 2002 the JIC concluded that Iraq had begun to develop missiles with a range of over 1,000 kilometres. If sanctions remained in place the Iraqis would not be able to produce such a missile before 2007. Sanctions and the earlier work of the inspectors had caused significant problems for Iraqi missile development. In the previous six months Iraqi foreign procurement efforts for the missile programme had been bolder. The JIC also assessed that Iraq retained up to 20 Al Hussein missiles from before the Gulf War.

The Iraqi ballistic missile programme since 1998

27. Since the Gulf War, Iraq has been openly developing two short-range missiles up to a range of 150km, which are permitted under UN Security Council Resolution 687. The Al-Samoud liquid propellant missile has been extensively tested and is being deployed to military units. **Intelligence indicates** that at least fifty have been produced. **Intelligence also indicates** that Iraq has worked on extending its range to at least 200km in breach of UN Security Resolution 687. Production of the solid propellant Ababil-100 (Figure 4) is also underway, probably as an unguided rocket at this stage. There are also plans to extend its range to at least 200km.

FIGURE 4: ABABIL-100

Compared to liquid propellant missiles, those powered by solid propellant offer greater ease of storage, handling and mobility. They are also quicker to take into and out of action and can stay at a high state of readiness for longer periods.

28. **According to intelligence**, Iraq has retained up to 20 Al Hussein missiles (Figure 5), in breach of UN Security Council Resolution 687. These missiles were either hidden from the UN as complete systems, or re-assembled using illegally retained engines and other components. We judge that the engineering expertise available would allow these missiles to be maintained effectively, although the fact that at least some require re-assembly makes it difficult to judge exactly how many could be available for use. They could be used with conventional, chemical or biological warheads and, with a range of up to 650km, are capable of reaching a number of countries in the region including Cyprus, Turkey, Saudi Arabia, Iran and Israel.

FIGURE 5: AL HUSSEIN

29. **Intelligence has confirmed** that Iraq wants to extend the range of its missile systems to over 1000km, enabling it to threaten other regional neighbours. This work began in 1998, although efforts to regenerate the long range ballistic missile programme probably began in 1995. Iraq's missile programmes employ hundreds of people. **Satellite imagery** (Figure 6) has shown a new engine test stand being constructed (A), which is larger than the current one used for Al Samoud (B), and that formerly used for testing SCUD engines (C) which was dismantled under UNSCOM supervision. This new stand will be capable of testing engines for missiles with ranges over 1000km, which are not permitted under UN Security Council Resolution 687. Such a facility would not be needed for systems that fall within the UN permitted range of 150km. The Iraqis have recently taken measures to conceal activities at this site.

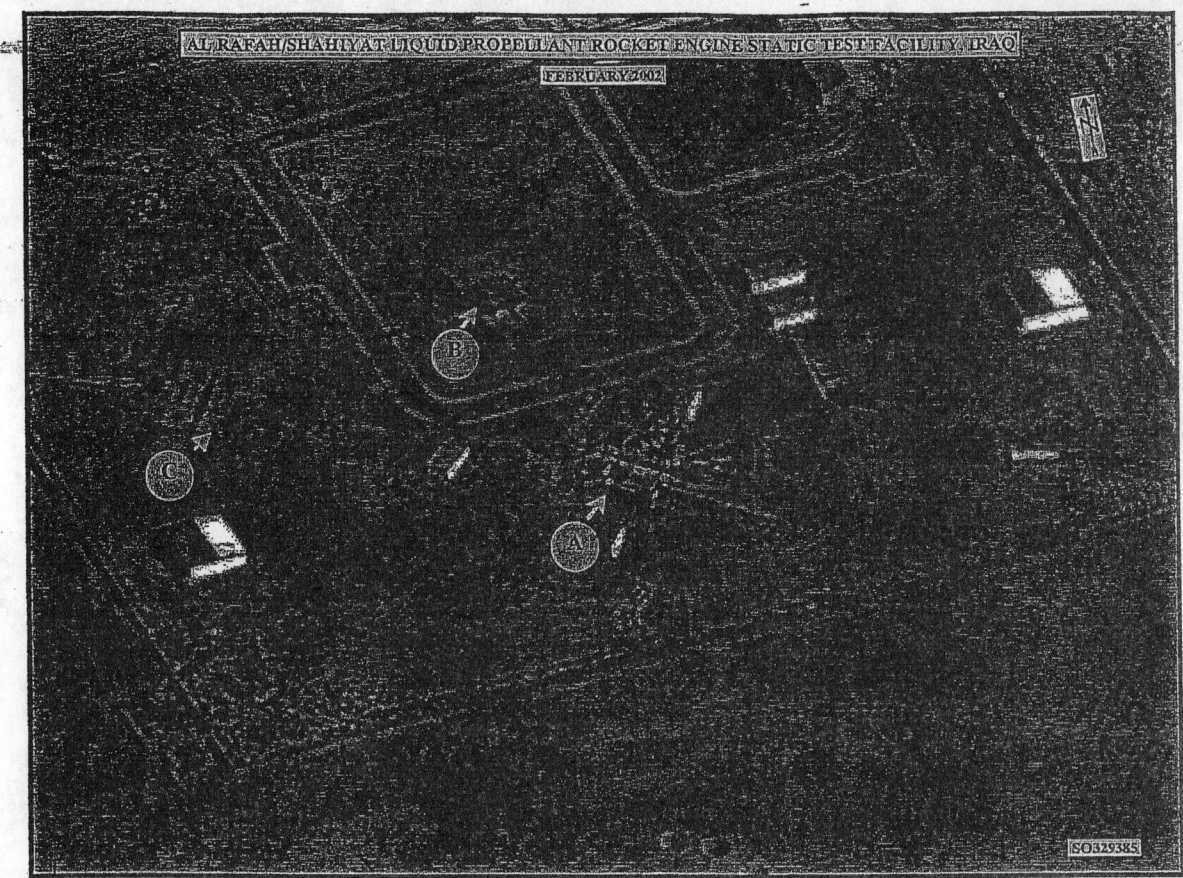

FIGURE 6: AL RAFAH/SHAHIYAT LIQUID PROPELLANT ENGINE STATIC TEST STAND

Iraq is also working to obtain improved guidance technology to increase missile accuracy.

30. The success of UN restrictions means the development of new longer-range missiles is likely to be a slow process. These restrictions impact particularly on the:

- availability of foreign expertise;

- conduct of test flights to ranges above 150km;

- acquisition of guidance and control technology.

DOS12|0080

Saddam remains committed to developing longer-range missiles. Even if sanctions remain effective, Iraq might achieve a missile capability of over 1000km within 5 years (Figure 4 shows the range of Iraq's various missiles).

31. Iraq has managed to rebuild much of the missile production infrastructure destroyed in the Gulf War and in Operation Desert Fox in 1998 (see Part 2). New missile-related infrastructure is also under construction. Some aspects of this, including rocket propellant mixing and casting facilities at the Al Mamoun Plant, appear to replicate those linked to the prohibited BADR-2000 programme (with a planned range of 700-1000km) which were destroyed in the Gulf War or dismantled by UNSCOM. A new plant at al-Mamoun for indigenously producing ammonium perchlorate, which is a key ingredient in the production of solid propellant rocket motors, has also been constructed. This has been provided illicitly by NEC Engineers Private Limited, an Indian chemical engineering firm with extensive links in Iraq, including to other suspect facilities such as the Fallujah 2 chlorine plant. After an extensive investigation, the Indian authorities have recently suspended its export licence, although affiliated individuals and companies in the Middle East are still illicitly procuring for Iraq.

32. Despite a UN embargo, Iraq has also made concerted efforts to acquire additional production technology, including machine tools and raw materials, in breach of UN Security Council Resolution 1051. The embargo has succeeded in blocking many of these attempts, such as requests to buy magnesium powder and ammonium chloride. But, despite the dual use nature of some of the items, we know from intelligence that some items have found their way to the Iraqi ballistic missile programme. More will inevitably continue to do so. **Intelligence makes it clear** that Iraqi procurement agents and front companies in third countries are seeking illicitly to acquire propellant chemicals for Iraq's ballistic missiles. This includes production level quantities of near complete sets of solid propellant motor ingredients such as aluminium powder, ammonium perchlorate and hydroxyl terminated polybutadiene. There have also been attempts to acquire large quantities of liquid propellant chemicals such as unsymmetrical dimethylhydrazine (UDMH) and diethylenetriamene. We judge this is intended to support production and deployment of the Al Samoud and Ababil-100 and development of longer range systems.

DOS/2/0081

Iraq: Current and Planned/Potential Ballistic Missiles

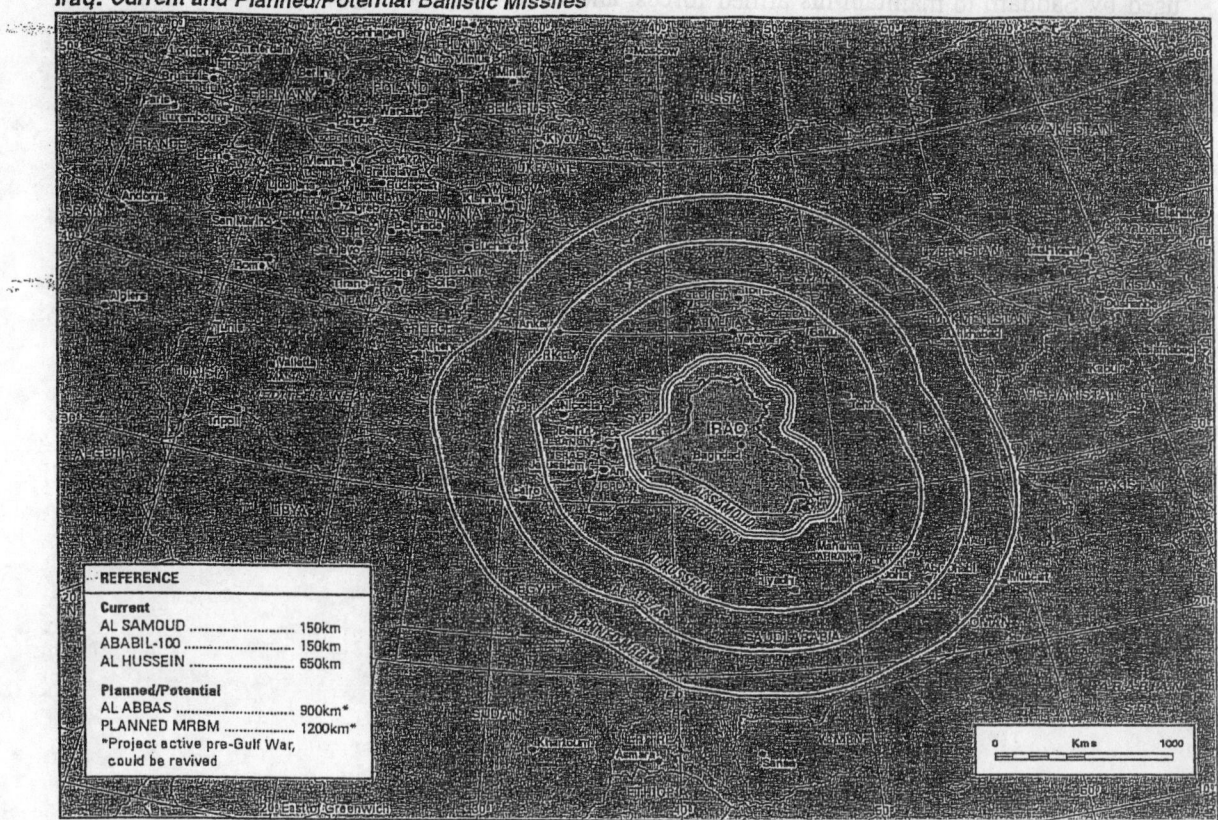

FIGURE 7: CURRENT AND PLANNED/POTENTIAL BALLISTIC MISSILES

FUNDING FOR THE WMD PROGRAMME

33. The UN has sought to restrict Iraq's ability to generate funds for its chemical, biological and other military programmes. For example, Iraq earns money legally under the UN Oil For Food Programme (OFF) established by UNSCR 986, whereby the proceeds of oil sold through the UN is used to buy humanitarian supplies for Iraq. This money remains under UN control, and cannot be used for military procurement. However, the Iraqi regime continues to generate income outside UN control, either in the form of hard currency, or barter goods (which in turn means existing Iraqi funds are freed up to be spent on other things). Iraq's illicit earnings amounted to around USD 3 billion during 2001. Compared to $....in 2002 and $.....in 1998 we assess that Iraq will generate up to a further USD 3 billion during 2002.

34. These illicit earnings go to the Iraqi regime. They are used for building new palaces, as well as purchasing luxury goods and other civilian goods outside OFF. Some of these funds are also

used by Saddam to maintain his armed forces, and to develop or acquire military equipment, including for chemical, biological and nuclear programmes. There is no indication as to what proportion of these funds may be used in this fashion. But we have seen no evidence that Iraqi attempts to develop its weapons of mass destruction and its ballistic missile programme, for example through covert procurement of equipment from abroad has been inhibited in any way by lack of funds. The steady increase over the last.....years in the availability of funds will enable Saddam to progress the programmes at a faster rate.

PART 2

HISTORY OF UN WEAPONS INSPECTIONS

1. During the 1990s, beginning in April 1991 immediately after the end of the Gulf War, the UN Security Council passed a series of resolutions [see box] establishing the authority of UNSCOM and the IAEA to carry out the work of dismantling Iraq's arsenal of chemical, biological and nuclear weapons programmes and long range ballistic missiles.

UN Security Council Resolutions (UNSCR) relating to WMD

UNSCR 687, April 1991 created the UN Special Commission (UNSCOM) and required Iraq to accept, unconditionally, "the destruction, removal or rendering harmless, under international supervision" of its chemical and biological weapons, ballistic missiles with a range greater than 150km, and their associated programmes, stocks, components, research and facilities. The International Atomic Energy Agency (IAEA) was charged with abolition of Iraq's nuclear weapons programme. UNSCOM and the IAEA must report that their mission has been achieved before the Security Council can end sanctions. They have not yet done so.

UNSCR 707, August 1991, stated that Iraq must provide full, final and complete disclosure of all its WMD programmes and provide unconditional and unrestricted access to UN inspectors. For over a decade Iraq has been in breach of this resolution. Iraq must also cease all nuclear activities of any kind other than civil use of isotopes.

UNSCR 715, October 1991 approved plans prepared by UNSCOM and IAEA for the ongoing monitoring and verification (OMV) arrangements to implement UNSCR 687. Iraq did not accede to this to November 1993. OMV was conducted from April 1995 to 15 December 1998, when the UN left Iraq.

UNSCR 1051, March 1996 stated that Iraq must declare the shipment of dual-use WMD goods.

These resolutions were passed under Chapter VII of the UN Charter which authorises the use of military force to enforce them.

2. As outlined in UNSCR 687, Iraq's chemical, biological and nuclear weapons programmes were also a breach of Iraq's commitments under:

- The Geneva Convention of 1925 – which bans the use of chemical weapons;

- the Biological and Toxin Weapons Convention – which bans the development, production, stockpiling, acquisition or retention of biological weapons;

- and the Nuclear Non-Proliferation Treaty (NPT) – which prohibits Iraq from manufacturing or otherwise acquiring nuclear weapons

3. UNSCR 687 obliged Iraq to provide declarations on all aspects of its WMD

> UNSCOM and the IAEA were given the remit to designate any locations for inspection at any time, review any document and interview any scientist, technician or other individual and seize any prohibited items for destruction.

programmes within 15 days and accept the destruction, removal or rendering harmless under international supervision of its chemical, biological and nuclear programmes, and all ballistic missiles with a range beyond 150 km. Iraq did not make a satisfactory declaration within the specified timeframe.

Iraq accepted the UNSCRs and agreed to co-operate with UNSCOM. The history of the UN weapons inspections was characterised by persistent Iraqi obstruction.

Iraqi Non-Co-operation with the Inspectors

4. The former Chairman of UNSCOM, Richard Butler, reported to the UN Security Council in January 1999, that in 1991 a decision was taken by a high-level Government committee to provide inspectors with only a portion of its proscribed weapons, components, production capabilities and stocks. UNSCOM concluded that Iraqi policy was based on the following actions:

- to provide only a portion of extant weapons stocks, releasing for destruction only those that were least modern;

DOS/2/0085

504

- to retain the production capability and documentation necessary to revive programmes when possible;

- to conceal the full extent of its chemical weapons programme, including the VX nerve agent project; to conceal the number and type of chemical and biological warheads for proscribed long –range missiles;

- and to conceal the existence of its massive biological weapons programme.

5. In December 1997 Richard Butler reported to the UN Security Council that Iraq had created a new category of sites – "Presidential" and "sovereign" – from which it claimed that UNSCOM inspectors would henceforth be barred. The terms of the ceasefire in 1991 foresaw no such limitation. However, Iraq consistently refused to

---

Iraq's policy of deception

Iraq has admitted having a large, effective, system for hiding proscribed material including documentation, components, production equipment and, possibly, biological and chemical agents and weapons from the UN. Shortly after the adoption of UNSCR 687 in April 1991, an Administrative Security Committee (ASC) was formed with responsibility for advising Saddam on the information which could be released to UNSCOM and the IAEA. The Committee consisted of senior Military Industrial Commission (MIC) scientists from all of Iraq's WMD programmes. The Higher Security Committee (HSC) of the Presidential Office was in overall command of deception operations. The system was directed from the very highest political levels within the Presidential Office and involved, if not Saddam himself, his youngest son, Qusai. The system for hiding proscribed material relies on high mobility and good command and control. It uses lorries to move items at short notice and most hide sites appear to be located close to good road links and telecommunications. The Baghdad area was particularly favoured. In addition to active measures to hide material from the UN, Iraq has attempted to monitor, delay and collect intelligence on UN operations to aid its overall deception plan.

---

allow UNSCOM inspectors access to any of these eight Presidential sites. Many of these so-called "palaces" are in fact large compounds which are an integral part of Iraqi counter-measures designed to hide weapons material (see photograph).

A photograph of a presidential site or what have been called "palaces".

Buckingham palace has been super-imposed to demonstrate their comparative size

Buckingham Palace and grounds

DOS/2/0087

506

Intimidation

6. Once inspectors had arrived in Iraq, it quickly became apparent that the Iraqi's would resort to a range of measures (including physical threats and psychological intimidation of inspectors) to prevent UNSCOM and the IAEA from fulfilling their mandate.

7. In response to such incidents, the President of the Security Council issued frequent statements calling on Iraq to comply with its disarmament and monitoring obligations.

Iraqi obstruction of UN weapons inspection teams.

- firing warning shots in the air to prevent IAEA inspectors from intercepting nuclear related equipment (June 1991);

- keeping IAEA inspectors in a car park for 4 days and refusing to allow them to leave with incriminating documents on Iraq's nuclear weapons programme (September 1991).

- announcing that UN monitoring and verification plans were "unlawful" (October 1991);

- refusing UNSCOM inspectors access to the Ministry of Agriculture. Threats were made to inspectors who remained on watch outside the building. The inspection team had reliable evidence that the site contained archives related to proscribed activities;

- refusing to allow UNSCOM the use of its own aircraft to fly into Iraq (January 1993). In 1991-2 Iraq objected to UNSCOM using its own helicopters and choosing its own flight plans;

- refusing to allow UNSCOM to install remote-controlled monitoring cameras at two key missile sites (June-July 1993);

- repeatedly denying access to inspection teams (1991- December 1998);

- interfering with UNSCOM's helicopter operations, threatening the safety of the aircraft and their crews (June 1997);

- demanding end of U2 overflights and the withdrawal of US UNSCOM staff (October 1997);

- destroying documentary evidence of WMD programmes (September 1997).

Obstruction

8. Iraq denied that it had pursued a biological weapons programme until July 1995.

DOS/2/0088

In July 1995, Iraq acknowledged that biological agents had been produced on an industrial scale at Al-Hakam. Following the defection in August 1995 of Hussein Kamel, Saddam's son-in-law and former Director of the Military Industrialisation Commission, Iraq released over 2 million documents relating to its WMD programmes and acknowledged that it had pursued a biological programme that led to the deployment of actual weapons. Iraq admitted producing in excess of 200 biological weapons with a reserve of agent to fill considerably more.

9. Iraq tried to obstruct UNSCOM's efforts to investigate the scale of its biological

---

Inspection of Iraq's biological weapons programme

In the course of the first biological weapons inspection in August 1991, Iraq claimed that it had merely conducted a military biological research programme. At the site visited, Al-Salman, Iraq had removed equipment, documents and even entire buildings. Later in the year, during a visit to the Al-Hakam site, Iraq declared to UNSCOM inspectors that the facility was used as a factory to produce proteins derived from yeast to feed animals. Inspectors subsequently discovered that the plant was a central site for the production of anthrax spores and botulinum toxin for weapons. The factory had also been sanitised by Iraqi officials to deceive inspectors.

Another key site, the Foot and Mouth Disease Vaccine Institute at Daura which produced botulinum toxin and probably anthrax, was not divulged as part of the programme. Five years later, after intense pressure, Iraq acknowledged that tens of tonnes of bacteriological warfare agent had been produced there and at Al-Hakam. Amazingly, Iraq *continued to develop* the Al-Hakam site into the 1990s, misleading UNSCOM about its true purpose.

As documents recovered in August 1995 were assessed, it became apparent that the full disclosure required by the UN was far from complete. Successive inspection teams went to Iraq to try to gain greater understanding of the programme and to obtain credible supporting evidence. In July 1996 Iraq refused to discuss its past programme and doctrine forcing the team to withdraw in protest. Monitoring teams were at the same time finding undisclosed equipment and materials associated with the past programme. In response, Iraq grudgingly provided successive disclosures of their programme which were judged by UNSCOM, and specially convened international panels, to be technically inadequate.

In late 1995, Iraq acknowledged weapons testing the biological agent ricin, but did not provide production information. Two years later – in early 1997 – UNSCOM discovered evidence that Iraq had produced ricin.

---

weapons programme. It created forged documents to account for bacterial growth media, imported in the late 1980s, specifically for the production of anthrax, botulinum toxin and probably plague. The documents were created to indicate that the material had been imported by the State Company for Drugs and Medical

DOS12 0089

Appliances Marketing for use in hospitals and distribution to local authorities. Iraq also censored documents and scientific papers provided to the first UN inspection team, removing all references to key individuals, weapons and industrial production of agents.

10. Iraq has yet to provide any documents concerning production of agent and subsequent weaponisation. Iraq destroyed, unilaterally and illegally, some biological weapons in 1991 and 1992 making accounting for these weapons impossible. In addition Iraq cleansed a key site at Al-Muthanna – its main research and development, production and weaponisation facility for chemical warfare agents - of all evidence of a biological programme in the toxicology department, the animal-house and weapons filling station.

11. Iraq refused to elaborate further on the programme during inspections in 1997 and 1998, confining discussion to previous topics. In July 1998, Tariq Aziz personally intervened in the inspection process stating that the biological programme was more secret and more closed than other WMD programmes. He also played down the significance of the programme. Iraq has presented the biological weapons programme as the personal undertaking of a few misguided scientists.

12. At the same time, Iraq tried to maintain its nuclear weapons programme via a concerted campaign to deceive IAEA inspectors. In 1997 the Agency's Director General stated that the IAEA was "severely hampered by Iraq's persistence in a policy of concealment and understatement of the programme's scope."

Achievements

13. Despite the conduct of the Iraqi authorities towards them, both UNSCOM and the IAEA Action Team have valuable records of achievement in discovering and exposing Iraq's biological weapons programme and destroying very large quantities of chemical weapons stocks, missiles as well as the infrastructure for Iraq's nuclear weapons programme.

UNSCOM and IAEA Achievements

UNSCOM surveyed 1015 sites in Iraq, carrying out 272 separate inspections. Despite Iraqi obstruction and intimidation, UN inspectors uncovered details of chemical, biological, nuclear and ballistic missile programmes. One of the main discoveries was that at the time of the Gulf War, [Iraq had been within 3 years - NPD checking UNSCOM language] of acquiring a nuclear weapon. Other major UNSCOM/IAEA achievements included:

- the destruction of 40,000 munitions for chemical weapons, 2,610 tonnes of chemical precursors and 411 tonnes of chemical warfare agent;

- the dismantling of Iraq's prime chemical weapons development and production complex at Al-Muthanna, and a range of key production equipment;

- the destruction of 48-SCUD type missiles, 11 mobile launchers and 56 sites, 30 warheads filled with chemical agents, and 20 conventional warheads;

- the destruction of the Al-Hakam biological weapons facility and a range of production equipment, seed stocks and growth media for biological weapons;

- the discovery in 1991 of 15 kg of highly enriched uranium, forcing Iraq's acknowledgement of uranium enrichment programmes and attempts to preserve key components of its prohibited nuclear weapons programme; and

- the removal and destruction of the infrastructure for the nuclear weapons programme, including the Al-Athir weaponisation/testing facility.

---

14. Despite UNSCOM's efforts, following the effective ejection of UN inspectors in December 1998, there remained a series of significant unresolved disarmament issues. In summarising the situation in a report to the Security Council, the UNSCOM Chairman, Richard Butler indicated that:

- contrary to the requirement that destruction be conducted under international supervision, "Iraq undertook extensive, unilateral and secret destruction of large quantities of proscribed weapons and items";

- and Iraq "also pursued a practice of concealment of proscribed items, including weapons, and a cover up of its activities in contravention of Council resolutions."

DOS/2/0091

Overall, Butler declared that obstructive Iraqi activity had had "a significant impact upon the Commission's disarmament work."

Withdrawal of the Inspectors

15. By the end of 1998 UNSCOM was in direct confrontation with the Iraqi Government which was refusing to co-operate. The US and the UK had made clear that anything short of full co-operation would make military action unavoidable. Richard Butler was requested to report to the UN Security Council in December 1998 and stated that, following a series of direct confrontations, coupled with the systematic refusal by Iraq to co-operate, UNSCOM was no longer able to perform its disarmament mandate. As a direct result, on December 16 the weapons inspectors were withdrawn and Operation Desert Fox was launched by the US and the UK a few hours afterwards.

Operation Desert Fox (16-19 December 1998):

Operation Desert Fox targeted industrial facilities related to Iraq's ballistic missile programme and a suspect biological warfare facility as well as military airfields and sites used by Iraq's security organisations which are involved in its weapons of mass destruction programmes. Key facilities associated with Saddam's Ballistic Missile programme were significantly degraded.

The Situation Since 1998

16. There have been no UN-mandated weapons inspections in Iraq since 1998. In an effort to enforce Iraqi compliance with its disarmament and monitoring obligations, the Security Council passed resolution 1284 in December 1999. This established the United Nations Monitoring, Verification and Inspection Commission (UNMOVIC) as a successor organisation to UNSCOM and called on Iraq to give UNMOVIC inspectors "immediate, unconditional and unrestricted access to any and all areas, facilities, equipment, records and means of transport". It also set out the steps Iraq needed to take to in return for the eventual suspension and lifting of sanctions. A key measure of Iraqi compliance would be full co-operation with UN inspectors, including unconditional, immediate and unrestricted access to any and all sites.

DOS12/0092

511

Given Iraq's track record of co-operation with UNSCOM and the IAEA between 1991-98, it is difficult to conclude other than that the prospects of Iraq meeting this standard are dim.

17. For the past three years, Iraq has allowed the IAEA to carry out an annual inspection of a stockpile of low-enriched uranium. This has led some countries and western commentators to conclude – erroneously – that Iraq is meeting its nuclear disarmament and monitoring obligations. As the IAEA has pointed out in recent weeks, this annual inspection does "not serve as a substitute for the verification activities required by the relevant resolutions of the UN Security Council."

18. Dr. Hans Blix, the Executive Chairman of UNMOVIC, and Dr. Mohammed El-Baradei, the Director General of the IAEA, have declared that in the absence of inspections it is impossible to verify Iraqi compliance with its UN disarmament and monitoring obligations. In April 1999, an independent UN panel of experts noted that "the longer inspection and monitoring activities remain suspended, the more difficult the comprehensive implementation of Security Council resolutions becomes, increasing the risk that Iraq might reconstitute its proscribed weapons programmes."

19. The departure of the Inspectors greatly diminished our ability to monitor and assess Iraq's continuing attempts to reconstitute its chemical, biological, nuclear and ballistic missile programmes.

DOS/2/0093

PART 3

IRAQ UNDER SADDAM

Introduction

1. The Republic of Iraq is bounded by Turkey, Iran, Kuwait, Saudia Arabia, Jordan, Syria and the Persian Gulf. Its population of around 23 million is ethnically and religiously diverse. Approximately 77% are Arabs. Sunni Muslims form around 17% of the Arab population and dominate the government. About 60% of Iraqis are Shias and 20% are Kurds. The remaining 3% of the population consists of Turkomans, Armenians, Assyrians, Christians and Jews.

2. Public life in Iraq is nominally dominated by the Ba'ath Party (see box on next page). But all real authority rests with Saddam Hussein and his immediate circle. Saddam's family, tribe and a small number of associates remain his most loyal supporters. He uses them to convey his orders, including to members of the government.

3. Saddam Hussein uses patronage and violence to

Saddam's rise to power

Saddam Hussein was born in 1937 in the Tikrit district, north of Baghdad. In 1957 he joined the Ba'ath Party. After taking part in a failed attempt to assassinate the Iraqi President, Abdul Karim Qasim, Saddam escaped, first to Syria and then to Egypt. In his absence he was sentenced to 15 years imprisonment.

Saddam returned to Baghdad in 1963 when the Ba'ath Party came to power. He went into hiding after the Ba'ath fell from power later that year. He was captured and imprisoned, but in 1967 escaped and took over responsibility for Ba'ath security. Saddam set about imposing his will on the Party and establishing himself at the centre of power.

The Ba'ath Party returned to power in 1968. In 1969 Saddam became Vice Chairman of the Revolutionary Command Council, Deputy to the President, and Deputy Secretary-General of the Regional Command of the Ba'ath. In 1970 he joined the Party's National Command and in 1977 was elected Assistant Secretary General. In July 1979, he took over the Presidency of Iraq. Within days, five fellow members of the Revolutionary Command Council were accused of involvement in a coup attempt. They and 17 others were summarily executed.

DOS/2/0094

motivate his supporters and to control or eliminate opposition. Potential rewards include social status, money and better access to goods. Saddam's extensive security apparatus and Ba'ath Party network provides oversight of Iraqi society, with

> **The Iraqi Ba'ath Party**
> The Ba'ath Party is the only legal political party in Iraq. It pervades all aspects of Iraqi life.
> Membership, around 700,000, is necessary for self advancement and confers benefits from the regime.

informants in social, government and military organisations. Saddam practises torture, execution and other forms of coercion against his enemies, real or suspected. His targets are not only those who have offended him, but also their families, friends or colleagues.

4. Saddam acts to ensure that no other centres of power in Iraq. He has crushed parties and tribes which might try to assert themselves, such as the communists and the Kurds. Members of the opposition abroad have been the targets of assassination attempts conducted by Iraqi security services.

Internal Repression – the Kurds and the Shias

5. Saddam has pursued a long-term programme of persecution of the Iraqi Kurds, including the use of chemical weapons. During the Iran/Iraq war, Saddam appointed his cousin, Ali Hassan al-Majid, as his deputy in the north. In 1987-88,

> **Saddam's security apparatus**
> Saddam relies on a long list of security organisations with overlapping responsibilities. The main ones are:
> - The **Special Security Organisation** oversees Saddam's security and monitors the loyalty of other security services. Its recruits are predominantly from Tikrit.
> - The **Special Republican Guard** is equipped with the best available military equipment. Its members are selected on the basis of loyalty to the regime.
> - The **Directorate of General Security** is primarily responsible for countering threats from the civilian population.
> - The **Directorate of General Intelligence** monitors and suppresses dissident activities at home and abroad.
> - The **Directorate of Military Intelligence**'s role includes the investigation of military personnel.
> - The **Saddam Fidayeen**, under the control of Udayy Hussein, has been used to deal with civil disturbances.

al-Majid led the "Anfal" campaign of attacks on Kurdish villages. Amnesty

DOS/2/0095

International estimates that more than 100,000 Kurds were killed or disappeared during this period.

6. After the Gulf War in 1991 Kurds in the north of Iraq rose up against Baghdad's rule. In response the Iraqi regime killed or imprisoned thousands, prompting a humanitarian crisis. Over a million Kurds fled into the mountains and tried to escape Iraq.

7. Persecution of Iraq's Kurds continues, although the protection provided by the northern No-Fly Zone has helped to curb the worst excesses. But outside this zone, the Baghdad regime has continued a policy of persecution and intimidation.

8. The regime has used chemical weapons against the Kurds, most notably in an attack on the city of Halabja in 1988. The implicit threat of the use of CW against the Kurds and others is an important part of Saddam's attempt to keep the civilian population under control.

9. The regime has tried to displace the traditional Kurdish and Turkoman populations of the areas under its control, primarily in order to weaken Kurdish claims to the oil-rich area

> **Repression and control: some examples**
> - A campaign of mass arrests and killing of Shia activists led to the execution of the Ayatollah Baqir al-Sadr and his sister in April 1980.
> - In 1983, 80 members of another leading Shia family were arrested. Six of them, all religious leaders, were executed.
> - A massive chemical weapons attack on Kurds in Halabja town in 1988, killing 5000 and injuring 10000 more.
> - A large number of officers from the Jabbur tribe were executed in the early 1990s for the alleged disloyalty of a few of them.

around the northern city of Kirkuk. Kurds and other non-Arabs are forcibly ejected to the three northern Iraqi governorates – Dohuk, Arbil and Sulaimaniyah – which are under de facto Kurdish control. According to the United Nations Commission on Human Rights (UNCHR) Special Rapporteur for Iraq, 94,000 individuals have been expelled since 1991. Agricultural land owned by Kurds has been confiscated and redistributed to Iraqi Arabs. Arabs from southern Iraq have been offered incentives to move into the Kirkuk area.

10. After the 1979 revolution that ousted the Shah in Iran, Saddam intensified a campaign against the Shia Muslim majority of Iraq, fearing that they might be encouraged by the new Shia regime.

11. In the wake of the Gulf War, riots broke out in the southern city of Basra on 1 March 1991, spreading quickly to other cities in Shia-dominated southern Iraq. The regime responded by killing thousands. Many Shia tried to escape to Iran and Saudi Arabia.

12. Some of the Shia hostile to the regime sought refuge in the marsh land of southern Iraq. In order to subjugate the area, Saddam embarked on a large-scale programme to drain the marshes to allow Iraqi ground forces to eliminate all opposition there. The rural population of the area fled or were forced to move to southern cities.

Human rights abuses – further examples
• About 2500 prisoners were executed between 1997 and 1999 in a "prison cleansing" campaign.
• 3000 prisoners were executed at the Mahjar Prison between 1993 and 1998.
• 4000 prisoners were executed at Abu Ghraib Prison in 1984.
• Prisoners are executed by machine gun.
• In October 2000, dozens of women accused of prostitution were beheaded without any judicial process. Some were accused for political reasons.
• Women prisoners at Mahjar are routinely raped by their guards.
• Prisoners at the Qurtiyya Prison in Baghdad and elsewhere are kept in metal boxes the size of tea chests. If they do not confess they are left to die.

DOS/2/0097

Internal Repression – human rights

13. Human rights abuses continue. People continue to be arrested and detained on suspicion of political or religious activities, or often because they are related to members of the opposition. Executions are carried out without due process of law. Relatives are often prevented from burying the victims in accordance with Islamic practice. Thousands of prisoners have been executed.

Human Rights – mistreatment in Abu Ghraib Prison

Abdallah, a member of the Ba'ath Party whose loyalty became suspect was imprisoned for four years at Abu Ghraib in the 1980s. On the second day of his imprisonment, the men were forced to walk between two rows of five guards each to receive their containers of food. While walking to get the food, they were beaten by the guards with plastic telephone cables. They had to return to their cells the same way, so that a walk to get breakfast resulted in twenty lashes. According to Abdallah, "It wasn't that bad going to get the food, but coming back the food was spilled when we were beaten." The same procedure was used when the men went to the bathroom. On the third day, the torture continued. "We were removed from our cells and beaten with plastic pipes. This surprised us, because we were asked no question. Possibly it was being done to break our morale", Abdallah speculated. The torture escalated to sixteen sessions daily. The treatment was organised and systematic. Abdallah was held alone in a 3x2-meter room that opened onto a corridor. "We were allowed to go to the toilet three times a day, then they reduced the toilet to once a day for only one minute. I went for four years without a shower or a wash", Abdallah said. He also learned to cope with the deprivation and the hunger that accompanied his detention: "I taught myself to drink a minimum amount of water because there was no placed to urinate. They used wooden sticks to beat us and sometimes the sticks would break. I found a piece of a stick, covered with blood, and managed to bring it back to my room. I ate it for three days. A person who is hungry can eat anything. Pieces of our bodies started falling off from the beatings and our skin was so dry that it began to fall off. I ate pieces of my own body. "No one, not Pushkin, not Mahfouz, can describe what happened to us. It is impossible to describe what living this day to day was like. I was totally naked the entire time. Half of the original groups [of about thirty men] died. It was a slow type of continuous physical and psychological torture. Sometimes, it seemed that orders came to kill one of us, and he would be beaten to death".

DOS|2|0098

14. Saddam has issued a series of decrees establishing severe penalties for criminal offences. These include amputation, branding, cutting off ears, and other forms of

> **Human Rights - individual testimony**
> "…I saw a friend of mine, al-Shaikh Nasser Taresh al-Sa'idi, naked. He was handcuffed and a piece of wood was placed between his elbows and his knees. Two ends of the wood were placed on two high chairs and al-Shaikh Nasser was being suspended like a chicken. This method of torture is know as *al-Khaygania* (a reference to a former security director known as al-Khaygani). An electric wire was attached to al-Shaikh Nasser's penis and another one attached to one of his toes. He was asked if he could identify me and he said "this is al-Shaikh Yahya". They took me to another room and then after about 10 minutes they stripped me of my clothes and a security officer said "the person you saw has confessed against you". He said to me "You followers of [Ayatollah] al-Sadr have carried out acts harmful to the security of the country and have been distributing anti-government statements coming from abroad". He asked if I have any contact with an Iraqi religious scholar based in Iran who has been signing these statements. I said "I do not have any contacts with him"… I was then left suspended in the same manner as al-Shaikh al-Sa'idi. My face was looking upward. They attached an electric wire on my penis and the other end of the wire is attached to an electric motor. One security man was hitting my feet with a cable. Electric shocks were applied every few minutes and were increased. I must have been suspended for more than an hour. I lost consciousness. They took me to another room and made me walk even though my feet were swollen from beating… They repeated this method a few times." (testimony to Amnesty International from an Iraqi theology student from Saddam City)

mutilation. Anyone found guilty of slandering the President has their tongue removed.

Saddam's family

15. Saddam's son Udayy maintained a private torture chamber known as the Red Room in a building on the banks of the Tigris disguised as an electricity installation. He ordered the Iraq football team to be caned on the soles of the feet for losing a World Cup match. He created a militia in 1994 which has used swords to execute victims outside their own homes. He has personally executed dissidents, for instance in the Shia uprising at Basra which followed the Gulf War.

DOS/2/0099

16. Members of Saddam's family are also subject to persecution. A cousin of Saddam called Ala Abd Al-Qadir Al-Majid fled to Jordan from Iraq, citing disagreements with the regime over business matters. He returned to Iraq after the Iraqi Ambassador in Jordan declared publicly that his life was not in danger. He was met at the border by Tahir Habbush, Head of the Iraqi Intelligence Service (the Mukhabarat), and taken to a farm owned by 'Ali Hasan Al-Majid. At the farm 'Ala was tied to a tree and executed by members of his immediate family who, following orders from Saddam, took it in turns to shoot him.

Human Rights - individual testimony

In December 1996, a Kurdish businessman from Baghdad was arrested outside his house by plainclothes security men. Initially his family did not know his whereabouts and went from one police station to another inquiring about him. Then they found out that he was being held in the headquarters of the General Security Directorate in Baghdad. The family was not allowed to visit him. Eleven months later the family was told by the authorities that he had been executed and that they should go and collect his body. His body bore evident signs of torture. His eyes were gouged out and the empty eye sockets filled with paper. His right wrist and left leg were broken. The family was not given any reason for his arrest and subsequent execution. However, they suspected that he was executed because of his friendship with a retired army general who had links with the Iraqi opposition outside the country and who was arrested just before his arrest and also executed.

---

17. Some 40 of Saddam's relatives, including women and children, have been killed. In February 1996, his sons-in-law Hussein Kamel and Saddam Kamel were executed. They had defected in 1995 and returned to Iraq from Jordan after the government had announced amnesties for them.

DOS/2/0100

Saddam's Wars

18. As well as ensuring his absolute control inside Iraq, Saddam has tried to make Iraq the dominant power of the region. In pursuit of these objectives he has led Iraq into two wars of aggression against neighbours, the Iran-Iraq war and the invasion of Kuwait.

19. With the fall of the Shah in Iran in 1979, relations between Iran and Iraq deteriorated sharply. In September 1980 Saddam renounced a border treaty he had agreed with Iran in 1975 ceding half of the Shatt al-Arab waterway to Iran. Shortly thereafter, Saddam launched a large-scale invasion of Iran. He believed that he could take advantage of the state of weakness, isolation and disorganisation he perceived in post-revolutionary Iran. He aimed to seize territory, including that ceded to Iran a few years earlier, and to assert Iraq's position as a leader of the Arab world. Saddam expected it to be a short, sharp campaign. But the conflict lasted for eight years.

20. It is estimated that the Iran/Iraq war cost the two sides a million casualties. Iraq used chemical weapons. Some twenty thousand Iranians were killed by mustard gas, and the

> **Opposition to Saddam during the Iran/Iraq war**
> During the war Saddam's security apparatus ensured any internal dissent or opposition was quickly eliminated. In 1982 he quickly purged a group within Iraq's ruling clique which suggested that the war might be brought to an end more quickly if Saddam stood down.

nerve agents tabun and sarin, all of which Iraq still possesses. Iraq also fired over 500 ballistic missiles at Iranian targets, including major cities.

21. The cost of the war ran into hundreds of billions of dollars for both sides. Iraq gained nothing. After the war ended, Saddam resumed his previous pursuit of primacy in the Gulf. His policies involved spending huge sums of money on new military equipment. But Iraq was burdened by debt incurred during the war and the price of oil, Iraq's only major export, was low.

DOS/2/0101

22. By 1990 Iraq's financial problems were severe. Saddam looked at ways to press the oil-producing states of the Gulf to force up the price of crude oil by limiting production and waive the $40 billion that they had loaned Iraq during its war with Iran. Kuwait had made some concessions over production ceilings. But Saddam blamed Kuwait for over production. When his threats and blandishments failed, Iraq invaded Kuwait on 2 August 1990. He believed that occupying Kuwait could prove profitable.

23. Saddam also sought to justify the conquest of Kuwait on other grounds. Like other Iraqi leaders before him, he claimed that, as Kuwait's rulers had come under the jurisdiction of the governors of Basra in the time of the Ottoman Empire, Kuwait should belong to Iraq.

24. During its occupation of Kuwait, Iraq denied access to the Red Cross, which has a mandate to provide protection and assistance to civilians affected by international armed conflict. The death penalty was extended to "crimes" such as looting and hoarding food.

25. In an attempt to deter military action to expel it from Kuwait, the Iraqi regime took hostage several hundred foreign nationals (including children) in Iraq and Kuwait, and prevented thousands more from leaving. Hostages were held as human shields at a number of strategic military and civilian sites.

> **Abuses by Iraqi forces in Kuwait**
> - Robbery and rape of Kuwaitis and expatriates.
> - Summary executions.
> - People dragged from their homes and held in improvised detention centres.
> - Amnesty International has listed 38 methods of torture used by the Iraqi occupiers. These included beatings, breaking of limbs, extracting finger and toenails, inserting bottle necks into the rectum, and subjecting detainees to mock executions.
> - Kuwaiti civilians arrested for "crimes" such as wearing beards.

DOS/2/0102

26. At the end of the Gulf War, the Iraqi army fleeing Kuwait set fire to over 1,160 Kuwaiti oil wells, with serious environmental consequences.

27. More than 600 Kuwaiti prisoners of war and missing persons are still unaccounted for. Iraq refuses to comply with its UN obligation to account for the missing. It has provided sufficient information to close only three case-files.

DOS/2/0103

522

CONCLUSION

1.   The record of Iraqi possession and use of weapons of mass destruction is clear and unequivocal. So too is Saddam's record of internal repression and external aggression, and his persistent flouting on UN resolutions.

2.   Our knowledge of Saddam's chemical, biological, nuclear and ballistic missile programmes is inevitably partial. Open sources of information add little to the picture after the de facto expulsion of UN inspection in 1998. But secret intelligence shows that these weapons programmes have continued. We judge that the current position is as follows:

Chemical and biological Weapons:	In breach of UNSCR 687: Chemical and biological agents stocks retained. Production has continued. Weapons available include bombs, airborne sprayer, artillery shells and rockets and ballistic missile warheads. Some weapons could be deployed within 45 minutes of an order.
Nuclear Weapons:	In breach of UNSCR 687 and Non Proliferation Treaty: Nuclear weapons programme being reconstituted; Large quantities of uranium obtained, despite absence of civil nuclear programme; Illicit procurement of equipment and special materials with potential role in nuclear weapons programmes. Nuclear experts recalled in 1998.

DO2 / 3 / 0002

Ballistic Missiles:	In breach of UNSCR 687: Retained up to 20 Al Hussein missiles with 650 km range. Developing missiles with range around 1000 km. Extending range of Al Samoud and Ababil-100 beyond 150 km limit laid down by UN.
Military planning:	Specifically envisages the use of chemical/biological weapons, including against his own population.

OOS/3/0007

19 September 2002

IRAQ'S PROGRAMME FOR WEAPONS OF MASS DESTRUCTION:

THE ASSESSMENT OF THE BRITISH GOVERNMENT

CAB/3/0022

CONTENTS

CAB/3/0023

EXECUTIVE SUMMARY

1. Under Saddam Hussein, Iraq has developed chemical and biological weapons, acquired missiles allowing it to attack neighbouring countries with these weapons, and persistently tried to develop a nuclear bomb. Iraq has had to admit to all these programmes to acquire weapons of mass destruction. And Saddam has used chemical weapons, both against Iran and against his own people.

2. Much information about Iraq's weapons of mass destruction is already in the public domain from UN reports and from Iraqi defectors. This points clearly to Iraq's continued possession of chemical and biological agents and weapons from before the Gulf War. It shows that Iraq has refurbished sites formerly associated with the production of chemical and biological agents. And it indicates a continuing Iraqi ability to manufacture these agents, and to use bombs, shells, artillery rockets and ballistic missiles to deliver them.

3. An independent and well researched overview of this public evidence was provided by the International Institute for Strategic Studies (IISS) on 9 September. This report also suggested that Iraq could assemble nuclear weapons within months of obtaining fissile material from foreign sources.

4. We endorse much of the IISS's analysis. As well as the public evidence, however, significant additional information is available to the government from secret intelligence sources, described in more detail in this paper. This intelligence cannot tell us about everything. But it provides a fuller picture of Iraqi plans and capabilities. It shows that Saddam Hussein attaches great importance to possessing weapons of mass destruction which he regards as the basis for Iraq's regional power. It shows that he does not regard them only as weapons of last resort. He is ready to use them, including against his own population, and is determined to retain them, in breach of United Nations Resolutions. Intelligence also shows that Iraq is preparing plans to conceal evidence of these weapons from renewed inspections, including by dispersing incriminating documents. And it

CAB|3|0024

527

confirms that despite sanctions and the policy of containment, Saddam has continued to make progress with his illicit weapons programmes.

5. As a result of this intelligence we judge that Iraq has:

-   continued to produce chemical and biological agents;

-   military plans for the use of chemical and biological weapons, some of which are deployable within 45 minutes of an order to use them. The authority to use chemical and biological weapons ultimately resides with Saddam, but he may have delegated this authority to his son Qusai;

-   developed mobile laboratories for military use, corroborating earlier reports about the mobile production of biological warfare agents;

-   pursued illegal programmes to procure controlled materials of potential use in the production of chemical and biological weapons programmes;

-   tried covertly to acquire technology and materials which could be used in the production of nuclear weapons;

-   sought significant quantities of uranium from Africa, despite having no active civil nuclear power programme that could require it;

-   recalled specialists to work on its nuclear programme;

-   retained up to 20 Al Hussein missiles, with a range of 650km, capable of carrying chemical or biological warheads;

-   started deploying its Al-Samoud liquid propellant missile, and has used the absence of weapons inspectors to work on extending its range to at least 200km, which is beyond the limit of 150km imposed by the United Nations;

-   started producing the solid-propellant missile Ababil-100, and is making efforts to extend its range to at least 200km, which is beyond the limit of 150km imposed by the United Nations;

-   constructed a new engine test stand for the development of missiles capable of reaching Israel and all Iraq's Gulf neighbours as well as the UK

CAB\3\0025

Sovereign Base Areas in Cyprus and NATO members (Greece and Turkey);

- pursued illegal programmes to procure materials for use in its illegal development of long range missiles;

- learnt lessons from previous UN weapons inspections and has already begun to conceal and disperse sensitive equipment and documentation in advance of the return of inspectors.

6. These judgements reflect the views of the Joint Intelligence Committee (JIC). More details on the judgements, and on the development of the JIC's assessments since 1998, are set out in Part 1 of this paper.

7. Iraq's weapons of mass destruction are in breach of international law. Under a series of Security Council Resolutions Iraq is obliged to destroy its holdings of these weapons under the supervision of UN inspectors. Part 2 of the paper sets out the key UN Resolutions. It also summarises the history of the UN inspection regime and Iraq's history of deception, intimidation and concealment in its dealings with the UN inspectors.

8. But the threat from Iraq does not depend solely on the capabilities we have described. It arises also because of the violent and aggressive nature of Saddam's regime. His record of internal repression and external aggression gives rise to unique concerns about the threat he poses. The paper briefly outlines in Part 3 his rise to power, the nature of his regime and his history of regional aggression. Saddam's human rights abuses are also catalogued, including his record of torture, mass arrests and summary executions.

9. The paper briefly sets out how Iraq is able to finance its weapons programme. Drawing on illicit earnings generated outside UN control, Iraq generated illegal income of some $3 billion in 2001.

10. This paper concludes that Saddam will use his weapons of mass destruction to protect and eventually project his power.

CAB/3/0027

530

PART 1

IRAQ'S CHEMICAL, BIOLOGICAL, NUCLEAR AND BALLISTIC MISSILE PROGRAMMES

CHAPTER 1: THE ROLE OF INTELLIGENCE

1. Since UN Inspectors were withdrawn from Iraq in 1998, there has been little overt information on Iraq's chemical, biological, nuclear and ballistic missile programmes. Much of the publicly available information about Iraqi capabilities and intentions is dated. But we also have available a range of secret intelligence about these programmes and Saddam's intentions. This comes principally from the United Kingdom's intelligence and analysis agencies – the Secret Intelligence Service (SIS), the Government Communications Headquarters (GCHQ), the Security Service, and the Defence Intelligence Staff (DIS). We also have access to intelligence from close allies.

2. Intelligence rarely offers a complete account of activities which are designed to remain concealed. The nature of Saddam's regime makes Iraq a difficult target for the intelligence services. Intelligence, however, has provided important insights into Iraqi programmes, and Iraqi military thinking. Taken together with what is already known from other sources, this intelligence builds our understanding of Iraq's capabilities, and adds significantly to the analysis already in the public domain. But intelligence sources need to be protected, and this limits the detail that can be made available.

3. Iraq's capabilities have been regularly reviewed by the Joint Intelligence Committee (JIC), which has provided advice to the Prime Minister and his senior colleagues on the developing assessment, drawing on all available sources. Part 1 of this paper includes some of the most significant views reached by the JIC between 1999 and 2002.

CAB|3|0028

> **Joint Intelligence Committee (JIC)**
> The JIC is a Cabinet Committee with a history dating back to 1936. The JIC brings together the Heads of the three Intelligence and Security Agencies (Secret Intelligence Service, Government Communications Headquarters and the Security Service), the Chief of Defence Intelligence and senior policy makers from the Foreign Office, the Ministry of Defence, the Home Office, the Treasury and the Department of Trade and Industry. It provides regular intelligence assessments to the Prime Minister, other Ministers and senior officials on a wide range of foreign policy and international security issues. The JIC meets each week in the Cabinet Office.

CAB/3/0029

CHAPTER 2: IRAQ'S PROGRAMMES: 1971-1998

1. Iraq has been involved in chemical and biological warfare research for over 30 years. Its **chemical warfare** research started in 1971 at a small, well guarded site at Rashad to the Northeast of Baghdad. Research was conducted there on a number of chemical agents including mustard gas, CS and tabun. Later, in 1974 a dedicated organisation called Al-Hassan Ibn Al-Haitham was established. At the same time

---

Effects of Chemical Weapons

Mustard is a liquid agent, which gives off a hazardous vapour, causing burns and blisters to exposed skin. When inhaled, mustard damages the respiratory tract; when ingested, it causes vomiting and diarrhoea. It attacks and damages the eyes, mucous membranes, lungs, skin, and blood-forming organs.

Tabun, sarin and VX are all nerve agents of which VX is the most toxic. They all damage the nervous system, producing muscular spasms and paralysis. As little as 10 milligrammes of VX on the skin can cause rapid death.

---

plans were made to build a large research and commercial-scale production facility in the desert some 70km Northwest of Baghdad under the Project cover of No 922. This was to become Muthanna State Establishment, also known as al-Muthanna, and operated under the front name of Iraq's State Establishment for Pesticide Production. It became partially operational in 1982-83. It had five research and development sections each tasked to pursue different programmes. In addition, the al-Muthanna site was the main chemical agent production facility, and it also took the lead in weaponising chemical and biological agents including all aspects of weapon development and testing, in association with the military. According to information, subsequently supplied by the Iraqis, the total production capacity in 1991 was 4,000 tonnes of agent per annum, but we assess it could have been higher. Al-Muthanna was supported by three separate storage and precursor production facilities known as Fallujah 1, 2 and 3 near Habbaniyah, north-west of Baghdad, parts of which were not completed before they were heavily bombed in the 1991 Gulf War.

CAB/3/0030

2. Iraq started **biological warfare** research in the mid-1970s. After small-scale research, a purpose-built research and development facility was authorised at al-Salman, also known as Salman Pak. This is surrounded on three sides by the Tigris

---

The effects of biological agents

Anthrax is a disease caused by the bacterium Bacillus anthracis. Inhalation anthrax is the manifestation of the disease likely to be expected in biological warfare. The symptoms may vary, but can include fever and internal bleeding. The incubation period for anthrax is 1 to 7 days, with most cases occurring within 2 days of exposure.

Botulinum toxin is one of the most toxic substances known to man. The first symptoms of poisoning may appear as early as 1 hour post exposure or as long as 8 days after exposure, with the incubation period between 12 and 22 hours. Paralysis leads to death by suffocation.

Aflatoxins are fungal toxins, which are potent carcinogens. Most symptoms take a long time to show. Food products contaminated by aflatoxin can cause liver inflammation and cancer. It can also affect pregnant women, leading to stillborn babies and children born with mutations.

Ricin is derived from the castor bean and can cause multiple organ failure leading to death within one or two days of inhalation.

---

river and situated some 35km South of Baghdad. Although some progress was made in biological weapons research at this early stage, Iraq decided to concentrate on developing chemical agents and their delivery systems at al-Muthanna. With the outbreak of the Iran-Iraq War, in the early 1980s, the biological weapons programme was revived. The appointment of Dr Rihab Taha in 1985, to head a small biological weapons research team at al-Muthanna, helped to develop the programme. At about the same time plans were made to develop the Salman Pak site into a secure biological warfare research facility. Dr Taha continued to work with her team at Muthanna until 1987 when it moved to Salman Pak, which was under the control of the Directorate of General Intelligence. Significant resources were provided for the programme, including the construction of a dedicated production facility, (Project 324) at al-Hakam. Agent production began in 1988 and weaponisation testing and later filling of munitions was conducted in association with the staff at Muthanna State Establishment. From mid-1990, other civilian facilities were taken over and some adapted for use in the production and research and development of biological agents. These included:

CAB\3\0031

- al-Dawrah Foot and Mouth Vaccination Plant which produced botulinum toxin and conducted virus research. There is some intelligence to suggest that work was also conducted on anthrax;

- al-Fudaliyah Agriculture and Water Research centre where Iraq admitted it undertook aflatoxin production and genetic engineering:

- Amariyah Sera and Vaccine institute which was used for the storage of biological agent seed stocks, and was involved in genetic engineering

3. By the time of the Gulf War Iraq was producing very large quantities of chemical and biological agents. From a series of Iraqi declarations to the UN during the 1990s we know that by 1991 they had produced at least:

- 19,000 litres of botulinum toxin, 8,500 litres of anthrax, 2,200 litres of aflatoxin, and were working on a number of other agents;

- 2,850 tonnes of mustard gas, 210 tonnes of tabun, 795 tonnes of sarin and cyclosarin, and 3.9 tonnes of VX.

4. Iraq's **nuclear programme** was established under the Iraqi Atomic Energy Commission in the 1950s. Under a nuclear co-operation agreement signed with the Soviet Union in 1959, a nuclear research centre, equipped with a research reactor, was built at Tuwaitha, the main Iraqi nuclear research centre. The research reactor worked up to 1991. The surge in Iraqi oil revenues in the early 1970s supported an expansion of the research programme. This was bolstered in the mid-1970s by the acquisition of two research reactors powered by highly enriched uranium fuel, and equipment for fuel fabrication and handling. By the end of 1984 Iraq was self-sufficient in uranium

CAB|3|0032

ore. One of the reactors was destroyed in an Israeli air attack in June 1981 shortly before it was to become operational, the other was never completed.

5. By the mid-1980s the deterioration of Iraq's position in the war with Iran prompted renewed interest in the military use of nuclear technology, and additional resources were put into developing technologies to enrich uranium as fissile material for use in nuclear weapons. Enriched uranium was preferred because it could be more easily produced covertly than the alternative, plutonium. Iraq followed parallel programmes to produce highly enriched uranium: electromagnetic isotope separation (EMIS) and gas centrifuge enrichment. By 1991 one EMIS enrichment facility was nearing completion and another was under construction. However, Iraq never succeeded in its EMIS technology, and the programme had been dropped by 1991. Iraq decided to concentrate on gas centrifuges as the means for producing the necessary fissile material. Centrifuge facilities were also under construction, but the centrifuge design was still being developed. In August 1990 Iraq instigated a crash programme to develop a single nuclear weapon within a year. This programme envisaged the rapid development of a small 50 machine gas centrifuge cascade to produce the highly enriched uranium required using fuel from the Soviet research reactor and unused fuel from the reactor bombed by the Israelis. By the time of the Gulf War, the crash programme had made little progress.

6. Iraq's declared aim was to produce a missile warhead with a 20-kiloton yield and weapons designs were produced for the simplest implosion weapons. These were similar to the device used at Nagasaki in 1945. Iraq was also working on more advanced concepts. By 1991 the programme was supported by a large body of Iraqi nuclear expertise, programme documentation and

> **Effect of a 20-kiloton nuclear detonation**
> A detonation of a 20-kiloton nuclear warhead over a city might flatten an area of approximately 3 square miles. Within 1.6 miles of detonation, blast damage and radiation would cause 80% casualties, three-quarters of which would be fatal. Between 1.6 and 3.1 miles from the detonation, there would still be 10% casualties.

CAB/3/0033

databases and manufacturing infrastructure. The International Atomic Energy Agency (IAEA) reported that Iraq had:

- experimented with high explosives to produce implosive shock waves;
- invested significant effort to understand the various options for neutron initiators;
- made significant progress in developing capabilities for the production, casting and machining of uranium metal.

The Head of the IAEA Action Team for Iraq concluded that at the time of Gulf War Iraq could have produced a nuclear weapon by the end of 1991.

> **SCUD missiles**
>
> The short-range mobile SCUD ballistic missile was developed by the Soviet Union in the 1950s, drawing on the technology of the German V-2 developed in World War II.
>
> For many years it was the mainstay of Soviet and Warsaw Pact tactical missile forces, and it was also widely exported.
> Recipients of Soviet-manufactured SCUDs included Iraq, North Korea, Iran, and Libya, although not all were sold directly by the Soviet Union.

7. Prior to the Gulf War, Iraq had a well-developed **ballistic missile** industry. Many of the missiles fired in the Gulf War were an Iraqi modified version of the SCUD missile, the Al Hussein, with an extended range of 650km. Iraq had about 250 imported SCUD-type missiles prior to the Gulf War plus an unknown number of indigenously produced engines and components. Iraq was working on other stretched SCUD variants, such as the Al Abbas, which had a range of 900km. Iraq was also seeking to reverse engineer the SCUD engine with a view to producing new missiles; recent intelligence indicates that they may have succeeded at that time. In particular Iraq had plans for a new SCUD-derived missile with a range of 1200km. Iraq also conducted a partial flight test of a multi-stage satellite launch vehicle based on SCUD technology, known as the Al Abid. Also during this period, Iraq was developing the BADR-2000, a 700-1000km range two-stage solid propellant missile (based on the Iraqi part of the 1980s CONDOR-2 programme run in co-operation with Argentina and Egypt). There were plans for 1200-1500km range solid propellant follow-on systems.

CAB|3|0034

The use of chemical and biological weapons

8. Iraq had made frequent use of a variety of chemical weapons during the Iran-Iraq War. (Many of the casualties are still in Iranian hospitals suffering from the long-term effects of numerous types of cancer and lung diseases.) In 1988 Saddam also used mustard and nerve agents against Iraqi Kurds at Halabja in northern Iraq (see box). Estimates vary, but according to Human Rights Watch up to 5,000 people were killed.

9. Iraq used significant quantities of mustard, tabun and sarin during the war with Iran resulting in over 20,000 Iranian casualties. A month after the attack on Halabja, Iraqi troops used over 100 tons of sarin nerve agent against Iranian troops on the Al Fao peninsula. Over the next three months Iraqi troops used sarin and other nerve agents on Iranian troops causing extensive casualties.

CAB/3/0035

The Attack on Halabja

Shortly before sunrise on Friday, 17th March 1988, the village of Halabja was bombarded by Iraqi warplanes. The raid was over in minutes. Saddam Hussein used chemical weapons against his own people. A Kurd described the effects of a chemical attack on another village:

"My brothers and my wife had blood and vomit running from their noses and their mouths. Their heads were tilted to one side. They were groaning. I couldn't do much, just clean up the blood and vomit from their mouths and try in every way to make them breathe again. I did artificial respiration on them and then I gave them two injections each. I also rubbed creams on my wife and two brothers."

(From "Crimes Against Humanity," Iraqi National Congress.)

Among the corpses at Halabja, children were found dead where they had been playing outside their homes. In places, streets were piled with corpses.

10. In 1991 Iraq used mustard gas to suppress the Shia uprising in Karbala, Southwest of Baghdad.

11. From Iraqi declarations to the UN after the Gulf War we know that by 1991 Iraq had produced a variety of delivery means for chemical and biological agents including over 16,000 free fall bombs and over 110,000 artillery rockets and shells. Iraq also admitted to UNSCOM that it had 50 chemical and 25 biological warheads available for its ballistic missiles.

CAB/3/0036

539

The use of ballistic missiles

12. Iraq fired over 500 SCUD-type missiles at Iran during the Iran-Iraq War at both civilian and military targets, and 93 SCUD-type missiles during the Gulf War. The latter were targeted at Israel and at Coalition forces stationed in the Gulf region

13. At the end of the Gulf War the international community was determined that Iraq's arsenal of chemical and biological weapons and ballistic missiles should be dismantled. The method chosen to achieve this aim was the establishment of the UN Special Commission (UNSCOM) to carry out intrusive inspections within Iraq and to eliminate its chemical and biological weapons and ballistic missiles with a range over 150km. The IAEA was charged with the abolition of Iraq's nuclear weapons programme. Between 1991 and 1998 UNSCOM succeeded in identifying and destroying very large quantities of chemical weapons and ballistic missiles as well as associated production facilities. The IAEA also destroyed the infrastructure for Iraq's nuclear weapons programme and removed key nuclear materials. This was achieved despite a continuous and sophisticated programme of harassment, obstruction and deception and denial (see Part 2). Because of this by 1998 UNSCOM concluded that they were unable to fulfil their mandate. The inspectors were withdrawn in December 1998.

14. Based on the UNSCOM report to the UN Security Council in January 1999 and earlier UNSCOM reports, we assess that when the UN inspectors left Iraq they were unable to account for:

- up to 360 tonnes of bulk chemical warfare agent, including 1.5 tonnes of VX nerve agent;

- up to 3,000 tonnes of precursor chemicals, including approximately 300 tonnes which, in the Iraqi CW programme, were unique to the production of VX;

CAB/3/0037

540

- growth media procured for biological agent production (enough to produce over three times the 8,500 litres of anthrax spores Iraq admits to having manufactured);

- over 30,000 special munitions for delivery of chemical and biological agents.

15. The departure of UNSCOM meant that the International Community was unable to establish the truth behind these large discrepancies and greatly diminished its ability to monitor and assess Iraq's continuing attempts to reconstitute its programmes.

16. While the enforcement of the sanctions regimes and the UN arms embargo and US/UK air operations in 1998 have impeded Iraq's efforts to reconstitute its weapons of mass destruction, they have not halted them. Much of Iraq's missile infrastructure has been rebuilt; the nuclear weapons programme is being reconstituted, albeit with difficulty; and Iraq continues to produce chemical and biological agents.

CAB|3|0038

CHAPTER 3: THE CURRENT POSITION: 1998-2002

1. This chapter sets out what we know of Saddam's chemical, biological, nuclear and ballistic missile programmes, drawing on all the available evidence. While it takes account of the results from UN inspections and other publicly available information, it also draws heavily on the latest intelligence about Iraqi efforts to develop their programmes and capabilities since 1998. The **main conclusions** are that:

- Iraq has a useable chemical and biological weapons capability, in breach of UNSCR 687, which has included recent production of chemical and biological agents;

- Saddam continues to attach great importance to the possession of weapons of mass destruction and ballistic missiles, which he regards as being the basis for Iraq's regional power. He is determined to retain these capabilities;

- Iraq can deliver chemical and biological agents using an extensive range of artillery shells, free-fall bombs, sprayers and ballistic missiles;

- Iraq continues to work on developing nuclear weapons, in breach of its obligations under the Non-Proliferation Treaty, and in breach of UNSCR 687. Uranium has been sought from Africa that has no civil nuclear application in Iraq;

- Iraq possesses extended-range versions of the SCUD ballistic missile in breach of UNSCR 687, which are capable of reaching Tehran, Eastern Turkey and Cyprus. It is also developing longer range ballistic missiles;

- Iraq's current military planning specifically envisages the use of chemical and biological weapons;

- Iraq's military forces are able to use chemical and biological weapons, with command, control and logistical arrangements in place. The Iraqi military are able to deploy these weapons within forty five minutes of a decision to do so;

CAB/3/0039

- Iraq has learnt lessons from previous UN weapons inspections and is already taking steps to conceal and disperse sensitive equipment and documentation in advance of the return of inspectors;

- Iraq's chemical, biological, nuclear and ballistic missiles programmes are well funded.

CHEMICAL AND BIOLOGICAL WEAPONS

JIC Assessment: 1999-2002

2. Since the withdrawal of the inspectors the Joint Intelligence Committee (JIC) has monitored evidence, including from secret intelligence, of continuing work on Iraqi offensive chemical and biological warfare capabilities. In the first half of 2000 the JIC noted intelligence on Iraqi attempts to procure dual-use chemicals; and on the reconstruction of civil chemical production at sites formerly associated with the chemical warfare programme. Iraq had also been trying to procure dual-use materials and equipment which could be used for a biological warfare programme. Personnel known to have been connected to the biological warfare programme up to the Gulf War had been conducting research into pathogens. There was intelligence that Iraq was starting to produce biological warfare agents in mobile production facilities. Planning for the project had begun in 1995 under Dr Rihab Taha, known to have been a central player in the pre-Gulf War programme. The JIC concluded that Iraq had sufficient expertise, equipment and material to produce biological warfare agents within weeks using its legitimate biotechnology facilities.

3. In mid-2001 the JIC assessed that Iraq retained some chemical warfare agents, precursors, production equipment and weapons from before the Gulf War. These stocks would enable Iraq to produce significant quantities of mustard gas within weeks and of nerve agent within months. The JIC concluded that intelligence on Iraqi former chemical and biological warfare facilities, their limited reconstruction and civil production pointed to a continuing research and development programme. These chemical and biological capabilities represented the most immediate threat from Iraqi weapons of mass destruction. Since 1998 Iraqi development of mass destruction weaponry had been helped by the absence of inspectors and the increase in illegal border trade, which was providing hard currency.

CAB|3|0040

4. In the last six months the JIC has confirmed its earlier judgements on Iraqi chemical and biological warfare capabilities and assessed that Iraq has the means to deliver chemical and biological weapons.

Recent Intelligence

5. Subsequently, intelligence has become available from reliable sources which complements and adds to previous intelligence and confirms the JIC assessment that Iraq has chemical and biological weapons. The intelligence also shows that the Iraqi leadership has been discussing a number of issues related to these weapons. This intelligence covers:

- **Confirmation that chemical and biological weapons play an important role in Iraqi military thinking.** Intelligence shows that Saddam attaches great importance to the possession of chemical and biological weapons, which he regards as being the basis for Iraqi regional power. He believes that respect for Iraq rests on its possession of these weapons and the missiles capable of delivering them. Intelligence indicates that Saddam is determined to retain this capability and recognises that Iraqi political weight would be diminished if Iraq's military power rested solely on its conventional military forces.

- **Iraqi attempts to retain its existing banned weapons systems:** Iraq is already taking steps to prevent UN weapons inspectors finding evidence of its chemical and biological weapons programme. Intelligence indicates that Saddam has learnt lessons from previous weapons inspections, has identified possible weak points in the inspections process and knows how to exploit them. Sensitive equipment and papers can easily be concealed, and in some cases this is already happening. The possession of mobile biological agent production facilities will also aid concealment efforts. Saddam is determined not to lose the capabilities that he has been able to develop further in the four years since inspectors left

- **Saddam's willingness to use chemical and biological weapons:** intelligence indicates that Saddam is prepared to use chemical and biological weapons if he believes his regime is under threat. We also know from intelligence that as part of Iraq's military planning, Saddam is willing to use chemical and biological weapons against an internal uprising by the Shia population. Intelligence indicates that the Iraqi military are able to deploy chemical or biological weapons within forty five minutes of an order to do so.

Chemical and biological agents: surviving stocks

6. When confronted with questions about the unaccounted stocks, Iraq has claimed, repeatedly, that if it had retained any chemical agents from before the Gulf War they would have deteriorated sufficiently to render them harmless. But Iraq has admitted to having the knowledge and capability to add stabiliser to nerve agent which would prevent such decomposition. In 1997 UNSCOM also examined some munitions which had been filled with mustard gas prior to 1991 and found that they remained very toxic and showed little sign of deterioration.

7. Iraq has claimed that all its biological agents and weapons have been destroyed. No convincing proof of any kind has been produced to support this claim. In particular, Iraq could not explain large discrepancies between the amount of growth media (nutrients required for the specialised growth of agent) it procured before 1991 and the amounts of agent it admits to having manufactured. The discrepancy is enough to produce more than three times the amount of anthrax allegedly manufactured.

Chemical agent: production capabilities

8. Intelligence shows that Iraq has continued to produce chemical agent. During the Gulf War a number of facilities which intelligence reporting indicated were directly or indirectly associated with Iraq's chemical weapons effort were attacked and damaged. Following the ceasefire UNSCOM destroyed or rendered harmless facilities and equipment used in Iraq's chemical weapons programme. Other equipment was released for civilian use either in industry or academic institutes, where it was tagged and regularly inspected and monitored, or else placed under camera monitoring, to ensure that it was not being misused. This monitoring ceased when UNSCOM withdrew from Iraq in 1998. However, capabilities remain and, although the main chemical weapon production facility at al-Muthanna was completely destroyed by UNSCOM and has not been rebuilt, other plants formerly associated with the chemical warfare programme have been rebuilt. This includes the chlorine and phenol plant at

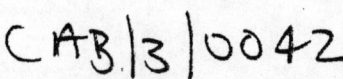

Fallujah 2 near Habbaniyah. In addition to their civilian uses, chlorine and phenol are used for precursor chemicals which contribute to the production of chemical agents.

9. Other dual use facilities, which are capable of being used to support the production of chemical agent and precursors, have been rebuilt and re-equipped. New chemical facilities have been built, some with illegal foreign assistance, and are probably fully operational or ready for production. These include the Ibn Sina Company at Tarmiyah (see figure 1), which is a chemical research centre. It undertakes research, development and production of chemicals previously imported but not now available and which are needed for Iraq's civil industry. The Director General of the research centre is Hickmat Na'im al-Jalu who, prior to the Gulf War worked in Iraq's nuclear weapons programme and after the war was responsible for preserving Iraq's chemical expertise.

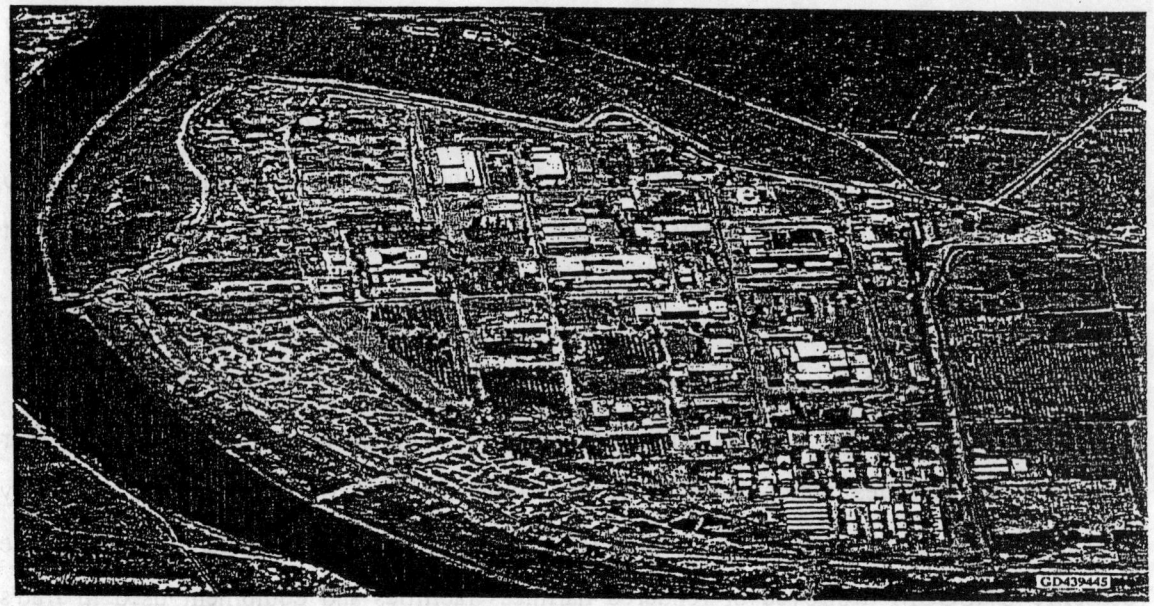

FIGURE 1: THE IBN SINA COMPANY AT TARMIYAH

10. Parts of the al-Qa'Qaa chemical complex damaged in the Gulf War have also been repaired and are operational. Of particular concern are elements of the phosgene production plant at Al Qa'Qaa. These were severely damaged during the Gulf War, and dismantled under UNSCOM supervision, but have since been rebuilt. While phosgene does have industrial uses it can also be used by itself as a chemical agent or as a precursor for nerve agents.

CAB/3/0043

546

11. Iraq has retained the expertise for chemical warfare research, agent production and weaponisation. Most of the personnel previously involved in the programme remain in country. While UNSCOM found a number of technical manuals (so called "cook books") for the production of chemical agents and critical precursors, Iraq's claim to have unilaterally destroyed the bulk of the documentation cannot be confirmed and is almost certainly untrue. Recent intelligence indicates that Iraq is still discussing methods of concealing such documentation in order to ensure that it is not discovered by any future UN inspections.

The Problem of Dual Use Facilities

Almost all components and supplies used in weapons of mass destruction and ballistic missile programmes are dual-use. For example, any major petrochemical or biotech industry, as well as public health organisations, will have legitimate need for most materials and equipment required to manufacture chemical and biological weapons. Without UN weapons inspectors it is very difficult therefore to be sure about the true nature of many of Iraq's facilities.

For example, Iraq has built a large new chemical complex, Project Baiji, in the desert in north west Iraq at Ash Sharqat (see figure 2). This site is a former uranium enrichment facility, which was damaged during the Gulf War, and rendered harmless under supervision of the IAEA. Part of the site has been rebuilt, with work starting in 1992, as a chemical production complex. Despite the site being far away from populated areas it is surrounded by a high wall with watch towers and guarded by armed guards. Intelligence reports indicate that it will produce nitric acid, which can be used in explosives, missile fuel, and in the purification of uranium.

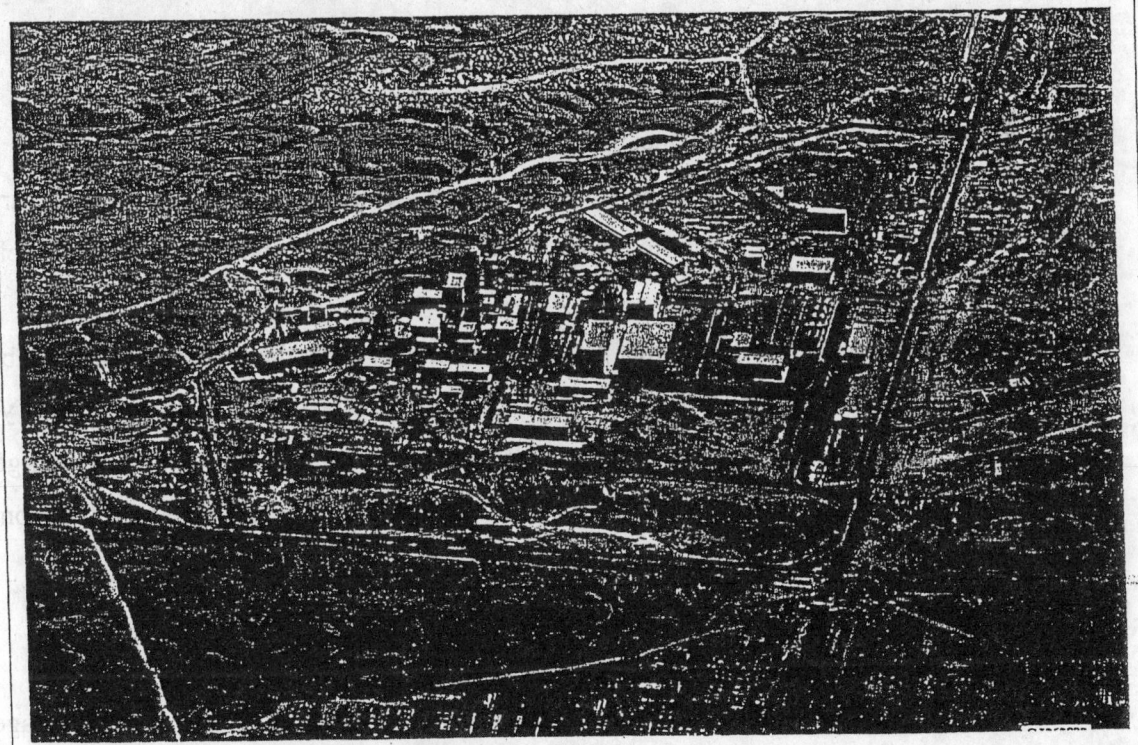

FIGURE 2: ASH SHARQAT CHEMICAL PRODUCTION FACILITY

CAB|3|0044

Biological agent: production capabilities

12. We know from intelligence that Iraq has continued to produce biological warfare agents. As with some chemical equipment, UNSCOM only destroyed equipment that could be directly linked to biological weapons production. Iraq also has its own engineering capability to design and construct biological agent associated fermenters, centrifuges, sprayer dryers and other equipment and is judged to be self-sufficient in the technology required to produce biological weapons. The experienced personnel who were active in the programme have largely remained in the country. Some dual-use equipment has also been purchased, but without monitoring by UN inspectors Iraq could have diverted it to their biological weapons programme. This newly purchased equipment and others previously subject to monitoring could be used in a resurgent BW programme. Facilities of concern include:

- the Castor Oil Production Plant at Fallujah: this was damaged in UK/US air attacks in 1998 (Operations Desert Fox) but has been rebuilt. The residue from the castor bean pulp can be used in the production of the biological agent ricin;

- the Al-Dawrah Foot and Mouth Disease Vaccine Plant, which was involved in biological agent production and research before the Gulf War;

- The Amariyah Sera and Vaccine plant at Abu Ghraib. UNSCOM established that this facility was used to produce biological agents, seed stocks and conduct biological warfare associated genetic research prior to the Gulf War. It has now expanded its storage capacity.

13. UNSCOM established that Iraq was planning to conceal from the inspectors the capability to produce biological warfare agents by developing mobile facilities. In the past two years evidence from defectors has indicated the existence of such facilities. Recent intelligence confirms that the Iraqi military have developed mobile facilities. These would help Iraq conceal and protect biological agent production from military attack or UN inspection.

Chemical and biological agents: delivery means

14. Iraq has a variety of delivery means available for both chemical and biological agents. These include:

CAB 13 0045

- free fall bombs - Iraq acknowledged to UNSCOM the deployment to two sites of free fall bombs filled with biological agent during 1990-91. These bombs were filled with anthrax, botulinum toxin and aflatoxin. Iraq also acknowledged possession of four types of aerial bomb with various chemical agent fills including sulphur mustard, tabun, sarin, cyclosarin, and VX;

- artillery shells and rockets - Iraq made extensive use of artillery munitions filled with chemical agents during the Iran-Iraq War. Mortars can also be used for chemical agent delivery. Iraq also claimed to have tested the use of shells and rockets filled with biological agents. Over 20,000 artillery munitions remain unaccounted for by UNSCOM;

- helicopter and aircraft borne sprayers - Iraq carried out studies into aerosol dissemination of biological agent using these platforms prior to 1991. UNSCOM was unable to account for many of these devices. It is probable that Iraq retains a capability for aerosol dispersal of both chemical and biological agent over a large area;

- Al Hussein ballistic missiles (range 650km) - Iraq told UNSCOM that it filled 25 warheads with anthrax, botulinum toxin and aflatoxin. Iraq also developed chemical agent warheads for Al Hussein. Iraq admitted to producing 50 chemical warheads for Al Hussein which were intended for the delivery of a mixture of sarin and cyclosarin. However, technical analysis of warhead remnants has shown traces of VX degradation product which indicate that some additional warheads were made and filled with VX;

- Al Samoud/Ababil-100 ballistic missiles (range 150km plus) - It is unclear if chemical and biological warheads have been developed for these systems, but given their experience on other missile systems, we judge that Iraq has the technical expertise for doing so;

FIGURE 3: THE L-29 JET TRAINER

- L-29 remotely piloted vehicle programme (see figure 3) - we know from intelligence that Iraq has

CAB/3/0046

attempted to modify the L-29 jet trainer to allow it to be used as a pilot-less aircraft (unmanned aerial vehicle - UAV), which is potentially capable of delivering chemical and biological agents over a large area.

Chemical and biological warfare: command and control

15. The authority to use chemical and biological weapons ultimately resides with Saddam, but intelligence indicates that he may have also delegated this authority to his son Qusai. Special Security Organisation (SSO) and Special Republican Guard (SRG) units would be involved in the movement of any chemical and biological weapons to military units. The Iraqi military holds artillery and missile systems at Corps level throughout the Armed Forces and conducts regular training with them. The Directorate of Rocket Forces has operational control of strategic missile systems and some Multiple Rocket Launcher Systems.

Chemical and biological weapons: summary

16. Intelligence shows that Iraq has covert chemical and biological weapons programmes, in breach of UN Security Council Resolution 687 and has continued to produce chemical and biological agents. Iraq has:

- chemical and biological agents and weapons available, both from pre-Gulf War stocks and more recent production;

- the capability to produce the chemical agents mustard gas, tabun, sarin, cyclosarin, and VX capable of producing mass casualties;

- a biological agent production capability and can produce at least anthrax, botulinum toxin, aflatoxin and ricin. Iraq has also developed mobile facilities to produce biological agents.

- a variety of delivery means available;

- military forces, which maintain the capability to use these weapons, with command, control and logistical arrangements in place.

CAB|3|0047

NUCLEAR WEAPONS

JIC Assessments: 1999-2001

17. Since 1999 the JIC has monitored Iraq's attempts to reconstitute its nuclear weapons programme. In mid-2001 the JIC assessed that Iraq had continued its nuclear research after 1998. The JIC drew attention to intelligence that Iraq had recalled its nuclear scientists to the programme in 1998. Since 1998 Iraq had been trying to procure items that could be for use in the construction of centrifuges for the enrichment of uranium.

Iraqi Nuclear Weapons Expertise

18. Paragraphs 5 and 6 of Chapter 2 describe the Iraqi nuclear weapons programme prior to the Gulf War. It is clear from IAEA inspections and Iraq's own declarations that by 1991 considerable progress had been made in both developing methods to produce fissile material and in weapons design. The IAEA dismantled the physical infrastructure of the Iraqi nuclear

---

Elements of a nuclear weapons programme

A typical nuclear fission weapon consists of:

- fissile material for the core, which gives out huge amounts of explosive energy from nuclear reactions when made "super critical", through extreme compression. Fissile material is usually either highly enriched uranium (HEU) or weapons-grade plutonium.
  - HEU can be made in gas centrifuges (see separate box).
  - plutonium is made by reprocessing fuel from a nuclear reactor.
- explosives are needed to compress the nuclear core. They also require:
  - a complex arrangement of detonators, explosive charges to produce an even and rapid compression of the core.
  - sophisticated electronics to fire the explosives.
  - a neutron initiator to provide initial burst of neutrons to start the nuclear reactions.

Weaponisation is the conversion of these concepts into a reliable weapon. It includes:

- developing a weapon design through sophisticated science and complex calculations;
- engineering design to integrate with the delivery system;
- specialised equipment to cast and machine safely the nuclear core.
- dedicated facilities to assemble the warheads.
- facilities to rigorously test all individual components and designs.

The complexity is much greater for a weapon that can fit into a missile warhead than for a larger Nagasaki-type bomb.

---

weapons programme, including the dedicated facilities and equipment for uranium separation and enrichment, and for weapon development and production, and removed the remaining highly enriched uranium. But Iraq retained, and retains, its experienced nuclear scientists and

CAB/3/0048

technicians, specialised in the production of fissile material and weapons design. Intelligence indicates that Iraq also retains the accompanying programme documentation and data.

Gas Centrifuge Uranium Enrichment
Uranium in the form of uranium hexafluoride is separated into its different isotopes in rapidly spinning rotor tubes of special centrifuges. Many hundreds or thousands of centrifuges are connected in cascades to enrich uranium. If the lighter U235 isotope is enriched to more than 90% it can be used in the core of a nuclear weapon.

19. Intelligence shows that the present Iraqi programme is almost certainly seeking an indigenous ability to enrich uranium to the level needed for a nuclear weapon. It indicates that the approach is based on gas centrifuge uranium enrichment, one of the routes Iraq was following for producing fissile material before the Gulf War. But Iraq needs certain key equipment, including gas centrifuge components, and components for the production of fissile material before a nuclear bomb could be developed.

20. Following the departure of weapons inspectors in 1998 there has been an accumulation of intelligence indicating that Iraq is making concerted covert efforts to acquire dual-use technology and materials with nuclear applications. Iraq's known holdings of processed uranium are under IAEA supervision. But there is intelligence that Iraq has sought the supply of significant quantities of uranium from Africa. Iraqi has no active civil nuclear power programme or nuclear power plants, and therefore has no legitimate reason to acquire uranium.

Iraq's civil nuclear programme
- Iraq's long-standing civil nuclear power programme is limited to small scale research. Activities that could be used for military purposes are prohibited by UNSCR 687 and 715.
- Iraq has no nuclear power plants and therefore no requirement for uranium as fuel.
- Iraq has a number of nuclear research programmes in the fields of agriculture, biology, chemistry, materials and pharmaceuticals. None of these activities require more than tiny amounts of uranium which Iraq could supply from its own resources.
- Iraq's research reactors are non-operational - one was bombed by the Israelis, one was never completed, and the other's fuel has been removed.

21. Other important procurement activity since 1998 includes attempts to purchase:

- vacuum pumps, which could be used to create and maintain pressures in a gas centrifuge cascade needed to enrich uranium;

CAB/3/0049

552

- an entire magnet production line of the correct specification for use in the motors and top bearings of gas centrifuges;

- anhydrous hydrogen fluoride (AHF) and fluorine gas. AHF is commonly used in the petrochemical industry and Iraq frequently imports significant amounts, but it is also used in the process of converting uranium into uranium hexafluoride for use in gas centrifuge cascades;

- one large filament winding-machine, which could be used to manufacture carbon fibre gas centrifuge rotors;

- a large balancing machine which could be used in initial centrifuge balancing work.

22. Iraq has also made repeated attempts to covertly acquire a very large quantity (60,000 or more) of specialised aluminium tubes. The specialised aluminium in question is subject to international export controls because of its potential application in the construction of gas centrifuges used to enrich uranium, although there is no definitive intelligence that it is destined for a nuclear programme. In the case of the magnets it appears that Iraq is attempting to acquire a capability to produce them on its own rather than rely on foreign procurement.

Nuclear weapons: timelines

23. In early 2002, the JIC assessed that UN sanctions on Iraq were hindering the import of crucial goods for the production of fissile material. The JIC judged that while sanctions remain effective, Iraq would not be able indigenously to produce a nuclear weapon. If they were removed or prove ineffective, it would take Iraq at least five years to produce a weapon. But we know that Iraq retains expertise and design data relating to nuclear weapons. We therefore judge that if Iraq obtained fissile material and other essential components from foreign sources, the timeline for production of a nuclear weapon would be shortened and Iraq could produce a nuclear weapon in between one and two years.

Radiological dispersal device

24. Iraq experimented with radiological dispersal devices (RDDs) during 1987. This programme never progressed beyond the research stage, and was dropped.

CAB/3/0050

> **Radiological dispersal device**
> A Radiological Dispersal Device (RDD) is designed to cause injury, or to deny access to an area through the dissemination of radioactive material. An RDD can be made using material from medical or industrial facilities, but makes an ineffective weapon. Very large amounts of highly radioactive material are required before an RDD will cause many fatalities or significant injuries.

BALLISTIC MISSILES

JIC Assessment: 1999-2002

25. In mid-2001 the JIC drew attention to what it described as a "step-change" in progress on Iraqi missile programme over the previous two years. It was clear from intelligence that the range of Iraqi missiles which was permitted by the UN and supposedly limited to 150kms was being extended and that work was under way on larger engines for longer-range missiles.

26. In early 2002 the JIC concluded that Iraq had begun to develop missiles with a range of over 1,000kms. The JIC assessed that if sanctions remained effective the Iraqis would not be able to produce such a missile before 2007. Sanctions and the earlier work of the inspectors had caused significant problems for Iraqi missile development. In the previous six months Iraqi foreign procurement efforts for the missile programme had been bolder. The JIC also assessed that Iraq retained up to 20 Al Hussein missiles from before the Gulf War.

The Iraqi ballistic missile programme since 1998

27. Since the Gulf War, Iraq has been openly developing two short-range missiles up to a range of 150km, which are permitted under UN Security Council Resolution 687. The Al-Samoud

FIGURE 4: ABABIL-100

liquid propellant missile has been extensively tested and is being deployed to military units. Intelligence indicates that at least fifty have been produced. Intelligence also indicates that Iraq has worked on extending its range to at least 200km in breach of UN Security Resolution 687. Production of the solid propellant Ababil-100 (Figure 4) is also underway, probably as an unguided rocket at this stage. There are also plans to extend its range to at least 200km. Compared to liquid propellant missiles, those powered by solid propellant offer greater ease of storage, handling and mobility. They are also quicker to take into and out of action and can stay at a high state of readiness for longer periods.

28. According to intelligence, Iraq has retained up to 20 Al Hussein missiles (Figure 5), in breach of UN Security Council Resolution 687. These missiles were either hidden from the UN as complete systems, or re-assembled using illegally retained engines and other components. We judge that the engineering expertise available would allow these missiles to be maintained effectively, although the fact that at least some require re-assembly makes it difficult to judge exactly how many could be available for use. They could be used with conventional, chemical or biological warheads and, with a range of up to 650km, are capable of reaching a number of countries in the region including Cyprus, Turkey, Saudi Arabia, Iran and Israel.

FIGURE 5: AL HUSSEIN

29. Intelligence has confirmed that Iraq wants to extend the range of its missile systems to over 1000km, enabling it to threaten other regional neighbours. This work began in 1998, although efforts to regenerate the long range ballistic missile programme probably began in 1995. Iraq's missile programmes employ hundreds of people. Satellite imagery (Figure 6) has shown a new engine test stand being constructed (A), which is larger than the current one used for Al Samoud (B), and that formerly used for testing SCUD engines (C) which was dismantled under UNSCOM supervision. This new stand will be capable of testing engines for missiles with ranges over 1000km, which are not permitted under UN Security Council Resolution 687. Such a facility would not be needed for systems that fall within the UN permitted range of 150km. The Iraqis have recently taken measures to conceal activities at this site.

CAB|3|0052

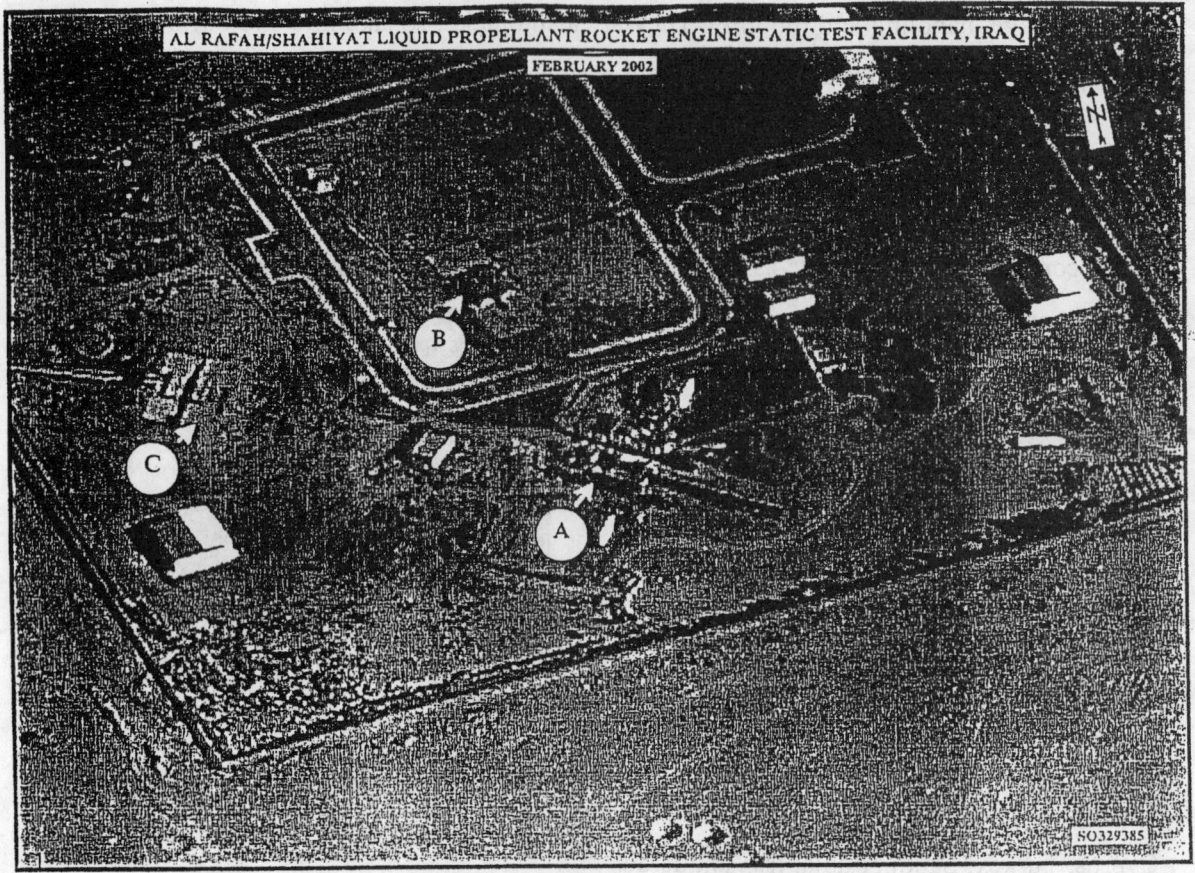

FIGURE 6: AL RAFAH/SHAHIYAT LIQUID PROPELLANT ENGINE STATIC TEST STAND

Iraq is also working to obtain improved guidance technology to increase missile accuracy.

30. The success of UN restrictions means the development of new longer-range missiles is likely to be a slow process. These restrictions impact particularly on the:

- availability of foreign expertise;

- conduct of test flights to ranges above 150km;

- acquisition of guidance and control technology.

CAB/3/0053

31. Saddam remains committed to developing longer-range missiles. Even if sanctions remain effective, Iraq might achieve a missile capability of over 1000km within 5 years (Figure 4 shows the range of Iraq's various missiles).

32. Iraq has managed to rebuild much of the missile production infrastructure destroyed in the Gulf War and in Operation Desert Fox in 1998 (see Part 2). New missile-related infrastructure is also under construction. Some aspects of this, including rocket propellant mixing and casting facilities at the Al Mamoun Plant, appear to replicate those linked to the prohibited BADR-2000 programme (with a planned range of 700-1000km) which were destroyed in the Gulf War or dismantled by UNSCOM. A new plant at al-Mamoun for indigenously producing ammonium perchlorate, which is a key ingredient in the production of solid propellant rocket motors, has also been constructed. This has been provided illicitly by NEC Engineers Private Limited, an Indian chemical engineering firm with extensive links in Iraq, including to other suspect facilities such as the Fallujah 2 chlorine plant. After an extensive investigation, the Indian authorities have recently suspended its export licence, although affiliated individuals and companies are still illicitly procuring for Iraq.

33.   Despite a UN embargo, Iraq has also made concerted efforts to acquire additional production technology, including machine tools and raw materials, in breach of UN Security Council Resolution 1051. The embargo has succeeded in blocking many of these attempts, such as requests to buy magnesium powder and ammonium chloride. But we know from intelligence that some items have found their way to the Iraqi ballistic missile programme. More will inevitably continue to do so. Intelligence makes it clear that Iraqi procurement agents and front companies in third countries are seeking illicitly to acquire propellant chemicals for Iraq's ballistic missiles. This includes production level quantities of near complete sets of solid propellant rocket motor ingredients such as aluminium powder, ammonium perchlorate and hydroxyl terminated polybutadiene. There have also been attempts to acquire large quantities of liquid propellant chemicals such as unsymmetrical dimethylhydrazine (UDMH) and diethylenetriamene. We judge this is intended to support production and deployment of the Al Samoud and development of longer range systems.

CAB\3\0054

Iraq: Current and Planned/Potential Ballistic Missiles

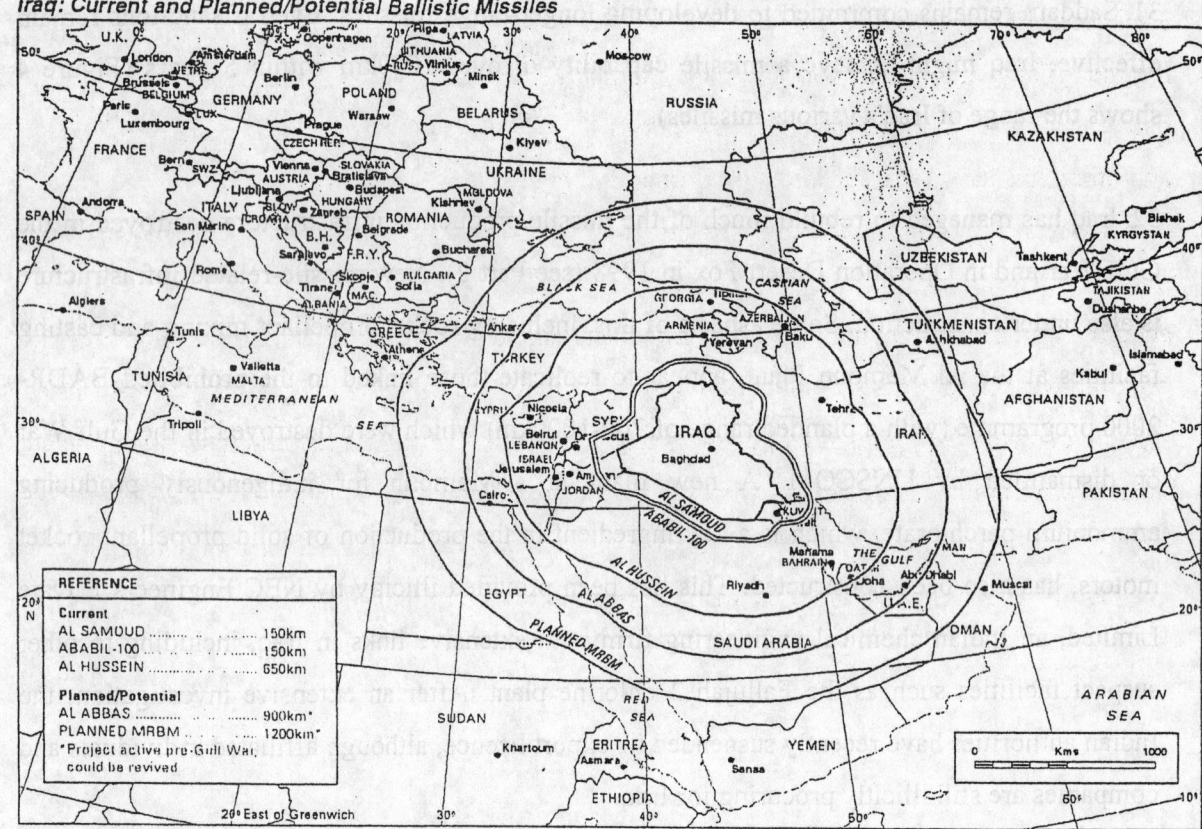

FIGURE 7: CURRENT AND PLANNED/POTENTIAL BALLISTIC MISSILES

FUNDING FOR THE WMD PROGRAMME

34. The UN has sought to restrict Iraq's ability to generate funds for its chemical, biological and other military programmes. For example, Iraq earns money legally under the UN Oil For Food Programme (OFF) established by UNSCR 986, whereby the proceeds of oil sold through the UN are used to buy humanitarian supplies for Iraq.

> **UN Sanctions**
> UN sanctions on Iraq prohibit all imports to and exports from Iraq. The UN must clear any goods entering or leaving. The UN also administers the Oil for Food (OFF) programme. Any imports entering Iraq under the OFF are checked against the Goods Review List for potential military or weapons of mass destruction utility.

This money remains under UN control, and cannot be used for military procurement. However, the Iraqi regime continues to generate income outside UN control, either in the form of hard currency, or barter goods (which in turn means existing Iraqi funds are freed up to be spent on other things).

CAB/3/0055

558

35. These illicit earnings go to the Iraqi regime. They are used for building new palaces, as well as purchasing luxury goods and other civilian goods outside OFF. Some of these funds are also used by Saddam to maintain his armed forces, and to develop or

Iraq's illicit earnings	
Year	Amount in $billions
1999	0.8 to 1
2000	1.5 to 2
2001	3
2002	3 (assessed)

acquire military equipment, including for chemical, biological, nuclear and ballistic missile programmes. We do not know what proportion of these funds is used in this way. But we have seen no evidence that Iraqi attempts to develop its weapons of mass destruction and its ballistic missile programme, for example through covert procurement of equipment from abroad has been inhibited in any way by lack of funds. The steady increase over the last three years in the availability of funds will enable Saddam to progress the programmes faster.

CAB|3|0056

PART 2

HISTORY OF UN WEAPONS INSPECTIONS

1. During the 1990s, beginning in April 1991 immediately after the end of the Gulf War, the UN Security Council passed a series of resolutions [see box] establishing the authority of UNSCOM and the IAEA to carry out the work of dismantling Iraq's arsenal of chemical, biological and nuclear weapons programmes and long range ballistic missiles.

UN Security Council Resolutions (UNSCR) relating to WMD

UNSCR 687, April 1991 created the UN Special Commission (UNSCOM) and required Iraq to accept, unconditionally, "the destruction, removal or rendering harmless, under international supervision" of its chemical and biological weapons, ballistic missiles with a range greater than 150km, and their associated programmes, stocks, components, research and facilities. The International Atomic Energy Agency (IAEA) was charged with abolition of Iraq's nuclear weapons programme. UNSCOM and the IAEA must report that their mission has been achieved before the Security Council can end sanctions. They have not yet done so.

UNSCR 707, August 1991, stated that Iraq must provide full, final and complete disclosure of all its WMD programmes and provide unconditional and unrestricted access to UN inspectors. For over a decade Iraq has been in breach of this resolution. Iraq must also cease all nuclear activities of any kind other than civil use of isotopes.

UNSCR 715, October 1991 approved plans prepared by UNSCOM and IAEA for the ongoing monitoring and verification (OMV) arrangements to implement UNSCR 687. Iraq did not accede to this to November 1993. OMV was conducted from April 1995 to 15 December 1998, when the UN left Iraq.

UNSCR 1051, March 1996 stated that Iraq must declare the shipment of dual-use WMD goods.

These resolutions were passed under Chapter VII of the UN Charter which is the instrument that allows the UN Security Council to authorise the use of military force to enforce its resolutions.

2. As outlined in UNSCR 687, Iraq's chemical, biological and nuclear weapons programmes were also a breach of Iraq's commitments under:

CAB/3/0057

- The Geneva Protocol of 1925 – which bans the use of chemical and biological weapons;

- the Biological and Toxin Weapons Convention – which bans the development, production, stockpiling, acquisition or retention of biological weapons;

- and the Nuclear Non-Proliferation Treaty (NPT) – which prohibits Iraq from manufacturing or otherwise acquiring nuclear weapons

3. UNSCR 687 obliged Iraq to provide declarations on all aspects of its WMD

> UNSCOM and the IAEA were given the remit to designate <u>any</u> locations for inspection at any time, review any document and interview any scientist, technician or other individual and seize any prohibited items for destruction.

programmes within 15 days and accept the destruction, removal or rendering harmless under international supervision of its chemical, biological and nuclear programmes, and all ballistic missiles with a range beyond 150km. Iraq did not make a satisfactory declaration within the specified timeframe.

Iraq accepted the UNSCRs and agreed to co-operate with UNSCOM. The history of the UN weapons inspections was characterised by persistent Iraqi obstruction.

Iraqi Non-Co-operation with the Inspectors

4. The former Chairman of UNSCOM, Richard Butler, reported to the UN Security Council in January 1999, that in 1991 a decision was taken by a high-level Government committee to provide inspectors with only a portion of its proscribed weapons, components, production capabilities and stocks. UNSCOM concluded that Iraqi policy was based on the following actions:

- to provide only a portion of extant weapons stocks, releasing for destruction only those that were least modern;

CAB/3/00J8

- to retain the production capability and documentation necessary to revive programmes when possible;

- to conceal the full extent of its chemical weapons programme, including the VX nerve agent project; to conceal the number and type of chemical and biological warheads for proscribed long-range missiles;

- and to conceal the existence of its biological weapons programme.

5. In December 1997 Richard Butler reported to the UN Security Council that Iraq had created a new category of sites – "Presidential" and "sovereign" – from which it claimed that UNSCOM inspectors would henceforth be barred. The terms of the ceasefire in 1991 foresaw no such limitation. However, Iraq consistently refused to

---

Iraq's policy of deception

Iraq has admitted having a large, effective, system for hiding proscribed material including documentation, components, production equipment and, possibly, biological and chemical agents and weapons from the UN. Shortly after the adoption of UNSCR 687 in April 1991, an Administrative Security Committee (ASC) was formed with responsibility for advising Saddam on the information which could be released to UNSCOM and the IAEA. The Committee consisted of senior Military Industrial Commission (MIC) scientists from all of Iraq's WMD programmes. The Higher Security Committee (HSC) of the Presidential Office was in overall command of deception operations. The system was directed from the very highest political levels within the Presidential Office and involved, if not Saddam himself, his youngest son, Qusai. The system for hiding proscribed material relies on high mobility and good command and control. It uses lorries to move items at short notice and most hide sites appear to be located close to good road links and telecommunications. The Baghdad area was particularly favoured. In addition to active measures to hide material from the UN, Iraq has attempted to monitor, delay and collect intelligence on UN operations to aid its overall deception plan.

---

allow UNSCOM inspectors access to any of these eight Presidential sites. Many of these so-called "palaces" are in fact large compounds which are an integral part of Iraqi counter-measures designed to hide weapons material (see photograph).

CAB/3/0059

A photograph of a presidential site or what have been called "palaces".

Buckingham palace has been super-imposed to demonstrate their comparative size

Buckingham Palace and grounds

CAB 13 10060

Intimidation

6. Once inspectors had arrived in Iraq, it quickly became apparent that the Iraqis would resort to a range of measures (including physical threats and psychological intimidation of inspectors) to prevent UNSCOM and the IAEA from fulfilling their mandate.

7. In response to such incidents, the President of the Security Council issued frequent statements calling on Iraq to comply with its disarmament and monitoring obligations.

Iraqi obstruction of UN weapons inspection teams.

- firing warning shots in the air to prevent IAEA inspectors from intercepting nuclear related equipment (June 1991);

- keeping IAEA inspectors in a car park for 4 days and refusing to allow them to leave with incriminating documents on Iraq's nuclear weapons programme (September 1991).

- announcing that UN monitoring and verification plans were "unlawful" (October 1991);

- refusing UNSCOM inspectors access to the Ministry of Agriculture. Threats were made to inspectors who remained on watch outside the building. The inspection team had reliable evidence that the site contained archives related to proscribed activities;

- In 1991-2 Iraq objected to UNSCOM using its own helicopters and choosing its own flight plans. In January 1993 it refused to allow UNSCOM the use of its own aircraft to fly into Iraq;

- refusing to allow UNSCOM to install remote-controlled monitoring cameras at two key missile sites (June-July 1993);

- repeatedly denying access to inspection teams (1991- December 1998);

- interfering with UNSCOM's helicopter operations, threatening the safety of the aircraft and their crews (June 1997);

- demanding the end of U2 overflights and the withdrawal of US UNSCOM staff (October 1997);

- destroying documentary evidence of WMD programmes (September 1997).

CAB/3/0061

Obstruction

8. Iraq denied that it had pursued a biological weapons programme until July 1995.

In July 1995, Iraq acknowledged that biological agents had been produced on an industrial scale at Al-Hakam. Following the defection in August 1995 of Hussein Kamel, Saddam's son-in-law and former Director of the Military Industrialisation Commission, Iraq released over 2 million documents relating to its WMD programmes and acknowledged that it had pursued a biological programme that led to the deployment of actual weapons. Iraq admitted producing in excess of 200 biological weapons with a reserve of agent to fill considerably more.

9. Iraq tried to obstruct UNSCOM's efforts to investigate the scale of its biological

---

Inspection of Iraq's biological weapons programme

In the course of the first biological weapons inspection in August 1991, Iraq claimed that it had merely conducted a military biological research programme. At the site visited, Al-Salman, Iraq had removed equipment, documents and even entire buildings. Later in the year, during a visit to the Al-Hakam site, Iraq declared to UNSCOM inspectors that the facility was used as a factory to produce proteins derived from yeast to feed animals. Inspectors subsequently discovered that the plant was a central site for the production of anthrax spores and botulinum toxin for weapons. The factory had also been sanitised by Iraqi officials to deceive inspectors. Iraq continued to develop the Al-Hakam site into the 1990s, misleading UNSCOM about its true purpose.

Another key site, the Foot and Mouth Disease Vaccine Institute at Dawrah which produced botulinum toxin and probably anthrax, was not divulged as part of the programme. Five years later, after intense pressure, Iraq acknowledged that tens of tonnes of bacteriological warfare agent had been produced there and at Al-Hakam.

As documents recovered in August 1995 were assessed, it became apparent that the full disclosure required by the UN was far from complete. Successive inspection teams went to Iraq to try to gain greater understanding of the programme and to obtain credible supporting evidence. In July 1996 Iraq refused to discuss it's past programme and doctrine forcing the team to withdraw in protest. Monitoring teams were at the same time finding undisclosed equipment and materials associated with the past programme. In response, Iraq grudgingly provided successive disclosures of their programme which were judged by UNSCOM, and specially convened international panels, to be technically inadequate.

In late 1995, Iraq acknowledged weapons testing the biological agent ricin, but did not provide production information. Two years later – in early 1997 – UNSCOM discovered evidence that Iraq had produced ricin.

CAB/3/0062

weapons programme. It created forged documents to account for bacterial growth media, imported in the late 1980s, specifically for the production of anthrax, botulinum toxin and probably plague. The documents were created to indicate that the material had been imported by the State Company for Drugs and Medical Appliances Marketing for use in hospitals and distribution to local authorities. Iraq also censored documents and scientific papers provided to the first UN inspection team, removing all references to key individuals, weapons and industrial production of agents.

10. Iraq has yet to provide any documents concerning production of agent and subsequent weaponisation. Iraq destroyed, unilaterally and illegally, some biological weapons in 1991 and 1992 making accounting for these weapons impossible. In addition Iraq cleansed a key site at Al-Muthanna – its main research and development, production and weaponisation facility for chemical warfare agents - of all evidence of a biological programme in the toxicology department, the animal-house and weapons filling station.

11. Iraq refused to elaborate further on the programme during inspections in 1997 and 1998, confining discussion to previous topics. In July 1998, Tariq Aziz personally intervened in the inspection process stating that the biological programme was more secret and more closed than other WMD programmes. He also played down the significance of the programme. Iraq has presented the biological weapons programme as the personal undertaking of a few misguided scientists.

12. At the same time, Iraq tried to maintain its nuclear weapons programme via a concerted campaign to deceive IAEA inspectors. In 1997 the Agency's Director General stated that the IAEA was "severely hampered by Iraq's persistence in a policy of concealment and understatement of the programme's scope."

Achievements

13. Despite the conduct of the Iraqi authorities towards them, both UNSCOM and the IAEA Action Team have valuable records of achievement in discovering and

CAB|3)0063

exposing Iraq's biological weapons programme and destroying very large quantities of chemical weapons stocks and missiles as well as the infrastructure for Iraq's nuclear weapons programme.

UNSCOM and IAEA Achievements

UNSCOM surveyed 1015 sites in Iraq, carrying out 272 separate inspections. Despite Iraqi obstruction and intimidation, UN inspectors uncovered details of chemical, biological, nuclear and ballistic missile programmes. One of the main discoveries was that at the time of the Gulf War, Iraq could have produced a nuclear weapon by the end of 1991. Other major UNSCOM/IAEA achievements included:

- the destruction of 40,000 munitions for chemical weapons, 2,610 tonnes of chemical precursors and 411 tonnes of chemical warfare agent;

- the dismantling of Iraq's prime chemical weapons development and production complex at Al-Muthanna, and a range of key production equipment;

- the destruction of 48-SCUD type missiles, 11 mobile launchers and 56 sites, 30 warheads filled with chemical agents, and 20 conventional warheads;

- the destruction of the Al-Hakam biological weapons facility and a range of production equipment, seed stocks and growth media for biological weapons;

- the discovery in 1991 of samples of indigenously-produced highly enriched uranium, forcing Iraq's acknowledgement of uranium enrichment programmes and attempts to preserve key components of its prohibited nuclear weapons programme; and

- the removal and destruction of the infrastructure for the nuclear weapons programme, including the Al-Athir weaponisation/testing facility.

---

14. Despite UNSCOM's efforts, following the effective ejection of UN inspectors in December 1998, there remained a series of significant unresolved disarmament issues. In summarising the situation in a report to the Security Council, the UNSCOM Chairman, Richard Butler indicated that:

- contrary to the requirement that destruction be conducted under international supervision, "Iraq undertook extensive, unilateral and secret destruction of large quantities of proscribed weapons and items";

LAB 13 0064

567

- and Iraq "also pursued a practice of concealment of proscribed items, including weapons, and a cover up of its activities in contravention of Council resolutions."

Overall, Butler declared that obstructive Iraqi activity had had "a significant impact upon the Commission's disarmament work."

Withdrawal of the Inspectors

15. By the end of 1998 UNSCOM was in direct confrontation with the Iraqi Government which was refusing to co-operate. The US and the UK had made clear that anything short of full co-operation would make military action unavoidable. Richard Butler was requested to report to the UN Security Council in December 1998 and stated that, following a series of direct confrontations, coupled with the systematic refusal by Iraq to co-operate, UNSCOM was no longer able to perform its disarmament mandate. As a direct result, on December 16 the weapons inspectors were withdrawn and Operation Desert Fox was launched by the US and the UK a few hours afterwards.

Operation Desert Fox (16-19 December 1998):

Operation Desert Fox targeted industrial facilities related to Iraq's ballistic missile programme and a suspect biological warfare facility as well as military airfields and sites used by Iraq's security organisations which are involved in its weapons of mass destruction programmes. Key facilities associated with Saddam's ballistic missile programme were significantly degraded.

The Situation Since 1998

16. There have been no UN-mandated weapons inspections in Iraq since 1998. In an effort to enforce Iraqi compliance with its disarmament and monitoring obligations, the Security Council passed resolution 1284 in December 1999. This established the United Nations Monitoring, Verification and Inspection Commission (UNMOVIC) as a successor organisation to UNSCOM and called on Iraq to give UNMOVIC inspectors "immediate, unconditional and unrestricted access to any and all areas, facilities, equipment, records and means of transport". It also set out the steps Iraq needed to take in return for the eventual suspension and lifting of sanctions. A key

CAB13/0065

measure of Iraqi compliance would be full co-operation with UN inspectors, including unconditional, immediate and unrestricted access to any and all sites. Given Iraq's track record of co-operation with UNSCOM and the IAEA between 1991-98, it is difficult to conclude other than that the prospects of Iraq meeting this standard are poor.

17. For the past three years, Iraq has allowed the IAEA to carry out an annual inspection of a stockpile of nuclear material (depleted natural and low-enriched uranium). This has led some countries and western commentators to conclude – erroneously – that Iraq is meeting its nuclear disarmament and monitoring obligations. As the IAEA has pointed out in recent weeks, this annual inspection does "not serve as a substitute for the verification activities required by the relevant resolutions of the UN Security Council."

18. Dr. Hans Blix, the Executive Chairman of UNMOVIC, and Dr. Mohammed El-Baradei, the Director General of the IAEA, have declared that in the absence of inspections it is impossible to verify Iraqi compliance with its UN disarmament and monitoring obligations. In April 1999, an independent UN panel of experts noted that "the longer inspection and monitoring activities remain suspended, the more difficult the comprehensive implementation of Security Council resolutions becomes, increasing the risk that Iraq might reconstitute its proscribed weapons programmes."

19. The departure of the Inspectors greatly diminished our ability to monitor and assess Iraq's continuing attempts to reconstitute its chemical, biological, nuclear and ballistic missile programmes.

CAB|3|0066

PART 3

IRAQ UNDER SADDAM

Introduction

1. The Republic of Iraq is bounded by Turkey, Iran, Kuwait, Saudia Arabia, Jordan, Syria and the Persian Gulf. Its population of around 23 million is ethnically and religiously diverse. Approximately 77% are Arabs. Sunni Muslims form around 17% of the Arab population and dominate the government. About 60% of Iraqis are Shias and 20% are Kurds. The remaining 3% of the population consists of Assyrians, Turkomans, Armenians, Christians and Yazidis.

2. Public life in Iraq is nominally dominated by the Ba'ath Party (see box on next page). But all real authority rests with Saddam Hussein and his immediate circle. Saddam's family, tribe and a small number of associates remain his most loyal supporters. He uses them to convey his orders, including to members of the government.

3. Saddam Hussein uses patronage and violence to motivate his

---

Saddam's rise to power

Saddam Hussein was born in 1937 in the Tikrit district, north of Baghdad. In 1957 he joined the Ba'ath Party. After taking part in a failed attempt to assassinate the Iraqi President, Abdul Karim Qasim, Saddam escaped, first to Syria and then to Egypt. In his absence he was sentenced to 15 years imprisonment.

Saddam returned to Baghdad in 1963 when the Ba'ath Party came to power. He went into hiding after the Ba'ath fell from power later that year. He was captured and imprisoned, but in 1967 escaped and took over responsibility for Ba'ath security. Saddam set about imposing his will on the Party and establishing himself at the centre of power.

The Ba'ath Party returned to power in 1968. In 1969 Saddam became Vice Chairman of the Revolutionary Command Council, Deputy to the President, and Deputy Secretary-General of the Regional Command of the Ba'ath. In 1970 he joined the Party's National Command and in 1977 was elected Assistant Secretary General. In July 1979, he took over the Presidency of Iraq. Within days, five fellow members of the Revolutionary Command Council were accused of involvement in a coup attempt. They and 17 others were summarily executed.

CAB/3/0067

supporters and to control or eliminate opposition. Potential rewards include social status, money and better access to goods. Saddam's extensive security apparatus and Ba'ath Party network provides oversight of Iraqi society, with informants in social,

> **The Iraqi Ba'ath Party**
> The Ba'ath Party is the only legal political party in Iraq. It pervades all aspects of Iraqi life.
> Membership, around 700,000, is necessary for self advancement and confers benefits from the regime.

government and military organisations. Saddam practises torture, execution and other forms of coercion against his enemies, real or suspected. His targets are not only those who have offended him, but also their families, friends or colleagues.

4. Saddam acts to ensure that there are no other centres of power in Iraq. He has crushed parties and ethnic groups which might try to assert themselves, such as the communists and the Kurds. Members of the opposition abroad have been the targets of assassination attempts conducted by Iraqi security services.

5. Army officers are an important part of the government's network of informers. Suspicion that officers have ambitions other than the service of the President leads to immediate execution. It is routine for Saddam to take pre-emptive action against those who he believes might conspire against him.

> **Saddam's security apparatus**
> Saddam relies on a long list of security organisations with overlapping responsibilities. The main ones are:
> - The **Special Security Organisation** oversees Saddam's security and monitors the loyalty of other security services. Its recruits are predominantly from Tikrit.
> - The **Special Republican Guard** is equipped with the best available military equipment. Its members are selected on the basis of loyalty to the regime.
> - The **Directorate of General Security** is primarily responsible for countering threats from the civilian population.
> - The **Directorate of General Intelligence** monitors and suppresses dissident activities at home and abroad.
> - The **Directorate of Military Intelligence**'s role includes the investigation of military personnel.
> - The **Saddam Fidayeen**, under the control of Udayy Hussein, has been used to deal with civil disturbances.

CAB/3/0068

Internal Repression – the Kurds and the Shias

6. Saddam has pursued a long-term programme of persecution of the Iraqi Kurds, including the use of chemical weapons. During the Iran/Iraq war, Saddam appointed his cousin, Ali Hassan al-Majid, as his deputy in the north. In 1987-88, al-Majid led the "Anfal" campaign of attacks on Kurdish villages. Amnesty International ¬estimates that more than 100,000 Kurds were killed or disappeared during this period.

> **Repression and control: some examples**
> - A campaign of mass arrests and killing of Shia activists led to the execution of the Ayatollah Baqir al-Sadr and his sister in April 1980.
> - In 1983, 80 members of another leading Shia family were arrested. Six of them, all religious leaders, were executed.
> - A massive chemical weapons attack on Kurds in Halabja town in March 1988, killing 5000 and injuring 10,000 more.
> - A large number of officers from the Jabbur tribe were executed in the early 1990s for the alleged disloyalty of a few of them.

7. After the Gulf War in 1991 Kurds in the north of Iraq rose up against Baghdad's rule. In response the Iraqi regime killed or imprisoned thousands, prompting a humanitarian crisis. Over a million Kurds fled into the mountains and tried to escape Iraq.

8. Persecution of Iraq's Kurds continues, although the protection provided by the northern No-Fly Zone has helped to curb the worst excesses. But outside this zone, the Baghdad regime has continued a policy of persecution and intimidation.

9. The regime has used chemical weapons against the Kurds, most notably in an attack on the town of Halabja in 1988. The implicit threat of the use of chemical weapons against the Kurds and others is an important part of Saddam's attempt to keep the civilian population under control.

10. The regime has tried to displace the traditional Kurdish and Turkoman populations of the areas under its control, primarily in order to weaken Kurdish claims to the oil-rich area around the northern city of Kirkuk. Kurds and other non-

CAB/3/0069

Arabs are forcibly ejected to the three northern Iraqi governorates – Dohuk, Arbil and Sulaimaniyah – which are under de facto Kurdish control. According to the United Nations Commission on Human Rights (UNCHR) Special Rapporteur for Iraq, 94,000 individuals have been expelled since 1991. Agricultural land owned by Kurds has been confiscated and redistributed to Iraqi Arabs. Arabs from southern Iraq have been offered incentives to move into the Kirkuk area.

11. After the 1979 revolution that ousted the Shah in Iran, Saddam intensified a campaign against the Shia Muslim majority of Iraq, fearing that they might be encouraged by the new Shia regime in Iran.

12. In the wake of the Gulf War, riots broke out in the southern city of Basra on 1 March 1991, spreading quickly to other cities in Shia-dominated southern Iraq. The regime responded by killing thousands. Many Shia tried to escape to Iran and Saudi Arabia.

13. Some of the Shia hostile to the regime sought refuge in the marshland of southern Iraq. In order to subjugate the area, Saddam embarked on a large-scale programme to drain the marshes to allow Iraqi ground forces to eliminate all opposition there. The rural population of the area fled or were forced to move to southern cities or across the border into Iran.

CAB 13 0070

Saddam's Wars

14. As well as ensuring his absolute control inside Iraq, Saddam has tried to make Iraq the dominant power of the region. In pursuit of these objectives he has led Iraq into two wars of aggression against neighbours, the Iran-Iraq war and the invasion of Kuwait.

15. With the fall of the Shah in Iran in 1979, relations between Iran and Iraq deteriorated sharply. In September 1980 Saddam renounced a border treaty he had agreed with Iran in 1975 ceding half of the Shatt al-Arab waterway to Iran. Shortly thereafter, Saddam launched a large-scale invasion of Iran. He believed that he could take advantage of the state of weakness, isolation and disorganisation he perceived in post-revolutionary Iran. He aimed to seize territory, including that ceded to Iran a few years earlier, and to assert Iraq's position as a leader of the Arab world. Saddam expected it to be a short, sharp campaign. But the conflict lasted for eight years. Iraq fired over 500 ballistic missiles at Iranian targets, including major cities.

16. It is estimated that the Iran/Iraq war cost the two sides a million casualties. Iraq used chemical weapons extensively from 1984. Some twenty thousand Iranians were killed by mustard gas, and the nerve agents tabun and sarin, all of

> **Opposition to Saddam during the Iran/Iraq war**
> During the war Saddam's security apparatus ensured any internal dissent or opposition was quickly eliminated. In 1982 he quickly purged a group within Iraq's ruling clique which suggested that the war might be brought to an end more quickly if Saddam stood down.

which Iraq still possesses. The UN Security Council considered the report prepared by a team of three specialists appointed by the UN Secretary General in March 1986, following which the President made a statement condemning Iraqi use of chemical weapons. This marked the first time a country had been named for violating the 1925 Geneva Convention banning the use of chemical weapons.

CAB 13 0071

17. The cost of the war ran into hundreds of billions of dollars for both sides. Iraq gained nothing. After the war ended, Saddam resumed his previous pursuit of primacy in the Gulf. His policies involved spending huge sums of money on new military equipment. But Iraq was burdened by debt incurred during the war and the price of oil, Iraq's only major export, was low.

18. By 1990 Iraq's financial problems were severe. Saddam looked at ways to press the oil-producing states of the Gulf to force up the price of crude oil by limiting production and waive the $40 billion that they had loaned Iraq during its war with Iran. Kuwait had made some concessions over production ceilings. But Saddam blamed Kuwait for over production. When his threats and blandishments failed, Iraq invaded Kuwait on 2 August 1990. He believed that occupying Kuwait could prove profitable.

19. Saddam also sought to justify the conquest of Kuwait on other grounds. Like other Iraqi leaders before him, he claimed that, as Kuwait's rulers had come under the jurisdiction of the governors of Basra in the time of the Ottoman Empire, Kuwait should belong to Iraq.

> **Abuses by Iraqi forces in Kuwait**
> - Robbery and rape of Kuwaitis and expatriates.
> - Summary executions.
> - People dragged from their homes and held in improvised detention centres.
> - Amnesty International has listed 38 methods of torture used by the Iraqi occupiers. These included beatings, breaking of limbs, extracting finger and toenails, inserting bottle necks into the rectum, and subjecting detainees to mock executions.
> - Kuwaiti civilians arrested for "crimes" such as wearing beards.

20. During its occupation of Kuwait, Iraq denied access to the Red Cross, which has a mandate to provide protection and assistance to civilians affected by international armed conflict. The death penalty was imposed for relatively minor "crimes" such as looting and hoarding food.

CAB|3|0072

21. In an attempt to deter military action to expel it from Kuwait, the Iraqi regime took hostage several hundred foreign nationals (including children) in Iraq and Kuwait, and prevented thousands more from leaving, in direct contravention of international humanitarian law. Hostages were held as human shields at a number of strategic military and civilian sites.

22. At the end of the Gulf War, the Iraqi army fleeing Kuwait set fire to over 1,160 Kuwaiti oil wells, with serious environmental consequences.

23. More than 600 Kuwaiti and other prisoners of war and missing persons are still unaccounted for. Iraq refuses to comply with its UN obligation to account for the missing. It has provided sufficient information to close only three case-files.

CAB 13/0073

Human rights

24. Human rights abuses continue within Iraq. People continue to be arrested and detained on suspicion of political or religious activities, or often because they are related to members of the opposition. Executions are carried out without due process of law. Relatives are often prevented from burying the victims in accordance with Islamic practice. Thousands of prisoners have been executed.

Human rights: abuses under Saddam

- 4000 prisoners were executed at Abu Ghraib Prison in 1984.
- 3000 prisoners were executed at the Mahjar Prison between 1993 and 1998.
- About 2500 prisoners were executed between 1997 and 1999 in a "prison cleansing" campaign.

- 122 male prisoners were executed at Abu Ghraib prison in February/ March 2000. A further 23 political prisoners were executed there in October 2001.
- Prisoners have been executed by machine gun.

- In October 2000, dozens of women accused of prostitution were beheaded without any judicial process. Some were accused for political reasons.
- Women prisoners at Mahjar are routinely raped by their guards.

- Methods of torture used in Iraqi jails include using electric drills to mutilate hands, pulling out fingernails, knife cuts, sexual attacks and 'official rape'.
- Prisoners at the Qurtiyya Prison in Baghdad and elsewhere are kept in metal boxes the size of tea chests. If they do not confess they are left to die.

---

25. Saddam has issued a series of decrees establishing severe penalties for criminal offences. These include amputation, branding, cutting off ears, and other forms of mutilation. Anyone found guilty of slandering the President has their tongue removed.

CAB 13/007

Human Rights – mistreatment in Abu Ghraib Prison

Abdallah, a member of the Ba'ath Party whose loyalty became suspect was imprisoned for four years at Abu Ghraib in the 1980s. On the second day of his imprisonment, the men were forced to walk between two rows of five guards each to receive their containers of food. While walking to get the food, they were beaten by the guards with plastic telephone cables. They had to return to their cells the same way, so that a walk to get breakfast resulted in twenty lashes. According to Abdallah, "It wasn't that bad going to get the food, but coming back the food was spilled when we were beaten." The same procedure was used when the men went to the bathroom. On the third day, the torture continued. "We were removed from our cells and beaten with plastic pipes. This surprised us, because we were asked no question. Possibly it was being done to break our morale", Abdallah speculated. The torture escalated to sixteen sessions daily. The treatment was organised and systematic. Abdallah was held alone in a 3x2-meter room that opened onto a corridor. "We were allowed to go to the toilet three times a day, then they reduced the toilet to once a day for only one minute. I went for four years without a shower or a wash", Abdallah said. He also learned to cope with the deprivation and the hunger that accompanied his detention: "I taught myself to drink a minimum amount of water because there was no placed to urinate. They used wooden sticks to beat us and sometimes the sticks would break. I found a piece of a stick, covered with blood, and managed to bring it back to my room. I ate it for three days. A person who is hungry can eat anything. Pieces of our bodies started falling off from the beatings and our skin was so dry that it began to fall off. I ate pieces of my own body. "No one, not Pushkin, not Mahfouz, can describe what happened to us. It is impossible to describe what living this day to day was like. I was totally naked the entire time. Half of the original groups [of about thirty men] died. It was a slow type of continuous physical and psychological torture. Sometimes, it seemed that orders came to kill one of us, and he would be beaten to death".

Saddam's family

26. Saddam's son Udayy maintained a private torture chamber known as the Red Room in a building on the banks of the Tigris disguised as an electricity installation. He ordered the Iraq football team to be caned on the soles of the feet for losing a World Cup match. He created a militia in 1994 which has used swords to execute victims outside their own homes. He has personally executed dissidents, for instance in the Shia uprising at Basra which followed the Gulf War.

CAB 13/0075

27. Members of Saddam's family are also subject to persecution. A cousin of Saddam called Ala Abd Al-Qadir Al-Majid fled to Jordan from Iraq, citing disagreements with the regime over business matters. He returned to Iraq after the Iraqi Ambassador in Jordan declared publicly that his life was not in danger. He was met at the border by Tahir Habbush, Head of the Iraqi Intelligence Service (the

---

Human Rights - individual testimony

In December 1996, a Kurdish businessman from Baghdad was arrested outside his house by plainclothes security men. Initially his family did not know his whereabouts and went from one police station to another inquiring about him. Then they found out that he was being held in the headquarters of the General Security Directorate in Baghdad. The family was not allowed to visit him. Eleven months later the family was told by the authorities that he had been executed and that they should go and collect his body. His body bore evident signs of torture. His eyes were gouged out and the empty eye sockets filled with paper. His right wrist and left leg were broken. The family was not given any reason for his arrest and subsequent execution. However, they suspected that he was executed because of his friendship with a retired army general who had links with the Iraqi opposition outside the country and who was arrested just before his arrest and also executed.

---

28. Mukhabarat), and taken to a farm owned by 'Ali Hasan Al-Majid. At the farm 'Ala was tied to a tree and executed by members of his immediate family who, following orders from Saddam, took it in turns to shoot him.

CAB/3/0071

> **Human Rights - individual testimony**
>
> "...I saw a friend of mine, al-Shaikh Nasser Taresh al-Sa'idi, naked. He was handcuffed and a piece of wood was placed between his elbows and his knees. Two ends of the wood were placed on two high chairs and al-Shaikh Nasser was being suspended like a chicken. This method of torture is known as *al-Khaygania* (a reference to a former security director known as al-Khaygani). An electric wire was attached to al-Shaikh Nasser's penis and another one attached to one of his toes. He was asked if he could identify me and he said "this is al-Shaikh Yahya". They took me to another room and then after about 10 minutes they stripped me of my clothes and a security officer said "the person you saw has confessed against you". He said to me "You followers of [Ayatollah] al-Sadr have carried out acts harmful to the security of the country and have been distributing anti-government statements coming from abroad". He asked if I have any contact with an Iraqi religious scholar based in Iran who has been signing these statements. I said "I do not have any contacts with him"... I was then left suspended in the same manner as al-Shaikh al-Sa'idi. My face was looking upward. They attached an electric wire on my penis and the other end of the wire is attached to an electric motor. One security man was hitting my feet with a cable. Electric shocks were applied every few minutes and were increased. I must have been suspended for more than an hour. I lost consciousness. They took me to another room and made me walk even though my feet were swollen from beating... They repeated this method a few times." (testimony to Amnesty International from an Iraqi theology student from Saddam City)

29. Some 40 of Saddam's relatives, including women and children, have been killed. His sons-in-law Hussein Kamel and Saddam had defected in 1995 and returned to Iraq from Jordan after the government had announced amnesties for them. They were executed in February 1996.

CAB 13 0077

CONCLUSION

1.   Four themes dominate even the most sober account of Saddam Hussein's rule in Iraq:

- Brutality as exercised against his own people;
- Aggression against neighbouring states;
- Cynicism in dealing with the Iraqi people, regional states and the International Community; and,
- Single minded pursuit of military power and above all weapons of mass destruction as the most effective means of exercising that power.

2.   This paper has set out our assessment of Saddam's current holding of chemical, biological and nuclear weapons and ballistic missile systems as well as his programmes for their development. Although our knowledge is partial, the paper concludes that he possesses mass destruction weapons and the means to produce them and to deliver them. His development programmes continue. An analysis of what he will do with these weapons now and in the future, must rest upon his record and our current information, including intelligence. It is reasonable to conclude that he will use whatever weaponry he has to hand to protect his power and eventually to project it when he feels strong enough to do so.

CAB|3|0078

ALASTAIR CAMPBELL

cc   Jonathan Powell
David Manning
David Omand
JIC Members

IRAQI WMD: PUBLIC PRESENTATION OF INTELLIGENCE MATERIAL

1.   I attach the final draft version of the dossier, taking account of additional comments from you and others received over the last 24 hours. The Prime Minister's Foreword is now incorporated within the overall document. The conclusion has been dropped.

2.   I am content that the text now reflects as fully and accurately as possible the intelligence picture on Saddam's mass destruction weapons.

JOHN SCARLETT

20 September 2002

IRAQ'S
WEAPONS OF MASS DESTRUCTION:

THE ASSESSMENT OF THE BRITISH
GOVERNMENT

CAB/33/0057

CONTENTS

CAB/33/0058

586

FOREWORD BY THE PRIME MINISTER, THE RIGHT HONOURABLE TONY BLAIR, MP

The document published today is based, in large part, on the work of the Joint Intelligence Committee (JIC). The JIC is at the heart of the British intelligence machinery. It is chaired by the Cabinet Office and made up of the heads of the UK's three Intelligence and Security Agencies, the Chief of Defence Intelligence, and senior officials from key government departments. For over 60 years the JIC has provided regular assessments to successive Prime Ministers and senior colleagues on a wide range of foreign policy and international security issues.

Its work, like the material it analyses, is largely secret. It is unprecedented for the Government to publish this kind of document. But in light of the debate about Iraq and Weapons of Mass Destruction (WMD), I wanted to share with the British public the reasons why I believe this issue to be a current and serious threat to the UK national interest.

In recent months, I have been increasingly alarmed by the evidence from inside Iraq that despite sanctions, despite the damage done to his capability in the past, despite the UNSCRs expressly outlawing it, and despite his denials, Saddam Hussein is continuing to develop WMD, and with them the ability to inflict real damage upon the region, and the stability of the world.

Gathering intelligence inside Iraq is not easy. Saddam's is one of the most secretive and dictatorial regimes in the world. So I believe people will understand why the Agencies cannot be specific about the sources, which have formed the judgements in this document, and why we cannot publish everything we know. We cannot of course publish the detailed raw intelligence. I and other Ministers have been briefed in detail on the intelligence and are satisfied as to its authority. I also want to pay tribute to our Intelligence and Security Services for the often extraordinary work that they do.

CAB/33/0059

What I believe the assessed intelligence has established beyond doubt is that Saddam has continued to produce chemical and biological weapons, that he continues in his efforts to develop nuclear weapons, and that he has been able to extend the range of his ballistic missile programme. I also believe that, as stated in the document, Saddam will now do his utmost to try to conceal his weapons from UN inspectors.

The picture presented by JIC papers in recent months has become more not less worrying. It is clear that despite sanctions, the policy of containment has not worked sufficiently well to prevent Saddam from developing these weapons.

I am in no doubt that the threat is serious, and current; that he has made progress on WMD, and that he has to be stopped.

Saddam has used chemical weapons, not only against an enemy state, but against his own people. Intelligence reports make clear that he sees the building up of his WMD capability, and the belief overseas that he would use these weapons, as vital to his strategic interests, and in particular his goal of regional domination. And the document discloses that his military planning allows for some of the WMD to be ready within 45 minutes of an order to use them.

I am quite clear that Saddam will go to extreme lengths, indeed has already done so, to hide these weapons and avoid giving them up.

In today's inter-dependent world, a major regional conflict does not stay confined to the region in question. Faced with someone who has shown himself capable of using WMD, I believe the international community has to stand up for itself and ensure its authority is upheld.

The threat posed to international peace and security, when WMD are in the hands of a brutal and aggressive regime like Saddam's, is real. Unless we face up to the threat, not only do we risk undermining the authority of the UN, whose resolutions he defies, but more important and in the longer term, we place at risk the lives and prosperity of our own people.

The case I make is that the UN resolutions demanding he stops his WMD programme are being flouted; that since the inspectors left four years ago, he has continued with this programme; that the inspectors must be allowed back in to do their job properly; and that if he refuses, or if he makes it impossible for them to do their job, as he has done in the past, the international community will have to act.

I believe that faced with the information available to me, the UK Government has been right to support the demands that this issue be confronted and dealt with. We must ensure that he does not get to use the weapons he has, or get hold of the weapons he wants.

589

EXECUTIVE SUMMARY

1. Under Saddam Hussein, Iraq developed chemical and biological weapons, acquired missiles allowing it to attack neighbouring countries with these weapons, and persistently tried to develop a nuclear bomb. Saddam has used chemical weapons, both against Iran and against his own people. Following the Gulf War, Iraq had to admit to all this. And in the ceasefire of 1991 Saddam agreed unconditionally to give up his weapons of mass destruction.

2. Much information about Iraq's mass destruction weaponry is already in the public domain from UN reports and from Iraqi defectors. This points clearly to Iraq's continuing possession, after 1991, of chemical and biological agents and weapons produced before the Gulf War. It shows that Iraq has refurbished sites formerly associated with the production of chemical and biological agents. And it indicates that Iraq remains able to manufacture these agents, and to use bombs, shells, artillery rockets and ballistic missiles to deliver them.

3. An independent and well researched overview of this public evidence was provided by the International Institute for Strategic Studies (IISS) on 9 September. The IISS report also suggested that Iraq could assemble nuclear weapons within months of obtaining fissile material from foreign sources.

4. As well as the public evidence, however, significant additional information is available to the government from secret intelligence sources, described in more detail in this paper. This intelligence cannot tell us about everything. However, it provides a fuller picture of Iraqi plans and capabilities. It shows that Saddam Hussein attaches great importance to possessing weapons of mass destruction which he regards as the basis for Iraq's regional power. It shows that he does not regard them only as weapons of last resort. He is ready to use them, including against his own population, and is determined to retain them, in breach of United Nations Security Council Resolutions.

590

5. Intelligence also shows that Iraq is preparing plans to conceal evidence of these weapons, including incriminating documents, from renewed inspections. And it confirms that despite sanctions and the policy of containment, Saddam has continued to make progress with his illicit weapons programmes.

6. As a result of the intelligence we judge that Iraq has:

- continued to produce chemical and biological agents;

- military plans for the use of chemical and biological weapons, including against its own Shia population. Some of these weapons are deployable within 45 minutes of an order to use them;

- command and control arrangements in place to use chemical and biological weapons. Authority ultimately resides with Saddam Hussein. (There is intelligence that he may have delegated this authority to his son Qusai);

- developed mobile laboratories for military use, corroborating earlier reports about the mobile production of biological warfare agents;

- pursued illegal programmes to procure controlled materials of potential use in the production of chemical and biological weapons programmes;

- tried covertly to acquire technology and materials which could be used in the production of nuclear weapons;

- sought significant quantities of uranium from Africa, despite having no active civil nuclear power programme that could require it;

- recalled specialists to work on its nuclear programme;

- retained up to 20 Al Hussein missiles, with a range of 650km, capable of carrying chemical or biological warheads;

- started deploying its Al-Samoud liquid propellant missile, and has used the absence of weapons inspectors to work on extending its range to at least 200km, which is beyond the limit of 150km imposed by the United Nations;

- started producing the solid-propellant Ababil-100, and is making efforts to extend its range to at least 200km, which is beyond the limit of 150km imposed by the United Nations;

- constructed a new engine test stand for the development of missiles capable of reaching the UK Sovereign Base Areas in Cyprus and NATO members (Greece and Turkey), as well as all Iraq's Gulf neighbours and Israel;

- pursued illegal programmes to procure materials for use in its illegal development of long range missiles;

- learnt lessons from previous UN weapons inspections and has already begun to conceal sensitive equipment and documentation in advance of the return of inspectors.

7. These judgements reflect the views of the Joint Intelligence Committee (JIC). More details on the judgements, and on the development of the JIC's assessments since 1998, are set out in Part 1 of this paper.

8. Iraq's weapons of mass destruction are in breach of international law. Under a series of United Nations Security Council Resolutions Iraq is obliged to destroy its holdings of these weapons under the supervision of UN inspectors. Part 2 of the paper sets out the key UN Security Council Resolutions. It also summarises the history of the UN inspection regime and Iraq's history of deception, intimidation and concealment in its dealings with the UN inspectors.

9. But the threat from Iraq does not depend solely on the capabilities we have described. It arises also because of the violent and aggressive nature of Saddam Hussein's regime. His record of internal repression and external aggression gives rise to unique concerns about the threat he poses. The paper briefly outlines in Part 3 Saddam's rise to power, the nature of his regime and his history of regional aggression. Saddam's human rights abuses are also catalogued, including his record of torture, mass arrests and summary executions.

CAR12310064

10. The paper briefly sets out how Iraq is able to finance its weapons programme. Drawing on illicit earnings generated outside UN control, Iraq generated illegal income of some $3 billion in 2001.

PART 1

IRAQ'S CHEMICAL, BIOLOGICAL, NUCLEAR AND BALLISTIC MISSILE PROGRAMMES

CHAPTER 1: THE ROLE OF INTELLIGENCE

1. Since UN Inspectors were withdrawn from Iraq in 1998, there has been little overt information on Iraq's chemical, biological, nuclear and ballistic missile programmes. Much of the publicly available information about Iraqi capabilities and intentions is dated. But we also have available a range of secret intelligence about these programmes and Saddam Hussein's intentions. This comes principally from the United Kingdom's intelligence and analysis agencies – the Secret Intelligence Service (SIS), the Government Communications Headquarters (GCHQ), the Security Service, and the Defence Intelligence Staff (DIS). We also have access to intelligence from close allies.

2. Intelligence rarely offers a complete account of activities which are designed to remain concealed. The nature of Saddam's regime makes Iraq a difficult target for the intelligence services. Intelligence, however, has provided important insights into Iraqi programmes, and Iraqi military thinking. Taken together with what is already known from other sources, this intelligence builds our understanding of Iraq's capabilities, and adds significantly to the analysis already in the public domain. But intelligence sources need to be protected, and this limits the detail that can be made available.

3. Iraq's capabilities have been regularly reviewed by the Joint Intelligence Committee (JIC), which has provided advice to the Prime Minister and his senior colleagues on the developing assessment, drawing on all available sources. Part 1 of this paper includes some of the most significant views reached by the JIC between 1999 and 2002.

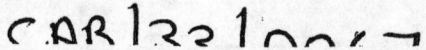

CHAPTER 2: IRAQ'S PROGRAMMES: 1971-1998

1. Iraq has been involved in chemical and biological warfare research for over 30 years. Its **chemical warfare** research started in 1971 at a small, well guarded site at Rashad to the Northeast of Baghdad. Research was conducted there on a number of chemical agents including mustard gas, CS and tabun. Later, in 1974 a dedicated organisation called Al-Hassan Ibn Al-Haitham was established. In the late 1970s

---

Effects of Chemical Weapons

Mustard is a liquid agent, which gives off a hazardous vapour, causing burns and blisters to exposed skin. When inhaled, mustard damages the respiratory tract; when ingested, it causes vomiting and diarrhoea. It attacks and damages the eyes, mucous membranes, lungs, skin, and blood-forming organs.

Tabun, sarin and VX are all nerve agents of which VX is the most toxic. They all damage the nervous system, producing muscular spasms and paralysis. As little as 10 milligrammes of VX on the skin can cause rapid death.

---

plans were made to build a large research and commercial-scale production facility in the desert some 70km Northwest of Baghdad under the Project cover of No 922. This was to become Muthanna State Establishment, also known as al-Muthanna, and operated under the front name of Iraq's State Establishment for Pesticide Production. It became operational in 1982-83. It had five research and development sections each tasked to pursue different programmes. In addition, the al-Muthanna site was the main chemical agent production facility, and it also took the lead in weaponising chemical and biological agents including all aspects of weapon development and testing, in association with the military. According to information, subsequently supplied by the Iraqis, the total production capacity in 1991 was 4,000 tonnes of agent per annum, but we assess it could have been higher. Al-Muthanna was supported by three separate storage and precursor production facilities known as Fallujah 1, 2 and 3 near Habbaniyah, north-west of Baghdad, parts of which were not completed before they were heavily bombed in the 1991 Gulf War.

2. Iraq started **biological warfare** research in the mid-1970s. After small-scale research, a purpose-built research and development facility was authorised at al-Salman, also known as Salman Pak. This is surrounded on three sides by the Tigris

---

The effects of biological agents

Anthrax is a disease caused by the bacterium Bacillus anthracis. Inhalation anthrax is the manifestation of the disease likely to be expected in biological warfare. The symptoms may vary, but can include fever and internal bleeding. The incubation period for anthrax is 1 to 7 days, with most cases occurring within 2 days of exposure.

Botulinum toxin is one of the most toxic substances known to man. The first symptoms of poisoning may appear as early as 1 hour post exposure or as long as 8 days after exposure, with the incubation period between 12 and 22 hours. Paralysis leads to death by suffocation.

Aflatoxins are fungal toxins, which are potent carcinogens. Most symptoms take a long time to show. Food products contaminated by aflatoxin can cause liver inflammation and cancer. It can also affect pregnant women, leading to stillborn babies and children born with mutations.

Ricin is derived from the castor bean and can cause multiple organ failure leading to death within one or two days of inhalation.

---

river and situated some 35km South of Baghdad. Although some progress was made in biological weapons research at this early stage, Iraq decided to concentrate on developing chemical agents and their delivery systems at al-Muthanna. With the outbreak of the Iran-Iraq War, in the early 1980s, the biological weapons programme was revived. The appointment of Dr Rihab Taha in 1985, to head a small biological weapons research team at al-Muthanna, helped to develop the programme. At about the same time plans were made to develop the Salman Pak site into a secure biological warfare research facility. Dr Taha continued to work with her team at al-Muthanna until 1987 when it moved to Salman Pak, which was under the control of the Directorate of General Intelligence. Significant resources were provided for the programme, including the construction of a dedicated production facility (Project 324) at al-Hakam. Agent production began in 1988 and weaponisation testing and later filling of munitions was conducted in association with the staff at Muthanna State Establishment. From mid-1990, other civilian facilities were taken over and some adapted for use in the production and research and development of biological agents. These included:

- al-Dawrah Foot and Mouth Vaccine Institute which produced botulinum toxin and conducted virus research. There is some intelligence to suggest that work was also conducted on anthrax;

- al-Fudaliyah Agriculture and Water Research centre where Iraq admitted it undertook aflatoxin production and genetic engineering;

- Amariyah Sera and Vaccine Institute which was used for the storage of biological agent seed stocks, and was involved in genetic engineering;

3. By the time of the Gulf War Iraq was producing very large quantities of chemical and biological agents. From a series of Iraqi declarations to the UN during the 1990s we know that by 1991 they had produced at least:

- 19,000 litres of botulinum toxin, 8,500 litres of anthrax, 2,200 litres of aflatoxin, and were working on a number of other agents;

- 2,850 tonnes of mustard gas, 210 tonnes of tabun, 795 tonnes of sarin and cyclosarin, and 3.9 tonnes of VX.

4. Iraq's **nuclear programme** was established under the Iraqi Atomic Energy Commission in the 1950s. Under a nuclear co-operation agreement signed with the Soviet Union in 1959, a nuclear research centre, equipped with a research reactor, was built at Tuwaitha, the main Iraqi nuclear research centre. The research reactor worked up to 1991. The surge in Iraqi oil revenues in the early 1970s supported an expansion of the research programme. This was bolstered in the mid-1970s by the acquisition of two research reactors powered by highly enriched uranium fuel, and equipment for fuel fabrication and handling. By the end of 1984 Iraq was self-sufficient in uranium ore. One of the reactors was destroyed in an Israeli air attack in June 1981 shortly before it was to become operational, the other was never completed.

5. By the mid-1980s the deterioration of Iraq's position in the war with Iran prompted renewed interest in the military use of nuclear technology, and additional resources were put into developing technologies to enrich uranium as fissile material (material that makes up the core of a nuclear weapon) for use in nuclear weapons. Enriched uranium was preferred because it could be more easily produced covertly than the alternative, plutonium. Iraq followed parallel programmes to produce highly enriched uranium (HEU): electromagnetic isotope separation (EMIS) and gas centrifuge enrichment. By 1991 one EMIS enrichment facility was nearing completion and another was under construction. However, Iraq never succeeded in its EMIS technology, and the programme had been dropped by 1991. Iraq decided to concentrate on gas centrifuges as the means for producing the necessary fissile material. Centrifuge facilities were also under construction, but the centrifuge design was still being developed. In August 1990 Iraq instigated a crash programme to develop a single nuclear weapon within a year. This programme envisaged the rapid development of a small 50 machine gas centrifuge cascade to produce weapons-grade HEU using fuel from the Soviet research reactor, which was already substantially enriched, and unused fuel from the reactor bombed by the Israelis. By the time of the Gulf War, the crash programme had made little progress.

6. Iraq's declared aim was to produce a missile warhead with a 20-kiloton yield and weapons designs were produced for the simplest implosion weapons. These were similar to the device used at Nagasaki in 1945. Iraq was also working on more advanced concepts. By 1991 the programme was supported by a large body of Iraqi nuclear expertise, programme documentation and databases and manufacturing infrastructure. The International Atomic Energy Agency (IAEA) reported that Iraq had:

> **Effect of a 20-kiloton nuclear detonation**
> A detonation of a 20-kiloton nuclear warhead over a city might flatten an area of approximately 3 square miles. Within 1.6 miles of detonation, blast damage and radiation would cause 80% casualties, three-quarters of which would be fatal. Between 1.6 and 3.1 miles from the detonation, there would still be 10% casualties.

CAB 133 | 0071

- experimented with high explosives to produce implosive shock waves;
- invested significant effort to understand the various options for neutron initiators;
- made significant progress in developing capabilities for the production, casting and machining of uranium metal.

> **SCUD missiles**
> The short-range mobile SCUD ballistic missile was developed by the Soviet Union in the 1950s, drawing on the technology of the German V-2 developed in World War II.
>
> For many years it was the mainstay of Soviet and Warsaw Pact tactical missile forces, and it was also widely exported.
> Recipients of Soviet-manufactured SCUDs included Iraq, North Korea, Iran, and Libya, although not all were sold directly by the Soviet Union.

7. Prior to the Gulf War, Iraq had a well-developed **ballistic missile** industry. Many of the missiles fired in the Gulf War were an Iraqi modified version of the SCUD missile, the Al Hussein, with an extended range of 650km. Iraq had about 250 imported SCUD-type missiles prior to the Gulf War plus an unknown number of indigenously produced engines and components. Iraq was working on other stretched SCUD variants, such as the Al Abbas, which had a range of 900km. Iraq was also seeking to reverse engineer the SCUD engine with a view to producing new missiles; recent intelligence indicates that they may have succeeded at that time. In particular Iraq had plans for a new SCUD-derived missile with a range of 1200km. Iraq also conducted a partial flight test of a multi-stage satellite launch vehicle based on SCUD technology, known as the Al Abid. Also during this period, Iraq was developing the BADR-2000, a 700-1000km range two-stage solid propellant missile (based on the Iraqi part of the 1980s CONDOR-2 programme run in co-operation with Argentina and Egypt). There were plans for 1200-1500km range solid propellant follow-on systems.

The use of chemical and biological weapons

8. Iraq had made frequent use of a variety of chemical weapons during the Iran-Iraq War. (Many of the casualties are still in Iranian hospitals suffering from the long-term effects of numerous types of cancer and lung diseases.) In 1988 Saddam also

used mustard and nerve agents against Iraqi Kurds at Halabja in northern Iraq (see box). Estimates vary, but according to Human Rights Watch up to 5,000 people were killed.

9. Iraq used significant quantities of mustard, tabun and sarin during the war with Iran resulting in over 20,000 Iranian casualties. A month after the attack on Halabja, Iraqi troops used over 100 tonnes of sarin nerve agent against Iranian troops on the Al Fao peninsula. Over the next three months Iraqi troops used sarin and other nerve agents on Iranian troops causing extensive casualties.

The Attack on Halabja

On Friday, 17th March 1988, the village of Halabja was bombarded by Iraqi warplanes. The raid was over in minutes. Saddam Hussein used chemical weapons against his own people. A Kurd described the effects of a chemical attack on another village:

"My brothers and my wife had blood and vomit running from their noses and their mouths. Their heads were tilted to one side. They were groaning. I couldn't do much, just clean up the blood and vomit from their mouths and try in every way to make them breathe again. I did artificial respiration on them and then I gave them two injections each. I also rubbed creams on my wife and two brothers."

(From "Crimes Against Humanity," Iraqi National Congress.)

Among the corpses at Halabja, children were found dead where they had been playing outside their homes. In places, streets were piled with corpses.

10. From Iraqi declarations to the UN after the Gulf War we know that by 1991 Iraq had produced a variety of delivery means for chemical and biological agents including over 16,000 free fall bombs and over 110,000 artillery rockets and shells. Iraq also admitted to the UN Special Commission (UNSCOM) that it had 50 chemical and 25 biological warheads available for its ballistic missiles.

The use of ballistic missiles

11. Iraq fired over 500 SCUD-type missiles at Iran during the Iran-Iraq War at both civilian and military targets, and 93 SCUD-type missiles during the Gulf War. The latter were targeted at Israel and at Coalition forces stationed in the Gulf region.

12. At the end of the Gulf War the international community was determined that Iraq's arsenal of chemical and biological weapons and ballistic missiles should be dismantled. The method chosen to achieve this aim was the establishment of UNSCOM to carry out intrusive inspections within Iraq and to eliminate its chemical and biological weapons and ballistic missiles with a range over 150km. The IAEA was charged with the abolition of Iraq's nuclear weapons programme. Between 1991 and 1998 UNSCOM succeeded in identifying and destroying very large quantities of chemical weapons and ballistic missiles as well as associated production facilities. The IAEA also destroyed the infrastructure for Iraq's nuclear weapons programme and removed key nuclear materials. This was achieved despite a continuous and sophisticated programme of harassment, obstruction and deception and denial (see Part 2). Because of this by 1998 UNSCOM concluded that they were unable to fulfil their mandate. The inspectors were withdrawn in December 1998.

13. Based on the UNSCOM report to the UN Security Council in January 1999 and earlier UNSCOM reports, we assess that when the UN inspectors left Iraq they were unable to account for:

- up to 360 tonnes of bulk chemical warfare agent, including 1.5 tonnes of VX nerve agent;

- up to 3,000 tonnes of precursor chemicals, including approximately 300 tonnes which, in the Iraqi ▓▓ programme, were unique to the production of VX;

- growth media procured for biological agent production (enough to produce over three times the 8,500 litres of anthrax spores Iraq admits to having manufactured);

- over 30,000 special munitions for delivery of chemical and biological agents.

14. The departure of UNSCOM meant that the International Community was unable to establish the truth behind these large discrepancies and greatly diminished its ability to monitor and assess Iraq's continuing attempts to reconstitute its programmes.

CHAPTER 3: THE CURRENT POSITION: 1998-2002

1. This chapter sets out what we know of Saddam's chemical, biological, nuclear and ballistic missile programmes, drawing on all the available evidence. While it takes account of the results from UN inspections and other publicly available information, it also draws heavily on the latest intelligence about Iraqi efforts to develop their programmes and capabilities since 1998. The **main conclusions** are that:

*   Iraq has a useable chemical and biological weapons capability, in breach of UNSCR 687, which has included recent production of chemical and biological agents;

*   Saddam continues to attach great importance to the possession of weapons of mass destruction and ballistic missiles, which he regards as being the basis for Iraq's regional power. He is determined to retain these capabilities;

*   Iraq can deliver chemical and biological agents using an extensive range of artillery shells, free-fall bombs, sprayers and ballistic missiles;

*   Iraq continues to work on developing nuclear weapons, in breach of its obligations under the Non-Proliferation Treaty, and in breach of UNSCR 687. Uranium has been sought from Africa that has no civil nuclear application in Iraq;

*   Iraq possesses extended-range versions of the SCUD ballistic missile in breach of UNSCR 687, which are capable of reaching Cyprus, Eastern Turkey, Tehran and Israel. It is also developing longer range ballistic missiles;

*   Iraq's current military planning specifically envisages the use of chemical and biological weapons;

*   Iraq's military forces are able to use chemical and biological weapons, with command, control and logistical arrangements in place. The Iraqi military are able to deploy these weapons within forty five minutes of a decision to do so;

604

- Iraq has learnt lessons from previous UN weapons inspections and is already taking steps to conceal and disperse sensitive equipment and documentation in advance of the return of inspectors;

- Iraq's chemical, biological, nuclear and ballistic missiles programmes are well funded.

CHEMICAL AND BIOLOGICAL WEAPONS

JIC Assessment: 1999-2002

2. Since the withdrawal of the inspectors the Joint Intelligence Committee (JIC) has monitored idence, including from secret intelligence, of continuing work on Iraqi offensive chemical and biological warfare capabilities. In the first half of 2000 the JIC noted intelligence on Iraqi attempts to procure dual-use chemicals; and on the reconstruction of civil chemical production at sites formerly associated with the chemical warfare programme. Iraq had also been trying to procure dual-use materials and equipment which could be used for a biological warfare programme. Personnel known to have been connected to the biological warfare programme up to the Gulf War had been conducting research into pathogens. There was intelligence that Iraq was starting to produce biological warfare agents in mobile production facilities. Planning for the project had begun in 1995 under Dr Rihab Taha, known to have been a central player in the pre-Gulf War programme. The JIC concluded that Iraq had sufficient expertise, equipment and material to produce biological warfare agents within weeks using its legitimate biotechnology facilities.

3. In mid-2001 the JIC assessed that Iraq retained some chemical warfare agents, precursors, production equipment and weapons from before the Gulf War. These stocks would enable Iraq to produce significant quantities of mustard gas within weeks and of nerve agent within months. The JIC concluded that intelligence on Iraqi former chemical and biological warfare facilities, their limited reconstruction and civil production pointed to a continuing research and development programme. These chemical and biological capabilities represented the most immediate threat from Iraqi weapons of mass destruction. Since 1998 Iraqi development of mass destruction weaponry had been helped by the absence of inspectors and the increase in illegal border trade, which was providing hard currency.

4. In the last six months the JIC has confirmed its earlier judgements on Iraqi chemical and biological warfare capabilities and assessed that Iraq has the means to deliver chemical and biological weapons.

Recent Intelligence

5. Subsequently, intelligence has become available from reliable sources which complements and adds to previous intelligence and confirms the JIC assessment that Iraq has chemical and biological weapons. The intelligence also shows that the Iraqi leadership has been discussing a number of issues related to these weapons. This intelligence covers:

- **Confirmation that chemical and biological weapons play an important role in Iraqi military thinking.** Intelligence shows that Saddam attaches great importance to the possession of chemical and biological weapons, which he regards as being the basis for Iraqi regional power. He believes that respect for Iraq rests on its possession of these weapons and the missiles capable of delivering them. Intelligence indicates that Saddam is determined to retain this capability and recognises that Iraqi political weight would be diminished if Iraq's military power rested solely on its conventional military forces.

- **Iraqi attempts to retain its existing banned weapons systems:** Iraq is already taking steps to prevent UN weapons inspectors finding evidence of its chemical and biological weapons programme. Intelligence indicates that Saddam has learnt lessons from previous weapons inspections, has identified possible weak points in the inspections process and knows how to exploit them. Sensitive equipment and papers can easily be concealed, and in some cases this is already happening. The possession of mobile biological agent production facilities will also aid concealment efforts. Saddam is determined not to lose the capabilities that he has been able to develop further in the four years since inspectors left.

- **Saddam's willingness to use chemical and biological weapons:** intelligence indicates that as part of Iraq's military planning, Saddam is willing to use chemical and biological weapons, including against an internal uprising by the Shia population. Intelligence

CAB/33/0077

indicates that the Iraqi military are able to deploy chemical or biological weapons within forty five minutes of an order to do so.

Chemical and biological agents: surviving stocks

6. When confronted with questions about the unaccounted stocks, Iraq has claimed, repeatedly, that if it had retained any chemical agents from before the Gulf War they would have deteriorated sufficiently to render them harmless. But Iraq has admitted to UNSCOM having the knowledge and capability to add stabiliser to nerve agent and other chemical warfare agents which would prevent such decomposition. In 1997 UNSCOM also examined some munitions which had been filled with mustard gas prior to 1991 and found that they remained ry toxic and showed little sign of deterioration.

7. Iraq has claimed that all its biological agents and weapons have been destroyed. No convincing proof of any kind has been produced to support this claim. In particular, Iraq could not explain large discrepancies between the amount of growth media (nutrients required for the specialised growth of agent) it procured before 1991 and the amounts of agent it admits to having manufactured. The discrepancy is enough to produce more than three times the amount of anthrax allegedly manufactured.

Chemical agent: production capabilities

8. Intelligence shows that Iraq has continued to produce chemical agent. During the Gulf War number of facilities which intelligence reporting indicated were directly or indirectly associated with Iraq's chemical weapons effort were attacked and damaged. Following the ceasefire UNSCOM destroyed or rendered harmless facilities and equipment used in Iraq's chemical weapons programme. Other equipment was released for civilian use either in industry or academic institutes, where it was tagged and regularly inspected and monitored, or else placed under camera monitoring, to ensure that it was not being misused. This monitoring ceased when UNSCOM withdrew from Iraq in 1998. However, capabilities remain and, although the main chemical weapon production facility at al-Muthanna was completely destroyed by UNSCOM and has not been rebuilt, other plants formerly associated with the chemical warfare programme have been rebuilt. This includes the chlorine and phenol plant at

CAB/33/0078

Fallujah 2 near Habbaniyah. In addition to their civilian uses, chlorine and phenol are used for precursor chemicals which contribute to the production of chemical agents.

9. Other dual use facilities, which are capable of being used to support the production of chemical agent and precursors, have been rebuilt and re-equipped. New chemical facilities have been built, some with illegal foreign assistance, and are probably fully operational or ready for production. These include the Ibn Sina Company at Tarmiyah (see figure 1), which is a chemical research centre. It undertakes research, development and production of chemicals previously imported but not now available and which are needed for Iraq's civil industry. The Director General of the research centre is Hickmat Na'im al-Jalu who, prior to the Gulf War, worked in Iraq's nuclear weapons programme and after the war was responsible for preserving Iraq's chemical expertise.

FIGURE 1: THE IBN SINA COMPANY AT TARMIYAH

10. Parts of the al-Qa'Qaa chemical complex damaged in the Gulf War have also been repaired and are operational. Of particular concern are elements of the phosgene production plant at Al Qa'Qaa. These were severely damaged during the Gulf War, and dismantled under UNSCOM supervision, but have since been rebuilt. While phosgene does have industrial uses it can also be used by itself as a chemical agent or as a precursor for nerve agents.

11. Iraq has retained the expertise for chemical warfare research, agent production and weaponisation. Most of the personnel previously involved in the programme remain in country. While UNSCOM found a number of technical manuals (so called "cook books") for the production of chemical agents and critical precursors, Iraq's claim to have unilaterally destroyed the bulk of the documentation cannot be confirmed and is almost certainly untrue. Recent intelligence indicates that Iraq is still discussing methods of concealing such documentation in order to ensure that it is not discovered by any future UN inspections.

The Problem of Dual Use Facilities

Almost all components and supplies used in weapons of mass destruction and ballistic missile programmes are dual-use. For example, any major petrochemical or biotech industry, as well as public health organisations, will have legitimate need for most materials and equipment required to manufacture chemical and biological weapons. Without UN weapons inspectors it is very difficult therefore to be sure about the true nature of many of Iraq's facilities.

For example, Iraq has built a large new chemical complex, Project Baiji, in the desert in north west Iraq at Ash Sharqat (see figure 2). This site is a former uranium enrichment facility, which was damaged during the Gulf War, and rendered harmless under supervision of the IAEA. Part of the site has been rebuilt, with work starting in 1992, as a chemical production complex. Despite the site being far away from populated areas it is surrounded by a high wall with watch towers and guarded by armed guards. Intelligence reports indicate that it will produce nitric acid, which can be used in explosives, missile fuel, and in the purification of uranium.

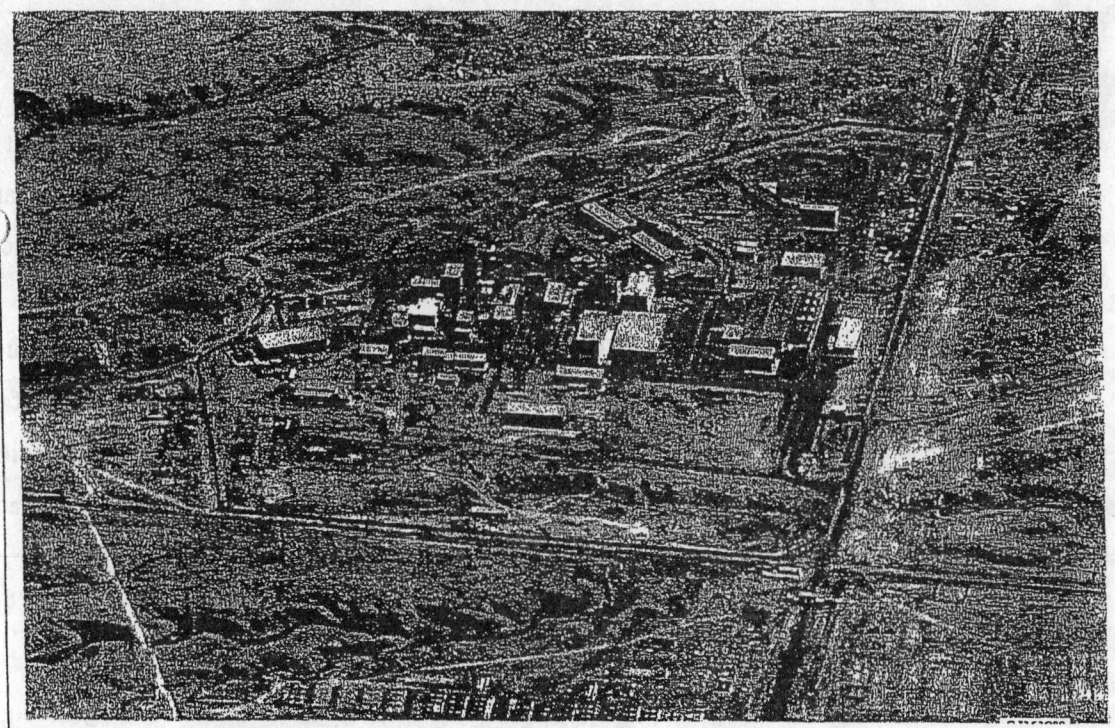

FIGURE 2: ASH SHARQAT CHEMICAL PRODUCTION FACILITY

609

Biological agent: production capabilities

12. We know from intelligence that Iraq has continued to produce biological warfare agents. As with some chemical equipment, UNSCOM only destroyed equipment that could be directly linked to biological weapons production. Iraq also has its own engineering capability to design and construct biological agent associated fermenters, centrifuges, sprayer dryers and other equipment and is judged to be self-sufficient in the technology required to produce biological weapons. The experienced personnel who were active in the programme have largely remained in the country. Some dual-use equipment has also been purchased, but without monitoring by UN inspectors Iraq could have diverted it to their biological weapons programme. This newly purchased equipment and others previously subject to monitoring could be used in a resurgent N programme. Facilities of concern include:

- The Castor Oil Production Plant at Fallujah: this was damaged in UK/US air attacks in 1998 (Operation Desert Fox) but has been rebuilt. The residue from the castor bean pulp can be used in the production of the biological agent ricin;

- the Al-Dawrah Foot and Mouth Disease Vaccine Institute, which was involved in biological agent production and research before the Gulf War;

- The Amariyah Sera and Vaccine plant at Abu Ghraib. UNSCOM established that this facility was used to store biological agents, seed stocks and conduct biological warfare associated genetic research prior to the Gulf War. It has now expanded its storage capacity.

13. UNSCOM established that Iraq considered the use of mobile biological agent production facilities. In the past two years evidence from defectors has indicated the existence of such facilities. Recent intelligence confirms that the Iraqi military have developed mobile facilities. These would help Iraq conceal and protect biological agent production from military attack or UN inspection.

Chemical and biological agents: delivery means

14. Iraq has a variety of delivery means available for both chemical and biological agents. These include:

CAB/33/0081

- free fall bombs - Iraq acknowledged to UNSCOM the deployment to two sites of free fall bombs filled with biological agent during 1990-91. These bombs were filled with anthrax, botulinum toxin and aflatoxin. Iraq also acknowledged possession of four types of aerial bomb with various chemical agent fills including sulphur mustard, tabun, sarin and cyclosarin;

- artillery shells and rockets - Iraq made extensive use of artillery munitions filled with chemical agents during the Iran-Iraq War. Mortars can also be used for chemical agent delivery. Iraq is known to have tested the use of shells and rockets filled with biological agents. Over 20,000 artillery munitions remain unaccounted for by UNSCOM;

- helicopter and aircraft borne sprayers - Iraq carried out studies into aerosol dissemination of biological agent using these platforms prior to 1991. UNSCOM was unable to account for many of these devices. It is probable that Iraq retains a capability for aerosol dispersal of both chemical and biological agent over a large area;

- Al Hussein ballistic missiles (range 650km) - Iraq told UNSCOM that it filled 25 warheads with anthrax, botulinum toxin and aflatoxin. Iraq also developed chemical agent warheads for Al Hussein. Iraq admitted to producing 50 chemical warheads for Al Hussein which were intended for the delivery of a mixture of sarin and cyclosarin. However, technical analysis of warhead remnants has shown traces of VX degradation product which indicate that some additional warheads were made and filled with VX;

- Al Samoud/Ababil-100 ballistic missiles (range 150km plus) - It is unclear if chemical and biological warheads have been developed for these systems, but given their experience on other missile systems, we judge that Iraq has the technical expertise for doing so;

FIGURE 3: THE L-29 JET TRAINER

- L-29 remotely piloted vehicle programme (see figure 3) - we know from intelligence that Iraq has

CAB/33/0082

611

attempted to modify the L-29 jet trainer to allow it to be used as a pilot-less aircraft (unmanned aerial vehicle - UAV), which is potentially capable of delivering chemical and biological agents over a large area.

Chemical and biological warfare: command and control

15. The authority to use chemical and biological weapons ultimately resides with Saddam, but intelligence indicates that he may have also delegated this authority to his son Qusai. Special Security Organisation (SSO) and Special Republican Guard (SRG) units would be involved in the movement of any chemical and biological weapons to military units. The Iraqi military holds artillery and missile systems at Corps level throughout the Armed Forces and conducts)gular training with them. The Directorate of Rocket Forces has operational control of strategic missile systems and some Multiple Rocket Launcher Systems.

Chemical and biological weapons: summary

16. Intelligence shows that Iraq has covert chemical and biological weapons programmes, in breach of UN Security Council Resolution 687 and has continued to produce chemical and biological agents. Iraq has:

- chemical and biological agents and weapons available, both from pre-Gulf War stocks and more recent production;

) the capability to produce the chemical agents mustard gas, tabun, sarin, cyclosarin, and VX capable of producing mass casualties;

- a biological agent production capability and can produce at least anthrax, botulinum toxin, aflatoxin and ricin. Iraq has also developed mobile facilities to produce biological agents/

- a variety of delivery means available;

- military forces, which maintain the capability to use these weapons, with command, control and logistical arrangements in place.

CAB133/0083

NUCLEAR WEAPONS

JIC Assessments: 1999-2001

17. Since 1999 the JIC has monitored Iraq's attempts to reconstitute its nuclear weapons programme. In mid-2001 the JIC assessed that Iraq had continued its nuclear research after 1998. The JIC drew attention to intelligence that Iraq had recalled its nuclear scientists to the programme in 1998. Since 1998 Iraq had been trying to procure items that could be for use in the construction of centrifuges for the enrichment of uranium.

Iraqi Nuclear Weapons Expertise

18. Paragraphs 5 and 6 of Chapter 2 describe the Iraqi nuclear weapons programme prior to the Gulf War. It is clear from IAEA inspections and Iraq's own declarations that by 1991 considerable progress had been made in both developing methods to produce fissile material and in weapons design. The IAEA dismantled the physical infrastructure of the Iraqi nuclear

Elements of a nuclear weapons programme

A typical nuclear fission weapon consists of:

- fissile material for the core, which gives out huge amounts of explosive energy from nuclear reactions when made "super critical", through extreme compression. Fissile material is usually either highly enriched uranium (HEU) or weapons-grade plutonium.
  - HEU can be made in gas centrifuges (see separate box).
- plutonium is made by reprocessing fuel from a nuclear reactor.
- explosives are needed to compress the nuclear core. They also require:
  - a complex arrangement of detonators, explosive charges to produce an even and rapid compression of the core.
  - sophisticated electronics to fire the explosives.
  - a neutron initiator to provide initial burst of neutrons to start the nuclear reactions.

Weaponisation is the conversion of these concepts into a reliable weapon. It includes:
- developing a weapon design through sophisticated science and complex calculations;
- engineering design to integrate with the delivery system;
- specialised equipment to cast and machine safely the nuclear core.
- dedicated facilities to assemble the warheads.
- facilities to rigorously test all individual components and designs.

The complexity is much greater for a weapon that can fit into a missile warhead than for a larger Nagasaki-type bomb.

---

weapons programme, including the dedicated facilities and equipment for uranium separation and enrichment, and for weapon development and production, and removed the remaining highly enriched uranium. But Iraq retained, and retains, many of its experienced nuclear scientists and technicians, who are specialised in the production of fissile material and weapons

CAB133 0084

613

design. Intelligence indicates that Iraq also retains the accompanying programme documentation and data.

Gas Centrifuge Uranium Enrichment
Uranium in the form of uranium hexafluoride is separated into its different isotopes in rapidly spinning rotor tubes of special centrifuges. Many hundreds or thousands of centrifuges are connected in cascades to enrich uranium. If the lighter U235 isotope is enriched to more than 90% it can be used in the core of a nuclear weapon.

19. Intelligence shows that the present Iraqi programme is almost certainly seeking an indigenous ability to enrich uranium to the level needed for a nuclear weapon. It indicates that the approach is based on gas centrifuge uranium enrichment, one of the routes Iraq was following for producing fissile material before the Gulf War. But Iraq needs certain key equipment, including gas centrifuge components, and components for the production of fissile material before a nuclear bomb could be developed.

20. Following the departure of weapons inspectors in 1998 there has been an accumulation of intelligence indicating that Iraq is making concerted covert efforts to acquire dual-use technology and materials with nuclear applications. Iraq's known holdings of processed uranium are under IAEA supervision. But there is intelligence that Iraq has sought the supply of significant quantities of uranium from Africa. Iraq has no active civil nuclear power programme or nuclear power plants, and therefore has no legitimate reason to acquire uranium.

Iraq's civil nuclear programme
- Iraq's long-standing civil nuclear power programme is limited to small scale research. Activities that could be used for military purposes are prohibited by UNSCR 687 and 715.
- Iraq has no nuclear power plants and therefore no requirement for uranium as fuel.
- Iraq has a number of nuclear research programmes in the fields of agriculture, biology, chemistry, materials and pharmaceuticals. None of these activities require more than tiny amounts of uranium which Iraq could supply from its own resources.
- Iraq's research reactors are non-operational - one was bombed by the Israelis, one was never completed, and the other's fuel has been removed.

21. Other important procurement activity since 1998 includes attempts to purchase:

- vacuum pumps, which could be used to create and maintain pressures in a gas centrifuge cascade needed to enrich uranium;

CAB/33/0085

- an entire magnet production line of the correct specification for use in the motors and top bearings of gas centrifuges. It appears that Iraq is attempting to acquire a capability to produce them on its own rather than rely on foreign procurement;

- anhydrous hydrogen fluoride (AHF) and fluorine gas. AHF is commonly used in the petrochemical industry and Iraq frequently imports significant amounts, but it is also used in the process of converting uranium into uranium hexafluoride for use in gas centrifuge cascades;

- one large filament winding machine, which could be used to manufacture carbon fibre gas centrifuge rotors;

- a large balancing machine which could be used in initial centrifuge balancing work.

22. Iraq has also made repeated attempts covertly to acquire a very large quantity (60,000 or more) of specialised aluminium tubes. The specialised aluminium in question is subject to international export controls because of its potential application in the construction of gas centrifuges used to enrich uranium, although there is no definitive intelligence that it is destined for a nuclear programme.

Nuclear weapons: timelines

. In early 2002, the JIC assessed that UN sanctions on Iraq were hindering the import of crucial goods for the production of fissile material. The JIC judged that while sanctions remain effective, Iraq would not be able to produce a nuclear weapon. If they were removed or prove ineffective, it would take Iraq at least five years to produce sufficient fissile material for a weapon indigenously. However, we know that Iraq retains expertise and design data relating to nuclear weapons. We therefore judge that if Iraq obtained fissile material and other essential components from foreign sources, the timeline for production of a nuclear weapon would be shortened and Iraq could produce a nuclear weapon in between one and two years.

CAB/33/0086

BALLISTIC MISSILES

JIC Assessment: 1999-2002

24. In mid-2001 the JIC drew attention to what it described as a "step-change" in progress on Iraqi missile programme over the previous two years. It was clear from intelligence that the range of Iraqi missiles which was permitted by the UN and supposedly limited to 150kms was being extended and that work was under way on larger engines for longer-range missiles.

25. In early 2002 the JIC concluded that Iraq had begun to develop missiles with a range of over 1,000kms. The JIC assessed that if sanctions remained effective the Iraqis would not be able to produce such a missile before 2007. Sanctions and the earlier work of the inspectors d caused significant problems for Iraqi missile development. In the previous six months Iraqi foreign procurement efforts for the missile programme had been bolder. The JIC also assessed that Iraq retained up to 20 Al Hussein missiles from before the Gulf War.

The Iraqi ballistic missile programme since 1998

FIGURE 4: ABABIL-100

26. Since the Gulf War, Iraq has been openly developing two short-range missiles up to a range of 150km, which are permitted under UN Security Council Resolution 687. The Al-Samoud liquid propellant missile has been extensively tested and is being deployed to military units. Intelligence indicates that at least fifty have been produced. Intelligence also indicates that Iraq has worked on extending its range to at least 200km in breach of UN Security Resolution 687. Production of the solid propellant Ababil-100 (Figure 4) is also underway, probably as an unguided rocket at this stage. There are also plans to extend its range to at least 200km. Compared to liquid propellant missiles, those powered by solid propellant offer greater ease of storage, handling and mobility. They are also quicker to take into and out of action and can stay at a high state of readiness for longer periods.

27. According to intelligence, Iraq has retained up to 20 Al Hussein missiles (Figure 5), in breach of UN Security Council Resolution 687. These missiles were either hidden from the

UN as complete systems, or re-assembled using illegally retained engines and other components. We judge that the engineering expertise available would allow these missiles to be maintained effectively, although the fact that at least some require re-assembly makes it difficult to judge exactly how many could be available for use. They could be used with conventional, chemical or biological warheads and, with a range of up to 650km, are capable of reaching a number of countries in the region including Cyprus, Turkey, Saudi Arabia, Iran and Israel.

FIGURE 5: AL HUSSEIN

28. Intelligence has confirmed that Iraq wants to extend the range of its missile systems to over 1000km, enabling it to threaten other regional neighbours. This work began in 1998, although efforts to regenerate the long range ballistic missile programme probably began in 1995. Iraq's missile programmes employ hundreds of people. Satellite imagery (Figure 6) has shown a new engine test stand being constructed (A), which is larger than the current one used for Al Samoud (B), and that formerly used for testing SCUD engines (C) which was dismantled under UNSCOM supervision. This new stand will be capable of testing engines for missiles with ranges over 1000km, which are not permitted under UN Security Council Resolution 687. Such facility would not be needed for systems that fall within the UN permitted range of 150km. The Iraqis have recently taken measures to conceal activities at this site.

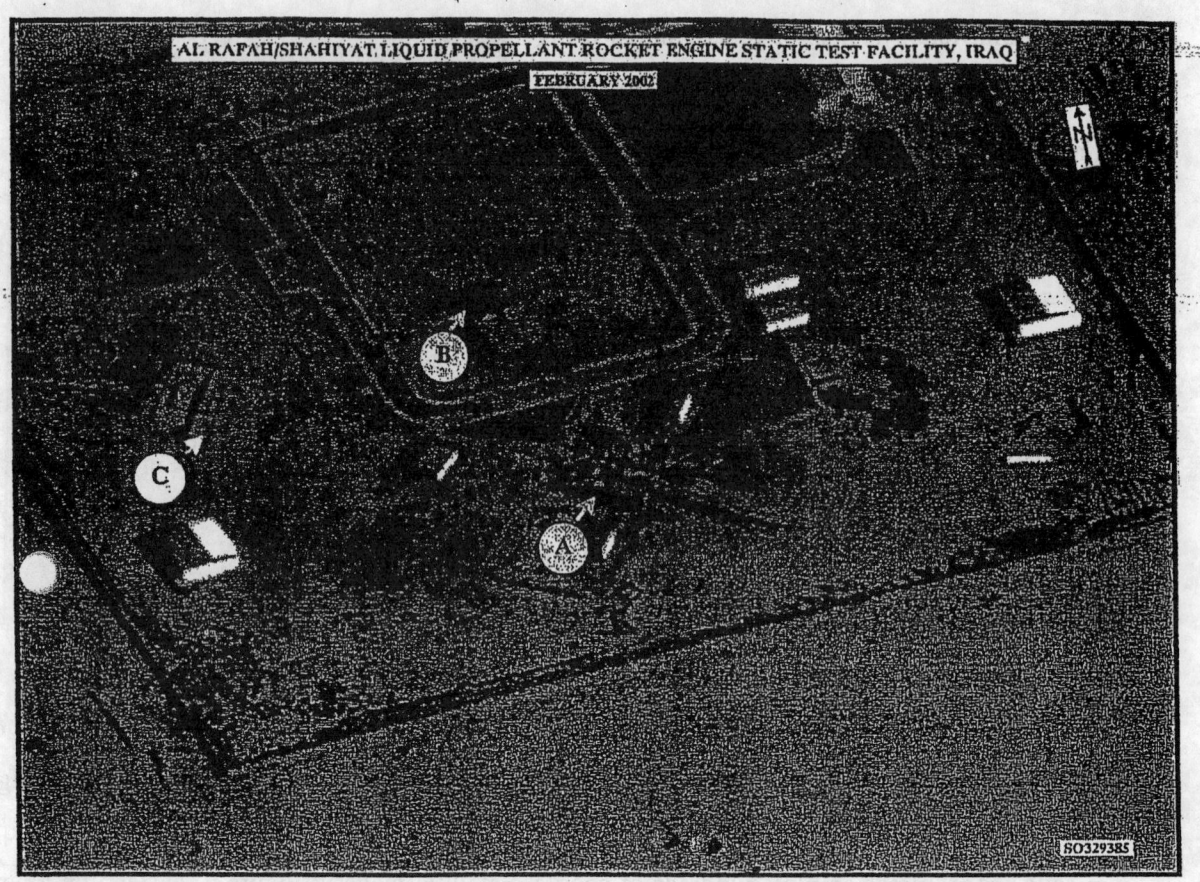

FIGURE 6: AL RAFAH/SHAHIYAT LIQUID PROPELLANT ENGINE STATIC TEST STAND

Iraq is also working to obtain improved guidance technology to increase missile accuracy.

29. The success of UN restrictions means the development of new longer-range missiles is likely to be a slow process. These restrictions impact particularly on the:

- availability of foreign expertise;

- conduct of test flights to ranges above 150km;

- acquisition of guidance and control technology.

CAB/33/0089

30. Saddam remains committed to developing longer-range missiles. Even if sanctions remain effective, Iraq might achieve a missile capability of over 1000km within 5 years (Figure 4 shows the range of Iraq's various missiles).

7 surely!

31. Iraq has managed to rebuild much of the missile production infrastructure destroyed in the Gulf War and in Operation Desert Fox in 1998 (see Part 2). New missile-related infrastructure is also under construction. Some aspects of this, including rocket propellant mixing and casting facilities at the Al Mamoun Plant, appear to replicate those linked to the prohibited BADR-2000 programme (with a planned range of 700-1000km) which were destroyed in the Gulf War or dismantled by UNSCOM. A new plant at al-Mamoun for indigenously producing ammonium perchlorate, which is a key ingredient in the production of solid propellant rocket motors, has also been constructed. This has been provided illicitly by NEC Engineers Private Limited, an Indian chemical engineering firm with extensive links in Iraq, including to other suspect facilities such as the Fallujah 2 chlorine plant. After an extensive investigation, the Indian authorities have recently suspended its export licence, although other individuals and companies are still illicitly procuring for Iraq.

32. Despite a UN embargo, Iraq has also made concerted efforts to acquire additional production technology, including machine tools and raw materials, in breach of UN Security Council Resolution 1051. The embargo has succeeded in blocking many of these attempts, such as requests to buy magnesium powder and ammonium chloride. But we know from intelligence that some items have found their way to the Iraqi ballistic missile programme. More will inevitably continue to do so. Intelligence makes it clear that Iraqi procurement agents and front companies in third countries are seeking illicitly to acquire propellant chemicals for Iraq's ballistic missiles. This includes production level quantities of near complete sets of solid propellant rocket motor ingredients such as aluminium powder, ammonium perchlorate and hydroxyl terminated polybutadiene. There have also been attempts to acquire large quantities of liquid propellant chemicals such as unsymmetrical dimethylhydrazine (UDMH) and diethylenetriamene. We judge this is intended to support production and deployment of the Al Samoud and development of longer range systems.

CAB/33/0090

Iraq: Current and Planned/Potential Ballistic Missiles

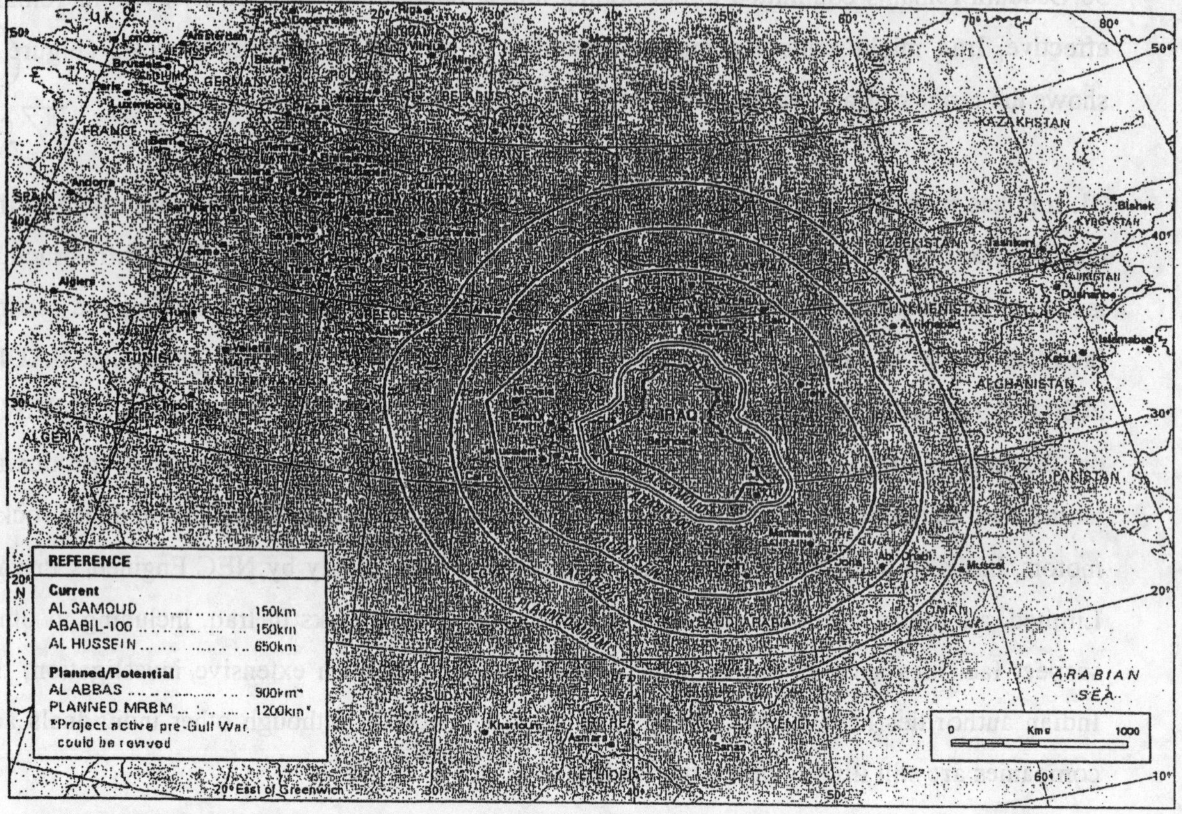

FIGURE 7: CURRENT AND PLANNED/POTENTIAL BALLISTIC MISSILES

FUNDING FOR THE WMD PROGRAMME

> **UN Sanctions**
> UN sanctions on Iraq prohibit all imports to and exports from Iraq. The UN must clear any goods entering or leaving. The UN also administers the Oil for Food (OFF) programme. Any imports entering Iraq under the OFF are checked against the Goods Review List for potential military or weapons of mass destruction utility.

33. The UN has sought to restrict Iraq's ability to)nerate funds for its chemical, biological and other military programmes. For example, Iraq earns money legally under the UN Oil For Food Programme (OFF) established by UNSCR 986, whereby the proceeds of oil sold through the UN are used to buy humanitarian supplies for Iraq. This money remains under UN control, and cannot be used for military procurement. However, the Iraqi regime continues to generate income outside UN control, either in the form of hard currency, or barter goods (which in turn means existing Iraqi funds are freed up to be spent on other things).

34. These illicit earnings go to the Iraqi regime. They are used for building new palaces, as well as purchasing luxury goods and other civilian goods outside OFF. Some of these funds are also used by Saddam to maintain his armed forces, and to develop or

Iraq's illicit earnings	
Year	Amount in $billions
1999	0.8 to 1
2000	1.5 to 2
2001	3
2002	3 (assessed)

acquire military equipment, including for chemical, biological, nuclear and ballistic missile programmes. We do not know what proportion of these funds is used in this way. But we have seen no evidence that Iraqi attempts to develop its weapons of mass destruction and its ballistic missile programme, for example through covert procurement of equipment from abroad has been inhibited in any way by lack of funds. The steady increase over the last three years in the availability of funds will enable Saddam to progress the programmes faster.

CAB/33/0092

PART 2

HISTORY OF UN WEAPONS INSPECTIONS

1. During the 1990s, beginning in April 1991 immediately after the end of the Gulf War, the UN Security Council passed a series of resolutions [see box] establishing the authority of UNSCOM and the IAEA to carry out the work of dismantling Iraq's arsenal of chemical, biological and nuclear weapons programmes and long range ballistic missiles.

UN Security Council Resolutions (UNSCR) relating to WMD

UNSCR 687, April 1991 created the UN Special Commission (UNSCOM) and required Iraq to accept, unconditionally, "the destruction, removal or rendering harmless, under international supervision" of its chemical and biological weapons, ballistic missiles with a range greater than 150km, and their associated programmes, stocks, components, research and facilities. The International Atomic Energy Agency (IAEA) was charged with abolition of Iraq's nuclear weapons programme. UNSCOM and the IAEA must report that their mission has been achieved before the Security Council can end sanctions. They have not yet done so.

UNSCR 707, August 1991, stated that Iraq must provide full, final and complete disclosure of all its WMD programmes and provide unconditional and unrestricted access to UN inspectors. For over a decade Iraq has been in breach of this resolution. Iraq must also cease all nuclear activities of any kind other than civil use of isotopes.

UNSCR 715, October 1991 approved plans prepared by UNSCOM and IAEA for the ongoing monitoring and verification (OMV) arrangements to implement UNSCR 687. Iraq did not accede to this to November 1993. OMV was conducted from April 1995 to 15 December 1998, when the UN left Iraq.

UNSCR 1051, March 1996 stated that Iraq must declare the shipment of dual-use WMD goods.

These resolutions were passed under Chapter VII of the UN Charter which is the instrument that allows the UN Security Council to authorise the use of military force to enforce its resolutions.

2. As outlined in UNSCR 687, Iraq's chemical, biological and nuclear weapons programmes were also a breach of Iraq's commitments under:

CAB/33/0092

622

- The Geneva Protocol of 1925 – which bans the use of chemical and biological weapons;

- the Biological and Toxin Weapons Convention – which bans the development, production, stockpiling, acquisition or retention of biological weapons;

- and the Nuclear Non-Proliferation Treaty (NPT) – which prohibits Iraq from manufacturing or otherwise acquiring nuclear weapons.

3. UNSCR 687 obliged Iraq to provide declarations on all aspects of its WMD

> UNSCOM and the IAEA were given the remit to designate <u>any</u> locations for inspection at any time, review any document and interview any scientist, technician or other individual and seize any prohibited items for destruction.

programmes within 15 days and accept the destruction, removal or rendering harmless under international supervision of its chemical, biological and nuclear programmes, and all ballistic missiles with a range beyond 150km. Iraq did not make a satisfactory declaration within the specified timeframe.

Iraq accepted the UNSCRs and agreed to co-operate with UNSCOM. The history of the UN weapons inspections was characterised by persistent Iraqi obstruction.

Iraqi Non-Co-operation with the Inspectors

4. The former Chairman of UNSCOM, Richard Butler, reported to the UN Security Council in January 1999, that in 1991 a decision was taken by a high-level Iraqi Government committee to provide inspectors with only a portion of its proscribed weapons, components, production capabilities and stocks. UNSCOM concluded that Iraqi policy was based on the following actions:

- to provide only a portion of extant weapons stocks, releasing for destruction only those that were least modern;

CAB/33/0094

- to retain the production capability and documentation necessary to revive programmes when possible;

- to conceal the full extent of its chemical weapons programme, including the VX nerve agent project; to conceal the number and type of chemical and biological warheads for proscribed long-range missiles;

- and to conceal the existence of its biological weapons programme.

5. In December 1997 Richard Butler reported to the UN Security Council that Iraq had created a new category of sites – "Presidential" and "sovereign" – from which it claimed that UNSCOM inspectors would henceforth be barred. The terms of the ceasefire in 1991 foresaw no such limitation. However, Iraq consistently refused to

---

Iraq's policy of deception

Iraq has admitted to UNSCOM having a large, effective, system for hiding proscribed material including documentation, components, production equipment and, possibly, biological and chemical agents and weapons from the UN. Shortly after the adoption of UNSCR 687 in April 1991, an Administrative Security Committee (ASC) was formed with responsibility for advising Saddam on the information which could be released to UNSCOM and the IAEA. The Committee consisted of senior Military Industrial Commission (MIC) scientists from all of Iraq's WMD programmes. The Higher Security Committee (HSC) of the Presidential Office was in overall command of deception operations. The system was directed from the very highest political levels within the Presidential Office and involved, if not Saddam himself, his youngest son, Qusai. The system for hiding proscribed material relies on high mobility and good command and control. It uses lorries to move items at short notice and most hide sites appear to be located close to good road links and telecommunications. The Baghdad area was particularly favoured. In addition to active measures to hide material from the UN, Iraq has attempted to monitor, delay and collect intelligence on UN operations to aid its overall deception plan.

---

allow UNSCOM inspectors access to any of these eight Presidential sites. Many of these so-called "palaces" are in fact large compounds which are an integral part of Iraqi counter-measures designed to hide weapons material (see photograph).

A photograph of a
presidential site or
what have been called
"palaces".

Buckingham palace
has been super-
imposed to
demonstrate their
comparative size

Buckingham Palace and grounds

CAB/33/0096

625

Intimidation

6. Once inspectors had arrived in Iraq, it quickly became apparent that the Iraqis would resort to a range of measures (including physical threats and psychological intimidation of inspectors) to prevent UNSCOM and the IAEA from fulfilling their mandate.

7. In response to such incidents, the President of the Security Council issued frequent statements calling on Iraq to comply with its disarmament and monitoring obligations.

Iraqi obstruction of UN weapons inspection teams.

- firing warning shots in the air to prevent IAEA inspectors from intercepting nuclear related equipment (June 1991);

- keeping IAEA inspectors in a car park for 4 days and refusing to allow them to leave with incriminating documents on Iraq's nuclear weapons programme (September 1991);

- announcing that UN monitoring and verification plans were "unlawful" (October 1991);

- refusing UNSCOM inspectors access to the Ministry of Agriculture. Threats were made to inspectors who remained on watch outside the building. The inspection team had reliable evidence that the site contained archives related to proscribed activities;

- In 1991-2 Iraq objected to UNSCOM using its own helicopters and choosing its own flight plans. In January 1993 it refused to allow UNSCOM the use of its own aircraft to fly into Iraq;

- refusing to allow UNSCOM to install remote-controlled monitoring cameras at two key missile sites (June-July 1993);

- repeatedly denying access to inspection teams (1991- December 1998);

- interfering with UNSCOM's helicopter operations, threatening the safety of the aircraft and their crews (June 1997);

- demanding the end of U2 overflights and the withdrawal of US UNSCOM staff (October 1997);

- destroying documentary evidence of WMD programmes (September 1997).

Obstruction

8. Iraq denied that it had pursued a biological weapons programme until July 1995.

CAB/33/0097

In July 1995, Iraq acknowledged that biological agents had been produced on an industrial scale at Al-Hakam. Following the defection in August 1995 of Hussein Kamel, Saddam's son-in-law and former Director of the Military Industrialisation Commission, Iraq released over 2 million documents relating to its WMD programmes and acknowledged that it had pursued a biological programme that led to the deployment of actual weapons. Iraq admitted producing 183 biological weapons with a reserve of agent to fill considerably more.

9. Iraq tried to obstruct UNSCOM's efforts to investigate the scale of its biological

---

Inspection of Iraq's biological weapons programme

In the course of the first biological weapons inspection in August 1991, Iraq claimed that it had merely conducted a military biological research programme. At the site visited, Al-Salman, Iraq had removed equipment, documents and even entire buildings. Later in the year, during a visit to the Al-Hakam site, Iraq declared to UNSCOM inspectors that the facility was used as a factory to produce proteins derived from yeast to feed animals. Inspectors subsequently discovered that the plant was a central site for the production of anthrax spores and botulinum toxin for weapons. The factory had also been sanitised by Iraqi officials to deceive inspectors. Iraq continued to develop the Al-Hakam site into the 1990s, misleading UNSCOM about its true purpose.

Another key site, the Foot and Mouth Disease Vaccine Institute at Dawrah which produced botulinum toxin and probably anthrax, was not divulged as part of the programme. Five years later, after intense pressure, Iraq acknowledged that tens of tonnes of bacteriological warfare agent had been produced there and at Al-Hakam.

As documents recovered in August 1995 were assessed, it became apparent that the full disclosure required by the UN was far from complete. Successive inspection teams went to Iraq to try to gain greater understanding of the programme and to obtain credible supporting evidence. In July 1996 Iraq refused to discuss it's past programme and doctrine forcing the team to withdraw in protest. Monitoring teams were at the same time finding undisclosed equipment and materials associated with the past programme. In response, Iraq grudgingly provided successive disclosures of their programme which were judged by UNSCOM, and specially convened international panels, to be technically inadequate.

In late 1995, Iraq acknowledged weapons testing the biological agent ricin, but did not provide production information. Two years later – in early 1997 – UNSCOM discovered evidence that Iraq had produced ricin.

---

weapons programme. It created forged documents to account for bacterial growth media, imported in the late 1980s, specifically for the production of anthrax, botulinum toxin and probably plague. The documents were created to indicate that the material had been imported by the State Company for Drugs and Medical

Appliances Marketing for use in hospitals and distribution to local authorities. Iraq also censored documents and scientific papers provided to the first UN inspection team, removing all references to key individuals, weapons and industrial production of agents.

10. Iraq has yet to provide <u>any</u> documents concerning production of agent and subsequent weaponisation. Iraq destroyed, unilaterally and illegally, some biological weapons in 1991 and 1992 making accounting for these weapons impossible. In addition Iraq cleansed a key site at Al-Muthanna – its main research and development, production and weaponisation facility for chemical warfare agents - of all evidence of a biological programme in the toxicology department, the animal-house and weapons filling station.

11. Iraq refused to elaborate further on the programme during inspections in 1997 and 1998, confining discussion to previous topics. In July 1998, Tariq Aziz personally intervened in the inspection process stating that the biological programme was more secret and more closed than other WMD programmes. He also played down the significance of the programme. Iraq has presented the biological weapons programme as the personal undertaking of a few misguided scientists.

12. At the same time, Iraq tried to maintain its nuclear weapons programme via a concerted campaign to deceive IAEA inspectors. In 1997 the Agency's Director General stated that the IAEA was "severely hampered by Iraq's persistence in a policy of concealment and understatement of the programme's scope."

Achievements

13. Despite the conduct of the Iraqi authorities towards them, both UNSCOM and the IAEA Action Team have valuable records of achievement in discovering and exposing Iraq's biological weapons programme and destroying very large quantities of chemical weapons stocks and missiles as well as the infrastructure for Iraq's nuclear weapons programme.

CAB|33|0099

UNSCOM and IAEA Achievements

UNSCOM surveyed 1015 sites in Iraq, carrying out 272 separate inspections. Despite Iraqi obstruction and intimidation, UN inspectors uncovered details of chemical, biological, nuclear and ballistic missile programmes. Major UNSCOM/IAEA achievements included:

- the destruction of 40,000 munitions for chemical weapons, 2,610 tonnes of chemical precursors and 411 tonnes of chemical warfare agent;

- the dismantling of Iraq's prime chemical weapons development and production complex at Al-Muthanna, and a range of key production equipment;

- the destruction of 48-SCUD type missiles, 11 mobile launchers and 56 sites, 30 warheads filled with chemical agents, and 20 conventional warheads;

- the destruction of the Al-Hakam biological weapons facility and a range of production equipment, seed stocks and growth media for biological weapons;

- the discovery in 1991 of samples of indigenously-produced highly enriched uranium, forcing Iraq's acknowledgement of uranium enrichment programmes and attempts to preserve key components of its prohibited nuclear weapons programme; and

- the removal and destruction of the infrastructure for the nuclear weapons programme, including the Al-Athir weaponisation/testing facility.

---

14. Despite UNSCOM's efforts, following the effective ejection of UN inspectors in December 1998, there remained a series of significant unresolved disarmament issues. In summarising the situation in a report to the Security Council, the UNSCOM Chairman, Richard Butler indicated that:

- contrary to the requirement that destruction be conducted under international supervision, "Iraq undertook extensive, unilateral and secret destruction of large quantities of proscribed weapons and items";

- and Iraq "also pursued a practice of concealment of proscribed items, including weapons, and a cover up of its activities in contravention of Council resolutions."

CAB/33/0100

Overall, Butler declared that obstructive Iraqi activity had had "a significant impact upon the Commission's disarmament work."

Withdrawal of the Inspectors

15. By the end of 1998 UNSCOM was in direct confrontation with the Iraqi Government which was refusing to co-operate. The US and the UK had made clear that anything short of full co-operation would make military action unavoidable. Richard Butler was requested to report to the UN Security Council in December 1998 and stated that, following a series of direct confrontations, coupled with the systematic refusal by Iraq to co-operate, UNSCOM was no longer able to perform its disarmament mandate. As a direct result, on December 16 the weapons inspectors were withdrawn and Operation Desert Fox was launched by the US and the UK a few hours afterwards.

Operation Desert Fox (16-19 December 1998):

Operation Desert Fox targeted industrial facilities related to Iraq's ballistic missile programme and a suspect biological warfare facility as well as military airfields and sites used by Iraq's security organisations which are involved in its weapons of mass destruction programmes. Key facilities associated with Saddam's ballistic missile programme were significantly degraded.

The Situation Since 1998

16. There have been no UN-mandated weapons inspections in Iraq since 1998. In an effort to enforce Iraqi compliance with its disarmament and monitoring obligations, the Security Council passed resolution 1284 in December 1999. This established the United Nations Monitoring, Verification and Inspection Commission (UNMOVIC) as a successor organisation to UNSCOM and called on Iraq to give UNMOVIC inspectors "immediate, unconditional and unrestricted access to any and all areas, facilities, equipment, records and means of transport". It also set out the steps Iraq needed to take in return for the eventual suspension and lifting of sanctions. A key measure of Iraqi compliance would be full co-operation with UN inspectors, including unconditional, immediate and unrestricted access to any and all sites, personnel and documents.

CAB/33/0101

17. For the past three years, Iraq has allowed the IAEA to carry out an annual inspection of a stockpile of nuclear material (depleted natural and low-enriched uranium). This has led some countries and western commentators to conclude – erroneously – that Iraq is meeting its nuclear disarmament and monitoring obligations. As the IAEA has pointed out in recent weeks, this annual inspection does "not serve as a substitute for the verification activities required by the relevant resolutions of the UN Security Council."

18. Dr. Hans Blix, the Executive Chairman of UNMOVIC, and Dr. Mohammed El-Baradei, the Director General of the IAEA, have declared that in the absence of inspections it is impossible to verify Iraqi compliance with its UN disarmament and monitoring obligations. In April 1999, an independent UN panel of experts noted that "the longer inspection and monitoring activities remain suspended, the more difficult the comprehensive implementation of Security Council resolutions becomes, increasing the risk that Iraq might reconstitute its proscribed weapons programmes."

19. The departure of the Inspectors greatly diminished our ability to monitor and assess Iraq's continuing attempts to reconstitute its chemical, biological, nuclear and ballistic missile programmes.

PART 3

IRAQ UNDER SADDAM HUSSEIN

Introduction

1. The Republic of Iraq is bounded by Turkey, Iran, Kuwait, Saudia Arabia, Jordan, Syria and the Persian Gulf. Its population of around 23 million is ethnically and religiously diverse. Approximately 77% are Arabs. Sunni Muslims form around 17% of the Arab population and dominate the government. About 60% of Iraqis are Shias and 20% are Kurds. The remaining 3% of the population consists of Assyrians, Turkomans, Armenians, Christians and Yazidis.

2. Public life in Iraq is nominally dominated by the Ba'ath Party (see box on next page). But all real authority rests with Saddam Hussein and his immediate circle. Saddam's family, tribe and a small number of associates remain his most loyal supporters. He uses them to convey his orders, including to members of the government.

Saddam Hussein's rise to power

Saddam Hussein was born in 1937 in the Tikrit district, north of Baghdad. In 1957 he joined the Ba'ath Party. After taking part in a failed attempt to assassinate the Iraqi President, Abdul Karim Qasim, Saddam escaped, first to Syria and then to Egypt. In his absence he was sentenced to 15 years imprisonment.

Saddam returned to Baghdad in 1963 when the Ba'ath Party came to power. He went into hiding after the Ba'ath fell from power later that year. He was captured and imprisoned, but in 1967 escaped and took over responsibility for Ba'ath security. Saddam set about imposing his will on the Party and establishing himself at the centre of power.

The Ba'ath Party returned to power in 1968. In 1969 Saddam became Vice Chairman of the Revolutionary Command Council, Deputy to the President, and Deputy Secretary-General of the Regional Command of the Ba'ath. In 1970 he joined the Party's National Command and in 1977 was elected Assistant Secretary General. In July 1979, he took over the Presidency of Iraq. Within days, five fellow members of the Revolutionary Command Council were accused of involvement in a coup attempt. They and 17 others were summarily executed.

CAB/33/0103

3. Saddam Hussein uses patronage and violence to motivate his supporters and to control or eliminate opposition. Potential rewards include social status, money and better access to goods. Saddam's extensive security apparatus and Ba'ath Party network provides oversight of Iraqi society, with informants in social, government and military organisations. Saddam practises torture, execution and other forms of coercion against his enemies, real or suspected. His targets are not only those who have offended him, but also their families, friends or colleagues.

> **The Iraqi Ba'ath Party**
> The Ba'ath Party is the only legal political party in Iraq. It pervades all aspects of Iraqi life.
> Membership, around 700,000, is necessary for self advancement and confers benefits from the regime.

4. Saddam acts to ensure that there are no other centres of power in Iraq. He has crushed parties and ethnic groups which might try to assert themselves, such as the communists and the Kurds. Members of the opposition abroad have been the targets of assassination attempts conducted by Iraqi security services.

5. Army officers are an important part of the government's network of informers. Suspicion that officers have ambitions other than the service of the President leads to immediate execution. It is routine for Saddam to take pre-emptive action against those who he

> **Saddam Hussein's security apparatus**
> Saddam relies on a long list of security organisations with overlapping responsibilities. The main ones are:
> - The **Special Security Organisation** oversees Saddam's security and monitors the loyalty of other security services. Its recruits are predominantly from Tikrit.
> - The **Special Republican Guard** is equipped with the best available military equipment. Its members are selected on the basis of loyalty to the regime.
> - The **Directorate of General Security** is primarily responsible for countering threats from the civilian population.
> - The **Directorate of General Intelligence** monitors and suppresses dissident activities at home and abroad.
> - The **Directorate of Military Intelligence**'s role includes the investigation of military personnel.
> - The **Saddam Fidayeen**, under the control of Udayy Hussein, has been used to deal with civil disturbances.

633

believes might conspire against him.

Internal Repression – the Kurds and the Shias

6. Saddam has pursued a long-term programme of persecution of the Iraqi Kurds, including the use of chemical weapons. During the Iran/Iraq war, Saddam appointed his cousin, Ali Hassan al-Majid, as his deputy in the north. In 1987-88, al-Majid led the "Anfal" campaign of attacks on Kurdish villages. Amnesty International estimates that more than 100,000 Kurds were killed or disappeared during this period.

> **Repression and control: some examples**
> * A campaign of mass arrests and killing of Shia activists led to the execution of the Ayatollah Baqir al-Sadr and his sister in April 1980.
> * In 1983, 80 members of another leading Shia family were arrested. Six of them, all religious leaders, were executed.
> * A massive chemical weapons attack on Kurds in Halabja town in March 1988, killing 5000 and injuring 10,000 more.
> * A large number of officers from the Jabbur tribe were executed in the early 1990s for the alleged disloyalty of a few of them.

7. After the Gulf War in 1991 Kurds in the north of Iraq rose up against Baghdad's rule. In response the Iraqi regime killed or imprisoned thousands, prompting a humanitarian crisis. Over a million Kurds fled into the mountains and tried to escape Iraq.

8. Persecution of Iraq's Kurds continues, although the protection provided by the northern No-Fly Zone has helped to curb the worst excesses. But outside this zone, the Baghdad regime has continued a policy of persecution and intimidation.

9. The regime has used chemical weapons against the Kurds, most notably in an attack on the town of Halabja in 1988 (see Part 1 Chapter 2 paragraph 9). The implicit threat of the use of chemical weapons against the Kurds and others is an important part of Saddam's attempt to keep the civilian population under control.

10. The regime has tried to displace the traditional Kurdish and Turkoman populations of the areas under its control, primarily in order to weaken Kurdish claims to the oil-rich area around the northern city of Kirkuk. Kurds and other non-Arabs are forcibly ejected to the three northern Iraqi governorates – Dohuk, Arbil and Sulaimaniyah – which are under de facto Kurdish control. According to the United Nations Commission on Human Rights (UNCHR) Special Rapporteur for Iraq, 94,000 individuals have been expelled since 1991. Agricultural land owned by Kurds has been confiscated and redistributed to Iraqi Arabs. Arabs from southern Iraq have been offered incentives to move into the Kirkuk area.

11. After the 1979 revolution that ousted the Shah in Iran, Saddam intensified a campaign against the Shia Muslim majority of Iraq, fearing that they might be encouraged by the new Shia regime in Iran.

12. In the wake of the Gulf War, riots broke out in the southern city of Basra on 1 March 1991, spreading quickly to other cities in Shia-dominated southern Iraq. The regime responded by killing thousands. Many Shia tried to escape to Iran and Saudi Arabia.

13. Some of the Shia hostile to the regime sought refuge in the marshland of southern Iraq. In order to subjugate the area, Saddam embarked on a large-scale programme to drain the marshes to allow Iraqi ground forces to eliminate all opposition there. The rural population of the area fled or were forced to move to southern cities or across the border into Iran.

Saddam Hussein's Wars

14. As well as ensuring his absolute control inside Iraq, Saddam has tried to make Iraq the dominant power of the region. In pursuit of these objectives he has led Iraq into two wars of aggression against neighbours, the Iran-Iraq war and the invasion of Kuwait.

15. With the fall of the Shah in Iran in 1979, relations between Iran and Iraq deteriorated sharply. In September 1980 Saddam renounced a border treaty he had agreed with Iran in 1975 ceding half of the Shatt al-Arab waterway to Iran. Shortly thereafter, Saddam launched a large-scale invasion of Iran. He believed that he could take advantage of the state of weakness, isolation and disorganisation he perceived in post-revolutionary Iran. He aimed to seize territory, including that ceded to Iran a few years earlier, and to assert Iraq's position as a leader of the Arab world. Saddam expected it to be a short, sharp campaign. But the conflict lasted for eight years. Iraq fired over 500 ballistic missiles at Iranian targets, including major cities.

16. It is estimated that the Iran/Iraq war cost the two sides a million casualties. Iraq used chemical weapons extensively from 1984. Some twenty thousand Iranians were killed by mustard gas, and the nerve agents tabun and sarin, all of

> **Opposition to Saddam during the Iran/Iraq war**
> During the war Saddam's security apparatus ensured any internal dissent or opposition was quickly eliminated. In 1982 he quickly purged a group within Iraq's ruling clique which suggested that the war might be brought to an end more quickly if Saddam stood down.

which Iraq still possesses. The UN Security Council considered the report prepared by a team of three specialists appointed by the UN Secretary General in March 1986, following which the President made a statement condemning Iraqi use of chemical weapons. This marked the first time a country had been named for violating the 1925 Geneva Convention banning the use of chemical weapons.

17. The cost of the war ran into hundreds of billions of dollars for both sides. Iraq gained nothing. After the war ended, Saddam resumed his previous pursuit of primacy in the Gulf. His policies involved spending huge sums of money on new military equipment. But Iraq was burdened by debt incurred during the war and the price of oil, Iraq's only major export, was low.

18. By 1990 Iraq's financial problems were severe. Saddam looked at ways to press the oil-producing states of the Gulf to force up the price of crude oil by limiting production and waive the $40 billion that they had loaned Iraq during its war with Iran. Kuwait had made some concessions over production ceilings. But Saddam blamed Kuwait for over production. When his threats and blandishments failed, Iraq invaded Kuwait on 2 August 1990. He believed that occupying Kuwait could prove profitable.

19. Saddam also sought to justify the conquest of Kuwait on other grounds. Like other Iraqi leaders before him, he claimed that, as Kuwait's rulers had come under the jurisdiction of the governors of Basra in the time of the Ottoman Empire, Kuwait should belong to Iraq.

> **Abuses by Iraqi forces in Kuwait**
> - Robbery and rape of Kuwaitis and expatriates.
> - Summary executions.
> - People dragged from their homes and held in improvised detention centres.
> - Amnesty International has listed 38 methods of torture used by the Iraqi occupiers. These included beatings, breaking of limbs, extracting finger and toenails, inserting bottle necks into the rectum, and subjecting detainees to mock executions.
> - Kuwaiti civilians arrested for "crimes" such as wearing beards.

20. During its occupation of Kuwait, Iraq denied access to the Red Cross, which has a mandate to provide protection and assistance to civilians affected by international armed conflict. The death penalty was imposed for relatively minor "crimes" such as looting and hoarding food.

21. In an attempt to deter military action to expel it from Kuwait, the Iraqi regime took hostage several hundred foreign nationals (including children) in Iraq and Kuwait, and prevented thousands more from leaving, in direct contravention of international humanitarian law. Hostages were held as human shields at a number of strategic military and civilian sites.

22. At the end of the Gulf War, the Iraqi army fleeing Kuwait set fire to over 1,160 Kuwaiti oil wells, with serious environmental consequences.

23. More than 600 Kuwaiti and other prisoners of war and missing persons are still unaccounted for. Iraq refuses to comply with its UN obligation to account for the missing. It has provided sufficient information to close only three case-files.

Abuse of human rights

24. Human rights abuses continue within Iraq. People continue to be arrested and detained on suspicion of political or religious activities, or often because they are related to members of the opposition. Executions are carried out without due process of law. Relatives are often prevented from burying the victims in accordance with Islamic practice. Thousands of prisoners have been executed.

Human rights: abuses under Saddam

- 4000 prisoners were executed at Abu Ghraib Prison in 1984.
- 3000 prisoners were executed at the Mahjar Prison between 1993 and 1998.
- About 2500 prisoners were executed between 1997 and 1999 in a "prison cleansing" campaign.
- 122 male prisoners were executed at Abu Ghraib prison in February/ March 2000. A further 23 political prisoners were executed there in October 2001.
- Prisoners have been executed by machine gun.
- In October 2000, dozens of women accused of prostitution were beheaded without any judicial process. Some were accused for political reasons.
- Women prisoners at Mahjar are routinely raped by their guards.
- Methods of torture used in Iraqi jails include using electric drills to mutilate hands, pulling out fingernails, knife cuts, sexual attacks and 'official rape'.
- Prisoners at the Qurtiyya Prison in Baghdad and elsewhere are kept in metal boxes the size of tea chests. If they do not confess they are left to die.

---

25. Saddam has issued a series of decrees establishing severe penalties for criminal offences. These include amputation, branding, cutting off ears, and other forms of mutilation. Anyone found guilty of slandering the President has their tongue removed.

CAB|33|0110

639

> **Human Rights – mistreatment in Abu Ghraib Prison**
>
> Abdallah, a member of the Ba'ath Party whose loyalty became suspect was imprisoned for four years at Abu Ghraib in the 1980s. On the second day of his imprisonment, the men were forced to walk between two rows of five guards each to receive their containers of food. While walking to get the food, they were beaten by the guards with plastic telephone cables. They had to return to their cells the same way, so that a walk to get breakfast resulted in twenty lashes. According to Abdallah, "It wasn't that bad going to get the food, but coming back the food was spilled when we were beaten." The same procedure was used when the men went to the bathroom. On the third day, the torture continued. "We were removed from our cells and beaten with plastic pipes. This surprised us, because we were asked no question. Possibly it was being done to break our morale", Abdallah speculated. The torture escalated to sixteen sessions daily. The treatment was organised and systematic. Abdallah was held alone in a 3x2-meter room that opened onto a corridor. "We were allowed to go to the toilet three times a day, then they reduced the toilet to once a day for only one minute. I went for four years without a shower or a wash", Abdallah said. He also learned to cope with the deprivation and the hunger that accompanied his detention: "I taught myself to drink a minimum amount of water because there was no placed to urinate. They used wooden sticks to beat us and sometimes the sticks would break. I found a piece of a stick, covered with blood, and managed to bring it back to my room. I ate it for three days. A person who is hungry can eat anything. Pieces of our bodies started falling off from the beatings and our skin was so dry that it began to fall off. I ate pieces of my own body. "No one, not Pushkin, not Mahfouz, can describe what happened to us. It is impossible to describe what living this day to day was like. I was totally naked the entire time. Half of the original groups [of about thirty men] died. It was a slow type of continuous physical and psychological torture. Sometimes, it seemed that orders came to kill one of us, and he would be beaten to death". *(Sourced to Human Rights Watch)*.

Saddam's family

26. Saddam's son Udayy maintained a private torture chamber known as the Red Room in a building on the banks of the Tigris disguised as an electricity installation. He ordered the Iraq football team to be caned on the soles of the feet for losing a World Cup match. He created a militia in 1994 which has used swords to execute victims outside their own homes. He has personally executed dissidents, for instance in the Shia uprising at Basra which followed the Gulf War.

27. Members of Saddam's family are also subject to persecution. A cousin of Saddam called Ala Abd Al-Qadir Al-Majid fled to Jordan from Iraq, citing disagreements with the regime over business matters. He returned to Iraq after the Iraqi Ambassador in Jordan declared publicly that his life was not in danger. He was met at the border by Tahir Habbush, Head of the Directorate of General Intelligence

---

Human Rights - individual testimony

In December 1996, a Kurdish businessman from Baghdad was arrested outside his house by plainclothes security men. Initially his family did not know his whereabouts and went from one police station to another inquiring about him. Then they found out that he was being held in the headquarters of the General Security Directorate in Baghdad. The family was not allowed to visit him. Eleven months later the family was told by the authorities that he had been executed and that they should go and collect his body. His body bore evident signs of torture. His eyes were gouged out and the empty eye sockets filled with paper. His right wrist and left leg were broken. The family was not given any reason for his arrest and subsequent execution. However, they suspected that he was executed because of his friendship with a retired army general who had links with the Iraqi opposition outside the country and who was arrested just before his arrest and also executed. *(General & Security [illegible])*.

(the Mukhabarat), and taken to a farm owned by 'Ali Hasan Al-Majid. At the farm 'Ala was tied to a tree and executed by members of his immediate family who, following orders from Saddam, took it in turns to shoot him.

CAB/33/0112

Human Rights - individual testimony

"...I saw a friend of mine, al-Shaikh Nasser Taresh al-Sa'idi, naked. He was handcuffed and a piece of wood was placed between his elbows and his knees. Two ends of the wood were placed on two high chairs and al-Shaikh Nasser was being suspended like a chicken. This method of torture is known as *al-Khaygania* (a reference to a former security director known as al-Khaygani). An electric wire was attached to al-Shaikh Nasser's penis and another one attached to one of his toes. He was asked if he could identify me and he said "this is al-Shaikh Yahya". They took me to another room and then after about 10 minutes they stripped me of my clothes and a security officer said "the person you saw has confessed against you". He said to me "You followers of [Ayatollah] al-Sadr have carried out acts harmful to the security of the country and have been distributing anti-government statements coming from abroad". He asked if I have any contact with an Iraqi religious scholar based in Iran who has been signing these statements. I said "I do not have any contacts with him"... I was then left suspended in the same manner as al-Shaikh al-Sa'idi. My face was looking upward. They attached an electric wire on my penis and the other end of the wire is attached to an electric motor. One security man was hitting my feet with a cable. Electric shocks were applied every few minutes and were increased. I must have been suspended for more than an hour. I lost consciousness. They took me to another room and made me walk even though my feet were swollen from beating... They repeated this method a few times." (testimony to Amnesty International from an Iraqi theology student from Saddam City)

28. Some 40 of Saddam's relatives, including women and children, have been killed. His sons-in-law Hussein Kamel and Saddam had defected in 1995 and returned to Iraq from Jordan after the government had announced amnesties for them. They were executed in February 1996.

APPENDIX 13

Alison Blackshaw

From: Daniel Pruce
Sent: 10 September 2002 12:25
To: 'Mark Matthews'
Cc: Matthew Rycroft; 'Paul Hamill'; Godric Smith; Alastair Campbell
Subject: DOSSIER

Mark,

I promised some quick thoughts on John's draft of 9 September.

On content:

- in general I think we should personalise the dossier, placing the focus on Saddam as much as possible. So I would proose that we replace most, if not all, of the references to Iraq with references to Saddam;

- the personal witness statements are very powerful. Are there more we can use to illustrate Saddam's repression of his own people through murder, rape and torture?;

- we make a number of statements about Saddam's intentions/attitudes. Can we insert a few quotes from speeches he has made which, even if they are not specific, demonstrate that he is a bad man with a general hostility towards his neighbours and the West?;

- in the public's mind the key difference between this text and the IISS text will be the access to intelligence material. I like the idea of the history of JIC assessments. Might we also include a general statement on the nature of the intelligence services and their role. This could be drawn from material that is already in the public domain. It's inclusion might help underline the fact that the services have contributed to the report, often in ways which, for perfectly fair reasons, are imperceptible;

On presentation:

- the text now reads as a single continuous narrative. This is fine - but I think we should look at breaking it up into the sections set out in Alastair's note of yesterday;

- much of the evidence we have is largely circumstantial so we need to convey to our readers that the cumulation of these facts demonstrates an intent on Saddam's part - the more they can be led to this conclusion themselves rather than have to accept judgements from us, the better;

On mechanics:

- I'd be grateful if you could discuss with the FCO Publications team production times and costs. I would envisage that most people would access this text over the web, but I would guess that 500 hard copies will be needed. We can look at design questions later - but I would envisage a fairly sober presentation with a very "official" flavour.

- we also need to think, once we have John's further draft tomorrow, how we prepare the ground for the launch of the text to get expectations in the right place.

Danny

CAB/11/0021

1

Clare Sumner

From:	Daniel Pruce
Sent:	14 August 2003 20:23
To:	Clare Sumner
Subject:	FW: DRAFT DOSSIER (J SCARLETT VERSION OF 10 SEPT)

-----Original Message-----
From:	Philip Bassett
Sent:	11 September 2002 15:27
To:	Godric Smith; Daniel Pruce; Alastair Campbell
Cc:	Matthew Rycroft
Subject:	RE: DRAFT DOSSIER (J SCARLETT VERSION OF 10 SEPT)

Agree with Godric

& also:
- think it needs to be written more in officialese; lots of it is too journalistic as it now stands, with some of it (eg opening chapter as a biog of Saddam !) reading like STimes at its worst eg para 11 "emeshed", "web" or para 13
- needs much more weight, writing, detail: even the stuff marked as new (section 6) is only 12 pages at best out of a bundle of 56 (& that's at best eg p35 is all old UNSCOM stuff). It needs to be at least good as IISS, which it isn't vet, and at least as good as things like *Saddam's Secrets*, the book on the hunt for Iraq's hidden weapons, by an ex-CO and ex-UNSCOM advsier, which I'm not sure it is
- pictures in the text don't get the right feel: what about making them look more report-like, less journo-like, by putting them all the end, as appendices ?
- crucially, though, it's intelligence-lite. It feels like this is the least possible intelligence material the intell people are prepared to let go (despite the fact that we say at a couple of points eg para 2 that it's <u>everything</u> the Govt knows on the issue - which it clearly isn't). All intelligence material tends to read like unevidenced assertion, and we have to find a way to get over this: a) by having <u>better</u> intelligence material~~ ~~; b) by having <u>more</u> material (and better flagged-up) and c) more <u>convincing</u> material (eg by printing some of it eg as appendices, with names, identifiers etc blacked out
- it needs to end. At the moment, it just stops (on p42). A conclusion, saying something - making a case which *is* compelling. At the moment, it isn't

-----Original Message-----
From:	Godric Smith
Sent:	11 September 2002 12:35
To:	Daniel Pruce; Alastair Campbell
Cc:	Matthew Rycroft; Philip Bassett
Subject:	RE: DRAFT DOSSIER (J SCARLETT VERSION OF 10 SEPT)

I think there is material here we can work with but it is a bit of a muddle and needs a lot more clarity in the guts of it in terms of what is new /old. In each area we need to distinguish between the two and better source (as much as we can) to intelligence. It needs to be more factual if anything, less assertion based, with the rhetoric stripped out as I think this undermines it.

-----Original Message-----
From:	Daniel Pruce
Sent:	11 September 2002 10:04
To:	Alastair Campbell
Cc:	Matthew Rycroft; Philip Bassett; Godric Smith
Subject:	DRAFT DOSSIER (J SCARLETT VERSION OF 10 SEPT)

It's getting there, but needs more work. My initial thoughts on this latest draft:

Ownership:

- the foreword is good but whose voice is it? Do we need a minister to sign it off? Probably not. Who will issue the text? Us? The Cabinet Office? Why don't we issue it in the name of the JIC? Makes it more interesting to the media;

Saddam:

1

CAB/11/0023

- I think we need to personalise the dossier onto Saddam as much as possible - for example by replacing references to Iraq with references to Saddam;

- in similar vein I think we need a device to convey that he is a bad and unstable man. The section on Saddam's Iraq (pp9-11) could be expanded into a psychological profile and presented as such;

- and a few quotes from Saddam to demonstrate his aggressive intent and hatred of his neighbours and the West would help too;

Feel:

- our aim should also be to convey the impression that things have not been static in Iraq but that over the past decade he has been aggressively and relentlessly pursuing WMD while brutally repressing his own people. Again the dossier gets close to this - but I think some drafting changes could bring this out more;

Intelligence:

- Section 6, the one based on intelligence, is the one that readers will go to first. This draft already plays up the nature of intelligence sourcing. I think we could play this up more. The more we advertise that unsupported assertions (eg. Saddam attaches great iportance to the possession of WMD) come from intelligence the better. The history of JIC Assessments will help too. And why not an annex on the work of the intelligence services (we could draw from material already in the public domain)?;

Witness accounts:

- the material in Annex A on HR abuses is powerful - we might bring elements of it into the body of the dossier;

- in similar vein can we add copies of original documentation, if necessary with parts blanked out, to add to the feeling that we are presenting real evidence?;

Weapons:

- wherever we refer to them (either what the inspectors found or what we thinnk he has) I think we should also describe their destructive capacity as well - eg. p 26 UNSCOM found enough chemical warfare agent to kill x thousand people or contaminate an area the size of Wales.

Do you want to meet and discuss today? Separately I'm in touch with the FCO on production and distribution. We also need to develop a handling plan to get expectations in the right place before we launch.

Danny

2

From: Daniel Pruce
Sent: 14 August 2003 20:17
To: Clare Sumner
Subject: FW: DRAFT DOSSIER (J SCARLETT VERSION OF 10 SEPT)

——Original Message——
From: Philip Bassett
Sent: 11 September 2002 10:34
To: Daniel Pruce; Alastair Campbell
Cc: Matthew Rycroft; Godric Smith
Subject: RE: DRAFT DOSSIER (J SCARLETT VERSION OF 10 SEPT)

Very long way to go, I think. Think we're in a lot of trouble with this as it stands now

——Original Message——
From: Daniel Pruce
Sent: 11 September 2002 10:04
To: Alastair Campbell
Cc: Matthew Rycroft; Philip Bassett; Godric Smith
Subject: DRAFT DOSSIER (J SCARLETT VERSION OF 10 SEPT)

It's getting there, but needs more work. My initial thoughts on this latest draft:

Ownership:

- the foreword is good but whose voice is it? Do we need a minister to sign it off? Probably not. Who will issue the text? Us? The Cabinet Office? Why don't we issue it in the name of the JIC? Makes it more interesting to the media;

Saddam:

- I think we need to personalise the dossier onto Saddam as much as possible - for example by replacing references to Iraq with references to Saddam;

- in similar vein I think we need a device to convey that he is a bad and unstable man. The section on Saddam's Iraq (pp9-11) could be expanded into a psychological profile and presented as such;

- and a few quotes from Saddam to demonstrate his aggressive intent and hatred of his neighbours and the West would help too;

Feel:

- our aim should also be to convey the impression that things have not been static in Iraq but that over the past decade he has been aggressively and relentlessly pursuing WMD while brutally repressing his own people. Again the dossier gets close to this - but I think some drafting changes could bring this out more;

Intelligence:

- Section 6, the one based on intelligence, is the one that readers will go to first. This draft already plays up the nature of intelligence sourcing. I think we could play this up more. The more we advertise that unsupported assertions (eg. Saddam attaches great iportance to the possession of WMD) come from intelligence the better. The history of JIC Assessments will help too. And why not an annex on the work of the intelligence services (we could draw from material already in the public domain)?;

Witness accounts:

- the material in Annex A on HR abuses is powerful - we might bring elements of it into the body of the dossier;

- in similar vein can we add copies of original documentation, if necessary with parts blanked out, to add to the feeling that we are presenting real evidence?;

Weapons:

1

CAB/11/0025

- wherever we refer to them (either what the inspectors found or what we thinnk he has) I think we should also describe their destructive capacity as well - eg p 26 UNSCOM found enough chemical warfare agent to kill x thousand people or contaminate an area the size of Wales

Do you want to meet and discuss today? Separately I'm in touch with the FCO on production and distribution. We also need to develop a handling plan to get expectations in the right place before we launch.

Danny

2

CAB│11│0026

647

Daniel Pruce

From: Matthew Rycroft
Sent: 11 September 2002 11:59
To: Tom Kelly; Alastair Campbell
Cc: Daniel Pruce; Godric Smith; Philip Bassett
Subject: RE: Dossier

yes, part of the answer to "why now?" is that the threat will only get worse if we don't act now - the threat that Saddam will use WMD, but also the threat that Iraq's WMD will somehow get into the hands of terrorists ~~the ...~~ ~~............... ....~~ This all links into the illicit money, since the more funds he has - and his cash pile is growing all the time - the more likely he is to buy fissile material etc.

——Original Message——
From: Tom Kelly
Sent: 11 September 2002 11:50
To: Alastair Campbell
Cc: Matthew Rycroft; Daniel Pruce; Godric Smith; Philip Bassett
Subject: Dossier

This does have some new elements to play with, but there is one central weakness - we do not differentiate enough between capacity and intent. we know that he is a bad man and has done bad things in the past. We know he is trying to get WMD - and this shows those attempts are intensifying. But can we show why we think he intends to use them aggressively, rather than in self-defence. We need that to counter the argument that Saddam is bad, but not mad. We also, I think, need more direct argument on why containment is breaking down. In other words, putting the emphasis as much (maybe more) on the present and future, as the past.

The key must be to show that Saddam has the capacity, and is intent on using it in ways that threaten world stability, and that our ability to stop him is increasingly threatened.

CAB/11/0027

Alison Blackshaw

From: Mark.Sedwill ██████████
Sent: 11 September 2002 12:28
To: Charles.Gray ██████████
Edward.Chaplin ██████████, ██████████
Ed.Owen@fco ██████████
Cc: dmanning ██████████; matthew.rycroft ██████████
acampbell ██████████
Subject: CONF: Dossier 10/9 Version - Comments

ATT08668.htm

Charles,

Handling and Timing

I have sent this out to the Foreign Sec's party to see whether they think it is along the right lines (tone, content etc). ████████████████████
████████████████████████████████████
████████████████

I spoke to Alastair Campbell earlier about timing. He agreed we need to keep our options open on briging forward publication from w/b 23 September (which would coincide with the possible recall of Parliament) to next week
████████████████████████████████
████████████████████████████████
████████████████████████████████
████████████████

Drafting Comments

The draft looks to me to be heading in the right direction and is much better than earlier drafts. I think the tone could move further in the direction of factual analysis.

Specific comments:

Foreword: Suggest we get upfront UNSCR 687's demand that Iraq disarm. We need to make a key issue Saddam's defiance of the UN (one thing which distinguishes him from other dictators and holders of WMD), his persistent obstruction of the weapons inspectors and the 23/27 obligations (and however many specifically on WMD) unmet.

Executive Summary: Looks pretty good. Could be tweaked a bit in places. The first bullet of para 6 (the importance of WMD) should be strengthened to explain the centrality of WMD to SH's rule - the projection of power etc. I am a supporter of para 8, although I would drop the last phrase which takes it into policy rather than analysis. This document needs to set out the problem rather than the solution. People should conclude that for themselves.

Sections 1 & 2: I would combine these. Most of Section 2 (paras 1-12) should go after para 7 of Section 1. Paras 13-15 of Section 2 should follow Para 10 of Section 1. The passage on Saddam's Iraq (paras 8-15 of Section 1) needs amplifying. A wiring diagram showing the structure of the regime, the role and nature of the SRG, SSA (explaining that they are modelled on the SS and Gestapo etc) and Saddam's fedayeen etc, pictures of Saddam in his various guises (para 14). Crucially this section should explain the role of WMD in the political mythology which has sustained the regime, implicitly why giving it up would amount to a change of regime and how responsibility for WMD rests with those parts of the apparatus on which Saddam depends for

1

CAB|11|0030

his own security. ████████████████████████████████
████████████████████████████

Section 3 looks pretty good. I would depersonalise it a bit. Maybe use "the regime" instead of "SH" more. Para 5 could become a text box explaining more vividly the effects of the various agents. It does not sit very easily amidst the narrative.

I would combine Sections 3 and 4 to demonstrate more explicitly the link between UNSC action and persistent Iraqi obstruction. I would put in a text box listing UNSCRs, Iraq's non-compliance or late compliance with them. I would expand the history of weapons inpsections. It is an interesting story and would give the media a better feel for the difficulties they faced and the persistence of the Iraqi obstruction - Hussein Kamal and the chicken farm etc. ██ We might also get a couple of ex-inspectors to recount their experiences. Could we get the UK's UNSCOM Commissioner to do a piece? The blocking by armed guards of Ritter's team's attempt to get access to the SSA in October 1997 to track BW after the Iraqis had trried to run off with documents would be a good vignette████████████████████████████ Include Annex C

Section 6 is the crux of this and needs to be as factual as possible. I would lose the sub-title "Why are we concerned?" We need a very simple table somewhere (perhaps to be repeated in the Executive Summary) bringing together the unaccounted stuff with what we know since. This should be brief enough to get onto the Sky wall ie, no more than 5 bullets.

Annex A. SUggest this is divided up into so it is obviously a set of case histories.

Annex B should come into the main text - probably into the amplified Section 2.

Annex C should be brought into the combined Section 3 & 4.

Hope this is useful.

Mark

Mark Sedwill
Private Secretary

████████████████████
+44 20 72██ 9██9 (M)
██ 20 72██ 2██
██ 7██ 8██222 (M)

CAB|11|003

Alison Blackshaw

From: Ed.Owen@~~fco.gsi.gov.uk~~
Sent: 11 September 2002 13:14
To: Mark.Sedwill@~~foreign.gov.uk~~; Charles.Gray@~~foreign.gov.uk~~;
Cc: Edward.Chaplin@fco.gsi.gov.uk; ~~jeremygreenstock@georges.gov.uk~~, dmanning@~~.......~~;
            matthew.rycroft@~~...........~~; acampbell@~~...........~~
Subject: RE: CONF: Dossier 10/9 Version - Comments

ATT08844.htm

      I have just looked at the latest draft, and agree with MS that it is a good deal better than earlier drafts. I also share most of Mark's particular comments, and will add further this afternoon. Meanwhile, here are a few thoughts:

The foreword needs to refer to the UN in the first sentences. This is, after all, about the authority of the UN and international law. This is the only way we can win the argument in Parliament and elsewhere. Kofi Annan made some very helpful remarks on the radio this morning about the unique aspect of Iraq's behaviour towards the UN.

It also needs to reiterate the number of UNSC resolutions, and separate obligations, Iraq continues to ignore. In that vain we need to enhance Section 4 - which should list point by point, the obligations on Iraq - and tick off those SH is flouting.

Section 1 is a little odd. It is far too personal about Saddam, particularly paragraphs 12 to 15.

I will make further comments later.

Ed

CAB|11|0033

Alison Blackshaw

From: Mark.Sedwill@~~████████~~
Sent: 11 September 2002 17:42
To: Charles.Gray@~~████████~~
Cc: ~~████████~~, DManning@~~████~~;
    mrycroft@~~████████~~; ACampbell@~~████~~;
    Edward.Chaplin@~~████████~~, Ed.Owen@~~████~~; julian.miller@~~████~~
    ~~████████~~, john.scarlett@~~████████~~; dpruce@~~████~~
Subject: URGENT: Iraq Dossier: 10/9 Version - Foreign Secretary's Comments

ATT00290.htm

Charles,

The Foreign Secretary has now had a chance to go through the draft dossier.
He has endorsed the comments I made earlier on it (see below) and has the
following additional points:

General:
  more graphics, photos, diagrams, textboxes (like the one on p 26)
- incidents etc should have dates - one or two don't

Foreword:
- should be in narrative form by the Prime Minister
- needs a killer para on Saddam's defiance of the UN, only annexation of
another member state and unprecedented use of WMD

Executive SUmmary: V good. No additional changes.

Section 1: Put up front the section on the nature of the regime with more
details on the means of oppression and control (aggression and violent
oppression are intrinsic to the regime's projection of itself)

Section 3: Draw more on external sources eg, detailed reports from
Liverpool University on Halabja or the ICRC on human rights. More
credibility.

Annex A: needs better intro to make clear that human rights violations are
of a sort different to anywhere else (CW against his own population). There
is good material from UN SPecial Rapporteur in a preliminary report from his
visit in Feb 2002.

Mark

· ·

CAB/11/0034

652

Alison Blackshaw

From:	Daniel Pruce
Sent:	17 September 2002 12:01
To:	Tom Kelly; Alastair Campbell; Godric Smith; Tanya Joseph
Subject:	Dossier - 16 September draft

I attended a further Cabinet Office read through this morning. They have:

- re-ordered the text, with the new intell nearer the front (might be able to bring it further forward);

- added a short chapter on JIC and intelligence. Good but could give more details;

- kept in the longer nuclear timelines (p24, para 18 estimates a weapon within 5 years if sanctions are lifted, or within 1-2 years if Iraq obtains fissile material). We need to think carefully about how these will appear to compare with the IISS figure of a weapon within a few months;

- added a short conclusions table - not sure this adds a lot to the Executive Summary.

The re-organised material paints a more convincing cumulative picture, but the facts remain thin on nuclear.

Julian Miller will take in a further round of comments this afternoon and send over a final draft to us this evening.

Separately, Tanya and I are calling on the FCO this afternoon to discuss the practicalities of production and distribution.

DP

CAB/11/0052

Alison Blackshaw

From: Jonathan Powell
Sent: 17 September 2002 13:36
To: Alastair Campbell; David Manning
Subject: RE: Revised dossier foreword

Three comments:

- I think it is worth explicitly stating what TB keeps saying: this is the advice to him from the JIC. On the basis of this advice what other action could he as PM take. Something like "I am today taking the exceptional step of publishing the JIC's advice to me because I want MPs and the British public to see the advice on which I am acting. When you have read this I ask you to consider what else a responsible PM could do than follow the course we have in the face of this advice?"

- We need to do more to back up the assertions. "We cannot of course publish the detailed raw intelligence on which this report is based without endangering the lives of agents. But all of the statements in this report are backed up by detailed intelligence reports, the veracity and the sources of which have been verified by the intelligence agencies". Is there any independent verification we can cite?

- In the penultimate para you need to make it clear Saddam could not attack us <u>at the moment</u>. The thesis is .e would be a threat to the UK in the future if we do not check him.

-----Original Message-----
From: Felicity Hatfield **On Behalf Of** Alastair Campbell
Sent: 17 September 2002 10:21
To: Jonathan Powell; David Manning
Subject: Revised dossier foreword

<< File: 020916 - AC - TB Foreword - dossier.doc >>

Alison Blackshaw

From: Ed.Owen█████████████████
Sent: 17 September 2002 15:41
To: ████████████████ jscarlet██████████████
Cc: Mark.Sedwill████████████ dpruce██████████████; akelly████████████
Edward.Chaplin█████████; richard.stagg███████████;
William.Ehrman█████████████████████████
██████Keeling█████████████Charles.Gray@fco.gsi.gov.uk;
Stephen.Pattison@fco.gsi.gov.uk; Tim.Dowse@fco.gsi.gov.uk;
███████████████████████████Watt@fco.gsi.gov.uk;
Christopher████████████████████; ████████@████████
mark.matthews███████████; █████████@████████k; █████████@████████k;
Andrew.Patrick███████████; █████████@████████
Elizabeth█████████@████████; jmiller@████████
████████████████████████

Subject: RE: Iraq - Dosseir

ATT02837.htm

I want to limit my remarks to the Executive Summary which I do not think reads well enough to give a sceptical reader the confidence to believe that this dossier provides the necessary information.

Para 2 should not include reference to the IISS (too defensive so early on) and should start:

"A huge amount of information about Iraq's weapons of mass destruction is already in the public domain from United Nations reports and from Iraqi defectors. This shows that Iraq continues to possess chemical and biological agents and weapons from the Gulf War ....etc

Delete last sentence and provide new par 3 which reads:

"An independent overview of this public evidence was provided by the IISS in its report , "xxx", on 9th September. This report also suggested that Iraq could assemble nuclear weapons within months of obtaining fissile material from foreign sources. We endorse the IISS's analysis.

New para 4 should then begin:

'As well as this publicly available evidence, significant additional information is available to the Government .... etc.

Then there should be a new par which follows and starts:

"As a result of this intelligence we judge that Iraq has:

- bullet points to follow.

I think there are too many bullet points. The first one repeats what we have said already and the fifth is pretty obvious. The 10th about Ababil-100 only makes sense to Jane's Weekly. The 12th again appears superfluous.

I think about eight bullet points which perhaps combine existing points would be far more persuasive.

I think it odd that we only mention UNSC resolutions until the end of the exec summary. It's also rather oddly written. Shouldn't it read something like:

"In continuing to develop weapons of mass destruction Iraq has flagrantly flouted international law. In a series of SC resolutions, Iraq is under an

1

obligation to destroy its arsenal of these weapons, under the supervision of UN's inspection regime. But, as this paper sets out, Iraq has a history of dishonesty, deception, intimidation and concealment in its dealings with UN inspectors which left in 1998.

Hope this helpful

Ed

Surely and 3 are long and dense. Par 2 is confusing and its reference to the IISS report somewhat odd

2

656

Alison Blackshaw

From:	Jonathan Powell
Sent:	17 September 2002 19:41
To:	Scarlett John - SEC - A
Cc:	Alastair Campbell; David Manning
Subject:	Dossier

The dossier is good and convincing for those who are prepared to be convinced:

I have only three points, none of which affect the way the document is drafted or presented.

First the document does nothing to demonstrate a threat, let alone an imminent threat from Saddam. In other words it shows he has the means but it does not demonstrate he has the motive to attack his neighbours let alone the west. We will need to make it clear in launching the document that we do not claim that we have evidence that he is an imminent threat. The case we are making is that he has continued to develop WMD since 1998, and is in breach of UN resolutions. The international community has to enforce those resolutions if the UN is to be taken seriously.

Second we will be asked about the connections with Al Quaeda. ~~The document says nothing about these and TB will need to find a line on these given the different positions the US is taking on this in public. But we don't ...~~ nce

Third, if I was Saddam I would take a party of western journalists to the Ibn Sina factory or one of the others pictured in the document to demonstrate there is nothing there. How do we close off that avenue to him in advance?

CAB/11/0069

From:	Scarlett John - ~~intelligence~~
Sent:	18 September 2002 08:36
To:	Powell Jonathan - No. 10 -
Cc:	Campbell Alastair - No. 10 -; Manning David - no10-
Subject:	RE: Dossier

We are now doing a note now giving the detail on Iraq and AQ. ~~redacted~~
~~redacted~~
~~redacted~~

The dossier mentions about eight sites. There are dozens more which could be relevant. At least one of the eight (the engine test stand for long range missiles) would not be easy to stage manage without dismantling the stand i.e. this would be progress. The dossier stresses the dual-use problem and the ease of concealment. This applies to trained inspectors let alone journalists. We ought to be able to work out lines to tackle this issue up front.

-----Original Message-----
From: Jonathan Powell ~~redacted~~
Sent: 17 September 2002 19:41
To: Scarlett John - SEC - A
Cc: Alastair Campbell; David Manning
Subject: Dossier

The dossier is good and convincing for those who are prepared to be convinced.
I have only three points, none of which affect the way the document is drafted or presented.
First the document does nothing to demonstrate a threat, let alone an imminent threat from Saddam. In other words it shows he has the means but it does not demonstrate he has the motive to attack his neighbours let alone the west. We will need to make it clear in launching the document that we do not claim that we have evidence that he is an imminent threat. The case we are making is that he has continued to develop WMD since 1998, and is in breach of UN resolutions. The international community has to enforce those resolutions if the UN is to be taken seriously.
Second we will be asked about the connections with Al Quaeda. ~~redacted~~
~~redacted~~
~~redacted~~

Third, if I was Saddam I would take a party of western journalists to the Ibn Sina factory or one of the others pictured in the document to demonstrate there is nothing there. How do we close off that avenue to him in advance?

****

The Cabinet Office's computer systems may be monitored and communications carried on them recorded, to secure the effective operation of the system and for other lawful purposes.

CAB/11/0072

Alison Blackshaw

From:	Mark.Sedwill@~~[redacted]~~
Sent:	18 September 2002 09:51
To:	julian.miller@~~[redacted]~~
Cc:	Edward.Chaplin@~~[redacted]~~; Charles.Gray@~~[redacted]~~; Ed.Owen@~~[redacted]~~; acampbell@~~[redacted]~~; john.scarlet@~~[redacted]~~; mrycroft@~~[redacted]~~
Subject:	RE: CONF: Dossier 10/9 Version - Comments

ATT04426.htm

The Foreign Sec has two small comments:

*   Para 1 of the Executive Summary - should say "Iraq had to admit ..." rather than "has admitted"

*   Para 3 of Par 1 should say "... Prime Minister and senior Ministers ..."

ateful if he could see the draft going to Alastair Campbell.

Mark

Mark Sedwill
Private Secretary

Alison Blackshaw

From: Jonathan Powell
Sent: 18 September 2002 10:45
To: Alastair Campbell; Scarlett John - SEC - A
Cc: David Manning
Subject: RE: Dossier

As I said last night I am not suggesting any changes to the dossier, just flagging up points where we are going to need to mould expectations in advance of publication and on publication and areas where we are going to need briefing for the statement and press afterwards.

A note on AQ would be useful ▆▆▆

On the sites we just need to flag up before publication that of course Saddam can tidy places up and take people there but that does not change what he has been doing there.

The threat argument will be a major problem in the press/parliamentary assault after the dossier comes out and we need to flag up the point in the preface at publication and during the debate. We need to set the test for ourselves at a level we can meet.

-----Original Message-----
From: Felicity Hatfield On Behalf Of Alastair Campbell
Sent: 18 September 2002 10:23
To: Scarlett John - SEC - A; Jonathan Powell
Cc: Alastair Campbell; David Manning
Subject: RE: Dossier

I think we risk complicating the issue if we get into links with Al-Qaida. The dossier, and the debate in Parliament, are explicitly about Iraq/WMD. On the question of sites, we should in our briefing make clear that we assume he will sanitise one of them for the media, and pull some stunt, but remain robust re our judgements. Re the "imminent threat" point, that is why TB's foreword sets out "the case I am making". John, I will show him you revisions and hopefully get the foreword signed off today.

-----Original Message-----
From: Scarlett John - ▆▆▆▆▆▆▆▆▆▆▆▆▆▆▆▆▆▆▆▆▆▆ -
[mailto:▆▆▆▆▆▆▆▆▆@cabinet-office.migon.gov.uk]
Sent: 18 September 2002 08:36
To: Powell Jonathan - No. 10 -
Cc: Campbell Alastair - No. 10 -; Manning David - no10-
Subject: RE: Dossier

We are now doing a note now giving the detail on Iraq and AQ. ▆▆▆▆▆▆▆▆ ▆▆▆▆▆▆▆▆▆▆▆▆▆▆▆▆▆▆▆▆▆▆▆▆▆▆▆▆▆▆▆▆▆

The dossier mentions about eight sites. There are dozens more which could be relevant. At least one of the eight (the engine test stand for long range missiles) would not be easy to stage manage without dismantling the stand i.e. this would be progress. The dossier stresses the dual-use problem and the ease of concealment. This applies to trained inspectors let alone journalists. We ought to be able to work out lines to tackle this issue up front.

-----Original Message-----
From: Jonathan Powell ▆▆▆▆▆▆▆▆▆▆▆▆▆▆▆▆▆▆
Sent: 17 September 2002 19:41
To: Scarlett John - SEC - A
Cc: Alastair Campbell; David Manning
Subject: Dossier

The dossier is good and convincing for those who are prepared to be convinced.

I have only three points, none of which affect the way the document is drafted or presented.

First the document does nothing to demonstrate a threat, let alone an imminent threat from Saddam. In other words it shows he has the means but it does not demonstrate he has the motive to attack his neighbours let alone

CAB111 0077

1

the west. We will need to make it clear in launching the document that we do not claim that we have evidence that he is an imminent threat. The case we are making is that he has continued to develop WMD since 1998, and is in breach of UN resolutions. The international community has to enforce those resolutions if the UN is to be taken seriously.

Second we will be asked about the connections with Al Quaeda. ~~Therefore~~ ~~something about these and TB will need to discuss~~ ~~how we use it~~ ~~given the difference in position with US, who do it more than this~~ and the ~~Americans~~ ~~think~~

Third, if I was Saddam I would take a party of western journalists to the Ibn Sina factory or one of the others pictured in the document to demonstrate there is nothing there. How do we close off that avenue to him in advance?

****

CAB|11|0078

Alison Blackshaw

From: Felicity Hatfield on behalf of Alastair Campbell
Sent: 18 September 2002 14:31
To: Scarlett John - SEC - A
Cc: 'Julian.Miller████████████████████
Subject: Another dossier memo!

I asked someone in my office, whose judgement I trust, who has nothing to do with this area, to read the dossier "cold", as it were, and give me impressions, which I want to pass on.

Overall, she found it convincing. CW/BW, in particular. "By the time I got to human rights, I was in no doubt he has to be dealt with ". Indeed she felt she could have read a lot more on human rights.

However, she found the nuclear section confusion and unconvincing. "It left me thinking there's nothing much to worry about". She felt the whole section lacked the clarity of the rest of the document. "It needs a section that sets out what you need to make a nuclear weapon, set alongside to what he has already". She also felt it could benefit from an explanation of sanctions, how they work, what they do.

Sorry to bombard on this point, but I do worry that the nuclear section will become the main focus and as currently drafted, is not in great shape. Do you have a new version yet?

A few minor points she made. (Page numbers refer to the one you gave me yesterday am)

- different spelling of Qusay/Qusai
- Edinburgh spelled wrong in the box on page 10
- an "S" missing on the end of "delivery mean", par. 11 and page 12
- par 10, page 19 can we have more details on "illegal foreign assistance"
- page 21, par 12 first block, UK - US has as aberrant question mark in the middle
- page 30, par 33 we say nobody can't be used for military procurement, yet elsewhere we say it has been so used for growth agents.
- top line, page 36, aberrant apostrophe in "Iraqi's" should be deleted
- page 43, par 4, the words "there are" should be inserted between "that" and "no" in the first line of that paragraph.

Finally she felt that the conclusion box on CW/BW should include a list of agents in possession and production. I agree with that.

Sorry about the earlier mix up re foreword. You should have the correct one now.

UAB/11/0088

Alison Blackshaw

From: Joanna Nadin
Sent: 18 September 2002 14:42
To: Alastair Campbell
Subject: intelligence

Another point I have just thought of - when it mentions "intelligence" - what exactly are they talking about?

Do they mean our people in Iraq (if there are any), do they mean defectors?

Saying "intelligence suggests that this factory has probably been rebuilt" is not entirely convincing - especially if you do not know what "intelligence" is.

I think it needs to make clear to whatever extent it can (there are restrictions I am sure) how good these sources are. No-one outside Whitehall will know.

CAB/11/0089

Alison Blackshaw

From: Scarlett John - ISS - ████████████████████████████████
Sent: 18 September 2002 15:06
To: Campbell Alastair - No. 10 -; Scarlett John - ISS -
Cc: Miller Julian - Intelligence and Security Secretariat -
Subject: RE: Another dossier memo!

████████████

John Scarlett has seen these comments and is taking account of them in the revisions now in the process of being incorporated. ████████████████ ████████████████ regular Wednesday JIC meeting ███████████████ ███████████████████████████████████. He will revert later. The aim remains to have the draft finalised in the course of this extended day.

CAB/11/0090

Alison Blackshaw

From:	Felicity Hatfield on behalf of Alastair Campbell
Sent:	19 September 2002 08:21
To:	Scarlett John - SEC - A
Cc:	David Manning; Jonathan Powell; 'Julian.Miller~~@cabinet-office.x.gsi.gov.uk~~
Subject:	Nuclear Section

As I said to Julian last night, I think it would be simpler to have just one clearer section on nuclear timelines, perhaps on the following lines. (This would delete par. 18 and replace 24).

It is impossible to be precise about nuclear timelines. We can be clear however, that provided sanctions and export controls remain in place and effective, it is not possible for Iraq to develop nuclear weapons. This is because although they have the expertise, the design data, the planning and the intent they do not have the material necessary for the production of fissile material. This contrasts with CW/BW, which they can produce indigenously. Even if sanctions were removed, we assess that it would take up to five years for them to develop nuclear weapons. The timelines are considerably shortened however if Iraq manages to obtain fissile material illegally from overseas. In these circumstances, the JIC assessed in early 2002 that they could produce nuclear weapons in between one and two years.

<< File: dossier draft.doc >> This is a rough draft of what could be a core script for Tuesday - whether we go up on Today, or do a briefing. I think the key point in our favour is the systematic nature of what Saddam is up to. The weakness, obviously, is our inability to say that he could pull the nuclear trigger any time soon. But the basic message of by then it would be too late does deal with that I think.

1

CAB/11/0092

666

Alison Blackshaw

From: Jonathan Powell
Sent: 19 September 2002 13:57
To: Alastair Campbell; Scarlett John - SEC - A
Cc: David Manning
Subject: RE:

Can I see it?

-----Original Message-----
From: Alison Blackshaw **On Behalf Of** Alastair Campbell
Sent: 19 September 2002 12:43
To: Scarlett John - SEC - A
Cc: Jonathan Powell; David Manning
Subject:
Importance: High

I had a quick skim and am now out of the office until 2.30pm.

Re the foreword, I don't like the first sentence which makes him sound a bit James Bond-y. Can we discuss?

I don't think the conclusion works. I would either revert to, and strengthen, the box idea, or drop. In a way, the foreword covers most of the points.

I'm not sure about the "protest and project" his power bit.

Could the Shia uprising point go in the executive summary?

P.26, para 17, line 4, can we say "required for", rather than "that could be for use in".

"May have" re Qusai is very weak.

Sorry this is so rushed.

From:	Jonathan Powell
Sent:	19 September 2002 15:45
To:	Alastair Campbell; Scarlett John - SEC - A
Cc:	David Manning
Subject:	RE:
Importance:	High

Found my copy. I think it is good.
I agree with Alastair you should drop the conclusion.
Alastair - what will be the headline in the Standard on day of publication?
What do we want it to be?
I think the statement on p19 that "Saddam is prepared to use chemical and
biological weapons if he believes his regime is under threat" is a bit of a
problem. It backs up the Don McIntyre argument that there is no CBW threat
and we will only create one if we attack him. I think you should redraft the
para. My memory of the intelligence is that he has set up plans to use CBW
on western forces and that these weapons are integrated into his military
planning.
It needs checking for typos, eg Iraqi in middle of page 27.

> ——Original Message——
> From: Alison Blackshaw On Behalf Of Alastair Campbell
> Sent: 19 September 2002 12:43
> To: Scarlett John - SEC - A
> Cc: Jonathan Powell; David Manning
> Subject:
> Importance: High
>
> I had a quick skim and am now out of the office until 2.30pm.
>
> Re the foreword, I don't like the first sentence which makes him sound a
> bit James Bond-y. Can we discuss?
>
> I don't think the conclusion works. I would either revert to, and
> strengthen, the box idea, or drop. In a way, the foreword covers most of
> the points.
>
> I'm not sure about the "protest and project" his power bit.
>
> Could the Shia uprising point go in the executive summary?
>
> P.26, para 17, line 4, can we say "required for", rather than "that could
> be for use in".
>
> "May have" re Qusai is very weak.

Sorry this is so rushed.

CAB/11/0103

From:	Alison Blackshaw on behalf of Alastair Campbell
Sent:	19 September 2002 17:03
To:	Scarlett John - SEC - A
Cc:	Clare Sumner; Matthew Rycroft; David Manning; Jonathan Powell
Subject:	FW: Re final points for your 5pm meeting.
Importance:	High

1) Re nuclear timelines. If we're saying that it would take between one and 2 years for them to build a nuclear weapon by illegal means, why would it take 5 years with no sanctions? A lay reader may assume that no sanctions would mean he could do what he wanted and therefore, presumably, what he needed between 1 and 2 years.

If the answer is that it would take 5 years to go from planning to reality, whereas he could purchase ready-made materials from overseas, and so cut the timelines, I think that should be made explicity clear

Sorry not to have spotted this earlier but it now seems an obvious point.

2) Do we really need the 2 sentences on radiological dispersal device? They add little.

3) Further up that page, on the 2 blob points, could we say "is required to" rather than "could be used to".

CAB/11/0104

Alison Blackshaw

From:	Robert Hill
Sent:	20 September 2002 09:27
To:	Alastair Campbell; Jonathan Powell
Cc:	Sally Morgan
Subject:	Dossier/Statement on tuesday

This may be blindingly obvious but in terms of giving credibility to the dossier are we making parallels with Afghanistan. People said then: 'Show us the evidence before you attack'. We did - we could not share it all or give chapter and verse for it all. But when we went in we were proved right - in fact the situation was worse than we had described.

1

APPENDIX 14

10 DOWNING STREET
LONDON SW1A 2AA

From the Prime Minister's Press Office   29 May 2003

Dear Mr. Damazar,

RADIO FOUR TODAY PROGRAMME

In the absence abroad of my colleague Tom Kelly, I would like to register our concern at the failure of this morning's Today programme to contact Downing Street for a response to Andrew Gilligan's story which made serious and untrue allegations about this office over the presentation of a dossier relating to Iraq.

What is of further concern is that Today continued to run these allegations, at the top of every news bulletin, without any reference to the firm denial provided voluntarily by Downing Street after we first heard the story. This absence of any balancing comment continued despite our duty press officer calling the programme no less than four times. While John Humphrys did finally refer to our statement in his two-way with Andrew Gilligan, this is not the same, as I am sure you will accept, as making clear we categorically denied the story in your news bulletins.

I am also concerned that the World at One declined to interview Adam Ingram, the Minister for the Armed Forces, on their programme today on the grounds that he is not a member of the Cabinet. He is, however, the Minister responding for the Government on this issue and without his appearance I am unclear how the programme thought it could present a balanced piece on this issue. I notice, too, that WATO also failed, for some reason, to carry Downing Street's quote that, 'Any suggestion that there was any pressure or intervention from Downing Street is entirely false' which had been used on other broadcasters and newspapers.

I should add that we categorically deny the allegations made. But our complaint goes beyond this. The BBC's guidelines spell out clearly your obligations to present balanced reporting. I would like to hear from you how you

CAB\1\0154   8

believe these standards have been met when your reporters failed to give this office a chance in advance to respond to allegations and ignored denials when they were provided.

I would be interested to receive your comments on these issues.

Yours sincerely,

ANNE SHEVAS

Mr. Mark Damazer
Deputy Director BBC News
By Fax: 0208 576 7120

CAB/1/0155

9

British Broadcasting Corpor 0208 624 9874 ision Centre Wood Lane London W12 7RJ
Telephone 020 8624 9859 Fax 020 8624 9874

BBC News

Head of Radio News

Ms Anne Shevas
Prime Minister's Press Office
10 Downing Street
London
SW1A 2AA

Fax.: 020 7930 2831

30 May 2003

Dear Anne Shevas,

Thank you for your fax of May 29th to Mark Damazer regarding coverage of the Iraq dossier published last year. Mr Damazer is out of the office today and has asked me to reply. You raise a series of issues which I will address in turn.

Firstly you complain that we failed to contact Downing Street for a response. In fact we set out the main aspects of the piece to Adam Ingrams assistant on the evening before transmission. No specific Government comment was made at that time and when your office contacted the programme at 0715 their comments were included verbatim in John Humphrys introduction to the main item shortly after 0730. And of course later in the programme Mr Ingram had the opportunity to outline the Governments case.

Secondly you complain that we "continued to run these allegations at the top of every news bulletin without any reference to the firm denial." In the bulletin at 8.00am the lead story was in fact a report on the Prime Ministers arrival in Iraq with only a brief mention of the intelligence dossier in the introduction, the Downing Street denial did feature in the news bulletins on Radio Four at 0900, 1000, 1100 and 1200.

Turning to The World at One, the headline at the top of the programme started with the words *"Downing Street has dismissed a claim that the Governments dossier on Saddam Husseins weapons of mass destruction was rewritten to make the threat appear more urgent."* This denial was repeated in the introduction to the report on the subject by Shaun Ley, as it was when the story was carried on other BBC networks during the day.

As to the general approach of The World at One, the programme was seeking to move forwards and explore the process by which intelligence reports are written rather than going over the original issue again. Hence there were interviews with Dame Pauline Neville Jones

CAB/1/0156 6

and Mr Tom King. They did seek a Cabinet Minister to join this discussion and declined to interview Adam Ingram again as he had already appeared on Radio Four that morning. Instead they used a clip from his Today appearance.

Yours sincerely,

STEPHEN MITCHELL

cc: Mark Damazer

10 DOWNING STREET
LONDON SW1A 2AA

Director of Communications and Strategy 6 June 2003

Dear Richard

I am writing to complain about Andrew Gilligan's irresponsible reporting of what he claims to be information from 'intelligence sources'.

As was clear from his report on the Today programme this morning, he continues to display an extraordinary ignorance about intelligence issues. He said, for example, that the Joint Intelligence Committee (JIC) is a "No. 10 committee" on which the intelligence Agencies are "represented". He should know, because this is public knowledge, that the JIC is a Cabinet Office committee. The current Chairman is a former SIS official. It brings together the Heads of the three Intelligence and Security Agencies (Secret Intelligence Service, Government Communications Headquarters and the Security Service), the Chief of Defence Intelligence and his Deputy with senior officials responsible for policy formulation from the Foreign Office, the MoD, the Home Office, the Treasury, the DTI, the Cabinet Office and representatives of other government departments and agencies. It is part of the Cabinet Office, meets each week in the Cabinet Office, and is under the authority of the Security and Intelligence Co-ordinator. To present it as anything other than the intelligence community is grossly misleading. The role and composition of the JIC would be known to anyone with an ounce of knowledge about their work. Indeed, it was set out in the WMD dossier and has been in the public domain since publication of the Government's "National Intelligence Machinery" booklet in 1993.

Andrew Gilligan also said: "The JIC is the Committee in which disputes between the intelligence services and Downing Street are mediated." This is

CAB/1/0244

simply untrue. The JIC provides regular intelligence assessments to the Prime Minister, other ministers and senior officials on a wide range of foreign policy and international security issues.

Andrew Gilligan said: "...there's absolutely no doubt that there was rather a major row in that Committee". This is false, whatever his "source" tells him. As the Prime Minister has made clear, all the intelligence in the September dossier was there with the complete authority of the JIC. There was no row.

Do you accept that what Gilligan said this morning about the composition and role of the JIC is inaccurate? What, if anything, do you intend to do about it?

The BBC's reporting on the WMD issue has been driven for days now by the false claim of a single uncorroborated source that Gilligan claims to be reliable. The Prime Minister, after consulting the Chairman of the JIC who was able to speak on behalf of the Agencies represented on it, has emphatically denied the claims made by this single uncorroborated source, yet your reporting continues to be driven by it, not just on the Today programme, but across the BBC. At no point has the reliability of Gilligan's source been questioned or discussed by the BBC.

Strategic intelligence assessments are presented to the government by the JIC who receive intelligence information on a continual basis. The JIC draw on a wide range of experience and expertise to assess the information for its reliability and strength. As the Prime Minister said in a speech on the subject, some of the raw intelligence is reliable; some of it may be misinformation; some of it will be gossip; other material will be based on technical intelligence gathering. Following a rigorous process of assessment and analysis this information is presented to the Prime Minister and other Ministers.

I would like to ask about the rigour of the process which the BBC applies to its reporting. Do you have a process to filter out potential misinformation, gossip, unreliable or uncorroborated information? What is that process?

In particular I would like to know what checks and balances have been applied to some of Mr Gilligan's reporting of information from 'anonymous intelligence sources' or indeed how the BBC's own Guidelines are applied. You cannot have missed the irony that one of the central (albeit false) charges agsint us (namely that the 45 minutes claim in the dossier was based on a single

CAB/1/0245

uncorroborated source) was itself broadcast on the word of single uncorroborated source; or that Gilligan chose on 24 September to present the government's assessment as saying little that was new (and claimed that he already knew about the 45 minutes readiness to deploy CB weapons) but subsequently (Mail on Sunday, 1 June) claimed it was "very revelatory indeed".

With regard to the report on the BBC Today programme last Thursday at 0607 (transcript enclosed), can you explain to me how it conforms with the BBC's own producer guidelines, in particular the following three.

1. "Programmes should be reluctant to rely on only one source."

At what level was the decision taken to run this story, based on only one uncorroborated source, and to continue to run this story after an official denial, made on the authority of the Prime Minister and the Agencies themselves?

2. "The authority of programmes can be undermined by the use of anonymous contributors whose status the audience cannot judge."

What actions did BBC editors and management take to ensure the authority of the Today programme was not put in question by the use of this anonymous contribution? Are you, or the editors of all the outlets which have run reports on Gilligan's claims, aware of the source's professional status, the organisation he works for, his seniority and credibility? Have you, or the editors made any inquiries?

3. "contributors' credentials may need to be checked and corroborated several times. Documentary evidence may be needed to validate both stories and contributors' identities. It will usually be appropriate to seek corroboration from sources other than those suggested by the contributor."

Prior to broadcast what actions did BBC editors and management take to ensure the above guideline was complied with? Mr Gilligan's own account of his 'source' in newspaper articles would suggest it was not. Do the BBC have documentary evidence to validate either the story or the source of this item? Did the BBC seek corroboration from other sources prior to broadcasting the story? Did you offer any opportunity for a reply to some very serious allegations being made about the reliability of the dossier produced by the JIC?

CAB\1\0246

In a rather pathetic attempt to stand up his story, Gilligan claimed subsequently that the story has also been subsequently corroborated by, among others, Clare Short and Robin Cook. Can you spell out which elements of Gilligan's original story they are on the record as having corroborated which have not been addressed by the Prime Minister?

Gilligan also cites Adam Ingram as having corroborated his story that the "45 minutes" claim was based on intelligence from only one source and that it was added into the dossier by me. However Adam Ingram and the Prime Minister, the latter having consulted the Chairman of the JIC, have made it absolutely clear that this piece of information was not inserted into the dossier by No10. It came from an established and reliable line of reporting and was consistent with previous intelligence assessments. Its use was approved by the JIC after going through the usual rigorous process of assessment. The Prime Minister, having again consulted theChairman of JIC, has confirmed this, and that the allegations made by Gilligan and his "source" are not true.

You will, I imagine, seek to defend your reporting, as you always do. In this case, you would be defending the indefensible. On the word of a single, uncorroborated source, you have allowed one reporter to drive the BBC's coverage. We are left wondering why you have guidelines at all, given that they are so persistently breached without any comeback whatsoever.

ALASTAIR CAMPBELL

Mr. Richard Sambrook
BBC

Enclosures

CAB 11 0247

BBC

From Director, News

Alastair Campbell, Esq.,
Director of Comunication and Strategy,
10 Downing Street,
LONDON.
SW1A 2AA

13 JUN 2003

11 June, 2003

Dear Alastair,

Thank you for your fax of 6 June regarding Andrew Gilligan and the reporting of WMD. I see no likelihood of us agreeing on this matter but I will briefly set out why I think your allegations about our journalism are misguided.

Much of what you write focuses on the question of sources. You are wrong to suggest that our journalism is being driven by a single source. Andrew Gilligan has made it clear that one *specific* concern about the September dossier's presentation of the Government's case derived from a single source - the claim that Saddam Hussein could launch a WMD within 45 minutes of the order being given. But the judgements that were made on the quality of the source and its usefulness were informed by a wider context. The fact is that a variety of sources, over a period of time, have indicated their concern about the way intelligence was used and presented in September and they have voiced this concern both to Andrew and also to other BBC journalists. And, for that matter, to non-BBC journalists. That is why we know there has been tension about the presentation of intelligence.

Further, if we had thought the single source incredible we would not have reported the allegation at all. You would not expect me to reveal the source (and I am gratified that you have not asked) but I can assure you that I am satisfied that the source knew what he/she was talking about. It is fanciful to imply that Andrew - or anyone

CAB/1/0248 ..../2

else for that matter - can simply put stories on air without discussion with his editorial management. Of course we would have preferred the source to have gone on the record - but neither you nor I can be surprised that he/she chose not to do so. In sum - neither the source's anonymity nor the fact that *for one particular piece of information* there was only one source made it wrong for us to use the information in the way we did. There was no breach of the producer guidelines.

You talk about a right of reply. I agree. Our programmes did give the Government a right of reply and will continue to do so. By 0730 on the morning that Andrew Gilligan broadcast his first report on the drafting of the dossier the Government reply was broadcast. It was inadvertently missed at 0800 (though not by Radio 5) and was then used throughout the day and across the piece. Ministers have gone in and out of studios to say there was no disagreement about the dossier, that Andrew (and the many others who have published similar stories) have got it wrong - and so on. They will be able to continue to say this - but that does not mean we do not stand by the story. We do.

On which point it is worth going back to stage 1. We have not suggested that the 45 minute point was invented by anyone in Downing Street against the wishes of anyone in the intelligence community. We have suggested that there are pertinent and serious questions to be asked about the *presentation* of the intelligence material - a rather different point and one which I am not convinced your letter recognises.

Yours sincerely,

(Richard Sambrook)

CAB/11/0249

10 DOWNING STREET
LONDON SW1A 2AA

12 June 2003

Thank you for your reply of 11 June 2003. There are several outstanding issues you have failed to address, to which I would like responses.

Firstly, you have not answered my questions about Andrew Gilligan's obvious ignorance about intelligence issues. So I repeat - do you accept that what Andrew Gilligan said last week about the composition and role of the JIC was inaccurate? What, if anything do you intend to do about it?

Secondly, on the '45 minute' claim, you acknowledge it was indeed from a single source, for which I am grateful. I therefore believe it <u>does</u> conflict with your guideline that *"programmes should be reluctant to rely on only one source"*. Given this acknowledgement please can you explain to me how you can reach the conclusion that this guideline has been upheld? As I know that the source of this specific piece of information is not a member of the JIC, nor was directly involved in the publication of the dossier, would you accept that an emphatic denial from the Chairman of the JIC carries more weight than Mr Gilligan's single uncorroborated anonymous source?

Furthermore, the Intelligence and Security Committee report, published this week, also confirms Mr Gilligan's story was wrong.

"In September 2002 some intelligence was declassified and used to produce a dossier on the Iraqi WMD programme. The Agencies were fully consulted in the

CAB/1/0250

681

*production of the dossier, which was assembled by the Assessments Staff, endorsed
by the JIC and issued by the Prime Minister. The Committee supports the
responsible use of intelligence and material collected by the Agencies to inform the
public on matters such as these."*
(Intelligence and Security Committee Annual Report 2002/03 para 81)

For your information, this report is available at:

http://www.cabinet-office.gov.uk/reports/intelligence/pdf/annualir0203.pdf

I was disappointed, though not surprised, to note that the BBC's coverage of
this report focused primarily on the February dossier with very little mention, and
in some broadcasts no mention at all, of the Committee's conclusions on the
September dossier (para 81 as above). When the September dossier was
mentioned, the report's conclusion that none of the allegations made were true was
dismissed, as if of no significance. I find this peculiar, given questions over the
reliability of the information in the September dossier and the process in which it
was produced had led BBC output for over a week. In fact, I think the lack of
prominence given to the September dossier this week compared to the huge
amount of coverage last week, has created confusion as to which dossier was the
subject of the ISC's concerns. I'm left wondering if there has been a deliberate
lack of clarity in reporting as the report's conclusions on the September dossier
make uncomfortable reading for the BBC, calling into question the reliability of
much of your recent output.

Given the conclusions of this report, and the questions it raises about
Andrew Gilligan's source, will the BBC be conducting an internal inquiry into how
one of its journalists could get it so wrong and be left unchallenged by his
colleagues and bosses?

You say in your letter that you have not made any allegations, but instead
merely suggested that there are pertinent and serious questions to be asked. I
disagree. You have made very serious allegations which, if true, would amount to
serious wrongdoing by me and my staff. Furthermore, you have continued to
repeat them with little reference to denials by the Chairman of the JIC and
vindication by the ISC.

Finally, the BBC gave considerable time on Sunday, including leading some
bulletins, to the Sunday Telegraph story that I had written a letter of apology to the
head of the SIS. Some of your reports stated this was a confirmation that we had
abused intelligence. I know I am just a single source so your guidelines may
prevent you from reporting my testimony, but the head of the SIS has also

CAB/1/0251

confirmed the story is untrue. I am currently seeking an apology from the Sunday Telegraph.

ALASTAIR CAMPBELL

Mr Richard Sambrook
BBC, By Fax: 0208 576 7120

CAB/1/0252

From Director, News

BBC Correspondence
With Sambrook

Alastair Campbell, Esq.,
Director of Communication and Strategy,
10 Downing Street,
LONDON.
SW1A 2AA

16 June, 2003

Dear Alastair,

Thank you for your latest fax. Let me try again to address your concerns.

You still complain that in one of his many pieces Andrew Gilligan referred to the Joint Intelligence Committee as "a Number 10 Committee" rather than a "Cabinet Office Committee." I can only find one such reference. I concede that the Cabinet Office is not the same as a Prime Ministerial Department though I note that the first objective of the CO is to "support the PM in leading the government." In this instance, Andrew was attempting to simplify a description of the administration of government. I hardly think that amounts to "obvious ignorance" about intelligence issues.

You continue to believe Andrew Gilligan is in conflict with the Producer Guidelines. The Guidelines do say that our programme makers should be reluctant to rely on only one source. This guideline is not an outright ban, and as I explained in my previous letter Andrew Gilligan's judgements about that source (and the judgement of others involved in the decision to broadcast the story) were taken in context. A variety of sources over a period of time had spoken to BBC journalists about their concerns on matters relating to intelligence and WMD. However, we made it plain to the audience that the concern about the dossier's presentation of the 45 minute WMD threat derived from a single source.

............/2

CAB/1/0253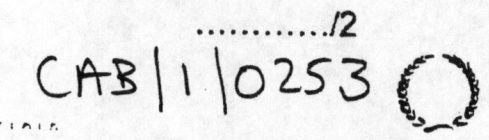

You also say that last week's Intelligence and Security Committee report "confirms Mr. Gilligan's story was wrong." The section of the report you quote does not do so. It states that the intelligence agencies were consulted in the production of the dossier, that the "Assessments Staff" assembled it, and that the JIC endorsed it. All of this is compatible with the dossier being rewritten before publication, and compatible too with the suggestion that some people in the intelligence community were still unhappy after publication as a result of changes in the presentation of the evidence. This is what Andrew Gilligan's source told him and is what we reported. As for your assertion that you know that the source of Andrew Gilligan's information is "not a member of the JIC or directly involved in compiling the dossier" I make no comment. Suffice to say that Andrew Gilligan had discussions with senior BBC colleagues in advance of broadcasting his piece and we are happy about the robustness of his source.

You have now queried our coverage of last week's ISC report generally, referring to "a deliberate lack of clarity." As you will know this coverage was in the hands of reporters other than Andrew Gilligan and it was their conclusion that the most significant areas in the report were the comments on the February dossier rather than the September one - together with the comments about Ministers needing to be better briefed.

You raise a new issue - about communications between yourself and the Intelligence agencies. I have read a number of fairly straightforward scripts quoting Downing Street on this matter which did not repeat the detail of the Sunday Telegraph's version of events. If you feel we got something wrong I would be happy to look into the specific report which gives you concern.

............/3

CAB\1\0254

I am sorry that we still seem far apart on the validity of our reporting on the concerns about the September dossier. I should remind you that we have a Programme Complaints Unit which functions completely separately from production arms of the BBC such as BBC News and reports to the Director General with a right of appeal to the Governors. If you feel it would help, you could make a formal complaint to the Head of the PCU, Fraser Steel.

Yours sincerely,

(Richard Sambrook)

CAB| 1|0255

10 DOWNING STREET
LONDON SW1A 2AA

Director of Communications and Strategy   26 June 2003

Dear Greg

I was sorry that I had to say what I said about the BBC, but I'm afraid
private discussion and correspondence on recent events have proved to be
pointless. I am regularly assured by Richard Sambrook that when the BBC
makes mistakes, you admit it. I'm afraid that is not the case and I have nine
years of experience of this phenomenon.

Put to one side our complaint about the BBC's coverage of Iraq recently
about which you were dismissive in your letter to the Prime Minister.

On the specific issue of the reporting of allegations about our and my
conduct in relation to the WMD dossier it has been a disgrace. I hope you take
time to read the entirety of my, and your correspondent's, evidence to the FAC.
I hope you note the contradictions between the latter's evidence and what he
broadcast and wrote, as a BBC journalist at the time. I hope you note the weight
of denial by the Agencies.

This story is 100% wrong. Every now and then the BBC might just admit
that it doesn't get everything right, and apologise. Today Richard said that the
BBC was not making allegations but reporting them. That is not accurate. And
if it were, it means you don't know if the story you broadcast was true. On the
basis on which you now say this was reported, it means that if a journalist is told
by a credible source in the BBC that you are involved in a terrible scandal, that
can be reported without corroboration provided the journalist makes clear that
this is what is being said, but not necessarily true. That is not journalism.

I am a huge admirer of the BBC, which is one of the UK's greatest
strengths and assets and which produced some exceptional journalism on Iraq.
But I really believe that if this story is not corrected, and an apology not given, it

BBC15/0092

687

- 2 -

renders pointless any attempt at meaningful discussion about how to resolve difficulties between us. It also underlines our concern that you are content to see BBC standards debased by agenda-driven journalism within parts of the Corporation. I think it's a big mistake. I also wonder whether your viewers and listeners really think they need to see and hear as much about this story as they've been force fed in recent days.

I just ask you, as someone whose career and commitment I've always admired, to think about it. I am copying this letter to Gavyn Davies, and regard it as private.

I have written separately to Richard Sambrook about questions that arise from his interview this morning, and I am releasing that letter to the press.

ALASTAIR CAMPBELL

Mr. Greg Dyke
Director General
BBC

10 DOWNING STREET
LONDON SW1A 2AA

Director of Communications and Strategy   26 June 2003

Dear Richard

    As you know, I have been engaged in private correspondence with you in recent weeks about the allegations on the BBC on the conduct of the Government, and of me, in relation to the WMD dossier of September 2002.

    I heard your interview on the Today programme this morning and would like now, in view of the continuing interest in this, to ask a number of questions. You said that the BBC had never alleged that we took the country into conflict on a false basis. I disagree. Indeed, could I point you to the introduction by John Humphreys before he spoke to your correspondent on the Today programme prior to my appearance at the FAC. He said:

> "Mr Campbell will answer questions about allegations made on this programme by Andrew Gilligan that the case for going to war was exaggerated, specifically that one of the dossiers presented by Mr. Blair had been sexed up to make it appear that Saddam was a greater threat to the West than the intelligence justified."

    That is one of many statements on the BBC by reporters and presenters making clear that Mr. Gilligan made these allegations, and that they amount to charges that the Government, from the Prime Minister down, misled Parliament and public about the case on which he had led the country into conflict.

    I think you will agree that this was certainly the allegation as MP's, press and public understood it at the time, as the voluminous coverage and the Parliamentary concern have shown. Could I have a response by the end of the day; given that is the time scale I am seeking to meet in relation to the issues the FAC has asked me further to address I think it is fair and reasonable. And of course, like me you will already be immersed in the detail as a result of our previous, thus far private exchanges.

CAB/11/0352

The questions are these:

- Does the BBC still stand by the allegation it made on 29th May that Number Ten added in the 45 minute claim to the dossier? Yes or no?
- Does it still stand by the allegation made on the same day that we did so again the wishes of the intelligence agencies? Yes or no?
- Does it still stand by the allegation made on that day that both we and the intelligence agencies knew the 45 minute claim to be wrong and inserted it despite knowing that? Yes or no?
- Does it still stand by the allegation, again on the same day, that we ordered th September dossier to be "sexed up" in the period leading up to its publication and that Gilligan had found what Humphreys called "evidence" that it was "cobbled together at the last minute with some unconfirmed material that had not been approved by the security services"? Yes or no?
- Does it still stand by the statement made on 6th June by Gilligan that the JIC i not part of the intelligence community, but a Number 10 Committee which exists to arbitrate between government and the intelligence agencies?
- Does it stand by the claim on the 3rd of June that the chairman of the JIC only "kind of bureaucratically signed off his report"? Yes or no?

Could I also ask:

- How many sources was the original "45 minute" allegation being added in based on? Was it one source or more than one source? You will be aware of the BBC Guidelines on this.
- Is that source on the JIC, and do you agree that any source not on the JIC did not have the full picture?
- Was the source, as Gilligan has said, "a senior official involved in drawing up the dossier", or is he, as _you_ said today, a source, "in the intelligence services I'm sure you at least understand the significance of the difference to which I : alluding.
- Is it now normal BBC practice not to seek to corroborate single source stories
- Finally do you believe that Gilligan's statement to the FAC that all he had ev alleged was that we gave "undue prominence" to the 45 minute point, or do y share my views that this is utterly inconsistent with what he and others or the BBC have said and what Gilligan has said, writing as a BBC journalist in the Mail on Sunday, the Sunday Telegraph, and The Spectator.

CAB/1/0353

the BBC's view? If it is a personal view, could you tell me what rule governs what BBC correspondents may or may not write in a freelance capacity to boost their BBC earnings? What are the procedures and were they followed in relation to this article? I am interested too, in respect of the many BBC journalists who boost their incomes by writing for national newspapers, what procedures govern their conduct and this writings? You will be aware that MP's have also expressed concern on this.

As our previous correspondence has achieved little on this subject, other than further exposing the BBC's refusal ever to apologise, even on a story that is potentially so damaging to the integrity of the Prime Minister, the Government and the political process, I am releasing this to the press. I look forward to your reply later today.

ALASTAIR CAMPBELL

Mr. Richard Sambrook

Alastair Campbell, Esq.,
Director of Communication and Strategy,
10 Downing Street,
LONDON.
SW1A 2AA

27 June, 2003

Dear Alastair

Thank you for your letter of 26th June. I chose not to reply yesterday
as I wanted time to examine fully the questions you asked and to
write a considered reply. That was not possible in the timescale you
gave me.

Before I answer the questions in detail I wish to explain the wider
context in which we came to broadcast the story in question. I will
summarise this under three headings:

- Your general claim that the BBC's reporting of the war and
  the events both before and after was biased.
- The impact of your February dossier being discredited.
- The general concern expressed by members of the security
  services that intelligence reports were being exaggerated.

1. Allegations of biased reporting

In your evidence to the Foreign Affairs Select Committee you made
it clear that you believed the BBC had an anti-war agenda. It is our
firm view that Number Ten tried to intimidate the BBC in its reporting
of events leading up to the war and during the course of the war
itself. As we told you in correspondence before the war started, our
responsibility was to present an impartial picture and you were not
best placed to judge what was impartial. This was particularly the
case given the widescale opposition to the war in the UK at that
time, including significant opposition inside the Parliamentary

............/2

CAB/1/0355

Labour Party. For example, you will remember when the key division on the war took place in the House of Commons in March you wrote to me to suggest that we had given too much prominence to the vote which recorded the largest backbench parliamentary revolt in modern history.

During the war you again accused us of unfairness - in particular criticising our reporting from Baghdad. You know that we strongly dispute that charge and the BBC's Board of Governors, after detailed discussion both during and after the war, have expressed their complete satisfaction with the impartiality of BBC News coverage.

In your evidence to the Select Committee you extended your attack on our journalism suggesting that we have been animated by a rationale "that the Prime Minister led the country to war on a false basis". It seems you have missed the many reports we have filed from Iraq about mass graves, torture and political repression - evidence which has been used to justify the war.

2. The February Dossier

It is impossible to discuss our reporting of the September 2002 dossier without seeing it in the context of what we knew by then of the February 2003 dossier - the dossier which even the Foreign Secretary described as "a complete Horlicks" earlier this week.

What was by then clear was that your department had plagiarised an article from the internet, based on an old University thesis, changed crucial parts of it and then used it unattributed to strengthen the case for Britain going to war. That was the provenance of the February dossier - which might still stand were it not for the intervention of a Cambridge academic.

The discrediting of the February dossier inevitably influenced questions asked about any similar dossiers. In these circumstances any decent journalist would inevitably question whether similar tactics had been used when writing the earlier dossier.

............/3

CAB/1/0356

In addition, in early March, the Director General of the IAEA, Dr Mohammed El Baradei, described the documents on which an important claim in the September dossier was based (the Niger uranium claim) as "not authentic" - and indeed cast doubt on other aspects of the September dossier's claims about a nuclear weapons programmes.

We thus made a judgement that the information provided by the source fitted into a pattern of concerns - and that it was perfectly proper to report the allegations made by Andrew Gilligan's source. Your correspondence and evidence to the FAC ignores this background - which is central to any understanding of the BBC's journalism.

3. Unease in the Security Services

As we have told you before, a number of BBC journalists who have close contact with both the military and the security services had reported that their contacts were concerned that intelligence reports were being exaggerated to strengthen the case against Saddam Hussein. In particular they were saying that whilst low scale Weapons of Mass Destruction existed they did not pose the level of threat the government was suggesting. Many journalists in other news organisations were receiving similar briefings.

For example:

Peter Beaumont and Gaby Hinsliff wrote (*Observer* 24 February 2003) of disagreement between the intelligence services and Downing Street - "the essence of the disagreement is said to have been that intelligence material should be presented 'straight' rather than spiced up to make a political argument." Their article also talks about "fairly serious rows" between at least one member of the JIC and Alastair Campbell.

............/3

CAB|1|0357

Raymond Whittaker (*Independent on Sunday* 27 April) wrote of "a high level UK source" saying that "intelligence agencies on both sides of the Atlantic were furious that briefings they gave political leaders were distorted". He went on to write: "You cannot just cherry-pick evidence that suits your case and ignore the rest. It is a cardinal rule of intelligence," said one aggrieved officer. "Yet that is what the PM is doing. "Another said: "What we have is a few strands of highly circumstantial evidence, and to justify an attack on Iraq it is being presented as a cast-iron case. That really is not good enough."

Richard Norton-Taylor, *Guardian* 30 May: "British intelligence sources expressed fury at Downing Street's behaviour. They were reluctant to allow Downing Street to use their intelligence assessment because they feared it would be manipulated for political ends....Caveats...were swept aside by Mr Blair, egged on by Mr Campbell, well-placed sources said."

Daniel McGrory, *Times* 30 May: "Senior sources say they received a barrage of phone calls from staff at No 10 demanding more evidence. Intelligence chiefs insist that the dossier was written by someone inside No 10 and not by British Intelligence...agents were wary that frightened defectors who wanted asylum would say what the British and Americans wanted to hear...there was debate amongst intelligence analysts whether the [45-minute source's] claims should have been passed to No 10, as senior figures doubted whether it was true, but were under pressure to deliver 'compelling evidence.'"

Glenn Frankell, *Washington Post* 30 May: "One official acknowledged that there had been what he described as 'pressured and superheated debates at the time' between Downing Street and intelligence officials over the contents of the dossier."

Peter Beaumont, Gaby Hinsliff, *Observer* 1 June: "What we are seeing is something very new, and very strange. MI6 is sticking its head over the parapet as much as it ever will...MI6 feels totally discredited and used." ("source")

............/5

CAB/1/0358

"MI6 feels that it has been pushed rather unwillingly into the limelight by the Government. It is a shot across the bows." (a second "source")

Nick Fielding, *Sunday Times* 1 June, reported that the dossier was the result of a "deal after months of bitter disagreements between intelligence chiefs and Blair's aides. Campbell had attempted to persuade the agencies to include hard-hitting conclusions. They were reluctant to agree because they said the case was not proven."

Furthermore on 22 March, the UN Chief Weapons Inspector, Hans Blix, criticised the manipulation of intelligence to make the case for war - accusing the coalition of using "shaky" evidence. Robin Cook - soon after his resignation - echoed that, questioning the Government's evidence (such as that in the September dossier) that Iraq presented an imminent threat: "it was difficult to believe that Saddam had the capacity to hit us."

It was in this context that we judged that reporting the claim made by Andrew Gilligan's source was in the public interest.

Having dealt with the context, let me turn now to the report on the Today programme. This week you have misrepresented our journalism.

- You have said we accused the Prime Minister, the Foreign Secretary and other ministers of lying. We have not.
- You have said the BBC deliberately accused the Prime Minister of misleading the House of Commons and of leading the country into war on a false basis. We have not.
- You have accused the BBC of damaging the integrity of the political process. We believe we have done the opposite.

The nub of what the BBC reported was:
- unease among some of the intelligence community about the use of intelligence in government dossiers
- the assertion of one senior and credible source – who has proved reliable in the past - that the "45 minute claim" was wrong and was inserted late into the dossier.

............/6

CAB/1/0359

CAB/11/0338

In response to this we have provided the Government with frequent and ample opportunities to state their position and rebut the allegations and this you have done. This is a perfectly fair and proper journalistic process which we stand by.

Now to your questions and I make no apology for repeating some of the points I have just made.

> ☐ *Does the BBC still stand by the allegation it made on 29th May that Number 10 added in the 45 minute claim to the dossier ?*

The allegation was not made by the BBC but by our source – a senior official involved in the compilation of the dossier - and the BBC stands by the reporting of it.

Andrew Gilligan made it clear that according to his source the 45 minute claim was real, but unreliable, intelligence information.

We do not report everything that every source tells us. In this instance we believe that the source is credible and that it was legitimate to place his concerns in the public domain given what we knew of the February dossier and the other points I have listed above. We stand by this decision.

> ☐ *Does it still stand by the allegation made on the same day that we did so against the wishes of the intelligence agencies?*

Again we reported accurately what we had been told by the source that the 45 minute claim was included in the dossier "against our wishes."

> ☐ *Does it still stand by the allegation made on that day that both we and the intelligence agencies knew the 45 minute claim to be wrong and inserted it despite knowing that.*

Andrew Gilligan accurately reported the source telling him that the government "probably knew that the 45 minute figure was wrong" and that the claim was "questionable." The basis for this assertion by Andrew Gilligan's source was that the information about the 45

............/7

CAB11 0360

697

minute claim had been derived from only one intelligence source - whereas most of the other claims in the dossier had at least two. Gilligan's source also believed this single Iraqi source had probably got the information wrong.

    ◻ *Does it still stand by the allegation, again on the same day, that we ordered the September dossier to be 'sexed up 'in the period leading up to its publication – and that Gilligan found what Humphreys (sic) called "evidence" that it was "cobbled together at the last minute with some unconfirmed material that had not been approved by the security services?"*

We stand by our reporting of the source as saying that the dossier was "sexed up " and that had happened at a late stage in its preparation – and that the "sexing up " relied on uncorroborated material not approved of by all in the intelligence agencies.

I note today that Mr Peter Ricketts, Director General of the Foreign and Commonwealth Office has told the Foreign Affairs Committee that the "45 minute" claim was not in the first draft of the dossier.

    ◻ *Does it still stand by the statement made on 6* June that the JIC is not part of the intelligence community , but a Number 10 committee which exists to arbitrate between government and the intelligence services?*

We never said that the JIC was not part of the intelligence community. What we actually said was the JIC is not the same thing as the intelligence services.

    ◻ *Does it still stand by the claim on 3rd June that the chairman of the JIC only kind of "bureaucratically signed off his report?"*

It would have been better if Andrew Gilligan had attributed this answer to his source and that was a slip on the day. However he had frequently reminded the audience that claims were derived from the source. What Andrew Gilligan did in this section of the report was to acknowledge that the JIC chairman had indeed 'signed off'

............/8

CAB/1/0361

on the dossier - but that did not of itself mean that all members of the intelligence services were happy with its contents. Further we know from other sources that some senior members of the intelligence community were reluctant to use intelligence material in this way.

   ☐ *How many sources was the original "45 minute." allegation being added in based on ? Was it one source or more than one source? You will be aware of the BBC Guidelines on this.*

I have repeatedly made it clear that the <u>particular</u> allegations made in Andrew Gilligan's report of the 29th May came from one source and I have outlined why we felt it appropriate to broadcast the information. The audience was told time and again on the 29th May that the criticism of the dossier's compilation was being made by one source. The source was credible and what he chose to tell Andrew Gilligan was highly plausible given what we knew by then about the preparation of the February "dodgy dossier". Other journalists, including some within the BBC, had been told of concerns held in the intelligence community about the way intelligence was used in the run-up to war in Iraq - and they had been told this by sources other than the one who spoke to Andrew Gilligan. In the light of this it would have been wrong for the BBC to decide not to put into the public domain the information provided to Andrew Gilligan by his source - and we did so with transparent attribution to a single source.

As for your point about the BBC Guidelines let me quote:

     "Programmes should be reluctant to rely on only one source."

That is true. The BBC would have preferred it if the source had been on the record. But you well know that in this field sources very rarely – if ever – choose to speak on the record. I do not accept your inference that means we cannot publish information on intelligence matters if only derived from one source – particularly in light of what we knew about the February dossier.

            ..../9

CAB/1/0362

There is a clear editorial procedure involving referral up to senior managers which was followed in this case.

We also note that Adam Ingram told us on May 29th that your "45 minute" claim is based on a single uncorroborated intelligence source.

> ☐ *Is that source on the JIC and do you agree that any source not on the JIC did not have the full picture?*

I do not intend to say anything more about our source. You well know that it is a matter of principle for us not to reveal our sources. I will do nothing to help you in this regard.

> ☐ *Was the source, as Gilligan has said, "a senior official involved in drawing up the dossier," or is he, as you said today, a source "in the intelligence services?" I'm sure you at least understand the significance of the difference to which I am alluding.*

I refer you to my previous answer.

> ☐ *Is it now normal BBC practice not to seek to corroborate single source stories?*

Of course we would prefer corroboration. The fact remains that we made a judgement about whether in the particular circumstances it was appropriate to place the allegations made by our source into the public domain. I have already outlined the context which justified this decision.

> ☐ *Finally do you believe that Gilligan's statement to the FAC that all he had ever alleged was that we gave "undue prominence" to the 45 minute point, or do you share my views that it is utterly inconsistent with what he and others or the BBC have said and what Gilligan has said, writing as a BBC journalist in the Mail on Sunday, The Sunday Telegraph and The Spectator?*

............./10

CAB/1/0363

It is incorrect to say all Andrew Gilligan ever said to the FAC was the single charge made by the source. His evidence was more wide ranging and it corresponds with what was broadcast. I quote from his evidence to the FAC:

Q450 Sir John Stanley: You are making, Mr Gilligan, a very, very serious allegation against the integrity of the JIC. The entire ---

Mr Gilligan: I am not making any allegations.

I would repeat, as I have said throughout, I am not making any allegations. My source made the allegations. We were reporting the charge of my source, who is a figure sufficiently senior and credible to be worth reporting.

I reported the source as saying there was unhappiness within the intelligence services, disquiet within the intelligence services."

Q455 Sir John Stanley: In terms of your evidence to this Committee, the only piece of evidence which you are specifying was allegedly made at the last minute subject to a political requirement to "sex it up", to use your phrase, is the 45 minute claim?

Mr Gilligan: That was the only specific piece of evidence that my source discussed, yes.

Sir John Stanley: Thank you.

Q456 Mr Olner: So the rest of the evidence that was in the dossier was reliable? By implication, if your source said he was not happy about the 45 minute thing then he was happy with the rest of it.

Mr Gilligan: The fact that my source was not specifically unhappy with other elements of the dossier does not necessarily mean that other elements of the dossier were reliable. Of course it might mean that, but I do not think anything can be drawn from it the other way.

Q552 Mr Chidgey: So the only degree of certainty that your source has or had was that he did not believe the 45 minutes?

............/11

CAB11\0364

Mr Gilligan: No, as I say, my source was reasonably sure, as are all the other intelligence people I have spoken to, that Iraq had a WMD programme of some description, but it was smaller and less of an imminent threat than that claimed by the Government. That was the view of my source and the view of several other people's sources in the rest of the media and indeed other sources I have spoken to, intelligence and non-intelligence.

The words of my source was that it was transformed in the week before it was published to make it sexier. Given all that you have said and given the other things I have described, I think that is a credible allegation.

As for newspaper articles – Andrew has not written on this subject for The Sunday Telegraph. The only significant difference in any piece he has written is when he wrote in the Mail on Sunday that the source had indicated your own involvement in the story.

> *Finally, have you seen today's Spectator, in which Mr Gilligan, writing not in a personal capacity but as a BBC correspondent writes an article concluding that the Prime Minister is a 'push over' in his relations with President Putin. Is that the BBC view? If it is a personal view, could you tell me what rule governs what BBC correspondents may or may not write in a freelance capacity to boost their BBC earnings? What are the procedures and were they followed in relation to this article? I am interested too, in respect of the many BBC journalists who boost their incomes by writing for national newspapers, what procedures govern their conducts and this writings? (sic) You will be aware that MPs have also expressed concern on this.*

This piece was submitted in advance to an appropriate editorial manager as is our procedure. Our guidelines on conflicts of interest cover what our journalists are allowed to write. These guidelines are in the public domain. As for this specific article the BBC does not impose a single view on its correspondents.

............/12

CAB/1/0365

Alastair, I have set out my views at considerable length. You will see that I do not accept the validity of your attacks on our journalism and on Andrew Gilligan in particular. We have to believe that you are conducting a personal vendetta against a particular journalist whose reports on a number of occasions have caused you discomfort.

Given the context described in the first part of my letter and given the credibility of our source are you really suggesting that an independent broadcaster should have suppressed this story because it only had one source?

In my previous letter to you (June 16th) I drew your attention to our complaints procedure and invited you to make a formal complaint if you so wished. You chose to ignore this. That avenue remains open. I should also say that *if* the information provided by our source is *proved* to be incorrect we would make the fact very clearly known to our audiences and we would express regret. As we stand today, that is simply not the case.

Yours sincerely,

(Richard Sambrook)
Director, BBC News

CAB/1/0366

Richard Sambrook's reply has been read to me. It confirms that the BBC broadcast a story that was hugely damaging to the integrity of the Government and the Prime Minister without knowing that story to be true and without any effort to check whether the story was true or not.

It confirms our central charge that they do not have a shred of evidence to justify their lie, broadcast many times on many BBC outlets, that we deliberately exaggerated and abused British intelligence and so misled Parliament and public.

The allegations were outrageous. So is Mr Sambrook's reply.

If the BBC are now saying that their journalism is based upon the principle that they can report what any source says, then BBC standards are now debased beyond belief. It means the BBC can broadcast anything and take responsibility for nothing.

I asked Mr Sambrook some very straightforward questions. He has not provided straightforward answers because he knows that this story is not true and that his journalist made no effort to check its veracity.

I do not want 12 pages of weasel words, sophistry and a defence of unethical journalism. Far better would be a 12 word apology that says "The BBC allegations were wholly false and we apologise sincerely for them.".

The story was a lie. It is a lie. Every day the BBC continues in its defence of the indefensible, it damages itself even more.

I am a huge admirer of the BBC which is responsible for some of the finest journalism and journalists in the world. Their reputation is being undermined by its institutional failure ever to admit it is wrong.

I will reply in detail to Mr Sambrook's letter after the weekend. In the meantime, I urge him to understand that the Government will not let this matter drop until an apology is delivered.

I have been encouraged by the response we have had, from journalists in the BBC and elsewhere, and from members of the public, at our determination to ensure that such a grave and false charge against the Government, the Prime Minister, the intelligence agencies and the political process does not go unchallenged.

APPENDIX 15

GICS
GOVERNMENT INFORMATION
& COMMUNICATION SERVICE

Page 1 of 5 - 030627 - Iraqdossier - Campbell - C4News - Part1 -ORD7747 -ORD7747

TRANSCRIPT

Programme(s)	The Channel Four News
Date & time	Friday 27th June 2003 1910
Subject / interviewee	Intelligence dossiers on Iraq – Alastair Campbell
Prepared by:	Paul Ellis
Contact numbers:	020 7276 1080 – Pager 07659 137 572 – 24hrs, every day

Jon Snow: *Well now we are joined by Alastair Campbell, a rare moment, thank you for, for coming in. This row between you and the BBC, I mean, many will see it as a diversionary tactic to prevent people actually seeing the real issue here which is that MPs are not getting to the root of whether in fact the intelligence we were provided with was the real intelligence provided by the intelligence services.*

Alastair Campbell: Well if people wish to see it as a diversionary tactic they may. The media are constantly telling people never to take things at face value. This isn't a row between me and the BBC this is an attempt by the Government to get the BBC to admit that a fundamental attack upon the integrity of the Government, the Prime Minister, the intelligence agencies, let alone people, the, sort of, evil spin doctors in the dark who do their dirty works in the minds of a lot of journalists, let them just accept for once they have got it wrong. The allegation, let's just understand what this allegation amounted to, and these weasel words in Richard Sambrook's letters, letter today (indistinct) says to me we didn't make the allegation we reported a source making the allegation. What does that say about journalism? You've been a journalism for decades, I was a journalist for quite a long time, I respect a huge number of journalists including many at the BBC ...

JS: *But I have to say ...*

AC: ... but they're now saying I, you can say anything you want on the television because somebody said it to you, doesn't matter if it's true ...

JS: *... yes ...*

AC: ... doesn't matter if you check it, doesn't matter if it's corroborated ...

JS: *... however the BBC's ...*

AC: ... you can say it.

JS: *... the BBC's riposte to you is very reasoned. It is set in the context of all the other information which was in the public domain, it's entirely consistent with that information. It credits the Guardian, the Observer, the Independent, the Times, I mean, most of Fleet Street had similar accounts of what intelligence sources were telling them. The BBC doesn't seem to be out of step with anybody else.*

AC: The BBC in their letter to me, and it's fascinating, they have post facto justification of a story by citing sources in newspapers which wrote stories subsequent to their, to the story that they had done. Some of those stories I know for a fact are incorrect. One of them, there's no point going through all the detail I think the public are probably bored rigid with this already, one

GICS Media Monitoring Unit
Room B18, Cabinet Office, 70 Whitehall, London SW1A 2AS
Fax: 020 7270 1030 e-mail: mmu@cabinet-office.x.gsi.gov.uk

CAB/1/0368

705

of those stories I know for a fact is wrong and I've addressed in evidence to the select committee.

JS: *I think the public is more likely to be concerned at the extraordinarily intemperate language which is coming out on behalf of the Prime Minister in your name. 'The story was a lie, it is a lie ...*

AC: Correct.

JS: *... weasel words', weasel not, incidentally, spelt correctly, in consistent terms with the original ...*

AC: Well as I understand it ...

JS: *... fake dossier which you produced.*

AC: ... if I may say so, the statement that you're reading from was read to the Press Association so that, that I wouldn't get hung up on a spelling mistake by somebody who's type it although I know that you, you also Jon reported the four people in my office were responsible for writing the so-called dodgy dossier when they were not. However put that to one side. The reason that is weasel words is it does not answer the questions that I put. I asked the BBC whether they were standing by the allegation they made, the BBC made as John Humphreys described it, the BBC made the allegation that we deliberately exaggerated, abused, distorted intelligence ...

JS: *And the answer to that question ...*

AC: ... the answer ...

JS: *... that you put to the BBC ...*

AC: ... to the question ...

JS: *... the answer to the question you put to the BBC, do they stand by it, the answer is yes. A robust yes.*

AC: ... the answer, excuse me, that letter is about as robust as Blackburn Rovers were when they played Trelleborges. I'll tell you the, the answer to the question yes or no did we abuse British intelligence, the answer to that question is no. It is a serious ...

JS: *We don't know, the answer to that question is we do not know.*

AC: ... excuse me, excuse me ...

JS: *And the reason we do not know is that there is obfuscation and diversion, part of which we're seeing right here played out before us. The fact is MPs want to question the chiefs of the intelligence services and should be allowed to do so instead you're preferring, you the Government, are preferring a hole in the corner operation with an intelligence committee which is not held in public and which is answerable to the Prime Minister.*

AC: Well part of the problem I alluded to in my evidence to the select committee is that a lot of journalists see their mission to discredit politicians and the political process. You describe people like Ann Taylor, who chairs the Intelligence and Security Committee, as a hole in the corner operation, you're talking (indistinct) intelligence agencies about people who do very difficult, brave jobs for this country.

JS: *You know very well that Ann Taylor was appointed by the Prime Minister ...*

AC: Correct.

JS: *... is answerable to the Prime Minister and accountable to the Prime Minister.*

AC: No she submits here reports to the Prime Minister.

JS: *He has the right to publish ...*

AC: The Prime Minister has to take judgements about what is published on security and intelligence grounds.

JS: *The point about the committee that is sitting here and that questioned you today, the day before ...*

AC: Wednesday ...

JS: *... on Wednesday and questioned the Foreign Secretary today is that it is one that is accountable to MPs selected by MPs and accountable to us as electors and that is the committee which should be allowed to get to the root of this issue and that surely is what the Government is preventing them doing?*

AC: Let me just say this about that. I'm not going to talk about the FAC's inquiry because I don't think I should until they've concluded it I will, however, say this. Donald Anderson as I understand it and his committee had a private session with Jack Straw today in which they will have discussed some of, some of these issues. I have submitted today to the committee, and I don't intend to discuss the contents at all, but I've submitted further answers to the questions that they asked me which go in some detail in to the intelligence issues and the specific question and the charge that I distorted British intelligence. That I inserted a claim that was not true, that I knew it not to be true. They are serious allegations and ...

JS: *But you've heard the Foreign Secretary himself tell that committee that that dossier was a Horlicks that the ...*

AC: No sorry, again, deliberate conflation of two things ...

JS: *... he said ...*

AC: ... (indistinct) correct yourself, correct yourself; it is not the same document do you accept that?

JS: *Which is not the same document?*

AC: You just said that the Foreign Secretary described the dossier as a Horlicks ...

JS: *The dodgy (indistinct) dossier?*

AC: Excuse me we were talking about the weapons of mass destruction dossier. This is the problem you, the people who ...

JS: *I, I ...*

AC: ... have been opposed to this conflict from the word go are now seeking to main, to change the ground and to say the Prime Minister led the country to, in to conflict on a false basis and you're deliberately conflating (indistinct).

JS: *... the issue in play here today is absolutely that this war was fought on the basis of intelligence information. That intelligence information, firstly the charges that in the first document in September there were serious errors of fact, we now know ...*

AC: Sorry the first document in September there were serious errors of fact, and what were they Jon?

JS: *The Niger allegation in which the minister who was supposed to have signed the nuclear purchasing order had himself resigned many years before ...*

AC: And do you know, you know do you Jon that the, that that was the basis on which British intelligence put that in the dossier, you know that do you because if you think that you are wrong. There were no errors of fact in the, the WMD dossier in September 200 (indistinct) ...

JS: *The, the Niger source was nothing to do with us?*

AC: ... excuse me it was another country's intelligence and the British intelligence put what they put in that dossier on the basis of British intelligence; get your facts right before you make serious allegations against Government and against intelligence agencies.

JS: *Well one, one fact is, one fact is absolutely incontrovertible and that is that the second dossier, the dodgy dossier, was indeed just that and the last question ...*

AC: As I have acknowledged ...

JS: *... and ...*

AC: ... as I have acknowledged ...

JS: *... but you've not acknowledged ...*

AC: ... as I have admitted, let me just, let me just draw this contrast between myselves, between the Government and the BBC. On Wednesday at that select committee I acknowledged we had made a mistake, I accepted responsibility for that on behalf of the junior, the, the official in my office who made ...

JS: *That, that is all a part of ...*

AC: ... let me finish the point ...

JS: *... that's, that's a matter of record.*

AC: ... can I finish the point? The BBC, I'm all in favour of senior management defending ...

JS: *I want to ask you one last question because I don't think ...*

AC: ... well I want to finish the sentence ...

JS: *... we're going to clarify this but I want one last question ...*

AC: ... I want to finish the sentence ...

JS: *... the last question is ...*

AC: ... well you can ask the question but I'm going to finish the question.

JS: *... you are now part of the story, when the Government's communications chief is himself part of the story isn't it time he resigned?*

AC: For heaven's sake the reason I am part of the story is that a BBC journalist made an allegation about me ...

JS: *Against whom the BBC believe you have a vendetta because he's caused you trouble.*

AC: ... I have never, I have never met the guy. I have never met Andrew Gilligan, I don't have a vendetta against him. I do believe that anybody with an interest in good, decent journalism of which there is a huge amount in this country should understand that when allegations are made, when lies are broadcast, when, as that letter shows, there is not a shred of evidence to substantiate the allegation they should apologise and then we can move on, we can get focusing on the things that really matter to your viewers out there which are the public services in the country, the economy of this country and the foreign policy of this country. And this distraction ...

JS: *Given, given ...*

AC: ... created ...

JS: *... given the mistake, given the mistake ...*

AC: ... created by the BBC ...

JS: *... that you've, you've admitted regarding the second dossier have you offered your resignation?*

AC: No I haven't Jon and what's more that's a further attempt to conflate the two issues. In contrast to the BBC I have acknowledged we made a mistake, I have apologised on behalf of the Government. Now the BBC should acknowledge they've made a mistake and they should apologise to the Government then we can move on.

JS: *Alastair Campbell thank you very much for joining us.*

End

CAB|1|0372

APPENDIX 16

Mr Richard Sambrook
Head of News
BBC

June 28th 2003

Dear Richard,

During my interview on the Today programme this morning your presenter, John Humphrys, asserted the BBC had checked out the allegation made by Andrew Gilligan on the Today Programme on May 29th beforehand with the Ministry of Defence.

I have spoken to the MOD at some length, including with the official the BBC claims was given the opportunity to respond to this allegation. The MOD remains certain that the only contact between the Today programme and the MOD press office related to an interview on the use of cluster bombs. Mr Gilligan was asked whether any other issues would be raised in the interview. He mentioned a separate story on WMD, gave no further details and, critically, made it clear that this was not an MOD issue and he was not seeking a response from them.

I would be grateful if on Monday morning the Today programme corrected the false statement that the MOD was given an opportunity to respond to this allegation prior to its broadcast.

With very best wishes,

Ben Bradshaw MP

LETTER FROM ALASTAIR CAMPBELL TO RICHARD SAMBROOK

Thank you for your letter of 27 June.

I am saddened that you have failed to answer the direct questions I put to you. One month to the day since you broadcast these allegations, surely you have been able to establish whether or not you are satisfied that they are true. I was also very surprised that your defence now rests on the principle that you can report anything that a source says, regardless of its veracity, provided that you report accurately what the source has told you.

I note in particular that you have been unable to substantiate the most damaging allegations – namely that we "sexed up" the WMD dossier by inserting, against the wishes of the Chairman of the Joint Intelligence Committee and the Intelligence Agencies, the 45 minute intelligence whilst knowing it to be untrue, and so helped the Prime Minister to persuade Parliament and the country to go to war on a false basis.

The BBC's report of 29 May – the allegations from which have been repeated by the BBC many times since and, thanks to the BBC have been repeated by broadcast and print media around the world - was wrong in every material respect. The BBC has, in effect, been standing by a single, uncorroborated anonymous source who gave you wholly false and inaccurate information – a source who seems, to put it at its kindest, to have been operating away from the centre of events.

Your editorial team showed poor professional judgement and competence in relying on such a source without making any further checks, or putting the allegations to the people against whom they were being made. You and other senior BBC executives, for your part, seem unwilling to grapple with the fact that you broadcast a manifestly inadequate piece of journalism; that you are standing by a story that is simply untrue.

I respect, however, the BBC's independence, if not in this instance its competence. Given how far apart we remain, I see little purpose in continuing our exchanges in advance of the Foreign Affairs Committee report being published. You will also be aware of the separate inquiry by the Intelligence and Security Committee which will also have a bearing on these issues. Let us first await the outcome of the Foreign Affairs Committee report. I reserve the right at that time, or subsequently, to pursue my case further, possibly, in the way that you suggest, through the BBC Programme Complaints Unit.

CAB/1/0373

British Broadcasting Corporation Room 3601 Stage 6 Television Centre Wood Lane London W12 7RJ Telephone 020 8576 7178 Fax 020 8576 7120

From Director, News

June 29ᵗʰ 2003

Dear Ben

Thank you for your letter yesterday asking for a correction to our assertion that the MOD were forewarned of the WMD story we broadcast on May 29ᵗʰ. My understanding, from contemporaneous programme notes, is as follows:

- At 5pm on May 28ᵗʰ the Today programme put in a bid to the MOD for an interview on cluster bombs.

- At 6.30pm Andrew Gilligan spoke to Kate O'Connor, the MOD press officer, about the Cluster bomb interview and added there would be another story running on WMD.

- Between 6.30pm and 7pm producer Martha Findlay spoke to MOD press officer Richard Walley and confirms the bid has widened from cluster bombs to include WMD

- Between 8 and 8.30pm the MOD calls the Today programme and confirms an interview with Adam Ingram on Cluster bombs but does not confirm that he will speak about WMD

- At 9.45 pm the MOD press office rings the Today programme to confirm Mr Ingram will speak about WMD as well.

As the transcript of his interview shows (see attached) Mr Ingram was well briefed in advance on the item and able to respond to questions with some detail. In light of this we see no need to correct John Humphrys assertion to you that the MOD was forewarned. Downing St's denial was also given prominence in the programme.

You also asserted yesterday that Andrew Gilligan's report in some way flouted the BBC's Producer Guidelines. It did not. I attach the relevant sections. An entirely proper editorial process was followed in advance of broadcast.

Given the prominence of your views yesterday I am releasing this letter to the press.

Best wishes,

Richard

Richard Sambrook
Director, BBC News

1

CAB/11/0390

Mr Richard Sambrook
Director of News
BBC

June 30th 2003

Dear Richard,

Thank you for your letter. It has done absolutely nothing to re-assure me about the standards of journalism on this story or your knowledge of the procedures followed.

There are, of course, serious worries about the use of a single anonymous source for such an important story. What I find most worrying, however, is your admission that no attempt whatsoever was made to give No 10 or the Government any chance to comment or deny the very serious allegations made before they were broadcast. This is indefensible.

Your letter makes clear that Andrew Gilligan had not, as John Humphrys claimed to me on Saturday, 'called the Ministry of Defence and told them the story was being run so they had an opportunity to rebut it'. All that Andrew Gilligan did was mention in passing that the programme was also running another story about Weapons of Mass Destruction.

No advance warning was given about the nature of the story, nor the specifics or seriousness of the allegations, let alone any chance to deny them before they were broadcast. No opportunity was given to rebut them as you suggest.

The only reason Adam Ingram was able to be briefed before his appearance after 8am was because your false allegations had been running since 6am. Neither Adam Ingram nor the MOD press officer had any knowledge of the allegations before the Today programme broadcast them.

Would you not agree that it is standard journalistic practice that the person or organisation against whom such grave allegations are being made should be given the chance to comment on or deny them prior to broadcast? Could you tell me why this did not happen?

As we are entering the second month of this controversy, could you also tell me whether you believe it is true that No 10 inserted the 45 minute intelligence against the wishes of the intelligence services and in the knowledge that this was probably wrong – the allegation broadcast on the Today programme on May 29th.

With very best wishes,

Ben Bradshaw MP

CAB/1/0391

From Director, News

Ben Bradshaw, Esq., MP.,
The House of Commons,
LONDON.
SW1A OAA

1 July, 2003

Dear Ben,

Thank you for your latest letter. We are clearly not going to agree. I suggest, in line with Alastair's last letter to me, that we now wait for the report of the Foreign Affairs Select Committee.

We appreciate the level of anger in Government about our report. I hope you appreciate the deep sense of injustice in the BBC that a disagreement about one report was used to traduce the whole organisation.

With best wishes.

Yours sincerely,

Richard

(Richard Sambrook)

CAB/1/0392

INVESTOR IN PEOPLE

HOUSE OF COMMONS
LONDON SW1A 0AA

Mr Richard Sambrook
Director of News
BBC

July 1st 2003

Dear Richard,

I was surprised by your desire to wait for the outcome of the Foreign Affairs select committee. The specific point that I have been making, namely that John Humpreys was wrong to claim in an interview with me the BBC checked Gilligan's allegation with the Government prior to broadcast, is not something I would expect the Foreign Affairs Select Committee to adjudicate on.

You will now know, as I do, John Humphreys' claim is untrue.

I have not traduced the whole of the BBC. In fact, I have gone out of my way to praise the superb journalism of the BBC.

All that needs to happen is an apology for broadcasting a false claim which, I note, you are no longer bothering to defend.

With very best wishes,

Pp LenShallcross

Ben Bradshaw MP

Ben	**Constituency Office**	**Parliamentary Office**
Bradshaw	Labour HQ	House of Commons
	26b Clifton Hill	Westminster
Labour	Exeter EX1 2DJ	London SW1A 0AA
Member of		
Parliament for	**Tel:** 01392 424 464	**Tel:** 020 7219 6597
	Fax: 01392 425 630	**Fax:** 020 7219 0950
Exeter	BBC15/0170	e-mail: bradshawb@parliament.uk

447

HOUSE OF COMMONS

LONDON SWIA 0AA

Mr Stephen Whittle
Controller of Editorial Policy
BBC

July 1st 2003

Dear Stephen,

As you may be aware, I have been engaged in correspondence with Richard Sambrook over the BBC's conduct on the Iraq Weapons of Mass Destruction dossier story - originally broadcast by the Today Programme on May 29ᵗʰ and repeated endlessly by the BBC in the following days and weeks.

I believe that the BBC has ignored or broken many of its own public guidelines on this story. I know that there are many journalists in the BBC who agree with me.

But despite the fact that the very grave allegations broadcast are false, that they were based on a single anonymous source, that no attempt was made to corroborate them, that no attempt was made to put the charges to the Government before they were broadcast, Richard continues to claim that the BBC acted properly. As such, there seems no point in continuing my correspondence with him.

As a great admirer of the BBC and a former BBC journalist myself, I remain seriously concerned at the damage that this controversy is doing to the Corporation's deserved reputation for accuracy, impartiality and fairness. It is, I'm afraid, only too clear that Richard is unable to admit even obvious errors of judgement and conduct - such as the failure to put any of the allegations to the Government before they were broadcast - for fear of the whole of the BBC's defence crumbling.

As you are both Controller of Editorial Policy and helped write the Producers' Guidelines, I would like you to investigate whether you agree with Richard's claim, in his letter to me, that "an entirely proper editorial process was followed in advance of the broadcast".

In particular, I would like you to consider the process followed against the following guidelines:

1) *General : All BBC programmes and services should be open-minded, fair and show a respect for the truth.* Do you believe it is fair that serious allegations can be broadcast without any effort being made to get a response from those who are accused prior to broadcast? Most importantly, do you believe the allegations are true?

2) *General: The Agreement accompanying the BBC's Charter specifies that the Corporation should treat controversial subjects with due accuracy and impartiality both in news programmes and other programmes that deal with matters of public policy or of political and industrial controversy.* Do you accept that there could hardly be a more controversial subject than the allegation broadcast by the BBC that

Richard's claims that the BBC behaved properly because it accurately reported someone's false allegations.

These are, in my view, clear instances where the processes followed on this story – a very serious story – flouted, ignored or pushed to the extreme the Producer Guidelines. I believe the more serious the story, the more seriously these guidelines should be followed. That was certainly the case when I worked at the BBC.

They were drawn up, as you will know better than me, to prevent the sort of damage done to the BBC's reputation as well as the unfair damage done to others that we have seen in the last few weeks. I look forward to your investigation and your reply. In the mean-time, I am releasing this letter to the press.

With very best wishes,

PP Lenny Shallcross

Ben Bradshaw MP

Ben Bradshaw

Labour Member of Parliament for Exeter

Constituency Office
Labour HQ
26b Clifton Hill
Exeter EX1 2DJ

Tel: 01392 424 464
Fax: 01392 425 630

Parliamentary Office
House of Commons
Westminster
London SW1A 0AA

Tel: 020 7219 6597
Fax: 020 7219 0950

e-mail: bradshawb@parliament.uk

 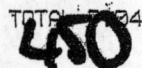

BBC

From Controller, Editorial Policy

Ben Bradshaw, MP
House of Commons
London
SW1A 0AA

1ˢᵗ July 2003

By Post and Fax: 020 7219 0950

Dear Ben,

Thank you for your letter.

Richard Sambrook has made a very detailed response to the questions that were posed to Alistair Campbell which covers many, if not most, of the points that you raise.

As to your specific questions about the Producers' Guidelines, I am satisfied that the reliance on a single source (provided that source is credible and in a position to know what they are talking about) is not in conflict with our guideline on accuracy. As you will know from your own experience as a journalist and politician, political journalism would virtually cease in both print and broadcast media if every report relied on several sources. The key test is rigorous editorial judgement based on a reliable journalistic process. The original report on the Today programme met that criterion, with Government ministers given the opportunity to respond then and subsequently.

Incidentally, the guideline that you cite on anonymity relates to situations where programmes are seeking to talk to people in trouble with the law.

The Guidelines are a public statement of our editorial values. I am confident from what I know of the circumstances that they were followed. We will, of course, go on reporting the responses of the government, the wider public debate, and the findings of committees of the House, fully, fairly, and impartially.

I am releasing this letter to the press.

Yours

Stephen Whittle
Controller, Editorial Policy
333 Henry Wood House
BBC
Tel. 020 7765 5655
mailto:stephen.whittle@bbc.co.uk

BBC15/0174 **451**

TOTAL P.02

DG. MD

HOUSE OF COMMONS

LONDON SW1A 0AA

Stephen Whittle
Controller of Editorial Policy
BBC

July 2nd 2003

Dear Stephen,

Thank you for your reply of today. It was not satisfactory.

If you are not prepared to address the number of serious issues I raised perhaps you could just try to answer one of my questions.

Did the BBC put the specific and grave allegation made by Andrew Gilligan on the Today programme on May 29th to the Government before it was broadcast, as claimed by John Humphrys in his interview with me on Saturday?

Please, no more dissembling, just a simple yes or no.

As things stand Humphrys, in effect, accused me of lying when I stated that the allegation had not been put to the Government before broadcast.

Despite repeated attempts I am still waiting for a reply to this simple question and would be grateful for one now.

I am releasing this letter to the press.

With very best wishes,

Ben Bradshaw MP

CC Richard Sambrook

Ben Bradshaw

*Labour
Member of
Parliament for*

Exeter

Constituency Office
Labour HQ
26b Clifton Hill
Exeter EX1 2DJ

Tel: 01392 424 464
Fax: 01392 425 630

Parliamentary Office
House of Commons
Westminster
London SW1A 0AA

Tel: 020 7219 6597
Fax: 020 7219 0950

BBC15/0179

e-mail: bradshawb@parliament.uk
website: www.benbradshaw.co.uk

456

720

SECRETARY OF STATE

MINISTRY OF DEFENCE
ROOM 205, OLD WAR OFFICE BUILDING
WHITEHALL LONDON SW1A 2EU

Telephone: 020 721 82111/2/3
Fax: 020 721 87140
Email: defencesecretary@defence.mod.uk

MO 6/17/15C

2 July 2003

Dear Richard,

My attention has been drawn to your letter of 29 June to Ben Bradshaw and I would like to correct a number of specific points relating to the MOD.

During his interview on the Today Programme with Ben Bradshaw on 28 June John Humphrys said that Andrew Gilligan 'checked with the Ministry of Defence' before broadcasting his story. This is simply not true, as the record below makes clear.

Shortly after that interview was broadcast, at 8.50am, Andrew Gilligan called the MOD duty press officer. Two press officers were present as this was during the handover period. Mr Gilligan said he was calling to 'note that he had spoken to the Chief Press Officer before the programme was broadcast and that was what he had said.' He then rang off without offering any explanation.

I deduce from this call that the basis for John Humphrys' claim that the story was 'checked with the MOD' is the conversation Mr Gilligan had with the Chief Press Officer at approximately 6.30pm on 28 May.

Richard Sambrook Esq
Director, BBC News
BBC TV Centre
Wood Lane
London
W12 7RJ

CAB/1/0403

As we have already made clear, the conversation on 28 May was actually about a piece on the use of cluster bombs in Iraq and a possible interview bid for Adam Ingram. Mr Gilligan did not discuss any other story. He was asked whether he was working on anything else for the programme. He then mentioned that he was working on something else about WMD. He did not discuss any detail of this story, he did not put any questions about it to the MOD and most importantly, he said that this was not a story for the MOD. By his own admission he did not regard MOD as the relevant Government department. I cannot see how this can be described as 'checking the story.'

Although Mr Gilligan has already told us that he believes this was the relevant conversation, your letter to Ben Bradshaw also lists other conversations between the MOD and the Today Programme on 28 May and suggests that these conversations were about WMD. The times and details of all out-of-hours calls to the MOD Press Office are logged. This record shows that your account is inaccurate:

    8.00pm -   call from Ian Watson confirming that the Today Programme definitely wanted Adam Ingram on the programme.

    10.30pm -   call from Chris Howard asking if Adam Ingram would do two minutes on WMD at the end of the interview on cluster bombs. The two running issues about WMD at the time were comments made by Donald Rumsfeld earlier and the second WMD briefing paper. He did not mention dossiers and he said he did not know the detail of the piece.

Finally, you suggest that Adam Ingram must have known about the piece in advance because he was able to answer questions on the programme. You will recall that Mr Gilligan's first item on the story ran at 6.07am. This broadcast was the first time anyone in MOD was aware of the 45 minutes/dossier story.

CAB/11/0404

722

This information shows that either you are deliberately misleading us or that you yourself are being misled. I would be grateful for a response once you have checked this information provided above with the relevant staff.

Yours sincerely

GEOFFREY HOON

723

From Director, News

Ben Bradshaw, Esq., MP.,
The House of Commons,
LONDON.
SW1A OAA

3 July, 2003

Dear Ben,

Further to your letter of 1 July I attach herewith a copy of a letter to
Geoff Hoon which I have sent today.

Yours sincerely,

(Richard Sambrook)

CAB/1/0399

TOTAL P.03

British Broadcasting Corporation Room 5601 Stage 6 Television Centre Wood Lane London W12 7RJ Telephone 020 8576 7178 Fax 020 8576 7120

From Director, News

Rt. Hon. Geoffrey Hoon MP.,
Ministry of Defence,
Room 205,
Old War Office Building,
WHITEHALL,
London.
SW1A 2EU

3 July, 2003

Dear Geoff,

Thank you for your letter. Clearly your version of what happened on the evening of 28 May differs from ours. I take that seriously and will again look at what happened together with the BBC's Controller of Editorial Policy who, as you know, is independent of the News Division. I will respond as soon as that is done.

If we fell short of what we believe to be acceptable we shall say so.

At no time in this dispute have I sought to in any way criticise the MoD Press Office with whom we have always enjoyed excellent relations.

With best wishes.

Yours sincerely,

(Richard Sambrook)

CAB/11/0406

British Broadcasting Corporation Broadcasting House Portland Place London W1A 1AA Telephone 020 7580 4468

From Controller, Editorial Policy

Ben Bradshaw, MP
House of Commons
London
SW1A 0AA

3rd July 2003

<u>**By Post and Fax: 020 7219 0950**</u>

Dear Ben,

Thank you for your letter of last night. You will have seen Richard Sambrook's response to
Geoff Hoon. We will therefore get back to you in due course.

Kind regards

Yours sincerely

Stephen Whittle

Controller, BBC Editorial Policy
Room 330, Henry Wood House
3-6 Langham Place
London W1A 1AA
Tel. 020 7765 5655
emailto:stephen.whittle@bbc.co.uk

1

TOTAL P.02

CAB/1/0400

Mr Richard Sambrook
Director of News
BBC

3 July 2003

Dear Richard,

On this morning's Today programme, Andrew Marr claimed that the central allegation about No 10's involvement in the September WMD dossier and the 45 minute intelligence "wasn't that they doctored it or fudged it or whatever but that simply that it had been inserted late in the process?" This is totally untrue.

The actual grave and false allegation made was that the 45 minute intelligence was inserted into the dossier by the Government, against the wishes of the intelligence services and despite the fact that the Government probably knew it was false.

Andrew Gilligan on the Today Programme of May 29, said: "What we have been told by one of the senior officials in charge of drawing up that dossier was that actually the Government probably knew that the 45 minute figure was wrong".

He went onto say that the original document prepared by the intelligence agencies was bland and that "Downing Street, our source says, a week before publication, ordered it to be sexed up, to be made more exciting and ordered more facts to be discovered."

On Radio 5, on the same day, Gilligan said intelligence sources 'mentioned a few things which they weren't happy with and at Downing Street's insistence those were written into the document. And one of the main things that they weren't happy with was this claim that Iraq could deploy its biological and chemical weapons within forty five minutes."

There is absolutely no doubt what the central charge broadcast by the BBC was and it was much more serious and specific than the BBC's Political Editor suggested this morning.

I am releasing this letter to the press.

With very best wishes,

Ben Bradshaw MP

CAB|1|0402

727

British Broadcasting Corporation Room 5601 Stage 6 Television Centre Wood Lane London W12 7RJ Telephone 020 8576 7179 Fax 020 8576 7120

From Director, News

Rt. Hon. Geoffrey Hoon MP.,
Ministry of Defence,
Room 205,
Old War Office Building,
WHITEHALL,
London.
SW1A 2EU

3 July, 2003

Dear Geoff,

I am sorry you were disappointed. So were we as we very much wanted to hear your views about reconstruction in Iraq. As I have just replied to you I am looking seriously at the discrepancy your letter last night highlighted, and will respond in due course.

We continue to stand by our view that we were justified in broadcasting the allegations of our source when we broadcast them. Since then we have been accused of saying many things which we simply have not said.

In light of that I would be interested for you to clarify which allegation you refer to in your final paragraph.

Yours sincerely,

Richard

(Richard Sambrook)

✳ Internal

DR

SECRETARY OF STATE

Copy to:
PS/Minister(AF)
PS/USofS
DGCC
D News
Sec(Iraq)
D News CPO
Special Advisers

MINISTRY OF DEFENCE
ROOM 205, OLD WAR OFFICE BUILDING
WHITEHALL LONDON SW1A 2EU

Telephone: 020 721 82111/2/3
Fax: 020 721 871 40
Email: defencesecretary@defence.mod.uk

MO 6/17/15C

4 July 2003

Dear Mr Sambrook,

Thank you for your letter of 3 July. I am not clear why you seek clarification of the allegation referred to in my letter of the same date. Our correspondence has related to one allegation only and it is highlighted again in the first paragraph of my letter. The allegation is that Andrew Gilligan's story of 29 May was 'checked with MOD.' This is not true.

You say that the BBC wants to hear my views on reconstruction in Iraq. I would welcome an opportunity to discuss this subject and to reply to the allegation that Mr Gilligan's story was 'checked with MOD'. You will be aware that, yesterday evening, the Today programme again asked to interview me about reconstruction in Iraq but withdrew the bid on learning that I would also wish to address the second point.

Yours sincerely,

Laurence Laxham
(Private Secretary)

GEOFFREY HOON

Approved by the Defence
Secretary and signed
in his absence.

Richard Sambrook Esq
Director, BBC News
BBC TV Centre
Wood Lane
London
W12 7RJ

CAB/1/0408

Recycled Pa

Rt. Hon. Geoffrey Hoon MP.,
Ministry of Defence,
Room 205,
Old War Office Building,
WHITEHALL,
London.
SW1A 2EU

7 July, 2003

Dear Geoff,

I am now in a position to respond to your letter of 2 July.

As you know, I asked Stephen Whittle, Controller, Editorial Policy, to look at what happened on the night of May 28th. The Today programme team again made clear to him that it is their belief that at least three calls were made to MOD press officers. They believe that between them those calls covered sufficiently both the allegations made by the source about WMD, as well as the extension of the bid for the interview with Adam Ingram. However, we acknowledge that it would have been better if our logs about this were more specific as there is a clear conflict over exactly what was said.

Your own account recognises that the bid was extended, but oddly does not include the confirmation at your end that the Minister would appear. In any event, it is clear from the programme that Adam Ingram was well briefed on the points. No one complained at the time that he had been bounced.

As you will know, the BBC Governors have taken the view "that the Today programme should have kept a clearer account of its dealings with the Ministry of Defence on this story and could have also asked the No 10 Press Office for a response prior to broadcasting the story. However, we note that firm government denials of the story were broadcast on the Today Programme within 90 minutes of the original broadcast by Andrew Gilligan, and these were followed soon after on the same programme by equally firm denials by a defence minister."

We can only apologise for any misunderstanding that may have occurred in the bidding process and have taken steps to tighten our procedures for the future.

We have always enjoyed excellent relations with the MOD press office and hope we will continue to do so.

Yours sincerely

Richard Sambrook

CAB/1/0409

Rt. Hon. Geoffrey Hoon MP.,
Ministry of Defence,
Room 205,
Old War Office Building,
WHITEHALL,
London.
SW1A 2EU

9 July, 2003

Dear Geoff

Thank you for the opportunity to meet yesterday. I am sorry, in the light of
subsequent events, you felt unable to be entirely frank with me.

Stephen Whittle has now finished looking at the issue of what advance warning
the Today programme gave the MoD about Andrew Gilligan's story.

The position is unchanged since my last letter to you. Our team genuinely
believe they outlined some details of the allegations but do not have written
notes to back that up. Your team, I am sure genuinely, believe insufficient detail
was given.

As you know the BBC Governors statement on Sunday evening, which received
widespread and detailed public attention, acknowledged that the programmes
record keeping should be better and that we could have put the allegations to
Downing St. Since then I have written to you to apologise for any
misunderstanding - a letter I am quite happy be put in the public domain.
However as there is still a difference of view about what was said which has not
been reconciled we are not prepared to broadcast an apology.

Best wishes,

Yours sincerely

Richard Sambrook

CAB/1/0410

Mr Richard Sambrook
Head of News
BBC

July 9th 2003

Dear Richard,

On the Today programme of June 26, you said the BBC had "one senior and credible source <u>in the intelligence services</u>" for the allegations contained in Andrew Gilligan's story.

Given that you are now perhaps the only person who knows the name of both Andrew Gilligan's source and the name of the Government official who believes he may be his – misreported – informant, could you tell me whether you can repeat the claim that Mr Gilligan's source is 'in the intelligence services' with confidence?

With very best wishes,

Ben Bradshaw MP

CAB/1/0411

British Broadcasting Corporation Room 5601 Stage 6 Television Centre Wood Lane London W12 7RJ Telephone 020 8576 7178 Fax 020 8576 7120

From Director, News

10 July 2003

Ben Bradshaw MP
House of Commons
Westminster
London SW1A OAA

Dear Ben

Thank you for your letters.

As you know we have said we are not going to make any further comment relating to our source so I am not going to provide the clarification you seek.

You are of course welcome to instigate an official complaint about John Humphrys on the Today programme on June 28th.

The BBC's Programme Complaints Unit, which as you know operates independently of production divisions, can be contacted at:-

Broadcasting House
Portland Place
London W1A 1AA

Yours sincerely

RICHARD SAMBROOK

INVESTOR IN PEOPLE
TOTAL P.01

CAB/1/0412

APPENDIX 17

Reynolds v Times Newspapers Ltd (HL(E)) [2001]2 AC

Lord Nicholls of Birkenhead (at page 200 D)

My starting point is freedom of expression. The high importance of freedom to impart and receive information and ideas has been stated so often and so eloquently that this point calls for no elaboration in this case. At a pragmatic level, freedom to disseminate and receive information on political matters is essential to the proper functioning of the system of parliamentary democracy cherished in this country. This freedom enables those who elect representatives to Parliament to make an informed choice, regarding individuals as well as policies, and those elected to make informed decisions. Freedom of expression will shortly be buttressed by statutory requirements. Under section 12 of the Human Rights Act 1998, expected to come into force in October 2000, the court is required, in relevant cases, to have particular regard to the importance of the right to freedom of expression. The common law is to be developed and applied in a manner consistent with article 10 of the European Convention for the Protection of Human Rights and Fundamental Freedoms (1953) (Cmd 8969), and the court must take into account relevant decisions of the European Court of Human Rights (sections 6 and 2). To be justified, any curtailment of freedom of expression must be convincingly established by a compelling countervailing consideration, and the means employed must be proportionate to the end sought to be achieved.

Likewise, there is no need to elaborate on the importance of the role discharged by the media in the expression and communication of information and comment on political matters. It is through the mass media that most people today obtain their information on political matters. Without freedom of expression by the media, freedom of expression would be a hollow concept. The interest of a democratic society in ensuring a free press weighs heavily in the balance in deciding whether any curtailment of this freedom bears a reasonable relationship to the purpose of the curtailment. In this regard it should be kept in mind that one of the contemporary functions of the media is investigative journalism. This activity, as much as the traditional activities of reporting and commenting, is part of the vital role of the press and the media generally.

1

Reputation is an integral and important part of the dignity of the individual. It also forms the basis of many decisions in a democratic society which are fundamental to its well-being: whom to employ or work for, whom to promote, whom to do business with or to vote for. Once besmirched by an unfounded allegation in a national newspaper, a reputation can be damaged for ever, especially if there is no opportunity to vindicate one's reputation. When this happens, society as well as the individual is the loser. For it should not be supposed that protection of reputation is a matter of importance only to the affected individual and his family. Protection of reputation is conducive to the public good. It is in the public interest that the reputation of public figures should not be debased falsely. In the political field, in order to make an informed, choice, the electorate needs to be able to identify the good as well as the bad. Consistently with these considerations, human rights conventions recognise that freedom of expression is not an absolute right. Its exercise may be subject to such restrictions as are prescribed by law and are necessary in a democratic society for the protection of the reputations of others.

The crux of this appeal, therefore, lies in identifying the restrictions which are fairly and reasonably necessary for the protection of reputation. Leaving aside the exceptional cases which attract absolute privilege, the common law denies protection to defamatory statements, whether of comment or fact, proved to be actuated by malice, in the *Horrocks v Lowe* [1975] AC 135 sense. This common law limitation on freedom of speech passes the "necessary" test with flying colours. This is an acceptable limitation. Freedom of speech does not embrace freedom to make defamatory statements out of personal spite or without having a positive belief in their truth.

In the case of statements of opinion on matters of public interest, that is the limit of what is necessary for protection of reputation. Readers and viewers and listeners can make up their own minds on whether they agree or disagree with defamatory statements which are recognisable as comment and which, expressly or implicitly, indicate in general terms the facts on which they are based.

2

With defamatory imputations of fact the position is different and more difficult. Those who read or hear such allegations are unlikely to have any means of knowing whether they are true or not. In respect of such imputations, a plaintiff's ability to obtain a remedy if he can prove malice is not formally a sufficient safeguard. Malice is notoriously difficult to prove. If a newspaper is understandably unwilling to disclose its sources, a plaintiff can be deprived of the material necessary to prove, or even allege, that the newspaper acted recklessly in publishing as it did without further verification. Thus, in the absence of any additional safeguard for reputation, a newspaper, anxious to be first with a "scoop", would in practice be free to publish seriously defamatory misstatements of fact based on the slenderest of materials. Unless the paper chose later to withdraw the allegations, the politician thus defamed would have no means of clearing his name, and the public would have no means of knowing where the truth lay. Some further protection for reputation is needed if this can be achieved without a disproportionate incursion into freedom of expression.

....

Lord Cooke of Thorndon (at page 220 D)

The existing balance between the right to personal reputation and freedom of speech has been carefully and gradually developed over the years by common law and statutes. It is true that the restrictions on freedom of speech that have been thought necessary to give reasonable protection to personal reputation may have a tendency to chill the publication, not only of untruths, but also of that which may be true but cannot be proved to be true. But there is nothing new in this. Nor, as far as I am aware, is there any way of assessing which tendency is the greater – although experience of libel litigation is apt to generate a suspicion that it is the former.

....

3

Lord Hobhouse of Woodborough (at page 237 H)

This case is concerned with the problems which arise from the publication of factual statements which are not correct – ie do not conform to the truth. This case is not concerned with freedom of expression and opinion. The citizen is at liberty to comment and take part in free discussion. It is of fundamental importance to a free society that this liberty be recognised and protected by the law.

The liberty to communicate (and receive) information has a similar place in a free society but it is important always to remember that it is the communication of information not misinformation which is the subject of this liberty. There is no human right to disseminate information that is not true. No public interest is served by publishing or communicating misinformation. The working of a democratic society depends on the members of that society, being informed not misinformed. Misleading people and the purveying as facts statement which are not true is destructive of the democratic society and should form no part of such a society. There is no duty to publish what is not true: there is no interest in being misinformed. These are general propositions going far beyond the mere protection of reputations.

4

APPENDIX 18

IN CONFIDENCE

Deputy Chief of Defence Intelligence
Defence Intelligence Staff
Ministry of Defence
Old War Office Building
Whitehall
LONDON
WC1A 2EU

8 July 2003

Dear DCDI

Having scanned the Foreign Affairs Committee report of its
"Inquiry into the Decision to Go to War with Iraq" I have some
concerns. I am not clear whether I have any obligations with
regard to these matters, nor the extent of any conflict which may
exist between my responsibilities to the Department and the
Government, and my responsibilities to Parliament. I write to
seek your advice on this issue.

Your records will show that as   and probably the most
senior and experienced intelligence community official working on
"WMD," I was so concerned about the manner in which intelligence
assessments for which I had some responsibility were being
presented in the dossier of 24 September 2002, that I was moved
to write formally to your predecessor, Tony Cragg, recording and
explaining my reservations.

The Foreign Affairs Committee appears to consider it important
that the Foreign Secretary told them, " that there had been no
formal complaint from members of the security and intelligence
services about the content of the [September 2002] dossier." I
believe his evidence was, in fact, that he was not *aware* of any
such complaint, and there is no reason to suppose he should have
become aware of mine. Nonetheless, it is now a matter of record,
and I feel very uneasy that my minute could be uncovered at some
future date, and that I might be judged culpable for not having
drawn attention to it.

I would be most grateful if you could consider this and advise me
accordingly.

MOD/4/0011

739

MINISTRY OF DEFENCE
Old War Office Building
Whitehall, London SW1A 2EU
Telephone (Direct Dialling) 020 7218 2407
(Switchboard) 020 7218 9000

From Mr Martin Howard
Deputy Chief of Defence Intelligence

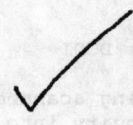

CDI 2/25, 4/2 & 4/3

23 July 2003

Thank you for your letter of 8 July (which for some reason did not reach me until the middle of last week).

I am grateful to you for drawing my attention to this I assume you are referring to the minute you wrote on 19 September to DIST, copy to Tony Cragg, my predecessor. I was aware of this and regard it as an entirely proper expression of your views at the time. The Defence Secretary and the former CDI have also been briefed on your note as part of the preparations for the evidence they gave this week to the Intelligence & Security Committee. There is, therefore, no question of your being found culpable in any way for what was, as I say, a perfectly legitimate action

I do not think you need take any further action, but if you would like to discuss the issue, please feel free to get in touch

Yours sincerely

Martin Howard

MOD\4\0012

Printed in the UK by The Stationery Office Limited
on behalf of the Controller of Her Majesty's Stationery Office
Id 163673   01/2004   019585   920173

ISBN 0-10-292715-4

9 780102 927153